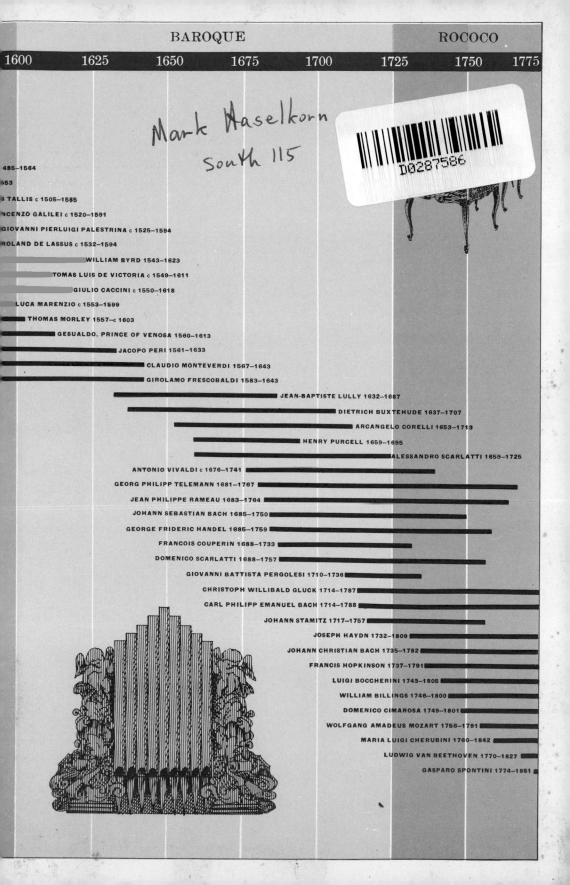

BAROQUE   ROCOCO

| 1600 | 1625 | 1650 | 1675 | 1700 | 1725 | 1750 | 1775 |

485–1564

553

TALLIS c 1505–1585

NCENZO GALILEI c 1520–1591

GIOVANNI PIERLUIGI PALESTRINA c 1525–1594

ROLAND DE LASSUS c 1532–1594

WILLIAM BYRD 1543–1623

TOMAS LUIS DE VICTORIA c 1549–1611

GIULIO CACCINI c 1550–1618

LUCA MARENZIO c 1553–1599

THOMAS MORLEY 1557–c 1603

GESUALDO, PRINCE OF VENOSA 1560–1613

JACOPO PERI 1561–1633

CLAUDIO MONTEVERDI 1567–1643

GIROLAMO FRESCOBALDI 1583–1643

JEAN-BAPTISTE LULLY 1632–1687

DIETRICH BUXTEHUDE 1637–1707

ARCANGELO CORELLI 1653–1713

HENRY PURCELL 1659–1695

ALESSANDRO SCARLATTI 1659–1725

ANTONIO VIVALDI c 1676–1741

GEORG PHILIPP TELEMANN 1681–1767

JEAN PHILIPPE RAMEAU 1683–1764

JOHANN SEBASTIAN BACH 1685–1750

GEORGE FRIDERIC HANDEL 1685–1759

FRANCOIS COUPERIN 1688–1733

DOMENICO SCARLATTI 1688–1757

GIOVANNI BATTISTA PERGOLESI 1710–1736

CHRISTOPH WILLIBALD GLUCK 1714–1787

CARL PHILIPP EMANUEL BACH 1714–1788

JOHANN STAMITZ 1717–1757

JOSEPH HAYDN 1732–1809

JOHANN CHRISTIAN BACH 1735–1782

FRANCIS HOPKINSON 1737–1791

LUIGI BOCCHERINI 1743–1805

WILLIAM BILLINGS 1746–1800

DOMENICO CIMAROSA 1749–1801

WOLFGANG AMADEUS MOZART 1756–1791

MARIA LUIGI CHERUBINI 1760–1842

LUDWIG VAN BEETHOVEN 1770–1827

GASPARO SPONTINI 1774–1851

The Enjoyment of Music

The Enjoyment

of Music

An Introduction to Perceptive Listening

By JOSEPH MACHLIS

PROFESSOR OF MUSIC, QUEENS COLLEGE
OF THE CITY UNIVERSITY OF NEW YORK

REVISED EDITION

W · W · NORTON & COMPANY · INC · *New York*

FOR
EARLE FENTON PALMER

Contents

Contents

x

Contents

Part Three. More Materials of Music

Part Four. Eighteenth-Century Classicism

Part Six. The Twentieth Century

Preface to the Revised Edition

THE ORIGINAL EDITION of this book grew out of the introductory course in music at Queens College of the City University of New York. Those of us who inaugurated and developed the course were working at a new college untrammeled by tradition or set procedures. We were able to experiment freely, to learn from our successes and our failures. Since the project in music appreciation embraces a thousand students a year, we have had as extensive a laboratory as could be desired in which to test both our theory and our practice.

Fairly early in our work we realized that the appreciation of an art is not the same thing as its history. We therefore abandoned chronological order in favor of a psychological approach. By beginning with pieces either familiar to the student or easily accessible to him, we strove to build up his confidence in his ability to enjoy music; and by proceeding gradually from the simplest level to a more advanced, to expand his horizons and develop his taste. For this reason, once the materials of music have been explained, the book starts with nineteenth-century romanticism, the style that is apt to be most accessible to a beginner. From there we move back to late eighteenth-century classicism, again back to the older music, and finally forward to the twentieth century. Thus Tchaikovsky, Beethoven, Bach, Debussy, and Stravinsky are encountered in a sequence that bears some relationship to the ascending order of difficulty represented by their music, rather than in a sequence depending exclusively on the dates of their birth.

My primary goal throughout has been to arouse the student's interest in and enjoyment of music; beyond that, to impart to him such knowledge as will help him respond to the works that constitute our musical heritage. This knowledge covers several areas in the territory loosely known as music appreciation. I have tried to explain in terms understandable to the layman how music is put together; to present the art against its social background, as part of the history of culture and in relation to parallel developments in the sister arts; to bring alive the great composers, both as artists and men; to analyze forms and styles; and to apply this combination of knowledges to an understanding of characteristic works. The book, naturally, covers a much wider field than the course; but it bears the lineaments of a method that never loses sight of the main goal—to create music lovers.

In the revision of the book I have tried to incorporate not only my own experience in teaching it during the years since its publication, but also the experience of the many colleagues throughout the country who were kind enough to respond to my request for suggestions. I received almost two hundred letters from those who had been using the text, containing many invaluable suggestions that I was able to follow. The text has been entirely re-set and re-checked for factual accuracy against the latest findings of musical scholarship. Certain parts have been entirely rewritten.

Dozens of additional musical examples enrich the text. A comprehensive chronological chart of composers has been affixed inside the front and back covers, to help the student orient himself in regard to the various historical periods. In addition, dates have been inserted after all the important works mentioned. Pictures have been added to underline the tie-up between music, painting, sculpture, and architecture during the different style-periods, and the book has been embellished by sixteen pages of full-color plates. I enlarged a number of chapters and changed the musical selections in others. For example, the chapter on Mozart was expanded to include a discussion of the classical piano concerto. The section on The Older Music was enlarged to include a number of works that had not been analyzed in the first edition. The choice of works in the chapter on Bach was changed to include the Suite No. 3, *Brandenburg Concerto* No. 2, and cantata *Wachet auf*. I expanded the chapters on impressionism and contemporary music; brought the chapters on Stravinsky and Schoenberg up to date; expanded the Schoenberg chapter to include an analysis of a large twelve-tone work, the Piano Concerto; expanded the section on Douglas Moore to include a discussion of an American opera—*The Ballad of Baby Doe;* added a chapter on Alban Berg and *Wozzeck*, a chapter on Ives, and an analysis of William Schuman's Third Symphony. The appendices have been expanded and brought up to date, especially the List of Records and the List of Books. A pronouncing list of basic musical terms has been added; the correct pronunciation of composers' names has been included in the Index; the Chronological List of Composers, with Parallel Tables of World Events and Principal Figures in Literature and the Arts, has been expanded to go back to the early Renaissance and, at the other end, has been brought up to the 1960s. I hope that these and similar changes will make the text more useful for both the teacher and the student. At the same time I have taken care to leave unchanged the structure and fundamental character of the original book.

I am heavily indebted to Nathan Broder, John Castellini, and Mary Ranney for their devoted reading of the manuscript. And I want very much to thank the colleagues who were sufficiently interested in the project of revision to send me their suggestions for making this a better book.

Joseph Machlis

Acknowledgments

THE BETTMANN ARCHIVE: Antoine-Jean Duclos, *Concert by Countess Sains Brisson*, p. 4; Moritz von Schwind, *A Schubert Evening*, p. 95; Robert and Clara Schumann, p. 104; Frédéric François Chopin, from a portrait by Eugène Delacroix, p. 113; Hector Berlioz, from a portrait by Honoré Daumier, p. 134; Franz Liszt at the piano, p. 142; César Franck, p. 173; Johannes Brahms, p. 178; Richard Wagner, p. 216; Georges Bizet, p. 237; Wolfgang Amadeus Mozart, p. 309; Ludwig van Beethoven, p. 328; Johann Sebastian Bach, p. 427; Giacomo Puccini, p. 472; Richard Strauss, p. 480; Claude Debussy, p. 496; Igor Stravinsky, a portrait by Pablo Picasso, p. 543; Béla Bartók, p. 564; Jenny Lind at Castle Garden, p. 597; Charles Ives, p. 608

FRATELLI ALINARI: Luca della Robbia, *Singing Boys, Relief for the Cantoria*, Museum of the Cathedral, Florence, p. 10; Raphael Sanzio, *The School of Athens*, p. 19; Donatello, Cantoria, Museum of the Cathedral, Florence, p. 29; Bernini, *The Ecstasy of Saint Theresa*, p. 389

PHOTOGRAPHIE GIRAUDON: Eugène Delacroix, *Liberty Leading the People*, p. 83 (Louvre); Veronese, *Wedding at Cana*, p. 375; detail from Veronese *Wedding at Cana*, p. 375

THE METROPOLITAN MUSEUM OF ART, New York: Apollo holding a Kithara (Gift of Mr. and Mrs. Leon Pomerance, 1953), p. 36; Jack Levine, *String Quartette* (Arthur H. Hearn Fund, 1942), p. 343; 17th century harpsichord (The Crosby Brown Collection of Musical Instruments, 1889), p. 400; J. M. W. Turner, *Grand Canal, Venice* (Bequest of Cornelius Vanderbilt, 1899), p. 84; George Frideric Handel, p. 447; Jean Antoine Watteau, *Embarkation for Cythera*, p. 460; Edgar Dégas, *The Foyer*, p. 489; Thomas Hart Benton, *The Cotton Pickers*, p. 602

THE DETROIT INSTITUTE OF ARTS: Pieter Brueghel, the Elder, *The Wedding Dance*, p. 11

STEINWAY AND SONS: A modern concert grand piano, p. 52

THE HOLTKAMP ORGAN COMPANY: A modern baroque organ, p. 53

FRENCH GOVERNMENT TOURIST OFFICE: The Paris Opera, p. 212; Amiens Cathedral, p. 369

THE METROPOLITAN OPERA: Photographs by Louis Melançon: *Tristan und Isolde*, love duet, p. 226; *Boris Godunov*, coronation scene, p. 250; *Don Giovanni*, final scene, p. 318. Photographs by Sedge Le Blang: *Aïda*, triumphal scene, p. 235; *Carmen*, card scene, p. 243

NATIONAL TOURIST ORGANIZATION OF GREECE: The Parthenon, Athens, p. 285

HENRY E. HUNTINGTON LIBRARY AND ART GALLERY, San Marino, California: Sir Joshua Reynolds, *Jane, Countess of Harrington*, p. 290

GERMAN TOURIST INFORMATION OFFICE: The high altar of the Theatine Church, Munich, p. 386

NATIONAL BROADCASTING COMPANY: *La Bohème*, four scenes, p. 475

LINCOLN CENTER FOR THE PERFORMING ARTS, Inc.: Metropolitan Opera House, Lincoln Center for the Performing Arts, p. 515

THE MUSEUM OF PRIMITIVE ART: African sculpture, *Fertility Figure: Standing Woman*, p. 517

ASCAP: George Gershwin, p. 633

PART ONE

The Materials of Music

"There are only twelve tones. You must treat them carefully."
Paul Hindemith

CHAPTER 1

By Way of Introduction

"Music to me is a power that justifies things."
Igor Stravinsky

The Art of Listening

WE INTEND it as a great compliment when we say of someone that he is a good listener. We mean that he not only listens passively to what we are telling him but that he enters actively into our tale, drawing us out, making us want to continue, somehow grasping the meaning behind the words. The very fact that we single out certain people as good listeners makes it clear that not everyone has mastered the art of listening.

The same goes for music. It is not enough to be in the same room with the sounds, or to listen intermittently while one's thoughts wander hither and yon. To listen perceptively requires that we fasten our whole attention upon the sounds as they come floating through the air; that we observe the patterns they form, and respond to the wellsprings of thought and feeling out of which those patterns have emerged. Responding to music is the most natural thing in the world, judging from the multitudes who sing, dance, hum, whistle, nod, and tap. But to listen perceptively to a great musical work—that is, really to hear it and understand it—is an art in itself: an art that may come more easily to some than to others, but that can be acquired through practice and application.

Our time, unfortunately, does not encourage the art of listening. Formerly it was not so easy to hear a symphony performed. You had to get to the concert hall and buy a ticket. Having invested the time and the effort, you were ready to listen when the orchestra finally struck up. Today you need only flick a knob, and the music comes pouring into the room. On Sunday morning millions of people flick that knob—and for the next ten hours are surrounded by music of one sort or another. They converse, eat, talk on the telephone, read the funnies, do crossword puzzles, and all the while that ceaseless tinkle, tinkle is sluicing past their ears, half-heeded, quarter-heeded, or unheeded. We are not only the beneficiaries of technology but also its victims. By a supreme irony, the very invention that brought music into every home in the land has all but ended the art of listening to it. People think they've been listening to music just because their ears happened to be

3

in the path of the sounds. They do not seem to realize that there is only
one way to listen to music, and that is—to listen!

As a matter of fact, we vary greatly in our way of responding to
music. During the playing, shall we say, of the Triumphal March from
Aïda, one listener will summon up a vision of ancient tombs and Pharaohs. Another floats off in a daydream equally far removed from the
music and the world. A third is filled with a strange sense of power at

Antoine-Jean Duclos, 1742–1795, *Concert.*

"People vary greatly in their way of responding to music."

the ringing tone of the trumpets. His neighbor for no apparent reason
recollects the half hour he spent in the dentist's chair. This one is
pleased with himself for having noticed the reappearance of Theme A.
That one has decided that the conductor is a shoemaker and wonders
how he ever managed to get an orchestra. The musicologist reflects
upon the contribution of Verdi to grand-opera style. The critic polishes
a phrase for his next review. The budding composer is oppressed by a
suspicion that he was born too late.

In all these ways of listening, one factor is constant—the ability of
the sounds to convey significant meaning. Music as an art bases its appeal on the sensuous beauty of musical sounds. But man is almost incapable of experiencing a physical stimulus without attaching to it a
deeper meaning. A sunset, a glass of wine, a summer breeze will awaken
associations that extend beyond the physical into the realm of thought
and feeling. Music begins as a disturbance in the air; yet it is a disturbance that reaches to the farthermost limits of man's emotional and

intellectual life.

For this reason it is idle to classify the listening experience (as writers on music used to do) as being on either the sensual, the emotional, or the intellectual level. Today it is recognized that such categories are extremely fluid. We listen differently to different kinds of music and we hear the same piece differently on different occasions. In art as in life the physical, emotional, and intellectual elements are too closely interwoven for us to be able to draw rigid boundaries between them. As newcomers to music we fall into the way of listening that comes natural to us. With practice and experience we learn other ways. The goal of our training in the art of listening must be to unite all three levels, so that we will apprehend the floating patterns of sound with all the joy of our senses, the freshness of our emotions, and the power of our understanding.

There are people who tell you that they prefer not to know anything about the music they hear. Technical information, they claim, spoils their enjoyment. But they would never suggest that the best way to enjoy a football match is to know nothing about the rules of the game. What they really fear, one suspects, is that knowledge of any kind might interfere with the fantasies they like to interpose between themselves and the sounds. They would rather immerse themselves in a tonal bubble bath, achieving thereby a state of hazy contentment.

The mature music lover has no such fear of knowledge. He realizes that the true source of the musical experience is not in himself but in the sounds. Consequently, whatever brings him closer to the sounds heightens his musical perceptions and his enjoyment. He is curious to know how the sounds are put together and why they do one thing rather than another. His information need not be as technical as that of the professional musician, but it demands some knowledge of the rules of the game.

"To understand," said Raphael, "is to equal." When we completely understand a great work of music we grasp the "moment of truth" that gave it birth. For the nonce we become, if not the equal of the master who created it, at least worthy to sit in his company. We receive his message, we fathom his intention. In effect, we listen perceptively; and that is the one sure road to the enjoyment of music.

The Meaning of Music

Music has been called the language of emotions. This is a not unreasonable metaphor; for music, like language, aims to communicate meaning. Like language too it possesses a grammar, a syntax, and a rhetoric. But it is a different kind of language. Words are concrete; tone is fluid and intangible. A word taken by itself has a fixed meaning; a tone assumes meaning only from its association with other tones. Words convey specific ideas; music suggests elusive states of mind.

Because of this elusiveness music has been subject to a constant attempt to translate its message into words. Writers of a former generation regaled their readers with personal interpretations of musical works. James Huneker saw in Chopin's G-minor Ballade "the slender-hipped girl with the eyes of midnight," while Romain Rolland heard in the first movement of Beethoven's *Appassionata* "a veritable ride to the abyss punctuated with laments." Serious musicians today reject such attempts to chain their art to concrete images. Such images destroy what is the unique glory of music: its freedom from literary—that is, from specific —meaning.

Suppose we say of Schubert's *Moment musical* in F minor that it is graceful, tender, expressive. Will this convey the remotest conception of the music to one who never heard it? The meaning of the piece cannot be translated into words. Precisely this constitutes its nature as music. We are able to define a word through other words. But we are not able to define a melody. It means—itself! Beyond that it will mean something different to each listener.

The *Moment musical* sprang out of a certain state of mind in Schubert that demanded tones for its expression and could be expressed in no other way. This state of mind included all the composer's experience as man and artist, his sensitivity to his time, his inheritance of certain traditions, his mastery of certain techniques. Above all, it represented his personal manner of speech as a musician, his unique and inimitable way of creating beauty through tones.

Even if we reject the possibility of translating the meaning of music into words, there still remains much for us to talk about. It will heighten our perception if we know something about the elements of which music is composed, and the way that composers go about organizing tones into patterns and forms. We may inquire into the forces that have shaped musical activity at various periods, the schools and movements within the art and their relationship to the social-cultural environment. We should have some knowledge of the men whose genius enriched the lives of their fellows, of their style, and of their contribution to the art. This information by no means constitutes the meaning of a musical work, but it will help each one of us to fathom that meaning for himself.

The practical musician is apt to distrust talk about music. This, he complains, is generally so complicated that it stands in the way of the music itself. Such mistrust is based on a valid intuition. There is only one way to learn to listen to music and that is—to listen, continually and intensively. It will help to focus our listening if we read and talk about music; but this is no more than a preliminary. The true meaning, the ultimate wisdom, is to be found in one place only: the sounds themselves.

Art as Experience

Music is an art dealing with the organization of tones into patterns. It is one of the great arts of our civilization, along with literature, painting, sculpture, architecture, and the dance. Wherever men have lived together, art has sprung up among them as a language charged with feeling and significance. The desire to create this language appears to be universal. It shows itself in primitive societies as in our own. It has become a very part of man's need to impose his will upon the universe; to bring order out of chaos; to endow his moments of highest awareness with enduring form and substance.

Art, like love, is easier to experience than define. It would be not easy to find two philosophers who agree on a definition. We may say that art concerns itself with the communication of certain ideas and feelings by means of a sensuous medium—color, sound, bronze, marble, words. This medium is fashioned into a symbolic language marked by beauty of design and coherence of form. It appeals to our mind, arouses our emotions, kindles our imagination, enchants our senses.

Children are artists. The world for them is a thing of wonder. They invent stories and poems, they make up songs, they paint. But as they grow up this creativity is dulled in them; they lose the magic touch. The artist is one who retains his wonder at the world as well as a childlike need to communicate his feelings. He possesses that natural ability to express himself in one medium or another which we call talent. He thus learns to project his creative impulse through the symbols of his art; to capture his visions within a stable form.

The artist is part of the world about him. He can emerge only in an environment that cultivates art. A man could hardly develop a gift for writing symphonies in a society that had no orchestras, no schools of composition, no interest in symphonic music. The artist also needs a public, for his work springs not only from his desire for self-expression but also from his need to communicate with his fellows. He is nourished by their approval and response; he has to feel that they will understand him. This hope sustains him in his struggle to set down his ideas. It helps free him from the loneliness of the creative act.

A work of art embodies a view of life. It brings us the artist's personal interpretation of human destiny, the essence of his experience both as artist and man. In order to comprehend the work we must enter the secret world out of which it sprang. The greater our understanding, the more complete our possession of the art work, and the better we capture the joy, the illumination that went into its making. In so doing we are carried to heights of awareness, to intensities of experience of which we had hardly thought ourselves capable.

The function of literature, André Malraux has said, is to reveal to man his hidden greatness. The art work begins by opening to us the land-scape of its creator's inner life. It ends by revealing us to ourselves.

⁂ CHAPTER 2 ⁂

Music and Life: The Sources of Musical Imagery

"Art is a human activity having for its purpose the transmission
to others of the highest and best feelings to which man has risen."
                                                            Tolstoi

THE BEGINNINGS of music are shrouded in prehistory. However, a num-ber of theories have been advanced to explain its origin. One derives music from the inflections of speech, another from mating calls, a third from the cries of battle and signals of the hunt, a fourth from the rhythms of collective labor. Some attribute the rise of music to the imitation of nature, others connect it with the play impulse, with magic and religious rites, or with the need for emotional expression. These explanations have one factor in common: they relate music to the pro-foundest experiences of the individual and the group. Underlying all is the fact that man possesses in his vocal cords a means of producing song, in his body an instrument for rhythm, and in his mind the capacity to imagine and perceive musical sounds.

Life in primitive society is saturated with emotion. Speech and body movement alike are intensely expressive. Speech heightened by musical inflection becomes song. Body movement enlivened by musical rhythm becomes dance. Song and dance—that is, melody and rhythm—con-stitute the primal sources of music. They are imbued with the imagery of life. Love, courtship, and marriage; sowing and reaping; hunting and war—each of these has its songs and dances, as have the rites of fertility, the exorcism of evil spirits, the burial of the dead. Primitive culture does not recognize the notion that art is a self-contained ex-perience apart from life. In tribal society music is the direct expression of human experience, and constitutes a powerful bond between the individual and his fellows.

The art of music has come a long way from its primitive stage; but it has retained its connection with the springs of human feeling, with the accents of joy and sorrow, tension and release. In this sense we may speak of music as a universal language, one that transcends the barriers men put up against each other. Its vocabulary has been shaped by thousands of years of human experience; its rhetoric mirrors man's existence, his place in nature and in society.

Song

Song is the most natural form of music. Issuing from within the body, it is projected by means of the most personal of all instruments, the human voice. From time immemorial, singing has been the most widespread and spontaneous way of making music.

We have in folk music a treasury of song that reflects all phases of life —work songs, love songs, drinking songs, cradle songs, patriotic songs, dance songs, songs of mourning, marching songs, play songs, narrative songs. Some are centuries old, others are of recent origin. A folk song originates with an individual, perhaps on the spur of the moment. It is taken up by others, a detail is changed, a stanza added. In the course of its wanderings it assumes a number of versions. It becomes the collective expression of a group.

One has but to listen to a love song like *Greensleeves* or *Black Is the Color of My True Love's Hair* to realize how compellingly a melody may capture the accent of tenderness and longing. Songs such as *Water Boy*, which sprang up among prisoners on the chain gang, or *Lord Randall*, with its theme of betrayal, are surcharged with emotion. Treating of basic human experience, they are understood everywhere. At the same time they are rooted in the speech rhythms, the soil, and the life of a particular place—which is why they possess the raciness and vivid local color that are among the prime attributes of folk song.

The same directness of expression is found on a more sophisticated level in the art song. Here the sentiment is more special, more sharply focused. Text and music are of known authorship, and bear the imprint of a personality. Whereas folk song usually reflects the pattern of life in rural areas, the art song issues from the culture of cities. Like the folk song, however, its musical content is shaped by man's experience and projects deeply human emotion. Schubert's famous *Serenade* has become the archetype of the love song, Brahms's *Lullaby* of the cradle song, Schumann's *Two Grenadiers* of the martial ballad. Such songs have universal appeal and exemplify the power of music to set forth

Luca della Robbia, c. 1400–1482, *Singing Boys, Relief for the Cantoria,*
Museum of the Cathedral, Florence.

"Song is the most natural form of music."

the imagery of life. The spirit of song lyricism is also to be found in
instrumental music. Mendelssohn understood this when he called his
popular piano pieces "songs without words." This title might also be
applied to many of the short piano pieces of Schubert, Chopin, and
Schumann. More ambitious in scope is the "song" for orchestra, which
is best known from the slow movements of various symphonies, where
the composer embodies the lyric impulse in an extended movement. In
any case, the spirit of song permeates all music, whether vocal or instrumental. It remains the vital link between tone art and man's emotional life.

The Dance

Dance springs from man's joy in his body, his love of expressive gesture, his release of tension through rhythmic movement. It heightens the

pleasure of being, and at the same time mirrors the life of society. The dance of the countryside is different from the city dance; both, throughout the ages, were set off from the court dance. Folk, popular, and court dances nourished centuries of European art music.

Pieter Brueghel, the Elder, c. 1520–1569, *The Wedding Dance.*
"Dance springs from man's joy in his body."

A dance piece may be intended for actual use in the ballroom, like the dance-songs of our commercial popular music. Such was the case with the waltzes of Johann Strauss, who brought to its height the most popular city dance of the nineteenth century. Or a dance rhythm may serve as the basis for an abstract composition. This type of piece evokes images of body movement on an imaginary plane. In this category is a whole group of dance pieces that retain their popularity with the public, such as the gavottes of Bach, the minuets of Mozart, the contredanses of Beethoven, and the waltzes and mazurkas of Chopin. That the twentieth century has retained a fondness for compositions based on dance patterns is evidenced by such works as the Rumanian Dances of Bartók, the *Pavane for a Dead Infanta* of Ravel, and the *Circus Polka* of Stravinsky.

Dance forms of various kinds were absorbed by the eighteenth-century suite and symphony. The courtly minuet, for example, figures prominently in the symphonies of Haydn and Mozart, where it takes on the formal beauty of the classical style. In these movements the imagery of body movement is sublimated into a pure and serene instrumental music. Certain dance pieces exude a peasant gusto, others idealize the spirit of the dance, but all testify to the persuasive power of rhythm. For it is through rhythm that music mirrors the patterns of man's activity in the physical world.

Other Types of Musical Imagery

The march, which is related to the dance, descends from the ceremonial processions of tribal life. Its music is associated with trumpets and drums, with the pageantry of great occasions, religious, military, or patriotic. Whether it be the quick march made popular by Sousa or a grand processional such as the Triumphal March from Verdi's *Aïda,* which is played when the conquering hero Radames is welcomed home, this type of music is imbued with the imagery of human experience.

March rhythm may serve too as the basis for an abstract piece that is not intended actually to be marched to. Characteristic is the *Marche militaire* of Schubert, which tempers the military mood with lyricism, or the polonaises of Chopin, which recreate the proud processional dance in which the nobles of Poland paid homage to their king. The march creates an atmosphere of pomp and ceremony. Like the dance, it unites appealing melody and decisive rhythm. Like the dance, too, the march captures for music something of the movement and gesture of man's activity in space and time.

The religious impulse has motivated a considerable amount of the world's great music. Most works in this category were composed expressly for use in the church service; others are concert pieces on sacred themes. In either case they hold an expressive content that music is particularly well able to achieve: the aura of spirituality that surrounds the Masses of Palestrina, or the quality of sublimity that we associate with the religious works of Bach and Handel.

The religious spirit animates various kinds of music. In the sphere of popular song there are the Lutheran chorales, those sturdy congregational hymns that nurtured centuries of German music. In America we have produced a rich store of religious folk song in the spirituals, Negro and white. Melodies such as *Go Down, Moses* or *Deep River* are as indestructible as any to be found in the domain of folk art. Both the art song and opera have reflected religious themes; one has but to mention such popular examples of the religious mood as Schubert's *Ave Maria,* the Prelude to Wagner's *Lohengrin,* with its evocation of the Holy Grail, or the Good Friday music from his last music drama, *Parsifal.* On a more abstract level the religious impulse found expression in many a symphonic movement of the nineteenth century. For example, the so-called "Pilgrim's March" from Mendelssohn's *Italian Symphony* has a devotional character, as does the final movement from his *Reformation Symphony*. In the works of the German romantic composers the religious impulse was often associated with the worship of nature, as in the first movement of Bruckner's Fourth Symphony (*Romantic*), or in Mahler's Third.

The opera forms another potent link between life and music. Its theme is man, his passions, his conflicts, his actions. Through opera, composers learned to transform into musical images the most varied sentiments and situations. In this way music was encouraged to draw its substance directly from the drama of human existence. Today, in their operas and ballets as in their music for the theater and films, composers are affirming anew the relationship between music and human experience.

The source of musical imagery, then, is life itself, whether in religious or dramatic music, in the dance, the love song, the lullaby, or the warriors' chorus. Nor do composers forget these images when they turn to abstract works such as symphonies and concertos. In these examples of "pure" or absolute music there are still present echoes of song and dance, moods of triumph and lamentation, images of drama and religious faith—but in sublimated form, lifted from the specific to the abstract, from the particular to the universal. Therefrom springs the dual nature of music. On the one hand it is an art of expressive content rooted in human experience. On the other it is an art of abstract patterns that follow purely musical procedures deriving from the nature of sound.

This fascinating dualism causes endless argument concerning the nature of music. At one extreme are those who look for a specific meaning, a "story," in every piece of music they hear. At the other are those who deny all connection between music and reality, proclaiming the art to be a self-contained experience whose purity is violated as soon as it is related to anything outside itself. Each of these factions represents half the truth. Music is related to human experience and it has expressive content, otherwise it could not have functioned for thousands of years as a spiritual force in the lives of men. At the same time it presents the stuff of life on a high level of abstraction, purified, removed from word meanings, picture meanings, story meanings: an art that obeys purely musical impulses and is truly a "song without words." Else it would not be music.

CHAPTER 3

Melody: Musical Line

"It is the melody which is the charm of music, and it is that which is most difficult to produce. The invention of a fine melody is a work of genius."

Joseph Haydn

MELODY is that element of music which makes the widest and most direct appeal. It has been called the soul of music. It is generally what we remember and whistle and hum. We know a good melody when we hear it and we recognize its unique power to move us, although we might be hard put to explain wherein its power lies. The world has always lavished a special affection upon the creators of melody; nothing is more intimately associated with inspiration, not only in the popular mind but also among musicians, as the quotation from Haydn makes clear.

A melody is a succession of tones perceived by the mind as an entity. Some modern theorists maintain that any succession of tones, if repeated sufficiently, will take on melodic significance. Be that as it may, in order to perceive a melody as an entity we must find a significant relationship among its constituent tones. This places a certain responsibility upon us. What is accepted as a melody by one listener may not be so for another. Similarly, at one stage of our development we may not grasp as an entity what will later take on melodic significance for us. The enterprising music lover does not limit his appreciation to melodies of one type or era, but continually expands his horizons and lays himself open to unfamiliar kinds of melody which with repeated hearing he comes to understand and enjoy. When we accept a succession of tones as a melody, we feel that they have not been thrown together in any old way. We derive from them an impression of conscious arrangement: the sense of a beginning, a middle, and an end. A good melody has something inevitable about it. It possesses a distinctive profile, a quality of aliveness.

We hear the words of a sentence not singly but in relation to the thought as a whole. So too we perceive tones not separately but in relationship to each other within a pattern. Tones move up and down, one being higher or lower than another in musical "space." They also move faster or slower in time, one claiming our attention for a longer or shorter duration than another. From the interaction of the two dimensions—musical space and time—emerges the total unit which is melody.

This is the musical line—or curve, if you prefer—which guides our ear through a composition. The melody is the plot, the theme of a musical work, the thread upon which hangs the tale. As Aaron Copland aptly puts it, "The melody is generally what the piece is about."

The Structure of Melody

Let us examine the pattern of a well-known tune.

We notice at once that the melody divides itself into two halves. Such symmetry is found frequently in melodies dating from the eighteenth and nineteenth centuries. Each half is called a *phrase*. In music, as in language, a phrase denotes a unit of meaning within a larger structure. Two phrases together form a sentence, a musical period.

Each phrase is rounded off by a *cadence*, a term applied to a kind of resting place in music. The first phrase of *London Bridge* ends in an upward inflection, like a question. This is an inconclusive type of cadence, indicating, like a comma in punctuation, that more is to come. The second phrase answers with a vigorous downward inflection on the word "la-dy." This is a full cadence and creates a sense of conclusion. In this question-and-answer formation, the second phrase grows out of the first and completes its meaning. We find here the quality of organic unity that is a prime value in art.

The composer unifies his structure by repeating some of his musical ideas. Thus both phrases of *London Bridge* begin in identical fashion. The necessary contrast is supplied by fresh material, which in our example comes on the words "my fair lady." Through repetition and contrast the composer achieves both unity and variety. This combination of traits is basic to musical architecture, for without unity there is chaos, without variety—boredom.

The melody line does not leave off haphazardly, as if it suddenly found something better to do. On the contrary, it gives the impression of having reached its goal. If you will hum the last phrase of several well-known tunes such as *The Star-Spangled Banner*, *America*, and *Old Black Joe*, you will notice they all end on a tone that produces this effect of finality. We encounter here what for centuries has been a cardinal principle in our music: one tone is singled out as the center of the group; it serves as a landmark that gives the other tones their direction and relationship. This central tone may be thought of as the point of departure and return.

A melody may move up or down along the steps of the scale; it may repeat tones; it may leap to a tone several degrees away. The leap may be narrow or wide, as may be the *range* of the melody (the distance from its lowest to highest tone). Traits such as these determine the character of the melodic line. Compare the narrow range and stepwise movement of *America* with the bold leaps and far-flung activity of *The Star-Spangled Banner*. Clearly *The Star-Spangled Banner* is the more vigorous melody.

The phrase as a whole may trace an upward or downward curve. When we sing the scale, going up—as on a staircase—is more strenuous than coming down. *The Farmer in the Dell* presents an ascending first phrase which is answered by a descending second phrase—that is, tension followed by relaxation.

The far - mer in the dell   The far - mer in the dell

Heigh ho! the mer - ry oh The far - mer in the dell.

The tones move forward in time, now faster, now slower, in a rhythmic pattern that holds our attention even as does their up-and-down movement in space. Without the rhythm the melody loses its aliveness. Try singing *London Bridge* or *The Farmer in the Dell* in tones of equal duration, and see how much is lost of the quality of the pattern. So too the rhythm organizes the melody into clear-cut (and very often, symmetrical) phrases, and determines the spacing of the cadences. Of great moment in fixing the character of a melody is its speed or pace. A rapid tune such as *Dixie* or *Oh Susannah!* creates an atmosphere of jaunty activity, whereas a slow and sustained melody like *Silent Night* suggests serenity and rest.

Our gestures when we speak are purely physical movements, yet they carry emotional meaning. In the same way, the physical facts that make up a melody take on psychological implications. The melodic line may be described as angular or smooth, tense or relaxed, energetic or languid. Above all, the melody must be interesting. We say of a painter that he has a sense of line, meaning that he is able to achieve eventfulness, to sustain movement over the whole of his canvas. The same holds for the unfolding melody line with its rising and falling, its peaks and valleys. A melody has to have what musicians call the "long line." It must build tension as it rises from one level to the next, and must retain its drive up to the final note.

Pablo Picasso, b. 1881, *Four Ballet Dancers*
Collection, The Museum of Modern Art, New York
Gift of Mrs. John D. Rockefeller, Jr.

"We say of a painter that he has a sense of line, meaning that he is able to sustain movement. The same holds for the unfolding melody line."

What is apt to make a striking effect on the listener is the climax. Representing the peak of intensity, the climax gives purpose and direction to the melody line. It creates the impression of crisis met and overcome. Our national anthem contains a fine climax in the last phrase, on the words "O'er the land of the free." There can be no doubt in anybody's mind that this song is about freedom. Clearly, too, freedom must be striven for, to judge from the effort we have to make to get up to the crucial tone.

The principles we have touched upon are to be encountered in the melodies of the masters. Let us take some familiar examples. Brahms's Hungarian Dance No. 5 opens with vigorous upward leaps. The impression of energy is reinforced by the swing of the rhythm. As is often the case with dance tunes, the phrases and cadences are both symmetrical and clearly marked. There is an abundance of repetition and contrast, unity and variety; and when the piece reaches the final cadence, we know for certain that its goal has been attained.

The activity of this melodic line contrasts with the gentle stepwise movement and serene flow of Schubert's *Ave Maria*. Similarly the soaring line of the March from *Aïda* contrasts with the restricted activity of the melody in Ravel's *Pavane*. The *Londonderry Air* builds to a particularly fine climax in the final phrase, as does Chopin's E-flat Nocturne. The Hallelujah Chorus from Handel's *Messiah* is an excellent example of the way in which rhythm can make a melody memorable. The rhythmic figure on the word "Hallelujah," repeated again and again in the course of the piece, stamps itself unforgettably on the mind.

The question arises: is the composer conscious of these principles or does the melody simply happen that way? One might ask the same about the rhymes and meters of a poem. These, needless to say, do not happen accidentally. Yet if the poet had to think constantly of rules he could not create a living work. The same applies to the composer. Through a combination of talent, training, and practice he learns to think spontaneously—or at least comfortably—within the rules of his art. His melodies uniquely combine the flash of inspiration and the effort that must follow it. Intuition and planning, rapturous vision and technical skill, are here inextricably intertwined.

"Melody," writes the composer Paul Hindemith, "is the element in which the personal characteristics of the composer are most clearly and most obviously revealed." For melody is the essential unit of communication in music: the direct bearer of meaning from composer to listener.

CHAPTER 4

Harmony: Musical Space

"The evolution of the harmonic idiom has resulted from the fact that musicians of all generations have sought new means of expression. Harmony is a constant stream of evolution, a constantly changing vocabulary and syntax."

Roger Sessions

WE ARE accustomed to hearing melodies against a background of *harmony*. To the movement of the melody, harmony adds another dimension—depth. It imparts richness and color to the melodic line,

Raphael Sanzio, 1483–1520, *The School of Athens,* Fresco in the Vatican Palace.

"Harmony is to music what perspective is to painting."

weight and body to the musical tissue. Harmony is to music what perspective is to painting. It introduces the impression of musical space. It clarifies direction and creates meaning. The supporting role of harmony is apparent when a singer accompanies his melody with chords on the guitar or banjo, or when the pianist plays the melody with his right hand while the left strikes the chords. We are jolted if the wrong chord is sounded, for at that point we become aware that the necessary unity of melody and harmony has been broken.

Harmony pertains to the movement and relationship of chords. (In a narrower sense, a harmony is a chord.) A *chord* may be defined as a combination of tones occurring simultaneously and conceived as an entity. Just as the vaulting arch rests upon columns, so the melody unfolds above the supporting chords, the harmony. Melody constitutes the horizontal aspects of music; harmony, the vertical.

The Function of Harmony

The chords may serve as the framework of a composition. They form the substructure that holds it together. They have meaning only in relation to other chords; that is, only as each leads into the next. Harmony therefore implies movement, progression. In the larger sense, harmony denotes the over-all organization of tones in a musical work in such a way as to achieve order and unity.

The most common chord in our music is a certain combination of three tones known as a *triad*. Such a chord may be built by combining the first, third, and fifth degrees of the do-re-mi-fa-sol-la-ti-do scale: do–mi–sol. A triad may be built on the second degree (steps 2–4–6 or re–fa–la); on the third degree (steps 3–5–7 or mi–sol–ti); and similarly on each of the other degrees of the scale. The triad is a basic formation in our music. "In the world of tones," observes one authority, "the triad corresponds to the force of gravity. It serves as our constant guiding point, our unit of measure, and our goal."

Although the triad is a vertical block of sound, its three tones often appear horizontally as a melody. The first three tones of the *Blue Danube Waltz* form a triad, as do the first three of our national anthem (on the words "O-oh-say"). When the lowest tone (or root) of the chord is duplicated an octave above, we have a four-tone version of the triad. This happens at the beginning of *The Star-Spangled Banner,* on the words "say can you see." It is apparent that melody and harmony do not function independently of one another. On the contrary, the melody implies the harmony that goes with it, and each constantly influences the other.

The white keys of the piano are named after the first seven letters of the alphabet. We may build a triad on C by playing C–E–G (every other tone). A triad with D as root reads D–F–A. The triad on E is E–G–B, and so on. These and other more intricate chords form the materials of our harmonic system. They play an important part in determining the character of our music, its sounds and its meanings.

Active and Rest Chords

Music is an art of movement. Movement to be purposeful must have a goal. The progressions of chords cannot be left to chance. In the course of centuries musicians have evolved procedures to regulate the movement of chords. These conventions are part of the logic that art imposes upon nature.

Purposeful movement implies a central point of departure and return. We noticed such a point in the final tone of melodies. This is the *do* which comes both first and last in the do-re-mi-fa-sol-la-ti-do scale. The triad on *do* (do–mi–sol) is the I chord or *Tonic*, which serves as the chord of rest. But rest has meaning only in relation to activity. The chord of rest is counterposed to other chords which are active. The active chords seek to be completed, or *resolved*, in the rest chord. This striving for resolution is the dynamic force in our music. It shapes the forward movement, imparting direction and goal.

The fifth step of the do-re-mi-fa-sol-la-ti-do scale is the chief representative of the active principle. We therefore obtain two focal points: the active triad on *sol* (sol–ti–re), the V chord or *Dominant*, which seeks to be resolved in the restful triad on *do*. Dominant moving to Tonic constitutes a compact formula of activity completed, of movement come to rest. Formerly children used to learn this formula at school when the two chords were sounded at assemblies for the group to rise or be seated. Dominant resolving to Tonic is the most common final cadence in our music. We hear it asserted over and over again at the end of many compositions dating from the eighteenth and nineteenth centuries. After generations of conditioning we feel a decided need to hear an active chord resolve to the chord of rest.

Following is the harmonic structure of *London Bridge*, involving a simple progression from Tonic to Dominant and back.

London Bridge is	falling down,	Falling down,	falling down;
I————	I————	V————	I————
London Bridge is	falling down,	My fair	la-dy.
I————	I————	V————	I————

It will be noticed that the Dominant-Tonic progression shapes the cadence at the end of each phrase.

The triad built on the fourth scale step *fa* (fa–la–do) is known as the IV chord or *Subdominant*. This too is an active chord, but less so than the Dominant. The progression IV–I creates a less decisive cadence than the other. It is familiar to us from the two Amen chords sounded by the organ at the end of many hymns.

These three triads, the basic ones of our system, suffice to harmonize many famous melodies.

Way down upon the	Swanee River,	Far, far a- way,
I————	IV————	I———————— V——
There's where my heart is	turning ever,	There's where the old folks stay.
I——— —————	IV————	I———— V——— I——
All the world is	sad and dreary,	Every- where I roam,
V————	I————	IV———————— I—(V)
Oh, brothers, how my	heart grows weary,	Far from the old folks at home.
I————	IV————	I———— V——— I——

Consonance and Dissonance

Harmonic movement, we saw, is generated by the tendency of the active chord to be resolved in the chord of rest. This movement receives its maximum impetus from the dissonance. *Dissonance* is restlessness and activity, *consonance* is relaxation and fulfillment. The dissonant chord creates tension. The consonant chord resolves it. As Walter Piston points out, "It cannot be too strongly emphasized that the essential quality of dissonance is its sense of movement and not, as sometimes erroneously assumed, its degree of unpleasantness to the ear."

It was during the nineteenth century that the term dissonance took on its inaccurate implication of unpleasantness—inaccurate because, if dissonance is unpleasant, why should every composer have made use of it? The answer is that dissonance introduces the necessary element of expressiveness into music. Without it, a work would be intolerably dull and insipid. What suspense and conflict are to the drama, dissonance is to music. It creates the areas of tension without which the areas of relaxation would have no meaning. Each complements the other; both are a necessary part of the artistic whole.

Why does one aggregate of tones sound reposeful while another does not? Because of a combination of factors, acoustical, psychological, and historical. Certain tones combine more smoothly than others, even as do chemical elements. Yet this is not as decisive a circumstance as one would suppose. Cultural conditioning plays a major part in the formation of our attitudes—how else explain the fact that tone combinations which we in the West perceive as consonant or dissonant have no such implications for hundreds of millions in the Orient who are brought up on systems of music different from our own? The listener's experience is important too. One who hears much twentieth-century music will develop a greater tolerance for dissonance than he who limits his diet to Bach, Mozart, and Beethoven.

The history of music teaches us that tone combinations regarded as dissonant in their own time come to be accepted by later generations as consonant. Man's capacity to tolerate novel chords has grown steadily in the last thousand years. The leader in this development was always the composer, whose imagination grasped the possibilities of new combinations while they were still unacceptable to his fellows; who dared break with tradition, only to be roundly abused; who by sheer force of will imposed his vision on the world; and who, after having expanded the artistic horizon of his time, became in his turn the venerated founder of a new tradition that had a new set of rules set forth by disciples who would attack the next innovator as zealously as once their idol had been attacked.

Six hundred years ago Jacob of Liège was protesting against the modernists of his time. "O great abuse, great ignorance, great bestiality whereby an ass parades as a man. . . . For they confound concord with discord, so that it becomes impossible to distinguish the one from the other!" Two and a half centuries later the theorist Artusi excoriated the modernists (especially Monteverdi) for creating "a tumult of sounds, a confusion of absurdities," and for being so enamored of themselves that they substitute their innovations for the traditional rules. How familiar the sentiment, how oft repeated through the ages.

Harmony is a much more sophisticated phenomenon than melody. Historically it appeared much later, about a thousand years ago. Its real development took place only in the West. The music of the Orient to this day is largely melodic. Indeed, we may consider the great achievement of Western music to be harmony (hearing in depth), even as in painting it is perspective (seeing in depth). Our harmonic system has advanced steadily over the past ten centuries. Today it is adjusting to new needs. These constitute the latest chapter in man's age-old attempt to impose law and order upon the raw material of sound; to perceive tones·as the manifestation of a unifying idea, a selective imagination, a reasoning will.

CHAPTER 5

Rhythm and Meter: Musical Time

"In the beginning was rhythm."
Hans von Bülow

RHYTHM—the word means "flow" in Greek—denotes the controlled movement of music in time. It is the principle of organization and design that regulates the duration of the tones. Rhythm is the element of music most closely allied to body movement, to physical action. Its simpler patterns when repeated over and over have a hypnotic effect on us. For this reason rhythm has been called the heartbeat of music, the pulse that betokens life. It is this aspect of rhythm that people have in mind when they say of a dance-band musician that "he's got rhythm," meaning an electrifying quality, an aliveness almost independent of the notes. Yet, since music is an art that exists solely in time, rhythm in the larger sense controls all the relationships within a composition, from the over-all unity of its architecture to the minutest detail. Hence Roger Sessions's remark that "an adequate definition of rhythm comes close to defining music itself."

The Nature of Rhythm

We distinguish between the rhythms of prose and those of metrical poetry. The former are flexible and free, the latter more strictly organized. In music we may draw a similar distinction between elastic rhythms based on song-speech and the stricter rhythms that derive from the dance. It is the second kind that people generally have in mind when they speak of rhythm, that causes them to fall in step when the band plays, to nod or tap with the beat.

Rhythm releases our motor reflexes even if we do not respond with physical movement. We feel it in ourselves as a kind of ideal motion; we dance without leaving our chairs. Rhythm is the most important element in primitive music, projected in marvelously complex patterns by the tribal drums. It is primal energy unleashed, motion controlled. Before its conquering surge the shapeless minutes take on significance. Time becomes dynamic. Through the organizing power of rhythm, time becomes music.

Rhythm springs from the need for order inherent in the human mind. Upon the tick-tock of the clock or the clacking of train wheels we auto-

24

matically impose a pattern. We hear the sounds as a regular pulsation of strong and weak beats. In brief, we organize our perception of time by means of rhythm.

The ancients discerned in rhythm the creative principle of the universe, manifested alike in the regular movement of planets, the cycle of seasons and tides, of night and day, desire and appeasement, life and death. Yet these rhythms framed an existence that all too often lacked design and meaning. Rivers overflowed for no good reason, lightning struck, enemies pillaged. Exposed to the caprice of a merciless destiny, man fashioned for himself an ideal universe where the unforeseen was excluded and divine order reigned. This universe was art; and its con-

Nave arcade and mosaics, S. Apollinari Nuovo, Ravenna, 504 A.D.
"Rhythm springs from the need for order inherent in the human mind."

trolling principle was rhythm. The symmetrical proportions of architecture, the balanced groupings of painting and sculpture, the patterns of the dance, the regular meters of poetry—each in its own sphere represents man's deep-seated need for rhythmical arrangement. But it is in music, the art of ideal movement, that rhythm finds its richest expression.

Meter

Meter pertains to the organization of musical time; specifically, to the arrangement of musical beats in units of time known as *measures*. The measures contain a fixed number of beats and are marked off by the recurrence of a strong accent. In much of the music that we hear, the measures are of equal duration; that is to say, they contain the same number of beats. Meter constitutes the basic scheme of accents in a composition.

Every hour is equal in duration to the next. In our lives, however, each hour differs from the next in terms of its eventfulness. One hour will seem short because we are interested in what we are doing, another lags because we are not. We therefore distinguish between the hour as a fixed measure of sixty minutes and the hour as a changing unit of activity—between physical and psychological time. A similar distinction may be drawn between rhythm and meter. Meter connotes the fixed time units within which musical events take place. Within these units the rhythm flows freely—now more, now less eventfully. Thus rhythm is the pattern of musical activity, while meter is the pattern of musical time within which that activity unfolds. Meter involves the arrangement of beats into measures, while rhythm pertains to the arrangement of time values within the measure. Every waltz has the same meter: ONE-two-three, ONE-two-three. Within that meter, each waltz follows its own rhythm.

The distinction may be noted too in the domain of poetry. In reading a poem metrically we bring out the pattern of accented and unaccented syllables:

> When tó the sés - sions óf sweet sí - lent thóught
> I súm - mon úp re - mém - brance óf things pást,

When we read rhythmically, on the other hand, we bring out the natural flow of the language within the basic meter and, more important, the expressive meaning of the words. It is this distinction between rhythm and meter that the English critic Fox-Strangways has in mind when he observes: "A melody—an Irish reel perhaps—is in strict time, or people could not dance to it correctly; but if it had not also rhythm, they would not dance to it passionately."

Metrical Patterns

The simpler metrical patterns, in music as in poetry, depend on the regular recurrence of accent. Simplest of all is a succession of beats in which a strong alternates with a weak: ONE-two ONE-two—or in marching, LEFT-right LEFT-right. This is known as duple meter and is generally encountered as two-four time ($\frac{2}{4}$). The pattern occurs in many nursery rhymes and marching songs.

Twín - kle	twín - kle	lít - tle	stár - - - - -,
ONE - two	ONE - two	ONE - two	ONE - two

Hów I - -	wón - der	whát you	áre - - - -.
ONE - two	ONE - two	ONE - two	ONE - two

The best way to perceive rhythm is through physical response. The above tune can be tapped, while singing, with a downward movement of the hand on ONE and an upward movement on *two*.

Duple meter, then, contains two beats to the measure, of which the first is generally accented. Within this meter a tune such as *Yankee Doodle* presents a somewhat more eventful rhythmic pattern than the above example; *Dixie* and *Oh Susannah!* still more so. In these songs there is more than one melody tone to the beat. The meter is the steady ONE-two ONE-two that constitutes the underlying beat, above which flows the rhythmic pattern of the melody.

Yánkee Doodle	wént to town	Ríding on a	pó - ny
ONE - two	ONE - two	ONE - two	ONE - two

Another basic metrical pattern is that of an accented beat followed by two unaccented: three beats to the measure, or triple meter. This is the pattern of three-four time ($\frac{3}{4}$) traditionally associated with the waltz and minuet.

Two celebrated examples of triple meter are *America* and *The Star-Spangled Banner*.

Mý coun- try	'tís of thee,
ONE - two - three	ONE - two - three

Swéet land of	lí - - ber- ty
ONE - two - three	ONE - two - three

Óf thee I	síng ——————
ONE - two - three	ONE - two - three

Oh	sáy can you	sée —————— by the
three	ONE - two - three	ONE - two - three

dáwn's ear - ly	líght ——
ONE - two - three	ONE - two

Quadruple meter, also known as common time, contains four beats to the measure. The primary accent falls on the first beat of the measure, with a secondary accent on the third: ÓNE-two-Thrée-four. Quadruple meter, generally encountered as four-four time ($\frac{4}{4}$), is found in some of our most widely sung melodies: *Old Folks at Home; Old Black Joe;* the *Battle Hymn of the Republic; Long, Long Ago; Auld Lang Syne,* and a host of others.

Wáy —— dówn u - pon the	Swá - nee Ríver ——
ONE two Three four	ONE two Three four
Fár, —— fár a -	wáy ————————
ONE - two - Three - four	ONE - two - Three - four

Duple, triple, and quadruple meter are regarded as the simple meters. The compound meters contain five, six, seven, or more beats to the measure, with primary and secondary accents articulating the metrical pattern. Most frequently encountered among the compound meters is *sextuple meter:* six-four or six-eight time. This is often marked by a gently flowing effect. Popular examples are *My Bonnie Lies over the Ocean, Sweet and Low, Silent Night, Believe Me if All Those Endearing Young Charms, Drink to Me Only with Thine Eyes.*

Drínk to me ón - - ly	wí - ith thine éy - es and
ONE - two - three - Four - five - six	ONE - two - three - Four - five - six
Í——— will plé - edge with	míne ————————
ONE - two - three - Four - five - six	ONE - two - three - Four - five - six

The four patterns just discussed are the ones most frequent in the music of the nineteenth century, a period when musical rhythm was strongly influenced by folk and popular dance. The bulk of the output of that century—an enormous amount of music—falls into the patterns of two-four, three-four, four-four, and six-eight time. It bespeaks the ingenuity of composers that within these four meters they were able to achieve such diversity of rhythm in their works.

It will suffice to mention a few familiar examples of each of the various meters. Of duple meter: Brahms's Hungarian Dances Nos. 5 and 6; Schubert's *Marche militaire;* the Polka of Shostakovich. Three-four time is well illustrated by the Minuet from Mozart's Symphony No. 39 and the waltzes of Johann Strauss. For examples of quadruple meter listen to the Triumphal March from *Aïda* and the March from the *Love for Three Oranges.* The characteristically flowing effect of sextuple meter is set forth in such familiar pieces as the three *Venetian Boat Songs* of Mendelssohn; *Morning* from the *Peer Gynt Suite* of Grieg; and *The Sea and the Ship of Sinbad,* the first movement of Rimsky-Korsakov's *Scheherazade.*

The traditional patterns of meter make it possible for us to anticipate musical events. Through the regular recurrence of accent they set up expectancies in us that are sure to be fulfilled. They spring from and minister to our basic need for security.

"The Tyranny of the Bar Line"

In written music the measures are separated by a vertical bar line. (Hence the measure—the distance between two bar lines—is also known as a bar.) The principal accent falls on the first beat of the measure; in other words, immediately after the bar line. In simple meters such as duple, triple, and quadruple meter the bar line is consequently a symbol of the regular recurrence of accent.

Such regular meters were of great value in helping a mass public to follow a piece of music. They also helped to make it possible for people to sing and play together in large choruses and orchestras. Toward the end of the nineteenth century, however, composers rebelled more and more against "the tyranny of the bar line"—the inevitable recurrence of the accented ONE at the beginning of each measure. What had begun as a support ended by becoming a restraint.

To escape what to them seemed monotony, they disguised the trip-hammer beat of the meter with ever more complex rhythmic patterns within the measure. They also allowed the rhythm to flow across the bar line, thereby weakening the accent. And they embraced the irregular meters that we shall encounter in twentieth-century music. At this time poetry turned from regular meter to the more elastic patterns of free verse and prose. Music did the same.

Donatello, c. 1386–1466, Cantoria, Museum of the Cathedral, Florence.

"Through the power of rhythm the composer achieves a dimension in time comparable to what painter, sculptor, and architect achieve in space."

Of the many procedures used for escaping the fixed metrical pattern, the most common is *syncopation*. This term denotes a deliberate upsetting of the normal accent. Instead of falling on what is supposed to be the strong beat of the measure, the ONE, the accent is shifted to an off-beat. Through this irregularity the accent is made to conflict with the pattern that has been set up in the listener's mind. The pleasure of satisfying his expectations is abandoned for the equally important pleasure of surprise. Syncopation is associated in the popular mind with the Negro dance rhythms out of which modern jazz developed; but it has figured in European art music for centuries and was used by the masters with great subtlety.

To sum up: music is an art of movement in time. Rhythm, the artistic organization of musical movement, permeates every aspect of the musical process. It shapes the melody, the harmony, the form of the music. It binds together the parts within the whole: the notes within the measure, the measures within the phrase, the phrases within the period. Through the power of rhythm the composer achieves a dimension in time comparable to what painter, sculptor, and architect achieve in space.

Time is the crucial dimension in music. And its first law is rhythm.

⚜ *CHAPTER 6* ⚜

Tempo: Musical Pace

"The whole duty of a conductor is comprised in his ability to indicate the right tempo."

Richard Wagner

Tempo as an Element of Rhythm

METER tells us how many beats there are in the measure, but it does not tell us whether these beats occur slowly or rapidly. The *tempo*, by which we mean the rate of speed, the pace of the music, provides the answer to this vital matter. Consequently the flow of the music in time involves three matters: meter, which organizes musical time into measures; rhythm, which organizes time values within the measure; and tempo, which determines the speed of the beats, their duration in actual time.

Tempo carries emotional implications. We hurry our speech in moments of agitation. Our bodies press forward in eagerness, hold back in lassitude. Vigor and gayety are associated with a brisk gait as surely as despair demands a slow one. In an art of movement such as music, the rate of movement is of prime importance. We respond to musical tempo physically and psychologically. Our pulse, our breathing, our entire being adjusts to the rate of movement and to the feeling engendered thereby on the conscious and subconscious levels. Wagner's statement about tempo is of course an exaggeration, for the conductor has many other duties besides setting the tempo. It makes clear, however, that when a conductor hits on "the right tempo," he has correctly gauged the meaning and intent of a given composition.

Because of the close connection between tempo and mood, tempo markings indicate the character of the music as well as the pace. The tempo terms are generally given in Italian, a survival from the time when the opera of that nation dominated the European scene. Most frequently encountered are the following:

Very slow: *Largo* (broad)
            Grave (solemn)

Slow: *Lento*
            Adagio (gently, leisurely, slowly)

Moderate: *Andante* (going—at a walking pace)
            Andantino (a little andante, somewhat faster than andante)
            Moderato

Fairly fast: *Allegretto* (a little lively—not as fast as allegro)

Fast: *Allegro* (happy, cheerful, lively)

Very fast: *Allegro molto* (very lively)
            Vivace (vivacious, lively)
            Presto (very quick)
            Prestissimo (as quick as possible)

(For the pronunciation of these and other terms see the glossary in Appendix V.)

Largo has come to imply breadth and dignity; *grave*, pathos and heaviness; *adagio*, a tender or elegiac quality. Owing to the fact that musical practice changed considerably from the eighteenth century to the nineteenth, some of these terms carry with them a certain ambiguity. To the earlier period *andante* meant a "going" pace—that is, a fair degree of movement. To the nineteenth century it implied a slowish gait. Both meanings came to be accepted, which caused some confusion. Beethoven was not sure whether andantino was to be understood as being a bit slower or faster than andante. The above terms may be modified by adverbs such as *molto* (very), *meno* (less), *poco* (a little), and *non troppo* (not too much).

Of great importance are the terms indicating a change of tempo. The principal ones are *accelerando* (getting faster) and *ritardando* (holding back, getting slower); *a tempo* (in time) indicates a return to the original tempo.

Since tempo is inextricably associated with the mood and character of music, composers—especially during the nineteenth century—expanded the basic tempo terms to suggest the character of a composition or of a section thereof. Frequently encountered are the following: *adagio lamentoso* (slow and lamenting), *adagio espressivo* (slow and expressive), *largo e mesto* (very slow and sad), *andante maestoso* (fairly slow and majestic), *andante cantabile* (fairly slow and songful), *andante amoroso* (fairly slow and loving), *allegretto con grazia* (fairly fast, with grace), *allegro con brio* (fast, with vigor), *allegro appassionato* (fast and impassioned), and *allegro con fuoco* (fast, with fire). These are only a few of an extensive vocabulary of Italian, German, and French terms used by the romantic composers to indicate the emotional character of their music.

Determining the Tempo

Since tempo terms are indefinite, we need some means of determining precisely the pace of a musical work. This can be done only by indicating the time values of the notes in terms of minutes. To that end was devised the *metronome,* a mechanism consisting of a freely swinging pendulum with a movable weight and a scale of numbers behind it. When we slide the weight up or down to a certain marking, the pendulum swings that many times per minute, making a clicking sound with each movement. By writing = 60, the composer informs us that the piece is to be played at the rate of sixty quarter notes per minute. To establish this tempo we fix the weight at 60 and count one quarter note for each click of the metronome.

Metronome

Although the metronome was invented in the time of Beethoven, nineteenth-century composers did not make use of the device as extensively as might be supposed. Such exactitude was against the trend of the romantic period, which placed maximum emphasis on the mood of the interpreter. The metronome marking seemed to impose the tempo from without instead of allowing it to spring from the performer's feelings. The majority of composers continued with the general terms, permitting each player to adjust the pace to his own understanding of the music. Modern composers, on the other hand, take a kindlier view of metronome markings, which substitute an objective standard for the performer's feelings; with the result that such markings are widely used in twentieth-century music.

There can be no question, of course, of the performer's playing with or like a metronome. Musical tempo is a much more elastic concept than physical time. The movement of a piece, like speech, is a live thing, now pressing forward, now holding back. No artist playing the same work on two occasions could possibly duplicate the tempo throughout, with its infinite nuances, its subtle accelerations and retardations. The musician adheres to the beat in order to project a clear picture of the meter, rhythm, and tempo; he also departs from the beat in order to achieve the necessary suppleness of movement. In this way he breathes life into what would otherwise be a mechanical thing, transforming the music into a free flow of thought and feeling.

✿✿✿ C H A P T E R 7 ✿✿✿

Timbre: Musical Color

"Lucidity is the first purpose of color in music."
Arnold Schoenberg

A TONE produced by a trumpet will have a certain quality; the same tone on a violin will sound quite different. The difference lies in the characteristic color, or *timbre*, of each instrument. (The word retains its French pronunciation, *tám'br*.) Timbre focuses our musical impressions. It imparts to the tonal image its special and inalienable character. By the way in which the composer chooses his timbres he creates the particular sound-world that a given piece inhabits.

The composer has at his disposal two basic media—human voices and musical instruments. He may write for any combination of these that suits his purpose. His selecting one medium rather than another is due to a number of circumstances, some of which may be wholly external. Stravinsky tells how, during the First World War when it was difficult to assemble and rehearse large orchestras, he turned to the small ensemble (and thereby gave impetus to one of the important trends in twentieth-century music). A composer may be commissioned to write in a specific medium—a piece for three instruments, or for chorus; or, having exploited certain media in his art, he may feel impelled to explore others. Certain composers have a natural affinity for one medium rather than another, as in the case of Chopin's devotion to the piano. Then again, an idea may come to a composer's mind clothed in a definite instrumental color, for which none other will do.

In essence the composer is motivated by the same principle that makes the painter choose now oils, now water colors or etching. The nature of the thing to be said demands one medium rather than another. The composer selects the medium that will best express the quality and the meaning of his ideas. Once he has made his choice—a choral piece, let us say, or a string quartet—the medium in turn imposes its character upon the musical conception, shaping it, focusing it, and quite often inspiring fresh ideas. Thus a mutual relationship is set up. The idea determines the choice of medium; the medium determines the fate of the idea.

The composer constantly keeps in mind the nature of the medium that he has chosen. He takes into account the capacities and limitations of each instrument; he tries to make it do the things for which it is best suited. To write idiomatically for an instrument means to function musically within its limitations—perhaps even to transmute these into fresh sources of beauty. There are, to begin with, the limits of each instrument's range—the distance from its lowest to its highest tone, beyond which it cannot go. There are also the limits of dynamics—the degree of softness or loudness beyond which it cannot be played. There are technical peculiarities native to its low, middle, and high register, as a result of which a certain formation of notes will be executed more easily on one instrument than another. An instrument like the tuba, for example, sustains tones well but is unwieldy in rapid scale passages. Another such as the piano is agile in rapid passages but does not sustain tone well. These and a host of similar considerations determine the composer's choice as he clothes his ideas in their instrumental garb.

Certain composers have a more vivid color sense than others. The great masters of orchestration possess it in the highest degree. One thing is clear: tone color is not something that is grafted on to the musical conception; it is part and parcel of the idea, as inseparable from it as are its harmony and rhythm. Timbre is more than an element of sensuous charm that is added to a work; it is one of the shaping forces in music.

CHAPTER 8

Instruments of the Orchestra

"With these artificial voices we sing in a manner such as our natural voices would never permit."

John Redfield: *Music—A Science and an Art*

INSTRUMENTS have always been a source of wonder to those who made, played, and listened to them. The ancients attributed their invention to gods—Apollo, Pan, Mercury—or to legendary figures. Those who mastered their secrets were said to possess supernatural powers. Amphion, when the walls of Thebes were built, charmed the stones into place with his lyre. Orpheus calmed the wild beasts and moved even the god of death to pity. Man's first instrument was his body, both for vocal melody and, through slapping and stamping, for rhythm. To enhance the effect, he created the rude rattles, drums, and clappers with which the history of musical instruments began.

The music produced by any culture is very much influenced by the instruments available to its musicians. The composer depends for the realization of his ideas on the performer, who in turn depends on the maker of instruments. In early times all three were apt to be the same individual. As technology advances, instrument makers turn out ever more responsive instruments. This stimulates the performer to greater virtuosity, which impels the composer to make greater demands upon both performers and instruments. The result is that instrumental technique rises steadily through the ages. Works of Gluck, Beethoven, Wagner, Richard Strauss, and Schoenberg were pronounced unplayable by those who first had to perform them. What seemed impossible at one time became the accepted procedure of a later age.

An instrument is a mechanism that is able to generate musical vibrations and launch them into the air. Each instrument, according to its capacities, enables us to control the four properties of musical sound: pitch, duration, volume, and color (timbre).

By *pitch* we mean the location of a tone in the musical scale in relation to high or low. The pitch is determined by the rate of vibration, which to a large extent depends on the length of the vibrating body. Other conditions being equal, the shorter a string or column of air, the more rapidly it vibrates and the higher the pitch. The longer a string or column of air, the fewer the vibrations per second and the lower the pitch. The width, thickness, density, and tension of the vibrating body also affect the outcome.

Duration depends on the length of time over which vibration is maintained. We hear tones as being not only high or low but also short or long.

Greek vase, fifth century B.C. Apollo holding a Kithara.

"The ancients attributed the invention of instruments to gods —Apollo, Pan, Mercury—or to legendary figures."

Volume (dynamics) depends on the degree of force of the vibrations, as a result of which the tone strikes us as being loud or soft. As for the timbre or tone color, that depends on how the instrument accentuates the overtones within the sound wave. This is influenced by a number of factors, such as the size, shape, and the proportions of the instrument, the material of which it is made, and the manner in which vibration is set up.

The oldest and still the most popular of all instruments is the human voice. In no other instrument is the contact between performer and medium so intimate. In none other is expression so personal and direct. The voice is the ideal exponent of lyric melody and has consistently been the model for those who make instruments as well as for those who play them. Instruments can do things that are impossible for the voice to execute, yet it is the highest praise we can bestow upon a performer to say that he makes his instrument sing.

Instruments figure in our music singly; in small groups (chamber music); and as part of that most spectacular of ensembles, the orchestra. In the orchestra they are divided into four sections: string, woodwind, brass, and percussion.

The String Section

The string section of the orchestra includes four instruments—violin, viola, violoncello (or cello), and double bass. These have four strings, which are set vibrating by drawing a bow across them. The hair of the bow is rubbed with rosin so that it will "grip" the strings. The player holds the bow in his right hand. He *stops* the string by pressing down a finger of his left hand at a particular point on the fingerboard, thereby leaving a certain portion of the string free to vibrate. By stopping the string at another point he changes the length of the vibrating portion, and with it the rate of vibration and the pitch.

The *violin* was brought to its present form by the brilliant instrument makers who flourished in Italy from around 1600 to 1750. Most famous among them were the Amati and Guarnieri families—in these dynasties the secrets of the craft were transmitted from father to son—and the master builder of them all, Antonio Stradivari (c. 1644–1737).

The violin is universally admired for its singing tone, which brings it of all instruments closest to the human voice. Pre-eminent in lyric melody, it is also capable of brilliance and dramatic effect, of subtle nuances from soft to loud, of the utmost rhythmic precision and great agility in rapid passages. The violin has an extremely wide range. (For the comparative range of the instruments and the tuning of the strings, see Appendix III.)

The *viola* is somewhat larger than the violin. Its strings are longer, thicker, heavier; it is lower in range. The tone is husky in the low register, somber and penetrating in the high. The viola is an effective melody instrument, particularly for themes of a mournful or passionate nature. It often serves as a foil for the more brilliant violin by playing a secondary melody. It usually fills in the harmony, or doubles—that is, reinforces by duplicating, usually at an octave—the other parts.

The *violoncello*, popularly known as cello, is lower in range than the viola and is notable for its lyric quality, which takes on a dark resonance in the low register. Composers value highly its expressive tone. In the orchestra the cellos perform functions similar to those of the violins

Above: Violin, Viola, bow and mute. *Below:* Cello, Double Bass and violas. They often carry the melody. They enrich the sonority with their full-throated songfulness. They accentuate the rhythm. And together with the basses they supply the foundation for the harmony of the string choir.

The *double bass,* known also as contrabass or bass viol, is the lowest in range of the string group. Accordingly, it plays the bass part—that is, the foundation of the harmony. Its deep indistinct tones come into focus when they are duplicated an octave higher, usually by the cello. When this is done, the double bass assumes great carrying power and furnishes basic support for the entire orchestra. In more recent music, the dark timbre of the instrument has also been much used to achieve special color effects.

The string instruments are pre-eminent in playing *legato* (smooth and connected), though they are capable too of the opposite quality of tone, *staccato* (short and detached). A special effect, *pizzicato* (plucked), is executed by the performer's plucking the string with his finger instead of using the bow. *Vibrato* denotes the rich, throbbing tone achieved when the player moves his finger slightly away from and back to the required spot. This enrichment of the tone heightens the expressiveness of the string instruments. In *glissando* the player moves a finger of his left hand rapidly along the string, sounding all the pitches of the scale. *Tremolo,* the rapid repetition of a tone through a quick up-and-down movement of the bow, is associated in the popular mind with suspense and excitement. No less important is the *trill,* a rapid alternation between a tone and its upper neighbor, often giving a birdlike effect. (The trill is not limited to string instruments.) *Double-stopping* involves playing two or more strings simultaneously. Thereby the members of the violin family, essentially melodic instruments, become capable of harmony. The *mute* is a small attachment that fits over the bridge, muffling (and changing) the sound. *Harmonics* are flutelike crystalline tones in the very high register. They are produced by lightly touching the string at certain points while the bow is drawn across the string. (See Appendix VII.)

The string section has come to be known as "the heart of the orchestra." The title indicates the versatility and general usefulness of this group. The strings also figure prominently as solo instruments and in chamber music: in duets, trios, quartets, quintets, and the like.

The Woodwind Section

The woodwind section of the orchestra consists of members of four different families: flute and piccolo; oboe and English horn; clarinet and bass clarinet; bassoon and contrabassoon. Saxophones are also included in this group. Besides being prominent in the orchestra, the woodwinds possess a solo literature and are widely used in chamber music.

The tone is produced by a column of air vibrating within a pipe that has little holes in its side. When one or another of these holes is opened or closed, the length of the vibrating air column within the pipe is changed. The woodwind instruments are capable of remarkable agility by means of an intricate mechanism of keys arranged so as to suit the natural position of the fingers.

The woodwinds have a long history. They are descended from the pipes and reeds of the ancient civilizations of the East. Introduced into Europe in early times, they gradually evolved into the forms we know today. They add a variety of striking timbres to the orchestral palette, and are invaluable in creating atmosphere and in presenting novel ideas. However, the woodwinds cannot be used as extensively as the more neutral strings; for the more distinctive the color of an instrument, the sooner the ear tires of it.

The *flute* is the coloratura soprano of the woodwind choir. Its timbre ranges from the poetic to the brilliant. Its tone is cool and velvety in the expressive low register, and smooth in the middle. In the upper part of the range the timbre is bright, birdlike, and stands out against the orchestral mass. The present-day flute, made of a silver alloy rather than wood, is a cylindrical tube that is held horizontally. It is closed at one end. The player blows across a mouth hole (embouchure) cut in the side of the pipe at the other end. The flute is much prized as a melody instrument and offers the player complete freedom in playing rapid repeated notes, scales, and trills.

The *piccolo* (from the Italian *flauto piccolo,* "little flute") has a piercing tone that produces the highest notes in the orchestra. In its upper register it takes on a shrillness that is easily heard even when the orchestra is playing full blast. For this reason the instrument contributes to many an orchestral climax. On the other hand, composers are coming more and more to make use of the limpid singing quality of its lower register.

The *oboe* is made of wood. The double reed in the mouthpiece consists of two slips of cane so shaped as to leave between them an extremely small passage for air. Because of this compression, the tone is focused and intense in all registers. Oboe timbre is generally described as plaintive, nasal, reedy. The instrument is associated with pastoral effects and with nostalgic melodies. The pitch of the oboe, once correctly established, is not readily subject to change, for which reason it is chosen to sound the A for the other instruments when the orchestra tunes up.

The *English horn* is in the nature of an alto oboe. Its wooden tube is wider and longer than that of the oboe and ends in a pear-shaped bell, which largely accounts for its soft, somewhat mournful timbre. The instrument would be well named were it not for the fact that it is neither English nor a horn. Its expressive, gently poignant tone made it a favorite with the nineteenth-century romantics. Berlioz, speaking of his *Symphonie fantastique*, explains that "the English horn repeats the phrases of the oboe in the lower octave, like the voice of a youth replying to a girl in a pastoral dialogue." His aim, he indicates, was a mood "of sorrowful loneliness."

The *clarinet* has a single reed, a small elastic piece of cane fastened against its chisel-shaped mouthpiece. The instrument possesses a beautiful liquid tone, clear and powerful in the high register, relaxed in the middle, cool and almost spectral in the low. It has a remarkably wide range from low to high and from soft to loud. The clarinet is a favorite

Piccolo   Flute   Oboe   English horn Clarinet   Bass clarinet

instrument when it comes to playing melody. Almost as agile as the flute, it has an easy command of rapid scales, trills, and repeated notes. The bass clarinet's range is one octave lower. Its rich singing tone, its flexibility and wide dynamic range make it an invaluable member of the orchestral community.

The *bassoon* belongs to the double-reed family. Its tone is weighty and thick in the low register, dry and sonorous in the middle, reedy and intense in the upper. It is one of the most flexible and useful of the bass instruments. Capable of a hollow-sounding staccato and wide leaps that

Bassoon   Contrabassoon   Saxophone

create a humorous effect, it is at the same time a highly expressive instrument. The contrabassoon, known also as double bassoon, produces the lowest tone in the orchestra. Its tube, over sixteen feet in length, is folded four times around to make it less unwieldy. Its function in the woodwind section may be compared to that of the double bass among the strings, in that it supplies a foundation for the harmony. In recent times the double bassoon has been much used for its tone color.

The *saxophone* is of fairly recent origin, having been invented by Adolphe Sax of Brussels in 1840. It was created by combining the features of several other instruments—the single reed of the clarinet, the conical tube of the oboe, and the metal body of the brass instruments. The saxophone blends well with either woodwinds or brass. In the 1920s it became the characteristic instrument of the jazz band. French composers have been partial to it from the first; but, although it figures prominently in a number of important modern scores, it has not yet established itself as a permanent member of the orchestra.

The woodwinds are a less homogeneous group than the strings. Nowadays they are not necessarily made of wood, and they represent several methods of setting up vibration: by blowing across a mouth hole (flute family); by blowing into a mouthpiece that has a single reed (clarinet and saxophone families); by blowing into a mouthpiece fitted with a double reed (oboe and bassoon families). They do, however, have two features in common: first, the holes in the side of the pipe; and second, their timbres, which are such that composers think of them and write for them as a group.

The Brass Section

The brass section consists of the trumpet, horn, trombone, and tuba. They are indispensable for melody, for sustaining harmony, for rhythmic accent, for the weight of their massed tone, and for the flamelike sonority they contribute to climaxes. These instruments have cup-shaped mouthpieces (except for the horn, whose mouthpiece is shaped like a funnel). The column of air within the tube is set vibrating by the tightly stretched lips of the player, which act as a kind of double reed. To go from one pitch to another requires not only mechanical means, such as a slide or valves, but also variation in the pressure of the lips and breath. This demands great muscular control.

Trumpets and horns were widely used in the ancient world. The primitive instruments were fashioned from the horns and tusks of animals, which at a more advanced stage of civilization were reproduced in metal. They were used chiefly for military signals and in religious ceremonies. Their tone was on the terrifying side, as is evidenced by what happened to the walls of Jericho.

Mechanical improvements introduced in the early nineteenth century made available a brass section more maneuverable than ever before. Although these instruments are not as maneuverable as either wood-winds or strings, succeeding generations of players have learned to handle them with ever greater virtuosity. Besides playing an important role in the orchestra, the members of the brass choir have come to figure prominently in twentieth-century chamber music and in the modern dance band.

Trumpet and mute

The *trumpet* possesses a firm, brilliant timbre that lends radiance to the orchestral mass. It is associated with martial pomp and vigor. Its hard, lean sonority appeals to the modern temper, with the result that twentieth-century composers have assigned to it some memorable solos in their works. Played softly, the instrument commands a lovely round tone. The muted trumpet is much used; the mute, a pear-shaped device of metal or cardboard, is inserted in the bell. When the muted tone is forced, a harsh snarling sound results that is not soon forgotten. Jazz trumpet players have experimented with various kinds of mutes, and these are gradually finding their way into the symphony orchestra.

The *horn,* generally called the French horn, is an evocative instrument. Descended from the hunting horn, the instrument was a favorite with nineteenth-century composers, who identified its timbre with the

French horn

sound of nature. Its golden resonance lends itself to a variety of uses: it can be mysteriously remote in soft passages, and nobly sonorous in loud. The timbre of the horn blends equally well with woodwinds, brass, and strings, for which reason it serves as the connecting link among them. Although capable of considerable agility, the horn is at its best in sustained utterance; for sheer majesty, nothing rivals the sound of several horns intoning a broadly flowing theme in unison. The muted horn has a poetic faraway sound; if the muted tone is forced, however, the result is an ominous rasping quality.

The *trombone*—the Italian word means "large trumpet"—has a grand sonorousness that combines the brilliance of the trumpet with the majesty of the horn. In place of valves it has a movable U-shaped slide that alters the length of the vibrating air column in the tube. (The valve trombone is used occasionally, but lacks the orotund tone

Trombone

of the slide trombone.) Composers consistently avail themselves of the trombone to achieve effects of nobility and grandeur. "Directed by the will of a master," writes Hector Berlioz, "the trombones can chant like a choir of priests, threaten, utter gloomy sighs, a mournful lament, or a bright hymn of glory."

The *tuba* is the bass of the brass choir. Like the string bass and contrabassoon, it furnishes the foundation for the harmonic fabric. It is surprisingly responsive for so unwieldy an instrument. To play it requires—among other things—good teeth and plenty of wind. The tuba adds body to the orchestral tone, and a dark resonance ranging from velvety softness to a growl.

Mention should be made, too, of the brass instruments used in military and outdoor bands. Most important of these is the *cornet*, which was developed early in the nineteenth century from the post-horn. The cornet has a shorter body than the trumpet and possesses greater agility. (It is basically an instrument of conical shape, whereas the body of the trumpet is cylindrical for the greater part of its length.) The tone of the cornet is rounder but less brilliant than that of the trumpet. Because of the comparative ease with which it is played, the cornet has become the mainstay of brass bands and small orchestras of

Tuba   Tenor tuba
                              (euphonium, baryton)

the music-hall type. Among the brass-band instruments are the *flügel-horn,* which is similar in shape to the cornet but wider; the *baritone* and *euphonium,* which are tenor tubas; and the *helicon,* which is a double bass tuba in circular form, so that the player is able to carry the instrument over his shoulder. (An American type of helicon is the sousaphone, named after John Philip Sousa, who suggested its specially designed bell.) The *bugle,* originally a hunter's horn, has a powerful tone that carries in the open air. Since it is not equipped with valves, it is able to sound only certain tones of the scale, which accounts for the familiar pattern of military duty calls.

Cornet

The Percussion Instruments

The percussion section comprises a variety of instruments that are made to sound by striking or shaking. Certain ones are made of metal or wood. In others, such as the drums, vibration is set up by striking a stretched skin.

The percussion section of the orchestra is sometimes referred to as "the battery." Its members accentuate the rhythm, generate excitement in climactic moments, and inject splashes of color into the orchestral sound. Like seasoning in food, they are most effective when used sparingly.

The percussion instruments fall into two categories, those of definite and those of indefinite pitch. In the former class are the kettledrums, or timpani, which are used in sets of two or three. The *kettledrum* is a

Kettledrum

hemispheric copper shell across which is stretched a "head" of calfskin held in place by a metal ring. Adjustable screws or a pedal mechanism enable the player to change the tension of the calfskin head, and with it the pitch. The instrument is played with two padded sticks, which may be either soft or hard. Its dynamic range extends from a mysterious rumble to a thunderous roll. The muffled drum frequently

Glockenspiel   Celesta

figures in passages that seek to evoke an atmosphere of mystery or mourning. The *glockenspiel* (German for a set of bells) consists of a series of horizontal tuned plates of various sizes, made of steel. The player strikes these with mallets, producing a bright metallic sound. The *celesta*, which in appearance resembles a miniature upright piano, is a kind of glockenspiel that is operated by a keyboard: the steel plates are struck by small hammers and produce an ethereal sound. The *xylophone* consists of tuned blocks of wood which produce a dry, crisp

Xylophone

timbre when struck. Expert xylophone players attain dazzling speed and accuracy. Contemporary composers are partial to the instrument's hollow, "objective" tone. The *marimba*, a xylophone of African and

Marimba

South American origin, is associated with exotic dance music. The *vibraphone* combines the principle of the xylophone with propellers, one to each note, which are driven by an electric motor. Its highly unusual tone is marked by a slow vibrato that can be controlled by chang-

Vibraphone

ing the speed of the motor. The instrument, also known as a *vibraharp* or metal xylophone, plays a prominent part in jazz, and has been used by a number of contemporary composers. *Chimes* consist of a set of tuned metal tubes of various lengths suspended from a frame and

Chimes

struck with a hammer. They have a broad dynamic range, from a metallic tinkle to a sonorous clang, and are frequently called upon to simulate church bells.

Bass drum

Side or Snare drum (snares are on the underside)   Tenor drum

Tambourine   Castanets

Triangle   Cymbals   Gong

Among the percussion instruments of indefinite pitch are the *bass drum;* the *side drum,* also known as *snare drum;* the *tenor drum; tambourine* and *castanets;* the *triangle, cymbals,* and *gong.*

Other Instruments

The *harp* is one of the oldest of musical instruments. It appears in its earliest form on Babylonian inscriptions of over four thousand years ago. It was the traditional instrument of the bards of ancient Britain

Harp

and Ireland, and became the national emblem of the latter country. Its strings are played by plucking and produce a crystalline tone that blends well with the orchestral timbres. The pedals are used to shorten the strings, hence to raise the pitch.

Chords on the harp are frequently played in broken form; that is, the tones are sounded one after another instead of simultaneously. From this circumstance comes the term *arpeggio,* which means a broken chord (*arpa* is the Italian for "harp"). Arpeggios occur in a variety of forms on many instruments. By breaking up the chord instead of sounding it in block formation, composers are able to extend a harmony over a period of time and to arrange it in diverse rhythmic figures.

The *piano,* a most popular instrument, is widely used in the home as well as on the concert stage. Whereas the violinist or clarinetist needs someone to accompany him, the pianist is able to play both melody and harmony. This self-sufficiency makes the piano an extremely useful instrument. It is indispensable for accompanying; is widely used in small orchestras and dance bands; and is of great assistance to musicians in the study of operatic and orchestral scores.

A modern concert grand piano.

The full name of the instrument is *pianoforte,* the Italian for "soft-loud," which indicates its wide dynamic range and its capacity for nuance. Its strings are struck with little hammers controlled by a keyboard mechanism. The piano cannot sustain tone as well as the string and wind instruments, but in the hands of a fine performer it is capable nonetheless of singing melody. Each string (except in the highest register) is covered by a damper that stops the tone when the finger releases the key. By pressing down a pedal the dampers are raised, so that the strings continue to vibrate together, thereby producing that luminous haze of sound which the great piano composers used to such advantage. The piano is pre-eminent for brilliant scales, arpeggios and trills, rapid passages and octaves. It has a wide range from lowest to highest tone and commands great rhythmic vitality. Nineteenth-century piano writing leaned toward sensuous beauty and lyricism. Present-day composers have found a new use for the piano as a rhythmic percussion instrument of crisp sonority, both solo and as a member of the orchestra.

The *organ*, once regarded as "the king of instruments," is a wind instrument; air is fed to its pipes by mechanical means. The pipes are controlled by two or more keyboards and a set of pedals. Gradations in the volume of tone are made possible on the modern organ by means of swell boxes. The organ possesses a multicolored sonority and majestic harmonies that fill a huge space. Organ builders of the nineteenth century tried to make the instrument imitate the orchestra as closely as possible. In recent years a reaction set in: many organ builders favor a return to the pure, transparent sonorities of the instrument for which Bach, Handel, and earlier masters wrote their works. Nowadays the electronic organ is coming into use. Here the sound is produced not

A modern
baroque organ.

by wind but by electrical oscillators.

The instruments described in this chapter form a vivid and diversified group. To composer, performer, and listener alike they offer a rich palette that embraces manifold possibilities of color and shades of expression.

CHAPTER 9

The Orchestra

"Orchestration is part of the very soul of the work. A work is thought out in terms of the orchestra, certain tone-colors being inseparable from it in the mind of its creator and native to it from the hour of its birth."

Nicholas Rimsky-Korsakov

FROM the group of approximately twenty that Bach had at his disposal or of the thirty-odd that Mozart knew, the modern orchestra has grown into an ensemble that may call for more than a hundred players. These musicians, many of artist stature, give their full time to rehearsal and performance, achieving a precision of ensemble playing unknown in former times.

The orchestra is constituted with a view to securing the best balance of tone. The performers are divided into the four sections we have described. In large orchestras approximately two thirds are string players, one third are wind players. From three to five men take care of the percussion. The following distribution is typical of the modern orchestra.

	18 first violins
	16 second violins
Strings, about 65:	12 violas
	10 violoncellos
	10 double basses
	3 flutes, 1 piccolo
Woodwinds, about 15:	3 oboes, 1 English horn
	3 clarinets, 1 bass clarinet
	3 bassoons, 1 double bassoon
	4 horns
Brass, 11:	3 trumpets
	3 trombones
	1 tuba

Percussion, 5:

2 kettledrum players
3 men for bass and side drum, glockenspiel, celesta, xylophone, triangle, cymbals, tambourine, etc.

It will be noticed that there are about 34 violins, which are divided into two groups, first and second. Each functions as a unit and plays a separate part. In the woodwind section one of the players of the principal instrument generally doubles on the related one. The third flutist, for example, also plays the piccolo. Saxophones are added when called for in the score. Certain works call for a larger brass section with additional horns and one or more extra trumpets. Included in these large ensembles are two harps and, for certain contemporary scores, a piano.

The instruments are arranged so as to secure effective blending and contrast. Most of the strings are up front. Brass and percussion are at the back. Following is a characteristic seating plan.

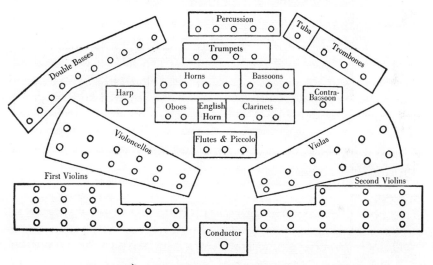

Typical seating plan of a symphony orchestra.

The arrangement shown above is modified in several of our major orchestras, in which first and second violins are grouped on the conductor's left, while cellos and violas sit on his right. In the back row, the percussion may be placed on the left, trombones and tuba in the center, double basses on the right.

The ensemble is directed by the conductor, who beats time and indicates the entrances of the various instruments, the shadings in the volume of tone, the principal and subordinate lines, and a host of related details that serve to make clear the structure of the work. Poised on the podium, baton raised—some prefer to do without—the con-

ductor may be likened to a commander at the head of his troops. It is
his task to bring the ensemble to life, to impose upon it a unifying
conception, and to mold the group into a perfectly coordinated body.

The conductor has before him the score of the work. This consists
of from a few to as many as twenty-five or more staves, each representing one or more instrumental parts. All the staves together comprise a single composite line. What is going on at any moment in the
orchestra is indicated at any given point straight down the page. It

A page from Stravinsky's *Petrushka*, showing the arrangement of instrumental parts in an orchestral score.

will be observed from the illustration that the instruments are grouped in families, the woodwinds on top, then the brass, percussion, and strings.

The Art of Orchestration

The composer bent over a page of score paper may be compared to a weaver intertwining strands of various hues or a painter mixing colors on his palette. He envisions the color scheme in his imagination as he blends and contrasts the timbres. He assigns his themes to the instruments that will present them most effectively. He fashions the score so that the melody will stand out clearly against the background. At the same time he sees to it that the accompanying lines are interesting in their own right. He distributes the material among the various instruments and groups, pitting one against the other and creating an interplay of the multicolored strands. He judges accurately the kind of sound he desires, be it powerful, caressing, or delicate; and he uses color to highlight the rhythmic patterns and the architectonic design, to set off the principal ideas from the subordinate, and to weld the innumerable details into a whole.

In solving the manifold problems of orchestration he is aided in the first place by that aptitude for overcoming difficulties which we call talent, in the second by years of study and careful listening to orchestral works. He is aided too by a tradition of more than three hundred years, the common practice of generations that transcends the wisdom of any one master in that it represents the cumulative experience of all. The tradition guides him through his apprenticeship and continues to stimulate him in his maturity.

The foregoing should dispel the widespread misconception that one man writes the music while another orchestrates it. This is true of popular dance music, the scores of the average musical comedy, and Hollywood. But in art music, as the quotation from Rimsky-Korsakov makes clear, the two functions cannot be separated. We could nò more imagine Brahms's music with Wagner's orchestration than picture a familiar face with someone else's nose. What the composer says and how he says it are part and parcel of his individual manner of conceiving sound, his musical physiognomy. So personal is this that we can often recognize the composer solely from the way the horns or strings are handled.

Erroneous too is the notion that the composer first writes his orchestral piece for the piano and then arranges it for instruments. An orchestral work, from its inception, is conceived in terms of the orchestra. Its shape and idiom derive from the nature of the instruments.

It cannot come to life in any other medium. If many composers like to
have a piano in the room while writing, it is primarily because this
gives them contact with the living sound. But the piano is no more
able to render a symphonic piece than a black-and-white reproduction
can reveal the quality of a Raphael or a Titian.

Listening to the orchestra is a favorite pastime of the musical public
today. Most of this listening is done via phonograph, radio, and television, so that many listeners never come in contact with the living
orchestral sound. A pity, for the best way to become familiar with the
orchestral instruments is to be in the concert hall, where one can see
as well as hear them. Recorded music plays a vital role in our musical
life, but it should be regarded as a preparation for the live performance,
not as a substitute.

The Orchestra in Action

We shall in the course of this book have ample occasion to comment
on how various composers wrote for the orchestra. At this point, however, the reader may find a helpful introduction to the orchestra in a
work such as Prokofiev's perennially popular *Peter and the Wolf*, a "symphonic tale for children young and old." In this work the Russian master
set himself the task of acquainting youngsters with the instruments of
the orchestra. He therefore associated each character in his tale with
a striking tone color and a characteristic theme. The wolf is represented
by the French horns, Peter by the strings, Peter's grandfather by the
bassoon, the bird by the flute, the duck by the oboe, the cat by the
clarinet in low register, and the shooting of the hunters by the kettle-

The New York Philharmonic Orchestra.

drums and bass drum. Each instrument is used characteristically, so that its nature and capacities are revealed. For those who have not had much experience in following the various strands of color in the orchestral web, this delightful work will serve as a fine guide to the orchestra in action. (For other works that illustrate the capacities of the orchestra, see the list of recordings for this chapter in Appendix I.)

Tchaikovsky's *Nutcracker Suite* is a particularly fine example of vivid orchestral sonorities. (The word *suite*, as the nineteenth century used it, indicates an instrumental work consisting of a number of short movements unified by a central idea. The suite may be either an independent work or a set of pieces drawn from a larger work.) The *Nutcracker Suite* was drawn from a Christmas Eve ballet concerning a little girl who dreams that the nutcracker she received as a gift has turned into a handsome prince. Russian nutcrackers are often shaped like a human head, hence the transformation. The fairy-tale atmosphere impelled Tchaikovsky to some enchanting music.

The Miniature Overture sets the mood. It is in $\frac{2}{4}$ time, marked Allegro giusto (fast, in strict time). To achieve an effect of lightness and grace Tchaikovsky omitted the bass instruments—cellos, double basses, trombones, tuba—as well as trumpets. The percussion section is represented only by the triangle. The dainty effect is enhanced by the use of staccato and the prevalence of the upper register. The sense of climax at the end is achieved through an increase in volume of tone and a rise in pitch.

There follows the March, in a lively $\frac{4}{4}$ time. The characteristic march rhythm is set forth by clarinets, horns, and trumpets. The triplet rhythm is widely associated with military flourishes, but in this setting takes on a fanciful quality. Winds are answered by strings—a widely used orchestral device. Worthy of note is the filigree work in the accompaniment, in this case presented by the cellos and double basses pizzicato, an effect dear to Tchaikovsky's heart. In the middle section a staccato theme in high register, presented by three flutes and clarinet, vividly conveys a suggestion of ballet movement.

"I have discovered a new instrument in Paris, something between a piano and a glockenspiel, with a divinely beautiful tone," wrote Tchaikovsky to his publisher in 1891. "I want to introduce this into the ballet." The instrument was the celesta, whose ethereal sound pervades the Dance of the Sugar-Plum Fairy. The piece, marked Andante non troppo (fairly slow, not too much so) is in $\frac{2}{4}$ time. It opens with four bars of pizzicato introduction, whereupon the celesta tone is effectively contrasted with that of the bass clarinet. There is a passage for celesta alone, after which the opening theme is repeated. In the theater this music is inevitably associated with a ballerina swathed in diaphanous veils.

The Trepak or Russian Dance, marked Molto vivace (very lively), is in $\frac{2}{4}$ time. The short measure and heavy accents create the suggestion of vigorous physical movement proper to a peasant dance. The full orchestral sonority is enlivened by the presence of the tambourine. Tchaikovsky, at the end, achieves a climax through an increase in the volume of sound (crescendo), and an acceleration of pace (accelerando).

The little girl and her prince are entertained by various sweetmeats in the castle of the Sugar-Plum Fairy. Coffee dances the Arab Dance, a subdued number marked Allegretto that forms an effective contrast with the Trepak that preceded. It is in $\frac{3}{8}$ time. Muted violas and cellos set up a rhythmic *ostinato*—that is, a rhythmic figure repeated over and over with an almost hypnotic insistence. Against this dark curtain of sound, after introductory chords in the woodwinds, the muted violins unfold an oriental-sounding melody. The steady throb of a tambourine adds the properly exotic touch. Striking is the long-drawn-out wail of the oboe, in upper register, over the quiet movement of the melody and harmony in the strings below. The music dies away at the end.

Tea, not to be outdone, presents the Chinese Dance, Allegro moderato, in $\frac{4}{4}$ time. Bassoons, playing staccato, establish a rhythmic ostinato against which flute and piccolo trace a somewhat shrill melody. Whether this music bears any resemblance to that heard in Peking is beside the point. It is sufficiently close to what Western ears have come popularly to regard as Chinese—which means that it is pleasantly exotic and colorful.

The Dance of the Toy Flutes, marked Moderato assai (very moderate) and in $\frac{2}{4}$ time, has always been a favorite with devotees of Tchaikovsky. Against a pizzicato accompaniment of violas, cellos, and double basses, three flutes outline a suave and beguiling melody. A short solo on the English horn arrests the ear, after which the opening theme returns. The middle section of the piece is devoted to a telling idea presented by the trumpets, with a slight swell as the melodic line ascends and a decrease in volume as it moves downward. After this the gracious melody of the flutes is heard again.

The Waltz of the Flowers that closes the suite displays to the full Tchaikovsky's gifts as a composer of ballet music. It is marked Tempo di Valse and is in $\frac{3}{4}$ time. Flowing melody and brilliancy of color are here associated with that sense of movement and gesture which are of the essence in the dance theater. The introduction alternates chords in the woodwinds and horns with arpeggios on the harp. The harp has a striking *cadenza* (an extended solo passage introduced into an orchestral work in order to display the virtuosity of the performer and the capacities of the instrument). The waltz proper begins with a phrase for the horns alternating with one for the solo clarinet. A contrasting melody emerges on the strings, punctuated by a measure on the wood-winds—always an effective orchestral procedure. The opening melody returns, now set off by ornamentation on the flutes. Notable, in the middle section, is the full-throated melody of the violas and cellos. The first section is repeated and works up to the climactic finale through a steady increase in pace and volume, together with a rise to the brilliant upper register. With its suggestion of swirling ballerinas, this music conjures up everything we have come to associate with the romantic ballet.

In a piece such as this, as in many that we will examine in later chapters, it is clear that color is at the heart of the conception. The orchestral timbre is used to highlight the melodies, harmonies, and rhythms; to balance these, one against the other; and to weld them into lucid and convincing forms. Beyond this purely structural use of color, the composer—being one who is fascinated by sound—indulges his sheer love of sonority, his sense of the orchestra as a thing of wonder and beauty.

With its amplitude of tonal resources, its range of dynamics and infinite variety of color, the modern orchestra offers a memorable experience, both to the musician and music lover. There is good reason for the widespread conviction that it is one of the wonders of our musical culture.

CHAPTER 10

Dynamics: Musical Volume

DYNAMICS denotes the degree of loudness or softness at which the music is played. In this area, as in that of tempo, certain responses seem to be rooted in the nature of our emotions. Mystery and fear call for a whisper, even as jubilation and vigorous activity go with full resonance. A lullaby or love song moves in another dynamic range than a triumphal march. Modern instruments place a wide gamut of dynamic effects at the composer's disposal.

The principal dynamic indications are:

Very soft: *pianissimo (pp)*
Soft: *piano (p)*

Moderately soft: *mezzo piano* (*mp*)
Moderately loud: *mezzo forte* (*mf*)
Loud: *forte* (*f*)
Very loud: *fortissimo* (*ff*)

Of special importance are the directions to change the dynamics. The commonest are:

Growing louder: *crescendo* (◁══)
Growing softer: *decrescendo* or *diminuendo* (══▷)
Sudden stress: *sforzando* (*sf*, forced)—accent on a single note or chord

The terms indicating dynamics are even less precise than those indicating tempo. No equivalent of the metronome exists to tell the player how many decibels of loudness he should inject into a tone, or how to shade a crescendo. He is guided in these matters by his taste and understanding, and by the natural capacity of his instrument. Performers sometimes go beyond that capacity, as is evident from the references to pounding and forcing the tone that one finds in reviews of concerts.

As the orchestra increased in size and precision, composers extended the range of dynamic shadings in both directions, so that we find *ppp* and *fff*. Ultimately four and even five p's or f's were used—an example of nineteenth-century extravagance in matters regarding musical expression.

The markings for tempo and dynamics are so many clues to the expressive content of a piece of music. These so-called "expression marks" steadily increased in number during the late eighteenth century and during the nineteenth, as composers tried ever more precisely to indicate their intentions. In this regard it is instructive to compare a page of Bach with one of Tchaikovsky. (See pp. 64–65.)

A number of terms embrace both tempo and dynamics. This is true especially of those used in the nineteenth century to fix the mood and character of a piece. *Andante maestoso* (fairly slow and majestic) implies a stately pace and full sonority. *Morendo* (dying away) indicates that the music is to become slower and softer. *Scherzando* (playful) requires a light tone and brisk movement. *Con brio* (with vigor) suggests an energetic pace and vibrant sonority.

Tempo and Dynamics as Elements of Musical Expression

Crescendo and diminuendo are among the important expressive effects available to the composer. Through the gradual swelling and diminishing of the tone volume, the illusion of distance enters music. It is as if the source of sound were approaching us and then receding. As orchestral style developed, composers quickly learned to take advantage of this procedure. Rossini, for example, was so addicted to employing a long-drawn-out swell of tone for the sake of dramatic effect that he was caricatured in Paris as "Monsieur Crescendo." The impact of such a crescendo can be little short of electrifying, as is apparent from the closing section of his Overture to *The Barber of Seville*. A similar effect is to be observed in Ravel's *Bolero*, in which an extended melody is repeated over and over while the music grows steadily louder. The crescendo is achieved, first, by piling on instruments one after the other; second, by causing the various instruments to play progressively louder. The work is a *tour de force* of orchestration.

In such cases the crescendo becomes the shaping force of the music, the element that determines the conception as a whole. This is true, too, of Wagner's Prelude to *Lohengrin*, which is intended to depict the descent from heaven of the Holy Grail. The image of a band of angels approaching from the distance and then receding is translated into what has become a basic pattern in music, the crescendo-and-decrescendo (◁▭▭ ▭▭▷). A stunning example of this dynamic scheme is to be found also in Debussy's nocturne for orchestra, *Fêtes* (Festivals).

Crescendo in conjunction with accelerando (louder and faster) creates excitement as surely as decrescendo together with ritardando (softer and slower) slackens it. The effect of an intensification of volume and pace is exemplified in Honegger's *Pacific 231*, in which the composer tries to suggest the sense of power conjured up by a locomotive as it gradually builds up momentum and tears through the night. Here crescendo and accelerando are translated into the imagery of motion, as is the case in the finale of Tchaikovsky's Waltz of the Flowers, which is designed to build up to a rousing curtain for the *Nutcracker* ballet. In the Tchaikovsky piece the music climbs steadily from the middle register to the bright and nervous high, so that the three elements—acceleration of pace, increase in volume, and rise in pitch—reinforce one another to create the climax.

Devices of this kind are infallible in their effect upon audiences, which would seem to indicate that they are not the arbitrary procedures of a single imagination but are rooted in certain basic responses inherent in our nature.

A page from the score of Bach's Brandenburg Concerto No. 2 (note the lack of expression marks)

A page from the score of Tchaikovsky's *Pathétique Symphony* (showing the profusion of expression marks in nineteenth-century scores)

CHAPTER 11

Form: Musical Structure and Design

"The principal function of form is to advance our understanding. It is the organization of a piece which helps the listener to keep the idea in mind, to follow its development, its growth, its elaboration, its fate."

Arnold Schoenberg

THE IDEA must have a visible embodiment, a dwelling not only beautiful in itself but suitable to the content. Out of this need comes form in art: the principle of organic unity that shapes the structure to the idea. Form and content, the *how* and the *what,* are as indissoluble as body and mind. Form is of decisive importance in architecture, painting, and sculpture; in poetry, drama, and the novel. But in music, where the material is so intangible, where an impression is no sooner received than it is succeeded by another, form is of the essence. How much so may be seen from the fact that the word "composing" was derived, in the Middle Ages, from the Latin *componere,* "to put together." For the musicians of old the problem was not so much to create elements as to weld them together.

Form is that quality in a work of art which presents to the mind of the beholder an impression of conscious choice and judicious arrangement. It represents law and order in art. It shows itself in the selection of certain details and the rejection of others. Form is manifest too in the relationship of the parts to the whole. It helps us to grasp the work of art as a unity. It can be as potent a source of beauty as the content itself.

Whether in the domestic arts—the setting of a table, the weaving of a basket—or in the loftier ones, a balance is required between unity and variety, between symmetry and asymmetry, activity and repose. Nor is this balance confined to art. Nature has embodied it in the forms of plant and animal life and in what man likes to think of as her supreme handiwork—his own form.

Form in Music

Our lives are composed of sameness and differentness: certain details are repeated again and again, others are new. Music mirrors this dualism. Its basic law of structure is repetition and contrast—unity and variety. Repetition fixes the material in our minds and ministers to our need for the familiar. Contrast sustains our interest and feeds our love of change. From the interaction of the familiar and the new, the repeated elements and the contrasting ones, result the lineaments of musical form. These are to be found in every type of musical organism, from the nursery rhyme to the symphony.

There is wisdom in the usage of language that calls an individual part of a symphony a movement. For a piece of music is precisely that. It sets out from a certain point and moves inexorably toward the conclusion of the piece. When it gets there the music ends. Throughout its course we must feel the music as a progression toward a goal. Rhythm, melody, harmony, timbre, tempo, and dynamics unite to give us this impression. When they succeed, it means that the form is convincing.

The principle of form is embodied in a variety of musical forms. These utilize procedures worked out by generations of composers. No matter how diverse, they are based in one way or another on repetition and contrast. The forms, however, are not fixed molds into which the composer pours his molten material. What gives a piece of music its aliveness is the fact that it adapts a general plan to its own requirements. All faces have two eyes, a nose, and a mouth. In each face, though, these features are to be found in a wholly individual combination. The forms that students in composition follow are readymade formulas set up for their guidance. The forms of the masters are living organisms in which external organization is delicately adjusted to inner content. No two symphonies of Haydn or Mozart, no two sonatas of Beethoven are exactly alike. Each is a fresh and unique solution of the problem of fashioning musical material into a logical and coherent form.

Three-Part or Ternary Form (A-B-A)

A basic pattern in music is three-part or ternary form. Here the composer presents a musical idea, next presents a contrasting idea, and then repeats the first. Hence this type of structure embodies the principle of "statement-departure-return" (A-B-A). The repetition safeguards the unity, while variety is supplied by the middle section.

It often happens that as soon as the idea is set forth it is repeated, so as to engrave it on the mind. In such cases the A-B-A pattern becomes A-A-B-A, as in the following song, Each of the four phrases ends in a cadence. The first two phrases constitute a *period* or sentence, as do the last two. Consequently the melody could be described as a double period,

A Way down upon the Swanee River, far, far, away,
A There's where my heart is turning ever, there's where the old folks stay.
B All the world is sad and dreary, everywhere I roam,
A Oh brothers, how my heart grows weary, far from the old folks at home.

This formation is to be found in many familiar melodies such as *Long, Long Ago; Believe Me if All Those Endearing Young Charms; Maryland, My Maryland; Ach du lieber Augustin;* and *Old Man River.* It is the standard formula for the tunes of Tin Pan Alley. Our need for repetition simplifies the composer's task: of the four phrases of the song, he has to compose only two.

The phrases do not have to follow the A-A-B-A pattern. Any number of variants are possible. For that matter, the phrases do not have to be four in number, although this formation prevails in the music of the eighteenth and nineteenth centuries. But no matter what their structure, most melodies will be found to repeat certain material and to intersperse this with fresh material. The principle of statement-departure-return is found in Gregorian chants of over a thousand years ago as well as in the popular songs of today. It figures in our music from the simple folk song to the elaborate movements of symphonies and sonatas.

The four phrases in the A-A-B-A formation make up a unit that corresponds roughly to a paragraph in prose. Such a unit may be built up, through repetition and expansion, into a larger formation. For instance, a contrasting section may be fashioned from new material, after which the composer repeats the first section, either as before or with some variation. There results what is known as a ternary form, consisting of three symmetrical sections. In the following diagram, capital letters indicate the independent sections, and small letters the distribution of phrases within the section.

A	B	A
a-a-b-a	c-c-d-c	Exact
or	or	repetition
a-b-b-a,	c-d-d-c,	or
a-b-a-b,	c-d-c-d,	
etc.	etc.	variation

Three-part form became the standard pattern for innumerable short pieces of a simple song or dance type—nocturnes, waltzes, marches, impromptus, romances, and the like. The pattern is clear in many familiar compositions such as Schubert's *Marche militaire;* Chopin's F-sharp Nocturne, Opus 15, No. 2; and Brahms's Hungarian Dance No. 5. Also the minuet of the classical symphony is in A-B-A form. The reader will have no difficulty recognizing in these pieces the underlying pattern of statement-departure-return.

So as not to interrupt the musical flow, a transition passage may be inserted to lead from one section to the next. All the same, each section is an independent unit, and the middle one must present a contrast to the first and last. This may show itself in a number of ways. An agitated first section may be opposed to a lyric middle part. A dynamic

Santuario de Ocotlan, Mexico (A-B-A or three-part form in architecture). "The middle section must present a contrast to the first and last sections."

rhythmic idea in the one section may be counterposed to a songlike idea in the other. The first part may lie in the dark lower register, the second in the middle or upper range. There may be contrasts in tempo and dynamics, in timbre and in the type of accompaniment. All of these serve to emphasize the contrast between the A and B sections.

With its attractive symmetry and its balancing of the outer sections against the contrasting middle one, the three-part or ternary form constitutes a simple, clear-cut formation that is a favorite in painting and architecture no less than in music.

Two-Part or Binary Form (A-B)

Two-part form is based on the question-and-answer or A-B formation observed in such tunes as *London Bridge, The Farmer in the Dell,* and *America.* A similar structure is to be observed in Brahms's *Lullaby,* the Italian folk song *Santa Lucia,* and the *Londonderry Air.* These are A-B forms which divide into two symmetrical periods, each of which subdivides into two four-bar phrases.

Binary form is much in evidence in the short pieces that made up the suite of the seventeenth and eighteenth centuries, a period of lively experimentation in the realm of musical structure. The harpsichord pieces of François Couperin exhibit this form, as do numerous pieces by Bach. In the late eighteenth and the nineteenth century binary form was not as popular as ternary; it is comparatively rare today.

We will examine in subsequent chapters the great forms of Western music. No matter how imposing their dimensions, they all show the principle of repetition and contrast, of unity in variety, that we have traced here. In all its manifestations our music displays the striving for organic form that binds together the individual tones within the phrase, the phrases within the musical sentence, the sentences within the section, the sections within the movement, and the movements within the work as a whole; even as, in a novel, the individual words are bound together in phrases, sentences, paragraphs, sections, chapters, and parts.

It has been said that architecture is frozen music. By the same token, music is floating architecture. Form is the architectural principle in music: it distributes the areas of activity and repose, tension and relaxation, light and shade, and integrates the multitudinous details, large and small, into the spacious and coherent structures that are the glory of Western music.

❧ *CHAPTER 12* ❧

Musical Style

"The style is the man."
Buffon

STYLE has been defined as "the distinctive or characteristic manner of presentation, construction, or execution in any art." For the musician the word embraces all the factors that determine the language in which a musical work is couched. These depend upon the procedures and devices of melody, harmony, rhythm, timbre, form, and other elements that make up its "characteristic manner of presentation."

The word may refer to the element of fitness that shapes each type of art work to its function. We distinguish between the style of the novel and that of the essay, between the style of the cathedral and that of the palace. Similarly, we draw distinctions in music between operatic and oratorio style, between symphonic and chamber-music style. The medium too imposes its characteristic manner of presentation, so that we speak of instrumental style, vocal style, keyboard style, orchestral style.

The word may also indicate an artist's personal manner of expression, i. e., the distinctive flavor that sets him apart from all others. Thus we speak of the style of Dickens or Thackeray, of Raphael or Michelangelo, of Wagner or Brahms. The word is used in a narrower sense to denote a certain work or period in the output of a master: the style of Beethoven's last period, the style of the Sistine Madonna, or the style of *Tannhäuser* as distinguished from that of *Tristan*. In a larger sense we often identify style with national culture, as when we speak of French, Italian, or German style; or with an entire civilization, as when we contrast the musical style of the West with that of the Orient.

We said that style includes the totality of devices and procedures that determine the musical language. But the language of music changes from one age to the next. For this reason, one very important use of the word is in connection with the various periods in the history of the art. Beyond that, we relate the leading schools and movements in music to parallel developments in literature, painting, sculpture, and architecture. Here the concept of style enables us to draw the proper connection between the artist and his time, so that the art work is placed in its social-historical frame. No matter how greatly the artists of a particular era may vary in personality and outlook, when seen in the perspective of time they turn out to have certain qualities in common. The age has put its stamp upon all. Because of this we can tell at once that a work of art dates from the Middle Ages or the Renaissance, from the eighteenth century or the nineteenth. Style in this sense sums up the goals and ideals of an epoch, its special way of thinking and feeling, its characteristic mode of expression. Style represents the common practice of an age, the procedures that each artist inherits and adapts to his individual needs. The style of a period, then, is the total art-language of all its artists as they react to the forces—artistic, political, economic, religious, philosophic—that shape their environment.

Scholars will always disagree as to precisely where one style period ends and the next begins. Culture is a dynamic process, and history is a continuous state of becoming. Each period leads by imperceptible de-

grees into the following one, dates and labels being merely convenient
signposts. The following outline shows the main style periods in the
history of Western music. Each represents a conception of form and
technique, an ideal of beauty, a manner of expression and performance
attuned to the cultural climate of the period; in a word—a style! (The
dates, naturally, are approximate.)

350–600 A.D.	Period of the Church Fathers.
600–850	Early Middle Ages. Gregorian Chant.
850–1150	Romanesque. Development of the staff in musical notation, about 1000.
1150–1450	Gothic.
1450–1600	Renaissance.
1600–1750	Baroque.
1725–1775	Rococo.
1775–1825	Classical.
1820–1900	Romantic.
1890–1915	Postromantic, including impressionism.
1910—	The New Music

Style in music, then, relates to type and form, to medium and function, to individuals and nations, to periods and schools. So broad a
concept is of necessity ambiguous. For example, under the heading
of operatic style we may include a work by Mozart and one by Puccini, yet the two operas will be separated by all the differences between the eighteenth- and nineteenth-century styles. Under the label
of twentieth-century style we admit both Stravinsky and Bartók, yet
there are enormous differences between the personal styles of the two
composers.

For all its vagueness, style is an invaluable concept in art. It takes in
all the factors that may possibly influence the grammar, the syntax,
and the rhetoric of the language of art. It is a concept that sharpens
our sensitivity to all that goes into a particular art work; that enables
us to see the individual work in relation to the total output of an artist,
and the individual artist in relation to the total output of his time.

CHAPTER 13

Musical Notation

> "Musical notation is so familiar to us that few are aware of the difficulty of the problems which had to be solved, and the innumerable experiments undertaken for the invention and perfection of a satisfactory method of recording musical sounds."
>
> Sylvia Townsend Warner

OUR MUSICAL notation is the result of an evolution that reaches back to antiquity. It has adapted itself to successive systems of musical thought, and continues to do so. It is by no means a perfect tool, but it has proved adequate to the constantly new demands made upon it.

Musical notation presents a kind of graph of the tones in regard to their pitch and duration. The notes are written on the *staff*, a series of five horizontal lines with four spaces between, each representing another degree of pitch. The lines and spaces are named after the first seven letters of the alphabet. From one C to the next is a distance of an octave. The series is duplicated in higher and lower octaves.

C D E F G A B C D E F G A B C

The pitch is altered by five signs known as accidentals. The sharp (♯) raises the pitch by a half tone (or semitone); the flat (♭) lowers the pitch by a half tone. The natural (♮) cancels these, restoring the original pitch. Also in use are the double sharp (✗) and double flat (♭♭) which respectively raise and lower the pitch by two half tones.

The piano keyboard exemplifies this arrangement of whole and half tones (see p. 74). From one key to the next is a distance of half a tone, as from C to its upper neighbor C-sharp or from B to its lower neighbor B-flat. It will be noticed that C-sharp is identical with D-flat, D-sharp with E-flat, F-sharp with G-flat, G-sharp with A-flat, and A-sharp with B-flat. Where the white keys have a black key between them, they are a whole tone (two semitones) apart, as at C–D, D–E, F–G, G–A, and A–B. Where the white keys have no black key between them they are a half tone (or semitone) apart, as at E–F and B–C. Where the black keys have one white key between them they are a whole tone apart: C♯–D♯, F♯–G♯, G♯–A♯. Where the black keys have two white keys between them they are a tone and a half (three semitones) apart, as from E♭ to F♯ and from B♭ to C♯. By playing the eight white keys from one C to the next we sound the do-re-mi-fa-sol-la-ti-do scale, which we will examine more closely in a later chapter.

Arrangement of the piano keyboard

The clef is a letter sign placed on the staff in order to indicate the pitch of the notes. It is written on a certain line from which are reckoned the others. The G or treble clef establishes the second line of the staff as G above middle C (counting the bottom line as the first). The F or bass clef establishes the fourth line as F below middle C. The treble clef is used in music for instruments of high range such as the violin or flute; in piano music, for the upper (generally the right-hand) part. The bass clef is used for instruments of low range such as the double bass and tuba; in piano music, for the lower (generally the left-hand) part. There is also a C clef for instruments of middle range, which establishes middle C either on the third line of the staff (alto or viola clef) or on the fourth line (tenor clef).

Time Values

The duration of the notes is indicated by a system of relative values. When the whole note receives four beats, a half note receives two, and a quarter note one beat. A quarter note is equivalent to two eighth notes; an eighth note equals two sixteenths. Smaller subdivisions such as thirty-second and sixty-fourth notes are also used.

A note may be divided into three equal notes of the next lower denomination, in which case we have a triplet.

A tie connects two successive notes of the same pitch, prolonging the first by the value of the second. A dot after a note prolongs its time value by half.

Dotted rhythms break up the musical flow, creating those terse, pointed patterns that composers have used extensively. A familiar example of dotted rhythm occurs in the opening strophe of *The Battle Hymn of the Republic,* on the words "Mine eyes have seen the glory of the coming of the Lord"; the dotted rhythm continues through the next two lines. (For other examples see the musical illustrations on p. 77.)

Time never stops in music, even when there is no sound. Silence is indicated by rests, which correspond in time value to the notes.

| whole | half | quarter | eighth | sixteenth | thirty - second | sixty - fourth |

The time signature indicates the meter. The upper numeral shows the number of beats in the measure; the lower shows the unit of value, the note value receiving one beat. The time signature $\frac{3}{4}$ means there are three beats to a measure, with a quarter note receiving one beat. In $\frac{6}{8}$ time there are six beats to the measure, an eighth note receiving one beat. Following are the most frequently encountered time signatures.

Duple meter	$\frac{2}{2}$	$\frac{2}{4}$	$\frac{2}{8}$	
Triple meter	$\frac{3}{2}$	$\frac{3}{4}$	$\frac{3}{8}$	$\frac{3}{16}$
Quadruple meter		$\frac{4}{4}$	$\frac{4}{8}$	
Sextuple meter		$\frac{6}{4}$	$\frac{6}{8}$	

Also in use are $\frac{9}{8}$ (3 groups of 3) and $\frac{12}{8}$ (4 groups of 3). Contemporary music shows a wide use of nonsymmetrical patterns such as $\frac{5}{4}$ or $\frac{5}{8}$ (3 + 2 or 2 + 3) and $\frac{7}{4}$ or $\frac{7}{8}$ (4 + 3, 3 + 4, 2 + 3 + 2, etc.).

Four-four ($\frac{4}{4}$) is known as *common* time and is often indicated by the sign C. A vertical line drawn through this sign ($\mathcal{C}$) indicates *alla breve* or duple time, generally quick, with the half note receiving one beat instead of the quarter; in other words, $\frac{2}{2}$ time instead of $\frac{4}{4}$.

The following examples show how the system works. It will be noticed that the measures are marked off by vertical bar lines. The bar line indicates the location of the primary accent, the ONE.

Lon - don Bridge is fall - ing down, Fall - ing down, fall - ing down,

Lon - don Bridge is fall - ing down, My fair la - dy

The far - mer in the dell __ The far - mer in the dell __

Heigh ho! the mer - ry oh The far - mer in the dell. __

My coun - try 'tis of thee Sweet land of li - ber - ty Of thee I sing

Oh! say can you see by the dawn's ear - ly light, What so

proud - ly we hail'd at the twi - light's last gleam - ing?

Notation and the Performer

The printed lines of a play do not indicate the many nuances of expression—the continual shifting of pace, the changes in emotional tension, the accenting of one word rather than another, the pauses, inflections, movements, and gestures—that create a living character. It is here that actor and director make their personal contribution, as a result of which one performer's interpretation of a role differs markedly from another's. The notation of music is even more limited in this regard than language. The composer is able to set down the pitches and their values in time; he indicates whether a passage should go fast or slow, soft or loud; and he may add other details that serve as clues to the character of the piece. But the life of the music, its mood and feeling, cannot be written down in symbols. This is where the sympathetic imagination of the performer comes into play, his intuition, his sense of timing, above all his understanding of style. The performer makes the notes come alive, he unlocks the composer's intention; his temperament serves as a kind of colored glass through which is refracted the creator's.

There is no single recipe for the proper performance of a work. Two great artists will differ in their interpretation of the same piece, yet each will be convincing on his own grounds. The great artist is one who strikes an exceedingly difficult balance. He asserts his own personality sufficiently to re-create and effectively project the music, while on the other hand he enters imaginatively into the spirit of the creator and reverently transmits the latter's intention.

It is the performer's high duty to transform the symbols on the page of music into glowing sound. To this task he brings the insights that talent, training, and years of experience have given him. When he discharges it well he makes a real contribution to our musical experience; he becomes the vital link between the composer and ourselves.

PART TWO

Nineteenth-Century Romanticism

"Music is the most romantic of all the arts—one might almost say, the only genuinely romantic one—for its sole subject is the infinite. Music discloses to man an unknown realm, a world in which he leaves behind him all definite feelings to surrender himself to an inexpressible longing."

E. T. A. Hoffmann (1776–1822)

CHAPTER 14

The Romantic Spirit

"Romanticism is beauty without bounds—the beautiful infinite."
Jean Paul Richter (1763–1825)

HISTORIANS of art observe that the life of style moves between two opposite poles. In one period art leans toward order, poise, serenity. In another it exalts strangeness and wonder and ecstasy. During one era the artist views life objectively; he participates in a common practice and expresses emotion through universal symbols. During another he becomes fiercely individualistic; he seeks a manner of expression that is personal and subjective. One generation of artists strives above all for beauty of design and proportion. Another loosens the established forms, enthroning in their place picturesque detail and striking color, mood and atmosphere. One type of artist accepts tradition; the other rebels against it. One art style embraces the rational, limiting itself to what can be thought and felt; another yearns for the irrational and the infinite. We call the one art classic, the other romantic.

Nietzsche in his writings on art dramatized the contrast between the two through the symbol of Apollo, god of light and measure, as opposed to Dionysus, god of intoxication and passion. Neither the Apollonian nor the Dionysian is confined to one epoch or country. The romantic impulse is to be found in Homer and Vergil, in the romances of the Middle Ages, and in the tragedies of Shakespeare. The classical temper, which achieved its golden age in ancient Greece, became a source of inspiration for the Renaissance, two thousand years later, and for every century after. Classic and romantic have alternated and even existed side by side from the beginning of time, for they correspond to two basic impulses in man's nature: on the one hand, his love of traditional standards, his need to have emotion purged and controlled; on the other, his desire for intoxication and ecstasy, his longing for the unknown and the unattainable.

It is important to avoid the common misconception that classical art is form without feeling while romantic art is feeling without form. _There can be no art without feeling, nor can there be art without form._ Every art work represents an amalgamation of inner idea and outer structure; the two are indissoluble. Every artist makes use to the full of all the expressive and all the technical resources available to his time. Thus classical art contains profound emotion and drama, just as romantic art often exhibits a most subtle sense of form. The difference between them

81

is one of emphasis; it has to do with the way in which form and content are fused. Classicism purifies emotion by subjecting it to the discipline of an all-embracing design. In romantic art the emotion often struggles against this discipline, it floods the form and threatens to burst it asunder. From this is derived the inner tension of romantic art, the sense of strain that is alien to the classical spirit.

Specifically, the classic and romantic labels are attached to two important periods in European art. The one held the stage in the last quarter of the eighteenth century and the early decades of the nineteenth. The other, stemming out of the social and political upheavals that followed in the wake of the French Revolution, came to the fore in the second quarter of the nineteenth century. Romanticism dominated the art output of the nineteenth century; gave its name to a movement and an era; and created a multitude of colorful, intensely lyrical works that are still very much with us.

The Romantic Movement

The French Revolution was the outcome of momentous social forces. It signalized the transfer of power from the feudal-agricultural aristocracy to the industrial middle class. The new society, based on free enterprise, emphasized the individual as never before. Freedom—political, economic, religious, personal—was its watchword. On the artistic front this urge for individualism found expression in the romantic movement.

The breakdown of the aristocratic way of life, with its formal code of behavior, opened the door to the unashamed expression of feeling. One of the prime traits of romantic art was its emphasis on emotion. The slogan of "Liberty, Fraternity, Equality" inspired hopes and visions to which few artists failed to respond. Love of nature, interest in simple folk and in children, sympathy with the oppressed, faith in man and his destiny—all these, so intimately associated with the time, point to the democratic character of the romantic movement.

For centuries the artist had functioned under the patronage of the Church or of princely courts. Under the patronage system he had been a commoner creating for aristocrats who were interested in his product rather than in him. Now he addressed an audience of his social and political equals. His joys and sorrows became a legitimate subject for his art, his personality grew to be his most important asset. "I am different from all the men I have seen," proclaimed Jean-Jacques Rousseau. "If I am not better, at least I am different." In an age of individualistic empire builders the artist too emerged as an individual. The change

Eugène Delacroix, 1799–1863, *Liberty Leading the People.*
"One of the prime traits of romantic art was its emphasis on emotion."

is apparent in poetry where, it has been well said, the pronoun "I" now
made its appearance. Gone were the elegant couplets of eighteenth-
century poetry. The new age responded with sighs and tears to the
passionate lyricism of Byron and Shelley, Keats, Heine, and de Musset.

The newly won freedom of the artist proved a not unmixed blessing.
He confronted a philistine world from which he felt himself more and
more cut off. A new type emerged—the artist as bohemian, the rejected
dreamer who starved in an attic and through peculiarities of dress and
behavior "shocked the bourgeois." This was the sensitive individual who
was both too good for the moneyed world about him and not good
enough. Increasingly the romantic artist found himself arrayed against
the established order. He was free from the social restraints imposed
by court life; but he paid dearly for his freedom in loneliness, in knowing himself apart from his fellows. Withdrawal from the world brought
a preoccupation with inner problems. Eternal longing, regret for the
lost happiness of childhood, an indefinable discontent that gnawed at
the soul—these were the ingredients of the romantic mood. Yet the
pessimism within was not without its cause in the reality without. It
became apparent that the high hopes fostered by the Revolution were

not to be realized overnight. Despite the brave slogans, men were not yet equal or free. The optimism of the Enlightenment had given way to doubt and disenchantment—"the illness of the century."

This malaise was reflected in the art of the time. Thus, Balzac's *Human Comedy* depicted the warping of human relationships in the new society. Hugo dedicated *Les Misérables* "to the unhappy ones of the earth." The nineteenth-century novel found its great theme in the conflict between the individual and society. Jean Valjean and Heathcliffe, Madame Bovary and Anna Karenina, Oliver Twist, Tess of the d'Urbervilles, and the Karamazovs—a varied company rises from those impassioned pages to point up the frustrations and guilts of the nineteenth-century world.

Hardly less persuasive was the art of those who sought escape. Some glamorized the past, as did Walter Scott and Alexandre Dumas. Longing for far-off lands inspired the exotic scenes that glow on the canvases of Turner and Delacroix. Whereas the eighteenth century had found its inspiration in ancient Greece, the romantics discovered the so-called Dark Ages. King Arthur and Siegfried, fairy tale and medieval saga usurped the place formerly held by the gods and heroes of antiquity.

J. M. W. Turner, 1775–1851, *Grand Canal, Venice.*

"Longing for far-off lands inspired the exotic scenes that glow on the canvases of Turner and Delacroix."

The romantics also discovered nature, but nature as a backdrop for the inner conflicts of man. Theirs was a world of "strangeness and wonder": the eerie landscape of a Coleridge or a Poe. The fantastic and the macabre, traits of the medieval imagination, had returned to European art.

For the aristocrats of the classical era, art had been an ornament of social life. The nineteenth century elevated art into a religion, a source of intoxication that compensated for all that life withheld. The great works of the eighteenth century were produced by craftsmen-artists on commission from a patron, a church, or an opera house. But the romantic artist increasingly discarded the craftsman's view, and instead saw himself impelled by "inspiration." He created for posterity, that ideal audience which would one day accord him the approval that the bourgeois failed to give.

Poetry and painting, drama and the novel fulfilled as best they might the demands laid upon them by the romantic temperament. But it was in music that the romantics found their fulfillment. Music by its very indefiniteness spoke directly to the heart. It alone could appease the longing for the happiness that was nowhere to be found. "Every passion," wrote Hoffmann, author of the fantastic *Tales*, "is clothed by music with the purple luster of romanticism." Music became *the* romantic art, to the condition of which—in Walter Pater's celebrated phrase—all the other arts aspired. The magic potion drunk by the lovers in the first act of *Tristan* was an apt symbol. Their public no less than they yearned for oblivion, the highest bliss; and this only music—romantic music— could give them.

Romanticism has a youthful exuberance. Its ardor, its idealism, and its discontents are the attributes of youth. An atmosphere of adolescence surrounds the lives and works of its leading figures. Significantly, some of the greatest among them died at what is ordinarily the threshold of maturity: Keats at twenty-six, Shelley at thirty, Schubert at thirty-one; Chopin, Mendelssohn, Byron, and Poe before they reached forty. They burned with the "hard gemlike flame" and were consumed.

Critics complain that romanticism has grown to be too loose a term to be used with any degree of accuracy. Partly this is because of the contradictory nature of the era to which the name is attached. The nineteenth century included many opposites: liberalism and reaction, idealism and the crassest materialism, bourgeois sentimentality and stark realism, mysticism and scientific inquiry, democratic revolution and royalist restoration, romantic optimism and no less romantic despair. No one label could hope to cover all these.

As with many great movements, nineteenth-century romanticism was guilty of excesses that left it open to criticism. It lent itself to bombast and rhetoric, to self-pity and straining for effect. Yet it achieved passionate utterance and brought art into intimate contact with the life of the heart. It glorified lyricism, and plumbed new depths in the human personality. Inheriting the Beethovenian desire to "embrace the millions," romanticism addressed itself to the world and created a mass audience larger than had ever existed before.

There is an immense excitement about the romantic era—the excitement of reaching for things that had never been attempted hitherto. Romantic art manifests a hunger for life and a fervor of emotion that are nothing short of formidable. It is an intensely expressive art that still holds millions in thrall.

CHAPTER 15

Romanticism in Music (c. 1820-1900)

"Music is the melody whose text is the world."
Schopenhauer

EMOTION in art differs in one important respect from the emotions of life: it is presented within a form. In the course of shaping his ideas into a form the artist endows them with beauty. He also lifts them from the personal level, where they would be of interest only to himself and his friends, to the enduring realm of art.

It is through the form, then, that the artist's private feelings are given to the public. The classical era evolved elaborate forms to effect this transformation: the solo sonata, symphony, concerto, and various types of chamber music. But the romantics, desiring to keep emotion at maximum intensity, loosened the classical design and flooded it with lyricism. Or they developed free supple forms that strove for direct contact with the listener.

The early nineteenth century therefore saw a departure from the grand form of the preceding age—the classical sonata-symphony. The romantic composers could no more follow the forms of Haydn, Mozart, and Beethoven than they could transport themselves back to the time of those masters. What they had to say—what the age demanded of them to say—constituted a new content that had to find its own form. Many critics regard the nineteenth century as the period that brought about the breakdown of design. But this implies that only

J. M. W. Turner, 1775-1851, *Valley of Aosta — Snow storm, Avalanche and Thunderstorm.* (The Art Institute of Chicago)

"The romantics discovered nature, but nature as a backdrop for the inner conflicts of man."

Eugène Delacroix, 1799-1863, *Women of Algiers in Their Apartment*. (The Louvre Museum, Paris)

". . . one of the most arresting offshoots of the romantic movement: the evoking of an exotic locale for the sake of picturesque effect."

Jacques Louis David, 1748-1825, *The Oath of the Horatii*. (The Toledo Museum of Art. Gift of Edward Drummond Libbey)

"The foremost painter of revolutionary France, Jacques Louis David, decked his huge commemorative canvases with the symbols of Athenian and Roman democracy."

one kind of design is correct, a debatable thesis. It was their very instinct for design that led the romantic composers to abandon the procedures of the past. Any diligent conservatory student can learn to construct a sonata "correctly." We can hardly suppose that musicians of the caliber of Berlioz, Schumann, or Liszt could not do as much. As a matter of fact, dozens of "correct" symphonies were written in the romantic period which today are forgotten. The works that have survived are precisely those that departed from the heritage of the past, and in so doing embodied a new vision.

The nineteenth century was vastly interested in instrumental music. Its melody, however, was molded to the lyricism of the human voice. This above all was the period when musicians strove to make their instruments "sing." It is no accident that the themes from romantic symphonies, concertos, and other instrumental works are today converted into popular songs; for romantic melody had a wide and immediate appeal, as is evidenced by the enduring popularity of the tunes of Schubert, Chopin, Verdi, and their fellows. It is the romantic concept of melody that is most familiar to our present-day public.

Of equal significance was the achievement of the romantic era in regard to harmony. Nineteenth-century musicians, in their attempt to expand the expressive powers of music, experimented widely in this domain. Especially they investigated the capacity of dissonant harmony to generate emotional tension. Chopin, Liszt, and Wagner were among the innovators who exerted a decisive effect on the further evolution of our harmonic system. Their piquant chord progressions lent the musical fabric a bewitching variety of colors. They revealed a new harmonic language that stands as one of the foremost achievements of the romantic era.

The interest in folklore and the rising tide of nationalism impelled the romantic musicians to utilize the folk songs and dances of their native lands. As a result, a number of national idioms—Hungarian, Polish, Russian, Bohemian, Scandinavian—came to the fore and opened up new areas to European music, greatly enriching its melody and harmony. At the same time the emphasis shifted from the universal to the special; from abstract musical ideas to local color and picturesque detail.

In the domain of tone color romanticism made what is perhaps its most signal contribution. Color, for the classical period, had been a means of clarifying the form, of bringing out the details of the architecture. In the romantic period orchestration became an art in itself. The musician finally had a palette comparable to the painter's. The romantics regarded color as the gateway to sensuous beauty, to tonal enchantment. Now the horn, the romantic instrument par excellence, came into its own; as did those expressive combinations of woodwinds and strings that were so dear to the romantic imagination. Richard Strauss remarked that Berlioz "was the first composer to derive his inspiration consistently from the nature of the instruments." In this regard the pioneering Frenchman was a true romantic.

Romanticism found a fresh and highly characteristic means of expression in the short lyric forms—the song and piano piece—which came to occupy a central place during the first phase of the romantic movement. But the desire for intimate lyricism was only part of the picture. The romantic interest in tone color went hand in hand with a steady growth in the size and importance of the orchestra. The center of musical life in the nineteenth century was no longer church or palace, but concert hall. The new patrons of music, the middle-class public, were ready to support large orchestras composed of full-time musicians. Interest came to center in the orchestra and, among musicians, in the art and science of orchestration. The nineteenth-century orchestra became a huge, colorful ensemble that offered composers an ideal medium for the large public forms of music, for the brilliant colorism and grandiose rhetoric that came to characterize the late romantic style.

The desire for direct communication led composers to use a large number of expressive terms intended to serve as clues to the mood of the music, with the result that a highly characteristic vocabulary sprang up. We mentioned several of these terms in Chapter 10. Among the directions frequently encountered in nineteenth-century scores are *espressivo* (expressively), *dolce* (sweetly), *cantabile* (songful); *pastorale, agitato, misterioso, lamentoso, trionfale; dolente* (weeping), *mesto* (sad), *maestoso* (majestic), *gioioso* (joyous); *con amore* (with love, tenderly), *con passione, con fuoco* (with fire). These suggest not only the character of the music but the frame of mind behind it.

The Union of the Arts

The romantic esthete wished to encompass all experience at its maximum intensity. He was enchanted in turn by poetry, music, painting. How much more intoxicating, he reasoned, would be the effect of combining all three. Music in the nineteenth century drew steadily closer to literature and painting—a typically romantic phenomenon. There was a practical reason for the story-and-picture approach to music. The abstract forms of the classical era had been developed for an audience of aristocratic connoisseurs. As large segments of the population began to join the ranks of music lovers, there arose the inevitable question concerning symphony and sonata: But what does it mean? Nothing answered the problem so well as to attach a label that conjured up for the listener a romantic story or scene.

Yet behind this practical consideration was a far more significant one: the attempt to bring music into touch with life. The romantics were unable to accept music as an abstract, purely esthetic experience. For them it was linked to dreams and passions; to philosophy and religious faith; to profound meditations on life, death, and destiny; to love of nature, pride in one's country, desire for freedom, and to the fierce political struggles of the age. The result was that music took on an intensely human content. It began to evoke moods and visions in a way that it never had before.

Romantic music, then, was marked on the one hand by intimate lyricism, on the other by the grand orchestral gesture. It developed harmony and color, exploited folklore and national sentiment, painted exotic scenes. It brought music close to literary and pictorial values, it exalted passion and intoxication. The romantic attitude enabled music to achieve a unique position in the nineteenth century: as a moral force, a vision of man's greatness, and as a direct link between his interior life and the outer world.

Song and Piano Piece

CHAPTER 16

The Short Lyric Forms as an Expression of Romanticism

"Out of my great sorrows I make my little songs."
Heinrich Heine

THROUGH the short lyric forms the romantic movement satisfied its need for intimate personal expression. Coming into prominence in the early decades of the century, the song and piano piece emerged as one of the purest manifestations of the new lyricism.

The Song

The repertory of song—folk, popular, and art—is more extensive than that of all other types of music. For song combines two musical elements of universal appeal—melody and the human voice. A song is a short lyric composition for solo voice based on a poetic text. The vocal melody is presented as a rule with an instrumental accompaniment. The melodic line is rooted in the natural inflections of the language. For this reason vocal music reflects the speech patterns of a nation and grows out of the native soil. It is this that makes Debussy's vocal line seem so French, Brahms's so German, Stephen Foster's so American.

The accompaniment furnishes harmonic background and support to the melody. It constitutes the framework of the song, creates the necessary atmosphere, and frequently offers a significant commentary on the words. It may also function independently of the words through purely instrumental passages such as a prelude, interludes, and a postlude.

In discussing the art song, writers on music like to point out that the music completes the poetry and reveals its inner meaning. Such a misconception is possible only to those whose training is musical rather

90

than literary. A great poem is complete in itself and needs nothing more to enhance it. It has a music of its own, a delicate arrangement of consonants and vowels that is wiped out as soon as music is added. Actually the music imposes a new set of values on the poem; the musical rhythm distorts the word rhythm, the musical harmony destroys the word harmony, the musical melody overwhelms the word melody. In short, music overpowers everything it is brought in contact with. Certain poets have so rich a music of their own that it is almost impossible to subjugate their verses to the imperious requirements of music. Shakespeare, Milton, and Shelley are infinitely more difficult to set to music than Scott, Byron, or Burns. The poem must be good enough to move the composer, but it must not be so great as to resist him.

All of which explains the mixed attitude of poets toward the composers who set their verses to music. On the one hand they are pleased with the greater fame thereby accorded their poetry, on the other they are concerned for the autonomy of their art. The greater the setting, the more surely it will overpower the poem. Tennyson's complaint, "Why do these damned musicians make me say a thing twice when I said it only once!" is a case in point.

A melody, too, is a thing complete in itself. It is shaped by laws and procedures having nothing to do with literature. Its meaning as a musical pattern has no specific connection with the meaning of particular words. There is nothing in the tune of *London Bridge* to suggest either a bridge or a fair lady. The musical meaning may even contradict the word meaning. In this nursery rhyme, for example, the words "falling down" are repeated three times on tones that actually move upward. In other words, the musical meaning takes precedence over the word meaning. A striking instance occurs in our national anthem. After the majestic opening strain is sung twice, the orchestra and the audience invariably go into a lyrical *piano*. This presents an effective contrast with the martial opening, and makes very good sense musically. Yet at this point the words are: "And the rocket's red glare, the bombs bursting in air . . ." So great is the ascendancy of music over words that the phrase continues to be performed lyrically without any sense of incongruity on anyone's part.

A song, then, is composed of two independent entities—words and music—that have to be reconciled. To do so is not as easy as the result would seem to suggest.

Types of Song Structure

We distinguish between two main types of song structure. In *strophic form* the same melody is repeated with every stanza, or strophe, of the poem. This formation, which occurs very frequently in folk and popular song, permits of no great closeness between words and music. Instead it sets up a general atmosphere or feeling-tone that accommodates itself equally well to all the stanzas. The first may tell of the lover's expectancy, the second of his joy at seeing his beloved, the third of her father's harshness in separating them, and the fourth of her sad death, all these being sung to the same tune. The prevalence of strophic song throughout the ages points to one conclusion: the folk learned early that a lovely tune is a joy in itself, and that it heightens emotion no matter what the content of a particular stanza.

The other type is what the Germans call *durchkomponiert*, literally "through-composed"—that is, composed throughout. Here the music follows the story line, changing with each stanza according to the text. This affords the possibility of subtle characterization that captures every shade of meaning in the words.

The strophic form is used for lyric moods, simple emotions, and songs in folk or popular style. Examples are Schubert's *Heidenröslein* (Hedge Rose) and Brahms's *Lullaby*. The "through-composed" song is suited for narrative, for dramatic ballads—as in Schubert's *Der Erlkönig* (The Erlking) and Schumann's *Die beiden Grenadiere* (The Two Grenadiers)—and for the introspective poetry that the romantic composers and their successors set with such refinement. An intermediate type combines the repetition of the strophic song with the freedom of the song that is through-composed. The same melody will be repeated for two or three stanzas, with new material introduced when the poem seems to require it, generally at the climax. Schubert's celebrated *Ständchen* (Serenade) is a fine example of this structure.

In any case the successful addition of music to poetry produces not simply the sum of the two but something new, different in quality from either of its elements. The music lifts the words to another plane of experience, endows them with another dimension. The words furnish the point of departure, the scaffolding. All else lies in the music.

The Art Song in the Romantic Period

Despite the prominence of song throughout the ages, the art song as we know it today was a product of the romantic era. It was created by the union of romantic poetry and music in the early nineteenth century. This union was consummated with such artistry by Franz Schubert and his successors, notably Robert Schumann and Johannes Brahms, that the new genre came to be known all over Europe by the German word for song—*Lied*.

The lied depended for its flowering on the upsurge of lyric poetry

that marked the rise of German romanticism. Goethe (1749–1832) and
Heine (1799–1856) are the two leading figures among a group of poets
who, like Wordsworth and Byron, Shelley and Keats in our literature,
cultivated a subjective mode of expression through the short lyric poem.
The lied brought to flower the romantic desire for the union of music
and poetry. Projected through the most expressive of instruments—the
human voice—the lied met the need of the age not only for subjective
expression but also for a type of emotion in music that was specific and
easy to identify. The lied ranged from tender sentiment to dramatic
balladry. Its favorite themes were love and longing, the beauty of
nature, the transience of human happiness.

The triumph of the romantic art song was made possible by the
emergence of the piano as the universal household instrument of the
nineteenth century. The piano accompaniment translated the poetic
images into musical ones. It engaged in dialogue with the voice part,
brought to completion what the latter left unsaid, and showed itself
capable of remarkable sophistication. Voice and piano together created
compact tone poems charged with feeling, suited alike for amateurs
and artists, for the home as for the concert room. Within a short time
the lied achieved immense popularity and made a durable contribution
to world art.

The Piano Piece

The short lyric piece was the instrumental equivalent of the song.
The favored medium was the piano, whose literature in this domain far
surpasses in interest and variety that for any other instrument. This
species of intimate composition, which illumines a particular mood
rather than a general idea, is known as a *characteristic piece* (or character piece). Among the titles most frequently used are *bagatelle* (literally, "a trifle"), *impromptu* (on the spur of the moment), *intermezzo*
(interlude), *nocturne* (night song), *novelette* (short story), *moment
musical, song without words, album leaf, prelude, romance, capriccio*
(caprice); and, of larger dimensions, the *rhapsody* and *ballade.* In the
dance category are the *waltz, mazurka, polka, écossaise* (Scottish
dance), *polonaise, march,* and *country dance.*

Many of these pieces follow a simple A-B-A structure that presents
two contrasting moods. The first may be rhythmic and the second lyric,
or the other way around. The return of the first section gives these
pieces a rounded form, imparting balance and symmetry to the design.
In time the general titles gave way to specific ones of a fanciful and
descriptive nature. Typical are Schumann's *In the Night, Soaring,
Whims;* Liszt's *Forest Murmurs* and *Fireflies.*

Before the romantic period, composers lavished their attention upon large musical forms—symphony, concerto, string quartet, and the like. These achieved their effects through the logical development of musical ideas. In such works intellectual factors played an important role. The character piece, on the other hand, emphasized new values in musical expression: freshness, simplicity, spontaneity, and the presentation of musical material in such a way as to underline the element of pure feeling. Yet even in the domain of the short lyric forms we find an urge for large-scale structure. This expressed itself in the cycle of songs or piano pieces joined together by a literary or musical idea, as in Schubert's *Die schöne Müllerin* (The Lovely Maid of the Mill) and Schumann's *Carnaval*. Such cycles may be compared to the series of short stories within a frame, such as *The Canterbury Tales* or *The Decameron,* that had been popular in European literature for centuries.

The short lyric forms occupied a central position in the musical output of the romantic era. They did so because the nineteenth-century composer recognized that size is no criterion in art, and that an exquisitely wrought miniature may contain as much beauty as a symphony. In the song and lyric piano piece romanticism, especially in its early phase, found one of its most characteristic means of expression.

❧❧❧ CHAPTER 17 ❧❧❧

Franz Schubert (1797-1828)

"When I wished to sing of love it turned to sorrow. And when I wished to sing of sorrow it was transformed for me into love."

IN THE popular mind Franz Schubert's life has become a romantic symbol of the artist's fate. He suffered poverty and was neglected during his lifetime. He died young. And after his death he was enshrined among the immortals.

His Life

He was born in a suburb of Vienna, the son of a schoolmaster. The boy learned the violin from his father, piano from an elder brother; his beautiful soprano voice gained him admittance to the imperial chapel and school where the court singers were trained. His creative gift asserted itself in boyhood, and his teachers were duly astonished at the musicality of the shy dreamy lad. One of them remarked that Franz seemed to learn "straight from Heaven."

His schooldays over, young Schubert tried to follow in his father's footsteps, but he was not cut out for the routine of the classroom. He found escape in the solitude of his attic, immersing himself in the lyric poets who were the first voices of German romanticism. "Everything he touched turned to song." With a spontaneity comparable to Mozart's, the melodies took shape that gave to the new romantic lyricism its ideal expression. *Gretchen at the Spinning Wheel,* to Goethe's verses, was

Moritz von Schwind, *A Schubert Evening*. Schubert is at the piano.

written in a single afternoon—when he was seventeen. A year later came his setting of the same poet's *Erlking*. One of his greatest songs, it was the work of a few hours.

Schubert's talent for friendship attracted to him a little band of followers. Their appreciation of his genius solaced him for the neglect and incomprehension of the world. Poets, painters, musicians, these young enthusiasts were the advance guard of the romantic movement. With their encouragement Schubert, not yet twenty, broke with the drudgery of his father's school. In the eleven years that were left him he occupied no official position (although he occasionally made half-hearted attempts to obtain one). He lived with one or another of his friends in that mixture of poverty and camaraderie, hope and despair, that operetta writers of a later age have found it all too easy to glamorize. And steadily, with an almost self-devouring intensity, the music came pouring from the bespectacled young man. "How do you compose?" he was asked. "I finish one piece," was the answer, "and begin the next."

Schubert was singularly unable to stand up to the world. Songs that in time sold in the hundreds of thousands he surrendered literally for the price of a meal. It was borne in upon him that the creative gift is not enough for an artist. "The state should support me," he remarked sadly, "so that I may be untroubled and free to compose." As the years passed, the buoyancy of youth gave way to a sense of loneliness, the tragic loneliness of the romantic artist. "No one feels another's grief," he wrote, "no one understands another's joy. People imagine that they can reach one another. In reality they only pass each other by." Yet he comprehended—and in this he was the romantic—that his very suffering must open to his art new layers of awareness. "My music is the product of my talent and my misery. And that which I have written in my greatest distress is what the world seems to like best."

Schubert

He still yielded to flurries of optimism when success appeared to lie within his grasp. Again and again he directed his efforts to opera. But he was not destined for success in the theater. His repeated defeats had a devastating effect upon his impressionable nature. He describes himself as "the most unfortunate, most miserable being on earth . . . whose brightest hopes have come to nought, to whom love and friendship are but torture, and whose enthusiasm for the beautiful is fast vanishing." There came to him an intimation that the struggle had been decided against him. "It seems to me at times that I no longer belong to this world."

This was the emotional climate of the magnificent song cycle *Die Winterreise* (The Winter Journey), in which he struck a note of somber lyricism new to music. Depressed by illness and poverty, he abandoned himself to the mournful images of Wilhelm Müller's poems. The long dark journey—was it not the symbol of his own life? Now he nerved himself to his last effort. To the earlier masterpieces was added, in that final year, an amazing list that includes the Symphony in C major, the Mass in E-flat, the String Quintet in C, the three posthumous piano sonatas, and thirteen of his finest songs, among them the ever-popular *Serenade*.

With the great C-major Symphony behind him he made arrangements to study counterpoint. "I see now how much I still have to learn." Ill with typhus, he managed to correct the proofs of the last part of *Die Winterreise*. The sense of defeat accompanied him through the final delirium; he fancied that he was being buried alive. "Do I not deserve a place above the ground?" His last wish was to be buried near the master he worshiped above all others—Beethoven.

He was thirty-one years old when he died. His possessions consisted of his clothing, his bedding, and "a pile of old music valued at ten florins": his unpublished manuscripts. In the memorable words of Sir George Grove, "There never has been one like him, and there never will be another."

His Music

Schubert stood at the confluence of the classic and romantic eras. His symphonic style bespeaks the heir of the classical tradition; but in his songs and piano pieces he was wholly the romantic, an artist whose magical lyricism impelled Liszt to call him "the most poetic musician that ever was." Like every composer of the nineteenth century, he was weighed down by the greatness of his predecessors. "Who can do anything more after Beethoven?" he complained. Yet within the orbit of that towering figure he developed a symphonic idiom of his own. His symphonies, for all their romantic ardor, are classical in their dramatic momentum and continuity. They rank with the finest since Beethoven.

Chamber music was Schubert's birthright as a Viennese. To the tradition of intimate social music he brought his own inwardness of spirit. The string quartets, the *Trout Quintet* (1819), the two trios (1827), and the transcendent Quintet in C (1828) bear the true Schubertian stamp. They end the line of Viennese classicism.

In the Impromptus and *Moments musicaux* (Musical Moments) the piano sings the new lyricism. Caprice, spontaneity, and the charm of the unexpected take their place as elements of romantic art. Of comparable freshness is the popular tone of the dance pieces, Waltzes, Ländlers, and Écossaises. As for his piano sonatas, they have never established themselves because of their length. Single movements are of surpassing loveliness, but on the whole they lack conciseness and unity.

Schubert's gregarious nature responded to the sound of many voices joined in song. His secular choruses represent a new genre of social music suited for the mass audience of the democratic age. A splendid example is his *Frühlingslied* (Spring Song) for male voices. His Masses and other religious works, rooted in the Catholic milieu in which he grew up, contain some of his most beautiful vocal writing.

Finally there are the songs, more than six hundred of them. Many were written down at white heat, sometimes five, six, seven in a single morning. In popular manuals Schubert has been named "Father of the Song." The title is misleading; it implies that he originated the art song, which he did not. But it does indicate how closely his genius is linked in the popular mind with the lyric song as we know it today. Certain of his melodies achieve the universality of folk song, others display the highest sophistication. In either case they issue directly

from the heart of the poem. Their eloquence, their freshness of feeling
has never been surpassed. Of special moment are the accompaniments:
a measure or two, and the rustling brook is conjured up, the dilapidated
hurdy-gurdy, or the post-horn announcing the eagerly awaited letter.
In his song cycles Schubert imaginatively extended the possibilities of
the lied. *Die schöne Müllerin* (1823) and *Die Winterreise* (1827) are
works of remarkable poignancy, in which the individual songs contribute to an artistic revelation of the highest order.

The themes treated by Schubert are as diverse as life itself. Upon
the poets whose verses he set he conferred a dubious immortality:
never again would their poems seem complete without his music.
Goethe sensed this when he preferred the settings of his poetry by
mediocre composers to Schubert's. The poet must have suspected that
his verses had been subjugated here to a higher end. Of Schubert's songs
may be said what Schumann remarked about the C-major Symphony:
"This music transports us to a region where we cannot remember ever
to have been before."

Der Erlkönig (*The Erlking*) — Art Song

This masterpiece of Schubert's youth (1815) captures the romantic
"strangeness and wonder" of Goethe's celebrated ballad, which is based
on the legend that whoever is touched by the King of the Elves must
die. The poem has four characters: the narrator, the father, the child,
and the seductive Elf.

Wer reitet so spät durch Nacht und Wind?	Who rides so late through night and wind?
Es ist der Vater mit seinem Kind;	It is the father with his child.
er hat den Knaben wohl in dem Arm,	He holds the boy within his arm,
er fasst ihn sicher, er hält ihn warm.	He clasps him tight, he keeps him warm.
"Mein Sohn, was birgst du so bang dein Gesicht?"	"My son, why hide your face in fear?"
"Siehst, Vater, du den Erlkönig nicht?	"See, father, the Erlking's near.
den Erlenkönig mit Kron' und Schweif?"	The Erlking with crown and wand."
"Mein Sohn, es ist ein Nebelstreif."	"Dear son, 'tis but a misty cloud."
"Du liebes Kind, komm, geh' mit mir!	"Ah, sweet child, come with me!
gar schöne Spiele spiel' ich mit dir;	Such pleasant games I'll play with thee!
manch' bunte Blumen sind an dem Strand,	Such pleasant flowers bloom in the field,
meine Mutter hat manch' gülden Gewand."	My mother has many a robe of gold."

she sings like the father

"Mein Vater, mein Vater, und hörest du nicht,
was Erlenkönig mir leise verspricht?"

"Oh father, father, do you not hear
What the Erlking whispers in my ear?"

"Sei ruhig, bleibe ruhig, mein Kind;
in dürren Blättern säuselt der Wind."

"Be still, my child, be calm;
'Tis but the withered leaves in the wind."

"Willst, feiner Knabe, du mit mir geh'n?
meine Töchter sollen dich warten schön;
meine Töchter führen den nächtlichen Reih'n
und wiegen und tanzen und singen dich ein."

"My lovely boy, wilt go with me?
My daughters fair shall wait on thee,
My daughters nightly revels keep,
They'll sing and dance and rock thee to sleep."

"Mein Vater, mein Vater, und siehst du nicht dort
Erlkönigs Töchter am düstern Ort?"

"Oh father, father, see you not
The Erlking's daughters in yon dark spot?"

"Mein Sohn, mein Sohn, ich seh' es genau,
es scheinen die alten Weiden so grau."

"My son, my son, the thing you see
Is only the old gray willow tree."

"Ich liebe dich, mich reizt deine schöne Gestalt,
und bist du nicht willig, so brauch' ich Gewalt."

"I love thee, thy form enflames my sense;
And art thou not willing, I'll take thee hence!"

"Mein Vater, mein Vater, jetzt fasst er mich an!
Erlkönig hat mir ein Leid's gethan!"

"Oh father, father, he grasps my arm,
The Erlking has done me harm!"

Dem Vater grauset's, er reitet geschwind,
er hält in Armen das ächzende Kind,

The father shudders, he speeds ahead,
He clasps to his bosom the sobbing child,

erreicht den Hof mit Müh' und Noth:

He reaches home with pain and dread:

in seinen Armen das Kind war todt!

In his arms the child lay dead!

The eerie atmosphere of the poem is established by the piano part. Galloping triplets are heard against a rumbling figure in the bass. This motive, so romantic in tone, pervades the canvas and imparts to it an astonishing unity.

The characters are vividly differentiated through changes in the melody, harmony, rhythm, and type of accompaniment. The child's terror is suggested by clashing dissonance, pitched higher each time. The father, allaying his son's fears, is represented by a more rounded vocal line. As for the Erlking, his cajoling is given in suavely melodious phrases.

The song is through-composed; the music follows the unfolding of the narrative with a steady building up of tension to the climax. Abruptly the obsessive triplet rhythm breaks off, giving way to declamation. "In his arms the child"—a pause—"lay dead."

The thing seems strangely simple, inevitable. The doing of it by a marvelous boy of eighteen was an event in the history of romanticism.

Heidenröslein (*Hedge Rose*)

The strophic song is well exemplified by this gem of Schubertian melody. Couched in the idiom of folk song, *Heidenröslein* (1815) displays the engaging traits of the romantic lied: simplicity of sentiment, feeling for nature, directness of communication, and spontaneous melody. Goethe's verses strike a vein of homely feeling which, with unerring intuition, Schubert translated into the popular tone.

Sah ein Knab' ein Röslein steh'n,	Saw a lad a rosebud there,
Röslein auf der Heiden,	Rosebud on the heather,
war so jung und morgenschön,	Young and fresh in morning light,
lief er schnell, es nah' zu seh'n,	She shed her charms upon the air.
sah's mit vielen Freuden.	He gazed upon her with delight.
Röslein, Röslein, Röslein roth,	Rosebud, rosebud, rosebud red,
Röslein auf der Heiden.	Rosebud on the heather.
Knabe sprach: "ich breche dich,	Said the boy: "I'll pluck thee,
Röslein auf der Heiden!"	Rosebud on the heather!"
Röslein sprach: "ich steche dich,	Said the rose: "I'll prick thee,
dass du ewig denkst an mich,	That thou may'st remember me,
und ich will's nicht leiden."	For I shall not suffer thee!"
Röslein, Röslein, Röslein roth,	Rosebud, rosebud, rosebud red,
Röslein auf der Heiden.	Rosebud on the heather.
Und der wilde Knabe brach	And the cruel boy plucked the rose,
's Röslein auf der Heiden;	Rosebud on the heather;
Röslein wehrte sich und stach,	She in vain sought to oppose;
half ihr doch kein Weh und Ach,	In vain alas her pain and woes,
musst' es eben leiden.	She had to yield and suffer.
Röslein, Röslein, Röslein roth,	Rosebud, rosebud, rosebud red,
Röslein auf der Heiden.	Rosebud on the heather.

The mood is indicated by the marking *lieblich* (graceful). The accompaniment is of the simplest. The charming nonsymmetry of Goethe's seven-line stanza is reflected in the music. The first two lines comprise one phrase, the next three another, while the last two serve as a refrain which is echoed by the piano in a little postlude after each stanza. The melody line is narrow in range, predominantly stepwise in movement, and of tripping gait. Delightful is the ascent along the scale to the climax, on the line, "Röslein, Röslein, Röslein roth."

This type of Schubert song occupies a position in Germany similar to that of Stephen Foster's melodies with us. As one critic well put it, "Schubert does not try to imitate folk song. He creates it."

Impromptu in A-Flat, Opus 90, No. 4

A publisher of Vienna hit on the title "Impromptu," thereby neatly fixing the quality of caprice that characterizes these piano pieces. The name accorded with the romantic notion that music came in a flash of inspiration. Yet the lyric pieces of Schubert manifest, together with their spontaneous emotion, a sure control of form and detail. As in the sonnets of Keats—in whom some have recognized an affinity with the Viennese master—art is here concealed by art.

One of Schubert's most widely played piano pieces, the Impromptu in A-flat, Opus 90, No. 4, was written in 1827. (*Opus*, abbreviated Op., the Latin for "work," is used in conjunction with a number to indicate the chronological position of a piece—or a group of pieces—in a composer's output. The opus number may refer to either the order of composition or the order of publication. The practice of using opus numbers was not fully established until the early nineteenth century.) The Impromptu in A-flat is an A-B-A form, with each section subdividing into symmetrical smaller sections. The piece is an Allegretto in $\frac{3}{4}$ time. The principal idea involves arpeggios that sweep down gently in a broad arc. Presently, beneath cascades of broken chords in the treble, a wisp of melody emerges in the bass (example on next page).

The middle part, a somber and sustained song accompanied by repeated chords, presents an effective contrast to the outer sections.

Tension builds in a steady line to the climax. The emotion is direct, concentrated, inescapable. As in the songs, the tight frame of the lyric piece guards Schubert from the diffuseness that beset him in his sonatas.

This little masterpiece was published in 1885, almost sixty years after it was composed. It was one of a series of manuscripts that kept coming to light throughout the century, recovered from the "pile of old music valued at ten florins" that was left behind at his death.

Moment musical *in F Minor, Opus 94, No. 3*

In title, form, and substance the most famous of the "Musical Moments" (c. 1825) epitomizes the short lyric piece. It is intimate and unassuming; one would almost say artless, were it not for the omnipresence of art. It bears the finest qualities of the miniature: chiseled line, fastidious speech, and epigrammatic thought.

The piece consists of brief symmetrical sections, each of them repeated. So small a frame does not allow for great contrasts. The mood of the opening prevails more or less throughout.

In this compact little work are manifest the qualities that set Schubert apart, in the eyes of his devotees, from all others: his charm of melody,

Michelangelo, 1475-1564, *The Libyan Sibyl*, Sistine Chapel ceiling. (Courtesy *Life* Magazine © 1955, Time, Inc.)

"Renaissance painting found its symbols in Greek and Roman antiquity."

Sandro Botticelli, c. 1444-1510, *Spring*. (The Uffizi Gallery, Florence)

"The Renaissance marks the passing of European society from an exclusively religious orientation to a secular."

Leonardo da Vinci, 1452-1519, *The Virgin and Child with Saint Anne.* (The Louvre Museum, Paris)

"The Renaissance created unified space and the simultaneous seeing of the whole. It discovered the landscape, created the illusion of distance, and opened up endless vistas upon the physical loveliness of the world."

Raphael, 1483-1520, *The Marriage of the Virgin.* (The Brera Museum, Milan)

his tenderness, his gentle sorrow, and that ineffably romantic longing which can only be described as Schubertian.

CHAPTER 18

Robert Schumann (1810-1856)

"Music is to me the perfect expression of the soul."

THE TURBULENCE of German romanticism, its fantasy and subjective emotion, found their voice in Robert Schumann. His music is German to the core, yet he is no local figure. A true lyric poet, he rose above the national to make his contribution to world culture.

His Life

Robert Schumann was born in Zwickau, a town in Saxony, son of a bookseller whose love of literature was reflected in the boy. At his mother's insistence he undertook the study of law, first at the University of Leipzig, then at Heidelberg. The youth daydreamed at the piano, steeped himself in Goethe and Byron, and attended only an occasional lecture. His aversion to the law kept pace with his passion for music; it was his ambition to become a pianist. At last he won his mother's consent and returned to Leipzig to study with Friedrich Wieck, one of the foremost pedagogues of the day. "I am so fresh in soul and spirit," he exulted, "that life gushes and bubbles around me in a thousand springs."

The young man practiced intensively to make up for his late start. In his eagerness to perfect his technique he devised a contrivance that held the fourth finger immobile while the others exercised. The gadget was so effective that he permanently injured the fourth finger of his right hand. The end of his hopes as a pianist turned his interest to composing. In a burst of creative energy he produced, while still in his twenties, his most important works for the piano.

The spontaneity of his production astonished him. "Everything comes to me of itself," he wrote, "and indeed, it sometimes seems as if I could play on eternally and never come to an end." He refers again and again to the almost automatic quality of his inspiration. "Often I feel such a compulsion to compose that even if I were on a lonely island in the middle of the sea I could not stop. . . . It makes me altogether happy, this art." Such intensity—the prime quality of the lyricist—carried with it a premonition of early doom. "Oh I cannot help it, I should like to sing myself to death like a nightingale. . . ."

He was engaged concurrently in an important literary venture. With a group of like-minded enthusiasts he founded a journal named *The New Magazine for Music*. The leading spirit in the enterprise, he regarded it as his mission "to help prepare and hasten the coming of a new poetic era." Schumann threw himself into his editorial activities as

Robert and Clara Schumann.

impetuously as he had into composing. Under his direction the periodical became one of the most important music journals in Europe.

Schumann's critical essays revealed the composer as a gifted literary man. Cast in the form of prose poems, imaginary dialogues, or letters, they were as personal as his music. He fought the taste of the bourgeois —the Philistines, as he liked to call them. He agitated for the great works of the past and for the new romanticism. In sketches that were half fact, half fiction he portrayed his friends and associates. Felix Meritis was Mendelssohn, whom at that time he admired above all living musicians. Master Raro was the judicious critic modeled after his teacher Friedrich Wieck. Chiarina was the latter's young daughter

Clara, already known as one of the gifted pianists of the time. Schumann himself assumed two pen names to express the two sides of his personality: Florestan was gay and impetuous, Eusebius dreamy and introspective. The two carried on great arguments that mirrored the conflict between exuberance and restraint, between rebellious content and controlling form: the basic conflict in the soul of the romantic artist.

The hectic quality of this decade was intensified by his courtship of Clara Wieck. When he first came to study with her father she was an eleven-year-old prodigy who forthwith lost her heart to the young man. She was about sixteen when Robert realized that he loved her. Wieck's opposition to the marriage bordered on the psychopathic. Clara was the supreme achievement of his life and he refused to surrender her to another. For several years she was cruelly torn between the father she revered and the man she loved. At length, since she was not yet of age, the couple was forced to appeal to the courts against Wieck. The marriage took place in 1840, when Clara was twenty-one and Robert thirty. His happiness overflowed into a medium more personal even than the piano. This was his "year of song," when he produced over a hundred of the lieder that represent his lyric gift at its purest.

The two artists settled in Leipzig, pursuing their careers side by side. Clara became the first interpreter of Robert's piano works and in the ensuing decade contributed substantially to the spreading of his fame. Yet neither her love nor that of their children could ward off his increasing withdrawal from the world. Moodiness and nervous exhaustion culminated, in 1844, in a severe breakdown. The doctors counseled a change of scene. The couple moved to Dresden, where Schumann seemingly made a full recovery. But the periods of depression returned ever more frequently. "In these years I have been very industrious. One must work as long as day lasts. . . ."

In 1850 Schumann was appointed music director at Düsseldorf. But he was ill-suited for public life; he could neither organize music festivals nor deal with masses of men, and was forced to relinquish the post. During a tour of Holland, where Clara and he were warmly received, he began to complain of "unnatural noises" in his head. His last letter to the violinist Joachim, two weeks before the final breakdown, is a farewell to his art. "The music is silent now . . . I will close. Already it grows dark."

He fell prey to auditory hallucinations, during which he was kept awake by a single maddening tone. Once he rose in the middle of the night to write down a theme that he imagined had been brought him by the spirits of Schubert and Mendelssohn. It was his last melody. A week later, in a fit of melancholia, he threw himself into the Rhine. He was rescued by fishermen and placed in a private asylum near Bonn. Despite occasional flashes of lucidity, the darkness did not lift. He died two years later at the age of forty-six.

His Music

Schumann's art exemplifies the conflict between classical form and romantic content that his generation was heir to. He fought to save for romanticism the heritage of Beethoven, and bravely tackled the great classical forms—symphony, sonata, concerto, and chamber music. But he was essentially a lyricist and made his major contribution in the romantic realm of the lied and the piano piece.

As a piano composer Schumann was one of the most original figures of the century. Whimsy and ardent expressiveness pervade his miniatures, which brim over with impassioned melody, novel harmonies, and vigorous rhythms. The titles of the collections strike the romantic note; among them we find *Fantasy Pieces, Papillons* (Butterflies), *Romances, Scenes from Childhood*. No less characteristic are the names affixed to individual numbers: *In the Night, Why?, The Poet Speaks*. Schumann emphasized that he added the titles *after* the music was written. All the same he illustrates the tendency of his time to "literarize" musical emotion, to associate it with specific images. He was less successful with the abstract forms. Although his three sonatas contain lovely things, they fall short of the organic unity that was the classical ideal. He did, however, succeed in producing three large works that stand in the top class of the repertory: the Fantasy in C, the Symphonic Etudes, and the Piano Concerto in A minor.

As a lieder writer he ranks second only to Schubert. His songs are finely wrought and rich in poetic suggestion. His favorite theme is love, particularly from the woman's point of view. His favored poet was Heine, for whom he had an affinity like that of Schubert for Goethe. The piano accompaniments are integrated with the vocal line in the highest degree. Schumann followed Schubert in cultivating the song cycle. Among his supreme achievements are the cycles *Frauenliebe und -Leben* (Woman's Love and Life, verses by Chamisso, 1840) and *Dichterliebe* (Poet's Love, by Heine, 1840).

Thoroughly romantic in feeling are the four symphonies. Schumann has been taken to task for his inability to develop thematic material and to orchestrate. The difficulty lies deeper, in the lyrical rather than symphonic nature of his thinking. Certain of the themes to which he accorded symphonic treatment would have come off better as piano pieces or songs. This accounts in part for the shortness of breath of which the critics speak. One often receives the impression from his symphonic music of listening to a piano piece that has been orchestrated. (He is not the only romantic composer of whom this can be said.) Yet even when his instrumental writing is awkward, it fits peculiarly his forceful ideas. The best of his symphonies, the First and Fourth, communicate a lyric freshness that has kept them alive long after many more adroitly fashioned works have fallen by the way. What could be closer to the essence of German romanticism than the "nature sound" of the horns and trumpets at the opening of the *Spring Symphony,* his First? "Could you infuse into the orchestra," he wrote the conductor, "a kind of longing for spring? At the first entrance of the trumpets I should like them to sound as from on high, like a call to awakening."

Through his writings on music he stands in the forefront of nineteenth-century critics. His propagandizing on behalf of Bach, Beethoven, and Schubert helped enormously to raise the level of public taste. And he singled out the creative forces of his own time with sure intuition. His first article, a review of a set of variations by an unknown young composer named Frédéric Chopin, began with the famous words: "Hats off, gentlemen—a genius!" More than twenty years later, in his last essay, he prophesied the future eminence of another unknown— Johannes Brahms. His writings prove, if proof were needed, that there is no better critic of music than the composer who is articulate. Many a paragraph applies amazingly to our own time.

Die beiden Grenadiere (*The Two Grenadiers*)

Heinrich Heine's ballad about two homecoming Napoleonic soldiers furnished the text for Schumann's most celebrated song (1840). Here is exemplified the vigorous, Florestan side of Schumann's genius.

Nach Frankreich zogen zwei Grenadier',	To France came from Russia two grenadiers
die waren in Russland gefangen,	Who had been captives in battle,
und als sie kamen in's deutsche Quartier,	And as they reached the German frontiers
sie liessen die Köpfe hangen.	Their heads were bowed with grief.
Da hörten sie beide die traurige Mähr,	For there they heard the sorrowful news
dass Frankreich verloren gegangen,	That France had been defeated,
besiegt und geschlagen das tapfere Heer,	Defeated and scattered her valiant army,
und der Kaiser, der Kaiser gefangen.	And the Emperor, the Emperor taken.
Da weinten zusammen die Grenadier'	Then wept the two grenadiers
wohl ob der kläglichen Kunde.	Such sorrowful tidings to learn;
Der Eine sprach: "Wie weh wird mir,	The first one said: "Woe is me,

wie brennt meine alte Wunde!"	Now fiercely my old wounds burn."
Der And're sprach: "Das Lied ist aus,	The other said: "My song is done,
auch ich möcht' mit dir sterben,	Would that I were dead,
doch hab' ich Weib und Kind zu Haus,	Yet I've a wife and child at home
die ohne mich verderben."	Who are helpless without me."
"Was schert mich Weib, was schert mich Kind	"What matters wife or child?
ich trage weit bess're Verlangen,	By nobler desires I am shaken,
lass sie betteln geh'n wenn sie hung- rig sind,	Let them go beg if they hungry be,
mein Kaiser, mein Kaiser gefangen!	My Emperor, my Emperor is taken.
Gewähr mir, Bruder, eine Bitt':	Grant me, brother, one request:
Wenn ich jetzt sterben werde,	If I now should die,
so nimm meine Leiche nach Frank- reich mit,	Take my body to France with you,
begrab' mich in Frankreichs Erde.	In my native soil let me lie.
Das Ehrenkreuz am rothen Band	My cross of honor with band of red
sollst du auf's Herz mir legen;	Lay upon my heart;
die Flinte gieb mir in die Hand,	My musket place in my hand,
und gürt mir um den Degen.	And my sword beside me.
So will ich liegen und horchen still,	So will I lie within the grave,
wie eine Schildwach', im Grabe,	A sentry still, and faithful,
bis einst ich höre Kanonengebrüll	Till I hear the roar of the cannon
und wiehernder Rosse Getrabe.	And the galloping hoofbeats.
Dann reitet mein Kaiser wohl über mein Grab,	Then over my grave will my Em- peror ride
viel Schwerter klirren und blitzen;	While swords flash and descend.
dann steig' ich gewaffnet hervor aus dem Grab,	Then armed to the teeth will I rise from the grave
den Kaiser, den Kaiser zu schützen!"	The Emperor, the Emperor to de- fend."

The song is an example of the dramatic ballad that is through-composed. A martial figure in the piano part, in $\frac{4}{4}$ time, immediately sets the mood (see the example).

This prelude, marked by the dotted rhythms beloved by Schumann, recurs. The little motive of sixteenth notes at its end is heard again and again throughout the song. There is a slackening of intensity as the soldiers learn the sorrowful news. Their mounting agitation is reflected in an acceleration of pace. The request of the second grenadier (stanzas 3 and 4) steadily builds up tension. The climax is very grand: as the soldier pictures himself in the grave, the vocal line rises to the strains of the *Marseillaise*. It is one of those exciting effects that never fail. In the final stanza Schumann repeats the line about the flashing swords—the only repetition of text in the whole song—to allow for the necessary musical expansion. A postlude of sustained chords in the piano part adds a thoughtful commentary.

The heroics of this ballad belong to a former era; but it would be difficult to surpass its sweeping line, its virile tone, and its effectiveness in the concert hall.

Ich grolle nicht (*I'll Not Complain*)
From Dichterliebe

The introspective side of Schumann's lyricism—Eusebius—predominates in what is probably his most powerful love song. Heine's lines fired the composer to a lied of brooding intensity.

Ich grolle nicht,	I'll not complain,
und wenn das Herz auch bricht,	E'en though my heart will break,
Ewig verlor'nes Lieb! Ich grolle nicht.	Love forever lost, I chide you not.
Wie du auch strahlst in Diamantenpracht,	You gleam in jeweled splendor bright,
Es fällt kein Strahl in deines Herzens Nacht,	There falls no ray into your heart's fierce night,
das weiss ich längst.	This well I know.

Ich grolle nicht,
und wenn das Herz auch bricht.
Ich sah dich ja im Traume,
und sah die Nacht in deines Herzens
    Raume,
und sah die Schlang', die dir am
    Herzen frisst,
Ich sah, mein Lieb, wie sehr du
    elend bist.
Ich grolle nicht, ich grolle nicht.

I'll not complain,
E'en though my heart will break.
I saw you in my dream,
The night within your heart I saw,

And saw the snake that at your heart
    doth gnaw,
My love, how all alone you are I
    saw.
I'll not complain, I'll not complain.

Schumann here achieves the supreme aim of the romantic lied—to give utterance to a state of soul. The soaring melody becomes a kind of graph that follows sensitively the rise and fall of emotion. Sustained dissonances in the accompaniment build harmonic and psychological tension.

Key lines in the text are repeated to allow for musical expansion. The form is a free variant of the strophic song, standing between that and the through-composed variety. Both stanzas start out identically. The first subsides to permit the music to return to the opening phrase. The second stanza builds up relentlessly to the tragic chords of the climax: "And saw the snake that at your heart doth gnaw . . ."

This is one of the great romantic songs.

Aufschwung (*Soaring*) *and Romance in F-Sharp*

Schumann's piano pieces exhibit his mastery of the miniature; also his capacity to translate into music the image, the emotion, or mood suggested by the title. Unhampered by the grand architecture of classical form, he functioned here in the lyric realm that was most congenial to his genius. The form is spontaneous, almost capricious, yet it is tightly organized and controlled. Within the pattern of statement-departure-return he found an ideal frame for what he had to say.

Aufschwung and the Romance again display the Florestan-Eusebius dualism in Schumann's nature. The first, Opus 12, No. 2, is one of the *Phantasiestücke* (Fantasy Pieces, 1837). Bold rhythmic patterns, ceaseless movement in the inner parts, and a flow of melodic ideas make this piece precisely what its name implies: a soaring, an upsurge of spirit. The meter is $\frac{6}{8}$, the tempo lively. The mood is fiery, as indicated by Schumann's marking *Sehr rasch* (very spirited).

The impetuous main idea recurs in contrast with subsidiary sections more quiet in nature, producing the structural pattern A-B-A-C-A-B-A. This arresting miniature embodies the spirit of the dance, and it also shows off Schumann's individual manner of writing for the instrument.

The Romance in F-sharp, Opus 28, No. 2 (1839), is a lied for piano. Schumann's lyricism takes shape in a flowing melody that moves either stepwise along the scale or with narrow leaps against a background of broken chords. The mood is tender, the harmonies expressive. Schumann directs that this piece be played *einfach* (simply).

After a somewhat agitated middle section the serene melody returns. At one point right and left hand engage in a tender dialogue, the one imitating the other. This interweaving of independent lines enriched the texture of Schumann's piano music and influenced a number of later composers. Wholly Schumannesque is the spinning out of the melody in broad sinuous curves; and the sense of incompletion at the end, where the music trails off into silence. The listener is left suspended in a dream, as it were—an effect much prized by the romantic composers. The Romance in F-sharp brings to piano literature the mood of tender avowal that was Schumann's finest vein.

"Music still devours me. I must often tear myself from it by violence." This remark indicates the passionate creativity of the decade and a half in which Schumann was at his peak. His peak was the spring tide of German romanticism, during which he nobly discharged what he conceived to be the artist's mission: "To send light into the depths of the human heart!"

⟡⟡⟡ *CHAPTER 19* ⟡⟡⟡

Frédéric François Chopin (1810-1849)

"My life . . . an episode without a beginning and with a sad end."

IN THE annals of his century Chopin is known as the "Poet of the Piano." The title is a valid one. His art, issuing from the heart of romanticism, constitutes the golden age of that instrument.

His Life

The national composer of Poland was half French. His father emigrated to Warsaw, where he married a lady-in-waiting to a countess and taught French to the sons of the nobility. Frédéric, who displayed his musical gifts in childhood, was educated at the recently founded Conservatory of Warsaw. His student years were climaxed by a mild infatuation with a young singer, Constantia Gladkowska, who inspired him with sighs and tears in the best nineteenth-century manner. "It was with thoughts of this beautiful creature that I composed the Adagio of my new concerto." The concerto was the one in F minor. Frédéric was nineteen.

After a concert at which Constantia sang and he played, the young artist set forth to make a name in the world. His comrades sang a farewell cantata in his honor. Frédéric wept, convinced he would never see his homeland again. In Vienna the news reached him that

Warsaw had risen in revolt against the Tsar. Gloomy visions tormented him; he saw his family and friends massacred. He left Vienna in the summer. On reaching Stuttgart he learned that the Polish capital had been captured by the Russians. The tidings precipitated a torrent of grief, and the flaming defiance that found expression in the *Revolutionary Etude.*

In September, 1831, the young man reached Paris. He thought of continuing to London, even to America. But he was introduced by a Polish prince into the aristocratic salons, and there created a sensation. His decision was made, and the rest of his career was linked to the

Frédéric François Chopin.
From a portrait by Delacroix.

artistic life of his adopted city. Chopin's letters indicate that musical success was as complicated a matter in that day as in this. "I have got into the highest society. I sit with ambassadors, princes, ministers. . . . This is a most necessary thing for me, since one's success is supposed to depend on it. At once you have a bigger talent if you have been heard at the English or Austrian Ambassador's. You play better if Princess Vaudmont was your patron—I can't say *is*, as the lady died a week ago . . . I have five lessons to give today. You think I am making a fortune? Carriages and white gloves cost more, and without them one would not be in good taste." The bantering tone should not mislead us. Chopin was a snob at twenty, and a snob he remained.

Paris in the 1830s was the center of the new romanticism. The circle in which Chopin moved included as brilliant a galaxy of artists as ever gathered anywhere. Among the musicians were Liszt and Berlioz, Rossini and Meyerbeer. The literary figures included Victor Hugo and

Balzac, Lamartine, George Sand, de Musset, Alexandre Dumas. Heinrich Heine was his friend, as was the painter Delacroix. Although Chopin was a man of emotions rather than ideas, he could not but be stimulated by his contact with the leading intellectuals of France.

He performed occasionally at concerts. But his music was too personal, he felt, to capture the public. "The crowd embarrasses me," he told Liszt. "I feel stifled by their hurried breathing, paralyzed by their curious glances." More congenial to him were the salons of countesses, in which rarefied atmosphere he unbent, drawing from the piano harmonies and rhythms that electrified his hearers. He was saying things in music that had never been said before. The frail young Pole avowed his "daring but noble resolve—to create a new era in art!" Only youth could set itself so lofty a goal; only genius achieve it.

Through Liszt he met Mme. Aurore Dudevant, "the lady with the somber eye," known to the world as the novelist George Sand. She was thirty-four, Chopin twenty-eight when the famous friendship began. Mme. Sand was brilliant and domineering; her need to dominate found its counterpart in Chopin's need to be ruled. She left a memorable account of this fastidious artist at work.

"His creative power was spontaneous, miraculous. It came to him without effort or warning. . . . But then began the most heartrending labor I have ever witnessed. It was a series of attempts, of fits of irresolution and impatience to recover certain details. He conceived a melody as a whole, but when he tried to write it down he analyzed it too much, and his regret at not recovering it in clear-cut form plunged him—by his own account—into a sort of despair. He would shut himself in his room for days, pacing up and down, breaking his pens, repeating and modifying one bar a hundred times . . . He would spend six weeks over a page, only to end by writing it out finally just as he had sketched it in the original draft."

For the next eight years Chopin spent his summers at Mme. Sand's chateau at Nohant, where she entertained the cream of France's intelligentsia. These were productive years for him, although his health grew progressively worse and his relationship with Mme. Sand ran its course from love to conflict, from jealousy to hostility and bitterness. She, born an aristocrat, had only contempt for her class. Opposed to the reactionary monarchy, she took an active part in the events that led to the Revolution of 1848. She resented Chopin's haughty reserve, his conventional social views, his lack of sympathy with the radical cause. They parted in bitterness.

According to his friend Liszt, "Chopin felt and often repeated that in breaking this long affection, this powerful bond, he had broken his life." Chopin's creative energy, which had lost its momentum in his middle thirties, came to an end. The "illness of the century," the lonely despair of the romantic artist pervades his last letters. "What has become of my art?" he writes during a visit to Scotland. "And my heart, where have I wasted it? I scarce remember any more how they sing at home. That world slips away from me somehow. I forget. I have no strength. If I rise a little I fall again, lower than ever."

He returned to Paris suffering from tuberculosis and died some months later at the age of thirty-nine. His funeral was his greatest triumph. Princesses and artists joined to pay him homage. Meyerbeer, Berlioz, and Delacroix were among the mourners. George Sand stayed away. His heart was returned to Poland, the rest of him remained in Paris. And on his grave a friendly hand scattered a gobletful of Polish earth.

His Music

Chopin was one of the most original artists of the romantic era. He decisively influenced the course of nineteenth-century music. His idiom is so entirely his own there is no mistaking it for any other. He was the only master of first rank whose creative life centered almost exclusively about the piano. From the first, his imagination was wedded to the keyboard, to create a universe within that narrow frame. His genius transformed even the limitations of the instrument into sources of beauty. (The prime limitation, of course, is the piano's inability to sustain tone for any length of time.) Chopin overcame these with such ingenuity that to him as much as to any individual is due the modern piano style. The widely spaced chords in the bass, sustained by pedal, set up masses of tone that wreathe the melody in enchantment. "Everything must be made to sing," he told his pupils. The delicate ornaments in his music—trills, grace notes, runs of gossamer lightness—magically prolong the single tones. And all this lies so well to hand that the music seems almost to play itself.

Yet it would be erroneous to suppose that Chopin dwells serenely within the limitations of the keyboard. There are moments in his larger works when he appears to struggle with his medium, to strain beyond its capacities. He gropes toward a vaster frame; he stands on the threshold of visions but dimly glimpsed. It is precisely then that he is at his greatest.

In harmony he was one of the daring innovators of the century, opening up to nineteenth-century music a wealth of iridescent color. His melodies are models of romantic lyricism; his rhythms are the idealization of body movement. So personal a message was hardly at home in the great classic forms. Chopin is a master of the miniature; his lyric forms draw their sustenance from the spirit of song and dance.

Slavic melancholy and French elegance—two distinguished strains mingle in his music.

It is remarkable that so many of his works have remained in the pianist's repertory. His Nocturnes—night songs, as the name implies —are tender avowals tinged with varying shades of melancholy. They are usually in A-B-A form. The Preludes are visionary fragments; some are only a page in length, several consist of two or three lines. Of these Schumann said, "In each piece we find in his own hand, 'Frédéric Chopin wrote it!' He is the boldest, the proudest poet of his time." The Etudes crown the literature of the study piece. The problems of piano technique are here transformed into poetry. The Impromptus are fanciful, capricious, yet they have a curious rightness about them. The Waltzes capture the brilliance and coquetry of the salon. They are veritable dances of the spirit. The Mazurkas, derived from a Polish peasant dance, with their elusive rhythms evoke the idealized landscape of his youth.

Among the larger forms are the four Ballades. These are epic poems of spacious structure, sagas related by a bard. The Polonaises revive the stately processional dance in which Poland's nobles were wont to hail their kings. Heroic in tone, they resound with the clangor of battle and grave deeds. In reminding his countrymen of their ancient glory the national poet strengthens their will to freedom. The *Berceuse* (Cradle Song), the *Barcarolle* (Boat Song), the Fantasy in F minor, and the dramatic Scherzos reveal the composer at the summit of his art. The Sonatas in B minor and B-flat minor are thoroughly romantic in spirit; they dissolve the outlines of sonata form in rhapsodic lyricism. The two concertos, one in E minor and one in F minor, are works of his youth. Chopin's was not an orchestral imagination, nor did the classical form specifically fit his musical ideas. Yet these contain some wonderfully felicitous moments, like the romantic sonority of horn and piano tone in the E-minor Concerto.

Chopin's style stands before us fully formed when he was twenty. It was not the result of an extended intellectual development, as was the case with masters like Beethoven or Wagner. In this he was the true lyricist, along with his contemporaries Schumann and Mendelssohn. All three died young, and all three reached their peak through the spontaneous lyricism of youth. In them the first period of romanticism—its idealist phase—found pure and noble expression.

Etude in E Major

A specific problem in pianoforte technique, the execution of double notes (two notes simultaneously) serves as the basis for the celebrated

Etude in E major, Opus 10, No. 3 (c. 1830). The upper fingers of the right hand play one of Chopin's most eloquent melodies while the lower fingers articulate an accompanying figure.

Characteristic is the rise to the climax and the gentle subsiding, a curve of tension and release much in favor with the romantics. The lyric middle section culminates in a sequence of double notes. There follows a brilliant passage based on extended broken chords that are the despair of pianists with small hands. When the excitement simmers down, the first section is heard again in curtailed form. A subtle touch, this. The composer implies that since we already know the material it suffices to touch upon it rather than restate it in its entirety.

Prelude in D Minor

Marked Allegro appassionato, the Prelude in D minor, Opus 28, No. 24 (1839), is steeped in Byronic pathos. Through it resounds the fevered restlessness of the romantic age. Noteworthy is Chopin's exploitation of the somber sonorities in the low register of the instrument. Merely the look of the notes on the page—extended arpeggios in the left hand against the clarionlike motive in the right—reveals the author.

The form expands freely from the initial motive. The latter returns in octaves. There is a steady accumulation of tension. The descent along the scale at the climax produces a demonic effect. The coda is brief and clangorous. A low D tolls thrice at the end. Strangeness and wonder, the essence of the romantic mood, pervade this music.

Polonaise in A-Flat

The heroic side of Chopin's art shows itself in the most popular of his Polonaises, the one in A-flat, Opus 53 (1842). The opening theme

is proud and chivalric. The octaves for the left hand in the following section approach the limits of what the piano can do. It seems as if only the full orchestra with its trumpets and drums could do justice to the conception. However, one has but to hear the piece in an orchestral arrangement to realize that this is pure piano music, an epic fashioned out of the clang and color of piano sonority.

The emotional temperature drops perceptibly after the octave episode, which is Chopin's way of building up tension against the return of the theme. The piece as a whole is rather rhetorical. A canvas painted with broad sweeps of the brush, it lacks Chopin's inwardness. In the hands of a virtuoso this Polonaise takes on surpassing brilliance; it is the epitome of the grand style.

His countrymen have enshrined Chopin as the national composer of Poland. Withal he is a spokesman of European culture. It is not without significance that despite his homesickness he spent the whole of his adult life in Paris. Thus Poland was idealized in his imagination as the symbol of that unappeasable longing which every romantic artist carries in his heart: the longing for the lost land of happiness that may never be found again. Heine, himself an expatriate, divined this when he wrote that Chopin is "neither a Pole, a Frenchman, nor a German.

He reveals a higher origin. He comes from the land of Mozart, Raphael, Goethe. His true country is the land of poetry."

❧ *CHAPTER 20* ❧

The Short Lyric Forms in the Late Romantic Period

The Song

THE INFLUENCE of the German lied spread through Europe in the second half of the nineteenth century. Although rooted in German romanticism, it proved itself adaptable to the tastes of other nations. The lied served as model for several non-German composers, some of whose songs established themselves firmly in the international repertory. Among the best known of these are Tchaikovsky's *None But the Lonely Heart,* Grieg's *I Love Thee,* and Dvořák's *Songs My Mother Taught Me.* It was a German composer, however, who did the most important work in this area. The songs of Johannes Brahms stand in direct line of descent from the lieder of Schubert and Schumann. He handled the short form with consummate ease and craftsmanship, bringing to his songs an inwardness of feeling and a manly, restrained fervor. The sensitiveness of the vocal line is matched by the eloquence of the accompaniment. Through his finest songs sounds the note of autumnal resignation that is so characteristic of this composer.

Die Mainacht (*May Night*)

This setting of a poem by Ludwig Hölty, one of Brahms's outstanding lieder (1868), well exemplifies the qualities of his song style.

Wann der silberne Mond
  durch die Gesträuche blinkt,
und sein schlummerndes Licht
  über den Rasen streut,
und die Nachtigall flötet,
wandl' ich traurig von Busch zu
  Busch.

Überhüllet vom Laub
  girret ein Taubenpaar

When the silvery moon
  shines through the rustling leaves,
And her pale languid light
  over the meadow pours;
When the nightingale warbles,
I wander sadly from glade to glade.

Hidden in the leaves
  I hear a pair of doves

sein Entzücken mir vor;   murmur in ecstasy.
aber ich wende mich,   I turn away,
suche dunklere Schatten,   Seeking darker shadows,
    und die einsame Träne rinnt.   and a lonely tear wells up.

Wann, o lächelndes Bild,   When, O lovely vision
    welches wie Morgenrot   whose smile streams through my
    durch die Seele mir strahlt,   soul like the flush of dawn,
find' ich auf Erden dich?   When on earth shall I find thee?
Und die einsame Träne bebt mir   And the lonely tear presses
    heisser die Wang' herab.   hotter upon my cheek.

The melody, marked *sehr langsam und ausdrucksvoll* (very slow and expressive), begins by outlining the tones of the Tonic chord, a characteristic procedure with Brahms. No less characteristic is the rich texture of the harmony, the accompaniment intertwining with the vocal line yet remaining independent of it. There is a nice balance in the melody between stepwise movement and narrow leaps, resulting in a broadly flowing line that is molded to the voice.

The mood changes with the second stanza. The mention of doves sends a tenderness through the music; the accompaniment shifts to the treble register. Expressive harmonies repeated in the left-hand part build up tension against the key line "I turn away, seeking darker shadows . . ." A wide and tragic downward leap marks the words "turn away." The emotional climax comes in the next phrase, with a long sustained note and a spinning out of the melody on the decisive word "tear."

At the third stanza we return to the melody of the first, with a resultant A-B-A form. The last line about the tear evokes the same music that was associated with this thought in the second stanza, and serves to round off the song. The accompaniment is now presented in triplet rhythm, as an element of intensification. In conjunction with the melody line it produces the effect of cross rhythm (three against two) of which Brahms was so fond.

Hölty's somewhat less than distinguished lines are lifted by the power of a distinguished musical imagination into the realm of the deeply felt, the inescapably romantic.

Vergebliches Ständchen (*Futile Serenade*)

The other side of Brahms's personality—extrovert, robust, and delighting in broad humor—is to be observed in the *Vergebliches Ständchen* (1881). It is his version of a folk song from the Lower Rhineland. One has but to compare his melody with the original to become aware of the artistic refinement that he brought to bear upon the rough-hewn folk tune.

Under the impact of nineteenth-century nationalism many composers turned to the folk idiom for inspiration. Some based their works upon actual folk songs; more frequently, however, the nationalist created his own melodies in the folk style. In the case of the *Vergebliches Ständchen* Brahms retained the words of the popular song and its general rhythmic scheme. Onto these he grafted a melody of his own mintage. What came out was a lusty and vivacious song in popular vein.

Er: Guten Abend, mein Schatz,
  guten Abend, mein Kind,
  guten Abend, mein Kind!
Ich komm' aus Lieb' zu dir,
ach, mach' mir auf die Tür,
mach' mir auf die Tür,
  mach' mir auf, mach' mir auf,
  mach' mir auf die Tür!

Sie: Mein' Tür ist verschlossen,
  ich lass' dich nicht ein,
  ich lass' dich nicht ein;
Mutter, die rät mir klug,
wärst du herein mit Fug,
wär's mit mir vorbei,
  wär's mit mir, wär's mit mir,
  wär's mit mir vorbei!

Er: So kalt ist die Nacht,
  so eisig der Wind,
  so eisig der Wind;
dass mir das Herz erfriert,
mein' Lieb' erlöschen wird,
öffne mir, mein Kind,
  öffne mir, öffne mir,
  öffne mir, mein Kind!

Sie: Löschet dein' Lieb',
  lass sie löschen nur,
  lass sie löschen nur!
Löschet sie immerzu,
geh' heim zu Bett, zur Ruh',

He: Good evening, my darling,
  good evening, my sweet,
  good evening, my sweet!
I come for love of you,
Open the door for me,
Open the door for me,
  Let me in, let me in,
  Open the door!

She: My door's firmly locked,
  I sha'n't let you in,
  I sha'n't let you in!
I heard my mother say,
That if you had your way
I well would rue the day,
  Rue the day, rue the day,
  I would rue the day!

He: The night is so cold,
  So icy the wind,
  So icy the wind!
My heart will be frozen through,
As will my love for you,
Let me in, my dear,
  Let me in, let me in,
  Let me in, my dear.

She: If your love flies away,
  Let it stray,
  Let it stray!
Let it stray, I said.
And so go home to bed.

gute Nacht, mein Knab',   Good night, my lad,
   gute Nacht, gute Nacht,   Good night, good night,
   gute Nacht, mein Knab'!   Good night, my lad!

The four stanzas call forth a regular strophic form. The melody outlines the common triads and moves in an animated ¾ time, achieving
the simplicity and naturalness of the folk mood. The opening phrase
contains the same little figure repeated three times, each time from a
lower note—a formation known as a descending sequence. The melody
is marked "lively and good-humored."

The relationship of folk song to the dance is underlined by the regularity of structure: four measures to the phrase, four phrases to the
stanza. Yet Brahms introduces a charming asymmetry with a six-bar
formation on the third phrase, the momentary waywardness setting off
the symmetry of the rest.

Charming too is the sudden change of color at the third stanza. The
melody takes on a plaintive tone as the lover beseeches: "The night
is so cold, so icy the wind!" This is achieved by flatting certain tones
(what we shall recognize in a later chapter as a change from major to
minor). The light-fingered accompaniment keeps the song moving and
creates an admirable frame for the spirited dialogue. Here is the thoroughly German aspect of Brahms—the soil from which flowered the
more cultivated blossoms of his art.

The Piano Piece

The enormous popularity of the piano as a household instrument in
the late romantic era kept the short lyric piece in the forefront of musical production. There sprang up a vast literature of pieces intended to
provide pleasant music for the home. Though much of this salon art
was of no more than ephemeral value, a few examples achieved international popularity—such as Tchaikovsky's *Barcarolle*, Dvořák's *Hu-
moresque*, and Grieg's *To Spring*—and have now become what is
known in certain circles as light classics.

In the realm of the piano piece it was again Brahms who did the most
serious work. He captured for the short piano piece something of the
quality it had achieved in the first half of the century. Compositions for
the piano extend through the whole of his career. His favorite form in
his mature years was the short lyric in A-B-A pattern, which he called

a capriccio when fast, an intermezzo when slow. He also wrote rhapsodies and ballades, these terms implying more extended flights of fancy.

Intermezzo in B-Flat Minor

Having begun his career as a pianist, Brahms was thoroughly aware of the nature and resources of his chosen instrument. That his writing has been labeled unpianistic by some is due to his effort to widen those resources, to push back the limits of what could be done on the keyboard. His piano music does not lie readily to the hand like that of Chopin or Liszt. It is rugged, even ungainly; but it makes up in power what it lacks in grace. He exploits especially the dark sonority of the instrument's lower register, its capacity for complex rhythms, widely spaced chords, and interweaving of independent lines.

The Intermezzo in B-flat minor, Opus 117, No. 2 (1892), is one of Brahms's late piano works. Couched in his characteristic vein of introspective lyricism, it has the manly tenderness, the tone of gentle contemplation that we associate with the German master. The piece is marked Andante non troppo e con molto espressione (not too slow and with much expression). Its melody traces a sinuous line—now falling, now rising, only to fall again—above broken chords. Distributed between both hands, the arpeggio accompaniment maintains a steady flow of harmony above which the melody unfolds.

In evidence is the composer's fondness for middle and low register, and the subdued coloring that results therefrom; also the pungent harmonies enriched by dissonance. The serene middle part balances the expressiveness of the first and third sections. It is this quieter mood that returns at the end to round off the piece.

The big public knows Brahms primarily as the composer of symphonies, concertos, and other large forms. In his songs and piano pieces he reveals himself a master of intimate lyricism. His short lyric forms breathe an end-of-the-century nostalgia; they look gently to the past, and constitute nothing less than a farewell to romanticism.

Program Music

CHAPTER 21

The Nature of Program Music

"More an expression of feeling than tone painting."
Beethoven (on the *Pastoral Symphony*)

FROM the mating of instrumental music with literature came the genre known as *program music,* which carries associations lying outside the realm of tone. The nature of these associations is indicated by a literary title or an explanatory note—the "program"—which is appended to the score. Program music is distinguished from *absolute* or *pure* music, which deals with musical patterns devoid of literary or pictorial connotations.

Program music has existed in one form or another for centuries. Every age has produced its quota of compositions intended to depict storms, battles, bird calls, the ringing of bells, the murmur of waterfalls, and the outlines of a story. However, it was only in the nineteenth century that this type of music came to play a major part in the output of an era.

Program music is of course not the only kind of music that is associated with story elements. Opera and song, oratorio and church music automatically have a "story" imposed upon them by the words. In instrumental music, however, the story element is far less concrete. The emergence of program music in the nineteenth century was associated with the conviction that the instruments—especially the orchestra—could now undertake the same tasks of poetic suggestion and description that vocal music had done for centuries.

The program serves an orchestral work in much the same way as the plot does an opera. It becomes the point of departure for the musical conception. It relates the music to certain poetic ideas or scenes that are capable of arousing emotion in the listener. The program stands as a link between the composer's experience as a musician and his experience as a human being. It represents his attempt to transplant

124

certain images of the external world into the ideal realm of music. However, once he is engaged in the task of composing, the musician takes over. He is preoccupied with the life of his themes, their unfolding and their development. In other words, the composer's primary aim is to make music. Whatever story-telling or pictorial aspects his composition may have are secondary to the music itself.

For this reason we should not listen to a piece of program music as though it were a kind of musical scenario or the accompaniment to an imaginary animated cartoon. Music is not a representational art like literature or painting. It is able to evoke scenes and suggest emotional states; but it cannot—to any important extent—depict the events of the external world. The program gives us a clue to the composer's frame of mind as he conceived the music, but the ultimate meaning lies in the music itself. In effect, we must never become so engrossed in the program that we do not hear the music. The program may lend interest to a composition and enhance its charm; yet no program, no matter how exciting, will ever succeed in making a dull piece interesting. Hence, composers of program music have repeatedly expressed the thought that, no matter how engaging the program, the piece must be able to stand on its own feet as music.

The program was of special importance in a period like the nineteenth century when musicians became sharply conscious of the connection between their art and the world about them. It helped them relate their work to the moral and political issues of their time. It also helped them to approach the classical forms of absolute music in a new way. All the same, the distinction between absolute and program music is not as rigid as many suppose. A work entitled Symphony No. 1 or Third String Quartet falls into the former category. Yet the composer in the course of writing it may very well have had in mind specific images and associations that he has not seen fit to divulge. Beethoven, whom we think of as the master of absolute music, confessed to a friend, "I have always a picture in my thoughts when I am composing, and work to it." Conversely, a piece called *Romeo and Juliet Overture* comes under the heading of program music. Yet if we were not told the title we would listen to it as a piece of pure music. This is what we are apt to do in any case once we get to know the work. What concerns us ultimately is the destiny not of the lovers but of the themes.

It is well for us to take note of the program, since this indicates the emotional and intellectual framework of the composition. But it is even better, with each rehearing of the work, to let the program recede into the background—where it belongs—and to concentrate on the music.

Varieties of Program Music

THE CONCERT OVERTURE

One impulse toward program music derived from the opera house. The overture at that time was a rousing orchestral piece in one movement designed to serve as an introduction to an opera (or a play). Many operatic overtures achieved an independent popularity as concert pieces. This pointed the way to a new type of overture much in favor with the romantic era: a one-movement concert piece for orchestra, based on a striking literary idea, such as Tchaikovsky's *Romeo and Juliet*. This type of composition might be descriptive, like Mendelssohn's seascape *Hebrides* (*Fingal's Cave*); or it could embody a patriotic idea, as does Tchaikovsky's *Overture 1812*. Works of this kind retained something of the tension of the theater, where the overture had originated.

The concert overture, despite its literary program, presented and developed its ideas in accordance with the procedures of absolute music. Its design, in fact, was the same as that of the first movement of the symphony, consisting of three sections—the Exposition, in which the main themes were introduced; the Development; and the Recapitulation (or Restatement). The concert overture offered the romantic composers an attractive genre midway between program and absolute music. On the one hand, they could avail themselves of the abstract musical procedures of the classical era. On the other, they were able to invest their music with poetic or pictorial images of a romantic cast.

INCIDENTAL MUSIC

An engaging species of program music is that written for plays, generally consisting of an overture and a series of numbers to be performed between the acts and during the important scenes. Music of this kind is not well named; it is not incidental at all. On the contrary, when successful it so enhances the drama as to become an integral part of the effect.

Nineteenth-century composers produced a number of works of this type that were notable for tone painting, characterization, and theater atmosphere. The most successful numbers were generally arranged into concert suites, certain of which became vastly popular. Mendelssohn's music for *A Midsummer Night's Dream* is one of the most felicitous works in this category. Hardly less appealing are the two suites from Bizet's music for Alphonse Daudet's play *L'Arlésienne* (The Woman of Arles) and the two from Grieg's music for Henrik Ibsen's poetic drama *Peer Gynt*.

THE PROGRAM SYMPHONY

The impulse toward program music was so strong that it invaded even the hallowed absolute form of the classical era—the symphony. In their attempt to reconcile classical form and romantic content, composers tried to retain the grand form of Beethoven and at the same time to associate it with a literary theme. Thus came into being the program symphony, a type best known through the works of Berlioz.

As the century advanced, it became apparent that the two modes of thought could not be successfully combined. The symphony was too firmly rooted in absolute music to take kindly to the infusion of a story. In the late romantic period the symphony abandoned literary content and returned to the abstract regions that constituted its natural habitat.

The last quarter of the century witnessed the triumph of what has been called the poematic symphony: a large work without a literary program but highly emotional in tone, retaining the imagery of nature worship and religious faith, of despair and affirmation, conflict and ultimate triumph, that appealed to the romantic mentality. As cultivated by César Franck, Tchaikovsky, Mahler, and Sibelius, this poetic but storyless type of symphony achieved immense popularity.

THE SYMPHONIC POEM

More and more the need was felt for a free form of orchestral music that would serve the romantic era as well as the symphony had served the classical. Toward the middle of the century the long-awaited step was taken with the creation of the symphonic poem, the nineteenth century's one original contribution to the large forms. This was the achievement of Liszt, who first employed the term in 1848.

A symphonic poem is a piece of program music for orchestra in one movement, which in the course of contrasting sections develops a poetic idea, suggests a scene, or creates a mood. The name is used interchangeably with *tone poem*. The symphonic poem as cultivated by Liszt and his disciples was an immensely flexible form that permitted its course to be shaped by the literary idea. The programs were drawn from poets and painters dear to the romantic temperament: Shakespeare, Dante, Petrarch; Goethe and Schiller; Michelangelo and Raphael; Byron and Victor Hugo. A strong influence was the "return to nature" that had been advocated by Rousseau. Before long the new form, assimilating the force of nationalism, turned to patriotic themes and native landscapes.

The symphonic poem differs in one important respect from the concert overture. The overture, as we saw, generally follows a specific musical design consisting of three sections—Exposition, Development, and Recapitulation. The symphonic poem is considerably freer in its form, which is shaped not only by musical considerations but also by the requirements of the literary program that is attached to the music.

Coming to maturity in the second half of the century, the symphonic poem assumed the traits that mark the later phase of the romantic movement: a penchant for theatrical effect; a love of impassioned lyricism and purple rhetoric; an emphasis on picturesque detail; and a fondness for subjects either intensely romantic or verging on the fantastic. More important, the symphonic poem gave composers the canvas they needed for a big single-movement form. It became the most widely cultivated type of program music throughout the second half of the century.

The varieties of program music just described—overture, incidental music, program symphony, and symphonic poem—comprise one of the striking manifestations of nineteenth-century romanticism. This type of music emphasized color, mood, and atmosphere; it impelled composers to try to express specific feelings; and it proclaimed the direct relationship of music to life.

❧❧ CHAPTER 22 ❧❧

Felix Mendelssohn (1809-1847)

"People often complain that music is too ambiguous; that what they should think when they hear it is so unclear, whereas everyone understands words. With me it is exactly the opposite, and not only with regard to an entire speech but also with individual words. These too seem to me so ambiguous, so vague, so easily misunderstood in comparison to genuine music which fills the soul with a thousand things better than words."

FELIX MENDELSSOHN stands out in the roster of musicians for the fortunate circumstances that attended his career: he was born to wealth; he found personal happiness; and he was the idol of a vast public.

His Life

Felix Mendelssohn was the grandson of Moses Mendelssohn, the Jewish philosopher who expounded Plato to the eighteenth century.

His father was an art-loving banker; his mother read Homer in the original. They joined the Protestant faith when Felix was still a child. The Mendelssohn home was a meeting place for the wit and intellect of Berlin. The garden house, seating several hundred guests, was the scene of memorable musicales where an orchestra under the boy's direction performed his numerous compositions. Here, when he was seventeen, his Overture to *A Midsummer Night's Dream* was presented to an enraptured audience.

The youth's education was thorough and well rounded. He visited the venerable Goethe at Weimar and attended Hegel's lectures at the University of Berlin. He worshiped Bach, Mozart, and Beethoven. In 1829 the twenty-year-old enthusiast organized a performance of the

Felix Mendelssohn.

St. Matthew Passion, which had lain neglected since the death of Bach. The event proved to be a turning point in the nineteenth-century revival of that master.

Mendelssohn's misfortune was that he excelled in a number of roles —as pianist, conductor, organizer of musical events, and educator. For the last fifteen years of his life his composing was carried on amid the distractions of a public career that taxed his energies and caused his early death even as poverty and neglect might have done. At twenty-six he was conductor of the Gewandhaus Orchestra at Leipzig, which he transformed into the finest in Europe. He was summoned to Berlin by Frederick William IV to carry out that monarch's plans for an Academy of Music. Later he founded the Conservatory of Leipzig, which set new standards for the training of musicians. He made ten visits to England, where his appearances elicited a frenzy of enthusiasm. All this in

addition to directing one or another of the provincial festivals that
formed the backbone of musical life in Germany. Mendelssohn composed with a speed and facility that invite comparison with Mozart
or Schubert, but he seldom allowed himself the inner repose that
might have imparted to much of his music the profundity it lacks.

His last major composition, the oratorio *Elijah,* was produced in 1846
at the Birmingham Festival and "touched off the emotional spring of
Victorian religious respectability as no other work had done." The following year he won fresh triumphs in England, appearing as pianist
and conductor of his works. He returned to Germany in a state of
nervous exhaustion. The happiness he found in the company of his wife
and children was shattered by a severe blow—the death of his sister
Fanny, to whom he was deeply attached. Six months later, at the age
of thirty-eight, he succumbed to a stroke. Huge throngs followed his
bier. Condolences came from all over Europe. A world figure had died.

His Music

Mendelssohn was dedicated to a mission: to preserve the purity of
the classical forms in an age that was turning from them. His fastidious
craftsmanship links him to the great tradition. Serene and elegant expression was the characteristic trait of a mind as orderly as it was conservative. Mendelssohn represents the classicist trend within the romantic movement. But it should not be supposed that he was untouched
by romanticism. In his early works he is the ardent poet of nature, a
landscape painter of gossamer brush. Tenderness and manly fervor
breathe from his music, and a gentle melancholy that is very much of
the age. As he matured, however, traditionalism permeated his outlook. Nor was this confined to music. Unlike many of the romantics,
he remained aloof from the revolutionary ferment of the time. He accepted the established order of things and viewed with dismay any
suggestion that this was not the best of all possible worlds. It is noteworthy that of the orchestral works by which he is remembered, the
greater number were produced before he was twenty-five.

Of his symphonies the best known are the Third, the *Scotch,* and
the Fourth, the *Italian*—mementos of his youthful travels. Both works
were begun in 1830, when he was twenty-one. His Fifth Symphony,
the *Reformation,* also dates from his early twenties. The Concerto for
Violin and Orchestra (1844) retains its position as one of the most popular ever written. The Octet for Strings, which he wrote when he was
sixteen, is much admired, as are the string quartets and the trios. As a
composer for the piano he was too conventional to attain the highest
rank, and his large works such as the Concerto in G minor have dropped

from the repertory. On the other hand, the short lyric pieces known as *Songs without Words* (1829–1842) enjoy undiminished popularity with young pianists. The titles appended by Mendelssohn's friends indicate the contents of the famous collection; among them are the *Spinning Song, Hunting Song, Consolation,* and the perennial *Spring Song.*

Mendelssohn was a prolific writer for the voice; his songs are suavely melodious. *Auf Flügeln des Gesanges* (On Wings of Song) and a few others are still performed. His choral music used to be widely sung, especially the psalms, hymns, anthems, and motets that pleased the religious taste of his time. The oratorio *Elijah* represents the peak of his achievement in this category.

Mendelssohn was particularly successful with the overture as an independent concert piece. His works in this category are vividly pictorial in character. Two—*A Midsummer Night's Dream* and *Hebrides* (*Fingal's Cave*)—are still vastly popular.

In England Mendelssohn was admired as no composer had been since Handel and Haydn. The first edition of Grove's Dictionary, the musical bible of the British, which appeared in 1880, devoted its longest article to him—sixty-eight pages. Bach received eight.

A Midsummer Night's Dream:
Overture and Incidental Music

The Overture (1826) to Shakespeare's fairy play is in Mendelssohn's happiest vein. The mood of elfin enchantment that the seventeen-year-old composer here achieved was to return again and again in his later music, but nowhere more felicitously. Four prolonged chords on the woodwinds open the portals to the realm of Oberon and Titania. The Exposition begins with the fairy music, which is introduced by the violins in high register, allegro di molto (very lively) and very softly. The dots over the notes indicate that they are to be played staccato (short and detached).

Allegro di molto

pp

The fairy music is expanded. There follows some vigorous subsidiary material, after which a transition leads into the second idea. This is a lyric theme presented by the strings, suggestive of the young lovers in the play. It provides an effective contrast to the rhythmic idea of the opening.

The third idea is the boisterous dance of the clowns. Energetic rhythm and wide leaps set the character of this theme, which is presented by the violins against a background of wind tone.

Now that the themes have been "exposed," there follows the middle section of the overture, the Development, which is an extended fantasy on the first theme. The composer gives free rein to his imagination in exploring a mood close to his heart. When the development of the idea has run its course the four mystic chords are heard again, introducing the Recapitulation, in which the thematic material is restated substantially as we heard it before. The coda ends the piece on a note of gentle retrospection. (A *coda*—the Italian word for "tail"—is a closing section that rounds off a musical work and brings it to its appointed end.) As the youthful composer explained, "After everything has been satisfactorily settled and the principal players have joyfully left the stage, the elves follow them, bless the house and disappear with the dawn. So ends the play, and my overture too."

A more experienced musician might have been briefer. Yet there is already in evidence here the mastery of form that was to be the mature Mendelssohn's most salient trait. Characteristic too are the elegance and limpidity of the orchestration, and the restrained lyricism. Withal, this music is steeped in the "nature sound" of German romanticism. In its evocation of the enchanted forest it reveals the romantic movement in its freshest, most ideal phase.

In 1842 Frederick William IV of Prussia decided on a production of Shakespeare's comedy at the royal theater and suggested to Mendelssohn that he write incidental music for the play. The composer added twelve numbers for this occasion, in which he recaptured the spirit of the Overture he had written sixteen years before. Three of the pieces —the Scherzo, Nocturne, and Wedding March—have achieved worldwide popularity and are frequently performed together with the Overture as a concert suite.

The Scherzo serves to launch Act II. To Puck's query, "How now, spirit? Whither wander you?" the Elf makes his famous reply: "Over hill, over dale, thorough bush, thorough brier . . ."

The *scherzo* (pronounced sker'tso)—the Italian word meaning

"jest," "joke"—had been elevated by Beethoven into a symphonic movement of great driving force. Mendelssohn transformed it into an independent piece compounded of elfin grace and humor. The Scherzo
from *A Midsummer Night's Dream* music is in ⅜ time and marked
Allegro vivace. The first idea is a staccato rhythmic pattern introduced
by the woodwinds softly in the upper register.

A contrasting second theme is presented pianissimo, in a low register,
by the strings. The two ideas alternate throughout the work. This
Scherzo is remarkable for its continuity of fabric. Tension is sustained
from first note to last. Characteristic is the pianissimo ending in which
an agile run on the flute trails off into the distance.

The Nocturne is played while the lovers, lost in the enchanted wood,
sleep. Here Mendelssohn is the poet of nature. The beauty of the forest
is evoked by the horn in a serenely tender melody.

Finally confusion is righted and all ends happily with the wedding
of the Duke. A fanfare on the trumpets introduces the March, without
which no bride considers herself happily married. The movement is
an Allegro vivace in ¼ time, for the most part forte.

Two sections of quieter character supply the necessary contrast to the
recurrent festive theme. The result is a well-rounded A-B-A-C-A form
with an abundance of melody right on to the ceremonious flourishes at
the end.

As the romantic tide swept over Europe, Mendelssohn was one of the
first idols to be engulfed. The late nineteenth century was as extreme
in its censure of him as the earlier had been in its adulation. His reserve
was disparaged as superficiality, his elegance as incapacity to feel. But
posterity is more changeable than we realize. Our generation, turning
away from the full-blown romanticism of its grandparents, has restored
Mendelssohn to favor. His particular virtues—sovereign command of
form, refinement of feeling, fastidious workmanship, and economy of
means—recommend him to an era that is not partial to the fervor of the
late romantics. The time is ripe for him again.

CHAPTER 23

Hector Berlioz (1803-1869)

"The prevailing characteristics of my music are passionate expression, intense ardor, rhythmic animation, and unexpected turns. To render my works properly requires a combination of extreme precision and irresistible verve, a regulated vehemence, a dreamy tenderness, and an almost morbid melancholy."

His Life

BERLIOZ was born in France in a small town near Grenoble. His father, a well-to-do physician, expected him to follow in his footsteps, and at nineteen Hector was dispatched to the medical school in Paris. The Conservatory and the Opéra, however, exercised an infinitely greater attraction than the dissecting room, and before long the fiery youth made a decision that horrified his upper-middle-class family: he quit medical school and entered the Conservatory.

The romantic revolution was brewing in Paris. Berlioz, along with Victor Hugo and the painter Delacroix, found himself in the camp of "young France." Having been cut off by his parents, he gave lessons, sang in a theater chorus, and turned to various musical chores. He fell under the spell of Beethoven, but hardly less powerful was the impact of Shakespeare, to whose art he was introduced by a visiting English

Hector Berlioz
From a portrait by Honoré Daumier, 1808–1879.

troupe. For the actress whose Ophelia and Juliet excited the admiration of the Parisians, young Berlioz conceived an overwhelming passion. In his *Memoirs*, which read like a romantic novel, he describes his infatuation for Harriet Smithson: "I became obsessed by an intense, overpowering sense of sadness. I could not sleep, I could not work, and I spent my time wandering aimlessly about Paris and its environs."

In 1830 came the first official recognition of Berlioz's gifts. He was awarded the coveted Prix de Rome, which gave him a stipend and an opportunity to live and work in the Eternal City. That year—he was twenty-seven—saw the composition of what has remained his most celebrated work, the *Symphonie fantastique*. Upon his return from Rome a hectic courtship of Miss Smithson ensued. There were strenuous objections on the part of both their families and violent scenes, during one of which the excitable Hector attempted suicide. He was revived. They were married.

Now that the unattainable ideal had become his wife, his ardor cooled. It was Shakespeare he had loved rather than Harriet, and in time he sought the ideal elsewhere. All the same, the first years of his marriage were the most fruitful of his life. By the time he was forty he had produced most of the works on which his fame rests.

To earn money he turned to music criticism, producing a stream of reviews and articles. His literary labors were a necessary part of his musical activity; he had to propagandize for his works and create an audience capable of understanding them. In so doing he found himself caught up in the journalistic whirlpool of Paris. Professing only contempt for politics, he shifted with the wind: from the reactionary monarchy of Charles X to the moderate monarchy of Louis Philippe to the opportunistic monarchy of Napoleon III. Every time he was on the threshold of success there seemed to be a revolution.

He had his triumphs, but the time was against him. The greatest French composer of the age had the misfortune to live during the lowest ebb of his country's taste. With the wrath of a prophet he hurled himself against the frivolity of his countrymen. As the heady romanticism of the 1830s gave way to the bourgeois tastes of the Second Empire he waged a losing battle. Inexorably the truth was borne in upon him. He had been born too soon—or too late.

In the latter part of his life he conducted his music in all the capitals of Europe. But Paris resisted him to the end. Year after year he dissipated his energies in reviewing the works of nonentities while his own were neglected. Disgust and misanthropy settled upon him. His last major work, the opera *Béatrice et Bénédict* (on his own libretto after Shakespeare's *Much Ado about Nothing*), shows a falling off of his powers. After this effort the flame was spent, and for the last seven years of his life the embittered master wrote no more.

The final chapters of his *Memoirs* breathe a colossal disenchantment. The "malady of the century" weighs heavily upon his self-portrait: "The same memories and regrets, the same yearning for the past, the same pitiable eagerness to retain the ever-flying present . . . I have neither hopes nor illusions nor great thoughts left. My son is nearly always absent. I am alone. My contempt for the stupidity and meanness of men, my hatred of their detestable ferocity are at their height. And I say hourly to death, 'When you will!' Why does he delay?"

He died at sixty-six, tormented to the end. "Some day," wrote Richard Wagner, "a grateful France will raise a proud monument on his tomb." The prophecy has been fulfilled.

His Music

Berlioz was one of the boldest innovators of the nineteenth century. His approach to music was wholly original, his sense of sound unique. There is some dispute among musicians as to the ultimate value of what he heard. But none can gainsay that it had never been heard before.

From the first he had an affinity for the literary program. His vivid imagination found outlet in a magnificent attempt to dramatize the symphony. Significantly, he called his symphonies instrumental dramas. For the abstract development of themes he substituted a luminous orchestral fabric shot through with literary meanings. In his choice of program Berlioz was the product of his age. The emotions are violent, the settings theatrical. Idyllic landscapes alternate with scenes of the supernatural and the macabre. Occasionally he fell into a realism that shocked the purists. But he was too much the musician to wish to imitate nature or tell a story in tone; he knew quite well, he stated, that "music is a substitute neither for speech nor for the art of painting." He never entertained "the absurd pretension of reproducing general ideas or moral qualities, but only passions and impressions."

His works exemplify the favorite literary influences of the romantic period. The overtures *Waverley* (c. 1827) and *Rob Roy* (1832) were inspired by novels of Walter Scott, *The Damnation of Faust* (1846) by Goethe. *Harold in Italy,* a program symphony with viola solo (1834) and *The Corsair,* an overture (1855), are after Byron. Shakespeare is the source for the overture *King Lear* (1831) and for the dramatic symphony for orchestra, soloists, and chorus, *Romeo and Juliet* (1839). Two other overtures, *Les Francs-Juges* (The Frankish Judges, c. 1827) and *Roman Carnival* (1844), conjure up respectively the Middle Ages and the Renaissance.

Berlioz never conquered the opera, the focal point of his ambitions.

His first operatic work was *Benvenuto Cellini* (1834–38), on a libretto
based on the Italian artist's famous autobiography. In 1859 he completed *Les Troyens* (The Trojans), on his own libretto based on Vergil.
Running beyond the confines of a single evening, the work consists of
two parts—*La Prise de Troie* (The Taking of Troy) and *Les Troyens
à Carthage* (The Trojans at Carthage). This broadly designed opera,
which contains some of the master's most powerful music, has been
successfully revived in recent years. *The Trojans* was followed, in
1862, by *Beatrice and Benedict.*

The Requiem (Mass for the Dead, 1837) and the *Te Deum* (Hymn
of Praise, 1849) are conceived on a grandiose scale. They testify to the
French love of the "big machine." For the depiction of Judgment Day
in the Requiem Berlioz required, in addition to a monster orchestra,
four brass choirs stationed at the four corners of the church (representing the four corners of the earth). This love of the gigantesque represents only one aspect of his personality. No less characteristic is the
tenderness that finds expression in the oratorio *L'Enfance du Christ*
(Childhood of Christ, 1854); the fine-spun lyricism that wells up in his
songs; the sensibility that fills his orchestra with Gallic clarity and grace.

It was in the domain of orchestration that Berlioz's genius asserted
itself most fully. His daring originality in handling the instruments
opened up a new world of romantic sonority. Until his time, as Aaron
Copland pointed out, "composers used instruments in order to make
them sound like themselves; the mixing of colors so as to produce a
new result was his achievement." He dreamed of a mammoth orchestra
of over four hundred and fifty players joined with a chorus of over
three hundred and fifty singers. Yet even when he uses large forces, his
texture is never opaque; his orchestra, as his admirer Camille Saint-
Saëns remarked, "is suffused with light, which sparkles like the facets
of a diamond." Berlioz's *Traité d'instrumentation et d'orchestration
modernes* (Treatise on Modern Instrumentation and Orchestration,
1844) was one of the most important musical texts of the nineteenth
century. Even more, his scores abound in novel effects and discoveries
that served as models to all who came after him. Indeed, the conductor
Felix Weingartner called Berlioz "the creator of the modern orchestra."

Symphonie fantastique

Berlioz's best-known symphony was written at the height of his infatuation with Harriet Smithson, when he was twenty-seven. The
program supplied by the composer reveals the sultry atmosphere
whence this work issued. In the *Symphonie fantastique* Berlioz summed
up not an unhappy love affair but all that he felt about life: his con-

ception of the artist as hero, his vision of human experience as longing
and fatality. It is hardly to be believed that this "novel in tones" was
conceived by a young man only three years after the death of Beethoven. "A young musician of morbid sensibility and ardent imagination
in a paroxysm of lovesick despair has poisoned himself with opium.
The drug, too weak to kill, plunges him into a heavy sleep accompanied
by strange visions. His sensations, feelings, and memories are translated
in his sick brain into musical images and ideas. The beloved one herself
becomes for him a melody, a recurrent theme [*idée fixe*] that haunts
him everywhere."

It is to be noted that this literary program is based on a musical
theme. The "fixed idea" that symbolizes the beloved—the basic theme
of the symphony—is subjected to variation in harmony, rhythm, meter,
and tempo; dynamics, register, and instrumental color. All this does not
differ in principle from the variation and development to which the
classical masters subjected their symphonic themes. What is new is the
fact that these transformations take on literary as well as musical significance. The basic motive, recurring by virtue of the literary program,
becomes a musical thread unifying five movements that are diverse in
mood and character.

I. *Reveries, Passions.* "He remembers the weariness of soul, the indefinable yearning he knew before meeting his beloved. Then, the volcanic love with which she at once inspired him, his delirious suffering
. . . his religious consolation."

A spacious introduction marked Largo establishes the atmosphere
of reverie. It establishes, too, the luminous resonance of Berlioz's orchestra, with its use of woodwinds and strings in upper register. The
movement proper is marked Allegro agitato e appassionato assai (lively,
agitated, and very impassioned). Solo flute and first violins announce
the "fixed idea," a broadly arching melody.

Characteristic is Berlioz's continual use of the orchestral crescendo;
also the chromatic-scale passages. (The chromatic scale takes in all
twelve tones of the octave. On the piano it includes the seven white
and five black keys. Chromatic scales became a favorite device of

the romantics for whipping up orchestral excitement.) At the climax
of the movement the "fixed idea" is intoned by full orchestra *ff*. A closing section consisting of sustained chords and marked *religiosamente*
suggests what Berlioz's program refers to as "his religious consolation."

II. *A Ball.* "Amid the tumult and excitement of a brilliant ball he
glimpses the loved one again." The dance movement of the symphony
is marked Valse Allegro non troppo (Waltz, not too fast). The introduction presents arpeggios on the harp against a string tremolo—an
enchanting sonority. The Waltz proper begins "sweet and tender."

The movement is in A-B-A form. In the middle section the "fixed idea"
reappears in waltz time, introduced by flute and oboe. Notable is the

climax at the end, which is built up through an increase in volume, an
acceleration of pace, and a rise in pitch.

III. *In the Fields.* "On a summer evening in the country he hears two
shepherds piping. The pastoral duet, the quiet surroundings . . . all
unite to fill his heart with a long absent calm. But *she* appears again.
His heart contracts. Painful forebodings fill his soul. . . . The sun sets
—the distant rumble of thunder—solitude—silence . . ."

The movement, marked Adagio, is an A-B-A form in $\frac{6}{8}$ time. The
famous dialogue between English horn and oboe in the introduction is
followed by a broadly spun melody that breathes a pastoral quiet.

The "fixed idea" appears in the middle section in a new version in $\frac{6}{8}$
time, introduced into this idyllic setting by solo flute and oboe. The
"distant rumble of thunder" is given on the kettledrums; the dynamic
markings in the score are very exact, ranging in subtle nuances from
ppp to *f* to *ppp*, while in the middle register the English horn suggests

the solitude of the unhappy lover.

IV. *March to the Scaffold.* "He dreams that he has killed his beloved, that he has been condemned to die and is being led to the scaffold. The procession moves to the sounds of a march now somber and wild, now brilliant and solemn. . . . At the very end the 'fixed idea' reappears for an instant, like a last thought of love interrupted by the fall of the axe."

Marked Allegretto non troppo in $\frac{4}{4}$, the march movement exemplifies the nineteenth-century love of the satanic. Not easily forgotten is the sound of the opening: muted horns, timpani, pizzicato chords on cellos and double basses. Richard Strauss did not forget it, nor did Mahler, nor Shostakovich. The lower strings play an energetic theme that strides down the scale. Then the diabolical march emerges in the woodwinds and brass.

Berlioz's orchestral imagination disports itself with the verve that is uniquely his. The theme of the beloved appears at the end, on the clarinet, and is cut off by a grim fortissimo chord. The effect ("a last thought of love interrupted by the fall of the axe") has been much criticized as being too realistic. One must remember, however, that when Berlioz wrote it he was opening up new fields of expression for his art.

V. *Dream of a Witches' Sabbath.* "He sees himself at a witches' sabbath surrounded by a host of fearsome specters who have gathered for his funeral. Unearthly sounds, groans, shrieks of laughter. . . . The melody of his beloved is heard, but it has lost its noble and reserved character. It has become a vulgar tune, trivial and grotesque. It is she who comes to the infernal orgy. A howl of joy greets her arrival. She joins the diabolical dance. Bells toll for the dead. A burlesque of the *Dies Irae.* Dance of the witches. The dance and the *Dies Irae* combined."

The movement opens with a Larghetto (not quite as slow as largo). Berlioz here exploits a vein that nourished a century of satanic operas, ballets, and symphonic poems. Flickering chromatic scales, *ppp*, on the violins and violas create the properly infernal atmosphere. In the Allegro that follows, the theme of the beloved is transformed into a "vulgar dance tune" played by a high-pitched clarinet.

The traditional Gregorian melody *Dies irae* (Day of Wrath), from the ancient Mass for the Dead, is given out by bassoons and tubas in a section in $\frac{6}{8}$ time marked Lontano (distant).

It is caricatured in shorter note values. In the *Ronde du sabat* (Witches' Dance), a driving tarantella rhythm ($\frac{6}{8}$) is heard in the cellos and basses, after which it is taken up in turn by various instrumental groups.

The interweaving of the various lines makes for an intricate orchestral fabric. Berlioz indicates the combining of the dance theme and the *Dies irae* in the score, not that anybody could miss it. This passage, of which he was so proud, leads to a rousingly theatrical ending for his theatrical subject.

The music of Berlioz is undergoing a widespread revival. He is admired not for the sulphurous eloquence that mirrored his time nor for the grandiose rhetoric that caused former generations to compare him to Victor Hugo. Twentieth-century musicians are won over rather by his elegance, by the luster and transparency of his orchestral sound and the verve of his rhythms. For all his flamboyance he never loses his refinement of thought and texture. It is the Latin—the classical—strain in him. Even the purple patches fall into the over-all scheme. There is a bigness of line and gesture about his music, an overflow of vitality and inventiveness. He is one of the major prophets in the romantic era.

꩜ *CHAPTER 24* ꩜

Franz Liszt (1811-1886)

"Sorrowful and great is the artist's destiny."

THE CAREER of Franz Liszt is one of the legends of the romantic era. As piano virtuoso he captured the imagination of Europe. As composer

and conductor, teacher, and organizer of musical events, he occupied
a central position in the artistic life of the century. Yet this fabulously
successful artist did not escape the romantic melancholy. "To die and
die young—" he once exclaimed, "—what happiness!"

His Life

Liszt was born in Hungary, son of a steward in the employ of a
wealthy family. A stipend from a group of Hungarian noblemen enabled him to pursue his musical studies in Paris. There he came under

Franz Liszt at the piano and his friends Alfred de Musset (1810–1857),
Victor Hugo (1802–1885), George Sand (1803–1876), Niccolò Paganini
(1782–1840), Gioacchino Rossini (1792–1868), and Marie d'Agoult (1805–
1876).

the spell of French romanticism, with whose leaders—Victor Hugo,
Delacroix, George Sand, Berlioz—he formed close friendships. The
Revolution of 1830 stirred the nineteen-year-old. He began at white
heat a *Revolutionary Symphony* which he never finished.

Young Liszt exemplified the new type of literary musician that came
to the fore in the romantic era. The essays he wrote in his twenties
evince an interest in socialism, an abundance of idealism, and a mysti-

cal conception of the artist as prophet and priest. Music, he preaches, is more than entertainment. Art is not for art's sake but for humanity's. "We believe as unshakably in art as in God and mankind, both of which find in it a means of noble expression. We believe in one unending progress, in an unconstrained social future for the musical artist. We believe in these with all the power of hope and love!"

The appearance in Paris of the sensational violinist Paganini, in 1831, made Liszt aware of the possibilities of virtuoso playing. The new mass public required spectacular soloists. Liszt met the need. He was one of the greatest of pianists—and showmen. An actor to his fingertips, he possessed the personal magnetism of which legends are made. Instead of sitting with his back to the audience or facing it, as had been the custom hitherto, he introduced the more effective arrangement that prevails today. It showed off his chiseled profile, which reminded people of Dante's. He crouched over the keys, he thundered, he caressed. Countesses swooned. Ladies less exalted fought for his snuffbox and tore his handkerchief to shreds. Liszt encouraged these antics as a necessary part of the legend. But behind the façade was a true musician. For his friends and disciples he played the last sonatas of Beethoven; they never forgot the experience.

Inseparable from the legend of the pianist was that of the lover. Liszt never married. His path for the better part of fifty years led through a thicket of sighs, tears, and threats of suicide. Among those briefly smitten were George Sand—they toured Switzerland for a summer— and Marie Duplessis, the original of Dumas's Lady of the Camellias. More important in his intellectual development was his relationship with Countess Marie d'Agoult, who wrote novels under the name of Daniel Stern. They eloped to an idyll in Switzerland that lasted for a number of years. Of their three children, Cosima subsequently became the wife of Wagner. Liszt and the Countess parted in bitterness. She satirized him in her novels.

He withdrew from the concert stage at the height of his fame in order to devote himself to composing. In 1848 he settled in Weimar, where he became court conductor to the Grand Duke. The Weimar period (1848–61) saw the production of his chief orchestral works. As director of the ducal opera house he was in a position to mold public taste. He used his influence unremittingly on behalf of the "Music of the Future," as he and Wagner named the type of program music, both dramatic and symphonic, that they, along with Berlioz, advocated. At Weimar Liszt directed the first performances of Wagner's *Lohengrin*, Berlioz's *Benvenuto Cellini*, and many other contemporary works. History records few instances of an artist so generous, so free from envy in his dealings with his fellow artists.

The most important of his friendships was that with Richard Wagner. At its beginning Liszt was the all-powerful director at Weimar while Wagner, a political exile from Germany, struggled with poverty and discouragement. Wagner found in Liszt his one hope of survival. Liszt for his part declared, "I dreamed of a new art period for Weimar, in which Wagner and I would have been the leaders as formerly were Goethe and Schiller." Liszt's exertions on behalf of his friend were decisive in establishing Wagner's fame. But as Wagner's star rose it became apparent to Liszt that in this ideal friendship he had given more than he had received. Toward the end, when Wagner's glory eclipsed his own, he remarked wryly: "Liszt once helped Wagner. Who will now help Liszt?"

The Weimar period saw his association with the woman who most decisively influenced his life. Princess Carolyne Sayn-Wittgenstein, wife of a powerful noble at the court of the Tsar, fell in love with Liszt during his last concert tour of Russia. Shortly thereafter she came to Weimar to unite her life with his. For years their home, the Altenburg, was a center of artistic activity. A woman of domineering will and intellect, the Princess assisted Liszt in his later literary efforts. These include a book on Gypsy music and a *Life of Chopin*. Both are eloquent and inaccurate.

In his last years Liszt sought peace in the bosom of the Church. He took minor orders and was known as Abbé Liszt. This was the period of his major religious works. He divided his time between Rome, Weimar, and Budapest, the friend of princes and cardinals. The gloom of old age was dispelled by fresh triumphs. At seventy-five he was received with enthusiasm in England, which had always been reluctant to recognize him as a composer. He journeyed to Bayreuth to visit the widowed Cosima and died during the festival of Wagner's works, with his last breath naming the masterpiece of the "Music of the Future"— Wagner's *Tristan*.

His Music

Liszt believed in "the renewal of music through its inner connection with poetry." But it was not his aim to make music usurp the function of the other arts. "The poorest of apprentice landscape painters," he wrote, "could give with a few chalk strokes a much more faithful picture than a musician with the best orchestra." The poetic idea served as point of departure for his fancy. Thenceforth the music developed according to its own laws. His goal was pure lyric expression, the projecting of a state of soul through what he called "the mysterious language of tone."

To give his lyricism free scope he created the symphonic poem. The form was held together by the continuous transformation of a few basic themes. But, as in the case of the "fixed idea" of Berlioz, this transformation took on a poetic symbolism from the program. By varying the melodic outline, the harmony and rhythm of a theme, by shifting it from soft to loud, from slow to fast, from low to high register, from strings to woodwinds or brass, he found it possible to transform its character so that it might suggest romantic love in one section, a pastoral scene in another, tension and conflict in a third, and triumph in the last. The symphonic poem as Liszt established it was a romantic species of theme and variations inspired by a poem, a painting, a landscape, or— what included the other three—a feeling about life.

His twelve symphonic poems (1848–57) exercised incalculable influence on the nineteenth century and were responsible for many a work that is still popular. His masterpiece for orchestra is the *Symphony after Goethe's Faust* (1854–57), comprising three portraits: *Faust, Gretchen, Mephistopheles.* A companion work is the *Symphony to Dante's Divine Comedy* (1855–56), also in three movements: *Inferno, Purgatory,* and *Vision of Paradise.* In these program symphonies he honored his companions in arms. The *Faust* is dedicated to Berlioz, the *Dante* to Wagner.

Liszt is one of the creators of modern piano technique. His exploitation of the resources of the instrument—octaves, trills, runs, arpeggios —is of the highest ingenuity. The piano in his hands became an orchestra, capable of colors and sonorities that were without precedent in his time. Through hundreds of arrangements and transcriptions, many of hair-raising difficulty (yet eminently playable), he extended the piano repertory to include a wealth of symphonic, operatic, organ, and vocal music. These transcriptions have dropped from view, but they performed yeoman service—in an age without radio or recordings— in bringing to a world-wide public the knowledge of Beethoven's symphonies, Schubert's songs, Bach's organ works, and Wagner's operas.

Having to conquer a public whose taste was not the most elevated, Liszt sometimes used his gifts to dazzle, overwhelm, and seduce instead of for the higher aims of art. But the best of his piano pieces, like his songs, are in the vein of true romantic lyricism. They are evocative tone poems, rich in sentiment, sweet, and utterly pianistic. Characteristic are *Sonneto 47 del Petrarca* (47th Sonnet of Petrarch, c. 1846); Concert Etude in D-flat, *Un Sospiro* (A Sigh, c. 1848); the vastly popular *Liebestraum* (Love Dream, c. 1850); *Mephisto Waltz* (1860), and *Trois Valses oubliées* (Three Forgotten Waltzes, 1881–83). The Hungarian Rhapsodies did much to advance the cause of musical nationalism. Into these celebrated pieces Liszt injected what he termed "the fantastically epic element." They are capricious, improvisational, flamboyant.

In a class apart is his chief work for the piano, the Sonata in B minor, a single movement of enormous dramatic tension (1853). Equally free in form and treatment are the two piano concertos, the brilliant one in E-flat, which reached its final version in the 1850s, and the more introspective one in A (final version, 1861). Here is the Liszt of impassioned rhetoric and grandiose gesture, the contemporary in every sense of Victor Hugo.

"The best of me," he declared, "is in my religious music." To this category belong the *Solemn Mass for Gran Cathedral* (1855), the *Hungarian Coronation Mass* (1867), and two mystical oratorios—*The Legend of St. Elizabeth* (1857–62) and *Christus* (1855–62). The passion and sensuousness of these works spring from Latin Catholicism. They have never established themselves in the Anglo-Saxon world.

A pioneer in respect to harmony, form, and orchestral color, Liszt had an abiding effect on the musical practice of the late nineteenth century. He was the first to give a full piano recital. (Before his time piano solos were interspersed with orchestral or vocal numbers.) He introduced the grand style in piano playing and established new standards of virtuosity. He injected the picturesque personality—embodiment of romantic individualism—into the concert hall, where it has remained ever since. A great teacher, he raised a generation of giants of the keyboard. He was a master of orchestral technique. His easily accessible music helped create the modern mass public. He influenced composers from Wagner and César Franck to Ravel and George Gershwin.

Les Préludes (*The Preludes*)

The most famous of the symphonic poems was written in 1854. It served as a warhorse for several generations. Few pieces of music sum up so well the temper of the mid-nineteenth century.

Liszt appended to the score a program note of his own devising that had some connection in his mind with one of the *Méditations poétiques* of the mystical poet Alphonse de Lamartine. "What is our life but a series of preludes to that unknown song whose first solemn note is tolled by Death? The enchanted dawn of every life is love. But where is the destiny on whose first delicious joys some storm does not break? . . . And what soul thus cruelly bruised, when the tempest rolls away, seeks not to rest its memories in the pleasant calm of pastoral life? Yet man does not long permit himself to taste the kindly quiet that first attracted him to Nature's lap. For when the trumpet sounds he hastens to danger's post, that in the struggle he may once more regain full

knowledge of himself and his strength." Such a program was vague
enough not to interfere with the musical conception. Liszt is said to
have written it after the piece was finished. At the same time it related
the music to one of the favorite themes of the age—the image of man
pitted against Fate—unfolding a series of moods, dramatic, lyric, pastoral, triumphal, that appealed immensely to the romantic mentality.

The work is fashioned from a basic motive of three notes presented
by the strings. The ascending interval of a fourth imparts to the motive
a questioning upward inflection. This becomes a characteristic feature
of the melodic material.

There follows a passage for full orchestra, Andante maestoso (at a
going pace, majestic), the "prelude to that unknown song." Notice that
the characteristic upward leap of a fourth is present both in the melody
and the accompaniment.

Two themes in Liszt's suavest manner evoke the image of love that he
calls "the enchanted dawn of every life." The first, espressivo cantando
(expressively, in singing style), is assigned to the second violins and
cellos. The germ motive (under bracket) is embedded in the melody.

The second amorous theme is played by muted violas and a quartet of
horns, espressivo ma tranquillo (expressive but tranquil). This melody
contrasts with the preceding. On closer examination, however, it too
turns out to be an ingenious expansion of the basic motive (notes
marked x).

espressivo ma tranquillo

Thus, behind all talk of the program and its literary associations we see the mind of the musician at work. What the piece is about, quite apart from love, nature, and destiny, is a three-note motive that contains an ascending leap. Out of these three notes is woven the musical tissue, by a process of continuous transformation.

The tempo quickens, tension mounts. The basic material is presented Allegro tempestoso. As in Berlioz, the atmosphere of struggle is associated with chromatic scales. The effect is a cliché to us, but was fresh then. Naturally the tempestuous passage features the brass.

An area of relaxation ensues with the Allegretto pastorale, a peaceful nature scene. The motive is now transformed into a bucolic theme scored for woodwinds and horn.

The return to the fray is marked by an Allegro marziale animato (fast, martial, animated). Through changes in pace, register, dynamics, and color, the two love themes are transformed into rousing battle calls.

Finally the mood of exaltation returns, to round off the action with the typically romantic "apotheosis." The basic motive has triumphed along with Man.

This music is frankly rhetorical. It exemplifies the grandiose phase of the romantic style. Its sweeping gesture may be encountered in the painting of Delacroix, the poetry of Byron, the plays and novels of Hugo. This type of art has maintained its popularity despite the enormous change in taste and outlook that separates our century from the nineteenth. What endears it to the big public is its essentially romantic nature.

Liszt's defect was one of character rather than genius. It lay in his too great eagerness to please, to dazzle, to be adored. This was the fatal flaw in an otherwise great man. His shortcomings have, for many people, obscured the qualities of a genuinely musical personality. The "Music of the Future" has become that of the past. Yet he remains—man and musician—the voice of an era. "In art," he said, "one must work on a grand scale." This he did.

𝕒𝕖𝕨 *C H A P T E R 2 5* 𝕨𝕖𝕒

Nationalism and the Romantic Movement

"There is no patriotic art and no patriotic science. Both belong, like everything nobly good, to the whole world."

Goethe

The Rise of Musical Nationalism

NATIONAL sentiment was an all-important factor in the political development of nineteenth-century Europe. Its influence extended to the sphere of art, where it became a determining force within the romantic movement. National tensions on the Continent—the pride of the conquering nations and the struggle for freedom of the subjugated ones—gave rise to emotions that found an ideal expression in music. What had been love of nature in the eighteenth century became, in the nineteenth, a glorification of the beauty of one's native land. What had begun as an interest in the common man turned into a romantic preoccupation with the folklore of one's own group. Romanticism exalted the popular tone and exploited picturesque local color, encouraging musicians to make use of the songs and dances of their people. The emphasis upon program music accorded with this trend. Composers focused their symphonic poems and operas on a national hero, or an event or place of patriotic significance. Romantic interest in the Middle Ages opened up to the musician a fanciful world of national legend and saga. In addition, the nationally conscious composer made a contribution to his country's art by uniting his music with the lyrics of a national poet.

The German war of liberation against Napoleon in the early part of the century released a surge of patriotic sentiment that created a receptive atmosphere for Carl Maria von Weber's folklore opera *Der Freischütz* (The Marksman, 1821). Weber's successor Richard Wagner reached the zenith of his career in the newly constituted German Empire, which viewed his epic dramas as a monument to national pride. Poland's struggle for freedom from tsarist rule aroused the national poet in Chopin. A united Italy seeking independence from Austria found her national artist in Giuseppe Verdi. Franz Liszt explored the Gypsy idiom of his native Hungary. A Czech national school headed by Bedřich Smetana and Antonín Dvořák came into prominence as part of Bohemia's attempt to achieve an indigenous culture. Russia and Scandinavia won their musical independence, to be followed at the turn of the century by England, Finland, Spain, and—some decades later—by the United States.

Examples of musical nationalism abound in the output of the romantic era. The folk idiom is prominent in the Mazurkas of Chopin, the Hungarian Rhapsodies of Liszt, the Slavonic Dances of Dvořák, and the Norwegian Dances of Grieg. The life of the peasantry furnishes the theme for Weber's *Freischütz*, Glinka's *A Life for the Tsar*, Smetana's *Bartered Bride*, as well as the fairy-tale operas and ballets of Tchaikovsky and Rimsky-Korsakov. Native scenes and place-names figure in any number of musical landscapes from Smetana's *The Moldau* to Musorgsky's *Night on Bald Mountain* and Johann Strauss's *Tales from the Vienna Woods*. The beauty of the Rhine, of German forest and mountain, pervades Wagner's *Ring of the Nibelung*. The gods and heroes of the ancient sagas live again in this vast epic that centers about the life and death of Siegfried. Tchaikovsky's *Overture 1812* commemorates a national victory. The symphonic poems of Smetana, Dvořák, and Sibelius glorify the exploits of national heroes. German art was enriched in the early romantic period by the settings of native poetry in the songs of Schubert and Schumann; as was French art in the postromantic period through the songs of Debussy and Ravel based on Baudelaire, Mallarmé, and Verlaine. Russia's national poet Alexander Pushkin (1799–1837) was the source of a number of operas by Tchaikovsky, Musorgsky, and Rimsky-Korsakov. Bizet wrote music for Alphonse Daudet's *L'Arlésienne*, Grieg for Henrik Ibsen's *Peer Gynt*.

The political implications of musical nationalism were not lost upon the authorities. Verdi's operas had to be altered again and again to suit the Austrian censor. Sibelius's tone poem *Finlandia* with its rousing trumpet calls was forbidden by the tsarist police when Finland was demanding her independence at the turn of the century. During World War II the Nazis forbade the playing of *The Moldau* in Prague and of Chopin's Polonaises in Warsaw because of the powerful symbolism residing in these works.

Nationalism encouraged the nations that had no established tradition of art music to develop their own manner of musical speech. It brought these newcomers to their rightful place in the concert of nations, alongside the older musical cultures of Italy, Germany, and France. The national impulse was naturally most prominent among the musically "young" nations, but the older ones felt it too. For national conscious-ness pervaded every manifestation of the European spirit in the nine-teenth century. The romantic movement is unthinkable without it.

Exoticism

Once nationalism showed the way, local color became a decorative element in musical art to be exploited for its own sake. This gave rise to one of the most arresting offshoots of the romantic movement: the evoking of a distant locale for the sake of picturesque effect. Exoticism glamorized the far-off and the unknown, "the land that never was." It was nourished by the romantic interest in atmosphere, in instrumental color and orchestration.

In the nineteenth century exoticism manifested itself, in the first place, as a longing of the northern nations for the warmth and color of the South; in the second, as a longing of the West for the fairy-tale splendors of the Orient. The former impulse found expression in the works of German, French, and Russian composers who turned for in-spiration to Italy and Spain. The long list stretches from Glinka's two Spanish Overtures and Mendelssohn's *Italian Symphony* to Tchai-kovsky's *Capriccio italien,* Rimsky-Korsakov's *Capriccio on Spanish Themes*, Chabrier's *España,* Lalo's *Symphonie espagnole,* and Richard Strauss's *Aus Italien.* The masterpiece in this category is of course Bizet's *Carmen.*

The glamor of the East was brought to international prominence by the Russian national school. In an empire that stretched to the borders of Persia, exoticism was really a form of nationalism. The fairy-tale back-ground of Asia pervades Russian music. Rimsky-Korsakov's orchestrally resplendent *Scheherazade* and his opera *Sadko,* Alexander Borodin's opera *Prince Igor* and symphonic poem *In the Steppes of Central Asia,* and Ippolitov-Ivanov's *Caucasian Sketches* are among the many orien-tally inspired works that for a time found favor throughout the world. A number of French composers also utilized exotic themes, as did Verdi in *Aïda* and Puccini in his operas *Madame Butterfly* and *Turandot.*

In giving voice to his personal view of life the artist expresses also the hopes and dreams of the group with which he is identified. It is this identification, seeping through from the profoundest layers of the unconscious, that makes Shakespeare and Dickens so English, Dos-toievsky so Russian, Proust so French. Yet to attain the highest level of art, this identification must reach out beyond the single group. Shakespeare, Dostoievsky, and Proust belong not only to their own nations but to the whole of culture. In depicting the life they knew they expressed what all men feel. The greatest art may be intensely national in form, but it must also be universal in content.

Under the impetus of nationalism, music turned from the universal to the particular. It exalted external picturesqueness above the inner spirit that endures beyond time and place. In so doing, it forfeited something of the embracing humanism it had achieved in the late eighteenth century, a humanism that reached its pinnacle in the age of Beethoven and Goethe. To compensate, nationalism added to the language of European music a variety of idioms of immense charm and vividness. By associating music with the love of homeland, nationalism aligned the art with the great social and political movements of the age, and enabled composers to give expression to the cherished aspirations of millions of people.

CHAPTER 26

Bedřich Smetana (1824-1884)

"I am no enemy of the old forms in the old music. But I do not hold that we now have to follow them. I have come to the conclusion that the forms of the past are finished. Absolute music is quite impossible for me."

BEDŘICH SMETANA was the founder of the Czech national school. As in the case of several nationalist composers, Smetana's career unfolded against a background of political agitation. Bohemia stirred restlessly under Hapsburg rule, caught up in a surge of nationalist fervor that culminated in the uprisings of 1848. Young Smetana aligned himself with the patriotic cause. After the revolution was crushed, the atmosphere in Prague was oppressive for those suspected of sympathy with the national cause. In 1856 Smetana accepted a post as conductor in Sweden.

A disciple of Berlioz and Liszt, Smetana turned to the writing of symphonic poems during his stay abroad. On his return to Bohemia in 1861 he resumed his career as a national artist and worked for the establishment of a theater in Prague where the performances would be given in the native tongue.

Although Smetana found happiness in his personal and professional life, he was afflicted by ill health in his later years. Like Beethoven, he became deaf. He suffered from severe noises in the head, attacks of depression, and loss of memory. His last works were achieved, as he wrote, "in spite of terrible and constant hindrances." In his Quartet in E minor—an autobiographical work subtitled *From My Life*—he evokes not only his happy youth, his characteristically Czech love of dance rhythm, the awakening of love in his early years, his reaching of maturity, but also, in the high, screeching note sustained by the violins in the final movement, the misfortunes that darkened his later years. He suffered a mental breakdown at the age of sixty and died shortly after.

The hope of national liberation that inspired his art was inseparable from his vision of a better life for his people. In giving expression to their desire for freedom, Smetana continued the tradition of the revolutionary epoch in which romanticism had its origin. Folklore and local color were never used by him as picturesque ends in themselves; they constituted the very soul of what he had to say.

Of his eight operas on patriotic themes, several still hold the boards in the theaters of his native land. One—*The Bartered Bride*—attained world-wide fame. Hardly less important in the establishing of Smetana's reputation was the cycle of six symphonic poems entitled *My Country* which occupied him from 1874 to 1879. These works are steeped in the beauty of Bohemia's countryside, in the pomp and pageantry of her legends. Best known of the series is the second, *The Moldau*, Smetana's finest achievement in the field of orchestral music.

Song and dance—the two inexhaustible sources of a folk musician's art—hold sway in Smetana's music. His work is suffused with spontaneous lyricism, with the insights of a fresh and positive temperament. It possesses, besides, an inveterate optimism and sturdiness of spirit that were not too common in the nineteenth century. This combination of traits made him a spokesman of his people and one of the characteristic nationalist composers of the romantic era.

Vltava (*The Moldau*)

In this tone poem the famous river becomes a poetic symbol that suffuses the musical imagery with patriotic associations. The program appended to the score explains the composer's intention. "Two springs pour forth in the shade of the Bohemian forest, one warm and gushing, the other cold and peaceful." These join in a brook that becomes the river Moldau. "Coursing through Bohemia's valleys, it grows into a mighty stream. Through thick woods it flows as the gay sounds of the hunt and the notes of the hunter's horn are heard ever closer. It flows through grass-grown pastures and lowlands where a wedding feast is being celebrated with song and dance. At night, wood and water nymphs revel in its sparkling waves. Reflected on its surface are fortresses and castles—witnesses of bygone days of knightly splendor and the vanished glory of martial times." The stream races ahead through the Rapids of St. John, "finally flowing on in majestic peace toward Prague and welcomed by historic Vysehrad"—the legendary site of the castle of the ancient Bohemian kings. "Then it vanishes far beyond the poet's gaze."

The opening is marked Allegro commodo non agitato (moderately fast, not agitated). A rippling figure is heard as a dialogue between two flutes against a pizzicato accompaniment by violins and harp. From this emerges a broadly flowing melody played by oboes and violins—the theme of the river—that describes a broad arc in its stepwise movement along the scale. Smetana adapted his melody from a Czech folk song.

After a suitable expansion of this idea, horn calls evoke a hunting scene. The section labeled *Peasant Wedding* is in the spirit of rustic dance. The mood changes to one of mystery. The score is marked *Moonlight—Nymphs' Revels*. Woodwinds, horn, and strings are used in a characteristically romantic way to conjure up a poetic landscape. The pace quickens as the music graphically depicts the seething rapids near Prague. As the river approaches the ancient site of the royal castle, the principal melody returns in an exultant mood with certain tones altered —what we will encounter in a later chapter as a change from minor to major. Now the brass intones a triumphal chorale, as if the composer were assuring his countrymen that their former glory will return. (A *chorale* is a hymn or a hymnlike tune.) There is a diminuendo to the end as the river "vanishes far beyond the poet's gaze."

The Czechs regard this symphonic landscape as a national tone poem that mirrors the very soul of their land. The rest of the world sees in it one of the more attractive examples of late romantic tone painting.

CHAPTER 27

The Awakening of Russia

> "I grew up in a quiet spot and was saturated from earliest child-
> hood with the wonderful beauty of Russian popular song. I
> am therefore passionately devoted to every expression of the
> Russian spirit. In short, I am a Russian through and through!"
>
> Tchaikovsky

THE ENTRANCE of Russia into the family of musically productive nations
was a striking phenomenon in the art life of the nineteenth century, and
one that had far-reaching effects. The Russians arrived on the scene too
late to be dominated by the Germanic tradition. Instead, they were in
the forefront of those who in the latter part of the century successfully
challenged the world supremacy of the German symphony.

Modern Russia began with the attempt of Peter the Great (1672–
1725) forcibly to westernize his empire. Throughout the eighteenth
century the Russian aristocracy imported French ideas, German tutors,
and Italian operas. It was Mikhail Glinka (1804–57) who launched the
national school with his folk opera A Life for the Tsar. The aristocratic
audience that gathered for its opening night in 1836 pronounced it to
be "music for coachmen." But the work accorded with the political
plans of Emperor Nicholas I, whose approval launched it on its triumphal career. Glinka continued his efforts with *Russlan and Ludmilla,*
based on a tale by Pushkin. He was ably seconded by Alexander
Dargomijsky (1813–69), composer of the operas *Russalka* and *The
Stone Guest.* The seed planted by these two gentlemen-composers
(they belonged to the landed gentry) brought a rich harvest.

The emancipation of the serfs by Alexander II in 1861 spelled the end
of feudal Russia. Some felt that the nation's future lay in a rapprochement with the West, others clung nostalgically to the old traditions.
This ferment of ideas is familiar to readers of the three leading Russian
novelists of the age. Ivan Turgeniev (1818–83) dealt with the problems
of the aristocracy, presenting the Western or cosmopolitan attitude.
Fedor Dostoievsky (1821–81), with his inspired depiction of the provincial gentry, merchants, and peasants, was the voice of pan-Slavic
mysticism. Leo Tolstoi (1828–1910) created in his vast canvases a
panorama of Russian society that encompassed both points of view.

The two attitudes were reflected in the group of gifted young musicians who appeared during the 1860s to create the Russian national
school. The cosmopolites advocated Western techniques and forms.

The Slavophiles demanded independence from the West, drawing inspiration from native folk song and religious music. Actually there was less distance between the two camps than their adherents supposed. The Russian composer had to function within the common practice of the West. In the absence of art forms specifically his own he had to take over those that had developed within the European tradition—symphony and concerto, opera and ballet, chamber music, piano piece, and song.

Coming to the classical forms rather late, the Russians never mastered the techniques that had made the symphony of Haydn, Mozart, and Beethoven a marvel of organic unity. From their folk song they evolved a simple technique of repeating and varying themes, which they used with great effectiveness. Their music echoed ancient scale patterns and bore the influence of Greek Orthodox chant. They were masters of melody; their rhythms, derived from native dance, had enormous verve; and they had a flair for sumptuous orchestral color. The emotional exuberance, exotic appeal, and brilliant coloring of their music struck a novel tone. They soon won a dominant position in the international repertory.

The Western camp was led by the pianist-composer Anton Rubinstein (1829–94), a disciple of the Mendelssohn-Schumann school. His operas, symphonies, and oratorios are no longer performed. To Americans he is known chiefly by his *Melody in F*. He was one of the first in his time to realize that the musical culture of his country would have to be built by thoroughly trained, full-time professionals, not by upperclass dilettantes who regarded music as a hobby. He founded the Conservatory of St. Petersburg (today's Leningrad), patterned after the Leipzig model. His brother, the pianist Nicholas Rubinstein, established the equally important Conservatory of Moscow. Out of the system of education inaugurated by these two came Russia's first native-trained professional composer, Peter Ilyich Tchaikovsky.

"The Mighty Five"

Russian nationalism fired the imaginations of a group of youthful enthusiasts who came to be known as "The Mighty Five." (It has become apparent since that the adjective applied to only one of their number.) Leader of this dedicated band was Mily Balakirev (1837–1910). A self-taught musician, he persuaded himself and his four disciples—César Cui, Alexander Borodin, Nicholas Rimsky-Korsakov, and Modest Musorgsky—that they had no need of exercises in German counterpoint to give expression to the pan-Slavic dream. The four youths—they were not much younger than their leader—came under the spell of Balakirev's fiery personality. Belonging as they did to the upper middle class, they were not averse to the notion of the gentle-man-composer established by Glinka and Dargcmijsky, as opposed to the strict professional training advocated by the Rubinsteins and Tchai-kovsky.

Of the five, Balakirev and Cui may be dismissed at once; they hardly rose above the level of the salon composer. Alexander Borodin (1834–87) was a gifted scientist who lectured at the Academy of Medicine and wrote important treatises in his field. He managed, amid the dis-tractions of a crowded life, to create several works that are still heard: the Second Symphony and the String Quartet No. 2; the national opera *Prince Igor*, notable for its fine choral writing and the exotic *Polovetsian Dances*; and the symphonic sketch *In the Steppes of Central Asia.* ——— *Borodin* Although Rimsky-Korsakov was the most successful of the group during his lifetime, it remained for the fifth among them to fathom the depths of his nation's soul. Modest Musorgsky was looked upon with conde-scension by his four comrades because of what they considered the technical ineptness of his writing. They never suspected that he was incomparably the greatest among them.

Russia's musical awakening, like her achievement in literature, was an expression on the artistic front of her coming of age as a European power. The Russian national school not only made a vital contribution to the musical culture of the nineteenth century but also—through its influence on Debussy, Ravel, and other moderns—strongly affected the twentieth-century scene.

✤✤✤ *CHAPTER 28* ✤✤✤

Nicholas Rimsky-Korsakov (1844-1908)

"Our epoch, the post-Wagnerian age, is the age of brilliance and imaginative quality in orchestral tone color."

RIMSKY-KORSAKOV is one of the chief representatives of nineteenth-century exoticism. His was an imagination haunted by fairy-tale land-scapes, by luminous seas and skies. His music has a picture-book quality and the gorgeousness of color that goes with it. The profounder emo-tions were unknown to this happy artist, but he was one of the great orchestrators of the nineteenth century. Certainly none was more influential in developing the picturesque and decorative aspects of the late romantic style.

Like Borodin, he began by regarding music as a side activity. His career as a naval officer was cut out for him by family tradition. The squadron to which he was assigned visited the United States in 1863. "Niagara Falls made the most marvelous impression on us," he records in his *Autobiography*. "We rowed in a boat as near as possible up to the falls." Since England during our Civil War espoused the Southern cause, her traditional enemy Russia sided with the North. "We followed the course of events with deep interest, though we kept exclusively within Northern territory. The expected war with England had not materialized, and we did not have to privateer and threaten English merchantmen in the Atlantic."

The flotilla proceeded to South America. In the tropics the young man was enchanted by the light and color that were later to vibrate through his music. "Wonderful is the tropical ocean with its azure color and phosphorescent light, wonderful are tropical sun and clouds. But the tropical night sky over the ocean is the most wonderful thing in the world!" During the three years of the cruise he wrote his First Symphony. This was performed upon his return to Russia, and brought him his first success as a composer. At twenty-seven he was appointed professor of composition and orchestration at the Conservatory of St. Petersburg. Two years later he resigned from the navy.

Rimsky-Korsakov was the first of "The Five" to realize the inadequacy of his professional training and to rebel against Balakirev's dilettantism. Although he had several symphonic works and a successful opera to his credit, he set himself to acquire the basic skills in which he felt himself deficient. He attended the counterpoint classes of a colleague at the Conservatory, alongside his own students, and called himself with justification "the best pupil in the school." This self-discipline resulted in a mastery of technique which at that time was indeed rare in Russia.

In his capacity as conductor and teacher Rimsky exercised a formidable influence on the course of Russian music. His pupils included Igor Stravinsky as well as a number of the leaders of the next generation —Glazunov, Ippolitov-Ivanov, Liadov, Gretchaninov. He is one of several nineteenth-century composers—Smetana is another, as is Grieg— who continue to occupy a central position in their native lands even though their importance on the international scene is waning. Russian musicians insist that we do not begin to appreciate his stature in this country because we are unfamiliar with his stage works. His fifteen operas continue to delight his countrymen. Almost all are based on subjects drawn from Russian history or fairy tale. The librettos of several are derived from the leading writers of his country: Pushkin (*The Golden Cockerel, Mozart and Salieri, Tsar Saltan*); Gogol (*May Night, Christmas Eve*); Ostrovsky (*Snow Maiden*). A few excerpts have caught the fancy of the American public: the *Song of India* from *Sadko*, *Hymn to the Sun* from *Le Coq d'Or* (The Golden Cockerel), and the *Flight of the Bumblebee* from *Tsar Saltan*.

Scheherazade

Rimsky-Korsakov is best known to the West through his orchestral evocation of *A Thousand and One Nights*, which for several decades was subjected to merciless overplaying. This symphonic suite (1888) displays all of Rimsky's charm and remains in point of orchestration one of the monumental scores of its time. One has but to hear Stravinsky's *Firebird* or Ravel's *Daphnis and Chloe* to realize how much the younger men learned from it.

The prefatory note tells of the Sultan Schahriar who, "convinced of the faithlessness of women, had resolved to put to death each of his wives after the wedding night. But the Sultana Scheherazade saved her life by diverting him with tales which she told him on a thousand and one nights. Conquered by his curiosity the Sultan postponed from one day to the next the execution of his wife and in the end renounced his bloody vow."

The introduction, marked Largo e maestoso (broad and majestic), presents two contrasting themes that conjure up the main characters. The brusque theme of the Sultan is announced fortissimo and pesante (heavily) in low register by most of the orchestra.

The motive of the Sultana (Narrator) is given by a solo violin in high register above arpeggios on the harp. It is an oriental-sounding melody that reappears throughout the four movements in various guises. It serves to identify the Sultana with each new tale; hence it becomes a unifying element in the work.

The movement proper, *The Sea and the Ship of Sinbad*, is an ample seascape in ⁶⁄₄ time, marked Allegro non troppo. This is frankly descriptive music, sensuous and atmospheric. The main theme is a vigorous idea derived from the Sultan theme. For contrast there is the relaxed sequence of chords presented by the woodwinds, which com-

mentators generally associate with the calm of the sea. An element of dramatic tension is supplied by the crescendo passages in which Rimsky whips up an exciting orchestral tempest. The movement is somewhat too long for the meager thematic material, which instead of being developed is simply repeated over and over again in the fairy-tale manner beloved by the Russian school. It is the orchestration that supplies the variety, now shot with flame as the brass give out their pronouncements, now silvered with the sheen of woodwinds and strings. Indeed, the movement, with its striking juxtaposition of flute, oboe, clarinet, horn, and violin tone, is a catalogue of orchestral effects.

The Tale of the Prince Kalender is an Arabian Nights narrative. This movement opens with the theme of the Sultana in her capacity as Narrator. An artless tune in the manner of a folk song, played by a solo bassoon andantino and capriccioso, gives an attractive picture of the happy-go-lucky prince who went disguised as a beggar. The melody contains several *grace notes,* marked by x in the following example. (A grace note is a very short note having no time value of its own, which is interpolated as an ornament before a longer note.)

Tension increases in the middle part of the movement. Tremolos on the strings and ominous pronouncements by trombones and trumpets suggest that our hero has run into trouble. But he extricates himself and proceeds on his untroubled way, satisfying both the listener and the demands of A-B-A form. Notable throughout is the naive folk tone that was much prized by the romantics.

The first movement is descriptive in character; the second, narrative. The third is lyric. *The Young Prince and Princess* is a love scene which is heard in A-B-A form. The movement unfolds at a moderate tempo. The Prince's song, first played by violins, is repeated by cellos and woodwinds. Notice the decorative runs that embellish the melody, played by a solo clarinet, then by a solo flute. The dance of the Princess is presented, at a slightly faster tempo, by solo clarinet against a strongly rhythmic accompaniment. Next we hear again the languorous melody of the opening. The restatement of the Prince's music is then interrupted by the Narrator, as if to remind the listener that the Sultana is finishing another of her tales. The movement ends on a tender note.

The finale, *Festival at Bagdad,* is a tumultuous dance scene. Marked Allegro molto, the movement inspired Debussy to the tart remark that Rimsky-Korsakov's music suggests a bazaar rather than the Orient. The

headlong dance in duple meter is interspersed with a procession of themes from the earlier movements—Scheherazade, the Sultan, the Kalender Prince, the Young Princess. This not only offers the listener the charm of reminiscence, but ties the work together, a procedure much in favor, we shall find, with nineteenth-century composers.

The movement mounts to a climax through a steady rise in pitch, volume, and pacing. At the height of the excitement there is a return to the broadly flowing $\frac{6}{4}$ time of the first movement. "The Ship is dashed to pieces against a rock surmounted by a Bronze Warrior." A graphic musical hurricane is whipped up by means of chromatic scales. Tumult builds inexorably to the point where stentorian trumpets pronounce the motive of doom. A great calm descends upon the orchestra. The coda strikes a note of reconciliation between the two primal themes, suggesting the Sultan's resolve to let Scheherazade keep her clever head. It is clear that they lived happily ever after.

Scheherazade occupies its own niche in the romantic heritage. Its position is analogous to certain literary classics such as *The Mill on the Floss* or *Oliver Twist.* We may not feel impelled to return to them in our maturity, yet we should be immeasurably the poorer for not having known them in our youth.

Peter Ilyich Tchaikovsky (1840-1893)

"Truly there would be reason to go mad were it not for music."

FEW COMPOSERS typify the end-of-the-century mood as does Peter Ilyich Tchaikovsky. He belonged to a generation that saw its truths crumble and found none to replace them. He expressed as did none other the pessimism that attended the final phase of the romantic movement.

His Life

Tchaikovsky was born at Votinsk in a distant province of Russia, son of a government official. His family intended him for a career in the government. He graduated at nineteen from the aristocratic School of Jurisprudence at St. Petersburg and obtained a minor post in the Ministry of Justice. Not till he was twenty-three did he reach the decision to resign his post and enter the newly founded Conservatory of St. Petersburg. "To be a good musician and earn my daily bread"—his was a modest goal.

He completed the course in three years and was immediately recommended by Anton Rubinstein, director of the school, for a teaching post at the new Conservatory of Moscow. Despite the long hours and large classes, the young professor of harmony applied himself assiduously to composition. His twelve years at Moscow saw the production of some of his most successful works.

Extremely sensitive by nature, Tchaikovsky was subject to attacks of depression aggravated by his irregular personal life. "Regretting the past and hoping for the future without ever being satisfied with the present—this is how my life is spent." Could there be a better characterization of the late romantic artist? In the hope of achieving some degree of stability Tchaikovsky entered into an ill-starred marriage with a student of the Conservatory, Antonina Miliukov, who was hopelessly in love with him. His sympathy for Antonina soon turned into uncontrollable aversion, and in a fit of despair he wandered into the icy waters of the Moscow River. Some days later he fled, on the verge of a serious breakdown, to his brothers in St. Petersburg.

In this desperate hour, as in one of the fairy tales he liked to turn into ballets, there appeared the kind benefactress who enabled him to go abroad until he had recovered his health, freed him from the drudgery

of teaching, and launched him on the most productive period of his
career. Nadezhda von Meck, widow of an industrialist, was an imperious and emotional woman. She lived the life of a recluse in her mansion
in Moscow, from which she ran her railroads, her estates, and the lives
of her eleven children. Her passion was music, especially Tchaikovsky's.
Bound by the rigid conventions of her time and her class, she had to be
certain that her enthusiasm was for the artist, not the man; hence she
stipulated that she was never to meet the recipient of her bounty.

Peter Ilyich Tchaikovsky.

Thus began the famous friendship by letter which soon assumed a
tone of passionate attachment. For the next thirteen years Mme. von
Meck made Tchaikovsky's career the focal point of her life, providing
for his needs with exquisite devotion and tact. She resisted all temptation to remove the relationship from its ideal plane. Save for an acci-
dental glimpse of one another at the opera or during a drive, they never
met.

The correspondence gives us an insight into Tchaikovsky's method of
work. "You ask me how I manage the instrumentation. I never compose
in the abstract. I invent the musical idea and its instrumentation simultaneously." Mme. von Meck inquires if the Fourth Symphony (which he
dedicated to her) has a definite meaning. Tchaikovsky replies, "How
can one express the indefinable sensations that one experiences while
writing an instrumental composition that has no definite subject? It is a
purely lyrical process. It is a musical confession of the soul, which un-
burdens itself through sounds just as a lyric poet expresses himself
through poetry. The difference lies in the fact that music has far richer
resources of expression and is a more subtle medium . . . As Heine
said, 'Where words leave off music begins.' "

There emerges from the letters the romantic view of music as an expression of personal sentiment; also the romantic view of art as a refuge from the difficulties of life. Tchaikovsky shows a remarkably sane attitude in regard to his position in history. "An artist should not be troubled by the indifference of his contemporaries. He should go on working and say all that he has been predestined to say. He should know that posterity alone can render a true verdict."

The years covered by the correspondence saw the spread of Tchaikovsky's fame. He was the first Russian whose music caught on in the West, and in 1891 he was invited to come to America to participate in the ceremonies that marked the opening of Carnegie Hall. From New York he wrote, "These Americans strike me as very remarkable. In this country the honesty, sincerity, generosity, cordiality, and readiness to help you without a second thought are extremely pleasant . . . The houses downtown are simply colossal. I cannot understand how anyone can live on the thirteenth floor. I went out on the roof of one such house. The view was splendid, but I felt quite giddy when I looked down on Broadway . . . I am convinced that I am ten times more famous in America than in Europe."

The letters of his final years breathe disenchantment and—that bugbear of middle-aged artists—the suspicion that he had nothing more to say. "Is it possible that I have completely written myself out? I have neither ideas nor inclinations!" But ahead of him lay his two finest symphonies.

Immediately after finishing his Sixth Symphony, the *Pathétique,* he went to St. Petersburg to conduct it. The work met with a lukewarm reception, due in part to the fact that Tchaikovsky, painfully shy in public, conducted his music without any semblance of conviction. Some days later, although he had been warned of the prevalence of cholera in the capital, he carelessly drank a glass of unboiled water and contracted the disease. He died within the week, at the age of fifty-three. The suddenness of his death and the tragic tone of his last work led to rumors that he had committed suicide, and almost immediately there accrued to the *Symphonie pathétique* the sensational popularity it has enjoyed ever since.

His Music

"He was the most Russian of us all!" said Stravinsky. In the eyes of his countrymen Tchaikovsky is a national artist. He himself laid great weight on the Russian element in his music. As in the case of Dvořák, his feeling for nature merged with attachment to the native soil. "Why is it that the simple Russian landscape, a walk in summer through Russian fields and forest or on the steppes at evening can affect me so that I have lain on the ground numb, overcome by a wave of love for nature." At the same time, in the putting together of his music Tchaikovsky was a cosmopolite. He came under the spell of Italian opera, French ballet, German symphony and song. These he assimilated to the strain of folk melody that was his heritage as a Russian, setting upon the mixture the stamp of a sharply defined personality. The exaggerated subjectivity that was a symptom of weakness in the man became a source of strength for the artist. He drew upon his innermost feelings, projecting these with a lack of inhibition that attracts many more than it repels. It is worthy of note that outside his native land Tchaikovsky's hyperemotional music has enjoyed its greatest success in England and the United States—precisely the two countries where Anglo-Saxon reserve puts a brake on the expression of personal feeling to a much greater degree than on the Continent.

Tchaikovsky cultivated all branches of music. Of prime importance are his last symphonies, the Fourth (1877), the Fifth (1888), and the Sixth (1893). These are rich in sentiment as in tension. They abound in purple passages and spectacular climaxes that endear them to the virtuoso conductor. It is hardly necessary to state that what Tchaikovsky had to say was too personal to fit easily into the architecture of the classical form. Yet there is no mistaking his melodic gift—that most precious possession of the composer—or his rhythmic vitality, his mastery of orchestral effect, his flair for the dramatic, his bigness of gesture.

In the domain of program music two symphonic poems continue to be played: the overture-fantasy *Romeo and Juliet* and the symphonic fantasy *Francesca da Rimini* (1876). Hardly less popular is the colorful *Capriccio italien* (1880). Of his eight operas, two hold the stage in his native land: *Eugene Onegin* (1877–78) and *Pique Dame* (Queen of Spades, 1890). Based on librettos derived from the national poet Pushkin, both are essentially lyric in character. Unlike the operas, Tchaikovsky's ballets maintain themselves on the international scene. *Swan Lake* (1876), *The Sleeping Beauty* (1889), and *The Nutcracker* (1892) are widely appreciated both in the ballet theater and in the concert hall.

The Piano Concerto in B-flat minor (1875) and the Violin Concerto in D major (1878) are staple display pieces of the virtuoso. The four suites for orchestra have dropped from sight. Tchaikovsky wrote a fair amount of chamber music. The First String Quartet is remembered because of the perennial *Andante cantabile;* the Trio for Piano, Violin, and Cello "In memory of a great artist"—Nicholas Rubinstein—represents his finest effort in this sphere. Tchaikovsky's piano pieces are of the salon variety. Several—*Romance, Barcarolle, Song without Words, Troika*—are firmly entrenched in the repertory of dinner music. Of his more than one hundred songs a single one—*None But the Lonely Heart,* in his familiar vein of romantic melancholy—has obscured many that are more representative of him at his best.

We shall in a later section consider Tchaikovsky as a symphonist. In this chapter we are concerned with his most successful effort in the domain of program music.

Overture-Fantasy Romeo and Juliet

Romeo and Juliet, the first work that fully revealed Tchaikovsky's gifts, was written in 1869, when the composer was twenty-nine. He thoroughly revised the piece afterward. The term *overture-fantasy* suggests his imaginative approach to the material. It also makes clear that this is not an overture to an opera but an independent concert piece. The form is similar to that we encountered in Mendelssohn's Overture to *A Midsummer Night's Dream:* a large three-section structure that allows for the presentation, development, and restatement of musical ideas (Exposition-Development-Recapitulation). In this case the form is enlarged by means of a spacious introduction. It was in no sense the composer's intent to give a musical depiction of the Shakespearean drama. Rather, he selected three salient images that lent themselves to musical treatment—the gentle Friar Laurence, the feud between the two noble families of Verona, and the lovers.

Ecclesiastical harmonies evoke the good friar. They are in the style of a chorale which is presented in four-part harmony by two clarinets and two bassoons, Andante non tanto quasi moderato (not too slow, almost moderate). Archaic in effect, the chords create a medieval atmosphere. They expand into a rather lengthy introduction, and return at the end of the piece in a prelude-postlude formation that encloses the action in a frame.

The Allegro giusto begins with the "Feud" theme.

The brusque rhythm with its strong syncopation suggests violent action, as do the full orchestral tone and explosive accompaniment. Characteristic of Tchaikovsky are the sweeping runs, ascending and descending, on the violins.

The love theme is a melody long of line and tenderly lyrical, sung by English horn and muted violas. The youthful composer created here a broadly spun song whose ardor is not unworthy of Shakespeare's lovers.

The mood is rounded off by a subsidiary idea of great expressiveness, played by the muted strings. With this the exposition section—that is, the presentation of the musical material—comes to an end.

The agitated development section is based mainly on the Feud theme, interspersed with references to the Friar Laurence music in the horns and trumpets. In the working out of his musical ideas Tchaikovsky achieves that building up of tension and momentum which is the essence of symphonic development. The Recapitulation brings back the feud theme substantially as before. The love music is now expanded and rises, wave upon wave of sumptuous orchestral sound, to one of those torrential climaxes that only an uninhibited romantic could achieve. Musicians have a healthy respect for Tchaikovsky's ability to spin out the musical line. Nothing better indicates the Russian master's command of his material.

The epilogue is fashioned out of the love theme. Muffled drums beat a dirge for the dead lovers, and the chorale of the opening is heard again, balancing the architecture. Arpeggios on the harp introduce the appropriately celestial note.

This is young man's music, fervid, communicative, and fashioned along broad simple lines. The work was received coldly at its first hearing in Moscow; it was hissed in Paris and Vienna—heaven knows why. Subsequently it became an international favorite. It captures a characteristic moment in the thought and feeling of the late romantic era. Beyond that it remains one of the more beguiling—and solidly wrought —examples of nineteenth-century program music.

Absolute Music

CHAPTER 30

The Symphony

"A great symphony is a man-made Mississippi down which we irresistibly flow from the instant of our leave-taking to a long foreseen destination."

Aaron Copland

WE HAVE in the past few chapters established two types of meaning that coexist in a musical work. On the one hand, music has an expressive content that may be associated in the composer's mind with certain emotions, scenes, or even an action. On the other, a composition exists as a piece of musical material that is fashioned into a balanced structure according to principles having to do solely with the nature of sound.

We now come to a class of music in which the two meanings are present in a somewhat different relationship. In the large forms of absolute music—symphony and concerto, sonata and chamber music—the expressive content is no longer chained to a program. The emotional content of the music is projected in abstract forms. Such music may lose something for the visual-minded listener who loves to have specific images and meanings as a crutch to lean on, but it gains as much for other listeners in that it leaves them free to find their own meanings. More important, such music follows its own laws untrammeled by story content. The musical ideas are rooted, of course, in the composer's way of feeling and his need to communicate that feeling. But they are organized in such a way that, without any aid at all from external images, they will give the listener a satisfying sense of order and continuity.

The Nature of the Symphony

A symphony is a large-scale work for orchestra, in several parts or movements. These generally are three or four in number, in the sequence fast, slow, fast; or fast, slow, moderately fast, fast. (There are

168

many exceptions to this pattern.) The movements contrast in character and mood. Taken together they form an architectural entity and establish the symphony as the most exalted type of absolute music.

We will postpone a detailed discussion of symphonic structure to a later part of this book. It will suffice for the present to establish the character of the first movement of the cycle as a large form based on three sections—Exposition, Development, and Recapitulation (or Restatement). Sometimes a slow introduction leads into the movement proper. The Exposition usually presents two contrasting themes— one strongly rhythmic, the other lyric—which expand into characteristic sections. There is a bridge or transitional passage that leads from the first theme group to the second. A codetta (little coda) rounds off the section. The Development is marked by a tremendous increase in tension. The themes may be broken into their component motives, recombined into fresh patterns, revealed in a new light. The potentialities of the material for dynamic growth and development are thoroughly explored. The character of this section is indicated in the names by which it is sometimes known—"free fantasia" or "working-out section." Conflict and drama are of the essence of the Development. In the Restatement or Recapitulation we hear again the themes of the Exposition more or less in their original guise, but with the wealth of new meaning that these have taken on in the course of the movement. There follows the coda, whose function it is to round off the action and to bring the movement to its appointed conclusion.

The first movement is generally the most dramatic of the cycle. It is written in what is known as sonata form, sonata-allegro form (because the tempo of this movement is almost always allegro), or first-movement form. This form may also be used for an independent piece such as the overture. We encountered first-movement form in the Midsummer Night's Dream Overture and the Romeo and Juliet Overture.

In contrast to the epic-dramatic character of the first movement, the second—in the nineteenth-century symphony—is generally a slow movement of tenderly lyric nature. It may, however, vary in mood from the whimsical, even playful, to the tragic and passionate. The tempo marking in most cases is andante, adagio, or largo. This movement may be in A-B-A form; sometimes it is a theme and variations. (Other possibilities are indicated in a later chapter.)

Third in the cycle, in the symphonies of the romantic period, is the strongly rhythmic and impetuous scherzo, with overtones of humor, surprise, whimsy, or folk dance. The tempo marking indicates a lively pace —allegro, allegro molto, vivace, or the like. The form is a large A-B-A, the middle section being of somewhat quieter nature. The reader will recall that scherzo is the Italian word for "jest"; but the mood may range from elfin lightness to demonic energy. In some symphonies the scherzo comes second.

The fourth and last member of the cycle is of a dimension and character to balance the first. It brings the symphony to a close, at any rate during the greater part of the nineteenth century, on a note of triumph —the glorification or "apotheosis" dear to the romantic temperament. The movement is generally a spirited allegro. In most of the romantic symphonies to be discussed in the next chapters the final movement, like the first, is based on the Exposition-Development-Recapitulation structure of sonata-allegro form.

We have here given the barest outline of symphonic form, not attempting a complete picture until after we shall have heard several representative symphonies. What is important at this point is to understand that the symphony is an ideal tone-drama whose several movements are concerned with the presentation of abstract musical ideas. The essence of its style is dramatic contrast and development within a tight frame of thematic continuity. It arouses emotion in the listener, but emotion not directed to any specific image. For the symphony is a highly charged communication in the language of absolute music, whose glory is its freedom from definiteness. From our knowledge of the romantic era, from the letters and statements of composers concerning their symphonic works, we may glean some idea of the emotional climate that a given symphony inhabits. Certain characteristic symbolisms recur, as the movement "from doubt to faith" of César Franck's Symphony, or the progression from conflict to triumphal affirmation that appealed to the nineteenth-century mind. However, what the doubt, faith, conflict, or triumph is about is unspecified. We may be specific about the formal content of a symphony—the disposition of the themes, their growth and development. The emotional content is left for each listener to determine for himself.

The word theme is apt to figure prominently in any discussion of musical form. By a theme we mean a distinctive musical idea that serves as a building block, a germinating element in a large musical work. The theme may be a fully rounded melody or it may be a compact melodic-harmonic-rhythmic kernel that is capable of further growth and flowering. The theme may be broken down into its constituent fragments which are known as motives. For example, the melody of London Bridge might serve as a theme in a large work. The first four notes (on the words "London Bridge is") could constitute one motive, the next three notes (on the words "falling down"), another. In the unfolding of a work this theme and its motives might undergo continual development, in the course of which their capacity for growth would be explored.

We shall have more to say on theme and motive when we discuss the classical form in detail.

The Symphony in the Romantic Era

The sonata form was the crowning achievement of eighteenth-century classicism. Brought to artistic maturity by Haydn, Mozart, and Beethoven, it embodied the thought and feeling of the classical age. The romantic composers were at a disadvantage: they tried to adapt the grand form to a content for which it had not been intended. The struggle between classical form and romantic content was the central issue of nineteenth-century music. As more than one composer complained, it was not easy to write a symphony after Beethoven.

The classical symphony was based on the clash of musical ideas; romanticism preferred the battle of emotions. Classical form called for careful planning, thematic logic, abstract thought; romanticism loved diffuseness and caprice, mood and atmosphere. Classicism favored absolute music; the romantic era favored program music. The classical symphony was a rational, tightly coherent form; romanticism was avid for lyricism. In the first flush of the romantic movement the symphony had to compete, on the one hand with the symphonic poem, on the other with short lyric forms such as the song and piano piece. To Liszt, Berlioz, Wagner, and other adherents of the "Music of the Future" it seemed that the symphony as the classical era had known it was a thing of the past.

Once the initial fervor of romanticism had subsided, however, the symphony regained its central position: its appeal to the purely musical instincts of composers was too great to be long ignored. Imperceptibly it accommodated itself to the needs of the new age. Its structure was loosened by lyricism and by the grand rhetoric of the nineteenth-century style. It absorbed the romantic love of spectacular effect and grandiose gesture. It could not recapture the ideal balance of form and content, the Olympian serenity of Haydn and Mozart, or the tightness of construction of Beethoven. But it became an intensely human document packed with action, with turbulent climax and spine-tingling proclamation, with purple patches and with upwellings of song.

The romantic symphony cannot be judged, strictly speaking, by the standards of the classical era. It aspired to something else. Only in this way could it truthfully reflect its own time. Only in this way were brought into being the exuberant works that continue to delight multitudes of music lovers.

CHAPTER 31

César Franck (1822-1890)

"What Wagner did for human love, I have done for divine."

CÉSAR FRANCK was the most important figure in French instrumental music of the late nineteenth century. He forged the link between France and the German symphonic tradition. (He was born, appropriately, in the country that lies between the two cultures—in Belgium, at Liège.) Confronted with a public for whom music in large measure was synonymous with opera, he was one of those who implanted in them an awareness of instrumental music and helped prepare the way for the emergence of a French school of symphonists.

His Life

Franck was for thirty years organist of the Church of St. Clotilde in Paris. His inspired improvisations on the instrument he loved constituted the summit of French achievement in this field. By nature kindly and retiring, this dedicated artist was unfit for the politics that bring important posts and power. Whatever official recognition he received— he held a professorship at the Conservatory—was given him in his capacity as organist rather than composer. Winter and summer he rose at five-thirty in the morning, devoting two hours to creative work before he began his teaching chores. He was on his way to a lesson when, crossing the street, he was struck by an omnibus. The injury, improperly treated, hastened his death in his sixty-ninth year.

Franck's music was steadfastly ignored by the official musical world of Paris. When a work of his did get a hearing, as like as not it suffered from an inadequate performance. This unassuming artist demanded very little from his contemporaries. On one occasion, when his pupils were furious at the way his music had been played, he remonstrated with them: "No no, you really are too exacting, dear boys. For my part I was quite satisfied." His first unqualified success came in the very last year of his life, with the performance of his String Quartet. "The next day," relates his disciple and biographer Vincent d'Indy, "he said to us quite naïvely, 'There, you see, the public is beginning to understand me.'"

The ultimate triumph of his ideas was helped by political events. The defeat of France by Germany in 1870 brought about a resurgence of national pride and created a favorable climate for the growth of a national school. There came into being the Société Nationale de Musique, whose aim it was to promote the performance of works by French musicians. Franck was one of the founders and for a time president

César Franck.

of the society. In the ensuing years there gathered about him the pupils who were to become the leaders of the next generation in French music, among them Vincent d'Indy, Ernest Chausson, Gabriel Pierné, and Henri Duparc. "Father Franck"—his pupils named him "Pater Seraphicus" because of his gentleness—also provided a stimulating example for other composers such as Camille Saint-Saëns, Gabriel Fauré, Emmanuel Chabrier, and Paul Dukas. Thus, although he was never in his lifetime the world figure he subsequently became, he exerted an invigorating influence on French musical life at a crucial moment in its development.

His Music

Franck was a religious mystic for whom music was an act of faith. His was a nature given to contemplation and ecstasy. He saw the movements of the sonata cycle as a progression from conflict to triumph; a spiritual advance from darkness to light, from inner struggle and doubt to the serenity of belief. His music dealt in symbolic meanings and states of soul. In this he was of the romantic age.

At the same time he was attuned to the classical heritage. He strove to inject into French music the constructional logic of the German tradition. During his earlier years he tried his hand at program music and opera. But he found his true expression, in the final period of his career, in the large forms of absolute music. The works by which he is remembered include one each of the important types: the Symphony, the Sonata in A for Violin and Piano (1886), the Quintet in F minor for Piano and Strings (1878–79); the String Quartet in D (1889); a concerto for piano and orchestra—the *Symphonic Variations* of 1885; and a large work for piano, *Prelude, Chorale, and Fugue* (1884). To this list may be added his oratorio *Les Béatitudes* (1869–79); *Rédemption,* a symphonic poem for soprano solo, male chorus, and orchestra (2nd version, 1874); and a number of compositions for the organ that laid the foundation of the modern French school of organ music.

The conflict between classical form and romantic content posed problems for Franck that he could not always solve, notwithstanding his skill in developing, varying, and intertwining musical themes. He sought to knit together the movements of the sonata structure through what is known as *cyclical form.* This involves the use of the same material in the different movements, often in the shape of a motto theme that comes back at a dramatic moment in each, to serve both as reminiscence and unifying thread. Franck carried the principle still farther by deriving all the material from a few basic themes, which appear in manifold transformations and disguises throughout the different movements. Cyclical form heightened the unity of the symphony in accordance with the needs of the romantic age. By the same token it weakened the opposition between the different movements and themes that was the basis of classical sonata form.

Romantic in the extreme was the rich sensuous harmony that Franck inherited from Wagner and Liszt, particularly the latter. His idiom is characterized by what is known as chromatic harmony. (The chromatic scale, it will be recalled, includes the twelve semitones or half tones into which the octave is divided.) Chromaticism met the need of the romantic age for an expressive language spiced with dissonance and with chords that generated tension. It is one of the prime characteristics of romantic music. The chromatic idiom imparts to Franck's style its hyperemotional quality, its high tension and excitement. As a result, his works present a special blend of the spiritual and the erotic, of the religious and the theatrical.

Symphony in D Minor

The D-minor Symphony (1886–88), Franck's most widely played work, displays the essential qualities of his style. It is an ample, communicative piece abounding in opulent harmonies and heaven-storming proclamation. The first movement is constructed out of three ideas. First is a germinal motive of upward inflection, whose intervals duplicate the three-note questioning motive that opens Liszt's *Les Préludes*.

Announced in the lower register by violas, cellos, and double basses, it flowers into an introduction rich in atmosphere.

The germ motive becomes the tempestuous first theme of the Allegro non troppo (not too lively). This is a vigorous idea characterized by dotted rhythms and wide leaps.

Introduced by the strings against a background of brusque chords in the winds, the main theme expands into a spacious section. The slow introduction and the allegro passage are restated at a higher pitch. This restatement has the effect both of postponing the action and of intensifying it.

The second idea counterposes lyricism to drama and constitutes an area of relaxation in the precipitous forward movement. It is marked molto cantabile, dolce (very songful, sweet), and is heard in the most caressing register of the violins. In contrast to the first theme, this melody moves quietly along the scale.

The third idea completes the progression from conflict to serenity to faith. Strings and woodwinds proclaim this "Faith" theme in high register. The melody, in true Franckian fashion, spirals about a central tone (at x).

The development section is charged with excitement. Franck marshals his impressive skill at combining themes and motives, interweaving these in an intricate texture suffused with chromatic harmonies

and seductive colors. He tries to revive the clash of ideas that marked
the classical form. Yet the Development is primarily a play of mood
and emotion. The questioning motive makes a spectacular return. Intoned by trombones and tuba, the theme is imitated in close order by
trumpets and cornets. From there on the Recapitulation pursues its
course to the coda and the soaring final cadence.

The second movement is an imaginatively conceived Allegretto,
which combines the principle of statement-departure-and-return with
that of theme transformation. Harp and pizzicato strings outline a sequence of chords that becomes a harmonic background for the famous melody sung by the English horn. Notice under the bracket the
germinal motive of the first movement, here presented in a new guise.

A contrasting melody is followed by the return of the first theme.
There follows a mysterious flickering figure in the violins which is a
subtle transformation of the opening theme. The clarinet introduces
one of Franck's most appealing melodies:

The relationship between the flickering motive and the main theme
becomes apparent when they are both combined, the one serving as
accompaniment to the other. The coda reminisces gently on the themes
of the movement.

The impetuous finale, marked Allegro non troppo, is in first-movement
(sonata-allegro) form. After a vigorous introduction, bassoons and cellos introduce a darkly colored theme whose capacity for growth is not

immediately apparent. The germinal motive reappears in new surroundings. The second subject is played by the brass—trumpets, cornets,
trombones, tuba. It is one of those Franckian tunes which for many
listeners is associated with spiritual aspiration.

Cyclical construction is much in evidence in the Development and Recapitulation. The English-horn melody returns, as does the Faith (third) theme of the first movement. The germinal motive of the opening is now revealed as the unifying thread of the work. It is when all Franck's themes are brought together in this fashion that we realize why they combine so well: they all bear a family resemblance. Thus, the cyclical method in this work involves much more than the reappearance in all the movements of a motto theme; it implies, really, that all the material is derived from a common source. The final movement of the symphony achieves a less unified effect than the preceding movements; too much seems to be going on. But the music is whipped up to a rousing climax and the work ends in a blaze of glory —the romantic "apotheosis."

The Symphony of César Franck is a memorial to the late romantic style. Its breadth of gesture, hymnic exaltation, and rich orchestral garb make it a favorite with the public. It is the work of a musician whose dedication to lofty ideals assures him a niche in the history of his art. For several decades Franck was regarded as a contemplative, severely classical artist. We see him today as an arch-romantic.

⁂ *CHAPTER 32* ⁂

Johannes Brahms (1833-1897)

"It is not hard to compose, but it is wonderfully hard to let the superfluous notes fall under the table."

AGAINST the colorful program art of Berlioz, Liszt, and Wagner there arose an austere, high-minded musician dedicated to the purity of the classical forms. His veneration for the past and his mastery of the architecture of absolute music brought him closer to the spirit of Beethoven than were any of his contemporaries.

His Life

Brahms was born in Hamburg, son of a double-bass player whose love of music was greater than his attainments. As a youngster of ten Johannes helped increase the family income by playing the piano in the dance halls of the slum district where he grew up. By the time he was twenty he had acquired sufficient reputation as a pianist to accompany the Hungarian violinist Eduard Reményi on a concert tour.

His first compositions made an impression on Joseph Joachim, leading violinist of the day, who made possible a visit to Robert Schumann at Düsseldorf. Schumann recognized in the shy young composer a future leader of the camp dedicated to absolute music. Just as at the beginning of his career he had hailed the genius of Chopin, he now at its close performed a similar service for Brahms. He published in his journal the famous essay entitled "New Paths," in which he named the

Johannes Brahms.

twenty-year-old "young eagle" as the one who "was called forth to give us the highest ideal expression of our time." Brahms awoke to find himself famous.

Robert and Clara took the fair-haired youth into their home. Their friendship opened up new horizons for him. Five months later came the tragedy of Schumann's mental collapse. Brahms hastened to Clara's side and, with a tenderness and strength he had not suspected in himself, tided her over the ordeal of Robert's illness.

The older man lingered for two years while the younger was shaken by the great love of his life. Clara Schumann was then at the peak of her fame. Fourteen years his senior and the mother of seven children, she appeared to young Brahms as the ideal of womanly and artistic perfection. What had begun as filial devotion ripened into romantic passion. She for her part found a necessary source of strength in the loyalty of the "young eagle." She watched his genius unfold as once she had watched Robert's. For Johannes this was the period of storm and stress, as his letters to her reveal. "I regret every word I write you which does not speak of love. You have taught me and every day teach me more and more to marvel at the nature of love, affection, and self-denial. I can do nothing but think of you." At the same time he was rent by feelings of guilt, for he loved and revered Schumann, his friend and benefactor, above all others. He thought of suicide and spoke of himself, as one may at twenty-two, as "a man for whom nothing is left."

This conflict was resolved the following year by Schumann's death; but another conflict took its place. Now that Clara was no longer the unattainable ideal, Brahms was faced with the choice between love and freedom. Time and again in the course of his life he was torn between the two, with the decision going always to freedom. His ardor subsided into a lifelong friendship. Two decades later he could still write her, "I love you more than myself and more than anybody and anything on earth." Toward the end of his life, when the forty-year-old relationship was almost broken because of a misunderstanding, he wrote to Clara, "Today you must allow me to repeat to you that you and your husband represent the most beautiful experience of my life, that you stand for its greatest wealth and noblest meaning."

His appointment as musician to the Prince of Detmold inaugurated his professional career. After four years at this post he returned to Hamburg to devote himself to composition. But he failed to obtain an official appointment in his native city—the directors of the Philharmonic never forgot that Johannes came from the waterfront—and settled in Vienna, which remained the center of his activities for thirty-five years. In the stronghold of the classical masters he found a favorable soil for his art, his northern seriousness refined by the grace and congeniality of the South. The time was ripe for him. His fame filled the world and he became the acknowledged heir of the Viennese masters.

This exacting artist had a curiously dual nature. He could be morose and withdrawn, yet he loved rough humor. A bohemian at heart, he craved bourgeois respectability. Behind a rough exterior he hid the tenderness that found expression in his music and his love of children. He fought the softness in himself and came to be feared for his caustic wit. To a musician fishing for compliments he remarked, "Yes, you have talent. But very little!" The elderly ladies whom he was rehearsing in *The Creation* were admonished: "Why do you drag it so? Surely you took this much faster under Haydn." When a renowned quartet played his work the viola player inquired if he was satisfied with the tempo.

Brahms snapped, "Yes—especially yours!" Thus the crotchety bachelor went his way through the middle-class circles of Vienna, the center of an adoring coterie. Although he complained of loneliness and on occasion fell in love, he was unable to accept the responsibility of a sustained relationship. His motto was *Free—but happy!* "It would be as difficult for me to marry," he explained, "as to write an opera. But after the first experience I should probably undertake a second!"

Just as in early manhood his mother's death had impelled him to complete *A German Requiem,* so the final illness of Clara Schumann in 1896 gave rise to the *Four Serious Songs.* Her death profoundly affected the composer, already ill with cancer. He died ten months later, at the age of sixty-four, and was buried not far from Beethoven and Schubert.

His Music

Hans von Bülow called Brahms's First Symphony the "Tenth." He thereby indicated its kinship with Beethoven's nine. From the same source came the remark about "the three B's—Bach, Beethoven, Brahms." Although both descriptions are meaningless from a historical point of view, they sum up what Brahms meant to his generation.

He was a traditionalist. His gaze was directed back to the classical era whose splendor it was no longer possible to resurrect. This sense of being a latecomer imparts to his music its gently retrospective flavor, its autumnal resignation. Endowed with the historic sense, Brahms looked upon himself as a preserver of the great tradition. His aim was to show that new and important things could still be said in the forms inherited from the classical masters. In this he differed from avowed innovators such as Berlioz, Liszt, and Wagner.

A romantic who was drawn to introspection and lyricism, he buttressed himself with the austere architecture of the large forms. "My themes come to me in a flash," he said. "Long after their arrival I take them up and work very hard over them." The romantic elements in his nature were brought under control and sublimated into a classical serenity, but the victory over himself was achieved not without struggle. His dual personality is felt in the specifically Brahmsian blend of tenderness and strength, of outgoing and reserve, that fascinates his admirers. In his large works the outlines are romantically veiled. He loses himself in transcendental visions, in a nostalgia generally wreathed in the mistiness of the horn. Nonetheless, he was one of the very few of his generation who came to grips with the main issues of classical structure and handled the large forms with something of the mastery of the past.

His melodies have a rugged strength. The harmonies are subtly archaic in quality, colored by his interest in old music. Certain progressions are recognizable at once as being his and no other's. His rhythm is vigorous, dynamic; he is fond of syncopations and cross rhythms. His loyalty is to idea rather than color; not for him the brilliant orchestration of Berlioz or Wagner. Woodwinds and brass are much used in their low register, blending with the strings in a silver-gray sonority that has a warmth all its own. The interweaving of the separate lines in his music gives it its intricate texture. He was a master at varying and combining themes.

Brahms's four symphonies (1876, 1877, 1883, 1885) are among the most important in the literature after Schubert. They are unsurpassed in the late romantic period for breadth of conception and design. Best known of the other orchestral works are the *Variations on a Theme by Haydn* (1873) and the concert overtures—the *Academic Festival* and the *Tragic* (1880). In the two concertos for piano and orchestra (1858, 1881) and the one for violin (1878), the solo instrument is integrated into a full-scale symphonic structure. The Double Concerto for Violin and Cello (1887) draws its inspiration from the age of Bach.

In greater degree than any of his contemporaries Brahms captured the tone of intimate communion that is the essence of chamber-music style. The duo sonatas, trios, quartets, quintets, and sextets for string and wind instruments, with and without piano, comprise a body of works marked by lyricism and a quality of introspection peculiarly his own. They are in the great tradition, even if Brahms shared the nineteenth-century tendency to allow orchestral thinking to invade the chamber style.

He is an important figure too in piano music. His style is marked by concentration of thought as by depth of feeling. The three sonatas (1852–53) are works of his youth. The *Variations and Fugue on a Theme by Handel* (1861) represents his top achievement in this field. A favorite with concert performers is the set of *Variations on a Theme by Paganini* (1863), a composition that requires supreme virtuoso playing. The romantic in Brahms also found expression in short lyric pieces; the Rhapsodies, Ballades, Capriccios, and lyrical meditations known as Intermezzi are among the treasures of the literature. On the popular level are the Hungarian Dances and the set of sixteen Waltzes for piano duet.

As a song writer Brahms stands in direct line of succession after Schubert and Schumann. His output includes about two hundred solo songs and an almost equal number for two, three, and four voices. The favorite themes are love, nature, death. The choral pieces, with and without accompaniment, continue the activity of Schubert, Mendelssohn, and Schumann in a branch of music that has always been especially popular in Germanic lands. His finest choral work is the *German Requiem* (1857–68), written to texts from the Bible selected by himself. A song of acceptance of death, this work more than any other spread his fame during his lifetime.

The national element is strong in Brahms. His lyricism was fed by German folk song. He spoke of himself as *echt Deutsch* (thoroughly German). When it was pointed out to him that art has no fatherland, "That is true," he retorted, "for those who listen but not for those who write." His love of the national inspired his arrangements of German folk and children's songs as well as the popular tone of many of his art songs. In his Waltzes he paid tribute to the popular dance of his beloved Vienna, but he knew he was too much the north German to capture the real Viennese flavor. When he gave his autograph to Johann Strauss's daughter—composers customarily inscribed a few bars of their music—he wrote the opening measures of the *Blue Danube Waltz* and noted beneath it, "Not, alas, by Johannes Brahms."

The Third Symphony

The Symphony No. 3 in F major, Opus 90, was completed in 1883 when Brahms was fifty years old. It is a picturesque work that serves well as an introduction to the composer's style. The first movement, Allegro con brio (lively, with vigor), is in sonata-allegro form. The opening three notes in the winds constitute a kind of motto that pervades the first movement and returns in the last.

The motto becomes an accompaniment to the principal idea. This is a downward striding, vigorous theme of commanding gesture. Played by the violins, it outlines the tones of the tonic chord.

The contrasting theme, pastoral in character, is presented by the clarinet grazioso and mezza voce (in half voice). The same pattern of notes recurs on different beats within the measure, a favorite device of Brahms that makes the melody appear to be "chasing its tail."

Brahms directs that the Exposition should be repeated. This practice of classical times was falling into discard in the late romantic period, when considerations of form were made subordinate to dramatic effectiveness. Brahms's adherence to the practice underlines his classicist bent.

The two themes are subjected to a brief and intense development, the motto theme serving as a unifying element. The Recapitulation is followed by an ample coda. Characteristic throughout is the prominence of horn tone, the warm but subdued resonance, the wide spacing of the harmonies, and the quality of reticent emotion that is Brahms's own.

The slow movement, an Andante in $\frac{4}{4}$ time, is an A-B-A structure that has assimilated certain developmental features of sonata form. The theme is announced espressivo and semplice (with simplicity) by

clarinets supported by bassoons and horns. A contrasting idea appears, marked by a triplet rhythm that is destined to take on significance in the final movement of the symphony. The first theme undergoes considerable development, and is restated with variation in rhythm, harmony, register, accompaniment, and orchestration. The movement ends on a serene note.

For the impetuous scherzo of Beethoven's symphony Brahms substituted a lyrical third movement in moderate tempo. The Poco allegretto is an impassioned, darkly colored orchestral song. The lyric

theme in the cellos is contrasted with a lighter idea in the middle part. The first section is restated, with the melody originally played by the cellos now given to the French horn, then to the oboe.

The finale is a dramatic sonata-allegro marked by concise themes and abrupt changes of mood. The first idea is a searching melody, narrow in range and with a well-defined curve. It is played in unison by bassoons and strings. The low register and the instrumentation combine to give it its somber coloration.

There follows a passage that is, as Sir Edward Elgar put it, "the tragic outcome of the wistful theme in the middle of the slow movement." Contrast is provided by a festive theme played by the horn and cellos in unison. The dark coloring is characteristic of the composer. The

movement proceeds with classical logic and impulsion. The principal theme is subjected to an exceedingly rich development. Here are three versions of the idea that figure prominently in the course of the movement:

A tender allusion by the violins to the opening theme of the symphony casts a nostalgic glow over the closing measures of the work.

The art of Brahms marks the close not only of a century but of a cultural epoch. As he saw about him the triumph of the "Music of the Future"—symphonic poem, symphonic drama, program symphony—it seemed as if everything he cherished was coming to an end. But in art there is neither beginning nor end, only unceasing change. Within a few decades after his death the impulse behind programmatic music had exhausted itself. Neoclassicism had conquered the twentieth century and brought about an extraordinary revival of the absolute forms of music whose purity he sought to preserve.

This lonely rhapsodist remains an impressive figure, one of the last representatives of nineteenth-century German idealism; a noble dreamer of dreams that were not always successfully realized, but at his best a profoundly musical voice—tender, searching, retrospective.

CHAPTER 33

Antonín Dvořák (1841-1904)

"In the Negro melodies of America I discover all that is needed for a great and noble school of music. These beautiful and varied themes are the product of the soil. They are American. They are the folk songs of America, and your composers must turn to them."

ANTONÍN DVOŘÁK is one of several late romantic composers who based their personal style on the songs and dances of their native lands. He stands alongside Bedřich Smetana as a founder of the Czech national school.

His Life

Dvořák was born in a village near Prague where his father kept an inn and butcher shop. Poverty for a time threatened to rule out a musical career. However, the boy managed to get to Prague when he was sixteen. There he mastered his craft and wound up as viola player in the orchestra of the Czech National Theater. Success as a composer came slowly, but in time he was able to resign his orchestra post and devote himself to composing, teaching, and conducting. By the time he was forty Dvořák had left behind the material cares that plagued the first years of his career. As professor of composition at the Conservatory of Prague he was able to exert an important influence on the musical life of his time.

The spontaneity and melodious character of his music assured its popularity; his works aroused much interest in Germany and England as well as in Vienna. When the last decade of the century arrived, Dvořák was known throughout Europe. In 1892 he was invited to become director of the National Conservatory of Music in New York City. He received fifteen thousand dollars a year at the Conservatory —a fabulous sum in those days—as compared with the six hundred dollars that made up his annual salary as a professor in Prague. His stay in the United States was fruitful. He produced what has remained his most successful symphony, *From the New World;* a number of chamber works, including the *American Quartet;* and the Concerto for Cello and Orchestra. Dvořák spent a summer at the Czech colony in Spillville, Iowa, in an atmosphere congenial to his simple tastes. Although every effort was made to induce him to continue at the Conservatory, his homesickness overrode all other considerations. After three years he returned to his beloved Bohemia. His joy at the prospect of going home found expression in a series of little Humoresques for piano, of which the seventh became one of the world's most overplayed pieces.

Dvořák spent his remaining years in Prague in the happy circle of his wife and children, students and friends. He was Director of the Conservatory and played an active part in training the younger generation of Czech composers. He died in his sixty-third year, revered as a national artist throughout his native land.

His Music

Dvořák was a natural musician, a type that has always been abundant in Bohemia. Songfulness was native to a temperament in which intuition predominated over the intellectual process. Having sprung from the village, he never lost touch with the soil that was the source of his strength. At the same time, he achieved a solid craftsmanship in his art that enabled him to shape his musical impulses into large forms notable for their clarity and rightness.

He responded to the chief influences of the nineteenth century— the classical form of Beethoven, the lyricism of Schubert, the seductive harmonies and colors of Liszt and Wagner, and the stylistic refinement of Brahms. In his hands, symphonic poem and concert overture became vehicles for Czech legend and folklore. His most successful operas were based on peasant life. Even more, into the abstract forms of symphony and string quartet he injected the racy songs and dances of the Bohemian countryside.

His music emanates from a robust personality. It is sane and wholesome, makes an immediate appeal, and never reaches for more than it can grasp. Joy in life, love of man and nature, are the topics of its discourse, as are faith in God, devotion to country, and the pleasures of rustic existence. In an age given to tortured emotions this happy music struck a welcome note. Dvořák's large output covered all branches of his art: operas, choral works, symphonies, concertos, chamber music, overtures, rhapsodies, symphonic poems, songs, piano pieces, Slavonic dances. The time had come for the international language of German classicism to receive an invigorating infusion of native dialects, and Dvořák—along with Edvard Grieg and the Russians—was a leader in this historic process.

Coming to the United States as one of the leading nationalists of Europe, Dvořák tried to influence his American pupils toward a national art. American musicians at that time went to study either at Leipzig, where they steeped themselves in the tradition of Mendelssohn, or at Weimar, where they absorbed the heritage of Liszt. Dvořák held up to them the necessity of creating a native music free from European influence. In the melodies of the Negroes, as in the cowboy tunes of the West, he discerned the raw material for such an art. One of his pupils was Henry T. Burleigh, the Negro baritone and arranger of spirituals. The melodies he heard from Burleigh stirred the folk poet in Dvořák, and strengthened him in his conviction that American composers would find themselves only when they had thrown off the European past and come to grips with the indigenous material of the New World.

The time was not ripe for his advice to be heeded. But his instinct did not mislead him concerning the future of American music. One has but to regard the rich harvest of contemporary American works based on folklore to realize how correct, in the main, was his view.

The New World Symphony

The subtitle *From the New World* defines the scope and intent of the Symphony No. 5, in E minor, Opus 95 (1893). Dvořák was too much the Czech to presume to write an American work. His aim was to record the impressions of a visitor, his response to the exuberance and vastness of a young and growing land. He wished also, as a folk composer, to pay homage to the spirit of Negro folk music even while he longingly evoked the landscape of his own Bohemia. The work is consequently a mixture of Czech and American elements. Above all it is the expression of Dvořák's personality functioning at its most direct and spontaneous level. "Omit the nonsense," he wrote to a Berlin conductor, "about my having made use of Indian and American motives . . . I tried only to write in the spirit of those national American melodies."

The symphony opens with an introduction marked Adagio which leads into a vigorous Allegro molto. This is a clearly wrought firstmovement form based on three themes. The first is an energetic idea that opens with an upthrusting arpeggio figure, wide of span and syncopated in rhythm.

It is presented against a curtain of string tone. The characteristic dotted rhythm persists throughout the bridge passage that leads into the next theme, unifying the fabric.

The second theme is a plaintive tune of Bohemian folk character

which is introduced by a flute and oboe. It has the narrow range and
repetition of tones associated with melodies born of the soil.

Third is a songful theme announced by flute solo and taken over, in
the answering phrase, by the violins. Its outlines were suggested by
Dvořák's favorite Negro spiritual, *Swing Low, Sweet Chariot.*

The Development is a fantasy on the first and third themes which is
held together by the dotted rhythm. It is brief, clear-cut, imbued with
forward drive. Its vivid contrasts of soft and loud, high and low, and
its broad crescendos and lively colors please ear and mind without tax-
ing either. The Recapitulation restates the thematic material. There is
a grandiose coda based on descending chromatic scales, culminating
in a fortissimo statement of the basic arpeggio figure.

The slow movement is the famous Largo, in $\frac{4}{4}$ time. Out of the
remote chords of the introduction, marked *ppp*, issues the nostalgic
melody assigned to the English horn. As the folk song *Going Home*
this has become famous in many lands, even as far away as China.
Dvořák here caught the accents of the weary ones of the earth. The
son of peasants set down what he felt. What he felt rings true.

The movement is in A-B-A form. The middle section is a kind of landscape piece whose darker coloring contrasts well with the outer sections. Just before the return of the Largo melody, the orchestra works
up a climax from which emerges, as an effective reminiscence, the
arpeggio figure of the first movement.

The Scherzo, marked Molto vivace (very lively), is a dance movement in $\frac{3}{4}$ time, unmistakably Czech in atmosphere. Its opening theme

is of an impetuously rhythmic character. This is contrasted with a suave
subject, replete with the charm of folk song, introduced by flute and

oboe; after which the first theme returns. The middle section of the
Scherzo reinforces the character of Czech folk song and dance. Then
the first section is heard again. In this movement, as in the Largo, Dvořák
uses cyclical form to unify his symphonic framework: there are a number of references to the first movement.

The finale, Allegro con fuoco (fast, with fire), is an ample sonata-
allegro form in $\frac{4}{4}$ time. The stormy introduction leads into a vigorous
melody, in the character of a march, played by trumpets and horns.

This is counterposed to a flowing lyric idea, a reverie sung by the

clarinet. The third theme is in the nature of a popular song. Its symmetrical phrases end in three descending notes that appear to be derived
from the familiar round, *Three Blind Mice*. This little figure takes on

prominence as it is bandied about by the various instrumental groups.

In the Development and Recapitulation we meet a grand procession
of themes from the earlier movements. In this instance cyclical form
somewhat weakens Dvořák's structure; the movement stops and starts
again. At the last there is the rousing sort of finale that we have come
to expect in works of this period.

The *New World Symphony* has always been a favorite in the United
States. Its continuity of thought, clarity of outline, and vivacity of detail command the respect of musicians; while its appealing melodies
and accessible ideas are such as make the popular classic.

CHAPTER 34

A Late Romantic Symphony

Tchaikovsky's Pathétique

"I have put my whole soul into this work."

TCHAIKOVSKY'S hospitality to Western ideas represented an important tendency in the development of Russian music. It was necessary for Russia's composers to assimilate the European tradition, to master in a short time not only the techniques of Italian opera and French ballet but—above all—of the Austro-German symphony. In the conquest of the large forms of absolute music Tchaikovsky played a leading role. His symphonies and concertos achieved a prominence in the international repertory rivaled by few works of the late romantic period.

Tchaikovsky's Sixth Symphony, the *Pathétique* (1893), is representative of his style and esthetic. Early in the last year of his life he wrote his nephew, to whom it was dedicated, that he was occupied with a new work. "This time with a program—but a program of the kind that will remain an enigma to all. Let them guess it who can. The work will be entitled *A Program Symphony*. The program is penetrated with subjective sentiment. During my journey, while composing it in my mind, I frequently shed tears."

He wrote down the first movement in less than four days. "There will be much in this work," he pointed out, "that is novel as regards form. The finale, for example, will not be a great allegro but an adagio of considerable dimensions." He finally shook off the fear of having outlived his creativeness. "You cannot imagine what joy I feel at the thought that my day is not yet over and that I may still accomplish much."

The introductory Adagio is somber in color and sets the tone of brooding intensity. A solo bassoon in low register moves sluggishly along the scale, foreshadowing the material of the Allegro proper.

The Allegro non troppo (not too fast) is a sonata-allegro form based upon two vividly contrasted ideas. First is a tense rhythmic theme penetrated, as Tchaikovsky put it, with subjective sentiment. Staccato figures

outline a nervous melodic line imbued with forward drive. Violas and
cellos play the opening phrase, to be answered by flutes and clarinets.

This idea expands into a frenzied passage. The area of relaxation
comes with the famous lyric theme sung by muted violins and cellos,
andante. Tchaikovsky marks the passage "tenderly, very songfully, ex-
pansively." These indications well describe the flowing melody whose
contours rise to the climactic point and subside gracefully therefrom.

This theme expands into an A-B-A formation within the spacious Exposition. A codetta rounds off the section on a note of tender retrospection.

An explosive chord, fortissimo, opens the Development. Based on the
first theme, this section is a veritable catalogue of Tchaikovsky's favorite orchestral devices. Violins sweep furiously up and down the scale.
Brusque accented chords spread across the orchestral gamut. The
richly colored tone mass is whipped up to excitement, thrusting its
way step by step to the higher register. Rhythmic figures are repeated
again and again with a kind of obsessive insistence, brass tone is hurled
against the busy strings and woodwinds, climax is piled upon climax in
ever-ascending terraces of sound.

The Recapitulation presents the two fundamental ideas with changes
in instrumental color. A new passage is introduced in which the massed
brass is pitted against woodwinds and strings in spectacular fashion.
The coda sounds the tragic tone. A descending scale reiterated in the
bass, pizzicato, invariably suggests to commentators the footfalls of fate.
The movement ends on a dramatic pianissimo.

Next is the Allegro con grazia (lively, with grace), a dance mood vivid and quite ballet-like in quality. This is an A-B-A form in what was, in the 1890s, a most unusual meter— $\frac{5}{4}$ time. The alternation within the measure of groups of two and three beats imparts to the movement a wayward charm. With this departure from the conventional, Tchaikovsky heralded the trend toward nonsymmetrical patterns that was to become a prime trait of twentieth-century music.

The melody returns in the woodwinds against a plucked-string accompaniment of ascending and descending filigree work, of a kind that appealed to Tchaikovsky's imagination. He used it again and again. The steady beat of the drum in the contrasting middle section creates an atmosphere of dramatic urgency, after which the lighter mood returns. A quiet coda rounds off the movement.

The third movement, Allegro molto vivace (very fast and lively), is an extraordinarily exciting scherzo-march. The first theme, characterized by staccato triplets, has a dancelike impulsion that well indicates Tchaikovsky's affinity for the ballet. The second theme, based on an incisive commanding rhythm ending with a syncopated "snap," takes on the character of an imperious march. From modest beginnings this characteristic pattern infiltrates the orchestral tissue and works up to an electrifying climax.

After an extended Exposition, the two themes are restated. The movement builds steadily to the dramatic coda.

Last is the Adagio lamentoso (very slow, lamenting) in $\frac{3}{4}$ time. The dolorous theme, introduced by the violins, unfolds a bleak landscape of the soul.

The atmosphere of sorrow is dispelled for a space by the consoling second theme, marked Andante. Presently the orchestral sound is lashed to a furious climax. The lament returns. An abbreviated version of the second theme serves as coda. At the end we hear a combination of bassoon and string tone similar to that with which the symphony opened. The music descends to the dark regions whence it issued.

Thus the arc of the nineteenth-century symphony is completed: from the optimism, the spirit of affirmation of a dawning revolutionary epoch that found its gesture in the triumphal finale of Beethoven's symphonies, to the twilight anguish of Tchaikovsky's last statement. The Beethovenian pathos celebrated man the master of his fate. The Tchaikovskian pathos was compounded of futile regret, impotent fury, torturing doubt. The artist is bound by mysterious threads to his age. In distilling the poison from his soul Tchaikovsky voiced the illness of an era.

Yet the Beethovenian vision of art as healing, of art as victory over life, sustained this end-of-the-century figure. Through art he conquered the forces of disunity within himself, he lifted himself above despair and won his place in history. He left his mark on the musical practice of the late romantic period. He established a kind of utterance that is unmistakably Tchaikovskian, in much the same way that we recognize another kind as Dickensian. He captured in his music the mood of a time and a place, endowed it with artistic form, and, by an act of will and imagination, made it comprehensible to men everywhere.

CHAPTER 35

The Concerto

The Nature of the Concerto

A concerto is generally a large-scale work in several movements for solo instrument and orchestra. Here the attention is focused upon the solo performer. This circumstance helps determine the style. The concerto has to be a "grateful" vehicle that will enable the artist to display his gifts as well as the capacities of the instrument. The dramatic tension between soloist and orchestra is analogous to that between protagonist and chorus in Greek tragedy. The massive harmonies of the piano, the sweetness of the violin, or the dark resonance of the cello may be pitted against the orchestra. This opposition of forces constitutes the essential nature of the concerto.

In its dimensions the concerto is comparable to a symphony. Most concertos are in three movements: a dramatic allegro in sonata form is followed by a songful slow movement and a brilliant finale. In the opening movement, as in the first movement of a symphony, contrasting themes are stated ("exposed"), developed, and restated. In this case, however, the tension is twofold: not only between the contrasting ideas but also between the opposing forces—that is, the solo instrument against the group. Each of the basic themes may be announced by the *tutti* (literally, "all"; i.e., the orchestra as a whole) and then taken up by the solo part. Or the latter may introduce the ideas and the orchestra expatiate upon them. A characteristic feature of the concerto is the *cadenza* which, the reader will recall, is a flowery solo passage in the manner of an improvisation that is interpolated into the movement. The term originally signified the display of trills and roulades indulged in by opera singers near the close, or cadence, of a scene in order to display their virtuosity and arouse the house to enthusiasm. The cadenza came out of a time when improvisation was an important element in art music, as it still is today in jazz. Taken over into the solo concerto, it made a dramatic effect: the orchestra fell silent and the soloist launched into a free play of fantasy on the themes of the movement.

Before the nineteenth century the performer was usually the composer; consequently the actual improvisation was apt to be of the highest caliber. With the rise of a class of professional players who interpreted the music of others but did not invent their own, the art of improvisation declined. Thus the cadenza came to be composed beforehand, either by the composer or by the performing artist. Beethoven was the first to write his own cadenzas as an integral part of a solo concerto, in his Fifth (*Emperor*) Piano Concerto. His example was followed by most of the composers who came after.

Virtuosity and the Concerto

The concerto as the nineteenth century knew it was essentially a display piece. Its rise to prominence was bound up with the increased emphasis on the virtuoso performer. Virtuosity was not, as is often implied, an invention of the nineteenth century. From the time when man first learned to play instruments he was fascinated by problems of technique. Virtuosity, vocal and instrumental, has flourished ever since the leading performers of ancient Greece competed in the Olympic games. It came into prominence whenever music moved from its amateur status in the home to the level of professional public performance, as in the opera house of the eighteenth century or the concert hall of the nineteenth.

Virtuosity is a legitimate element in art when it serves the expression of thought and feeling. As an end in itself it may have entertainment value but does not stand much higher, artistically, than does mechanical agility in any direction. The passionate interest in virtuosity manifested by the nineteenth-century public confronted composers with a real problem. On the one hand they were eager to take advantage of the new resources opened up by the great advance in instrumental technique. On the other, they had to make the new technique a legitimate part of what they had to express. The best minds of the century grappled with the problem. They harnessed brilliance of technique to the musical idea and made it an integral part of artistic form. In their finest works they succeeded in reconciling virtuosity and expression.

CHAPTER 36

Three Romantic Concertos

Mendelssohn: Concerto for Violin and Orchestra

THE VIOLIN CONCERTO in E minor, Opus 64 (1844), a staple of the repertory, dates from the latter part of Mendelssohn's career. As was frequently the case with this class of work, Mendelssohn composed it with a definite soloist in mind. In 1838 he wrote Ferdinand David, concertmaster of the Gewandhaus Orchestra in Leipzig, "I should like to write a violin concerto for you next winter. One in E minor is running through my head, and the beginning does not leave me in peace." The following year he informed David that "the whole of the first solo is to be for the E string." While writing the work he often consulted the violinist as to what was congenial to the instrument and lay well for the hand.

The work reveals Mendelssohn's gifts: clarity of form and grace of utterance, a subtle orchestral palette, and a vein of sentiment that is tender but reserved. Virtuosity throughout is assimilated to idea and feeling. The first movement, Allegro molto appassionato (very fast and impassioned), is a spacious example of sonata-allegro form. The customary orchestral introduction is omitted; the violin announces the main idea of the movement. This is a resilient and active melody in the upper register, marked by decisive rhythm and a broad arch, which unfolds in symmetrical phrases.

The expansion of this idea gives the violinist opportunity for brilliant passage work, much of it in the triplet rhythm that serves as a unifying element throughout the movement. The theme is then proclaimed by full orchestra (tutti).

A transitional idea appears. This leads to the contrasting lyric theme, narrow of range and characterized by stepwise movement along the scale and narrow leaps. It is introduced by clarinets and flutes, tranquillo and pianissimo over a sustained tone on the open G string of the solo instrument. Such a sustained tone in one part while the harmonies change in the other parts is known as a *pedal point* (or organ point, from the fact that it occurs frequently in organ music as a note sustained by one of the pedal keys). The lyric theme provides an area of relaxation in the precipitous forward drive of the movement.

The development section is marked by genuine symphonic momentum, culminating in the cadenza which, instead of coming at the end of the movement as is customary, serves as a link between the Development and a shortened Recapitulation. Under a curtain of widely spaced arpeggios on the violin the opening theme emerges in the orchestra. From here to the coda the movement gains steadily in power and is exemplary for its elegant handling of the large form.

A brief transitional passage ushers in the Andante, a large A-B-A form in ⁶⁄₈ time. Mendelssohn could not command the pathos of the

Beethovenian slow movement. Within his own limits he was able, however, to create an atmosphere of calm meditative sentiment. The middle section in somber elegiac vein marks the romantic in him; after which the serene opening melody returns.

An interlude marked Allegretto non troppo (fairly fast, not too much so) leads to brave flourishes scored for oboes, bassoons, horns, and trumpets, *ff*. The finale, an Allegro molto vivace (very fast and lively) in ⁴⁄₄ time, is a sonata-allegro form in the light breezy manner that is

Mendelssohn's most characteristic vein. The movement demands agile fingers and high spirits, a crisp staccato and brilliance of tone. The violin traces lightning arabesques against the scherzo-like background. Mendelssohn elaborates on the chief theme and, in the Recapitulation, combines it with a singing countermelody in the orchestra. Excitement builds steadily to the pyrotechnics of the coda.

Felicitous in melody, form, and texture, the Concerto displays the Mendelssohnian blend of tender sentiment and classic moderation. It springs from the romantic style in its earlier, purer phase.

Schumann: Concerto for Piano and Orchestra

Schumann's celebrated Piano Concerto in A minor, Opus 54, has its full share of romantic fervor. Yet it stems out of the classical tradition of absolute music, and displays the qualities that ranged Mendelssohn, Schumann, and Brahms—as guardians of the heritage of the past— against Berlioz, Liszt, Wagner, and their "Music of the Future." The first movement was written in 1841 as an independent Phantasie for Piano and Orchestra, to which the second and third movements were added four years later.

The Allegro affettuoso (lively and with feeling) opens with an imperious sequence of chords in dotted rhythms on the piano. The oboe announces the lyric theme from which the movement germinates. The piano answers. The first half of the melody for the most part moves

stepwise along the scale. The leap of an octave to the topmost note (at
x) makes an arresting climax, from which the melodic curve gently
subsides. Two motives (A and B) are to be distinguished which assume
importance not only in this but also in the subsequent movements.

A somber melody in the violins, in the nature of a transition, ends in
a third motive (C) which assumes great structural significance in the
course of the movement.

The second theme of the movement is not a new idea at all, but an
imaginative transformation of the first theme. It is played by the clarinet

against impetuous descending arpeggios on the piano. After a triumphal
tutti, the principal theme is heard in a new transformation, as a tender
dialogue between piano and clarinet in $\frac{6}{4}$ time, Andante espressivo.
The fantasy-like character of the movement permits the composer to
achieve an effect of spontaneity and caprice within the frame of sonata-
allegro form, which he handles with the freedom of a poet. The thematic
material is stated, developed, and restated. There is a steady drive to
the rhapsodic cadenza, which is woven in whole out of the germinal
theme. The latter appears in a new transformation in the coda, as a
vigorous march in $\frac{2}{4}$ time, Allegro molto.

The slow movement is an Intermezzo in $\frac{2}{4}$ marked Andantino grazioso (at a going pace, gracefully). This meditative song starts out as a
gracious colloquy between piano and orchestra. Notice that the material
is derived from the B motive of the first movement.

The middle section is based on a broadly flowing melody in the cellos, to which the piano responds with arabesques spun out in true Schumannesque manner. The opening section returns to round out the A-B-A form, and a fleeting reference to the first movement acts as a transition to the third.

The finale is an Allegro vivace in ¾ time. A vigorous theme on the piano is seconded by the orchestra. The B motive of the germinal theme appears in a new context. There is an outdoor atmosphere about this

Allegro, a quality of vigorous movement; it abounds in elaborate passage work for the solo instrument. A contrasting theme appears which through clever shifting of accent produces the cross rhythm of which Schumann was so fond. The result is to create a phrase of slower motion without actually changing either the meter or the tempo.

In this concerto Schumann for once achieved the perfect fusion of dramatic and lyric elements. Piano and orchestra commune with exemplary freedom and mobility. The orchestration is fresh, limpid, delicately colored. The compact themes lend themselves to symphonic development. The piano writing is masterly. There is nothing here of the miniature; the music is full-size in conception as in execution. The work, universally regarded as Schumann's masterpiece, is beyond question the finest piano concerto of the earlier romantic period—the finest, that is, to be produced between Beethoven and Brahms.

Brahms: Concerto No. 2 for Piano and Orchestra

There are many who consider the Piano Concerto No. 2, in B-flat major, Opus 83 (1878–81), Brahms's most perfectly realized composition. It is the outstanding piano concerto of the second half of the nineteenth century.

The germinal theme of the Allegro non troppo flowers out of two phrases that are introduced by the horn and are inseparable from the timbre of that romantic instrument. They move for the most part stepwise along the scale, both ending in a questioning upward inflection. Taken together they form a spacious curve of melody.

From this indescribably serene opening there unfolds a canvas that is compelling and alive. Piano virtuosity is in evidence throughout, but never as an end in itself; it is always made subservient to the idea. There is throughout an extraordinary homogeneity of thought and feeling, form and substance. The solo part is wholly integrated into the orchestral texture. Rarely in his symphonies did Brahms achieve the symphonic tension, the logic and élan of this memorable first movement. Unforgettable is the return of the theme at the Recapitulation. A rippling arpeggio figure in the upper register of the piano creates a cloud of sound out of which the horn theme emerges as from afar. The effect is sheer magic.

The Scherzo, marked Allegro appassionato, comes second in this cycle of movements. The writing for solo instrument is most complex. One becomes aware of how much Brahms did to broaden the conventional notion of what is pianistic. The movement nicely balances rhythmic and lyric elements. The impetuous first theme has the true symphonic impulsion. This is set off against one of those songful ideas so characteristic of Brahms; it is introduced by the strings and echoed by the piano.

There follows the slow movement, an Andante, which opens with a broadly spun melody for cello solo. One of the great lyric meditations of Brahms, it suffers from the ambiguity attaching to the word "andante." Almost invariably it is taken at a dragging adagio that neatly breaks the spine of the melody. Notable in this movement is the rhythmic flexibility that the composer achieves within the conventional metrical patterns.

The finale is an Allegretto grazioso whose gayety is marked by an aristocratic refinement. The absence of trumpets and drums throughout the movement contributes to a mood of utter serenity.

The second theme is one of Brahms's most inspired tunes. As we hear it first, a phrase on the woodwinds is answered by one on the strings.

The movement, in a modified sonata-allegro form, is an example of how a late nineteenth-century composer adapted the classical structure to his own needs. The result is a spiritualized dance mood in the classical style, on the plane of pure lyric expression.

 ≉⁂⁎ CHAPTER 37 ⁂⁎≉

Edvard Grieg (1843-1907)

"The fundamental trait of Norwegian folk song is a deep melancholy that may suddenly change to a wild unrestrained gayety. Our traditional tunes, handed down from an age when the Norwegian peasantry was isolated from the world in its solitary mountain valleys, bear the stamp of an imagination as daring as it is bizarre."

His Life and Music

EDVARD GRIEG occupies a position in his homeland similar to that of Dvořák in his. To the international music public he came to represent "the Voice of Norway." The nationalist movement of which his music was an expression had a political background. Agitation for independence from Sweden came to a head during the last quarter of the nineteenth century. This cause, to which Grieg was devoted with all his heart, was crowned with success not long before his final illness. "What has happened in our country this year," he wrote, "seems like a fairy tale. The hopes and longings of my youth have been fulfilled. I am deeply grateful that I was privileged to live to see this."

Scandinavia's art music, up to the time of Grieg, remained within the orbit of German musical culture. Her composers studied in Leipzig or Weimar and came home to continue the traditions of Mendelssohn and Schumann or Wagner and Liszt. Grieg's first attempts at composition, after several years at the Leipzig Conservatory, followed the formula that has been well described as "Mendelssohnacid Schumannoxide." It was only when he returned to Norway that he became aware of the need for a national art. In so doing he found his personal tone. "The more he sang about his land the more truly he spoke about himself."

Grieg was essentially a miniaturist. The architecture of the large forms—symphony, sonata, concerto, opera—was too ponderous for this poetic musician. The few full-length works by which he is known, such as the Piano Concerto and the sonatas for violin and piano, all date from the early years of his career when his inspiration was at its peak. As time went on he confined himself to the short lyric forms—songs, dances, piano pieces. These made an ideal music for the home that found favor with amateurs the world over; with the result that his works entered the musical life of Europe and America in the most direct way and he became, during his lifetime, one of the most widely loved of composers. Yet he suffered from a sense of failure at not being able to produce the symphonies and operas that he felt were expected of him. He blamed his poor health for his inability to undertake large works—he suffered from asthma. However, his asthma did not prevent him from sailing the fiords and climbing the mountains of his picturesque land. His ailment, one suspects, was not so much the cause as the excuse. Yet he needed no excuse, for the miniature has a valid place in art alongside the larger forms.

The final decades of his life were spent at his villa Troldhaugen (Hill of the Trolls), overlooking the fiords outside his native town of Bergen. In these years he was much in demand all over Europe as an interpreter of his works, and appeared in the various capitals as conductor and pianist. He received many tempting offers to visit the United States, but declined because of his uncertain health. His death at the age of sixty-four was mourned throughout the world. For his compatriots it was in the nature of a personal loss.

The Piano Concerto

Grieg was one of a rather large group of artists who start off with a lucky hit that they never quite duplicate. He was twenty-five when he wrote the Piano Concerto in A minor (1868). It remained his masterpiece.

The first movement, Allegro molto moderato (moderately lively), is in sonata form. It opens with a dramatic roll on the kettledrum and precipitously descending octaves in the solo part. The opening melody is introduced by the woodwinds, and with its subdued emotional coloring evokes the northern scene. We find here one of Grieg's mannerisms: a fragment of melody is repeated at once on a higher degree of the scale. This procedure, which is known as a *sequence*, is one of the marks of the miniaturist.

An animated bridge passage leads to the contrasting idea, which is played by the piano tranquillo e cantabile (tranquil and songful). This shows the same construction by fragments as the first theme. Set forth by the cellos and taken over by the piano, this lyric melody is in Grieg's characteristic vein.

The development section is brief and intense. The harmonies are familiar to us now, but they sounded altogether novel to Grieg's contemporaries. The Recapitulation is climaxed by an impressive cadenza that presents the main theme embellished by ornate runs, massed chords, and octaves. The movement ends with a coda marked Poco più allegro (a little faster).

The Adagio, an A-B-A form in ⅜ time, captures the lyric charm of

a Grieg song. The middle section is characterized by delicate filigree work on the piano, after which the first theme is repeated in a mood of romantic pathos.

A brief transition leads into the finale, Poco animato (somewhat animated). This movement, in A-B-A form, opens with a vigorously rhythmic theme of folk-dance character which is presented with bravura effect on the piano.

An effective contrast is supplied by the theme of the middle section, a dreamlike lyrical melody marked Poco più tranquillo (somewhat

calmer), which is introduced by a solo flute. After the restatement of the section, a brief cadenza leads into the coda, at the climax of which the songful second theme is transformed into a sumptuous Andante maestoso. This characteristically romantic "apotheosis" brings the work to a triumphal close.

The writing for solo instrument is idiomatic throughout. The style combines Lisztian brilliance with the strain of romantic lyricism stemming from the German romantics, notably Schumann. But the essential component that imparts to the work its individual tone is Grieg's Norwegian heritage, by turn dramatic and idyllic-pastoral, to which he brought his picturesque harmony, subtlety of color, and refinement of feeling.

It was given to Edvard Grieg to reveal to the world the Norwegian landscape and the musical imagery of its people. He fulfilled his mission with taste and imagination. Overshadowed by the more robust figures of his time, this attractive artist continues to exercise his own wistful charm.

Opera

CHAPTER 38

The Nature of Opera

"It is better to invent reality than to copy it."
Giuseppe Verdi

FOR WELL over three hundred years the opera has been one of the most alluring forms of musical entertainment. A special glamor attaches to everything connected with it—its arias, singers, and roles, not to mention its opening nights. Carmen, Mimi, Aïda, Tristan—what character in fact or fiction can claim, generation after generation, so constant a public?

An opera is a drama that is sung. It combines the resources of vocal and instrumental music, soloists, ensembles, and chorus, orchestra and ballet, with poetry and drama, acting and pantomime, scenery and costumes. To weld the diverse elements into a unity is a problem that has exercised some of the best minds in the history of music.

The addition of music to drama creates something more than the sum of the parts. Verdi's *Otello* is not Shakespeare's play with music added; it is another order of art, as valid in its own right as it is different from the original. A vast distance separates the two dramas—the distance between two kinds of theater and two kinds of illusion, each offering a profoundly emotional experience within its own conventions and laws.

Opera and Reality

At first glance opera would seem to make impossible demands on the credulity of the spectator. It presents us with human beings caught up in dramatic situations, who sing to each other instead of speaking. The reasonable question is (and it was asked most pointedly throughout the history of opera by literary men): how can an art form based on so unnatural a procedure be convincing? How can it bring about that "suspension of disbelief" which is the essence of the theater experience? The question ignores what must always remain the fundamental aspiration of art: not to copy nature but to heighten our awareness of it. True enough, people in real life do not sing to each other. Neither do they converse in blank verse, as Shakespeare's characters do; nor live in rooms of which one wall is conveniently missing so that the audience may look in.

All the arts employ conventions that are accepted both by the artist and his audience. Lyric poetry gives the impression of being a spontaneous utterance; yet much of it is arranged in the most artful patterns of meter and rhyme. We respond to the illusion of depth in a painting even though we know that the canvas is flat. We accept a motion picture as a slice of life, although the action has been carefully plotted to begin at a certain point, reach its climax at another, and come to a satisfying conclusion at the end of the sixth reel. Art is the grand illusion; the adorable lie and the penetrating truth. The conventions of opera are more in evidence than those of poetry, painting, drama, or film, but they are not different in kind. Once we have accepted the fact that the carpet can fly, how simple to believe that it is also capable of carrying the prince's luggage.

Opera functions in the domain of the poetic drama, which prevailed for centuries before the realism that holds sway in our theater and films today. It uses the human voice to impinge upon the spectator the basic emotions—love, hate, jealousy, joy, grief—with an elemental force possible only to itself. The logic of reality gives way on the operatic stage to the transcendent logic of art, and to the power of music over the life of the heart.

The Components of Opera

In the classic type of opera the explanations necessary to plot and action are presented in a kind of musical declamation known as recitative (reh-chee-ta-teev'). This vocal style imitates and emphasizes the natural inflections of speech; its rhythm is curved to the rhythm of the language. Instead of a purely musical line, recitative is often characterized by a rapid patter and "talky" repetition of the same note; also by rapid question-and-answer dialogue that builds dramatic tension in the theater. In short, recitative constitutes a style in which the purely musical factors are subordinated to a speechlike vividness.

Recitative gives way at the lyric moments to the aria, which releases the emotional tension accumulated in the course of the action. The aria is pure melody. It is what audiences wait for, what they cheer, and what

they remember. An aria, because of its beauty, may be effective even
when removed from its context. Many arias are familiar to multitudes
who never heard the operas from which they are excerpts.

The eighteenth-century opera developed two types of recitative. One
was the *secco* or "dry" recitative that had a very slight instrumental
support in the form of chords on the harpsichord. This was the out-and-
out "talky" style that served for dialogue and explanation. Then there
was the more elaborate type of recitative with an expressive orchestral
accompaniment (*accompagnato*). Here prevailed a flowing musical
line and genuine dramatic power. Indeed, the accompanied recitative
became the supreme vehicle of musical-dramatic speech. Mention
should be made too of the *arioso* (from the Italian for "like an aria"),
a style midway between recitative and aria, combining the supple
vocal line of the first with the set rhythms of the second. Many a recitative with orchestral accompaniment is in the nature of an arioso.

Grand opera is sung throughout. In opera of the more popular variety
the recitative is generally replaced by spoken dialogue. This is the type
known among us as operetta or musical comedy, which has its counterpart in the French *opéra-comique* and German *Singspiel*. Interestingly
enough, in Italy—the home of opera—even the comic variety, the
opera buffa, is sung throughout.

The emotional conflicts in opera are linked to universal types and
projected through the contrasting voices. Soprano, mezzo-soprano, and
contralto are counterposed to tenor, baritone, and bass. The dramatic
soprano is preferred for dynamic range and striking characterization, the lyric for gentler types. The coloratura has the highest range
and greatest agility in the execution of trills and rapid passages. Corresponding to these are the dramatic tenor and the lyric tenor. German
opera has popularized the *Heldentenor* (heroic tenor) who, whether
as Siegfried or Tristan, is required to display endurance, brilliance, and
expressive power. The palette is completed by the rich resonance of the
bass, a figure often associated with age and royal dignity.

An opera may contain ensemble numbers—trios, quartets, quintets,
sextets, septets. In these the characters pour out their respective emotions, creating a rich interplay of independent melody lines. The ensembles are not only musically decorative but are also a most potent
dramatic device, for they bring into focus the conflict between the
personages on stage. In the eighteenth-century opera the finale is a
composite ensemble that brings the work to a fitting close.

The chorus is used in conjunction with the solo voices or it may
function independently in the mass scenes. It may comment and reflect upon the action, in the manner of the chorus in Greek tragedy.
Or it may be integrated into the action. In either case choral song offers

the composer rich opportunities for varied musical-dramatic effects.

The orchestra provides the accompaniment. It sets the mood and creates the atmosphere for the different scenes. It also functions independently, in the overture, preludes to the acts, interludes, and postludes. It may take over the role of commentator, reminisce over things past, warn of those to come, and reveal what has been left unsaid. As with the piano part in the art song, the operatic orchestra may be subordinate to the voices, it may be equally important or—as happened in the latter half of the nineteenth century—even more so.

The ballet proves an eye-filling diversion in the scenes of pageantry that are an essential feature of grand opera. In the folk operas of the nineteenth century the ballet was used to present peasant and national dances. True, the ballet holds up the action; but it is so effective in creating atmosphere and theater excitement that composers have eagerly availed themselves of its possibilities.

The libretto or book of an opera must be devised so as to give the composer his opportunity for the set numbers—the arias, duets, ensembles, choruses, marches, ballets, and finales that are the traditional features of this art form. The librettist must not only create characters and plot with some semblance of dramatic insight, but he has also to present these in terms of the lyric theater, fashioning situations that justify the use of music and could not be fully realized without it. Not many librettists have succeeded in meeting these difficult requirements. We can understand why Mozart considered it the greatest good fortune when "a good composer who knows the theater and is himself able to contribute something and a clever poet, like a true phoenix, come together."

Opera lends itself to the grand style. The pomp and splendor of its great scenes are survivals from a time when opera was the chief diversion of princely courts. To this studied majesty of movement and gesture has been added the surcharged atmosphere of nineteenth-century poetic drama. The emotions are intense, the characters drawn with broad strokes of the brush. The operatic is an exuberant style. Everything is presented in vivid colors, larger than life-size. The spoken drama may concern itself with the clash of ideas; the opera concentrates on sentiments and passions.

The description just given applies to many operas of the late eighteenth century and of the nineteenth that form the core of the present-day repertory—from, let us say, Mozart's *Marriage of Figaro* to Verdi's *Aïda* and *Otello*. There were significant departures from the traditional plan, such as that represented by the music dramas of Richard Wagner, which we will examine later on.

Opera appeals primarily to those composers and music lovers who are given to the magic of the theater. It exerts its fascination upon those who love to hear singing. Thousands who do not feel at home with the abstract instrumental forms warm to opera, find there a graphic kind of music linked to action and dialogue, whose meaning it is impossible to mistake. Countless others are attracted for the very good reason that opera contains some of the grandest music ever written.

The Language Problem

The composer of opera translates the imagery of life into music in the most direct and immediate way. The drama transforms itself in his mind, line by line, into sound. One has but to read the letters of composers to their librettists to realize how close is the connection between the verbal and the musical meaning, how the masters extended themselves to capture in their music every nuance of the dialogue.

It is no less true that the vocal line takes its shape from the contours of the language. The composer releases the music inherent in its vowels and consonants; he reveals the melody of the language. That is one reason why opera is so intimately connected with national culture. What could be more German than Wagner, more Italian than Verdi?

A difficult problem arises when opera is exported to foreign lands. If it is given in the original tongue, the spectators lose the connection between text and music. They have of course a general idea of what is happening on the stage, but they cannot follow the relationship between text and music, the very thing that shaped the course of the work in the composer's mind; nor can they experience the line-by-line unfolding of the drama. If on the other hand the libretto is translated into the language of the audience, the authentic relationship between speech melody and vocal melody is destroyed. Wagner in French, Verdi in German—such shifts make the drama intelligible but destroy the authentic ring of the work.

Most European nations have preferred to sacrifice authenticity to the pleasure of understanding the proceedings on stage. Paris listens to Wagner in French, Berlin hears Verdi in German. Vienna, Prague, Moscow, Budapest translate opera into their respective tongues, thereby making it possible for the audience to participate in the dramatic experience. England and the United States, on the other hand, retain the original language. In these countries audiences do not understand what the characters are saying, nor—seemingly—do they care.

There are opera lovers who tell you that they prefer not to know what the characters are singing about. For such listeners, the meticulous effort of the great masters to render accurately the sentiments and the passions is transformed into a series of pear-shaped tones that might just as well be sung in Sanskrit or to a string of la-la-la's. Such listeners may have themselves a wonderful time at the opera, but they most certainly are not participating in the composer's dramatic intention. More than two hundred years ago Joseph Addison summed up the operatic situation in England in an observation that holds good today: "There is no Question but our great Grand-children will be very curious to know the Reason why their Forefathers used to sit together like an audience of foreigners in their own Country, and to hear whole Plays acted before them in a Tongue which they did not understand."

Two steps are necessary before opera can become a living part of a nation's culture. First, foreign operas have to be translated and presented in the native tongue, so that the audience will understand what is happening on the stage. Second, operatic tradition and technique have to be thoroughly absorbed by the nation's composers, so that they will be able to create operatic works of their own. Opera began as an international form imported from Italy. Then one nation after another adapted it to its own genius—first France, subsequently Germany, Russia, Bohemia, Hungary, England. Today in our own country we witness successful attempts to present the great operas of the past in English, in lively and literate translations. We are seeing the beginnings of a native school of opera written by American composers for American singers and audiences. And we already have, of course, a tradition of popular opera in the musical shows of Broadway and Hollywood which, like the popular operas of former times in France, Germany, and England, contain spoken dialogue, spirited action, broad humor, and pointed allusions to the topics of the day.

The future of opera in America lies not with the one or two celebrated opera houses that serve as repositories of the European tradition, but with the small lyric theaters and opera workshops scattered throughout the country. It rests also with the television studios that are beginning to bring opera into the American home in a form more closely related to our theater tradition than has been the case hitherto. Out of these and our popular musical theater will emerge a specifically American operatic culture. Signs are not lacking that it is on its way.

CHAPTER 39

Opera in the Romantic Period

"It is at the Théâtre-Français, from the lips of the great actors, that declamation accompanied by theatrical illusion gives us ineffaceable impressions. It is there that the musician learns to interrogate the passions, to sound the depths of the human heart."

André Grétry (1742–1813)

THROUGHOUT its history the opera house was a center of novel ideas and experimentation whose influence permeated every branch of music. It was in the opera house that composers of the romantic period strove for the union of the arts so ardently desired by their time. All the elements of the romantic style here found their focus: nationalism, exoticism, nature worship; folklore, historical drama, medieval epic; sensuous melody, colorful harmony, opulent orchestration, virtuoso singing; the grandiose, the grotesque, the supernatural, the expressive. Impelled by a hunger to encompass all facets of human experience, the romantic opera—like the world of which it was the bejeweled mirror—offered to eye and ear a feast of color, movement, and sound.

France

The grand opera that ruled the lyric stage in the post-Napoleonic era was very grand indeed. It was a conglomerate work based on heroic plots and "strong" situations drawn from history, abounding in purple rhetoric, brilliant solos and ensembles, spectacular ballets and décor— very much what the French call "the big machine." The masters of the new bourgeois society desired to feel heroic in their leisure hours. In this aggregation of battles and massacres, shipwrecks and coronations, amidst which hero and heroine were torn between love and honor, they found the last word in noble pathos.

Parisian grand opera was an exportable commodity whose triumphs extended to Berlin, London, and New York. Acknowledged master of the style was Giacomo Meyerbeer (1791–1864), a resourceful man of the theater whose dramatic power, striking declamation, and original orchestration exerted a more widespread influence than is generally realized. Meyerbeer's life work is summed up in three heroic operas: *Les Huguenots* (1836), based on the massacre of St. Bartholomew's Eve; *Le Prophète* (1849), dealing with the uprising of the Anabaptists of Münster and one of the most dramatic themes in literature—the false prophet; and *L'Africaine* (1864), laid in an exotic setting and centering about the explorer Vasco da Gama. To the same category of operas belongs *La Juive* (The Jewess) by Jacques Halévy (1799–1862), the climax of which turns on an auto-da-fé of the Inquisition. These admirably suited the taste of their time. They held the stage into the first quarter of the twentieth century, but have now disappeared.

Paris had two famous opera houses. The Opéra was reserved for works sung throughout. Those containing spoken dialogue were pre-

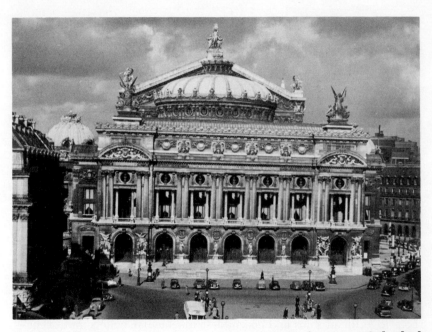

The Paris Opera, an outstanding example of the architecture of the high romantic period.

sented at a more intimate house, the Opéra-Comique. This type of opera outgrew its humble beginnings in the popular theater and took over certain traits of grand opera. The masters of this very French genre, much admired in their time, have not survived in the international repertory, but they strongly affected the course of nineteenth-century music in France. And it was out of the *opéra-comique* tradition that there came a work which captured the imagination of the world— *Carmen*.

Several composers of French opera achieved more than passing fame in the latter part of the century. Charles Gounod (1818–93) is remembered today chiefly for *Faust* (1859), one of the most phenomenally successful operas of the century. In this work he extracted elements from Goethe's philosophic drama and fashioned them into a grand opera well within the reach of his public. His *Roméo et Juliette* (1867) was also a favorite in the romantic repertory. Camille Saint-Saëns (1835–1921) scored a hit with his spectacular biblical opera *Samson and Delilah* (1877). Witty, cultivated, and urbane, this prolific musician produced several pieces that for a time enjoyed world-wide popularity. To this group belongs also Jules Massenet (1842–1912), an elegant and assured craftsman who created for the international operatic stage a gallery of beautiful sinners—Mary Magdalen, Herodias, Sappho, Thaïs. His masterpiece is of course *Manon* (1884), after the touching novel of Abbé Prévost.

On the comic side, none is more intimately associated with the spirit of Paris than Jacques Offenbach (1819–80), a spirited musician of German-Jewish parentage. His saucy operettas presented to French society of the era of Napoleon III the mirror in which it could laugh at its foibles. Parody and satire, comedy high and low intermingle in these works with titillating melodies and the rhythm of the cancan. The Paris of Offenbach was perhaps no more real than the Vienna of Johann Strauss. Each created a legendary city that became a symbol of delight to millions. They extended the limits of the musical public to include the lower middle and working classes, and thus helped prepare the way for the mass public of our time.

Italy

Italy was affected by romanticism to a lesser degree than either England, Germany, or France. Her classical heritage weakened the impact of the new movement, as did the continuity of her operatic tradition.

The most important figure of the first part of the century was Gioacchino Rossini (1792–1868), whose infectious melodies made him the idol of the musical world. His deft and transparent orchestration bespeaks a master. *The Barber of Seville* (1816), his finest work, was derived from the comedy of the same name by Beaumarchais. This was the play whose companion piece, *The Marriage of Figaro*, had supplied the libretto for Mozart's opera thirty years before. In the *Barber* Rossini produced an *opera buffa* not unworthy of its predecessor. His music displays a vitality and electrical excitement that stamp him one of the great musicians of the theater.

Of the many composers active in Italian opera at this time only two others are known to the American public. Gaetano Donizetti (1797–1848) was endowed with a facility of invention bordering on the legendary. He could turn out an opera in a week. The last act of *La Favorita* was tossed off in a few hours. He is remembered for his tragic opera *Lucia di Lammermoor* (1835) based on Walter Scott's novel *The Bride of Lammermoor;* the *opera buffa, Don Pasquale;* and the *opéra-comique, La Fille du régiment* (Daughter of the Regiment). Vincenzo Bellini (1801–35) was an artist of poetic temperament. His supple melodic line, refined and tenderly elegiac, exerted an influence on Chopin. He is best known for *Norma* and *La Sonnambula* (The Sleepwalker), both composed in 1831, and the historical opera *I Puritani* (The Puritans), written in the last year of his life. His untimely death prevented him from leading Italian opera toward the romantic lyricism that was native to his temperament.

Rossini, Donizetti, and Bellini left a rich legacy to their successors. They set the stage for developments that were to carry the national art form of Italy to new heights.

Weber and German Romantic Opera

In Germany the most important opera composer of his time was Carl Maria von Weber (1786–1826), who is called the father of German romantic opera with greater justice than usually attends such allegations of paternity. Weber leaped to fame with his *Songs of War and Fatherland* (1814), in which he set the lyrics of Theodor Körner, the poet of Young Germany who fell in battle during the Napoleonic invasion, at the age of twenty-two. With these stirring melodies Weber became the first national artist of the new age.

In 1817 the King of Saxony appointed him conductor of the German wing of the opera in Dresden. His ten years in this post were spent in a constant struggle to lift German music to an equal footing with the Italian opera patronized by the court. The middle classes were avid for a national art that reflected their own attitudes; but popular enthusiasm was suspect in the eyes of the rulers, since it was linked to the democratic movement. Amid the vexations of his official career, his strength sapped by tuberculosis, Weber composed his major works.

In *Der Freischütz* (The Marksman) he produced a folklore opera rooted in popular legend, a work pervaded by the beauty and mystery of the German forest. Presented in 1821, *Der Freischütz* scored one of the most spectacular successes in operatic history. *Euryanthe* (1823) was less successful. He accepted an invitation to London to conduct his *Oberon* (1826), which had been commissioned by Covent Garden. Already mortally ill, he experienced the final triumph of his career. He conducted the first twelve performances of the opera and died in London shortly after.

Weber exerted a most potent influence upon Richard Wagner, who worshiped his memory. Weber's important works exemplify major trends in the romantic movement. *Euryanthe* evokes the world of medieval chivalry, *Oberon* the landscape of elfin enchantment. His incidental music to *Preciosa* is Spanish in character, an early example of nineteenth-century exoticism. His piano music is on the virtuoso side, brilliant rather than profound. *Invitation to the Dance* transplants into the concert room the captivating rhythm of the waltz. Widely appreciated too is the *Konzertstück* (Concert Piece) for piano and orchestra.

Weber's realm lies at the confluence of the classic and romantic streams. The refinement of his art bespeaks the admirer of Mozart and the heir of the classical tradition. Carried to fame on the rising tide of nationalism, he retained the breadth of view and humanism of an earlier period. The favorite maxim of this most German of composers might have been uttered by Beethoven or Goethe. "Art has no fatherland; and we ought to value whatever is beautiful no matter what clime or region produced it."

CHAPTER 40

Richard Wagner (1813-1883)

"The error in the art genre of opera consists in the fact that a means of expression—music—has been made the object, while the object of expression—the drama—has been made the means."

RICHARD WAGNER looms as probably the single most important phenomenon in the artistic life of the latter half of the nineteenth century. Historians, not without justice, divide the period into "Before" and "After" Wagner. The course of postromantic music is unthinkable without the impact of this complex and fascinating figure.

His Life

He was born in Leipzig, son of a minor police official who died when Richard was still an infant. A year later the widow married Ludwig Geyer, a talented actor, playwright, and painter, who encouraged the artistic inclinations of his little stepson. The future composer was almost entirely self-taught. He had in all about six months of instruction in music theory. At twenty he abandoned his academic studies at the University of Leipzig and obtained a post as chorus master in a small opera house. In the next six years he gained practical experience conducting in provincial theaters. He fell in love with the actress Minna Planer, whom he married when he was twenty-three. He absorbed the current repertory that centered about Meyerbeer, Bellini, and Donizetti. Under these influences he produced his first operas, *Die Feen* (The Fairies, 1834) and *Das Liebesverbot* (Love Prohibited, 1836, after Shakespeare's *Measure for Measure*). As with all his later works, he wrote the librettos himself. He was in this way able to achieve a unity of the musical-dramatic conception beyond anything that had been known before.

Richard Wagner.

While conducting at the theater in Riga he began a grand opera based on Bulwer-Lytton's historical novel *Rienzi, Last of the Tribunes*. This dealt with the heroic figure who in the fourteenth century led the Roman populace against the tyrannical nobles and perished in the struggle. With the first two acts of *Rienzi* under his arm he set out with Minna to conquer the world. His destination was Paris. But the world, then as now, was not easily conquered; Wagner failed to gain a foothold at the Opéra.

The two and a half years spent in Paris (1839–42) were fruitful nevertheless. He completed *Rienzi* and produced *A Faust Overture,* the first works that bear the imprint of his genius. To keep alive he did hack work such as arranging popular arias for the cornet, and turned out a number of articles, essays, and semifictional sketches. He also wrote the poem and music of *The Flying Dutchman.* All this despite poverty and daily discouragement.

Just as the harassed young musician was beginning to lose heart a lucky turn rescued him from his plight: *Rienzi* was accepted by the Dresden Opera. Suddenly his native land was wreathed in the same rosy mist as had formerly enveloped Paris. He started for Dresden, gazed on the Rhine for the first time, and "with great tears in his eyes swore eternal fidelity to the German fatherland." *Rienzi,* which satisfied the taste of the public for historical grand opera of the Meyerbeer stripe, was extremely successful. As a result, its composer in his thirtieth year found himself appointed conductor to the King of Saxony.

With *The Flying Dutchman* Wagner had taken an important step from the drama of historical intrigue to the idealized folk legend. He continued on this path with the two dramas of the Dresden period—*Tannhäuser* (1843–45) and *Lohengrin* (1846–48)—which bring to its peak the German romantic opera as established by Weber, his revered model. The operas use subjects derived from folklore, display a profound feeling for nature, employ the supernatural as an element of the drama, and glorify the German land and people. But the Dresden public was not prepared for *Tannhäuser.* They had come to see another *Rienzi* and were disappointed.

A dedicated artist who made no concessions to popular taste, Wagner dreamed of achieving for opera something of the grandeur that had characterized the ancient Greek tragedy. To this task he addressed himself with the fanaticism of the born reformer. He was increasingly alienated from a frivolous court that regarded opera as an amusement; from the bureaucrats in control of the royal theaters, who thwarted his plans; and from Minna, his wife, who was delighted with their social position in Dresden and had no patience with what she considered his utopian schemes. He was persuaded that the theater was corrupt because the society around it was corrupt. His beliefs as an artist led him into the camp of those who, as the fateful year 1848 approached, dreamed of a revolution in Europe that would end the power of the reactionary rulers. He came under the influence of August Röckel, a musician turned revolutionary, and of the Russian anarchist Bakunin, who was then in Dresden. With reckless disregard of the consequences, Wagner appeared as speaker at a club of radical workingmen. He published two articles in Röckel's journal: "Man and Existing Society" and "The Revolution." "The present order," he wrote, "is inimical to the destiny and the rights of man. The old world is crumbling to ruin. A new world will be born from it!"

The revolution broke out in Dresden in May 1849. King and court fled. Troops dispatched by the King of Prussia crushed the insurrection. Röckel and Bakunin were captured. Wagner escaped to his friend Liszt at Weimar, where he learned that a warrant had been issued for his arrest. With the aid of Liszt he was spirited across the border and found refuge in Switzerland.

In the eyes of the world—and of Minna—he was a ruined man; but Wagner did not in the least share this opinion. "It is impossible to de-

scribe my delight when I felt free at last—free from the world of torturing and ever unsatisfied desires, free from the distressing surroundings that had called forth such desires." He settled in Zurich and entered
on the most productive period of his career. He had first to clarify his
ideas to himself, and to prepare the public for the novel conceptions
toward which he was finding his way. For four years he wrote no
music, producing instead his most important literary works, *Art and
Revolution, The Art Work of the Future,* and the two-volume *Opera
and Drama* which sets forth his theories of the music drama, as he
named his type of opera. He next proceeded to put theory into practice
in the cycle of music dramas called *The Ring of the Nibelung.* He began
with the poem on Siegfried's death that came to be known as *Götterdämmerung* (Dusk of the Gods). Realizing that the circumstances prior
to this action required explaining, he added the drama on the hero's
youth, *Siegfried.* The need for still further explanation led to a poetic
drama concerning the hero's parents, *Die Walküre* (The Valkyrie).
Finally, the trilogy was prefaced with *Das Rheingold* (The Rhinegold),
a drama revolving about the curse of gold out of which the action stems.

At this juncture Although he wrote the four librettos in reverse order he composed the
operas in sequence. When he reached the second act of *Siegfried* he
grew tired, as he said, "of heaping one silent score upon the other," and
laid aside the gigantic task. There followed his two finest works—
Tristan und Isolde (1857–59) and *Die Meistersinger von Nürnberg*
(The Mastersingers of Nuremberg, 1862–67). The years following the
completion of *Tristan* were the darkest of his life. The mighty scores
accumulated in his drawer without hope of performance: Europe contained neither theater nor singers capable of presenting them. Wagner
succumbed to Schopenhauer's philosophy of pessimism and renuncia-
tion—he who could never renounce anything. He was estranged from
Minna, who failed utterly to understand his artistic aims. His involve-
ment with a series of women who did understand him—but whose
husbands objected—obtruded the *Tristan* situation into his own life
and catapulted him into lonely despair. As he passed his fiftieth year,
his indomitable will was broken at last. He contemplated in turn suicide,
emigration to America, escape to the East.

At this juncture intervened a miraculous twist of events. An eighteen-
year-old boy who was a passionate admirer of his music ascended the
throne of Bavaria as Ludwig II. One of the young monarch's first acts
was to summon the composer to Munich. The King commissioned him
to complete *The Ring,* and Wagner took up the second act of *Siegfried*
where he had left off a number of years before. A theater was planned
especially for the presentation of his music dramas, which ultimately
resulted in the festival playhouse at Bayreuth. And to crown his happi-

ness he found, to share his empire, a woman his equal in will and courage—Cosima, the daughter of his old friend Liszt. For the last time the
Tristan pattern thrust itself upon him. Cosima was the wife of his
fervent disciple, the conductor Hans von Bülow. She left her husband
and children in order to join her life with Wagner's. They were married
some years later, after Minna's death. Their son was named Siegfried
and their home in Bayreuth, like a dwelling out of the sagas of *The Ring*,
Wahnfried.

The Wagnerian gospel spread across Europe, a new art-religion.
Wagner societies throughout the world gathered funds to raise the
temple at Bayreuth. The radical of 1848 found himself, after the Franco-
Prussian War, the national artist of Bismarck's German Empire. The
Ring cycle was completed, twenty-six years after Wagner had begun it,
and the four dramas were presented to worshipful audiences at the first
Bayreuth festival in 1876.

One task remained. To make good the financial deficit of the festival
the master undertook his last work, *Parsifal*, a "consecrational festival
drama" based on the legend of the Holy Grail. He finished it as he approached seventy. He died shortly after, in every sense a conqueror,
and was buried at Bayreuth.

His Music

Wagner gave shape to the desire of the romantic era for the closest
possible connection between music and dramatic expression; and beyond that, for the closest connection between music and life. "Every bar
of dramatic music," he maintained, "is justified only by the fact that it
explains something in the action or in the character of the actor." Nature
worship, national feeling, and the painting of specific moods and emotions find in his art their ultimate embodiment.

He insisted that music in the theater is not an end in itself, only a
means of achieving dramatic effect. His theories notwithstanding, the
music dwarfs all the other elements in his stage works; for he was
a musician first and a dramatist afterward. He did away with the old
"number" opera with its arias, duets, ensembles, choruses, and ballets.
His aim was a continuous tissue of melody that would never allow the
emotions to cool. This meant abandoning the old distinction between
recitative and aria. He evolved instead an "endless melody" that was
molded to the natural inflection of the German language, more melodious than traditional recitative, more flexible and free than traditional
aria. Wagner's endless melody was a step toward realistic dramatic
expression. By moving away from the formal tune based on four-measure
phrases, he brought his listeners to a broader conception of what mel-

ody is. Whenever possible he avoided definite cadences and sections, achieving a continuous flow and the highest degree of musical-dramatic unity.

The focal point of Wagnerian music drama, however, is not the melody but the orchestra. Here is the nub of his operatic reform. He had inherited the orchestral language and the symphonic art of Beethoven, and it became his mission to introduce these into the lyric theater. In so doing he developed a type of symphonic opera as native to the German genius as vocal opera is to the Italian. The orchestra is the unifying principle of his music drama. It is both participant and ideal spectator; it remembers, prophesies, reveals, comments. The orchestra is fate and primal force, flooding the action, the characters, and the audience in a torrent of sound that incarnates the sensuous ideal of the romantic era: a sumptuous sound shot with color and light, which for sheer imaginativeness is unsurpassed in nineteenth-century art.

The orchestral tissue is fashioned out of concise themes, the *leitmotifs,* or "leading motives"—Wagner called them basic themes—that recur throughout the work, undergoing variation and development even as the themes and motives of a symphony. The leitmotifs carry specific meanings, like the "fixed idea" of Berlioz or the germ theme in a symphonic poem of Liszt. They have an uncanny power of suggesting in a few strokes a personage, an emotion, or an idea; an object—the Gold, the Ring, the Sword; or a landscape—the Rhine, Valhalla, the lonely shore of Tristan's home. They are rooted in a kind of magical thinking which confers even upon inanimate objects the quality of life and will. Wagner united in himself the concrete pictorial imagination of the stage composer and the pure musical instinct of the symphonist. Once the leitmotifs are brought into being by the dramatic idea, the abstract musician in him takes over and weaves them into a symphonic fabric. Through a process of continual transformation the leitmotifs trace the course of the drama, the changes in the characters, their experiences and memories, their thoughts and hidden desires. As the leitmotifs accumulate layer upon layer of meaning, they themselves become characters in the drama, symbols of the relentless process of growth and decay that rules the destinies of gods and heroes.

The orchestra, in Wagnerian usage, is the sea of harmony over which rises and falls the wave of melody. Here harmony usurps the prime position previously held by melody and rhythm. Wagner tied together the harmonic discoveries of his age into a personal style. *Tristan* represents the farthermost limit of chromatic harmony. Its poignant dissonances voice the longing and the unfulfillment of an era. Never before had the unstable tone combinations been used so eloquently to portray states of soul. The active chord seeking resolution in the chord of rest—

Dominant moving to Tonic—became in Wagner's hands the most romantic of symbols: the lonely man—Flying Dutchman, Lohengrin, Siegmund, Tristan—seeking redemption through love, the love of the ideal
woman, named now Senta, now Elsa, Sieglinde, or Isolde.

A cardinal tenet of Wagner's philosophy was his desire to merge the
different arts into one super-experience. He believed his music drama to
be the "universal art work" in which were combined on an equal basis
music, poetry, drama, acting, dance, painting (the scenery), architecture, and sculpture (the plastic poses of the actors). He prophesied that
once the music drama had established itself the different arts would
never again exist separately. Such a notion could occur only to one who
had no real appreciation of either painting, sculpture, or poetry. He
never suspected that each art is most fully itself precisely when it does
the things that are impossible for the others. All the same, he was able
at Bayreuth to lavish attention upon every phase of the "art work of the
future," as he mistakenly called his music drama. There resulted a unity
of conception and effect until then unknown in the European theater.

Probably the most provocative part of his doctrine is that relating to
the social function of art. He regarded culture as a reflection of the
drives, goals, and conflicts of the social order. He conceived of art as
embodying man's highest creative impulse and as being intimately
linked to his moral nature. The theater was the temple where this impulse reached its fulfillment. The notion of art for art's or entertainment's sake was wholly repugnant to this view. It was the high office
of the drama to set forth the ideals of a nation. The Wagnerian drama
exhibited a seriousness and majesty of conception that were new in the
lyric theater. To this was added his German love of "deep" meanings, of
metaphysical obscurity and poetic symbols. His music dramas are static
occasionally and they have their tedious moments, but at their greatest
they possess a sweep and a grandeur uniquely their own.

Overture to Tannhäuser

In *Tannhäuser and the Contest of Song on the Wartburg*, as the full
title of the opera reads, Wagner invoked hallowed elements from the
German past. The castle of the Wartburg in Thuringia had been a center
of culture in the thirteenth century. The chief characters of the opera
were drawn from late medieval legends about the minnesingers (singers
of love), those courtly poet-musicians who were the German counterpart of the French troubadours. The notion of a tournament of song
at the court of a Thuringian prince was combined in the composer's
mind with the age-old theme of the repentant sinner, and with the
romantic concept of redemption through love that runs through all

Wagner's works.

The pagan deities who were vanquished when Christianity spread over Europe did not vanish from the imagination of the folk. They retired to the hills and forests to live on as elves, goblins, and pixies. Thus Venus and her train have withdrawn to a magic grotto beneath the Venusberg where they hold their unholy revels, tempting the unwary traveler—to the eternal damnation of his soul. Tannhäuser, a leading minstrel at the court of the Landgrave of Thuringia, has been so tempted and has dwelt with the goddess in the pleasures of pagan love. He now longs to return to earth. Venus tries to dissuade him, warning him that he will never find peace save in her arms. But he is firm in his resolve. The goddess, bitter, releases him.

Upon returning to the court, Tannhäuser is welcomed by his old comrades and by Elisabeth, niece of the Landgrave, who has long awaited his return. Once again the hall of song echoes to jubilant strains as the knights and their ladies assemble for a tournament of minstrels. Wolfram von Eschenbach (he was one of the great poets of the minnesinger period) hymns the Christian ideal of love as spiritual experience and self-abnegation. Tannhäuser listens with mounting impatience, the spell of Venus reasserting itself. Finally, in greatest agitation, he seizes his harp and sings in praise of the goddess who initiated him into the delights of carnal love. The assemblage is horrified at this impiety. Drawing their swords, the knights rush upon the blasphemer. But Elisabeth intercedes for him: the sinner must be allowed to live and repent. Tannhäuser is banished by the Landgrave. As though awaking from an evil dream, he is overwhelmed with remorse and joins the pilgrims who are on their way to Rome to seek from the Pope forgiveness for their sins.

The Pope absolves many, but when he hears Tannhäuser confess his sin he denies him pardon. The dead staff in his hand, he tells the suppliant, can sooner grow leaves than Tannhäuser win salvation. The unhappy knight, having made his way back to Thuringia, would return to Venus and damnation. A rosy glow suffuses the horizon; the goddess appears, delighted to take him back. But Wolfram invokes the name of Elisabeth. Tannhäuser comes to his senses and forever rejects Venus.

Now the bells begin to toll for the saintly Elisabeth, who has died still praying for the redemption of Tannhäuser's soul. The funeral procession descends from the Wartburg. Tannhäuser, repentant, dies beside Elisabeth's bier. A band of pilgrims return from Rome bearing in their midst a staff covered with fresh green leaves. They sing in praise of the miracle: God reigns on high and no man, no matter how great his sin, shall call upon Him in vain.

The Overture sets forth in clear-cut fashion the central conflict of

the drama between spiritual and sensual love. The piece is an A-B-A
form based on the opposition between the two outer sections and the
middle part. The spiritual element of the drama is presented in the symbol of the Pilgrims' Chorus, scored for clarinets, horns, and bassoons,
with which the Overture opens. Here is one of those granitic melodies
that, as so often in Wagner, begins by outlining the Tonic chord.

The music swells to a powerful climax and dies away, the dynamic design conjuring up the image of a band of pilgrims drawing ever closer,
their song reaching its zenith and then receding in the distance.

The middle part, an Allegro, is given over to music suggestive of the
Venusberg. The contrast between this section and the preceding one
is underlined in a number of ways besides the obvious change of tempo:
through the use of melodies that weave along the chromatic scale;
through emphasis on chromatic harmonies and dissonance; through
exciting, sharply dotted rhythms; and through the use of the upper register, which injects a bright nervous quality of tone. Woodwind color predominates, evoking the nature sound so appropriate to the rites of
pleasure that the music is intended to suggest. Wagner also uses extensively one of his favorite devices for whipping up excitement: the repetition over and over of a short motive, each time at a higher pitch—
what is known as an ascending sequence.

Three themes stand out in the middle part of the work. First, there is
an impetuous figure in the violas suggesting the revels in the Venusberg.

There follows the vigorous hymn in praise of Venus, that will play an
important part in the opera, presented in full orchestral sonority.

Third is the plea of Venus, the melody sung by the goddess when she beseeches the knight to stay with her, here presented by the clarinet against a tremolo in the violins.

An exciting passage of chromatic harmony prepares the way for the return of the Pilgrims' Chorus which, heard softly at first, grows steadily until it is proclaimed in stentorian tones by trumpets and trombones. In this version the Overture has established itself as a favorite in the concert hall. Wagner subsequently reworked the piece (the Paris version, 1861) so that, instead of returning to the theme of the Pilgrims' Chorus, the Overture leads directly into the Venusberg scene.

In *Tannhäuser* Wagner, at thirty, still functioned within the frame of the traditional grand opera with its set numbers—arias, duets, ensembles, choruses, and stately processionals. The rhythms are often of a square cut: four measures to a phrase, four phrases to a strophe. There are frequent lapses into conventional modes of expression. Withal, the richness of the choral and orchestral writing points toward the ample musical-dramatic style of the master's maturity.

Excerpts *from* Tristan und Isolde

For unity of mood, sustained inspiration, and intensity of feeling *Tristan und Isolde* is the most perfectly realized of Wagner's lyric tragedies. He overcame here the diffuseness and awkward plot construction that mar the dramas of *The Ring*. In *Tristan*, he wrote, "Life and death, the whole significance of existence of the external world, turn on nothing but the inner movements of the soul." Certainly no more eloquent tribute has ever been offered to consuming passion.

Isolde, proud princess of Ireland, has been promised in marriage to the elderly King Mark of Cornwall. Tristan, the King's nephew and first knight of his court, is sent to bring her to her new home. They had met before when Tristan fought against her country. What had begun as hate, wounded pride, and desire for revenge turns to overpowering love.

The Prelude to the drama depicts the passion that enmeshes them. This extraordinary tone poem evolves from a leitmotif that recurs throughout the opera. Used always to suggest the yearning, tenderness, and rapture of the lovers, the famous progression is the epitome of Wagnerian (that is, of romantic) harmony.

Langsam und schmachtend (Slow and languid)

leitmotif

Prelude, in Wagner's use of the term, indicates a freer and more flexible form than overture. It is more in the character of a fantasy, lyric rather than dramatic, contemplative rather than narrative. "There can be no greater pleasure," Wagner wrote in regard to *Tristan*, "than an artist's perfect abandon while composing." Abandon is possible only when one has achieved complete control over the means of expression. It is the quality that brings this prelude as close as any piece ever came to those twin goals of musical romanticism, intoxication and ecstasy.

The Love Duet is from Act II, which takes place outside King Mark's castle. The King leaves, ostensibly on a hunt. Tristan and Isolde meet in the garden. The scene between them is one of the high points of Wagnerian drama. The lovers hymn the night: "O rest upon us, night of love, Grant us forgetfulness of life. Take us within thine embrace, Free us forever from the world." Day represents the loathed reality that stands between them, the pretense and hopelessness of their worldly existence. Night is the symbol of their inner life—the real life. In this scene is consummated the great romantic theme of the individual estranged from society. Love is the dream and the search; the longing for oblivion. Since happiness is not to be attained in life, love leads beyond its confines, becoming the ultimate escape. Thus the impulse that generates life is transformed, by a magnificently romantic gesture, into the self-destroying passion whose fulfillment is death. The use of horn and woodwinds that envelop man and woman in the nature sound of German romanticism; the interpolation of Brangäne, Isolde's confidante, as she stands watch on the tower; the intangible suggestion of the beauty of the night; the sustained exaltation—it is Wagner at his most compelling.

At the high point of the Duet, King and retinue burst in upon the lovers. Tristan has been betrayed by his false friend Melot. He takes leave of Isolde and in the ensuing scuffle suffers himself to be mortally wounded. The doom they knew was inescapable is now upon them.

Act III is laid before Tristan's castle in Brittany, where he has been brought by his faithful servant Kurvenal. In his delirium he fancies himself back in the garden with Isolde. She arrives in time to see him die. The opera culminates in her hymn to love and death, the *Liebestod*. She envisions herself united with Tristan, the obstacles that kept them apart in life surmounted at last. Transfigured, she sinks lifeless on Tristan's body.

The Love Death follows a basic design in music. Beginning softly and

from a low pitch it builds up in a steadily mounting line to the torrential climax, whence it subsides. The aria—and aria it is, although the perfect Wagnerite would never call it that—is fashioned from a motive first heard during the love scene in Act II. There it was cruelly interrupted by the arrival of the King. Now, ascending wave upon wave, it achieves its resolution. "In the billowing air, in the resounding blare, in the world's encompassing breath—To drown, to sink, unknowing—Highest bliss!"

Wagner satisfied the need of an era for sensuous beauty and intoxication, for the heroic, the mystical, the grandiloquent. He glorified the medieval past, he sang the womanly woman and the manly man, he upheld intuition against reason, he mused upon mighty issues, and he commanded a wider public than composer ever had before. Rarely have the time, the place, and the personality come together so fortunately to create an international career. He found a means, wrote Nietzsche, of stimulating tired nerves "and in this way he made music ill." But this was the illness of a century, for which he furnished the magic potion.

Tristan und Isolde: love scene in the garden of King Mark's castle.

Greatness in music as in other spheres proceeds from the supreme height of spiritual tension. Wagner justly stands among the giants of his art. Yet his music issues from a lower level of spirituality than theirs. He knew hate and ruthlessness, lust for power and devouring passion. The creative energy of that imperious soul hid profoundly destructive forces. His music, rooted in the irrational, is truly demonic; by the same token it is not always healing. It enchants and overpowers the senses, but it does not always reach the secret places of the heart.

His impact upon his own time and the half century that followed was nothing short of overwhelming. Indeed, we are the first generation that is able to view him objectively. He takes his place in history as the most commanding figure of the romantic era; a master whose achievements have become part and parcel of our musical heritage.

CHAPTER 41

Giuseppe Verdi (1813-1901)

"Success is impossible for me if I cannot write as my heart dictates!"

IN THE case of Giuseppe Verdi, the most widely loved of operatic composers, it happened too—as with Wagner—that the time, the place, and the personality were happily met. He inherited a rich tradition, his capacity for growth was matched by masterful energy and will, and he was granted a long span of life in which his gifts attained their full flower.

His Life

Born in a hamlet in northern Italy where his father kept a little inn, the shy taciturn lad grew up amid the poverty of village life. His talent attracted the attention of a prosperous merchant in the neighboring town of Busseto, a music lover who made it possible for the youth to pursue his studies. After two years in Milan he returned to Busseto to fill a post as organist. When he fell in love with his benefactor's daughter, the merchant in wholly untraditional fashion accepted the penniless young musician as his son-in-law. Verdi was twenty-three, Margherita sixteen.

Three years later he returned to the conquest of Milan with the manuscript of an opera. *Oberto, Count of San Bonifacio* was produced at La Scala in 1839 with fair success. The work brought him a commission to write three others. Shortly after, Verdi faced the first crisis of his career. He had lost his first child, a daughter, before coming to Milan. The second, a baby boy, was carried off by fever, a catastrophe followed several weeks later by the death of his young wife. "My family had been destroyed, and in the midst of these trials I had to fulfill my engagement and write a comic opera!" *Un Giorno di regno* (King for a Day) failed miserably. "In a sudden moment of despondency I despaired of finding any comfort in my art and resolved to give up composing."

The months passed; the distraught young composer adhered to his decision. One night he happened to meet the impresario of La Scala, who forced him to take home the libretto of *Nabucco* (Nebuchadnezzar, King of Babylon). "I came into my room and throwing the manuscript angrily on the writing table, I stood for a moment motionless before it. The book opened as I threw it down. My eyes fell on the page and I read the line *Va pensiero sull' ali dorate* ["Go, my thought, on golden wings" —first line of the chorus of captive Jews who by the waters of Babylon mourn their ravished land]. Resolved as I was never to write again,

Giuseppe Verdi.

I stifled my emotion, shut the book, went to bed, and put out the candle. I tried to sleep, but *Nabucco* was running a mad course through my brain." In this fashion the musician was restored to his art. *Nabucco*, presented at La Scala the following season, was a triumph for the twenty-nine-year-old composer; it inaugurated a spectacular career.

Italy at this time was in the process of birth as a nation. The patriotic party aimed at liberation from the Habsburg yoke and the establishment of a united kingdom under the House of Savoy. Verdi from the beginning identified himself with the national cause. "I am first of all an Italian!" In this charged atmosphere his works took on special meaning for his countrymen. No matter in what time or place the opera was laid, they interpreted it as an allegory of their plight. The chorus of exiled Jews from *Nabucco* became a patriotic song. As the revolutionary year

1848 approached, Verdi's works—despite the precautions of the Austrian censor—continued to nourish the zeal of the nationalists. In *Attila* the line of the Roman envoy to the leader of the Huns, "Take thou the universe—but leave me Italy!" provoked frenzied demonstrations. When, in *The Battle of Legnano,* a chorus of medieval Italian knights vowed to drive the German invaders beyond the Alps, audiences were aroused to indescribable enthusiasm.

But the impact of Verdi's operas went deeper than the implications of the plot. The music itself had a dynamic force, a virility that was new in the Italian theater. This was truly, as one writer called it, "agitator's music." It happened too that the letters of Verdi's name coincided with the initials of the nationalist slogan—*Vittorio Emmanuele Re d'Italia* (Victor Emmanuel King of Italy). The cries of *Viva Verdi* that rang through Italian theaters not only hailed the composer but voiced the national dream. Rarely has a musician more ideally filled the role of a people's artist.

Although he was now a world-renowned figure, Verdi retained the simplicity that was at the core both of the artist and man. He returned to his roots, acquiring an estate at Busseto where he settled with his second wife, the singer Giuseppina Strepponi. She was a sensitive and intelligent woman who had created the leading roles in his early operas and who was his devoted companion for half a century. He acquired in later life an interest in agriculture and developed a model farm that gave employment to two hundred workers and their families, in whose welfare he displayed a patriarchal interest. During the period of economic distress that caused a mass emigration of Italians to America, Verdi declared with pride that from his district they did not emigrate. After Italy had won independence he was urged to stand for election to the first parliament because of the prestige his name would bring the new state. The task conformed neither to his talents nor inclinations, but he accepted and sat in the chamber of deputies for some years.

The outer activities of this upright man framed an inner life of extraordinary richness. It was this that enabled him to move with unflagging creative tension from one masterpiece to the next. He was fifty-seven when he wrote *Aïda*. At seventy-three he completed *Otello,* his greatest lyric tragedy. On the threshold of eighty he astonished the world with *Falstaff.* Such sustained productivity invites comparison with the old masters, with a Monteverdi, Michelangelo, or Titian.

His death at eighty-eight was mourned throughout the world. He bequeathed the bulk of his fortune to a home for aged musicians founded by him in Milan. Italy accorded him the rites reserved for a national hero. From the thousands who followed his bier there sprang up a melody—*Va pensiero sull' ali dorate* . . . It was the chorus from *Nabucco* that he had given his countrymen as a song of solace sixty years before.

His Music

Verdi's music struck his contemporaries as the epitome of dramatic energy and passion. Endowed with an imagination that saw all emotion in terms of action and conflict—that is, in terms of the theater—he was able to imbue a dramatic situation with shattering expressiveness. True Italian that he was, he based his art on melody, which to him was the most immediate expression of human feeling. Using rhythm, harmony, and orchestration with a sure hand, he never permitted these to overshadow the soaring line—now soulful, now explosive—of those tense indestructible tunes that have survived several generations of organ grinders. He sought dramatic truth with all the strength of his uncompromising nature. The element of variety in Verdi's scores derives from the fact that each character speaks his own language, and speaks it with the utmost directness. "Art without spontaneity, naturalness, and simplicity," he maintained, "is no art."

He was thoroughly aware of the nature of his task. "Opera is opera and symphony is symphony. Our music differs from German music. Their symphonies can live in halls, their chamber music can live in the home. Our music, I say, lives mainly in the theater." Again and again he demands of his librettists "a short drama, swift-moving and full of passion . . . Passions above all!" Although he appreciated the greatness of Wagner—an appreciation that was not reciprocated—he saw it as his mission to safeguard the Italian tradition from the influence of the symphonic music drama. "If the Germans, proceeding from Bach, have come to Wagner they do so as good Germans and all is well. But when we, descendants of Palestrina, imitate Wagner we commit a musical crime." And to the same point: "Think you that under this sun and this sky I could have written *Tristan* or the *Ring*?"

The maxims scattered through his letters could furnish a practical manual for the dramatic composer. "In the theater lengthy is synonymous with boring. And of all styles the boring is the worst . . . Style and language are worth nothing in a play without action . . . In the theater poets and musicians must know when it is necessary to throw over both poetry and music . . . The artist must look into the future, perceive new worlds amid the chaos." When a work failed: "Was it my fault or the singers'? Time will tell!"

Of his first fifteen operas the most important is *Macbeth,* in which for the first time he derived his story material from Shakespeare, whom he called "the great searcher of the human heart." There followed in close succession the three operas that established his international fame: *Rigoletto* in 1851, based on Victor Hugo's drama *Le Roi s'amuse* (The King is Amused); *Il Trovatore* (The Troubadour) in 1853, derived from a fanciful Spanish play; and *La Traviata* (The Lost One) also produced in 1853, which he adapted from the younger Dumas' play *La Dame aux camélias* (Camille). In these works of sustained pathos the musical dramatist stands before us in full stature.

The operas of the middle period are on a more ambitious scale, showing Verdi's attempt to assimilate elements of the French grand opera. The three most important are *Un Ballo in maschera* (A Masked Ball, 1859), *La Forza del destino* (The Force of Destiny, 1862), and *Don Carlos* (1867). In these the master fights his way to a higher conception of dramatic unity. "After *La Traviata*," he declared, "I could have taken things easy and written an opera every year on the tried and true model. But I had other artistic aims."

These aims came to fruition in *Aïda,* the work that ushers in his final period (1870–93). *Aïda* was commissioned by the Khedive of Egypt to mark the opening of the Suez Canal in 1870. Delayed by the outbreak of the Franco-Prussian War, the production was mounted with great splendor in Cairo the following year. In 1874 came the Requiem Mass in memory of Alessandro Manzoni, the novelist and patriot whom Verdi revered as a national artist. Although the composer was, as his devout wife put it, a man of little faith, he employed the dramatic ritual of the Church with the naturalness that was his birthright as an Italian.

Verdi found his ideal librettist in Arrigo Boito (1842–1918), himself a composer whose opera *Mefistofele* was popular in Italy for years. For their first collaboration they turned to Shakespeare. The result was *Otello* (1887), the apex of three hundred years of Italian lyric tragedy. After its opening night the seventy-four-year-old composer declared, "I feel as if I had fired my last cartridge. Music needs youthfulness of the senses, impetuous blood, fullness of life." He disproved his words when six years later, again with Boito, he completed *Falstaff* (1893). Fitting crown to the labors of a lifetime, this luminous comic opera ranks with Mozart's *Figaro*, Rossini's *Barber of Seville,* and Wagner's *Meistersinger.* Shakespeare's bedraggled knight, whom Verdi called "the eternally true type of jovial scoundrel," cavorts before us in all his glory—but given a new realization through music. When the action is resolved in the magical scene in Windsor Forest, the concluding fugue tells us that "man is born a clown and all the world's a jest." On this note the aged enchanter bade farewell to his art.

Aïda

In *Aïda* Verdi achieved an ideal fusion of the diverse elements that comprise grand opera. The dramatic story revolves about emotions that lend themselves to musical treatment. The libretto by Antonio Ghislanzoni exploits all the resources of the opera house in terms of picturesque scenery, spectacular display, ballets and striking mass scenes. Characters and situations are conceived in the grand manner, and the exotic setting admirably frames the inner experiences of the protagonists. Verdi worked within the traditional set numbers of opera—recitative and aria, duet and ensemble, dance, march, and chorus. But he injected into these the vitality of his genius and brought them into line with the needs of his time. He struck a balance between theatrical effect and dramatic truth. He availed himself of picturesque atmosphere without sacrificing universality, and made full use of the orchestra without threatening the supremacy of the voice. He created a lyric drama remarkable for unity and nobility of conception. It has been called "the perfect grand opera."

The action is laid in Egypt in the time of the Pharaohs during a war with the Ethiopians. Aïda, princess of Ethiopia, has been captured and is slave to Amneris, the Egyptian princess. The latter is in love with the conquering general Radames but rightly suspects that he loves Aïda rather than herself. Aïda's father Amonasro, the Ethiopian king, is brought into captivity, his identity unknown to his enemies. He still hopes to break the Egyptian power. Radames, torn between his passion for the enemy princess and devotion to his country, is induced to flee with Aïda and her father. The plan is foiled by the jealous Amneris. Aïda and Amonasro make their escape, Radames surrenders to the High Priest. He is sentenced to die by being entombed in a subterranean vault. Amonasro having been killed while leading the revolt, Aïda returns in time to make her way into the crypt. The lovers die together.

The Prelude is evolved from the lyrical phrase associated with Aïda

throughout the opera. Act I is in two scenes, the first of which is laid in the palace of the Pharaohs at Memphis. The famous *romanza*, *Celeste Aïda* (Celestial Aïda), in which Radames reveals his love, displays the composer's preference for melodies that move along the scale with occasional effective leaps along the chord.

*love song to aida
between aida &
Radames*

The basic conflict is established in a dramatic trio in which Amneris voices her jealousy, Radames fears she suspects the truth, and Aïda is torn between love and her devotion to the Ethiopian cause. The entrance of the King and court introduces the note of pomp that alternates throughout the play with the expression of personal emotion. Radames is appointed leader of the Egyptian forces against the Ethiopians. Aïda, alone, is tormented by the knowledge that the man she loves is to war against her father. She appeals to the gods in a grand *scena*.

The second scene takes place in the temple at Memphis. Priests in-

*Act II.
Priests prayers over
arms of Radames*

voke the god Ptah. The music assumes an oriental coloring as priestesses perform a sacred dance. Radames receives the consecrated arms and is blessed by the High Priest.

Act II opens in the royal palace. Moorish slaves perform a lively dance to distract the Princess. Aïda enters. A tense scene ensues between both women, at the climax of which Amneris in a jealous rage threatens to destroy her rival.

There follows the great scene at the gates of Thebes where the returning hero is welcomed by King, court, and populace. Trumpets sound the theme of the Triumphal March.

*Triumphal
March
① very dramatic
② Return of Radames (hero)*

Ablaze with color and movement, the tableau culminates in a stirring sextet. Amneris and the High Priest demand death for the prisoners. Amonasro, in chains, implores the King to be merciful. Pharaoh in a magnanimous mood releases the prisoners—all except Amonasro—and bestows the hand of his daughter upon the victorious general. Radames and Aïda hide their consternation. This mass scene, with its interplay of personal drama and regal splendor, has come to represent everything we associate with grand opera.

Act III is packed with action of the kind that Verdi needed for the full deploying of his powers. The scene—"Night: stars and a bright

Triumphal Scene from *Aïda*.

"This mass scene, with its interplay of personal drama and regal splendor, has come to represent everything we associate with grand opera."

moon"—is on the bank of the Nile. Amneris, accompanied by the High Priest, arrives to pray in the temple of Isis on the eve of her marriage. Events move swiftly and with ever mounting intensity. Aïda's aria *O patria mia* (O my native land), in which she bemoans her fate, leads to a furious encounter with her father. Amonasro orders her to find out from her lover the plan of the forthcoming campaign. He curses her when she refuses, and his rage breaks her will. Amonasro conceals himself at the approach of Radames. In the rapturous duet of the lovers Aïda persuades him that they can never find happiness within reach of the vengeful Amneris. He consents to fly with her, and divulges the plan of attack against Ethiopia. Amonasro appears and reveals himself as the enemy king, and Radames realizes that he has betrayed his country. At this point Amneris, who has come out of the temple, grasps the situation and accuses Radames of treason. Amonasro, drawing his knife, rushes upon her, but Radames interposes and saves her life. He implores Aïda and her father to save themselves. Soldiers appear before the temple and give pursuit. Radames, lost, surrenders to the implacable High Priest.

Act IV opens in a hall in the palace. Amneris orders Radames to be brought before her. She tells him she can save him if he will renounce Aïda. He spurns her offer and is led back to his cell. Overcome with remorse, the Princess curses the jealousy that has brought ruin to her beloved and endless misery to herself. The priests are heard pronouncing the death sentence.

In the final scene we see the subterranean vault and the temple above it. As the fatal stone is lowered Radames voices his hope that Aïda will never learn his fate. Then he discovers her in the crypt. Against the chorus of the priests in the temple above, the eerie chant of the priestesses, and the lamenting of Amneris, the lovers sing their final duet, a farewell to earth, a vision of eternal bliss to come.

[handwritten margin note: Radames tries to escape with Aïda & her father. Radames gets caught & sent to dungeon. Aïda goes to him to die with him]

Meno mosso

O ter-ra ad-di-o ad-di-o val-le di pian-ti
Fare-well, oh earth, fare-well thou vale ____ of sor-row

etc.

The creator of this majestic drama incarnated the soul of his nation. Boito recognized this when he saluted in Verdi "the genius of our race. He revealed to the world the ardor, the dash, the affection, the force of the Italian spirit."

꙳ C H A P T E R   4 2 ꙳

Georges Bizet (1838-1875)

"The composer gives the best of himself to the making of a work. He believes, doubts, enthuses, despairs, rejoices, and suffers in turn."

BLAZING with color and passion, *Carmen* is one of the rare works that enjoy the admiration of musicians no less than that of a world-wide public. It exemplifies the Gallic genius at its best. "Without form, no style; without style, no art," wrote Bizet in his youth. His masterpiece is rich in all three.

His Life and Works

Georges Bizet was born and raised in Paris. A student at the Conservatory, in his twentieth year he won the highest award of the school, the Prix de Rome, which made possible a three-year stay in the Italian capital. The rest of his career was passed in his native city. He was influenced by his teachers Gounod and Halévy. In 1869 he married the latter's daughter. Bizet was a practical man of the theater who functioned within the conventions of the Opéra-Comique. He was also an

Georges Bizet.

instinctive musician of the highest order who was destined to transcend those conventions.

"The very good is so difficult that a whole lifetime is not sufficient for achieving it," Georges wrote his parents from Rome. His all too brief career was a continuous preparation for his "very good." The works of his youth were followed by three operas that display the composer's power of evoking exotic atmosphere. *Les Pêcheurs de perles* (The Pearl Fishers, 1863) is a drama of love and ritual in Ceylon. Four years later came *La jolie fille de Perth* (The Fair Maid of Perth, after Walter Scott's novel), which takes place in a romanticized Scotland. *Djamileh* (1872) is laid in Cairo. Although none of these was an overwhelming success, they established Bizet's reputation as a composer to be reckoned with.

The greater Bizet emerges in the incidental music to Alphonse Daudet's somber drama *L'Arlésienne* (The Woman of Arles, 1872). He revealed himself here as the master of a limpid style with a tenderness all his own. Bizet was now offered the libretto that Meilhac and Halévy had fashioned from Prosper Mérimée's celebrated story of Gypsy life and love. (His librettist had the same name as, but is not to be confused with, his father-in-law.) He was ready for his appointed task. There resulted the greatest French opera of the century.

Mérimée's tale belonged to a new type of literature dealing with elemental beings and raw passions. It exemplified the interest in the lower classes that was part of the romantic desire to bring literature closer to the realities of life. Mérimée's Gypsies, smugglers, and brigands were depicted with an honesty that heralded the new realism. The opera softened the naked fury of the original story. But enough remained to disturb the audience that assembled for the opening night on the third of March, 1875. The Opéra-Comique was a "family theater" where the bourgeois of Paris brought their wives and marriageable daughters. Passion on the stage was acceptable as long as it concerned kings and duchesses long dead; Carmen and her unsavory companions were too close for comfort.

In its outer structure the work followed the *opéra-comique* tradition. That is, the set numbers—arias, duets, ensembles, marches, ballets, and choruses—were connected by passages of spoken dialogue. The content and imagery of *Carmen*, however, were far removed from the trifles that made up the usual fare at the Opéra-Comique. The tragic ending, the violent changes from gayety to inner drama, the realism and intensity constitute Bizet's contribution. Hardly less novel is the brilliant orchestration. In *Carmen* he created a music drama that brought the *opéra-comique* to its culmination. By so doing he transformed it into something more powerful and more profound. (The spoken dialogue was turned into musical recitative after Bizet's death by his friend Ernest Guiraud, so that the work might be presented at the Opéra. It is in this grand-opera version that *Carmen* is heard in the United States.)

The opera was not the fiasco that popular legend makes it out to have been. It did fail, incomprehensibly, to conquer its first audience. Vincent d'Indy relates how he and a friend—they were students then, and enraptured with the work—"went in search of Bizet in order to thank him and tell him of our joy. To our enthusiastic declarations he replied sadly, 'My dear fellows, you are the first to tell me this. And I am afraid you will be the last tonight!' "

The rumor that the piece was not quite respectable helped give it a run of thirty-seven performances in the next three months, an average of three a week. In addition the manager offered the composer and his librettists a contract for their next work. The failure of *Carmen* was only in Bizet's mind. He had put every ounce of his genius into the score. Its reception was a bitter disappointment. His delicate constitution, worn out by months of rehearsals and by the emotional tension that had attended the production, was ill-prepared to take the blow. Exactly three months after the première he succumbed to a heart attack, at the age of thirty-seven. His death came just when he had found his mature style.

The work was immediately dropped by the Opéra-Comique. Yet within three years it had made its way to Vienna and Brussels, London and New York. Five years later it returned to Paris, was received rapturously, and embarked on its fabulously successful career. Along with Verdi's *Aïda* and Puccini's *La Bohème* it remains one of the best-loved operas of the world.

Carmen

The power of this lyric drama stems from the impact with which it projects love, hate, desire. The story line follows one of the most compelling themes literature has to offer—the disintegration of a personality. The action is swift and unfaltering as the characters are carried step by step to their doom. The libretto is a tightly knit affair revolving around a few key words—love, fate, death, nevermore—all of them eminently singable. Carmen dominates the action, by turn tender, cruel, seductive, imperious, sensual, arch. She remains one of the great characters of operatic fiction. Invested with Bizet's music, Mérimée's heartless heroine takes on a certain nobility. She is fearless in the face of death. Even then she must be free. As for Don José, the simple soldier who is brought to ruin through his obsessive love, he is caught in a web not of his making, in which he is held by the deepest forces of his nature. Escamillo, the bull-fighter who supplants José in Carmen's fickle affections, is properly vain and swaggering. Micaela, José's childhood sweetheart who seeks in vain to lead him back to the wholesome life of his village, is the incarnation of goodness and devotion. (As frequently happens, she comes off less vividly than the questionable characters.) These personages and their conflicts are realized on the highest level of operatic art. They come to life through the music; they are unthinkable without it.

Remarkable is the meridional quality of Bizet's music, its suggestion of transparent air and sun-drenched landscape. Bizet's Spain is a place of splendor. Whether or not it resembles the real Spain is beside the point. He never saw the country, nor are his melodies derived from authentic Spanish song. But his is a Latin temperament evoking a Latin scene. As a student in Rome he wrote, "My senses are enthralled by Italian music—facile, idle, amorous, lascivious, and passionate all at once." Precisely these qualities permeate his Spanish—better, Mediterranean—music. *Carmen* is a drama of enormous vitality, ranging from poetic melancholy to savage passion. It creates a reality of its own.

The Prelude foreshadows the contrasting moods of the opera. The opening theme is the one that returns in the final scene outside the bull ring at Seville: a melody gay, external, charged with excitement and pleasure-seeking, its character accentuated by the pounding rhythm and the bright orchestration.

There follows the suave melody of the Toreador Song.

Against this is posed the motive of Fate. Beneath a tremolo on the strings is heard the ominous phrase, played by clarinet, bassoon, trumpet, and cellos, that runs like a dark thread through the score.

The curtain rises on a square in Seville. Soldiers loiter before the guard house. Micaela appears, inquiring for Don José. Abashed by the flirtatious young men, she withdraws. A trumpet in the distance announces the changing of the guard. The relieving company, led by Lieutenant Zuniga and Corporal Don José, is preceded by a crowd of urchins who enter to the strains of a captivating march. The clock strikes twelve. The girls emerge from the cigarette factory, which attracts the young blades of Seville. Carmen's entrance is heralded by a rhythmic transformation of the Fate motive.

Her character is established at once by the Habanera, based on a teasing tango rhythm. Bizet rewrote it thirteen times before he was satisfied. "Love is fickle and wild and free, A bird that none may ever tame. . . . If you love me not, I love you. And if I love—beware!" The

refrain is enhanced by the emphasis of the chorus on the crucial word
—*l'amour*.

Allegretto, quasi andantino

L'amour est un oi - seau re - bel- le Que nul ne
Love is fick - le and wild and free, A bird that

eto.

"*habanera*"
Carmen enters

Don José, waiting for Micaela to return, is absorbed in his thoughts.
Piqued by his indifference, Carmen takes the flower from her dress and
throws it to him. José, bewildered, picks it up. The orchestra sounds the
motive of Fate. Meanwhile, the clock having struck in the factory, the
girls withdraw. Micaela enters with a letter from José's mother. The
ensuing duet establishes José and Micaela as the "good people" in the
play.

Micaela's exit is followed by a quarrel in the factory between Carmen
and another girl. At once the stage is filled with two factions of chatter-
ing women. Carmen is led in, insolent, self-assured. She tries to strike
one of the women who demands that she be sent to jail. Zuniga and his
men go off to obtain an order for her arrest. Carmen, hands tied behind
her back, is left in the custody of José.

She loses no time in exerting her wiles. "Near the ramparts of Seville, at
the inn of my friend Lillas Pastia, I shall soon dance the gay seguidilla."
What is more, she will dance it with him. Only two steps are necessary
for them to achieve this delightful prospect: that he set her free and that
he join her there. José manfully resists her allurements, but the outcome is assured. By the time the lieutenant returns, the rope around
Carmen's wrists has been loosened. She is marched off to jail guarded by
José. At the bridge, as prearranged, she knocks him down and escapes.

The Entr'acte (Prelude to the second act) opens with a lonely melody, Moorish in coloring, played by two bassoons accompanied by
strings and drum. The curtain rises on Lillas Pastia's tavern. Carmen's
song celebrates the joys of Gypsy life. She is joined in the refrain by her
friends Mercedes and Frasquita. Lieutenant Zuniga presses his atten-
tions on Carmen. She learns from him that José, who received two

months in jail for helping her escape, has just been set free. Escamillo
arrives, his musical portrait being given by the swaggering opening of
the Toreador Song. He is taken with Carmen, which does not in the
slightest please Lieutenant Zuniga. Both men leave, the lieutenant
promising to return.

The Quintet follows, a brilliant ensemble number in which two of
the smugglers invite Carmen and her friends to join them in a little
matter of contraband that evening. Mercedes and Frasquita accept with
delight. Carmen declines. Her reason? She awaits Don José. His voice is
heard in the distance, singing the plaintive melody of the Entr'acte. The
Gypsies leave, suggesting that Carmen recruit her new lover into the
smugglers' band.

The scene between her and José covers a wide range of emotions. She
begins by dancing for him, accompanying herself on the castanets. José
is enchanted. When the retreat sounds from the distant barracks he
prepares to leave. Carmen, infuriated at a lover who puts duty above
her, mocks him as a dullard and bids him go. José, sadly drawing from
his pocket the flower he has treasured these many weeks, sings an aria
that is a favorite: "Here is the flower that you gave me, I kept it still
while I was jailed. In dead of night I saw your face. I had but one
desire, one hope—to see you once again."

Carmen, realizing her power over him, decides to lure José into the
smugglers' band. She holds out to him the attractions of a life of freedom. José implores her not to tempt him. He begins to realize that he
must renounce her. At this point there is a knocking at the door. Lieutenant Zuniga demands admittance, breaks in, and scoffs at Carmen for
taking a common soldier when she can have an officer. He orders José
to leave. The latter, mad with jealousy, draws his saber. The two men
fight and are separated by the Gypsies. Zuniga is hustled out by Carmen's friends. For José the die is cast: he has attacked an officer and
may return no more to the life he knew. The smugglers welcome the
deserter into their midst with a rousing finale that hails the freedom of
their lawless life.

The Prelude to the third act affords a breathing spell in the unfolding tragedy. A flute solo over harp accompaniment evokes the quietude of a mountain fastness. The curtain rises on the hide-out of the smugglers, who enter to an eerie march. Don José gloomily reflects on his situation. His mother still thinks him an honest man. If she but knew. Carmen, already tired of him, suggests that perhaps he had better return to her. They quarrel. The orchestra comments with the motive of Fate.

The Card Trio is one of the highlights of the opera. Frasquita and Mercedes tell their fortunes. The cards promise each what her heart desires—to Frasquita a handsome young lover, to Mercedes a rich old husband who will die and leave her his money. Carmen cuts the cards and draws the ace of spades. "Death! I've read it well. First I, then he."

Carmen, Card Scene.
"Death! I've read it well. First I, then he . . ."

In a monologue of great pathos she accepts her fate. "In vain you shuffle the cards to avoid the answer you dread to hear. To no avail—the cards remain sincere . . . Though you try twenty times, the pitiless cards repeat—Death!" One must hear it in the opera house to realize the explosive power of that word *mort.*

There follows the famous aria of Micaela, who comes seeking José, hoping still to rescue him from his madness. The horn adds romantic luster to the melody.

Je dis, ___ que rien ne m'é - pou - van - te   Je ___ dis, ___ hé -
I say ___ that no fear shall dis - may me   I ___ say, ___ a -

las! que je ré - ponds ___ de moi
las, fear shall not make me de - part

Escamillo arrives, eager to join Carmen. A fight develops between him and the jealous José. The men draw knives but are separated. José learns from Micaela that his mother is dying and is persuaded to leave with her. "We will meet again!" he warns Carmen as the motive of Fate is heard.

The Prelude to the last act, with its somber melody on the oboe above an accompaniment of strings and drum, has a quality of foreboding. The curtain goes up on a brilliant scene outside the arena in Seville. The crowd hails the various groups of bullfighters who march in to the blatant tune of the Overture. Finally Escamillo enters, with a radiant Carmen on his arm. There is a tender exchange between them. The crowd accompanies him into the ring. Carmen remains to face José.

The encounter is taut, volcanic. Each is driven by the basic law of his nature: José cannot give up his love, she cannot surrender her freedom. He entreats her to go with him—there is still time to begin anew. She refuses. "Then you love me no more?" "No, I love you no more." "But I, Carmen, I love you still!" He reaches the breaking point against the jubilant strains of the chorus in the arena. "For the last time, you fiend, will you come with me?" "No!" He stabs her as the Toreador Song rises from the crowd pouring out of the arena. José, dazed, kneels beside her body. The orchestra sounds the motive of Fate.

It was a German philosopher who, awakening from the intoxication of Wagnerian music drama, discovered in *Carmen* the ideal lyric tragedy. Nietzsche, after his break with Wagner—whom he had idolized—found in this swift-moving, all too human opera the antidote to the involved sagas of gods and heroes; the embodiment of Latin clarity and directness as against the ponderousness of the Teuton. "It is necessary to Mediterraneanize music!" he declared in one of the most eloquent tributes ever penned to a work of art. "Yesterday—would you believe it?—I heard Bizet's masterpiece for the twentieth time. Once again I attended with the same gentle reverence. How such a work completes one! One becomes a masterpiece oneself . . . This music is wicked, refined, fatalistic. Yet it remains popular. It possesses the refinement not of an individual but of a race.

"I envy Bizet for having had the courage of this sensitiveness—this southern, tawny, sunburnt sensitiveness—which hitherto in the music of European culture had found no means of expression. I know of no case in which the tragic irony that constitutes the kernel of love is expressed with such severity or in so terrible a formula as in the last cry of Don José: 'Yes, it is I who killed her— Ah, my adored Carmen!' "

CHAPTER 43

Modest Musorgsky (1839-1881)

"The artist believes in the future because he lives in it."

His Life

THE MOST unmistakably Russian of composers was born in the town of Karevo, in the province of Pskov. He prepared for a military career, in accordance with the family tradition, and was commissioned an officer in a fashionable regiment of Guards. At eighteen he came under the influence of Balakirev, made friends with Cui, Borodin, and Rimsky-Korsakov, and before long knew that he must devote his life to music.

As his talents developed, the young officer found his duties irksome and resolved to withdraw from the military. The other members of "The Five," not yet having accepted music as a full-time profession, counseled

Modest Musorgsky.
Portrait by Ilya Repin.

prudence. But the ardent youth, confident of his powers, was not to be dissuaded, and at the age of twenty-two resigned his commission.

History intervened at this point. The emancipation of the serfs in 1861 proved disastrous to the smaller landowners. Instead of being free to devote himself to art the young aristocrat was obliged to seek employment. He established himself in St. Petersburg, where a post at the Ministry of Transport gave him a modest subsistence. Evenings were devoted to reading, musical sessions with his four comrades, and his first attempts at composition.

There asserted itself almost immediately a personality that would accept neither tradition nor guidance. He was one of those who must find their own path. His path led to an uncompromisingly realistic approach to life and art: "To trace the finest traits in man's nature and in the mass of humanity, digging resolutely through these unexplored regions and conquering them—that is the true mission of the artist!" How close in spirit to the credo of Dostoievsky, that other interpreter of "the insulted and the injured": "My function is to portray the soul of man in all its profundity."

Musorgsky at twenty-nine was ready for the great task of his life. In *Boris Godunov* he found a worthy theme out of his country's past. He fashioned the libretto himself, after Pushkin's drama and the old chronicles. The years spent in the composition of this drama were the happiest he was ever to know. He was sustained by the fellowship of "The Mighty Five" and was especially close to Rimsky-Korsakov. When *Boris* was submitted to the imperial Opera, it was rejected on the ground that it lacked a leading woman's part. Musorgsky revised the work, adding the role of Marina. Finally all obstacles were overcome and the opera presented in 1874. The critics damned it but the public was impressed. Nor were its political implications lost on the young intelligentsia, at that time seething with unrest under the tsarist regime. The choruses depicting the revolt against Tsar Boris were soon heard on the streets of St. Petersburg. Despite its success—or because of it—the opera was regarded with suspicion by the censor and, it was rumored, aroused the displeasure of the imperial family. In the following season it was presented with drastic cuts and ultimately dropped from the repertory.

The withdrawal of *Boris* ushered in the bitter period of Musorgsky's life. In the six years that remained to him he moved ever farther from his comrades of the "invincible band." He had outgrown his admiration of Balakirev. Cui, by now an influential critic, had betrayed him by attacking *Boris*. Rimsky and Borodin, he felt, had sold out for success, capitulating to the academic spirit that he regarded as the enemy of true art. He remained alone, a rebel to the end.

But the lonely struggle demanded sterner stuff than he was made of. Moods of exuberant belief in himself alternated with periods of depression. Poverty, lack of recognition, and the drudgery of his clerical post played their part. His need for escape revived a craving for stimulants that he had kept more or less under control since early manhood. Increasingly his life lost its direction and followed the erratic course of the alcoholic.

To these years of despair belong his greatest songs, the cycles *Sunless* and the *Songs and Dances of Death.* The major work of this period was the national opera *Khovanshtchina,* on his own libretto, dealing with the revolt of the imperial bodyguard against Peter the Great. But the creative force that had carried him through *Boris* was spent. He worked at this somber drama until his death, refashioning it again and again. He left it unfinished.

As his former comrades rose higher in the social scale, Musorgsky sank lower. He who since childhood had identified himself with the humble of the earth now joined their ranks. The arc was complete, from the debonair young officer of the Guards to the slovenly tragic figure of Repin's famous portrait. Yet the spirit of the fighter remained with him to the end. In the last year of his life, when his friends had abandoned all hope of saving him, he still was able to write, "My motto remains unchanged. 'Boldly on! Forward to new shores!' . . . To seek untiringly, fearlessly, and without confusion, and to enter with firm step into the promised land—there's a great and beautiful task! One must give oneself wholly to mankind."

To give himself wholly he left his post and tried to support himself by accompanying singers. He was soon destitute. While attending a musical evening he collapsed and was placed in a hospital, suffering from delirium tremens. His comrades rallied to his side. But he died—as he had lived—alone, on his forty-second birthday, crying out, "All is ended. Ah, how wretched I am!"

His Music

Musorgsky appeared at a time when the initial force of romanticism had spent itself. He regarded it as his mission to seek fresh modes of expression. The romantic dictum that truth is beauty, beauty truth, had encouraged artists, he maintained, to prettify reality. He strove to rescue truth from the academic formulas that were beginning to pass for beauty. The theme runs through his letters. "*Life* wherever it shows itself, *truth* no matter how bitter—to speak out to people boldly, sincerely, point-blank—this is what excites me, this is what I want! . . . Art must embody more than beauty alone. Let us look life boldly in the eye!" The dignity of man was too great a thing to need prettying. "I love man in art. With lifted head, bravely and happily, I will go forth toward a genuine art that loves man."

By man he meant neither the aristocrat nor the habitué of the salons but the simple peasant whose face beckoned to him from the millions of huts of his vast land. In this mysterious identification with the downtrodden he was a true son of the 1860s in Russia. His hunger for truth opened up new areas of expression to art music. A gallery of characters drawn from Russian serfdom appears in his songs: the village idiot striving to declare his love; the young peasant who sees wife and children in rags and remembers the cradle song his mother sang him promising a carefree life; the soldier lying on the field of battle, crows wheeling above, while his wife at home tells their little son that father will soon return. A fresh and powerful imagination manifested itself in his songs, for many of which he wrote his own texts. In effect, Musorgsky created a profoundly realistic type of song that ended the supremacy of the romantic lied, and that in its profoundly human expressiveness embodied his dictum: "Art is not an end in itself but a means of addressing mankind."

Inevitably terms like realism and naturalism attach to Musorgsky's music. But such labels must be used with caution in regard to music, "the most romantic of all the arts." Musorgsky was a tone poet in the great line. He penetrated to the secret depths, the irrational layers of the human personality; to levels of awareness beyond the reach of Tchaikovsky's subjective emotion or the fairy-tale exoticism of Rimsky-Korsakov. He alone of the musicians of his country may be compared to Dostoievsky. He too was driven. And from the dark journey he brought back glimpses of the lonely regions of the soul; the stark landscape of *The Brothers Karamazov, The Idiot, The Possessed.*

Musorgsky's opposition to every trace of the academic spirit stemmed from the nature of both the artist and man. What he had to say demanded qualities other than the fluent part-writing and smooth progressions on which professors set such store. The bleak dissonances, the novel chord sequences, the "prose rhythms" based on groups of five, seven, or eleven beats, the telegraphic conciseness and rough-hewn structure were inseparable from his intensely personal manner of speech. He was thirty years ahead of his time. Rimsky-Korsakov took him to task for his roughness of style, his "meaningless disconnected harmonies, incorrect modulations," and general amateurishness. Yet it was Musorgsky rather than his comrades who influenced the twentieth century, when the rules he violated had been set aside. What his contemporaries took for the ineptitude of a dilettante was recognized by a later age as strangely prophetic vision.

A number of works were left incomplete at his death. His friends accepted it as their responsibility to bring these into finished form. Rimsky-Korsakov revised and orchestrated *Khovanshtchina*, which had remained in piano score. He also completed the final scene. In addition he arranged the present version of *Night on Bald Mountain*, a symphonic poem Musorgsky had never put into final shape. Three decades after Musorgsky's death César Cui made amends for his attack on *Boris* by completing *The Fair at Sorotchinsk*, a comic opera based on a folk tale of Gogol. In a different class was Rimsky-Korsakov's revision of *Boris*, a questionable undertaking in view of the fact that the opera had been completed and produced. Rimsky's intention was praiseworthy—to make *Boris* palatable to the opera public of that time. He corrected Musorgsky's "mistakes" in much the same spirit as he corrected the exercises submitted to him in class at the Conservatory. He smoothed out what seemed to him the strange harmonies and rhythms, changed the orchestration, and subjected the entire work to the very process of prettification against which Musorgsky's whole life was a protest. However, he achieved his aim. It was in Rimsky's version that *Boris* triumphed in the opera houses of the world. Now that we see Musorgsky in truer perspective, the desire is gaining ground to hear the opera either as he wrote it or—since he occasionally miscalculated an effect in the orchestra—with only such changes as are absolutely essential.

Boris Godunov

In *Boris Godunov* (first version 1868–69, second version 1871–72) Musorgsky gave his country its great national drama. It has been said that the real hero of the opera is the Russian people. In the magnificent choral tableaux we encounter, instead of the conventional operatic chorus, vivid types drawn from the peasantry. Musorgsky's genius for dramatic characterization reveals itself in the delineation of the main personages. Lyric song forms, many in folk style, are balanced by the dramatic recitative. The latter consists of a flexible declamation—what he called "musical prose"—that captures the intonations of living speech. "Whenever I hear people speaking, no matter who it is or what they say, my brain immediately gets to work to translate what I have heard into music." Nowhere is Musorgsky's instinct for dramatic truth more apparent than in his recitative.

The drama (in four acts with a prologue), which covers the years 1598–1605, centers about the guilt of a usurper. Boris Godunov, having contrived the murder of the boy Dmitri, rightful heir to the throne, has himself proclaimed Tsar. As the years pass he is tormented by remorse.

An adventurous young monk named Gregory resolves to pass himself off as the murdered Dmitri. He escapes to the Lithuanian frontier and proclaims himself heir to the throne. Welcomed by the Polish nobility who are opposed to Boris, he falls in love with the haughty Marina, daughter of the noble house of Mnishek. Marina knows that his claims are false, but she sees in him a means of becoming Empress and encourages him to aspire to her hand. The Pretender, back in Russia, rallies to his standard all who are discontented with Boris's rule. Boris, a prey to his guilt, is obsessed by hallucinations in which he sees the ghost of the murdered Tsarevich advancing toward him. He dies as the victorious Gregory-Dmitri marches on the Kremlin.

The Prologue, which takes place some years before the drama proper, consists of two great choral scenes. In the first the people gather before a monastery outside Moscow imploring Boris to accept the crown. They are egged on by a police officer who threatens them for not evincing sufficient enthusiasm. There follows the Coronation Scene, in which Musorgsky captures the majesty of tone and movement appropriate to a national drama. The bells of the Kremlin peal as the boyars proceed into the cathedral. The people sing a hymn of praise based on an ancient folk tune.

Boris Godunov, Coronation Scene.

Hail the sun in bright splen - dor ris -ing in glo - ry, glo - ry

In the first scene of Act I the aged monk Pimen works through the night on his chronicle, "that future generations of the Faithful may know the fateful story of their land." (This line was chosen by Musorgsky's friends to be carved on his tomb.) Gregory, awaking from a troubled dream in which he saw himself raised above all the world, muses on the usurper in the Kremlin. None dares remind Boris of the murdered child, yet in this cell an unknown hermit records the terrible truth. The powerful archaic harmonies that Musorgsky loved evoke a distant, troubled time.

The second scene takes place in an inn on the Lithuanian frontier. Song is interspersed with action. The mistress of the inn, as she darns, sings the Song of the Drake. Missail and Varlaam enter, two vagabonds masquerading as mendicant friars. With them is Gregory, anxious to cross the frontier. Warmed by the mistress's wine, Varlaam sings a ballad in old folk style of how Tsar Ivan smote the Tartars at Kazan. When the patrol arrives seeking the runaway monk, Gregory manages to divert their suspicion to Varlaam and makes his escape.

The second act, laid in the royal apartment in the Kremlin, sets off lyric song forms against dramatic recitative. Xenia, daughter of Boris, mourns her betrothed who has fallen in battle. To distract her the old nurse—the familiar Mamka of Russian tradition—sings the Song of the Gnat. The little Tsarevich responds with a "clapping song"—a worthy companion to Musorgsky's *Songs of Childhood*. Counterposed to these is the great monologue of the guilt-ridden Tsar. "I stand supreme in power . . . and yet all happiness eludes my tortured soul."

I stand su - preme in pow - er.   Five years I've reigned, and

kept   my coun - try peace - ful.

The scene in which the agonized Tsar struggles with his hallucination is on the level of Shakespearean tragedy. "O conscience, thou art cruel . . ." In his horror Boris becomes aware of the supreme irony: he, the all-powerful, is helpless against his fears.

Act III opens in the castle of the Mnisheks in Poland. Marina is char-

acterized from the start—beautiful, proud, calculating. She dismisses
the song of her maidens in praise of her beauty; for her, only songs of
brave deeds. The rhythms of mazurka and polonaise are associated
with the princess throughout. She has a short and violent encounter
with the Jesuit Rangoni, who orders her to gain the throne through the
Pretender in order to lead Russia back to the true faith.

The second scene takes place in the garden where Gregory, tormented
by love, awaits her. Marina and her guests issue from the castle to the

strains of a spirited polonaise. In the ensuing love scene Musorgsky
worked closer to the tradition of French grand opera than that ardent
Slavophile realized. Although less original than the Russian parts of
the opera, the scene is admirable for its characterization of Gregory and
Marina, the dramatic interplay between them, and the love melody—
which makes a capital effect in the theater.

Act IV opens outside a convent near Moscow. The people await
Boris and his retinue. They entreat the Tsar for bread; his boyars distribute alms. The village idiot, tormented by boys, appeals to Boris:
"These boys took my only coin away. Why don't you have them murdered, as long ago you murdered our Tsarevich!" The courtiers would
arrest the simpleton; but Boris, shaken, restrains them. "Go, pray for
your Tsar, poor idiot . . ." The second scene takes place in the throne
room of the Kremlin. Boris, half crazed by guilt, appears before the
Council of Boyars. The old monk Pimen tells of a vision in which he
heard the voice of the murdered Tsarevich. Boris, overcome, falls into
the arms of the boyars. Feeling his end approach, he calls for his son.
The boyars coldly eye the dying monarch as he takes leave of the little
Tsarevich. Musorgsky's recitative rises to the heights of lyric tragedy.
"O bitter death! How cruel is thy clutch. Not yet, not yet—I still am
Tsar! Death, be merciful . . ."

The closing scene is set in a forest clearing. Peasants revolting against Boris's authority bind one of his noblemen and make sport of him. The Pretender appears at the head of his army and is acclaimed by the people. All leave save the village idiot who, seated on a stone, sings to himself. "Flow, silent tears, flow, bitter tears . . . Weep, Russian folk. Weep, hungry folk." It is a surpassingly eloquent ending. (Rimsky-Korsakov, seeking a "stronger" one, reversed the two last scenes so as to finish with Boris's death.) The curtain falls as Musorgsky—crowning audacity!—ends his work on an incomplete cadence.

The creator of this profound drama of conscience was forgotten by his countrymen for several decades after his death. It was in the Paris of the Nineties that his work first came to be understood. Musicians of a new generation, among them Debussy and Ravel, discovered in him the first exponent of the modern temper, and found in his audacious harmonies an inspiration for their own. His poetic realism became a nourishing force in the formation of the contemporary style. From France appreciation of the forgotten master spread to Germany and finally to his native land.

The twentieth century has made amends for the incomprehension of the nineteenth. He who died so abjectly is recognized today as one of the towering figures of the late romantic period. As far as certain contemporary musicians are concerned, he is Russia's greatest composer.

PART THREE

More Materials of Music

"In any narrative—epic, dramatic or musical—every word or tone should be like a soldier marching towards the one, common, final goal: *conquest of the material.* The way the artist makes every phrase of his story such a soldier, serving to unfold it, to support its structure and development, to build plot and counterplot, to distribute light and shade, to point incessantly and lead up gradually to the climax—in short, the way every fragment is impregnated with its mission towards the whole, makes up this delicate and so essential objective which we call FORM."

Ernst Toch

CHAPTER 44

The Organization of Musical Sounds: Key and Scale

"All music is nothing more than a succession of impulses that converge towards a definite point of repose."

Igor Stravinsky

AT THE beginning of this book we discussed various elements of music. Now that we have had occasion to hear how these are interwoven in a number of works, we are ready to consider the materials of music on a more advanced level, particularly as they relate to the organization of the large classical forms.

Tonality

A system of music must have set procedures for organizing tones into intelligible relationships. One of the first steps in this direction is to select certain tones and arrange them in a family or group. In such a group one tone assumes greater importance than the rest. This is the *do,* the Tonic or keynote around which the others revolve and to which they ultimately gravitate.

By a *key* we mean a group of related tones with a common center or Tonic. The tones of the key serve as basic material for a given composition. When we listen to a composition in the key of A we hear a piece based in large part upon the family of tones that revolve around and gravitate to the common center A.

This "loyalty to the Tonic" is inculcated in us by most of the music we hear. It is the unifying force in the do-re-mi-fa-sol-la-ti-do scale that was taught us in our childhood. The reader can test for himself how strong is the pull to the Tonic by singing the first seven tones of this pattern, stopping on *ti.* He will experience an almost physical compulsion to resolve the *ti* up to *do.*

This sense of relatedness to a central tone is known as *tonality.* This sense, needless to say, resides in our minds rather than in the tones themselves. Tonality underlies the whole system of relationships among tones as embodied in keys, scales, and the harmonies based on those, such relationships converging upon the "definite point of repose." Specifically, tonality refers to those relationships as they were manifest in Western music from around 1600 to 1900. As Roger Sessions put it,

257

"Tonality should be understood as the principal means which the composers of the seventeenth, eighteenth, and nineteenth centuries evolved of organizing musical sounds and giving them coherent shape."

The "Miracle of the Octave"

A string of a certain length, when set in motion, vibrates at a certain rate per second and produces a certain pitch. Under the same conditions a string half as long will vibrate twice as fast and sound an octave above. A string twice as long will vibrate half as fast and sound an octave below. An octave is the distance from one tone to the next tone of the same name above or below. There is an octave from one C to the next, from D to D, from E to E, and so on. In the series do-re-mi-fa-sol-la-ti-do there is the interval of an octave from the lower *do* to the upper. By an *interval* we mean the distance and the relationship between two tones. For example, from C to E is a third (C-D-E). From C to G is a fifth (C-D-E-F-G).

When we sound together on the piano two tones other than an octave, say, C-D or C-F, the ear distinctly hears two different tones. But when we strike an octave the ear recognizes a very strong similarity between the two tones. Indeed, if one were not listening carefully one would almost believe that he was hearing a single tone. This "miracle of the octave" was observed at an early stage in all musical cultures, with the result that the octave became the basic interval in music.

The method of dividing the octave determines the scales and the character of a musical system. It is precisely in this particular that one system differs from another. In Western music the octave is divided into twelve parts. The fact is apparent from the look of the piano keyboard, where from any tone to its octave we find twelve keys—seven white and five black. These twelve tones are a half tone (or semitone) apart. That is, from C to C-sharp is a half tone; from C-sharp to D the same. From C to D is a whole tone. The half step and the whole step are the units of distance in our musical system.

Oriental music is based on other units. In India, for example, quarter-tone scales are used. The Javanese divide the octave into five nearly equal parts. Arabic music contains a scale that divides the octave into seventeen parts. We are not able to play oriental music on the piano, which is tuned in half and whole tones. Nor could we readily sing it, since we have been trained to think in terms of the whole- and half-tone intervals of our system.

The twelve semitones into which Western music divides the octave constitute what is known as the *chromatic scale*. They are duplicated in higher and lower octaves. No matter how vast and intricate a musical work, it is made up of the twelve basic tones and their higher and lower duplications.

Note: The black keys are named in relation to their white neighbors. When the black key between C and D is thought of as a semitone higher than C, it is known as C-sharp. When it is regarded as a semitone lower than D, the same key is called D-flat. Thus D-sharp is the same tone as E-flat, F-sharp is the same tone as G-flat, and G-sharp is the same tone as A-flat. Which of these names is used depends upon the scale and key in which a particular sharp or flat appears.

The Major Scale

A *scale* is an arrangement of a series of tones. Specifically, a scale presents the tones of the key in consecutive order, ascending or descending. It is, consequently, a statement of movement. The word is derived from the Italian *scala,* "ladder." In the widest sense a scale is a musical alphabet revealing at a glance the principle whereby tones are selected and related to one another in a given system. It is an abstraction that sums up a certain way of conceiving music, just as an alphabet is an abstraction that sums up a certain way of conceiving language. The scale is derived from actual musical practice. That is, the songs and dances come first. From this living music the theorist extracts and codifies his scales.

The music of the classic-romantic period is based on two contrasting scales, the *major* and the *minor.* These consist of seven different tones, with the octave *do* added at the end of the series. The major scale has the familiar do-re-mi-fa-sol-la-ti-do pattern. Its seven tones are picked out of the possible twelve in order to form a centralized family or key out of which musical compositions may be fashioned. It becomes clear that compositions based on the major scale represent a "seven out of twelve" way of hearing music.

We have thus far established two basic patterns on the piano keyboard. The seven white and five black keys from one C to the next constitute the twelve tones of the *chromatic* scale. The white keys alone from C to C give the tones of the major scale—in other words, the familiar do-re-mi-fa-sol-la-ti-do series. Let us examine this series a little more closely.

We notice that there is no black key on the piano between E-F (*mi-fa*) and B-C (*ti-do*). These tones, therefore, are a semitone apart, while the others are a whole tone apart. Consequently, when we sing the do-re-mi-fa-sol-la-ti-do sequence we are measuring off a pattern of eight tones that are a whole tone apart except steps 3–4 (*mi-fa*) and 7–8 (*ti-do*). The reader will find it instructive to sing this scale trying to distinguish between the half- and whole-tone distances.

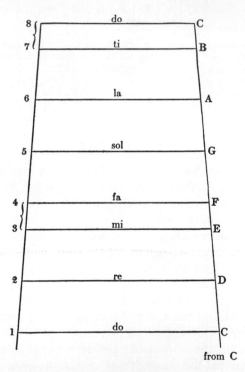

from C

This scale implies certain relationships based upon tension and resolution. We have already indicated one of the most important of these—the thrust of the seventh step to the eighth (*ti* seeking to be resolved to *do*). There are others: if we sing *do-re* we are left with a sense of incompleteness which is resolved when *re* moves back to *do*; *fa* gravitates to *mi*; *la* descends to *sol*. These tendencies, we saw, reside not in the tones but in our minds. They are the meanings attached by our musical culture to the raw material of nature.

Most important of all, the major scale defines the two poles of classical harmony: the *do* or Tonic, the point of ultimate rest; and the *sol* or Dominant, representative of the active harmony. Upon the trackless sea of sound this relationship imposes direction and goal. Tonic going to Dominant and returning to Tonic becomes a basic progression of classical harmony. It will also serve, we shall find, as a basic principle of classical form.

The Key as an Area in Musical Space

The major scale, we said, is a "ladder" of whole and half tones. A ladder may be placed on high ground or low, but the distance between its steps remains the same. So too the major scale may be measured off from one starting point or another without affecting the sequence of whole and half steps within the pattern.

Any one of the twelve tones of our octave may serve as starting point for the scale. Whichever it is, that tone at once assumes the function of the Tonic or key center. The other tones are chosen according to the pattern of the ladder. They immediately assume the functions of activity and rest implicit in the major scale. Most important, they all take on the impulse of gravitating more or less directly to the Tonic.

With each different Tonic we get another group of seven tones out of the possible twelve. In other words, every major scale has a different number of sharps or flats. The scale of C major is the only one that has no sharps or flats. If we build the major scale from G we must include an F-sharp in order to conform to the pattern of whole and half steps. (Try building the pattern whole step, whole step, half step, whole step, whole step, whole step, half step, from G. You will find that there is no F in this group.) If we build the major-scale pattern from D, we get a group of seven that includes two sharps. If F is our starting point the scale includes B-flat. (The twelve major scales are listed in Appendix IV.) When we play a simple tune like *America* on the piano with C as keynote—that is, in the key of C major—we use only the white keys. Should we play it with G as a keynote—that is, in the key of G major—we should in the course of it have to sound F-sharp, not F. Were we to play F we would be off key.

It becomes clear that the meaning of a tone, its direction and drive are determined not by its intrinsic nature but by its position in the scale. The tone C may be the Tonic or point of rest in one scale. In another it may be the seventh step seeking to be resolved by ascending to the eighth. In still another it may be the second step thrusting down to the first. In any case its impulse of activity or rest depends not on its character as the tone C but on its function as the *do*, the *ti*, or the *re* —the 1, 7, or 2—of that particular key and scale. The classical system is based on the eminently social doctrine that the significance of a tone depends not upon itself but upon its relationship to other tones.

The key serves as a means of identification. The title Symphony in A major refers to a work based in large measure upon the tones of the A-major scale and the harmonies fashioned from those, with the key-note A serving as the central tone to which the others gravitate. This group of seven is the one that includes three sharps.

The key signature at the head of a piece announces the number of sharps or flats that prevail in that particular composition.

G major   D major   A major   E major   F major   Bb major   Eb major   Ab major

To sum up: When we sing the series do-re-mi-fa-sol-la-ti-do we are marking off a series of whole and half steps that constitute the basic units of measurement in our musical system. We are setting forth these whole and half steps according to the pattern of the major scale. We are selecting seven tones out of twelve to constitute a key with a common center or keynote. We are setting up among these seven tones certain relationships of tension and resolution; especially the Tonic and Dominant as the two poles of rest and activity within the group. Finally, we are marking off an area in musical space that has the characteristics of geographical space—distance, direction, a fixed point of departure and return. Behind this sequence of eight tones stands the sense of tonality that has been basic to our music for centuries. And behind that is man's eternal quest for certainty, his need to impose order and meaning upon the raw material of the physical world.

The Minor Scale

Whether the major scale begins on C, D, E, or any other tone, it follows the same pattern in the arrangement of the whole and half steps. Such a pattern is known as a *mode*. Thus, all the major scales exemplify the major mode of arranging whole and half steps.

There is also a minor mode, which complements and serves as a foil to the major. It differs primarily from the major in that its third degree is lowered; that is, the scale of C minor has E-flat instead of E. In the pure or natural minor scale the sixth and seventh steps are also lowered: C-D-Eb-F-G-Ab-Bb-C. (For two other versions of the minor scale—harmonic and melodic—see Appendix IV.) The minor is pronouncedly different from the major in mood and coloring. *Minor*, the Latin word for "smaller," refers to the fact that the distinguishing interval C-E♭ is smaller than the corresponding interval C-E in the major ("larger") scale.

Like the major, the pattern of the minor scale may begin on each of the twelve tones of the octave. In each case there will be a different group of seven tones out of twelve; that is, each scale will include a different number of sharps or flats. It becomes clear that every tone in the octave may serve as starting point or keynote for a major and a minor scale. This gives us twelve keys according to the major mode and twelve keys according to the minor mode. There are of course other modes of arranging whole and half steps besides the major and minor patterns. Such scales have been appearing ever more frequently in our music in the past fifty years, enriching the harmonic resources of the traditional system. If the mode is not specified, the major is implied; as when we speak of the Melody in F, Minuet in G, or Symphony in A. The minor is always specified, as in the case of Schubert's Symphony in B minor or Mendelssohn's Violin Concerto in E minor.

Is the minor "sadder" than the major? Such connotations exist only in reference to the music of a particular time and place. The nineteenth century seems to have regarded the minor as more somber than the major. The funeral music of Beethoven, Mendelssohn, Chopin, Wagner, and Grieg is conspicuously in the minor, while the triumphal finales of a number of symphonies and overtures of the same period are as conspicuously in the major.

The minor mode has a certain exotic ring to Western ears and is associated in the popular view with oriental and east European music. This aspect of the minor is prominent in such works as the *Turkish Rondo* of Mozart; in a number of pieces in Hungarian style by Schubert, Liszt, and Brahms; in the main theme of Rimsky-Korsakov's *Scheherazade*, César Cui's *Orientale*, and similar exotica. The folk songs of certain regions appear to incline to the major while others lean toward the minor. There are, however, so many exceptions that such a generalization must be viewed with caution.

The contrast between minor and major became an element of musical structure during the classic-romantic period. For example, in A-B-A form, the outer sections might be in one mode and the contrasting middle section in the other. Or a symphony might start out in the minor and shift to the major in an access of triumph, as in Beethoven's Fifth, Franck's D-minor, and Tchaikovsky's Fifth. Thus the distinction between major and minor lent itself to contrasts of color, mood, and emotional intensity.

We have in this chapter explained a system of harmony based upon the division of the octave into twelve tones. Each of these tones may be the keynote of a scale according to the major mode and of a scale according to the minor mode. Each of these twenty-four scales has a different number of sharps or flats; that is, it contains a different group of seven tones out of the possible twelve. The twelve major and twelve minor keys make up the classical harmonic system.

There had to come into existence an art form that would mobilize the resources of this system, that would bring into focus its capacities for dramatic conflict and architectural expanse. It was the great achievement of the eighteenth century to evolve and perfect this form.

ᶠᵉᵃ *C H A P T E R   4 5* *ᵃᶠᵉ*

The Major-Minor System

"Form follows function."
Louis Sullivan

Transposition

SUPPOSE a certain melody begins on G. If one felt that the song lay a little too high for his voice, he might begin on F instead of G and shift all the tones of the melody one step lower. Someone else might find that the song lay too low for his voice. He would begin on A and sing each tone of the melody one step higher than it was written. The process of shifting all the notes of a musical composition to a higher or lower pitch is called *transposition*.

When we transpose a piece we shift it to another key. The level of pitch and the keynote are different, as are the number of sharps or flats. But the melody line remains the same because the pattern of its whole and half steps has been retained in the new key as in the old. That is why the same song can be published in various keys for soprano, alto, tenor, and bass.

We have all transposed melodies without being aware of it. For example, a group of children will begin a song from a certain note. If the melody moves too high or too low for comfort, their teacher will stop them and have them begin again from another tone. On an instrument, transposing is a more complicated matter. The player must adjust his fingers to another arrangement of sharps or flats. If he is a pianist or organist he must shift not only the melody but the harmonies as well. The ability to transpose a piece at sight is a skill that musicians regard with respect. It is a necessity for professional accompanists, who are constantly required to transpose songs to higher or lower keys to suit the range of singers.

Why does a composer choose one key rather than another for his piece? In former times external factors strongly influenced this choice. Up to the time of Beethoven, for example, the brass instruments were not able to change keys as readily as they are now. In writing for the string instruments composers considered the fact that certain effects, such as playing on the open strings, could be achieved in one key rather than another. Certain composers of the romantic period seemed to associate a certain emotional atmosphere or color with various keys. Characteristic was Mendelssohn's fondness for E minor, Chopin's for C-sharp minor. A composer's choice of key for a particular piece is determined by a variety of factors. The most important of these, probably, is his desire to retain the key in which he first imagined the music in his mind.

Modulation

If a piece of music can be played in one key as in another, why not put all music in the key of C and be done with it? Because the contrast between keys and the movement from one key to another is an essential element of musical structure. We have seen that the tones of the key form a closed circle of "seven out of twelve" that imparts coherence and focus to the music. But the circle may be opened up, in which case we are shifted—either gently or abruptly—to another area centering about another keynote. Such a change gives us a heightened sense of activity. It is an expressive gesture of prime importance.

The act of passing from one key to another is known as *modulation*. There is no way to describe in words something that can be experienced only in the domain of sound. Suffice it to say that the composer has at his disposal a number of ways of modulating; therewith he "lifts" the listener from one tonal area to another. As Arnold Schoenberg put it, "Modulation is like a change of scenery."

The twelve major and twelve minor keys of the classical harmonic system may be compared to so many rooms in a house, with the modulations equivalent to corridors leading from one to the next. The "rooms" were arranged in ascending order of sharps and flats: C major with none, G major with one sharp, D major with two, A major with three, and so on. The eighteenth-century composer firmly established the home key, then embarked on a leisurely journey to the next related key.

There resulted a spaciousness of structure that was the musical counterpart of the rolling sentences of the eighteenth-century novel and the balanced façades of eighteenth-century architecture.

Nineteenth-century romanticism, on the other hand, demanded a whipping-up of emotions, an intensifying of all musical processes. In the late romantic era the corridors between the "rooms" steadily shrank; modulations were ever more frequent and more daring. There came into being a hyperemotional music that wandered restlessly from key to key in accord with the need for excitement of the mid- and late-romantic era. By the same token, the balanced structure of the classical system, with its key areas neatly marked off one from the other, began to disintegrate.

Chromaticism

When seven tones out of twelve are selected to form a key, the other five become extraneous in relation to that particular Tonic. They enter the composition as transients, mainly to embellish the melody or harmony. Their status is summed up in the term *accidentals,* meaning the sharped or flatted notes that appear in the course of a piece without belonging to the prevailing key.

If the piece is to sound firmly rooted in the key, the seven tones that are directly related to the Tonic must prevail. Should the composer allow the five foreign tones—the accidentals—to become too prominent in his melody and harmony, the relationship to the key center would be weakened and the key feeling become ambiguous. The distinction between the tones that do not belong within the key area and those that do is made explicit in the contrasting terms *chromatic* and *diatonic.* "Chromatic" refers to the twelve-tone scale that includes all the semitones of the octave. Chromatic melody or harmony moves by half steps, taking in the tones that are extraneous to the key. The word comes from the Greek *chroma,* which means "color." "Diatonic," on the other hand, refers to musical progression based on the seven tones of a major or minor scale, and to harmonies that are firmly rooted in the key.

Diatonic harmony went hand in hand with the clear-cut key feeling that marked the late eighteenth-century style. We may say that the music of Haydn, Mozart, and Beethoven tends to be diatonic. (There are of course many passages in their music, especially in their late works, that belie this generalization.) Chromatic harmony, on the other hand, characterized the ceaseless modulation and surcharged emotional atmosphere of nineteenth-century music. From Schubert to Wagner and on to Richard Strauss and Mahler, the romantic and post-romantic composers indefatigably explored the possibilities of chromaticism. In an earlier section of this book we described the musical traits of nineteenth-century romanticism. We may now isolate its most important characteristic: the predominance of chromatic harmony.

The classical major-minor system required the separation of key areas. Wagner and his followers, by emphasizing chromatic harmony —that is, the in-between or borderline tones—weakened this separation. With Debussy, music moved into twilight regions where the outlines of key were increasingly veiled. The five chromatic or extraneous tones were no longer regarded as accidentals or embellishments of the harmony. They had established themselves on a footing of equal importance with the basic seven tones. Thus the twentieth century witnessed the disintegration of the classical major-minor system. The "seven out of twelve" way of hearing music was supplanted by a "twelve out of twelve."

The Key as a Form-Building Element

By marking off an area in musical space with a fixed center, the key provides the framework within which musical growth and development take place. The three main harmonies of the key—Tonic (I), Dominant (V), and Subdominant (IV)—become the focal points over which melodies and chord progressions unfold. In brief, the key is the neighborhood inhabited by a tune and its harmonies. Thus the key becomes a prime factor for musical unity.

At the same time the contrast between keys may further the cause of variety. The classical composer pitted one key against another, thereby achieving a dramatic opposition between them. He began by establishing his home key. Presently he modulated to a related key, generally that of the Dominant (for example, from C major with no sharps or flats to G major, one sharp; or from G major to D major, two sharps). In so doing he established a tension, since the Dominant key was unstable compared to the Tonic. This tension required resolution, which was provided by the return to the home key.

The progression from home key to contrasting key and back outlined the basic musical pattern of statement-departure-return. Through such a progression the movement came to do precisely what its name implied: it moved! The home key was the anchorage, the safe harbor; the foreign key represented adventure. The home key was the symbol of unity; the foreign key ensured variety and contrast.

The tension between two keys and their ultimate reconciliation became the motive power of the music of the classical era. This conflict-and-resolution found its frame in the grand form of the latter half of the eighteenth century—the ideal tone-drama known as the sonata.

✾✾ *CHAPTER 46* ✾✾

The Development of Themes: Musical Logic

> "I alter some things, eliminate and try again until I am satisfied. Then begins the mental working out of this material in its breadth, its narrowness, its height and depth."
>
> Ludwig van Beethoven

THINKING, whether in words or tones, demands continuity and sequence. Every thought must flow out of the one before and lead logically into the next. In this way is created a sense of steady progression toward a goal. If we were to join the beginning of one sentence to the end of another, it would not make any more sense than if we united the first phrase of one melody and the second of another. In our discussion of melody we compared the two phrases of *London Bridge* to a question-and-answer formation. A similar impression of cause and effect, of natural flow and continuity, must pervade the whole musical fabric.

When a melodic idea, we noted, is used as a building block in the construction of a larger work it is known as a theme or subject. The theme is the first in a chain of musical situations. All of these must grow out of the basic idea as naturally as does the plant from the seed. Hence the term *germ theme*, which indicates the capacity of the initial idea to flower, to expand, and to develop in such a way as to create an effect of organic unity. The net result of this expansion and development is to make the audience feel, as they would in the case of a convincing drama or novel, that each situation is a necessary link in the chain: given this particular premise, what happens at any point is inevitable; or must seem so.

The process of spinning out a theme, of weaving and reweaving the threads of which it is composed, is the essence of musical thinking. This process of expansion has its parallel in prose writing, where an idea stated at the beginning of a paragraph is embroidered and enlarged upon until all its aspects appear in view. Each sentence leads smoothly into the one that follows. In similar fashion, every measure takes up where the one before left off and brings us inexorably to the next.

The most tightly knit kind of expansion in our music is known as *thematic development*. To develop a theme means to unfold its latent energies, to search out its capacities for growth and bring them to fruition. Thematic development represents the constructional element in music. It is one of the most important techniques in musical composition, demanding of the composer imagination, master craftsmanship, and intellectual power.

In expanding and manipulating his ideas the composer treats the tone material in the manner of the sculptor or goldsmith: he molds the material, deriving inspiration from the stuff in his hands, allowing it to dictate forms and shapes peculiar to itself. He is engaged in a kind of thinking possible only in music, one that has its own logic, its own procedures and meanings; a thinking that cannot be duplicated in any other medium. For this reason is it so repugnant to most musicians to have literary interpretations forced upon a piece of abstract music. Any attempt to translate purely musical thinking into words seems to them a vulgarizing of the composer's intention, a distortion of his meaning. For this reason too we find whole sections in a large instrumental work to which it is neither necessary nor desirable to attach even such general labels as "joyous" or "melancholy." The composer is indulging his joy in expanding and working out the themes. What he feels at this point and what he intends his listeners to feel may perhaps best be described as the emotion of music, with no other labels attached.

In the process of development, certain procedures have proved to be particularly effective. The simplest is repetition, which may occur either at the same pitch or at another. For example, in *America,* the melodic idea on the words "Land where my fathers died" is duplicated immediately, but a tone lower, on the words "Land of the pilgrims' pride." Such a repetition on a higher or lower pitch is known as a *sequence*. The repetition may be either exact or with variations in the melody, harmony, rhythm, timbre, dynamics, and register. It may be attended by expansion or contraction of the note values as well as by bold and frequent changes of key.

A basic technique in thematic development is the breaking up of the theme into its constituent fragments, the *motives*. A motive is the smallest fragment of a theme that forms a melodic-rhythmic unit. The motives are the germ cells of musical growth. Through fragmentation of themes, through repeating and varying the motives and combining them in ever fresh patterns, the composer imparts to the musical organism the quality of dynamic evolution and growth.

Development may also proceed by imitation—that is, the theme may be presented by one instrument and forthwith imitated by another. Or the theme may be combined with other melody lines or fragments in an intricate texture. Through these and kindred devices the theme takes on fresh forms and displays unsuspected facets of its personality. As we watch this process of flowering and growth we experience the joy of recognizing the basic idea throughout its ever-changing manifestations.

Thematic development is too complex a technique to appear to advantage in short lyric pieces, songs, or dances. In such compositions a simple contrast between sections and a modest expansion within each section supplies the necessary continuity. By the same token, thematic development finds its proper frame in the large forms of music. To those forms it furnishes an epic-dramatic quality, along with the clarity, coherence, and logic that are the indispensable attributes of this most advanced type of musical thinking.

༿༺ CHAPTER 47 ༻༾

The Sonata: The First Movement

"The history of the sonata is the history of an attempt to cope with one of the most singular problems ever presented to the mind of man, and its solution is one of the most successful achievements of his artistic instincts."

Hubert Parry

WE REGARD the sonata as a musical form. It might perhaps be closer to the truth to speak of sonata style—that is, to consider the sonata as a manner of thinking; specifically, a manner of thinking for instruments that combines in the highest degree logical continuity, dynamic development, and emotional intensity. The sonata represents a certain type of musical material and the ideas struggling for expression through that material. We must understand its form not as an ingenious formula superimposed on Themes 1 and 2 but as the organic result of all the forces inherent in the musical thought of the classical era.

The name sonata comes from the Italian *suonare*, "to sound," indicating a piece to be sounded on instruments, as distinct from cantata, a piece to be sung. A sonata is an instrumental work consisting of a cycle of contrasting movements, generally three or four in number. The name sonata is used when the piece is intended for one or two instruments. If more than two are involved the work is called, as the case may be, a trio, quartet, quintet, sextet, septet, octet, or nonet. A sonata for solo instrument and orchestra is called a concerto; a sonata for the whole orchestra, a symphony. The sonata cycle, clearly, accounts for a large part of the instrumental music we hear.

Sonata-Allegro Form

The most highly organized and characteristic member of the several movements that make up the sonata cycle is the opening movement. This is in what is variously known as *first-movement form, sonata-allegro form,* or *sonata form.* Each of these names is useful but somewhat misleading. "First-movement form" is good provided we remember that this form may also be used for the other movements of the cycle. "Sonata-allegro form" is appropriate, since this type of movement is at its most characteristic in a <u>lively</u> or allegro movement. Unfortunately, the name fails to take into account that slow movements were sometimes cast in this form, especially in the eighteenth century. "Sonata form" is correct, and is much used by modern writers; but it is too easily confused with the term "sonata," which indicates the cycle as a whole—that is, all the movements. We will henceforth use sonata-allegro form or sonata form interchangeably, for both are met with constantly in the literature.

A movement in sonata-allegro form is based on two assumptions. The first is that a musical movement takes on direction and goal if, after establishing itself in the home key, it modulates to other areas and ultimately returns to the home key. We may therefore regard sonata form as a drama between two contrasting key areas. The "plot," the action, and the tension derive from this contrast. Sonata-allegro form, in brief, is an <u>artistic embodiment of the principles underlying the major-minor</u> <u>system</u>—the establishment, that is, of different key areas which serve as points of reference for a statement, a departure, and a return.

Second is the assumption that a theme may have its latent energies released through the development of its constituent motives. Most useful for this purpose is a brief incisive theme, one that has momentum and tension, and that promises more than at first sight it reveals. The themes will be stated or "exposed" in the first section; developed in the second; and restated or "recapitulated" in the third.

In a drama or novel, the various human traits—courage, cowardice, love, avarice—are presented not abstractly but as embodied in specific characters. So, too, the home key and the related key are associated with two contrasting themes. In this way the opposition between the two key areas is sharpened—dramatized, as it were—and presented to the listener as a conflict between two ideas. The contrasting themes furnish the composer with a basic store of material for expansion and development. From this he fashions an extended structure comprising areas of tension and relaxation, activity and rest, light and shade.

The first movement may open with a slow introduction that sets the stage for the allegro proper, or it may plunge directly into the allegro.

The Exposition (Statement) *of Sonata-Allegro form*

The opening section, the Exposition or Statement, sets forth the two opposing themes and their respective keys. The first theme and its expansion establish the home key. A transition or bridge leads into the contrasting key; in other words, the function of the bridge is to modulate. The second theme and its expansion establish the contrasting key. A closing section or codetta rounds off the Exposition and establishes a cadence in the contrasting key. Sometimes the closing section takes on the character of a third theme. In the classical sonata form the Exposition is repeated.

2 keys

The adventurous quality of the Exposition derives in no small measure from the fact that it "lifts" us from the home key to another area. The cadence in the contrasting key promises that much is to happen before we get back.

We become aware at this point of two types of musical material: that which comprises the ideas themselves—the main theater of action; and the subsidiary material that acts as connective tissue, that introduces an idea, leads us from one idea to the next, and concludes or rounds off the idea.

The Development

By wandering farther afield through a series of foreign keys, the music builds up tension against the inevitable return home. Hence, throughout the Development, temperature is kept at fever pitch through continual modulation. There results a sense of breathless activity and excitement.

At the same time the composer proceeds to reveal the potentialities of his themes. He breaks them into their component motives; recombines them into fresh patterns; and releases their latent energies, their explosive force. Conflict and action are the essence of drama. In the development section the conflict erupts, the action reaches maximum intensity. The protagonists of the drama are hurled one against another; their worlds collide. Emotion is transformed into motion. We hear a fragment of a theme thrown out by one group of instruments.

imitated by another, turned upside down (*inversion*), expanded to longer note values (*augmentation*), contracted into shorter note values (*diminution*), combined with other motives or even with new material. Now it appears in a remote key in the upper register, now deep in the bass. Suddenly a hitherto inconspicuous motive joins the fray and flowers into a fanciful design. The manifold transformations of the themes appear to grow inevitably out of the material. They turn out to have been implicit therein from the start, waiting for the master hand to release them. In the development section the composer marshals all his resources of imagination and ingenuity. He functions as the supreme architect, or as the general hurling his forces into battle. Each measure seems to grow out of the preceding by an inescapable law of cause and effect. Each adds to the drive and the momentum. Unity and diversity, logic and passion fuse at white heat to create much out of little.

The Recapitulation (Restatement)

When the developmental surge has run its course, the tension abates. A transition passage leads back to the home key. The beginning of the third section, the Recapitulation or Restatement, is in a sense the psychological climax of sonata form, just as the peak of many a journey is the return home. The first theme appears as we first heard it, in the home key, proclaiming the victory of unity over diversity, of continuity over change.

The Recapitulation follows the general path of the Exposition, restating the first and second themes more or less in their original form, but with the wealth of new meaning that these have taken on in the course of their wanderings. We experience the charm of returning to familiar ground, of recognizing old friends who have grown immeasurably since first we knew them. With the pleasure of recognition mingles a curious sense of many events having intervened; a sense of the passage of time.

Most important of all, in the Recapitulation the opposing elements are reconciled, the home key emerges triumphant. For this reason, the third section differs in one important detail from the Exposition: the composer must now remain in the home key. He therefore has to shift the second theme, which was originally in the contrasting key, to the home area (or as close to it as possible). In other words, although the second theme and its expansion unfold in substantially the same way as before, we now hear this material transposed into the home key. There follows the final pronouncement, the coda, in the home key. This is fashioned from material previously heard to which new matter is sometimes added. The coda rounds off the movement and asserts the victory of the home key with a vigorous final cadence.

The procedure just described is summed up in the following outline.

SONATA-ALLEGRO FORM (SONATA FORM)

Exposition * (or Statement)	Development	Recapitulation (or Restatement)
First theme and its expansion in home key	Builds up tension against the return to home key by	First theme and its expansion in home key
Bridge—modulates	(1) Frequent modulation to foreign keys	Bridge
Second theme and its expansion in contrasting key	(2) Fragmentation and manipulation of themes	Second theme and its expansion transposed to home area
Codetta. Cadence in contrasting key	Transition back to home key	Coda. Cadence in home key.

* May be preceded by a slow introduction.

An outline such as this is an oversimplification. It implies a ready-made mold into which the material is poured, whereas living form springs out of the material itself. The main features of the above outline are present in one shape or another in innumerable sonata-allegro movements. Yet no two are exactly alike in their disposition of the material. Each constitutes a unique solution of the problem in terms of character, mood, and relation of forces, just as every novel, play, or sonnet—and every living organism besides—is a particular and unique example of general structural principles. Sonata-allegro or first-movement form has proved capable of being adapted to the most diverse temperaments and ideas. The true artist—and it is his work alone that endures—allows the content to shape the form; so that what looks on paper like a fixed plan becomes, when transformed into living sound, a supple framework of infinite variety.

Even as the dramatist creates opposing personalities as the chief characters of his work, so the composer achieves a vivid contrast between the musical ideas that form the basis of the movement. The opposition between two themes may be underlined in a number of ways. Through a contrast in dynamics—loud against soft; in register—low against high; timbre—strings against winds, one instrumental combination against another; rhythm and tempo—an animated pattern against one that is sustained; tone production—legato against staccato; type of melody—an active melody line with wide range and leaps against one that is quieter; type of harmony—consonance against dissonance, diatonic harmony against chromatic; type of accompaniment—quietly moving chords against extended arpeggios. Only some of these may appear in any given work. One contrast is required, being the basis of the form: the contrast of key. And the opposition may be further intensified by putting one theme in the major and the other in minor.

From the interaction of all these emerged the conception of a first theme vigorously rhythmic and energetic, imparting to the movement its forward propulsion, as against a quietly lyrical second theme. Writers of the romantic era, partial to literary symbols, compared the two themes to the aggressively masculine as against the tenderly feminine. Such comparisons, needless to say, are farfetched; yet on one count this comparison is not entirely without validity. The novelist, by juxtaposing the masculine and the feminine, brings together the two creative forces in human life. In similar fashion the composer, by pitting against each other an idea based on rhythm and one based on melody, brings together within the grand form the two primal forces of music.

The novel is distinguished from the short story by its development of characters over a spacious canvas. Similarly, sonata-allegro is distinguished from the simple lyric forms by its development of themes over a large canvas. In a well-devised novel the characters are motivated by the inner forces of their personality. They seem at every juncture to have a choice; yet in the profoundest sense their decisions are inevitable. So in first-movement form the action springs inevitably from the germinal themes. The music follows one course rather than another not because the composer arbitrarily wills it so but because, given these premises, it must be so.

Sonata form has been a living force in our music for two hundred years, and in that time has survived vast changes in musical taste and thought. It has done so because it gives the composer so rich an opportunity to work out purely musical ideas in a purely musical way. It is an epic whose emotional content is rooted in life itself, yet whose action is projected without reference to anything outside music. It issues from the fertile soil of human experience, but it purifies that experience and lifts it to the ideal plane of abstraction.

The reader should be cautioned, in conclusion, against a widespread misconception. The conventional description of sonata-allegro form, by its emphasis upon the few themes that serve as building blocks for an instrumental movement, seems to imply that everything between these themes is in the nature of transitional material. Unfortunately many people listen in precisely this way to a symphonic movement, waiting for the themes—that is, the melodies they recognize—just as, in another context, they wait for the arias in an opera. But from everything we have said it is clear that the sonata-allegro movement is an organic unity in which the growth, the development, the destiny of a theme is no less important than the theme itself (just as, in assessing a human action, we consider its consequences no less than the deed proper).

It is equally clear that the masters evolved the sonata form precisely because it enabled them to establish an idea in time-space and afforded them room to investigate its consequences. From the structural point of view the theme includes not only the germinal idea but also its expansion and development. The musical examples in the past chapters and in those to come represent what is generally regarded as "Theme 1" or "Theme 2" of a sonata movement. They are actually only the kernels, the beginnings of themes. The theme, in the profoundly musical sense, must be considered to include not only the few notes on the page but also the "etc."—that is, the passage or section that constitutes the flowering of the idea. It is only when we take this larger view of the theme that we come to understand the symphonic movement for what it is: a continuous expansion and growth of musical ideas from first note to last, from which not a measure may be omitted without disturbing the equilibrium and the organic oneness of the whole. Only by listening to the movement in this way do we apprehend the essential qualities of symphonic style, its concentration, its continuity, its unflagging dynamism.

꠸꠸꠸ *CHAPTER 48* *꠸꠸꠸*

The Sonata, Continued:
The Other Movements

"To write a symphony means, to me, to construct a world."
                                    Gustav Mahler

WE now consider the other types of musical structure that came to be included in the cycle of movements.

Theme and Variations

Repetition, we saw, is a basic element of musical structure. This being so, composers devised ways of varying an idea when they repeated it. Variation is an important procedure that is to be found in every

species of music. But there is one type of piece in which it constitutes
the ruling principle—the *theme and variations*. The theme is stated
at the outset, so that the audience will know the basic idea that
serves as the point of departure. The melody may be of the composer's
invention, as in the second movement of Haydn's *Surprise Symphony;*
or one that he has borrowed from another, as in the case of Brahms's
Variations on a Theme by Paganini. The theme is apt to be a small two-
or three-part form, simple in character so as to allow room for elaboration. There follows a series of variations in which certain features of
the original idea are retained while others are altered. Each variation
sets forth the idea with some new modification—one might say in a
new disguise—through which the listener glimpses something of the
original theme.

To the process of variation the composer brings all the techniques
of musical embellishment. He may, to begin with, vary the melody. To
indicate the simplest way that this is done, suppose a melody to move
from C to E. One may ornament it by including the intermediate notes,
transforming the melodic progression into C-D-E, C-D-D♯-E or C-C♯-
D-D♯-E. In this way a more florid line results, although the melody is
not fundamentally changed. Conversely, one may omit certain notes
and thereby reduce the melody to its skeletal outline. Melodic variation is a favorite procedure in the jazz band, where the solo player
embellishes a popular tune with a series of arabesques.

In harmonic variation the chords that accompany a melody are replaced by others. Diatonic harmonies may give way to chromatic, simple triads to complex dissonances. Or the melody may be entirely
omitted, the variation being based on the harmonic skeleton. Or the
type of accompaniment may be changed; for example, from chords in
block formation to decorative broken chords (arpeggios). The melody
may be shifted to a lower register with the harmony sounding above
it. This is a favorite type of variation in piano music, where the melody
is transferred to the left hand while the right plays the harmonic figuration.

So too the rhythm, meter, and tempo may be varied, with interesting
changes in the nature of the tune. This may take on the guise of a
waltz, a polka, a minuet, a march. The texture may be enriched by
interweaving the melody with new themes. Or the original theme may
itself become an accompaniment for a new melody. By combining these
methods with changes in dynamics and tone color, the expressive content of the theme may be changed, so that it is presented now as a funeral
march, now as a serenade, folk dance, caprice, or boat song. This type
of character variation was much in favor in the romantic era.

Eighteenth-century composers in general retained the structural outlines of the theme. What the listener heard was a series of separate sections, each of which revealed another possibility of variation. In the nineteenth century the outlines of the separate variations were veiled, the form was tightened and unified. Composers departed more freely from the theme, welding the parts into a whole and accumulating tension through a steady building up from the simple to the complex.

The theme with variations challenges the composer's inventiveness and craftsmanship. It gives him the opportunity to manipulate purely musical material in a purely musical way, and enables him to achieve a high degree of unity in diversity. One therefore understands why variation form has attracted composers for the last three hundred years. The theme with variations was widely cultivated as an independent piece. In the second half of the eighteenth century it was taken over as one of the movements of the sonata cycle. There it served as the second or slow movement (as in Haydn's *Surprise Symphony*); as the fourth or final movement (Mozart, Clarinet Quintet); and in some instances as the first movement (Beethoven, Piano Sonata in A-flat, Opus 26).

Minuet and Trio

The minuet originated in the French court in the mid-seventeenth century; its stately ³ time embodied the ideal of grace of an aristocratic age. In the eighteenth century the minuet was taken over into the sonata cycle, where it served as the third movement, or occasionally the second.

Since dance music lends itself to symmetrical construction, we often find in the minuet a clear-cut structure based on phrases of four and eight measures. (All the same, the minuets of Haydn and Mozart reveal an abundance of nonsymmetrical phrases.) In tempo the minuet ranges from stateliness to a lively pace and whimsical character. As a matter of fact, certain of Haydn's minuets are closer in spirit to the village green than to the palace ballroom.

The custom prevailed in the seventeenth century of presenting two dances as a group, the first being repeated at the end of the second (A-B-A). The one in the middle was frequently arranged for only three instruments; hence the name *trio,* which persisted even after the customary setting for three was abandoned. The trio as a rule is lighter in texture and quieter of gait. Frequently woodwind tone figures prominently in this section, creating an out-of-doors atmosphere that lends it a special charm. At the end of the trio we find *da capo* or D.C. (from the beginning), signifying that the first section is to be played over again. Minuet and trio, then, is a symmetrical

three-part (A-B-A) structure in which each part in turn is a small a-b-a
or ternary form.

A   B   A

a-b-a   c-d-c   a-b-a

This structure is elaborated through repetition of the subsections,
a procedure that the composer indicates with a repeat sign (:||:).
However, when the minuet returns after the trio the repeat signs are
customarily ignored. A codetta may round off each section.

A   B   A

a:||:b-a:||:   c:||:d-c:|| a-b-a

In the nineteenth-century symphony the minuet was displaced by the
scherzo. The name had made its appearance in certain quartets of Haydn
and in the sonatas and symphonies of Beethoven. The scherzo is generally the third movement, occasionally the second. It is usually in $\frac{3}{4}$ time.
Like the minuet, it is a three-part form (scherzo-trio-scherzo), the first
section being repeated after the middle part. But it differs from the minuet in its headlong pace and vigorous rhythm. The scherzo—the name,
it will be recalled, is the Italian word for "jest"—is marked by abrupt
changes of mood ranging from the humorous or the whimsical to the
mysterious and even demonic. In the hands of Beethoven the scherzo
became a movement of immense driving force.

The Rondo

The rondo is a lively movement suffused with the spirit of the dance.
Its distinguishing characteristic is the recurrence of a central idea—the
rondo theme—in alternation with one or more subsidiary themes. Its
symmetrical sections create a balanced architecture that is satisfying
esthetically and easy to grasp. In its simplest form, A-B-A-B-A, the
rondo is an extension of the A-B-A principle. If there are two subordinate themes the sections may follow an A-B-A-C-A or similar pattern.

The true rondo as developed by the classical masters was more ambitious in scope. Characteristic was the formation A-B-A-C-A-B-A. The
first A-B-A was in the nature of an exposition and the corresponding
A-B-A at the end was a recapitulation. Between them was the C section,
which served as a kind of development. What with contrasts of key and
elaborate transitional passages, this type of rondo took on the spaciousness of sonata form and came to be known as a rondo-sonata.

Actually one may speak of rondo style as well as rondo form, for the
essence of the rondo—at any rate as Haydn and Mozart cultivated it—
is its vivacity and good humor. Because the theme is to be heard over

and over again it must be catchy and relaxing. One should point out, however, that not every movement that follows the rondo form has the spirit of the gay classical rondo. The rondo figured in eighteenth- and nineteenth-century music both as an independent piece and as a member of the sonata cycle. In the sonata it served as the final movement.

The Sonata Cycle as a Whole

The four-movement cycle of the classical masters, as found in their symphonies, concertos, sonatas, string quartets, and other types of chamber music, became the vehicle for their most important instrumental music. The following outline sums up the common practice of the classic-romantic era. It will be helpful to the reader, provided he remembers that it is no more than a general scheme and does not necessarily apply to all works of this kind. In Beethoven's Ninth Symphony, for example, the scherzo is the second movement while the Adagio comes third.

| | | | Tempo | |
Move-ment	Character	Form	Mozart: Symphony No. 40	Beethoven: Symphony No. 5
First	Epic-dramatic	Sonata-allegro form (Sonata form)	Allegro molto	Allegro con brio
Second	Slow and lyrical. In the 19th century may range from the tragic to the whimsical.	Theme and variations Sonata form A-B-A	Andante	Andante con moto
Third	Dancelike: Minuet (18th century) Scherzo (19th century)	Minuet and trio (A-B-A) Scherzo and trio (A-B-A)	Allegretto	Allegro
Fourth	Lively (18th century) Triumphal: the romantic "apotheosis" (19th century)	Sonata-allegro Rondo Rondo-sonata Theme and variations	Allegro molto	Allegro

The classical masters of the sonata thought of the four movements of the cycle as self-contained entities connected by identity of key. First, third, and fourth movements were in the home key, with the second movement in a contrasting key. The nineteenth century sought a more obvious connection between movements—a thematic connection. This need was met by cyclical structure, in which a theme from the earlier movements appeared in the later ones as a kind of motto or unifying thread.

The sonata cycle satisfied the need of composers for an extended instrumental work of an abstract character. It derived its being from the nature of the instruments. It mobilized the contrasts of key and mode inherent in the major-minor system. It created a spacious frame that encompassed the utmost diversity within a unity. Upon the insubstantial stuff of sound it implanted the heroic dimensions of architecture—length, width, and depth; spaciousness and symmetry. And it achieved all this according to principles deriving exclusively from the nature of sound. The sonata cycle has an epic-dramatic quality, leaving the listener with the sense of a vast action consummated, an eventful journey brought to its predestined conclusion. With its fusion of sensuous, emotional, and intellectual elements, its intermingling of lyric contemplation and action, the sonata cycle may justly claim to be one of the most ingenious art forms ever devised by man.

PART FOUR

Eighteenth-Century Classicism

"When a nation brings its innermost nature to consummate expression in arts and letters we speak of its classic period. Classicism stands for experience, for spiritual and human maturity which has deep roots in the cultural soil of the nation, for the mastery of the means of expression in technique and form, and for a definite conception of the world and of life; the final compression of the artistic values of a people."

Paul Henry Lang: *Music in Western Civilization*

CHAPTER 49

The Classical Spirit

'Tis more to guide, than spur the Muse's steed;
Restrain his fury, than provoke his speed;
The winged courser, like a gen'rous horse,
Shows most true mettle when you check his course.
                    Alexander Pope: *Essay on Criticism*

IN OUR discussion of nineteenth-century romanticism we cautioned the reader against the misconception that classical art is all form and no feeling, while romantic art is all feeling and no form. Let us emphasize again that there can be no art without emotion, since the work of art is born out of the artist's need to communicate his own experience to his fellow men. So too there can be no art without form, since the creative act by its very nature implies choice, the selection of certain details and the exclusion of others. The artist makes use of the emotions he feels and the forms he knows, striving always to find the form that will best suit what he has to say.

Where the classic and romantic approaches to art differ is in their emphasis; that is, in the nature of the relationship between content and form, between the emotion and the discipline necessary to give it shape. The romantic artist, we saw, values the expression of feeling above all. Hence in romantic art the emotion often struggles against the discipline of form. From this struggle stems the surcharged emotional atmosphere that surrounds so many romantic works. The classical artist, on the other hand, seeks the ideal balance between form and content. He is apt to exercise greater control over the emotional forces behind

The Parthenon, Athens.
"In classical art every detail receives its meaning from the whole."
285

his art. He tries to reconcile the claims of reason and emotion, to bring into harmony the impulses of the head and of the heart. Out of this harmony comes the poise, the serenity, the controlled quality of classical art.

The Nature of Classicism

The dictionary defines classicism in two ways: in general terms, as pertaining to the highest order of excellence in literature and art; specifically, pertaining to the culture of the ancient Greeks and Romans. Implicit in the classical attitude is the notion that supreme excellence has been reached in the past and may be attained again through adherence to tradition and discipline. In this regard classicism is opposed to the romantic revolt against the heritage of the past.

Being part of a tradition implies a relationship to something outside oneself. The classical artist participates in the common practice of his time. Unlike the romantic, he neither glories in nor emphasizes his apartness from other men. His prime aim is to achieve the highest with the materials and procedures at his disposal. The romantic is preoccupied with self-expression; the classicist is more interested in universal values.

The power of art to express emotion is self-evident to the classicist, whereas to the romantic it is a constant source of wonder. The classical artist regards neither his individuality nor his personal experience as the primary material of his art. The work itself exists for him as an entity, rather than as an emanation of his ego. His attention is directed rather to clarity of form, strength of line, and solid craftsmanship. He strives for an objective view of reality, invoking beauty and reason: what the senses can enjoy and the mind accept. To the uninhibited exuberance of romanticism he opposes an urbane maturity. Freed from the urgencies of the self, he strives to present the ideal in its essential purity; he therefore seeks symbols that will have universal validity. This wholeness of view encourages the qualities of order, stability, control, and harmonious proportion that we associate with the classical style. In romantic art the detail often leads its own life, independent of the whole. In classical art, on the other hand, every part subserves the over-all line. Every detail receives its meaning from the whole.

Classical art is dynamic; but its drama, going beyond the personal, derives from the artist's identification with man and nature. In classical art the emotion is purified, transfigured under the aegis of beauty into an ideal serenity. The particular is raised to the level of the collective-universal. Romanticism exploits the wonder and ecstasy of art, its daemonic force, its intimations of the unknown and the irrational. Clas-

Classicism, old and new. Ancient Roman sculpture, *Ariadne Sleeping*.
Madame Récamier by Jacques Louis David, 1748–1825.
"An art of noble simplicity . . ."

sicism explores the order and discipline of art, its potentialities for rational expression and exquisite workmanship. It affirms the victory of man's ordering will and reason over the chaotic forces of the subconscious. In J. B. Priestley's fine phrase, "The Classical depends upon the conscious mind, the Romantic upon the unconscious." Both the classic and the romantic spring from the nature of man; both, in turn, minister to his nature.

As we pointed out in our discussion of romanticism, neither the classical nor the romantic spirit is limited to any one time. Both have alternated throughout the history of culture. However, just as conditions in the nineteenth century were favorable for a longer and more individualistic period of romanticism than any other, so the social climate of the eighteenth century favored the emergence of the classical spirit in its purest phase.

Eighteenth-Century Classicism

The culture of the eighteenth century was under the patronage of an aristocracy for whom the arts were a necessary adornment of life. Art was part of the elaborate ritual that surrounded the existence of princes. In such a society, where the ruling caste enjoys its power through hereditary right, tradition is apt to be prized and the past revered. The center of art life is the palace and the privileged minority residing therein. In these high places the emphasis is on elegance of manner and beauty of style.

The art of the eighteenth century bears the imprint of the spacious palaces and formal gardens, with their balanced proportions and finely wrought detail, that formed the setting for enlightened despotism. As the second half of the century got under way, Louis XV presided over the extravagant fetes in Versailles (although he foresaw the deluge). Frederick the Great ruled in Prussia, Maria Theresa in Austria, Catherine the Great in Russia. Yet disruptive forces were swiftly gathering beneath the glittering surface. The American Revolution dealt a shattering blow to the doctrine of the divine right of kings. And before the century had ended, Europe was convulsed by the French Revolution.

The second half of the eighteenth century, consequently, witnessed both the twilight of the *ancien régime* and the dawn of a new political-economic alignment in Europe; specifically, the transfer of power from the aristocracy to the middle class, whose wealth was based on a rapidly expanding capitalism, on mines and factories, steam power and railroads. This shift was made possible by the Industrial Revolution, which gathered momentum in the mid-eighteenth century with a series of important inventions, from Watt's steam engine and Hargreaves's spinning jenny in the 1760s to Cartwright's power loom in 1785 and Eli Whitney's cotton gin in 1793.

The second half of the eighteenth century saw significant advances in science. Benjamin Franklin discovered electricity in 1752, Priestley discovered oxygen in 1774, Jenner perfected vaccination in 1796, Laplace advanced his mechanistic view of the universe and Volta invented the voltaic pile in 1800. There were important events in intellectual life, such as the publication of Winckelmann's *History of Ancient Art* (1764), of the French *Encyclopédie* (1751–72), and the first edition of the *Encyclopaedia Britannica* (1771). The final quarter of the century produced such landmarks as Adam Smith's *The Wealth of Nations*, Kant's *Critique of Pure Reason*, Rousseau's *Confessions*, Gibbon's *Decline and Fall of the Roman Empire*, Boswell's *Life of Johnson*, and Malthus's *Essay on Population*.

The intellectual climate of the classical era, consequently, was nourished by two opposing streams. On the one hand classical art captured the exquisite refinement of a way of life that was drawing to a close. On the other it caught the intimations of a new way of life that was struggling to emerge. This dualism is of the essence in the classical era and pervades all its attitudes. For example, the eighteenth century has been called the Age of Reason; but the two opposing camps invoked reason in diametrically opposite ways. The apologists of the status quo appealed to reason in order to justify the existing order. Early in the century Leibnitz taught that this was "the best of all possible worlds," and Pope proclaimed that "Whatever is, is right." As the century wore on, however, this spurious optimism became ever more difficult to maintain. The opponents of the established order, the *philosophes* who created the *Grande Encyclopédie* as an instrument of the Enlightenment—Voltaire, Diderot, Rousseau, Condorcet, d'Alembert and their comrades—also invoked reason, but for the purpose of attacking the existing order. Therewith these ideologues of the rising middle class became the prophets of the approaching upheaval.

The romantics, we saw, idealized the Middle Ages. But to eighteenth-century thinkers the medieval period represented a thousand years of barbarism—the Dark Ages. The term *Gothic* represented everything that was opposed to what they regarded as rational and cultivated. Their ideal was the civilization of ancient Greece and Rome. To the Gothic cathedral, with its stained-glass windows, its bizarre gargoyles, its ribbed columns soaring heavenward in passionate mysticism, they opposed the Greek temple, a thing of beauty, unity and proportion, lightness and grace.

Sir Joshua Reynolds, 1723–1792, *Jane, Countess of Harrington.*

"The fashionable painters of mid-eighteenth-century England included Greek urns and ruins in their portraits of the aristocracy."

Yet here too the revival of interest in classical antiquity meant different things to the opposing camps. The aristocrats and their spokesmen exalted Hellenism as the symbol of a rational, objective attitude that guarded one against becoming too deeply involved with the issues of life. They saw the ancient gods, kings, and heroes as a reflection of themselves—themselves ennobled, transfigured. Sir Joshua Reynolds, the most fashionable painter of mid-eighteenth-century England and the first president of its Royal Academy, included Greek urns and ruins in his portraits of the aristocracy, and advised the portrait painter to dress his figure "something with the general air of the antique for the sake of dignity." But to the protagonists of the middle class, Greece and Rome represented city-states that had rebelled against tyrants and thrown off despotism. It was in this spirit that the foremost painter of revolutionary France, Jacques Louis David, decked his huge commemorative canvases with the symbols of Athenian and Roman democracy. In this spirit, too, Thomas Jefferson lauded David for having "ennobled the contemporary countenance with the classical quality of ancient republican virtue," and proceeded to pattern both the Capitol and the University of Virginia after Greek and Roman temples.

The classical point of view held sway in English letters to such an extent that the mid-eighteenth century has come to be called the Augustan Age. Its arbiter was Samuel Johnson, whose position of leadership in literature was as undisputed as was that of his friend Reynolds in painting. Both men belonged to an influential circle that helped to determine the style of the Augustan Age: in prose, the stately sentence of balanced construction and rolling cadence; in poetry, a preference for the general rather than the particular, for social sentiment rather than personal passion, for the polished couplet that was the legacy of Pope; in painting, a reasoned approach to the problems of spatial organization, with emphasis upon correctness of line, balance and symmetry, the whole resulting in a pleasing formalism.

But this essentially aristocratic type of art was not the only one that flourished in this paradoxical age. The English novel, which captured a foremost position in European literature during the first half of the eighteenth century, came out of a humbler sphere. The novels of Samuel Richardson, Henry Fielding, Laurence Sterne, and Tobias Smollett were suffused with homely bourgeois sentiment; for the Age of Reason was also, curiously, the Age of Sensibility. Sense and sensibility, to borrow Jane Austen's title, increasingly permeate the art of the time, as is apparent from the work of such poets as Thomas Gray, George Crabbe, Oliver Goldsmith, and William Cowper; and the sensibility steadily broadens into a trend toward the romantic. Within the formal stream of Augustan classicism we become aware of a current of tender sentiment that constitutes an early manifestation of the romantic spirit.

Thus it is that the Age of Reason begins to give way to the Age of Romance considerably earlier than is commonly supposed. In the 1760s there already appeared a number of works that clearly indicate the new preoccupation with a picturesque and romantic medievalism: Macpherson's *Ossian*, Percy's *Reliques of Ancient English Poetry*, and the new "Gothic" novel as exemplified by Horace Walpole's *Castle of Otranto*. Akin to the spirit of these was Walpole's house at Strawberry Hill. In the same decade Rousseau, the "father of romanticism," produced some of his most significant writings. His celebrated dictum, "Man is born free and everywhere he is in chains," epitomizes the temper of the time. So too the first outcropping of the romantic spirit in Germany, the movement known as *Sturm und Drang* ("Storm and Stress"), took shape in the 1770s, when it produced two characteristic works by its most significant young writers—the *Sorrows of Werther* by Goethe and *The Robbers* by Schiller. (Goethe, it will be remembered, became a favorite lyric poet of the romantic composers.) By the end of the century the atmosphere had completely changed. The two most important English poets of the late eighteenth century—

Robert Burns and William Blake—stand entirely outside the classical stream. As does the greatest end-of-the-century painter, Goya, whose passionate realism anticipates a later age.

Late eighteenth-century culture, therefore, is neither as exclusively aristocratic nor as exclusively classical as we like to believe. It assimilated and was nourished by both democratic and pre-romantic elements. Precisely its dual nature lends it its subtle and pervasive charm.

The Artist Under Patronage

The eighteenth-century artist generally functioned under the system of aristocratic patronage. He created for a public high above him in social rank; his patrons were interested in his product rather than in his personality. To be personal in such circumstances would have been an impertinence. He was therefore inevitably directed toward a classical objectivity and reserve.

The artist under patronage was a master craftsman, an artisan working on direct commission from his patron. He was not concerned, as was his nineteenth-century counterpart, with posterity, with the nature of genius or inspiration. His art was neither miracle nor mystery; or better, it was so much of both that no one ever stopped to labor the point. The artist of the classical era produced works for immediate use, sustained by daily contact with his public. This was a public of connoisseurs for whom familiarity with art was part of their birthright. He could be as fastidious, as subtle as he pleased. No trouble he might take was too great, no detail too nice for so knowing an audience.

In point of social status the artist in livery was little better than a servant. This was not quite as depressing as it sounds, for in that society everybody was a servant of the prince save other princes. The patronage system gave artists economic security and a social framework within which they could function. They had to avoid ideas that might disturb or bewilder their princely patrons; but within the common practice of their time they were free to follow the dictates of their fancy. The patronage system offered important advantages to the great artists who successfully adjusted to its requirements, as the career of Haydn richly shows. On the other hand, Mozart's tragic end illustrates how heavy was the penalty exacted from one who was unable to make that adjustment.

Eighteenth-century classicism, then, mirrored the unique moment in history when the old world was dying and the new was in process of being born. From the meeting of two historic forces emerged an art of noble simplicity whose achievement in music constitutes one of the pinnacles of Western culture.

CHAPTER 50

Classicism in Music (c. 1775-1825)

"Ought not the musician, quite as much as the poet and painter, to study nature? In nature he can study man, its noblest creature."

Johann Friedrich Reichardt (1774)

CLASSICISM in music differs in one important respect from classicism in the other arts. In poetry and drama, painting, sculpture, and architecture, the classically minded artist drew inspiration from the models of ancient Greece and Rome. Composers had no such models, for the music of antiquity had not survived into modern times. In its most immediate sense the term *classicism,* consequently, applies to music by analogy rather than directly.

The classical period in music centers about the major achievements of the four masters of the Viennese school—Haydn, Mozart, Beethoven, and Schubert—and their contemporaries. Their art reached its flowering in a time of great musical experimentation and discovery, when musicians were confronted by three challenging problems: first, to explore to the full the possibilities offered by the major-minor system; second, to perfect a large form of absolute instrumental music that would mobilize those possibilities to the fullest degree; and third, having found this ideal form in the sonata cycle, to differentiate between its various types—the solo and duo sonata, trio, quartet, and other kinds of chamber music, the concerto, and the symphony. The classical masters solved these problems so brilliantly that their symphonies and concertos, piano sonatas, duo sonatas, string quartets, and similar works remain unsurpassed models for those who have come after. They evolved a dynamic instrumental language that was the perfect expression in sound of the processes of thematic growth and development which lay at the core of their thinking. In so doing they created a new world of musical thought and sound. At the same time we should remember that they perfected their art at a time when the forces of romanticism were gathering strength. Their works, consequently—especially the late ones—are not devoid of romantic elements.

If by classical we mean adherence to traditional forms, we certainly cannot apply the term to the composers of the Viennese school. They experimented boldly and ceaselessly with the materials at their dis-

293

posal. An enormous distance separates Haydn's early symphonies and string quartets from his later ones; the same is true of Mozart, Beethoven, and Schubert. Nor can we call these masters classical if by doing so we identify them with the eighteenth-century world. Beethoven and Schubert were men of the nineteenth century, their careers unfolded after the French Revolution, they inhabited a different social climate than Haydn and Mozart had known. Indeed, though Schubert's symphonies and chamber music are in the classical orbit, his songs and piano pieces—as we saw in an earlier section of this book—stamp him as a romantic.

What is classical about these four composers, who rank among the greatest that ever lived, is the perfect fusion of form and content in their work, the infallible control of the emotion within the form. What is classical, too, is the subordination of every detail to the over-all design. For the romantic composer color and harmony, melody and rhythm often existed as ends in themselves. For the classicist these functioned in the closest possible relationship, serving a single goal: unity of design; design as the principle of artistic law and order, born of the mating of reason and emotion. Out of this union came the chiseled structures of the Viennese masters, which offered a perfect frame for the classical impulse toward logical organization of the parts within the whole. In their works the form sprang out of the material, the material demanded the form. It is this unparalleled unity of form and content, of the idea and its one inevitable expression, that constitutes the truly classical element in eighteenth-century music in general, and in the music of the Viennese school in particular.

We have made reference before to Nietzsche's distinction between the Dionysian and the Apollonian. The classical temper finds a fit symbol in the god of light, whose sculptured beauty so eloquently proclaims the cult of harmonious proportion.

Main Currents in Classical Music

Musical classicism is in many respects the direct opposite of musical romanticism. Whereas the romantic composers sought to bring instrumental music into close relation with literature and painting, the classicists upheld the independence of music as a self-contained art. Hence romanticism leaned toward program music, classicism toward absolute. Romanticism glorified folklore and exploited peasant song and dance; the music of classicism came out of the culture of cities and the sophistication of princely courts. Romantic art is a democratic art; classical art is basically aristocratic (even though the popular tone, significantly, makes its appearance in the dance forms of Haydn). Romantic art was intensely national; classical music created a universal style disseminated through two international art forms—Italian opera and Viennese symphony. Romantic music favored exotic atmosphere and picturesque detail, whereas classical music concentrated on the development of largely abstract musical ideas.

Romantic music sounded the nature tone in its landscapes and sea scenes. Classical music on the whole ignored the scenic element, fastening instead upon the landscape of the spirit. For the romantics music was an enchantment, a religion. The classical era enjoyed music as an embellishment of gracious living. Romantic pessimism is alien to this urbane and essentially optimistic art.

Vocal Music

The opera house was a focal point of musical activity and experimentation in the classical era. Opera was the most important branch of musical entertainment and the one that reached the widest public. It offered a composer the most lucrative returns and the surest path to success. Classical opera was based on principles directly opposite to those that prevailed in the romantic music drama. The music was the point of departure and imposed its forms on the drama. Each scene was a closed musical unit. The separate numbers were conceived as parts of the whole and held together in a carefully planned framework. There was the greatest possible distinction between the rapid patter of recitative and the lyric curve of aria. The voice reigned supreme, yet the orchestra displayed all the vivacity of the classical instrumental style.

A significant development was the importance of comic opera (*opera buffa*), which adopted certain features of the serious opera and in turn influenced the latter. Far from being an escapist form of entertainment, comic opera was directly related to the life of the time. Its emphasis was on the affairs of "little people," on swift action, pointed situations, spontaneous emotion, and sharpness of characterization. This popular lyric theater showed an abundance of racy melody, brilliant orchestration, and lively rhythms. Characteristic were the ensemble numbers at the end of the act, of a verve and drive that influenced all branches of music. Classical *opera buffa* steadily expanded its scope until it culminated in the works of the greatest musical dramatist of the eighteenth century—Mozart.

As a center of music making, the Church retained its importance alongside opera house and aristocratic salon. Whereas the first half of the century had seen the high point of Protestant music in the art of Bach, the Catholic countries now assumed first place, especially the Habsburg domains. The masters of the classical Viennese school produced a great deal of church music, Masses, vespers, litanies, and the like. The notion has been advanced that the Masses of the classical era are not true church music because of their operatic and symphonic elements. Such reasoning sets up a distinction between church and secular style—between religion and life—that simply did not exist for the musicians of the classical period. They did as composers had done for centuries before them: they used the living idiom of their day (an idiom based on opera and symphony) to express their faith in God and man.

Instrumental Music

As we have indicated, constant experimenting in the field of instrumental music throughout the eighteenth century led to a clear distinction between the sonata for one medium and that for another. The piano sonata became the most ambitious form of solo music. The piano was supplanting the harpsichord and clavichord as an instrument for the home. Through the piano sonata, composers worked out new conceptions of keyboard style and sonata structure, creating a rich literature for both amateur and virtuoso.

Chamber music enjoyed a great flowering in the classical era, as did a type of composition that stood midway between chamber music and symphony, known as *divertimento*. The title fixes the character of this category of music as sociable diversion or entertainment. Closely related were the serenade, the *notturno* (night piece), and the *cassation* (a term of obscure origin probably referring to something in the streets or out-of-doors). Contemporary accounts tell of groups of street musicians who performed these works—for strings, winds, or both—outside the homes of the wealthy or in a quiet square before an appreciative audience of their townsmen. Salzburg and Vienna were pre-eminent in the richness and variety of their street music. The unique distinction of this popular music lies in the fact that its literature was enriched by the great masters. For once, "popular" and "classical" were united, giving rise to one of the most attractive species of eighteenth-century music.

The classical masters established the orchestra as we know it today. They based the ensemble on the blending of the four instrumental groups. The heart of this orchestra was the string choir. Woodwinds, used with great imagination, ably seconded the strings. The brass sustained the harmonies and contributed body to the tone mass, while the kettledrums supplied rhythmic life and vitality. The eighteenth-century orchestra numbered from thirty to forty players. The volume of sound was still considered in relation to the salon rather than the concert hall. (It was toward the end of the classical period that musical life began to move from the one to the other.) Foreign to classical art were the swollen sonorities of the late nineteenth century. The orchestra of Haydn and Mozart lent itself to delicate nuances in which each timbre stood out radiantly. The masters used their medium with surpassing economy, attaining a variety of color, a transparency and lightness of texture that are among the most enchanting manifestations of the classical temper.

The classical orchestra brought to absolute music a number of effects long familiar in the opera house. The gradual crescendo and decrescendo established themselves as staples of the new symphonic style. Hardly less conspicuous were the abrupt alternations of soft and loud, sudden accents, dramatic pauses; the use of tremolo, pizzicato, and similar devices of operatic music. The classical masters created an expressive and dynamic style of orchestral writing in which all the instruments participated actively. The interchange and imitation of themes among the various instrumental groups assumed the excitement of a witty conversation. The classical orchestral style did not exist as a value in itself; it sprang from the nature of the things it had to say and was perfectly suited to those.

Within the orchestral domain, the sonata cycle took on ample proportions. Of paramount importance was the sonata for solo instrument and orchestra—the concerto, which combined a virtuoso part for the featured player with the full symphonic resources of the instrumental ensemble. The piano concerto was the chief type, although other solo instruments were not neglected. But the central place in instrumental music was reserved, naturally, for the "sonata for orchestra"—the symphony. This grew rapidly in dimension and significance until, with the final works of Mozart and Haydn, it became the most important type of absolute music. Within its spacious outlines the masters of the classical era worked out all those problems of musical organization that we discussed in the chapters on sonata form. In so doing they achieved the true symphonic style, projected in a musical language of such expressiveness and élan that musicians everywhere still regard it as an unsurpassable ideal.

The classical sonata form was based upon a clear-cut opposition of keys. This demanded a harmony well rooted in the key (diatonic). By the same token romanticism aspired to dissolve all boundaries, favoring a harmony that veiled the contours of the key (chromatic). We have here an important distinction between the classical symphony and its romantic counterpart. The grand design of the Viennese masters was suffused, in the nineteenth century, with lyricism and chromaticism —in literary terms, with infinite longing.

Further Aspects of Musical Classicism

Audiences of the classical era differed from those of our time in one important respect. Their attention was directed mainly to the hearing of new works by living composers; whereas our public shies away from contemporary music but flocks to hear the standard repertory reinterpreted again and again. Such ancestor worship was unknown in the eighteenth century. The public then had only a mild interest in the music of earlier times. People were interested primarily in *what* was played; we are concerned primarily with *how* it is played. The star of the classical scene was the creator of music. The spotlight in our scene belongs, as far as the general public is concerned, to the performer. During the classical era there had not yet arisen a class of virtuoso pianists, violinists, and conductors who would serve as middlemen between composer and public, and whose contribution would be solely their personal way of performing the master's work. Composers were directly involved in the playing of their music—indeed, they were virtuosos too. Beethoven and Mozart were outstanding pianists in their time; Haydn appeared in England as conductor of his symphonies. Eighteenth-century eagerness for new music may be compared to the present-day appetite for new films—a situation, needless to say, most stimulating to production. The classical era, in brief, was an ideal climate for the living composer; whereas ours is pre-eminently devoted to the dead one.

The classical era created an all-European culture that transcended national boundaries. In this it reflected the international character of the two most powerful institutions in social life: the aristocracy and the Church. Indeed, the eighteenth century was the last stronghold of internationalism in art (until the twentieth began). German, French, and Italian influences intermingled in the art of Haydn and Mozart. These masters were not German in the way that Wagner was, or Schumann, or Brahms. Romantic nationalism, we saw, opened up new dialects to composers. By the same token something was lost of the breadth of view that made artists like Beethoven or Goethe in the highest sense citizens of the world.

This inter-European language was shared by all the contemporaries, greater and lesser, of Haydn and Mozart, in Austria and Germany, Italy and France. We have but to hear a few bars of their music to recognize that they spoke the same idiom as the two Viennese masters. They did not speak it as profoundly or as eloquently, which is why many of them have survived only in the history books; but they spoke it with utter assurance, for it was the one musical language of the age. The cult of personality had not yet come to the fore. We do not find in the eighteenth century so marked a difference between contemporaries as we do in the nineteenth between say, Wagner and Brahms; or, in the twentieth, between Bartók and Stravinsky.

Classicism achieved the final synthesis of the intellectual currents of eighteenth-century life. The great theme of this pure and Apollonian art was man, the measure of all things: a rational creature working out his destiny in an ordered universe whose outer garment was the beauty of nature and whose inner law was the clarity of reason. Eighteenth-century classicism struck the ideal balance between external form and inner content. So delicate an equilibrium springs only from the perfect fusion of matter and spirit. It is as rare in art as in life.

CHAPTER 51

Joseph Haydn (1732-1809)

"I have only just learned in my old age how to use the wind instruments, and now that I do understand them I must leave the world."

THE LONG career of Joseph Haydn spanned the critical decades of the classic era. He absorbed all that the eighteenth century had achieved and succeeded in bringing its diverse elements into a remarkable unity of style. The legacy he left was a contribution to music in scope and significance second to none.

His Life

He was born in a village in Lower Austria, son of a wheelwright. Folk song and dance were his natural heritage. Displaying uncommon musical aptitude as a child, he was taught the rudiments by a distant relative, a schoolmaster. In later life Haydn was grateful for the rigid discipline to which he had been subjected. "Almighty God, to whom I give thanks for His many mercies, gave me such facility in music that by the time I was six I stood up like a man and sang Masses in the church choir and could play a little on the keyboard and violin."

The beauty of his voice secured him a place as chorister in St.

Stephen's Cathedral in Vienna, where he remained till he was sixteen. With the breaking of his voice his days at the choir school came to an end. He established himself in an attic in Vienna, managed to obtain a dilapidated clavier, and set himself to master his craft. Those were the lean years. He eked out a living through teaching and accompanying, and often joined the roving bands of musicians who performed in the streets. In this way the popular Viennese idiom entered his style along with the folk idiom he had absorbed in childhood.

Joseph Haydn.

He was accompanist for a time to the pupils of Nicola Porpora, an Italian composer and teacher of singing who aided the young man's artistic development. Haydn before long attracted the notice of the music-loving aristocracy of Vienna, and was invited to the country house of a nobleman who maintained a small group of musicians. Here Haydn's attention was directed to the divertimento and string quartet. His next patron kept a small orchestra, so that he was able to experiment with more ample resources. In 1761, when he was twenty-nine, he entered the service of the Esterházys, a family of enormously wealthy Hungarian princes famous for their patronage of the arts. He remained in their service for almost thirty years—that is, for the greater part of his creative career.

The palace of the Esterházys was one of the most splendid in Europe, and music played a central part in the constant round of festivities there. The musical establishment under Haydn's direction included an orchestra, an opera company, a marionette theater, and the chapel. His creativity was stimulated by a constant demand for new works and by the intelligent appreciation of his patron. The agreement between prince and composer sheds light on the social status of the eighteenth-century artist. Haydn is required to abstain "from undue familiarity and from vulgarity in eating, drinking, and conversation." He is enjoined to act uprightly and to influence his subordinates "to preserve such harmony as is becoming in them, remembering how displeasing any discord or dispute would be to His Serene Highness. . . . It is especially to be observed that when the orchestra shall be summoned to perform before company the said Joseph Heyden shall take care that he and all the members of his orchestra do follow the instructions given and appear in white stockings, white linen, powdered, and with a pigtail or tie-wig."

Haydn's life is the classic example of the patronage system operating at its best. Though he chafed occasionally at the restrictions imposed on him by court life, he inhabited a world that questioned neither the supremacy of princes nor the spectacle of a great artist in livery. His final estimate of his position in the Esterházy household was that the advantages outweighed the disadvantages. "My Prince was always satisfied with my works. I not only had the encouragement of constant approval but as conductor of an orchestra I could make experiments, observe what produced an effect and what weakened it, and was thus in a position to improve, alter, make additions or omissions, and be as bold as I pleased. I was cut off from the world, there was no one to confuse or torment me, and I was forced to become *original*."

Haydn had married when still a young man, but did not get on with his wife. They separated, and he found consolation elsewhere. By the time he reached middle age his music had brought him fame throughout Europe. He was asked to appear at various capitals but accepted none of these invitations as long as his patron was alive. After the Prince's death he made two visits to England (1791, 1794–95), where he conducted his works with phenomenal success. The acclaim he received in England, comparable to that accorded Handel before and Mendelssohn after him, assured the triumph of German music in that country. He returned to his native Austria laden with honors and financially well off.

When he was seventy-six a memorable performance of *The Creation* was organized in his honor by the leading musicians of Vienna and members of the aristocracy. At the words "And there was light"—who that has heard the work can forget the grandeur of the C-major chord on the word "light"?—the old man was deeply stirred. Pointing upward he exclaimed, "It came from there!" His agitation increased as the performance advanced, so that it was necessary to take him home at the end of the first part of the oratorio. As he was carried out in his armchair

his admirers thronged about him. Beethoven, who had briefly been his
pupil, kissed his hands and forehead. At the door he turned around and
lifted his hands as if in blessing. It was his farewell to the public.

He died a year later, revered by his countrymen and acknowledged
throughout Europe as the premier musician of his time.

His Music

Haydn set himself to master a new instrumental language and to
adapt it to the new things that music had to say: specifically, to achieve
the dynamic development of themes and motives that was the kernel
of the new symphonic style, and to mold those high-strung themes of
his into convincing forms. These goals he encompassed with such success that for the next hundred years he was represented in popular
manuals as the "father" of the symphony, of the string quartet, of the
modern orchestra, and of instrumental music in general. Such allegations of paternity, it goes without saying, are vastly exaggerated. The
sonata was the product of an age, not an individual. Haydn's pre-
eminence stems from the fact that he solved its problems with greater
force and brilliance of imagination than did most of his contemporaries.
The mature classical idiom seemed to be fully realized for the first time
in his terse, highly personal style with its angular themes and nervous
rhythms, its expressive harmony, structural logic, and endlessly varied
moods.

The string quartet occupied a central position in Haydn's art. The
eighty-three examples he left are an indispensable part of the repertory.
The works of his middle and late years contain notable experiments in
sonority and form. Remarkable are the dramatic modulations, the
weighty codas in which he seems to anticipate Beethoven, the peasant
humor of the minuets and finales, the profound introspection of the
adagios. One understands Mozart's remark, "It was from Haydn that I
first learned the true way to compose quartets."

The friendship between the two greatest musicians of the age bene-
fited both. Mozart, younger by almost a quarter century, was stimulated
by Haydn's audacity in regard to form and structure. Haydn in turn
learned from the tonal opulence, masterly orchestration, and melodic
beauty of Mozart's writing. His last and greatest works were written
after Mozart's death, when the younger man's final symphonies had
revealed to him new possibilities in this medium. The relationship between the two was untouched by the rivalry which, in that day as in
this, caused enmity among artists. "I declare to you on my honor,"
Haydn told Mozart's father, "that I consider your son the greatest composer I know either personally or by name."

Like the quartets, the symphonies—over a hundred in number—extend across the whole of Haydn's career. In them he solved what he considered to be the basic problem of large-scale musical architecture: the unity of the idea. "This is where so many young composers fail," he declared. "They string together a number of fragments, they break off almost as soon as they have begun. And so at the end the listener carries away no definite impression." His fame as a symphonist rests mainly on the twelve works that he wrote in the 1790s, in two sets of six, for his appearances in England. Known as the Salomon Symphonies, after the impresario who arranged the concerts, they abound in effects that the public associates with later composers—syncopation, sudden crescendos and accents, dramatic contrasts of soft and loud, daring modulation, and an imaginative color scheme in which each choir and instrument plays its allotted part. Of Haydn's symphonies it may be said, as it has been of his quartets, that they are the spiritual birthplace of Beethoven.

Haydn was a prolific composer of church music. His fourteen Masses form the chief item in this category. The prevailing cheerfulness of these works reflects a trusting faith undisturbed by inner travail or doubt. "At the thought of God," he said, "my heart leaps for joy and I cannot help my music doing the same." *The Creation* (1798), written in his mid-sixties after his return from England, is a hymn to nature and its Creator. In this oratorio, based on Genesis and Milton's *Paradise Lost*, the earth and its beauties are described with that capacity for wonder which only children and artists know. "I never was so pious as when composing *The Creation*. I knelt down every day and prayed God to strengthen me for my work." Again, concerning the optimism of this music, "God gave me a cheerful heart, so He will surely forgive me if I serve Him cheerfully." That *The Creation* occupied a special place in the master's affections is evident from his excitement at the first performance. "One moment I was as cold as ice, the next I seemed on fire. More than once I feared I would have a stroke." The oratorio attained a popularity second only to that of Handel's *Messiah*. Haydn followed it with another on a text drawn from English literature—*The Seasons* (1801), based on James Thomson's celebrated nature poem. Completed when the composer was on the threshold of seventy, it was his last major work.

Haydn's tone imagery was instrumental in character. Yet he recognized that a good melody must be rooted in the nature of the human voice. "If you want to know whether you have written anything worth preserving," he counseled, "sing it to yourself without any accompaniment." His attitude toward his work shows that the time was passing when pieces were written for a single occasion or season. "I never was a quick writer and always composed with care and deliberation. That alone is the way to compose works that will last." His ceaseless experimenting with form should dispel the notion that the classicist adheres unquestionably to tradition. On the contrary, he chafed against the arbitrary restrictions of the theorists. "What is the good of such rules? Art is free and should be fettered by no such mechanical regulations. The educated ear is the sole authority on all these questions, and I think I have as much right to lay down the law as anyone." He upheld the expressive power of music against all rules. "Supposing an idea struck me as good and thoroughly satisfactory both to the ear and the heart, I would far rather pass over some slight grammatical error than sacrifice what seemed to me beautiful to any mere pedantic trifling." So, too, when his attention was called to an unconventional passage in a string quartet of Mozart's, he retorted, "If Mozart wrote it so he must have had good reason."

Haydn enriched the literature of the divertimento, the concerto, and the song. His piano sonatas, of late years unjustly neglected, are returning to favor. His numerous operas and marionette plays were designed specifically for the entertainment needs of the Esterházy court. "My operas are calculated exclusively for our own company and would not produce their effect elsewhere." But several, revived in recent years, have given delight. The symphonies, string quartets, and oratorios attained immense popularity in his lifetime, and innumerable amateur and professional groups were formed expressly to present them. They became an integral part of the musical culture of the age and helped shape the taste of the new mass public.

Haydn had the humility and striving for perfection of the true artist, but he knew the value of his works. "There are some bad ones among the good," he said. "Some of my children are well-bred, some ill-bred, and here and there is a changeling among them." How touching is the remark of the aged master quoted at the head of this chapter. Finally, in summing up his life's work: "I think I have done my duty and been of use in my generation by my works. Let others do the same."

The Surprise Symphony

The best known of Haydn's symphonies, the *Surprise,* in G major, is one of the set of six written for his first visit to London in 1791. The orchestra that presented these compositions to the world consisted of about thirty-five players: a full string section; two each of flutes, oboes, bassoons, horns, trumpets, and timpani.

The first movement opens with a brief introduction marked Adagio cantabile. This passage in Haydn's most reflective mood is notable for its limpid scoring for winds and strings. The movement proper is a forceful Vivace assai (very lively) in sonata-allegro form, imbued with the symphonic drive and forthrightness of the classical style.

The first theme, assigned to the first violins, establishes the home key, G major.

It expands into a vigorous section, after which a bridge passage leads to the contrasting key, D major. This is set forth by the second theme, which is played by the first violins.

As often happens in Haydn, the two basic ideas do not present a marked contrast to one another. The movement is built rather on the opposition between home and contrasting key. One theme flowers into the next in a continuous self-evolving fabric that is the essence of Haydn's symphonic thinking. A graceful closing theme rounds off the Exposition. The transparent orchestration and economy of means are characteristic traits of his style, as are the spaciousness of design and the prevailing good humor.

The Development opens with a reference to the main theme. The frequent modulations give that sense of excitement, of releasing hidden energies, which makes the classical development. Motives are expanded and developed, each measure seeming to give rise to the next. The abrupt changes from p to f impart a dynamic quality to the music. They are characteristic of Haydn's orchestral writing, and look ahead to Beethoven's dramatic style.

The Recapitulation presents the material in shortened form. The second theme is transposed from the contrasting to the home key—that is, from the Dominant key to the Tonic. A shapely coda brings the movement to an affirmative cadence in the home key.

The second movement is the Andante, a theme and variations in C major. The theme is of a folk-song simplicity. It is announced by the violins, staccato.

The eight-bar phrase is repeated pianissimo and ends in an abrupt fortissimo crash—the "surprise" that gives the symphony its name. "There," Haydn told a friend, "all the ladies will scream." But despite the famous anecdote, in an artist of Haydn's stature one must seek a deeper motivation for the effect. The contrast between soft and loud was one of the dynamic elements of the new orchestral language and was bound to fascinate an innovative artist like Haydn, quite apart from the ladies.

Haydn's variations are notable for their ease, taste, humor, and workmanship. Variation 1. The theme is combined with arabesques in the first violins.

Variation 2. The theme is shifted into the minor, and is played fortissimo.

Variation 3 returns to the major. The theme is heard in a new rhythm.

In the second half of this variation the theme is heard underneath countermelodies traced by solo flute and oboe.

Variation 4. The theme is heard with a change in dynamics, register, orchestration, and type of accompaniment. The second half of this variation introduces a new version of the melody. This striking variation ends on a sustained chord which leads into the coda. The theme is wreathed in new harmonies. The final measures, which are in the nature of a gentle summing up, have a wonderful sound.

Third is the Minuet in G major, a rollicking Allegro molto that leaves far behind it the manner of the courtly dance. Peasant humor and the high spirits of folk dance permeate this movement. It is earthy, vital, symphonic.

The A section opens with one of Haydn's delicious irregularities in structure: an eight-bar phrase is answered by a phrase of ten. Just before the return of the principal phrase, flute and oboe in high register are answered by bassoon and cello in low, with inimitable droll effect. This A section shows the typical structure of the classical minuet: a:‖:b-a-codetta:‖. The B or middle part, the Trio, is quieter in movement, combining bassoon and string tone. The Minuet proper is repeated da capo, giving a clear-cut A-B-A form.

Fourth is the Allegro di molto (very lively), a brisk, vigorous movement in sonata-allegro form. Like the first and third movements, it is in G major. Imbued with the popular tone, this Allegro has all the verve and charm of the Haydn finale. The principal theme establishes the home key of G.

An energetic bridge passage leads to a roguish little tune and codetta in the contrasting key, D major. The first theme undergoes a forceful development, in the course of which the music touches upon various major and minor keys. In the Restatement, the second theme is transposed into the home key. A jovial coda leads to the energetic cadence in G major.

The manner is the manner of a courtly age, but the voice is the voice of the people. Prince Esterházy's devoutly religious court composer was far removed from the slogans of the French Revolution. He would sternly have disapproved the doctrines of Rousseau and other leaders of the Enlightenment. Yet he caught in his music the naturalness and simplicity they prized. Like every great artist he stood both within his time and beyond it.

Haydn's is the music of a man rooted in the world, an optimistic music that even in its darker moments accepts life and finds it good. His serenity stems from conquest of self and from a clear vision of his goal. "Often when I was struggling against obstacles of all kinds, often when strength of mind and body failed me and it was difficult to persevere in the course on which I had set out, an inner feeling whispered to me, 'There are so few happy and contented people here below. Everywhere men are burdened with sorrow. Perhaps your work may be a source from which those oppressed by care may draw a moment's relief and relaxation.' Here was a powerful reason for going on!"

The nineteenth century with its love of the grandiose was not overly responsive to this clean, sensible music. Thus was created the stereotype of an amiable "Papa Haydn" in court dress and powdered wig who purveyed harmless pleasantries to the lords of the old regime. It has remained for the twentieth century to rescue this great musician from such incomprehension and to restore to its rightful place his deeply felt, finely wrought art—an art of moderation and humor, polished and lucid, profoundly human and unfadingly fresh.

CHAPTER 52

Wolfgang Amadeus Mozart (1756-1791)

"People make a mistake who think that my art has come easily to me. Nobody has devoted so much time and thought to composition as I. There is not a famous master whose music I have not studied over and over."

SOMETHING of the miraculous hovers about the music of Mozart. One sees how it is put together, whither it is bound, and how it gets there; but its beauty of sound and perfection of style, its poignancy and grace defy analysis and beggar description. For one moment in the history of music all opposites were reconciled, all tensions resolved. That luminous moment was Mozart.

Wolfgang Amadeus Mozart.

His Life

He was born in Salzburg, son of Leopold Mozart, an esteemed composer-violinist attached to the court of the Archbishop. The child's career presents the most extraordinary example of precociousness in the history of art. He began to compose before he was five, and performed at the court of the Empress Maria Theresa at the age of six. The following year his ambitious father organized a grand tour that included Paris, London, and Munich. By the time he was thirteen the boy had written sonatas, concertos, symphonies, religious works, an *opera buffa* and the operetta *Bastien and Bastienne*.

He reached manhood having attained a mastery of all forms of his art. The speed and sureness of his creative power, unrivaled by any other composer, is best described by himself: "Though it be long, the work is complete and finished in my mind. I take out of the bag of my memory what has previously been collected into it. For this reason the committing to paper is done quickly enough. For everything is already finished, and it rarely differs on paper from what it was in my imagination. At this work I can therefore allow myself to be disturbed. Whatever may be going on about me, I write and even talk." In similar vein he writes to his father: "You know that I am, so to speak, immersed in music, that I am busy with it all day—speculating, studying, considering."

His relations with his patron, Hieronymus von Colloredo, Prince-

Archbishop of Salzburg, were most unhappy. The high-spirited young artist rebelled against the social restrictions imposed by the patronage system. "The two valets sit at the head of the table," he writes his father. "I at least have the honor of sitting above the cooks." At length he could endure his position no longer. He quarreled with the Archbishop, was dismissed, and at twenty-five established himself in Vienna to pursue the career of a free artist, the while he sought an official appointment. Ten years remained to him. These were spent in a tragic struggle to achieve financial security and to find again the lost serenity of his childhood. Worldly success depended on the protection of the court. But the Emperor Joseph II—who referred to him as "a decided talent" —either passed him by in favor of lesser men or, when he finally took Mozart into his service, assigned him to tasks unworthy of his genius such as composing dances for the court balls. Of his remuneration for this work Mozart remarked with bitterness, "Too much for what I do, too little for what I could do."

In 1782 he married Constanze Weber, against his father's wishes. The step signalized Mozart's liberation from the close ties that had bound him to the well-meaning but domineering parent who strove so futilely to ensure the happiness of the son. Constanze brought her husband neither the strength of character nor the wherewithal that might have shielded him from the struggle with the world for which he was singularly unequipped. She was an undistinguished woman to whom Mozart, despite occasional lapses, was strongly attached. It was not till many years after his death that she appears to have realized, from the adulation of the world, the stature of her husband.

With the opera *The Marriage of Figaro*, written in 1786 on a libretto by Lorenzo da Ponte, Mozart reached the peak of his career as far as success was concerned. The work made a sensation in Vienna and in Prague, and his letters from the latter city testify to his pleasure at its reception. Noteworthy is his cheerful acceptance of the fact that the main arias of the opera had been transformed into popular dance tunes, a practice that people today regard as an irreverence. "At six o'clock I drove with Count Canal to the so-called Bretfeld ball, where the cream of Prague's beauties gather. I neither danced nor flirted with any of them, the former because I was too tired, the latter owing to my natural timidity. I looked on however with the greatest pleasure while all these people flew about in sheer delight to the music of my *Figaro* arranged for quadrilles and waltzes. Here they talk about nothing but *Figaro*. Nothing is played, sung, or whistled but *Figaro*. No opera is drawing like *Figaro*. Nothing, nothing but *Figaro*!"

He was commissioned to do another work for the following year. With da Ponte again as librettist he produced *Don Giovanni*. The opera baffled the Viennese. His vogue had passed. The composer whom we regard as the epitome of clarity and grace was, in the view of the frivolous public of his time, difficult to understand. His music, it was said, had to be heard several times in order to be grasped. What better proof of its inaccessibility? In truth, Mozart was entering regions beyond the aristocratic entertainment level of the day. He was straining toward an intensity of utterance that was new in the world. Of *Don Giovanni* Joseph II declared, "The opera is heavenly, perhaps even more beautiful than *Figaro*. But no food for the teeth of my Viennese." Upon which Mozart commented, "Then give them time to chew it." One publisher advised him to write in a more popular style. "In that case I can make no more by my pen," he answered. "I had better starve and die at once."

The last years of his life were spent in growing want. The frequent appeals to his friends for aid mirror his despair and helplessness. He describes himself as "always hovering between hope and anxiety." He speaks of the black thoughts that he must "repel by a tremendous effort." He asks for a loan so that he may work "with a mind *more free* from care and *with a lighter heart* and thus *earn more* . . . If only I had at least 600 gulden I should be able to compose with a fairly easy mind. Ah! I must have peace of mind." The love of life that had sustained him through earlier disappointments began to desert him. Again and again he embarked on a journey that seemed to promise a solution to all his difficulties, only to return empty-handed. A note of defeat crept into the gay tender letters he wrote his wife. "I cannot describe what I have been feeling. A kind of emptiness that hurts me dreadfully— a kind of longing that is never satisfied, that never ceases, that persists —no, rather increases daily."

In the last year of his life, after a falling off in his production, he nerved himself to the final effort. For the popular Viennese theater he wrote *The Magic Flute*, on a libretto by the actor-impresario-poetaster Emanuel Schikaneder. Then a flurry of hope sent him off to Prague for the coronation of the new Emperor, Leopold II, as King of Bohemia. The festival opera he composed for this event, *The Clemency of Titus*, failed to impress a court exhausted by the protracted ceremonies of the coronation. Mozart returned to Vienna broken in body and spirit. With a kind of fevered desperation he turned to his last task, the Requiem. It had been commissioned by a music-loving count who fancied himself a composer and intended to pass off the work as his own. Mozart in his overwrought state became obsessed with the notion that this Mass for the Dead was intended for himself and that he would not live to finish it. A tragic race with time began as he whipped his faculties to this masterwork steeped in visions of death.

The gentle resignation that many find in his music comes through in the letter he supposedly wrote da Ponte in England, in response to the latter's suggestion that he join him there.

I wish I could follow your advice, but how can I do so? My mind is confused, I reason with difficulty and cannot free myself from the image of this stranger. I see him perpetually entreating me, pressing me and impatiently demanding the work. I go on writing because composition tires me less than resting. Otherwise I have nothing more to fear. I know from what I suffer that the hour has come. I am at the point of death. I have come to the end without having had the enjoyment of my talent. Life was so beautiful, my career began under such fortunate auspices. But no one can change his destiny. No one can measure his days. One must resign oneself, it will be as providence wills. I must close. Here is my death-song. I must not leave it incomplete.

His last days were cheered by the growing popularity of *The Magic Flute*. The gravely ill composer, watch in hand, would follow the performance in his mind. "Now the first act is over . . . Now comes the aria of the Queen of Night . . ." His premonition concerning the Requiem came true. He failed rapidly while in the midst of the work. His favorite pupil, Süssmayr, completed the Mass from the master's sketches, with some additions of his own.

Mozart died shortly before his thirty-sixth birthday. In view of his debts he was given "the poorest class of funeral." His friends followed to the city gates; but the weather being inclement, they turned back, leaving the hearse to proceed alone. "Thus, without a note of music, forsaken by all he held dear, the remains of this prince of harmony were committed to the earth—not even in a grave of his own but in the common paupers' grave."

His Music

Mozart's art sprang from the European culture of his time. He assimilated the suave, sensuous vocal melody of the Italians, the advanced orchestral-symphonic conception of the Germans, the elegance and lucidity of the French. His music acknowledged no national boundaries. Like Haydn and Beethoven he addressed the world.

Many picture Mozart as one in whom the dainty elegance of court art reached its apogee. To others he represents the spirit of artless youth untouched by life. Both views are equally far from the truth. Neither the simplicity of his forms nor the crystalline clarity of his texture can dispel the intensity of feeling that pervades the works of his maturity. Because of the mastery with which everything is carried out, the most complex operations of the musical mind are made to appear effortless. This deceptive simplicity is truly the art that conceals art.

It has been said that Mozart taught the instruments to sing. Into his exquisitely wrought instrumental forms he poured the lyricism of the great vocal art of the past. There resulted a pure and spiritualized idiom. The peasant touch is missing from Mozart's music, which draws its inspiration neither from folk song nor nature. It is an indoor art, sophisticated, rooted in the culture of two musical cities—Salzburg and Vienna. Haydn, who adjusted both his life and music to the needs of the aristocracy, was the natural man and the democratic artist; while Mozart, whose life was one long gesture of rebellion against the old regime, in his art was essentially aristocratic. His music is the acme of refinement, the product of a ripe civilization lifted to universality through the profoundly human insights of its creator.

The Salzburg years saw the composition of a quantity of social music, divertimentos and serenades of great variety. In chamber music he favored the string quartet. His works in this form range in expression from the buoyantly songful to the austerely tragic. The last ten quartets rank with the finest specimens in the literature, among them being the set of six dedicated to Haydn, his "most celebrated and very dear friend." Worthy companions to these are the string quintets, in which he invariably used two violas. The somber Quintet in G minor represents the peak of his achievement in this medium.

One of the outstanding pianists of his time, Mozart wrote copiously for his favorite instrument. Among his finest solo works are the Fantasia and Sonata in C minor (K. 475 and 457; the K followed by a number that is included in the listing of Mozart's works refers to the catalogue of Ludwig Koechel, who enumerated them all in what he took to be the order of their composition). Mozart was less experimental than Haydn in regard to formal structure, yet he led the way in developing one important form: the concerto for piano and orchestra. He wrote more than twenty works in this medium. They possess the perfection of detail inseparable from his style. With these works the piano concerto achieved a leading position in the art of the classical era.

The more than forty symphonies—their exact number has not been determined—that extend across his career tend toward ever greater richness of orchestration, freedom of part writing, and depth of emotion. The most important are the six written in the final decade of his life—the *Haffner* in D (1782), the *Linz* in C (1783), the *Prague* in D (1786), and the three composed in 1788. With these works the symphony ceases to be a brilliant occasional piece suitable for opening or closing a program. It moves to the center as the most weighty form of abstract music. The last three, significantly, were never performed during Mozart's lifetime. They were composed for no specific occasion but from inner necessity—a momentous departure in an age when artists wrote only on commission. They came into being because the composer had something in him that had to be said, no matter who heard.

But the central current in Mozart's art that nourished all the others was opera. Here were embodied his joy in life, his melancholy, all the impulses of his many-faceted personality. None has ever surpassed his power to delineate character in music and to make his puppets come alive. No one solved more masterfully the age-old problems of opera—the marriage of music and text, the balance of voice and orchestra, of recitative and aria, solos and ensembles, dramatic action and musical expressiveness. His lyric gift, molded to the curve of the human voice, created a wealth of melody whose sensuous loveliness sets it apart in music. His orchestra, although it never obtrudes upon the voice, becomes the magical framework within which the action unfolds. His mastery of symphonic thinking enabled him to shape a broadly arched structure held together by relationship of keys and development of themes. Within this arch all the elements of the drama are brought into a convincing unity. Rooted in the great Italian tradition, Mozart understood what no amount of theorizing has ever been able to disprove —that in the lyric theater the music is the miraculous, the all-pervading element.

In Lorenzo da Ponte, an Italian-Jewish adventurer and poet who was one of the picturesque figures of the age (he ultimately emigrated to America, operated a distillery, taught Italian at Columbia College, and wrote a fascinating book of memoirs), Mozart found a librettist whose dramatic vitality was akin to his own. The collaboration produced three works: *The Marriage of Figaro* (1786), which da Ponte adapted from the comedy of Beaumarchais satirizing the old regime; *Don Giovanni* (1787), "the opera of all operas"; and *Così fan tutte* (1790), which has been translated in a variety of ways from "So do all women" to "Girls will be girls!" These crown the history of classical *opera buffa;* just as *The Abduction from the Seraglio* (1782) and *The Magic Flute* (1791), a gigantic fantasy steeped in the symbolism of Freemasonry, bring to its apex the German *Singspiel* (song-play). The grandly human conception of Mozart's lyric theater unfolds under the mask of comedy— but comedy elevated, as in *Don Giovanni,* to encompass all human experience. Mozart's music brings to life the eighteenth-century world with its class distinctions, its amorous intrigue, its molding of the individual to a set pattern. Abounding in irony and satire, these master-works reach beyond the gallant world of satin and lace whence they issued. They achieve what da Ponte set forth as his and Mozart's intention: "To paint faithfully and in full color the divers passions."

Mozart is the only composer that ever lived who achieved success in every branch of his art. In addition to the works we have mentioned,

his output includes some sixty pieces of church music, among which
are Masses, offertories, vespers, litanies, and the like; also more than
fifty arias with orchestra, songs for voice and piano, and choral works
with orchestra.

Excerpts from Don Giovanni

Conceived in the tradition of the *opera buffa, Don Giovanni* oversteps
that tradition into the realm covered by our term tragicomedy. Da
Ponte called it a "jocose drama." The opera is unique for its range of
emotions. As the great scenes unfold before us they take on the contours
of rounded musical forms that allow full scope for vocal melody, vivid
characterization, and swiftly paced action. Mozart reconciled the demands of pure music and the requirements of the stage in a degree
unparalleled either before or since. It was after looking through the
score of *Don Giovanni* that Rossini called him "the only composer who
had as much science as genius and as much genius as science."

The figure of Don Juan, the profligate-blasphemer who dies unre-
pentant, has attracted artists for centuries. The list includes Tirso de
Molina, Molière, and Thomas Shadwell in the seventeenth; Goldoni,
Gluck, and da Ponte (who borrowed liberally from other versions) in
the eighteenth; Byron and Richard Strauss in the nineteenth; Bernard
Shaw in the twentieth. Da Ponte's Don heralds a new type in literature
as in society: the supreme individualist who brooks no restraints and
brushes aside every obstacle in the way of his self-realization. Don Juan
is the eternal type of libertine for whom the pursuit of pleasure has become the final assertion of will. He so loves women that he must possess
them all. Or better, he so hates them that he must conquer and degrade
them all. He is cynical and cruel, but courageous. Even in the face of
mortal peril he remains true to himself—he refuses to repent. His ob-
liviousness of other human beings condemns him to the loneliness that
is his real punishment, a loneliness he forever seeks to escape. This
demonic creature is driven by a magnificent obsession. Mozart's music
humanizes him, transforms him into one of the boldest conceptions in
the entire range of the lyric theater. He defies all moral law. He dares
what lesser—or should one say more normal—men only dream of. He
fascinates as only a transgressor can. One feels guilty for identifying
with him; then one hears the music and is absolved from guilt.

Mozart put off writing the Overture until the last moment. He had to
sit up the night before the dress rehearsal, Constanze telling him stories
to keep him awake, in order to set it down. The parts were copied that
day and read at sight by the orchestra. Mozart, who conducted, remarked that "plenty of notes fell under the table." From the statement

quoted earlier in the chapter it is clear that we must amend this famous story in one detail. He did not compose the Overture that night; he committed to paper what was already finished in his mind.

The Overture begins with an Andante in ₵ time that establishes the home key of the opera—D minor. The opening measures are of an impressive dignity that will be associated at the climax of the work with the ghost of the Commandant. There follows a sonata-allegro movement that serves to introduce the opera without being related to it by

theme. The richness of sound and free interweaving of orchestral parts bespeak the high classical style.

The curtain rises on Don Giovanni's servant Leporello, who is standing outside the residence of Donna Anna bemoaning his fate: "Night and day I slave for one who's never pleased. I have to bear wind and rain, am fed badly, and sleep badly. I'd like to play the gentleman and serve no more. A fine gentleman you are, in there making sport with beauty while I stand watch outside . . ."

Don Giovanni, who had broken into Donna Anna's chamber, rushes out of the house struggling with her and concealing his face. Donna Anna, determined to discover the identity of her assailant, calls for help. Her father the Commandant appears, drawing his sword. Donna Anna withdraws into the house. The Don does not wish to fight the old man but is goaded into a duel in the course of which he mortally wounds the Commandant. The conversation between Don Giovanni and Leporello establishes the moral climate they inhabit. "Who is dead, you or the old man?" "Silly question. The old man." "Bravo. Nice work—attacking the daughter and murdering the father." "He asked for it." "And Donna Anna, what did she ask for?" "Shut up and come away. Unless you too are asking for something." "Oh no, master. I shan't say another word." They escape. Donna Anna comes out of the house with Don Ottavio, her betrothed. She discovers her father's body and is overcome by grief. In the ensuing duet she and Don Ottavio swear to track down the murderer and make him pay for his crime.

The opening *scena* has a swiftness of pace and action that derives from *opera buffa* and is here placed in the service of sheer drama. The action is held together by the expansion of themes and motives. Enhanced by the momentum of Mozart's orchestral style, this takes on all the continuity and drive of a symphonic movement. It is significant that

the richness of Mozart's orchestra disturbed contemporary opera goers
even as did that of Wagner's a century later.

The dialogue between Don Giovanni and Leporello is given in *reci-
tativo secco*—the dry, unadorned type of declamation which in classical
opera was accompanied by the harpsichord. The more expressive recitative of Donna Anna and Don Ottavio has an orchestral background.
Donna Anna is established forthwith as the great lady, noble of bearing
and somewhat remote, who throughout the work represents the aristocracy; even as the middle station in life and the peasantry have their
representatives. Conspicuous is the repetition of lines and phrases of
the text, which allows space for the necessary expansion and repetition
of musical material. This accords with Mozart's dictum that in opera
the poetry must be the obedient daughter of the music. As in the symphony, large units are given shape and coherence through the unifying
power of key. The opening scene ends in the home key of D minor,
forming a rounded musical entity that launches the dramatic-musical
action.

Leporello's Catalogue Aria, the fourth number of the opera, is sung to
Donna Elvira, who has been abandoned by the Don but still loves him.
To persuade her of the futility of her passion Leporello reads her the list

of his master's amours. "In Italy six hundred and forty. In Germany two
hundred and thirty-one. A hundred in France, in Turkey ninety-one.
But in Spain it's already one thousand and three ('*mille e tre*'). Country girls, servant girls, city girls, countesses, baronesses, princesses. All
ranks, all shapes, all ages . . ."

What is left unsaid in the vocal line is filled in by the saucy accompaniment. Theatrical in its brusqueness is the change from animated
allegro to lyric andante: "With blondes he praises their kindness, with
dark ones their constancy, with the fair ones their sweetness. In winter
he prefers them fat, in summer he likes them lean." This *buffo* aria, in
which the singer with a knowing wink takes the audience into his confidence, is in the great tradition of the theater of buffoons. To that tradition belong also Figaro's spirited outpourings and the *Largo al factotum*
of Rossini's *Barber of Seville*.

Là ci darem la mano, the seventh number—a little duet, as Mozart
called it—is sung by Don Giovanni and Zerlina, the artless peasant

Là ci da - rem la ma - no là di -   mi sì
Give me your hand sweet maid- en Whis - per a gen - tle "yes,"

maid who has momentarily caught his fancy. He succeeds in detaching
her from the country bumpkin Masetto, assures her that he intends to
marry her, and invites her to come with him to his villa. The voices
alternate, the phrases becoming ever shorter as he grows more ardent
and she more amenable. "I should feel happy. What if he's only making
sport of me . . . Come, my delight . . . I'm sorry for Masetto . . .
I'll change your life . . . How quickly I yield . . ." The tempo
changes from andante to allegro, $\frac{2}{4}$ time giving way to $\frac{6}{8}$ as she
throws herself into his arms. Together they sing, "Let us go, my
dearest, and ease the pangs of innocent love." There is much repetition
of the key word *andiam* (let us go) to allow for musical expansion. The
melody is Mozart at his suavest and most Italianate.

Don Giovanni, the final scene. The Don at supper before the arrival of
the Commandant.

In the course of the opera Donna Anna realizes that Don Giovanni is
the man who broke into her room on the fatal night. She and Don
Ottavio plan to deliver him to justice. Don Giovanni, meanwhile, during
one of his escapades takes refuge in the dead of night in the cemetery

where stands the statue of the Commandant. The stone figure chides
Don Giovanni for disturbing the peace of the dead. Enjoying Leporello's
terror, the Don now commits the crowning blasphemy. He invites the
Statue to sup with him that evening. The stone figure nods acceptance.

The final scene is the momentous supper in Don Giovanni's mansion.
He directs his musicians to play while he eats. They perform two ex-
cerpts from popular operas of the day. Their third number is the
Marching Song from *Figaro*, at which Leporello comments, "That one
I know only too well." The interplay between master and servant, com-
pounded of comedy and hostility, is interrupted by the arrival of Donna
Elvira, who pleads with Giovanni to mend his ways before it is too late.

The entrance of the Commandant's statue is one of the supreme moments in opera. The music returns to the home key of D minor; the arch
is completed. Three trombones join the *tutti* (the whole orchestra) to
herald the entrance of the specter.

The awesome pronouncement is heard against the harmonies that
opened the Overture. The melodic line, based on the downward leap of
an octave, is of a supernatural dignity.

The Statue asks the Don to repay the visit and take supper with him.
Leporello, shaking with fear, implores his master to decline. "He hasn't
the time—please excuse him!" But the Don will not be accused of cowardice. "I have no fear. I'll come." "Give me your hand in pledge."
"Take it!" He holds out his hand and feels the Statue's icy clasp. "Repent!
Change your life before it is too late." The Don struggles to free himself. Yet even now his courage does not desert him. He cannot renounce
his destiny. "No, I will not repent, you old fool!" "Then it is too late."
Flames shoot up. The demons of hell rise to claim their prey. They drag
the sinner to his doom.

There follows a sextet in which Leporello describes Don Giovanni's
fate to the interested parties—Donna Anna and Don Ottavio, Elvira,
Zerlina and Masetto—who moralize melodiously on the wages of sin.
This finale restores the *opera buffa* character of the work. It is heavenly
music.

Symphony No. 40, in G Minor

It was in the summer of 1788, during the darkest period of his life, that Mozart in the space of a little over six weeks composed his last three symphonies: in E-flat (K. 543); in G minor (K. 550); and in C, the *Jupiter* (K. 551). They are popularly known as Nos. 39, 40, and 41.

The G-minor Symphony represents that aspect of Mozart's art which pointed to a new expressive goal in music. Along with several important works that preceded it, the Symphony strikes a tenderly impassioned note. This music finely reflects the Age of Sensibility, and that interpenetration of classic and romantic elements of which we have spoken. The fact that Mozart, throughout his maturity, moved steadily closer to this expressive goal played its part in losing him the favor of an aristocracy to whom his music spoke in new and disquieting accents.

The first movement, in sonata form, plunges immediately into the Allegro molto. The Exposition opens with an intense theme which is played by the violins and establishes the home key of G minor. It flowers out of a three-note germ motive that is genuinely symphonic in its capacity for growth and development.

A vigorous bridge passage leads into the contrasting key, the related major—B-flat. The second theme, shared by woodwinds and strings, provides an area of comparative relaxation in the headlong drive of the movement. This melody is in direct contrast with the restlessness of the first subject.

The codetta, in which we hear echoings of the germ motive, establishes the cadence in the contrasting key. In most recordings of this work the Exposition is repeated, which is as it should be.

The Development is brief and packed with action. It searches out the possibilities of the opening theme, concentrating on the three-note motive. The music wanders far afield, modulating rapidly from one foreign key to the next. The principal melody appears in altered guise, as in the following example, revealing unsuspected aspects of its na-

ture. Now it is heard in the bass, given out by bassoon and lower strings against a countermelody high above. Now it appears in the upper register. Now the germ motive becomes the subject of a dialogue between violins and woodwinds. Suddenly we hear it in inversion. Never slackening in its course, the Development is crowned by the transition to the Recapitulation, one of those miraculous passages that only one figure in all of music could have written. With the reappearance of the initial theme we are back in the home key.

The Recapitulation follows the course of the first section. The bridge is expanded and circles about the home key. The second theme is shifted into G minor, taking on a strangely tender tone. The coda energetically confirms the home key.

The second movement, an Andante in E-flat in sonata-allegro form, is pitched on a less subjective level. It is almost as if the composer, having revealed more than he had intended, were retreating behind the formal elegance of the eighteenth-century style. The classical masters did not find it incongruous to cast a slow movement in the form so closely identified with the first (allegro) movement. Violas, second violins, then first violins enter in turn with the first theme in the home key.

Horn tone provides a background for the strings. There is Viennese grace in the characteristic dip of the melody in the answering phrase, which is heard in the first violins.

The theme unfolds amid an abundance of ornament in thirty-second notes, a kind of musical scrollwork in which flute, clarinet, and bassoon take part. This is not the kind of sonata movement that depends

on a dynamic contrast between first and second themes. The composer
contents himself with the opposition between home and contrasting key
in the Exposition and modulates actively in the Development, which
has the dynamic quality that goes with the growth of themes. The
transition to the Recapitulation is accomplished through a dialogue for
woodwinds—bassoon, clarinets, flutes. Andante here, as in the case
of the Haydn symphonies, is to be understood in the eighteenth-century
sense, meaning a "going" pace. With its ceremonious gestures and
embellishments, this movement reflects the courtly refinement of an
era that was drawing to a close.

The third movement, in G minor, recaptures the emotional tension
of the first. The Minuet is remarkable for its vigor and onrush. In this

minuet Mozart reaches out beyond the aristocratic dance that gave the
movement its name. The opening section is marked by a type of nonsymmetrical phrase structure that appears in Mozart, as in Haydn,
more frequently than is generally realized. Two phrases of three bars
each are followed by a phrase of five measures and one of three. This
A section is characteristic of the minuet of the classical symphony:
a:||: b-a-codetta:||.

The Trio, in G major, is in a relaxed mood. Color becomes an element of form as oboe, flute, and bassoon in turn take the phrase. The horn

outlines the melody when it is restated by the strings. The use of woodwinds and horns as melody instruments was well known in the opera
house, but it was a comparatively new thing in the symphony. Mozart's
subtly shaded sonorities became the model for succeeding generations.
The subsections of the Trio are repeated in the customary manner,
after which the Minuet is heard again, but without repeats. There
results a beautifully rounded A-B-A form.

The finale, Allegro assai (very fast), is a compact sonata form, abrupt
and imperious. A tragic restlessness lurks beneath its polished surface. The first subject, in G minor, is presented by the first violins. It

is of the upward-bounding type dear to the classical era and known as a *rocket theme*.

The contrasting theme, in the related key of B-flat major, sung by the first violins, provides the necessary foil in point of serenity and grace.

It is repeated, with subtle embellishments, by the clarinet.

The Development is highly dramatic. The rocket motive is bandied about by various instruments that crowd upon one another in hurried imitation as they spin out a complex orchestral fabric. Tension is maintained at maximum pitch by the rapid modulations through foreign keys. With its tightly knit expansion of motives, this section is the epitome of classical thinking. The Recapitulation presents the material again with certain changes, most important of which is the shifting of the second theme into the home key. From that moment of enchantment until the final cadence we witness the exciting spectacle of a great artist functioning at the summit of his powers.

Piano Concerto in D Minor

Mozart played a crucial role in the development of the piano concerto. His concertos were written primarily as display pieces for his own public performances. They abound in the brilliant flourishes and ceremonious gestures characteristic of eighteenth-century social music.

It is interesting to observe that in the piano concertos of his maturity Mozart took all sorts of liberties in regard to form. The piano concerto presented him with a special problem. The opposition between home key and contrasting key that was the basis of sonata form had to be combined here with the contrast between the two opposing entities —the piano and the orchestra. We can observe the artist's instinct for architectonic logic responding to the challenge as he adapts the sonata-allegro structure to the requirements of this double contrast. The orchestral tutti serve as the pillars of a grandly imposing architecture.

Around them unfolds a plastic form in which Mozart explores all the possibilities of texture: the orchestra alone, the piano alone, and the innumerable varieties of interplay possible between them. The two sonorous forces exchange themes and share themes; sometimes each holds to its own ideas. Heavenly melodies alternate with virtuoso passages for the soloist abounding in exposed scales, arpeggios, and broken octaves that demand the highest order of pianism.

Of the seventeen piano concertos that Mozart wrote during his years in Vienna, only two are in minor. These are marked by a brooding intensity and a lofty pathos that strike a new tone in what was generally a brilliant, extrovert type of music. The Piano Concerto in D minor (K. 466, 1785) is one of Mozart's greatest works. The opening theme, based on an ascending triplet figure, suggests—to paraphrase Nietzsche—the birth of orchestral music from the spirit of opera; for it evokes the same combination of mystery and drama as is present in the dark opening scene—also in D minor—of *Don Giovanni*. (The opera was written two years later.) Presented by cellos and double basses against a string background, this theme strikes the note of passionate expressivity that informs the movement.

A bridge passage leads to the contrasting theme in F major.

The closing section brings the orchestral Exposition to a cadence in D minor. Notice how clearly this passage accords with what is the structural function of codetta material: to round off what has gone before.

The piano enters. Its first theme is in the home key (D minor). The

mysterious opening theme then returns in the orchestra, with the piano playing figuration against it. The piano shares briefly in the second theme of the orchestra, then presents its own theme in F, which is immediately restated in the orchestra.

The closing theme is an exciting expansion of the one previously played by the orchestra. We have here, accordingly, a double Exposition based on two orchestral and two piano themes with a closing theme common to both. These constitute the basic material of the movement.

An orchestral tutti launches the Development, which is based on the first orchestral theme and the first piano theme. This section sustains the grandly pathetic tone of what has preceded. After an eventful journey through a series of foreign keys, a brief passage on the piano ushers in the Recapitulation, in which both piano and orchestra are heard, one in the home key of D minor, and the other in the relative key of F major, as before, but with all manner of subtle variations in the material in order to allow for the proper interplay between piano and orchestra. The first piano theme is omitted in this Restatement; the second is transposed from F major to D minor. A series of chords in the orchestra announces the cadenza. (As we noted in our discussion of the concerto in Chapter 35, the cadenza was not written out in the eighteenth century; it was a free improvisation on the themes of the movement.) An agitated coda leads to a pianissimo ending.

The second movement, the Romanze, is in B-flat major. The piano opens with an expressive melody in Mozart's suavest manner.

etc.

This movement is an A-B-A form in which each section in turn approximates an a-b-a pattern.

The provenance of this music must be sought, again, in the opera house. The model for an Andante like this is the operatic aria, in which the orchestra creates a frame for the lyric line of the voice, here sung by the piano. In the middle section Mozart returns to the darkly emotional mood of the first movement, with the piano executing figuration in agitated triplets against an orchestral background. Then the melody of the opening returns, to round off the movement on a note of magical serenity.

The last movement, an Allegro assai (very fast), is an example of the classical rondo finale at its best. The recurrent idea on which the movement is based is an upward-leaping rocket theme, of the type we found in the final movement of the G-minor Symphony. It is announced by the piano in the home key of D minor.

Contrasting ideas serve to set off the main theme. The most important of these is introduced by the piano in F minor.

This is followed by a saucy little tune in which there lives again the spirit of the *opera buffa*. It is presented by the orchestra in F major and

taken over by the piano. The themes are laid out in expansive key areas, which gives this Allegro an architectural firmness beneath the surface animation. Thematic development and modulation introduce an element of sonata style into the rondo framework. Provision is made for a cadenza. Mozart depends on the possibilities for light and shade inherent in the contrast between minor and major, especially in the closing section, which moves into D major. The *opera-buffa* tune provides a happy ending to this glorious work.

Eine kleine Nachtmusik (A *Little Night Music*)

The elegance and delicacy of touch commonly associated with Mozart are embodied in this serenade for strings. The piece was composed,

or at any rate written down, in a single day in August 1787. Intended
for a festive occasion, it stems from the tradition of Viennese social
music exemplified in the divertimento. The score calls for first and
second violin, viola, cello, and bass, the last two doubling the same part.
In performance there were probably several players to each part, so
that this work (K. 525) stands between chamber and orchestral music.
It is in four movements, compact, intimate, and beautifully propor-
tioned.

The opening Allegro is a sonata form in $\frac{4}{4}$ time in G major. As was
customary in music of this type, the first movement has a marchlike
character—as if the musicians were arriving for their cheerful task.

Second is the Romanza, an eighteenth-century andante that maintains
the balance between lyricism and a pleasant reserve. The key is C, the
meter ₵; symmetrical sections are arranged in an A-B-A-C-A structure.
The Minuet, marked Allegretto, is in G major and in regular four-bar
structure. The Trio, which is marked sotto voce (in an undertone, subdued), traces a soaring curve of Mozartean melody; after which the
Minuet is repeated.

The rondo finale, Allegro, is in ₵ in the home key of G. It is based
on a vivacious principal theme that alternates with a subordinate idea.

The movement displays certain features of sonata form—opposition between home and contrasting key, development of the rondo theme, and
modulation far afield. We have said that there is a rondo style as well
as a rondo form. This is the perfect example, bright, jovial, and—a trait
inseparable from this master—stamped with an aristocratic refinement.

In the music of Mozart subjective emotion is elevated to the plane of
the universal. The restlessness and the longing are exorcised by the
ideal loveliness of Apollonian art. It is the duality of this music, its trembling between laughter and tears, its noble serenity amid grief and
pain, that constitutes its special magic. The classic and the romantic,
the impassioned and the elegant fuse in a style of miraculous unity and
control. Mozart is one of the supreme artists of all time; the voice of
pure beauty in music, and probably the most sheerly musical composer
that ever lived.

CHAPTER 53

Ludwig van Beethoven (1770-1827)

"Freedom above all!"

BEETHOVEN belonged to the generation that received the full impact of the French Revolution. He was nourished by its vision of the freedom and dignity of the individual. The time, the place, and the personality combined to produce an artist sensitive in the highest degree to the impulses of the new century. He created the music of a heroic age and in accents never to be forgotten proclaimed its faith in the power of man to shape his destiny.

His Life

He was born in Bonn, in the Rhineland, where his father and grandfather were singers at the court of the Elector. The family situation was unhappy, the father being addicted to drink, and Ludwig at an

Ludwig van Beethoven.

early age was forced to take over the support of his mother and two younger brothers. At eleven and a half he was assistant organist in the court chapel. A year later he became harpsichordist in the Elector's orchestra. A visit to Vienna in his seventeenth year enabled him to play for Mozart. The youth improvised so brilliantly on a theme given him by the master that the latter remarked to his friends, "Keep an eye on him—he will make a noise in the world some day."

Arrangements were made some years later for him to study with Haydn in Vienna at the Elector's expense. He left his native town when he was twenty-two, never to return. One of his admirers, Count Waldstein, inscribed in his album at parting, "Work well and receive the spirit of Mozart from the hands of Haydn." Despite this sound advice the relationship between pupil and teacher left much to be desired. The aging Haydn was ruffled by the young man's volcanic temperament and independence of spirit. Beethoven worked with other masters, the most academic of whom declared that "he has learned nothing and will never do anything in decent style."

Meanwhile his powers as a pianist took the music-loving aristocracy by storm. He was made welcome in the great houses of Vienna by the powerful patrons whose names appear in the dedications of his works —Prince Lichnowsky, Prince Lobkowitz, Count Razumovsky, and the rest. Archduke Rudolph, brother of the Emperor, became his pupil and devoted friend. These connoisseurs, no less than the public, were transported by his highly personal style of improvisation, by the wealth of his ideas, the novelty of their treatment, and the surging emotion behind them.

To this "princely rabble," as he called them, the young genius came —in an era of revolution—as a passionate rebel, forcing them to receive him as an equal and friend. "It is good to move among the aristocracy," he observed, "but it is first necessary to make them respect you." The day had passed of the artist in livery waiting in the antechamber for his instructions. Beethoven, sensitive and irascible, stood up for his rights as an artist. When a nobleman at the home of Count von Browne persisted in talking during his performance, he left off and in a loud voice remarked, "For such pigs I do not play!" Prince Lichnowsky, during the Napoleonic invasion, insisted that he play for some French officers. Beethoven stormed out of the palace in a rage, demolished a bust of Lichnowsky that was in his possession, and wrote to his exalted friend: "Prince! what you are, you are through the accident of birth. What I am, I am through my own efforts. There have been many princes and there will be thousands more. But there is only one Beethoven!" Such was the force of his personality that he was able to make the aristocrats about him accept this interesting proposition. Beneath the rough exterior they recognized an elemental power akin to a force of nature.

Beethoven functioned under a modified form of the patronage system. He was not attached to the court of a prince. Instead, the music-

loving aristocrats of Vienna helped him in various ways—by paying
him handsomely for lessons, or through gifts. He was also aided by
the emergence of a middle-class public and the growth of concert life
and music publishing. At the age of thirty-one he was able to write,
"I have six or seven publishers for each of my works and could have
more if I chose. No more bargaining. I name my terms and they pay."
A youthful exuberance pervades the first decade of his career, an almost
arrogant consciousness of his strength. "Power is the morality of men
who stand out from the mass, and it is also mine!" Thus spoke the individual, in the new era of individualism.

Then, as the young eagle was spreading his wings, fate struck in a
vulnerable spot: he began to lose his hearing. His helplessness in the
face of this affliction dealt a shattering blow to his pride. "Ah, how
could I possibly admit an infirmity in the one sense that should have
been more perfect in me than in others. A sense I once possessed in
highest perfection. Oh I cannot do it!" As his deafness closed in on
him—the first symptoms appeared when he was in his late twenties—it
became the symbol of his terrible sense of apartness from other men,
of all the defiance and insecurity and hunger for love that had rent
him for as long as he could remember. "Forgive me when you see me
draw back when I would gladly mingle with you. My misfortune is
doubly painful because it must lead to my being misunderstood. For
me there can be no recreation in the society of my fellows. I must live
like an exile." His malady brought to a focus what was to become one
of the main themes of the nineteenth century—the loneliness of man.
Upon the mistaken advice of his doctors he retired in 1802 to the
oppressive solitude of a summer resort outside Vienna called Heiligen-
stadt. A titanic struggle shook him, between the destructive forces in
his soul and his desire to live and create. It was one of those searing
experiences that either break a man or leave him stronger. "But little
more and I would have put an end to my life. Only art it was that
withheld me. Ah, it seemed impossible to leave the world until I had
produced all that I felt called upon to produce, and so I endured this
wretched existence."

It was slowly borne in on him that art must henceforth give him the
happiness life withheld. Only through creation could he attain the victory of which fate had threatened to rob him. The will to struggle asserted itself; he fought his way back to health. "I am resolved to rise
superior to every obstacle. With whom need I be afraid of measuring
my strength? If possible I will bid defiance to my fate, although there
will be moments in life when I will be the unhappiest of God's creatures
. . . I will take Fate by the throat. It shall not overcome me. Oh how
beautiful it is to be alive—would that I could live a thousand times!"

Having conquered the chaos within himself he came to believe that man could conquer chaos. This became the epic theme of his music: the progression from despair to conflict, from conflict to serenity, from serenity to triumph and joy. The revelation that had come to him through suffering was a welcome message to the world that was struggling to be born. The concept of man the master of his fate hit off the temper of the new middle-class society in its most dynamic phase. In giving expression to his personal faith Beethoven said what his generation most wanted to hear. He became the major prophet of the nineteenth century, the architect of its heroic vision of life. "I am the Bacchus who presses out the glorious wine for mankind. Whoever truly understands my music is freed thereby from the miseries that others carry about in them." He had stumbled on an idea that was to play a decisive part in nineteenth-century thought: the concept of art as refuge, as compensation for the shortcomings of reality; art as sublimation, atonement, faith—the idealized experience, the ultimate victory over life.

The remainder of his career was spent in an unremitting effort to subjugate the elements of his art to the expressive ideal he had set himself. Fellow musicians and critics might carp at the daring of his thoughts, but his victory was assured. A growing public, especially among the younger generation, responded to the powerful thrust of his music. His life was outwardly uneventful. There were the interminable quarrels with associates and friends—he grew increasingly suspicious and irritable, especially in his last years when he became totally deaf. There were the complicated dealings with his publishers, in which he displayed an impressive shrewdness; his turbulent love affairs (he never married); his high-handed interference in the affairs of his brothers; his tortured relationship with his nephew Carl, an ordinary young man upon whom he fastened a tyrannical affection. All these framed an inner life of extraordinary intensity, an unceasing spiritual development that reached down to ever profounder levels of insight and opened up new domains to tonal art.

Biographers and painters have made familiar the squat sturdy figure —he was five foot four, the same as that other conqueror of the age, Napoleon—walking hatless through the environs of Vienna, the bulging brow furrowed in thought, stopping now and again to jot down an idea in his sketchbook; an idea that, because he was forever deprived of its sonorous beauty, he envisioned all the more vividly in his mind. A ride in an open carriage in inclement weather brought on an attack of dropsy that proved fatal. He died in his fifty-seventh year, famous and revered.

His Music

Beethoven is the supreme architect in music. His genius found expression in the structural type of thinking embodied in the sonata-symphony. His was an instrumental conception. In this respect he differs from the masters who infused into the instruments the spirit of vocal melody. (It is no accident that his name is missing from the list of composers whose symphonic themes are converted year after year into popular songs.) The sketchbooks in which he worked out his ideas show how gradually they reached their final shape and how painstakingly he molded the material into its one inevitable form. It is significant that when he describes the creative process in himself he stresses the development of the idea. "I carry my thoughts within me long, often very long before I write them down. In doing this my memory stands me in such good stead that even years afterward I am sure not to forget a theme I have once grasped . . . As I know what I want, the fundamental idea never deserts me. It mounts, it grows in stature. I hear, I see the picture in its whole extent standing all of a piece before my spirit, and there remains for me only the task of writing it down."

Significant too is his comment regarding the source of his material. "You will ask where I get my ideas. I am not able to answer that question positively. They come directly, indirectly; I can grasp them with my hands. Out amid the freedom of nature, in the woods, on walks, in the silence of the night, early in the morning, called forth by such moods as in the minds of poets translate themselves into words, but in mine into tones that ring, roar, storm until at last they stand as notes before me."

Inheriting the grand form from Haydn and Mozart, he transformed it into a spacious frame for his ideas. He expanded the dimensions of the first movement, especially of the coda, which became an ample section, designed to balance the proportions of the movement. Like Haydn and Mozart, he treated the Development section as the dynamic center of sonata form. His short incisive themes offer limitless opportunity for expansion and development. They unfold with volcanic energy and momentum. The slow movement became in his hands a hymnic adagio, the embodiment of Beethovenian pathos. He transformed minuet into scherzo, making it a movement of rhythmic energy ranging from "cosmic laughter" to mystery and wonder. He enlarged the finale into a movement comparable in size and scope to the first, ending the symphony—as the new age required—on a note of triumph.

The piano occupied a central position in Beethoven's art. His thirty-two sonatas are an indispensable part of its literature, whether for the amateur pianist or concert artist. They are well called the pianist's New Testament (the Old being the *Well-Tempered Clavier* of Bach). Dynamic contrasts, explosive accents, opposition of low and high register, syncopation, and powerful crescendos are essential features of his idiom. Characteristic is his fondness for the theme and variations. Here he becomes the master builder, marshaling his inexhaustible wealth of ideas to fashion out of the simplest material a towering edifice.

In the symphony Beethoven found the ideal medium wherein to address mankind. His nine symphonies are spiritual dramas of universal appeal. Their sweep and tumultuous affirmation of life mark them a pinnacle of the rising democratic art. They are conceived on a scale too grand for the aristocratic salon; they demand the amplitude of the concert hall. For Beethoven the beauty of instrumental timbre was not an end but a means for expressing ideas. Color—in this he was the classicist—served to clarify the design. "Does he imagine I think of his miserable violin when the spirit is upon me?" he retorted when the complaint reached him that he did not write gratefully for the instrument. When the idea demanded it he wrote against the instrument, or beyond it—as in his final piano sonatas. Someone pointed out to him that the cello part of a certain quartet did not lie within the hand. "It must lie!" he answered.

With his Third Symphony, the *Eroica* (1803), Beethoven achieved the expanded architecture of his mature style. The work was originally dedicated to Napoleon, First Consul of the Republic, in whom he saw incarnated the spirit of revolution and the freedom of man. When the news came that Napoleon had proclaimed himself Emperor he was disenchanted. "He too is just like any other! Now he will trample on the rights of man and serve nothing but his own ambition." The embittered composer tore up the dedicatory page of the just-completed work and renamed it "Heroic Symphony to celebrate the memory of a great man." A conqueror himself—did he not once declare, "I too am a king!"—he understood the Corsican. "It is a great pity I do not comprehend the art of war as well as I do the art of music. I would conquer him!"

The Fifth Symphony (1805–07) has fixed itself in the popular mind as the archetype of all that a symphony is. The Seventh (1812) was regarded by Wagner as "the apotheosis of the dance." The Ninth, the *Choral Symphony* (1817–23), strikes the searching tone of Beethoven's last period. Its finale, in which soloists and chorus join with the orchestra, contains the famous line, "Be embraced, ye millions!" The choral movement is a setting of Schiller's *Ode to Joy*, a ringing prophecy of the time when "all men shall be brothers." In these works there sounds the rhetoric of the new century. Complementing them are the

Fourth (1806) and Eighth (1812), two buoyant and serene symphonies; and the Sixth, the hymn to nature known as the *Pastorale* (1808). Beethoven's conception of nature was closer to Rousseau's than to Byron's. "I am as happy as a child at the thought of roaming in the woods, among the trees and flowers and rocks. No man loves the country more than I. Forest, trees, and rocks re-echo all that mankind longs for. Every tree seems to speak to me saying, 'Holy! Holy!' " It is this pantheistic view of the universe that pervades the *Pastorale*.

The concerto offered Beethoven a congenial public form in which he combined virtuosity with symphonic architecture. Most popular of his works in this medium are the Fourth Piano Concerto, in G (1806); the Fifth, in E-flat (the *Emperor*, 1809); and the noble Concerto for Violin in D (1806). He wrote much chamber music, the string quartet being closest to his heart. The six quartets Opus 18 and the three Opus 59, the latter dedicated to Count Razumovsky, are pre-eminent for profundity of feeling and technical mastery. His supreme achievements in this area are the last five quartets, which together with the Grand Fugue, Op. 133, occupied the final years of his life. In these, as in the last five piano sonatas, Beethoven found his way to a skeletal language from which all nonessentials had been rigidly pared—a language far transcending his time. The master's gaze is focused within, encompassing depths that music never before had plumbed. To these works, which constitute the inner citadel of his art, may be applied the remark he made when a puzzled violinist asked him concerning one of the Razumovsky quartets, "But surely you do not consider this to be music?" He replied, "It is not for you but for a later age!"

Although his most important victories were won in the instrumental field, Beethoven enriched the main types of vocal music. Of his songs the best known is the cycle of six, *An die ferne Geliebte* (To the Distant Beloved). His sole opera *Fidelio* (originally called *Leonora*, completed in 1805) centers about wifely devotion, human freedom, and the defeat of those who would destroy it. There is much memorable music in it. All the same, Beethoven's imagination was hampered by the trappings of the stage. He is at his most dramatic in abstract forms. Although the pious Haydn considered him an atheist, he hymned "Nature's God" through the traditional form of religious music. The *Missa solemnis* (Solemn Mass in D, 1818–23) ranks in importance with the Ninth Symphony and the final quartets. The work transcends the limits of any specific creed or dogma. Beethoven's altar is the world, his faith embraces all creeds. Above the Kyrie of the Mass he wrote a sentence that applies to the whole of his music: "From the heart . . . may it find its way to the heart."

His creative activity, extending over a span of thirty-five years, bears witness to a ceaseless striving after perfection. "I feel as if I had written scarcely more than a few notes," he remarked at the end of his career. And a year before his death: "I hope still to bring a few great works into the world." Despite his faith in his destiny he knew the humility of the truly great. "The real artist has no pride. Unfortunately he sees that his art has no limits, he feels obscurely how far he is from the goal. And while he is perhaps being admired by others he mourns the fact that he has not yet reached the point to which his better genius like a distant sun ever beckons him."

Chronologically Beethoven's life fell in almost equal parts in the eighteenth and nineteenth centuries. His career bridged the transition from the old society to the new. The romantics, responding to the grand rhetoric and sweep of his music, claimed him as one of their own. It is a mistake to regard him thus. He was not "the man who freed music" —presumably from the shackles imposed on it by Haydn and Mozart. On the contrary, he brought the great classical forms to their ultimate development in terms of logical structure and power. However, into these forms he injected the dynamic force and expressiveness that were the essence of the new century. He was the spokesman of the rising age of individualism. The sum of his message was freedom. By freedom, though, he understood not romantic license but the Hegelian "recognition of necessity," not romantic revolt but the inner discipline that alone constitutes freedom. This exalted conception he projected with such intensity of vision and mastery of means that his shadow lengthened across the next hundred years.

The Fifth Symphony

The most popular of all symphonies, Beethoven's Fifth, in C minor, Opus 67, is also the most concentrated expression of the frame of mind and spirit that we have come to call Beethovenian. It embodies in supreme degree the basic principle of symphonic thinking—the flowering of an extended composition from a kernel or germ theme by a process of organic growth. The popular story that Beethoven, when asked for the meaning of the opening theme, replied, "Thus Fate knocks at the door," is probably not authentic. Such literalness seems unlikely in one who was so completely the tone poet. If the work continues to be associated with Fate it is rather because of the inevitable, the relentless logic of its unfolding.

The first movement, marked Allegro con brio (lively, with vigor), springs out of the rhythmic idea of "three shorts and a long" that dominates the symphony. Announced in unison by strings and clarinet (Beethoven holds his full forces in reserve), the motive establishes the home key of C minor. It is the most compact and commanding gesture in the whole symphonic literature.

Out of this motive flowers the first theme, which is nothing more than a repetition, at different levels of the scale and with altered intervals, of the germinating rhythm.

The power of the movement springs from the almost terrifying single-mindedness with which the underlying idea is pursued. It is rhythm, torrential yet superbly controlled, that is the generating force behind this "storm and stress." Beethoven here achieved a vehemence that was new in music. We reach an area of relaxation in the lyric second theme, in the related key of E-flat major. Yet even here the headlong course of the movement does not slacken. As the violins, clarinet, and flute sound the gentle melody in turn, the cellos and double basses persist with the "three shorts and a long" in the bass.

Basic rhythm

The Development is a tightly knit fabric woven out of the basic rhythm. The crescendo here becomes an element of form, imparting to the movement its relentless drive. No less characteristic of Beethoven's style are the powerful contrasts between soft and loud. The transition back to the home key culminates in a fortissimo proclamation of the underlying rhythm by full orchestra. The Restatement is interrupted when an oboe solo introduces a note of pathos, momentarily slackening the tension. The second theme is transposed into C major. Beethoven balances the formal structure with an extended coda in which the basic rhythm reveals a new fund of explosive energy.

Beethovenian serenity and strength imbue the second movement, Andante con moto (at a going pace, with movement). The key is A-flat; the form, a theme and variations. There are two melodic ideas. First is a broadly spun theme sung by violas and cellos. It is followed by one of

those hymnic upward-thrusting subjects so characteristic of the master, which echoes the "three shorts and a long" of the opening movement.

In this Andante the constructive impulse prevails over the lyrical. It is not a romantic slow movement; rather is it classical in its reserve, its symphonic drive, its architectural cohesion.

Beethoven varies the opening melody by embellishing it first in six-

teenth notes, then in thirty-seconds. The second theme is varied in color, dynamics, register, and type of accompaniment, gathering strength until it is proclaimed by the full orchestra. The coda, marked Più mosso (faster), opens with a motive on the bassoon against syncopated chords in the strings. A dynamic crescendo rounds off the movement.

Third in the cycle of movements is the Allegro in ¾ which returns to the somber C minor that is the home key of the work. In its rhythmic drive and élan, this is a genuinely symphonic scherzo. From the depths

of the bass rises a characteristic subject, a rocket theme introduced by
cellos and double basses.

The pattern of the first eight notes is identical with those of the last
movement of Mozart's G-minor Symphony. Beethoven was aware of the
resemblance, for he copied out the Mozart theme in his sketchbook opposite his own. Our "tune detectives" who specialize in such discoveries
fail to point out that the important thing in such cases is not the theme
but its destiny—what the composer does with it. Because of differences in rhythm, mood, and treatment, Beethoven's movement is as far
removed as could be from Mozart's.

The "three shorts and a long" reappear fortissimo in the horns. Nourished by the crescendo, the movement steadily accumulates force and
drive. The Trio is based on a gruffly humorous motive of running eighth
notes stated in the bass by cellos and double basses and imitated in
turn, in ever higher register, by violas, second violins, and first violins.

The motive of the double basses was described by Berlioz in a celebrated phrase as the "gambols of a frolicsome elephant." Beethoven's
cosmic laughter resounds through these measures: a laughter that
shakes—and builds—a world.

The Scherzo returns in a modified version, followed by a transition
that leads directly into the fourth movement. This highly dramatic
passage, punctuated by the mysterious tapping of the kettledrum, is
spun out of the scherzo theme and the basic rhythm. There is a steady
accumulation of tension until the orchestra, in a blaze of light, surges
into the triumphal Allegro in C major.

Beethoven achieves dramatic contrasts of color through his changes
of mode. The first movement is in a somber minor. The second, with its
classical serenity, is in major. The third, save for the jovial Trio, returns
to minor. Then the dark C minor is dispelled for good with the upsurge
of the finale. At this point three instruments make their appearance for
the first time in the symphonies of the classical Viennese school—piccolo, double bassoon, and trombone, lending brilliance and body to the
orchestral sound.

The fourth movement is a monumental sonata form in which Beethoven overcomes what would seem to be an insuperable difficulty: to

fashion an ending that will sustain the tension of what has gone before. Actually the ideas are less distinguished than those of the earlier
movements. What carries the work to its victorious end is the rhythmic
energy, the bigness of conception, and the orchestral sonority. The
main idea, in C major, is based on a chord-and-scale pattern. This

is followed by a theme that serves as a bridge from C to G major.

The contrasting key is represented by a vigorous theme containing
triplets:

There follows a decisive closing theme. The Development is marked by
dynamic rhythm and free modulation. Then—an amazing stroke!—
Beethoven brings back the "three shorts and a long" as they appeared in the third movement, deliberately allowing the momentum
to slacken so that he may build up tension against the upsurge of the
Recapitulation. This is followed by an extensive coda fashioned from
materials already heard. The pace accelerates steadily up to the concluding Presto. There is a final outcropping of the basic rhythm. The
symphonic stream at the very end becomes an overpowering torrent
as the Tonic chord—prime source and goal of all activity—is hurled
forth by the orchestra again and again.

The Appassionata

As in the case of the *Moonlight,* the title of the Piano Sonata in F
minor, Opus 57—*Appassionata*—was not Beethoven's. Would he not
have considered each of his sonatas impassioned? Such fanciful names
were sometimes appended by music publishers in order to stimulate
sales. Nonetheless, these labels are not without significance. If they

caught on as they did, it was because they expressed something of what this music meant to those who heard it.

The solo sonata took its rise from the spirit of chamber music. It was an ideal form for the home. In this respect Beethoven's early sonatas adhered to the model established by Haydn and Mozart. As music moved from salon to public concert hall the sonata expanded in scope and dimension, along with the other forms of absolute music. In the *Appassionata* (1804–06) we encounter a new type of concert sonata conceived on a scale extending beyond the private circle of listeners. The violence of its drama, the brilliance of its rhetoric, and the amplitude of its canvas demand an audience. This was music for a new age.

The work is in three movements. The first, Allegro assai (very fast), opens in a brooding F minor. The opening subject is an expansion of the F-minor chord. Harmony was now so potent a factor in music that it could shape the melody. A simple chord line, transformed by rhythm, becomes the basis of a memorable theme.

Interesting is the appearance in the opening passage of a rhythm that was soon to become famous in another context—the "three shorts and a long." The pattern obviously pervaded Beethoven's thinking at that period of his life. This is a tempestuous movement, couched in the "tenderly passionate" language that made his improvisations on the piano a thing of wonder to his contemporaries. Characteristic are the violent contrasts between pianissimo and fortissimo. The heavenly second theme, in the related major key of A-flat, stands out against its darker surroundings. Despite the contrast of mood it is related to the first theme; it arises from an inversion of the opening motive and ad-

heres to the same rhythmic pattern. A dramatic closing theme rounds off the Exposition.

The Development is without precedent in piano music for its breadth and impact. The material is drawn from both subjects and from the bridge between. Beethoven makes striking use throughout of arpeggio figures. With the return to the home key we hear the principal theme against a new accompaniment. The material is freely altered. The coda is tempestuous.

The serene Andante con moto, in $\frac{2}{4}$ time, is in D-flat major. It opens with a searching theme that serves as basis for a set of three variations. The melodic outline is retained, while the harmonic figuration becomes ever more elaborate. Most effective, after the process of embellishment has been completed, is the coda, in which the theme returns in all its original simplicity. The emotion is powerful and profound, yet kept well within the confines of the form. This is a truly classical slow movement.

A brief transition leads into the Allegro ma non troppo (not too fast) which is in sonata-allegro form. As volcanic a finale as ever was written, this is one of those "perpetual motions" whose secret is absolutely unrelenting tension. Only a master of musical architecture could have created so homogeneous a tissue. Beethoven calls for the repeat of the Development and Recapitulation. He underestimated the demands that this movement makes upon the player (and the listener). Even without the repeat the movement taxes the endurance, both technical and emotional, of all but the virtuoso performer. Pianists generally play it—in spite of Beethoven's direction—at a breakneck speed that all but obliterates its meaning. That the music manages to survive such mauling is due to the fund of emotion and intellect of which it is compounded.

Overture to Coriolan (Coriolanus)

Sonata form has one important element in common with the drama. The classical tragedy centered about the conflict within the hero between two opposing forces such as love and honor. Classical sonata form centered about a conflict between two opposing keys and theme groups. Sooner or later composers were bound to adjust the musical drama to the literary one. It was Beethoven who consummated this adjustment. In his Overtures to Collin's *Coriolan* (1807) and Goethe's *Egmont* (1810), as in the four Overtures to his opera *Fidelio*, the opposition between a rhythmically aggressive theme and a lyrically yielding theme was harnessed to the dramatic conflicts of the theater. In this way sonata-allegro form—the grand form of absolute music—was laid open to the influence of a literary program, a development of great significance for the nineteenth century. One may of course listen to these overtures as absolute music, disregarding the story behind them. At the same time it is of interest to see how Beethoven reconciled abstract form with poetic content.

The hero of Collin's tragedy, as of Shakespeare's, is the Roman patrician Coriolanus, whose opposition to the tribunes of the people results in his being exiled from Rome. He goes over to the enemy Volscians,

gathers a huge army, and marches on his native city, determined to lay
it waste. A deputation of his countrymen pleads with him to spare
Rome, but he turns a deaf ear. As a last resort his mother, wife, and
little son are dispatched to his camp. Their entreaties finally move him
to desist from his purpose. In Plutarch's account as in Shakespeare's,
Coriolanus is murdered by the infuriated Volscians. In Collin's play the
remorseful general commits suicide.

Beethoven, we saw, was at his most dramatic in instrumental music.
The Overture to *Coriolan*, Opus 62, projects the essence of the tragedy.
After a brief introduction we hear a fateful motive that establishes the
home key of C minor. Its expressive content suggests the somber state
of mind of the hero of the play.

This essentially rhythmic subject, presented by the first violins and
violas, is opposed to the tender, supplicating melody in the contrasting
key of E-flat. Here, because of the story, one may possibly accept the
nineteenth-century view of the first theme as masculine and the second as feminine.

The Development is a powerful drama fashioned from the closing
theme of the Exposition. The Recapitulation presents the material in
shortened form and departs in certain details from the traditional pattern of sonata-allegro. The first theme, for example, returns not in the
home key of C minor but in F minor. There is a stirring coda. The tense
motive with which the piece began slackens to a somber ending. Beethoven, we know, was concerned with the hero as the supreme representative of mankind. *Coriolan* is one of several works in which his
heroic conception of man receives its ideal expression.

Beethoven has aptly been called the orator of the democratic era.
His music stems from a Promethean struggle for self-realization. It is
the expression of a titanic force, the affirmation of an all-conquering
will.

CHAPTER 54

Classical Chamber Music

"No other form of music can delight our senses with such exquisite beauty of sound, or display so clearly to our intelligence the intricacies and adventures of its design."

Henry Hadow

By *chamber music* is meant ensemble music for from two to about eight or nine instruments with one player to the part, as distinct from orchestral music in which a single instrumental part may be presented by anywhere from two to eighteen players. The essential trait of chamber music is its intimacy and refinement; its natural setting is the home. In this domain we find neither the surge and thunder of the symphony nor the grand gesture of the operatic stage. The drama is of an inward kind. Each instrument represents an ideal type and is expected to assert itself to the full; but the style of playing differs from that of the solo virtuoso. The soloist is encouraged to exalt his own personality. In

Jack Levine, b. 1915, *String Quartette*.
"The essential trait of chamber music is its intimacy and refinement."

343

chamber music, on the other hand, the various instruments are part of an ensemble and try to blend into a perfect whole. It has been said that in no other kind of music is it so difficult to create a masterpiece. Certainly in no other kind is the texture (and the composer) so exposed.

The classical era saw the golden age of chamber music. Haydn and Mozart, Beethoven and Schubert established the true chamber-music style, which is in the nature of a friendly conversation among equals. Limpid harmony and chiseled form, clarity of thought and freshness of feeling characterize their enchantingly subtle art. In their chamber music the Viennese masters addressed themselves to a limited audience of friends and connoisseurs of music. They attained thereby a degree of personal utterance not possible in the large public forms of musical communication such as the opera and oratorio, symphony and concerto. Some of their profoundest thoughts are to be discovered in their chamber works.

The central position in classical chamber music was held by the string quartet. Consisting of first and second violins, viola, and cello, this group came to represent the ideal type of happy comradeship among instruments, lending itself to music of exquisite detail and purity of style. Other favored combinations were the duo sonata—piano and violin or piano and cello; the trio—piano, violin, and cello; and the quintet, usually consisting of a combination of string instruments, or a string quartet and solo instrument such as the piano or clarinet. The age produced, too, some memorable examples of chamber music for the larger groups—sextet, septet, and octet.

Haydn: String Quartet in F, Opus 3, No. 5

Haydn was in his early twenties when he wrote his first string quartet. He was past seventy when he commenced his last. His eighty-three works in this medium testify to a half-century of artistic growth. The early ones issue from a time when the difference between orchestral and chamber style had not yet been clearly established. The composer is finding his way to the four-movement form and to a texture in which all four instruments share equally. He has not yet achieved the independence of part writing that characterizes the later quartets. But his gifts are in evidence in the abundance of spontaneous melody and the simple clear forms of these youthful works.

The six quartets of Opus 3 were written some time after 1760, during his first years in the service of the Esterházys. They mark the transition from his early manner to a more mature style. The fifth of the set contains an Andante cantabile that for generations has been a favorite with the public. Often heard separately and known as the Serenade, the movement is based on one of those indestructible tunes that bear the

imprint of a composer's melodic genius. The first violin, muted, carries
the melody against a pizzicato accompaniment by the other strings. The

Andante cantabile

𝆏 *dolce*

movement, in $\frac{4}{4}$ time, is in two-part form. The first part proceeds from
C major to G, the second returns to C. Each is repeated. One has but
to hear it to realize how important an element of Haydn's art was Austrian popular song.

This Andante is the second movement. The first is a Presto in F in
$\frac{3}{8}$, bright, gay, and uncomplicated, with a flow of artless melody within
a sonata-allegro form. The Development and Recapitulation are repeated as well as the Exposition. The third movement, the Minuet,
is in F. It opens with a four-bar phrase which is answered by one of six.
Such a nonsymmetrical formation, we have noticed, is as closely related
to the classical style as are the usual symmetries of four-bar construction. The finale, in F major, is in $\frac{2}{4}$ time. It is marked Scherzando
(gaily, jestingly), and is in sonata-allegro form. Here the spirit of
opera buffa holds sway. In a movement such as this may be discerned,
fully formed, the line of thought and feeling that culminated in the
great finales of the master's last period.

Mozart: Quintet for Clarinet and Strings

The spirit of Viennese house-music pervades this celebrated quintet
(K. 581). The combination of instruments used shapes the conception.
The work is based on the opposition between two protagonists—the
clarinet, which because of its striking tone is the center of attention,
and the string quartet. Mozart brings into play all the qualities of the
clarinet, its capacity for broad singing melody as well as its agility in
ornate virtuoso passages that run the gamut from low to high register.

The first movement is an ample Allegro in sonata form. It is in $\frac{4}{4}$
time, in A major. The opening theme has a sweet serenity. Introduced
by the strings, it is set off by arpeggios on the clarinet. The second
theme, in E, displays the exquisite songfulness of the Mozartean cantabile. It is presented by the first violin and shifted into minor when the
clarinet takes it over, imparting to the movement a romantic tone. The

Allegro   *etc.*

𝆏 *dolce*

development section lends itself to animated rivalry between clarinet
and strings, after which the thematic material is restated.

The Larghetto, in D, is a broadly spun song for clarinet against a background of muted strings. Mozart here captures the spirit of his great operatic arias. The middle section contains an exciting dialogue between clarinet and first violin. Then the aria returns.

The Menuetto, in the home key of A major, has two trios instead of one. After each, the Minuet proper is played da capo without repeats. The first, in A minor, is for strings alone. The second trio, in A major, emphasizes the clarinet and is based on one of those bouncy arpeggio themes that so vividly capture the buoyancy of Austrian popular dance. Here is the spirit of the *Ländler*, the peasant dance from which descended the Viennese waltz.

The Finale, an Allegretto in A, in ₵ time, is a theme and variations. The melody is of utmost simplicity, to allow room for elaboration; yet it is stamped with aristocratic refinement. The variations include embellishment of the melody; a change to triplet rhythm in the accompaniment; a new melody spun over the harmonies of the old; the original theme heard against florid arabesques; and a change of pace—and character—first to adagio, finally to allegro. This is music in the great tradition.

Beethoven: String Quartet in C Minor, Opus 18, No. 4

Beethoven did not undertake the writing of string quartets until he was almost thirty. The six quartets of Opus 18 date from 1798–1800. As might be expected, they show traces of the influence of Haydn and Mozart, the acknowledged masters of the form. Yet in far greater degree they bear the imprint of Beethoven's personal language.

The fourth of the set, in C minor, strikes the impassioned tone familiar from the piano sonata in the same key, the so-called *Pathétique*. The first movement, a tightly constructed sonata-allegro, opens sonorously with a somber theme that is presented by the

first violin. The contrasting theme, introduced by the second violin, is suavely melodious and relaxed; it is in the related key of E-flat major. Characteristic are the resounding chords produced by double, triple, and quadruple stopping; the abrupt contrasts of soft and loud; the sudden accents and syncopations.

The second movement, in C major and in ⅜ time, is marked Andante scherzoso, quasi Allegretto (fairly slow and playful, almost Allegretto).

A staccato theme enters on each instrument in turn, the four lines interweaving in a neatly threaded fabric. This independence of parts marks the entire movement. Yet Beethoven wears his learning lightly; the music trips along in real scherzando fashion. "Andante" is used here in the eighteenth-century sense, indicating a fairly movemented pace. To make sure that this was understood, Beethoven added "quasi allegretto."

Third is a Minuet marked Allegretto, in the home key of C minor. As in Mozart's G-minor Symphony, the movement is of a gravity not envisaged in the term "minuet." The Trio makes up for this with a melody in popular style that leaps along the tones of the chord. Charming is the dialogue between second violin and cello at the end of the Trio, in which a fragment of melody played by the one is immediately imitated by the other. Beethoven directed that when the first section is repeated it should be taken faster.

The final Allegro, a rondo in C minor in ¢ time, is akin in spirit to the movements that the Viennese masters customarily labeled *All' Ongarese* (in Hungarian style). The impetuous rondo theme recurs in alternation with subsidiary material of a more relaxed character. The capricious rhythms of Hungarian folk dance are suggested in the sudden pause in the second phrase, which is indicated by a *fermata* or hold. The coda, marked Prestissimo, brings the work to a tumultuous close.

Schubert: The Trout Quintet

One of the most popular of Schubert's chamber works, the *Trout Quintet* dates from 1819, when the composer was twenty-two. He had spent the summer before in Hungary, a circumstance that may have influenced him to mark the finale of this work *All' Ongarese.* He had just completed a happy journey through upper Austria, whose landscape pervades this music. In the course of the trip he was asked to make his song *Die Forelle* (The Trout) available to players of chamber music. Schubert responded with the Quintet in A major for piano and strings, whose fourth movement consists of a set of variations on the melody of the song.

The addition of piano to the ensemble expands the frame of a chamber-music work and introduces the element of virtuosity. A natural opposition ensues between the piano sound and that of the string mass. Schubert, significantly, strengthened the string group. Instead of writing for the usual quartet he employed a violin, viola, cello, and double bass. The work dates from a period when he had become interested in exploring the resources of the piano both as solo and ensemble instrument. The *Trout Quintet* was one of the first fruits of this preoccupation.

The opening Allegro vivace is a cheerful movement of ample dimensions in which the voices interweave with truly Schubertian felicity. The Andante looks back to the quietude of the eighteenth-century slow movement, and is marked by striking changes of key. The Scherzo places Schubert in the great Viennese lineage. Out of the spirit of the dance he conjures up, as did his illustrious predecessors, the surging rhythm that creates forms and molds ideas.

The most popular movement, the fourth, is the set of variations on the song. The theme is announced by first violin against a background of

string tone. The first variation allots it to the piano against arpeggios in the strings, the second to cello against exciting arabesques in the upper register of the violin. In Variation 3 the melody is carried by double bass against elaborate running passages on the piano. The tune hitherto has remained unchanged. The next two variations present it with changes of register, dynamics, harmony, melodic outline, rhythm, and type of accompaniment: the fourth variation shifts to the minor, the fifth is Schubert at his grandest. In the sixth and final variation he returns to the mood of the song by setting forth the melody against the rippling figure of the original piano accompaniment. The quintet concludes with a beguiling fifth movement, a rondo that is an idealized dance in Hungarian style.

The prevailing optimism of Schubert's early twenties is reflected throughout the work. Alien to it is the tragic tone of the later string quartets and of the great Quintet for Strings in C. The *Trout Quintet* springs out of the finest tradition of Viennese social music. It in turn had a robust progeny in the chamber music with piano of Schumann and Brahms.

Chamber music, because of its nature, has never commanded the wide public of symphony, opera, or oratorio. There was a time not so long ago when it was considered to be accessible only to the connoisseur. But the impact of radio and recordings upon our musical life has helped to change all this. Recognized as an ideal music for the home, it has been made familiar to the American public through frequent broadcasts of both live and recorded chamber groups, with the result that it now occupies its rightful place in our musical scene. It holds out to the listener a quite special musical experience, and offers him delights that no other branch of music can duplicate.

↝ *C H A P T E R 5 5* ↜

From Classic to Romantic:
Schubert's *Unfinished*

"I am very greatly obliged by the diploma of honorary membership you so kindly sent me. May it be the reward of my devotion to the art of music to become wholly worthy of such a distinction one day. In order to give musical expression to my sincere gratitude as well, I shall take the liberty before long of presenting your honorable Society with one of my symphonies in full score."

WE DISCUSSED the songs and piano pieces of Franz Schubert in connection with the romantic movement, whose first stirrings found in them so vivid an expression. In his symphonies, however, as in his chamber music, Schubert was the heir of the classical Viennese tradition. For this reason we consider his most celebrated symphony in a section devoted to the achievements of Haydn, Mozart, and Beethoven. The work forms the natural link between their music and the romantic era.

The title *Unfinished* which attaches to Schubert's Symphony No. 8, in B minor, is somewhat unfortunate, suggesting as it does that the composer was snatched away by death before he could complete it. Actually the work was written when Schubert was twenty-five years old, in 1822, and was sent to the Styrian Musical Society in the town of Graz in fulfillment of the promise made in the letter just quoted. He completed two movements and sketched the opening measures of a scherzo. Given his facility, a work was no sooner conceived than written down; if he abandoned the task in this instance it was probably because he had said all that he had to say. The Symphony in B minor is no more unfinished than those sonatas of Beethoven that contain only two movements. It is a superb artistic entity in which Schubert adapts the conventional symphonic scheme to his own purpose.

The work displays his radiant orchestral sonority, his power of making the instruments sing, his unique handling of woodwinds and brass,

The wonder is all the greater when we remember that Schubert never heard his finest symphonic scores. The B-minor Symphony, for example, was never performed during his lifetime. The manuscript lay gathering dust for more than thirty-five years after his death.

The first movement, Allegro moderato, is based on three ideas. The first, in the nature of an introductory theme, establishes the home key of B minor. It emerges out of the lower register in a mysterious pianissimo, played by cellos and double basses.

Allegro moderato

The second is a broadly curved melody in the home key, given out by an oboe and clarinet over the restless accompaniment of the strings. The downward leap from the opening note imparts to the melodic line a characteristically Schubertian poignancy.

Third is the great lyric theme in G major, sung by cellos against syncopated chords in the clarinets and violas. Extraordinary is the broad arch traced by the forward surge of this melody, yet how simple is its pattern.

A codetta derived from this theme rounds off the Exposition and establishes the contrasting key of G major.

The development section is remarkable for its architectonic force, its dramatic intensity and momentum. With sure symphonic instinct Schubert picks what seems like the least promising of his themes—the first— for expansion and working out. The idea reveals its latent energies in a symphonic fabric that grows steadily in power and impetus. Now it is presented by the lower strings and imitated in the upper. Now a fragment flowers into new lines of thought. The violent contrasts between loud and soft, between high and low intensify a drama that is conceived and executed in wholly symphonic terms. Characteristic is the way that ideas are broken off abruptly, only to resume with greater force. Altogether novel is Schubert's use of the sumptuous resonance of the trombones, which he pits against the woodwinds, the one answering the other against a turbulent string background. Harmonic and rhythmic tension builds steadily to the return home. The constructive logic and symphonic verve of this Development bespeak the high classical tradition.

The Recapitulation restates the material of the first section. The lyric theme of the cellos is transposed to D major, which is related to the home key of B minor. The coda brings back the opening idea, so that the movement ends with the germ theme out of which it flowered.

The second movement in E major is marked Andante con moto (at a going pace, with motion), in spite of which conductors persist in taking it at a drawn-out adagio that is utterly out of character. This Andante is in abbreviated sonata form; that is, an Exposition and Recapitulation without a Development. How sheerly romantic is the sonority of the opening chords, played by bassoons and horns against a descending pizzicato on the double basses, out of which emerges the principal motive in the strings.

An orchestral crescendo leads to the next idea in the related key of C-sharp minor. This is a long-breathed song introduced by clarinet

and answered by oboe against syncopated chords in the strings. The closing section of the Exposition undergoes an exciting symphonic expansion. Then the two ideas return in the Recapitulation, with subtle changes of color. This time, for example, it is the oboe that introduces the broadly curved second idea and the clarinet that answers. The coda looks back to the opening measures, and closes the movement on a note of dreamy retrospection.

Schubert's *Unfinished* reveals, in relation to the classical age, nothing less than a new world of sound. Its harmonies are poetically expressive; its delicate coloring stems from a most subtle differentiation between the different instrumental voices. Its melodic imagery is of surpassing power and breadth. The prodigal creator of this music passed his uneventful life in the city of Beethoven; too diffident to approach the great man, he worshiped from afar. He could not know that of all the composers of his time, his name alone would be linked to that of his idol. They who far surpassed him in fame and worldly success are long forgotten. Today we speak of the four masters of the classical Viennese school: Haydn, Mozart, Beethoven—and Schubert.

PART FIVE

The Older Music

"Music was originally discreet, seemly, simple, masculine, and of good morals. Have not the moderns rendered it lascivious beyond measure?"

Jacob of Liège (fourteenth century)

Harmony and Counterpoint: Musical Texture

IN WRITINGS on music we encounter frequent references to the fabric or texture. Such comparisons between music and cloth are not as unreasonable as may at first appear. Both are composed of threads woven together in such a way as to create patterns against a background. The weave of the musical fabric may be one of several types.

Monophonic Texture

The simplest is *monophonic or single-voice texture*. Here the melody is heard without either a harmonic accompaniment or other vocal lines. Attention is focused on the single line. All music up to about a thousand years ago, of which we have any knowledge, was monophonic. The great heritage of the monophonic period in Western music is Gregorian chant, the age-old liturgical music of the Catholic Church, which was conceived as a pure vocal line without a harmonic background.

To this day the music of the oriental world—of China, Japan, India, Java, Bali, and the Arab nations—is largely monophonic. The melody may be accompanied by a variety of rhythm and percussion instruments that embellish it, but there is no third dimension of depth or perspective such as harmony alone confers upon a melody. To make up for this lack the single line, being the sole bearer of musical meaning, takes on great complexity and finesse. The monophonic music of the Orient boasts subtleties of pitch and refinements of rhythm unknown in our music.

Polyphonic Texture

When two or more melodic lines are combined we have a *polyphonic or many-voiced texture*. Here the music derives its expressive power and its interest from the interplay of the several lines. Polyphonic texture is based on counterpoint. This term comes from the Latin *punctus contra punctum*, "dot against dot" or "note against note"—that is to say, one line against the other. Counterpoint is the art and science of combining several lines or voices into a unified musical fabric. "Contrapuntal" and "polyphonic" are used in a general sense as interchangeable. Strictly speaking, they are not. We have polyphonic music when several people harmonize a melody. It is only when each of the parts has a melodic and rhythmic life of its own that we have true counterpoint.

355

It was a little over a thousand years ago that European musicians hit upon the device of combining two or more lines simultaneously. (Folk music appears to have known this procedure a long time before.) At this point Western art music parted company from the monophonic Orient. There ensued a magnificent flowering of polyphonic art that came to its high point in the fifteenth and sixteenth centuries. This development of contrapuntal technique was tied up with the predominance of religious choral music.

Homophonic Texture

In the third type of texture a single voice takes over the melodic interest while the accompanying voices surrender their individuality and become blocks of harmony, the chords that support, color, and enhance the principal part. Here we have a single-melody-with-chords or homophonic texture. Again the listener's interest is directed to a single line; but this line, unlike that of oriental music, is conceived in relation to a harmonic background. Homophonic texture is familiar to all; we hear it when the pianist plays the melody with his right hand while the left sounds the chords, or when the singer or violinist carries the tune against a harmonic accompaniment on the piano.

We have said that melody is the horizontal aspect of music while harmony is the vertical. The comparison with the warp and woof of a fabric consequently has real validity. The horizontal threads, the melodies, are held together by the vertical threads, the harmonies. Out of their interaction comes a weave that may be light or heavy, coarse or fine.

The several types of texture are apparent from the look of the music on the page. (See opposite page.)

Although we draw a distinction between the contrapuntal and harmonic aspects of music, they exist side by side. Suppose a vocal quartet to be harmonizing a tune. We hear a single melody with chords underneath—that is to say, vertical blocks of sound. Yet each of the singers as he moves from one chord to the next follows his own horizontal line. Similarly in polyphonic music, no matter how intricate the interplay of the horizontal lines, at any given point they all form a vertical block or chord. The difference between the two textures is one of emphasis. When the composer centers interest on the movement of the separate voices, the texture is said to be polyphonic. When he gives precedence to the harmonic or vertical aspect, we have homophonic or chordal texture. Needless to say there are innumerable gradations between the two extremes.

A composition need not be exclusively in one texture or the other. For

a) Monophonic Gregorian Chant

Do - mi - ne De - us Rex coe - le - stis De - us Pa -

ter om - ni - po - tens

b) Polyphonic - Chorus, *Behold the Lamb of God,* from Handel's *Messiah*

c) Homophonic - Chopin, Waltz in B minor, Opus 69, No. 2

example, a symphonic movement may present a theme against a homophonic texture. In the development section, however, the texture is apt
to become increasingly contrapuntal. So, too, in a homophonic piece the
composer may enhance the effect of the principal melody through an
interesting play of counterthemes and counter-rhythms in the accompanying parts. This is the case in the best orchestral music of the classic-
romantic period.

Texture helps to determine the over-all effect of the music. On the
one hand the composer avoids a fabric that will be too simple and lacking in interest. On the other he exercises caution lest the texture grow
so complex that it will distract from or even overshadow the main line.
The music of certain composers is noted for lightness and transparency
of texture: Mozart in the eighteenth century, Mendelssohn in the nineteenth, Stravinsky in the twentieth. The music of others, such as Brahms
and Sibelius, is characterized by a heavy texture. The problem of texture is related too to the general style of an era. There was a great shift-

ing of interest from polyphonic to homophonic music around the year 1600. Contrapuntal and harmonic texture existed side by side, the one influencing the other. After 1750 and throughout the classic-romantic period, composers emphasized the harmonic aspect of music over the contrapuntal. The late nineteenth-century composers, notably Richard Strauss, were inclined toward an overly rich texture. A reaction set in with the twentieth century, which turned back to the classical ideal of limpid sound and independent part writing. We may sum up the various periods of music history, from the standpoint of texture, as follows.

Before the tenth century A.D.:   monophonic
From around 1000 to 1600:   polyphonic
1600–1750:   polyphonic-homophonic
1750–1900:   homophonic. Contrapuntal procedures ab-
                                 sorbed into orchestral and chamber-music
                                 style, and of course choral music
Since 1900:   revival of interest in polyphonic texture

We have studied the sonata-symphony and other forms that stemmed out of the homophonic-harmonic period. In subsequent chapters we will examine the great forms of polyphonic music.

Devices of Counterpoint

When several independent lines are combined, composers try to give unity and shape to the texture. A basic procedure for achieving this end is imitation, in which a subject or motive is presented in one voice and then restated in another. While the imitating voice restates the theme, the first voice continues with counterpoint. This repetition of an idea— at different times and pitches—by all the voices is musically most effective. It is of the essence in contrapuntal thinking. We have spoken of the vertical and horizontal threads in musical texture. To these imitation adds a third, the diagonal, as is apparent from the following example.

How long is the statement that is to be imitated? This varies considerably. It may be the entire length of a melodic line that runs from the beginning to end of a piece. Or the imitation may occur intermittently. When the whole length of a line is imitated, we have a strict type of composition known as a *canon.* The name comes from the Greek word for "law" or "order." Each phrase heard in the leading voice is repeated almost immediately in an imitating voice throughout the length of the work. The most popular form of canon is the round, in which each voice enters in succession with the same melody. Composers do not often cast an entire piece or movement in the shape of a canon. What they do is to use canonic devices as an effect in all sorts of pieces. The example of diagonal texture just given shows canonic imitation as it occurs in the final movement of César Franck's Sonata for Violin and Piano.

The imitation may be strict, in which case the duplicating voice follows note for note the course laid out by the leading voice. Or it may be approximate or free imitation, in which the composer is allowed more leeway. Many development sections in the string quartets and symphonies of the classic-romantic period contain passages of free imitation. In such passages the composer weaves themes and motives into an imaginative contrapuntal fabric.

Contrapuntal writing is marked by a number of devices that have flourished for centuries. *Inversion* is a species of imitation in which the melody is turned upside down; that is, it follows the same intervals but in the opposite direction. Where the melody originally moved up by a third, the inversion moves down a third. Where it descended by a fourth, it now ascends a fourth. Thus, D-E-F inverted becomes D-C-B. *Augmentation* consists of imitating a theme in longer time values. A quarter note may become a half, a half note a whole, and so on. In consequence, the theme in its new version sounds slower. *Diminution* consists of imitating a theme in shorter time values. A whole note may become a half, a half note a quarter; which makes the theme in its new version sound faster. *Retrograde,* also known as *cancrizans* or *crab motion,* means to imitate the melody backwards. If the original sequence of notes reads B-D-G-F, the imitation reads F-G-D-B. Retrograde-and-inversion imitates the theme by turning it upside down and backwards. These devices of sixteenth-century counterpoint have been revived in contemporary music, especially by Arnold Schoenberg and his school.

It is apparent that the formal element plays a prominent part in contrapuntal music. Form, we noted, is what stands between the artist's initial emotion and its ultimate realization as a work of art. The more elaborate the form, the more thorough this process of purification is apt to be, the greater the "distance" from the first impulse to its final expression. Counterpoint has always been regarded as one of the most advanced of compositional techniques. It represents the intellectual, the objective and structural element in music. It has appealed to certain composers and listeners as the purest type of musical expression, the ultimate in abstraction and refinement of thought.

Nor need it be supposed that the procedures we have outlined reduce

Josquin

music to a cut-and-dried manipulation of notes. True, one may build a contrapuntal structure by applying the correct technical procedures, but to fill such a construction with poetry and emotion requires an imagination of the first order and sovereign mastery of the means of musical expression.

Musical Texture and the Listener

The different types of texture require different kinds of listening. Homophonic music poses no special problem to the music lover. He is able to differentiate between the principal melody and its attendant harmonies, and to follow their interrelation. He is helped in this by the fact that most of the music he has heard from the time of his childhood consists of melody and chords.

The case is different with polyphonic music, which is not apt to appeal to those who listen with half an ear. Here we must be aware of the independent lines as they flow alongside each other. Polyphonic music requires greater concentration on the part of the listener. Only by dint of repeated hearings do we learn to follow the individual voices and to separate each within the contrapuntal web.

As an exercise in listening contrapuntally let us take a simple example, the chorale *Wachet auf, ruft uns die Stimme* (Awake, a Voice Is Calling) as it is presented in the third verse of Bach's cantata of that name. The tenors are singing the chorale in the middle register, mostly in quarter notes. Above them the violins are playing a florid counterpoint of a livelier nature. Below them the cellos and double basses are carrying the bass line, mostly in quarter and eighth notes. Thus the three lines are distinct not only in register but also in rhythm and color. It is well to listen to the piece several times, concentrating first on each voice alone, then on any two, finally on all three. One becomes aware, in following the three planes of movement, of the illusion of space which it is the unique capacity of counterpoint to create; of the fascinating tensions, both musical and psychological, brought into being by the simultaneous unfolding of several lines.

Contrapuntal music does not yield its secrets as readily as do the less complex kinds. By the same token it challenges our attention and holds our interest. With each rehearing we seem to discover another of its facets.

CHAPTER 57

The Remote Past

"Nothing is more characteristic of human nature than to be soothed by sweet modes and stirred up by their opposites. Infants, youths, and old people as well are so naturally attuned to musical modes by a kind of spontaneous feeling that no age is without delight in sweet song."

Boethius (c. 480–524)

THE RELICS of the ancient civilizations—Sumer, Babylonia, Egypt—bear witness to a flourishing musical art. In the antique world, religious myth and tradition ascribed divine powers to music. The walls of Thebes rose and those of Jericho fell to the sound of music. David played his lyre to cure the melancholy of Saul. In the temple at Jerusalem the Levites, who were the musicians, "being arrayed in fine linen, having cymbals and psalteries and harps, stood at the east end of the altar, and with them an hundred and twenty priests sounding with trumpets."

Only a few fragments have descended to us of the music of antiquity. The centuries have forever silenced the sounds that echoed through the Athenian amphitheater and the Roman circus. Those sounds and the attitudes they reflected, in Greece and throughout the Mediterranean world, formed the subsoil out of which flowered the music of later ages. They became part of the heritage of the West.

Gregorian Chant

Music functioned in the Church from its earliest days. St. Paul exhorted the Ephesians to let sound "psalms and hymns and spiritual songs, singing and making melody in your hearts to the Lord." The music of the Church absorbed Greek, Hebrew, and Syrian influences. It became necessary in time to assemble the ever growing body of chants into an organized liturgy. The task extended over several generations but is associated chiefly with Pope Gregory the Great, who reigned from 590 to 604.

Like the music of the Greeks and Hebrews from which it descended, Gregorian chant (also known as plainchant or plainsong) consists of single-line melody. It stems from the monophonic period of music and knows not the third dimension of harmony and counterpoint. It consists

361

Detail from Romanesque ivory carving.

"The undulating vocal line of Gregorian chant is the counterpart in sound of the sinuous traceries of Romanesque art."

of a freely flowing vocal line subtly attuned to the inflections of the Latin text. Gregorian melody is free from regular accent. It embodies what may be called prose rhythm in music, or free-verse rhythm, as distinguished from metrical-poetry rhythm such as we find in the regularly accented measures of two-four or three-four time.

The Gregorian melodies, numbering more than three thousand, were worked over in the course of generations until they took on their traditional shape. They formed a body of anonymous melody whose roots stretched deep into the spiritual life of the folk; a treasure of religious song which, as someone well said, relates to "Everyman rather than Me." Gregorian chant avoids the excitement of wide leaps and dynamic contrasts. Its gentle rise and fall constitutes a kind of disembodied musical speech, "a prayer on pitch." Free from the shackles of regular phrase structure, the continuous, undulating vocal line is the counterpart in sound of the sinuous traceries of Romanesque art and architecture.

Characteristic of the Gregorian style is the setting of a single syllable of text to an expressive line of notes, as on the syllables of the word "Alleluia." Such a florid passage is known as a *melisma,* and the style of setting is said to be *melismatic.* This extending of a single syllable over several notes is congenial to the rhapsodic improvisations of the Orient. Through Gregorian chant the melismatic style entered Western music and remained a prominent feature of the art works of later times.

At first the Gregorian chants were handed down orally from one generation to the next. As the number of chants increased, singers needed to be reminded of the general outlines of the different melodies. Thus came into being the *neumes,* little ascending and descending signs that were written above the words to suggest the course of the melody. As time passed the neumes were placed at various heights above the text in order to secure greater accuracy. Lacking a staff of horizontal lines, the neumes could indicate the position of the tones not precisely but only in relation to each other. Yet they served the Gregorian style more effectively than is generally supposed.

With the passing of centuries the true Gregorian tradition was lost. The ancient melodies were corrupted; they were forced into regular rhythms fitted with harmonies. In the nineteenth century a movement took shape, headed by the Benedictine Monks of Solesmes in France, to restore the pure Gregorian art. Their work has done much to spread an appreciation of the authentic manner of performing the ancient chants.

Gregorian chant embodies the ideal of religious expression through music. "Its beauty, its nobility," writes one authority, "come from the fact that it borrows nothing or as little as possible from the world of the senses." The sacred text is set phrase by phrase, with occasional repetition of words. The music subserves the text, which is clearly heard throughout. Striking is the simplicity and forthrightness of the musical setting of the Mass, in view of the elaborate settings of the same text by the great composers of later times. "Everything in this music combines to give peace."

A page of Gregorian chant from an Anglo-Saxon manuscript of the tenth century.

The Gregorian melodies constitute our richest legacy from the period of pure monophonic melody. They nourished fifteen hundred years of European folk, popular, and art music. They bring us as close as we shall ever come to the lost musical art of the ancient Mediterranean culture—the art of Greece, Syria, and Palestine.

The Medieval Modes

The melody patterns of Gregorian chant were classified according to *modes*. (A mode, it will be recalled, is a specific pattern of whole and half steps.) The medieval or church modes were groups of eight tones, each of which had its central or final tone. These can be played on the white keys of the piano. In the following example the principal tone is indicated by a half note.

The church modes served as the basis for European art music for a thousand years. With the development of polyphony, or many-voiced music, a harmonic system evolved based on the modes. The adjective *modal* consequently refers to the type of melody and harmony that prevailed in the early and later Middle Ages. It is frequently used in opposition to *tonal*, which refers to the harmony based on the major-minor tonality that supplanted the modes. Toward the beginning of the twentieth century, composers began to look for fresh musical resources outside the major-minor system. They were intrigued by the archaic charm of the music of the fifteenth and sixteenth centuries, with the result that modal harmony became an important element of modern musical style.

🌿 CHAPTER 58 🌿

The Later Middle Ages

WITHIN THE Romanesque period (c. 850–1150) took place the single most important development in the history of Western music: the rise of polyphony. Counterpoint and harmony, like perspective in painting —hearing and seeing in depth—must be accounted among the most significant products of the new European culture.

Once several melodic lines proceeded side by side, there could no longer be the flexible prose rhythms of single-line music. Polyphony brought about the emergence of regular meters that enabled the different voices to keep together. This music had to be written down with exact indication of pitch and rhythm; thus evolved our modern staff of lines and spaces on which pitch and duration could be represented with a reasonable degree of accuracy.

With exact notation, music took a long step from being an art of improvisation and oral tradition to one that was carefully planned and that could be preserved accurately. Henceforth a musical work could be studied by many musicians; the creative experience of one could nourish all the rest. The period of anonymous creation characteristic of folk art drew to a close. The individual composer appeared upon the scene.

This development took shape during the Gothic era (c. 1150–1450). The period saw a flourishing secular music in the art of the minstrels and troubadours of the feudal courts. More important, it witnessed the rise of the cathedrals with their choirs and organs. The mastery of construction that made possible the building of those mighty edifices had its counterpart in music. The new science of counterpoint was brought to heights of virtuosity. The learned musicians, for the most part monks and priests, mastered the art of constructing extended musical works through the various devices of counterpoint. Their prime interest at this point was in the structural combining of musical elements, which explains the derivation of the word "composer" from the Latin *componere*, "to put together." The creative musician of the late Gothic period thought of himself primarily as a master builder.

The earlier forms of medieval music have not survived in our present-day concert life and therefore do not come within the province of this book. Among the many highly developed genres that were cultivated at this time, none was of more lasting importance than the setting of the Mass, which became the central musical art form of the fifteenth and sixteenth centuries.

The Mass

The Mass is the most solemn ritual of the Roman Catholic Church. It constitutes a re-enactment of the sacrifice of Christ. The name is derived from the Latin *missa*, "dismissal" (of the congregation at the end of the service).

The aggregation of prayers that make up the Mass falls into two categories: those that vary from day to day throughout the church year, the Proper; and those that remain the same in every Mass, the Ordinary. The liturgy, which reached its present form about nine hundred years ago, provides Gregorian melodies for each item of the ceremony. With the rise of polyphony composers began to weave additional voices around the plainchant. They concentrated on the prayers that were an invariable part of the service rather than on the variable items that were

TENTH CENTURY

Magnus cesar otto que hic modus refert
in nomine ottine dict quada nocte membra
sua dum collocat palatio casu subito inflamat

ELEVENTH CENTURY

Mira lege miro modo deus format ominem mire magis hunc

TWELFTH CENTURY

Laudes crucis attollant de sca Cruce.

THIRTEENTH CENTURY

Alle lu ia Si Mag nus sanctus

FOURTEENTH CENTURY

ain se leua sire ganh li do sade

SEVENTEENTH CENTURY

Bei guardi che m'incendono i begl'occhi che risplendo no Com'i

EIGHTEENTH CENTURY

Allegretto e innocente
SONATA

The evolution of notation in Western Music.

heard only once during the liturgical year. Thus came into prominence the five sections that the public knows as the musical setting of the Mass: Kyrie, Gloria, Credo, Sanctus, and Agnus Dei. The opening section, the Kyrie—a prayer for mercy—contains the only Greek words left in the service and dates from the early centuries of Christianity. It is an A-B-A form that consists of nine invocations: three *Kyrie eleison* (Lord, have mercy upon us), three *Christe eleison* (Christ, have mercy upon us), and again three *Kyrie eleison*. There follows the *Gloria in excelsis Deo* (Glory be to God on high). This is a joyful hymn of praise which is omitted in the penitential seasons, Advent and Lent. The third movement is the confession of faith, *Credo in unum Deum, Patrem omnipotentem* (I believe in one God, the omnipotent Father). It includes also the *Et incarnatus est* (And He was incarnate), the *Crucifixus* (He was crucified), and the *Et resurrexit* (And He arose). Fourth is *Sanctus Sanctus Sanctus* (Holy Holy Holy), which concludes with the *Hosanna in excelsis* (Praise in the highest) and the *Benedictus qui venit in nomine Domini* (Blessed is He who cometh in the name of the Lord), after which the *Hosanna in excelsis* is repeated as a kind of refrain. The fifth and last part, *Agnus Dei qui tollis peccata mundi* (Lamb of God who taketh away the sins of the world), is sung three times. Twice it concludes with *Miserere nobis* (Have mercy on us), and the third time with the prayer *Dona nobis pacem* (Give us peace).

The polyphonic setting of the Mass was generally based on a fragment of Gregorian chant. This was sung in long-drawn-out notes by the tenor while the other voices wove florid designs around it, and was known as the *cantus firmus* (fixed melody). The cantus firmus served as the skeletal structure of the work and, when used in all the movements of a Mass, welded it into a unity. The combining of a composer's original creation with a pre-existing melody appealed to the medieval mind. It provided him with the fixed element that he could embellish with all the resources of his artistry; somewhat as, centuries later, did the theme and variations. Of the Masses for special services the most important is the Mass for the Dead, which is sung at funeral and memorial services. It is known as the Requiem, from the opening verse *Requiem aeternam dona eis, Domine* (Rest eternal grant them, O Lord). Included are prayers in keeping with the solemnity of the occasion, among them the awesome evocation of the Last Judgment, *Dies irae* (That Day of Wrath).

The history of the Mass as an art form extends over the better part of eight hundred years. In that time it garnered for itself some of the greatest music ever written.

Amiens Cathedral.

"The mastery of construction that made possible the building of those mighty edifices had its counterpart in music. The composer of the late Gothic period thought of himself primarily as a master builder."

Between Gothic and Renaissance

At the waning of the Middle Ages stands the Burgundian School that flourished in the fifteenth century in the duchy of Charles the Bold. The Burgundian masters abandoned the complexities of Gothic counterpoint in favor of a simpler and more appealing style. They established the four-part harmonization that has been standard ever since. They based all movements of the Mass on the same melody, thereby achieving a large-scale architecture. They used the voices in high register along with a mixture of contrasting instruments—double reeds, recorders, viols, trombones—to achieve a bright, lustrous tone.

Chief figure of the Burgundian School was Guillaume Dufay (c. 1400–1474). Sprung from the peasantry, he brought into art music the charm of folk song. Dufay was a master of intimate lyric forms. He bridged the gap between the late Gothic in France and the Renaissance in Italy, where he lived for nine years. He has been "discovered" by the twentieth century and is much admired by contemporary musicians.

By the time of Dufay the pre-existing melody, the cantus firmus on which the Mass was based, was often drawn from a popular song that gave its name to a particular Mass. This mingling of the sacred and the secular would prove disturbing to believers today; but it was in keeping with the spirit of an age whose faith was so complete as to embrace all aspects of life. Instruments play a prominent part in Dufay's music, both in support of the voices and in independent interludes. The point is worthy of note in view of the widespread notion that old music is exclusively vocal. The words of the Mass are dissolved in music, with one syllable of text extending over many notes. Characteristic are the sweetly expressive harmonies, the transparent texture, and the radiant sonority of the interweaving voices. This euphony was new to music. It was one of the signal achievements of Dufay's serene art, an art that stands at the culmination of one era and the threshold of another.

The Gothic—early, middle, and late—extended over centuries, during which the heritage of the ancient Mediterranean culture was fused with the genius of the rude northern tribes. Out of the union came a new thing into the world: the European tradition.

CHAPTER 59

The Renaissance

"I am not pleased with the Courtier if he be not also a musician, and besides his understanding and cunning [in singing] upon the book, have skill in like manner on sundry instruments."

Baldassare Castiglione: *The Courtier* (1528)

THE RENAISSANCE (c. 1450–1600) is one of the beautiful if misleading names in the history of culture: beautiful because it implies an awakening of intellectual awareness, misleading because it suggests a sudden rebirth of learning and art after the presumed stagnation of the Middle Ages. History moves continuously rather than by leaps and bounds. The Renaissance was the next phase of a cultural process that, under the leadership of the universities and princely courts, had begun long before.

What the Renaissance does mark is the passing of European society from an exclusively religious orientation to a secular; from an age of unquestioning faith and mysticism to one of belief in reason and scientific inquiry. The focus of man's destiny was seen to be his life on earth rather than in the hereafter. There was a new reliance on the evidence of the senses rather than on tradition and authority. Implied was a new confidence in man's ability to solve his problems and rationally order his world. This awakening found its symbol in the culture of Greek and Roman antiquity. The men of the Renaissance discovered the summit of human wisdom not only in the Church fathers and saints, as their ancestors had done, but also in Homer and Vergil and the ancient philosophers.

Historians used to date the Renaissance from the fall of Constantinople to the Turks in 1453 and the emigration of Greek scholars to the West. It were better, if a date is needed, to pick that of the invention of printing and paper around the year 1440. Several momentous events set off the new era from the old. The introduction of gunpowder brought to an end the age of knighthood. The development of the compass made possible the voyages of discovery that opened up a new world and demolished old superstitions. The revival of ancient letters was associated with the humanists. This revival had its counterpart in architecture, painting, and sculpture. If the Romanesque found its grand

Villa Valmarana, called "The Rotunda," by Andrea Palladio, 1518–1580.

"The gloomy fortified castles of the medieval barons gave way to spacious edifices that displayed the harmonious proportions of the antique style."

architectural form in the monastery and the Gothic in the cathedral, the Renaissance lavished its constructive energy upon palace and château. The gloomy fortified castles of the medieval barons gave way to spacious edifices that displayed the harmonious proportions of the antique style. Athenian temple was posed against Gothic cathedral: balance and symmetry against fantasy and caprice; simple lines against crowded traceries and details; Hellenic clarity and restraint against the passionate spirituality of the Gothic style. In effect, renaissance architecture embodied the striving for a gracious and reasoned existence that was the great gesture of the age.

So, too, the elongated saints and martyrs of medieval painting and sculpture were replaced by the Venus of Botticelli and the Athenian sages of Raphael. Even where artists retained the religious atmosphere, the Mother of Sorrow and the symbols of grief gave way to smiling madonnas—often posed for by very secular ladies—and dimpled cherubs. The human form, denied for centuries, was revealed as a thing of beauty; also as an object of anatomical study. Nature entered painting along with the nude, and with it an intense preoccupation with the laws of perspective and composition. Medieval painting had presented life as an allegory; the Renaissance preferred realism. The medieval painters posed their figures frontally, impersonally; the Renaissance developed psychological characterization and the art of portraiture. Medieval painting dealt in types; the Renaissance concerned itself with individuals. Space in medieval painting was organized in a succession of planes over which the eye traveled as over a series of episodes. The Renaissance created unified space and the simultaneous seeing of the whole. It discovered the landscape, created the illusion of distance, and opened up endless vistas upon the physical loveliness of the world.

The Renaissance came to flower in the nation that stood closest to the classical Roman culture. Understandably the great names we associate with its painting and sculpture are predominantly Italian: Donatello (1386–1466), Luca della Robbia (1400–82), Masaccio (1401–28), Verrocchio (1435–88), Botticelli (1447–1510), Leonardo da Vinci (1452–1519), Michelangelo (1475–1564), Titian (1477–1576), and Raphael (1483–1520). With the masters who lived in the second half of the century, such as Tintoretto (1518–94) and Veronese (1528–88), we approach the world of the early Baroque.

The Renaissance achieved a heightened awareness of the human personality. Its turbulence and dynamic force were in marked contrast to the static nature of medieval society. To medieval submissiveness it opposed aggressive individualism. The rulers of the Italian city-states, Medici, Borgias, Sforzas—bankers and brigands, courtiers, merchant princes, and adventurers all in one—represented a new concept of

power. They engaged in ruthless intrigue with the rulers of the new
centralized European states. Even more, they were involved in a vast
struggle against the temporal power of the Pope. Against a universal,
politically supreme Church they opposed the concept of national states.
Against the universal culture of the Church they encouraged the spirit
of nationalism, which found expression in a new pride in the native
tongue and its literature.

The Renaissance, then, gave impetus to the twin currents of rationalism and realism that have prevailed in European culture ever since.
Granted that its love of art and beauty existed side by side with
tyranny, ignorance, superstition; that its humanism took shape in a
scene dominated by treachery and lust. It is the noble usage of history
to judge an age by its finest. By that measure this period ranks high.
From the multicolored tapestry of renaissance life emerge figures that
have captured the imagination of the world: Lorenzo de' Medici and
Ludovico Sforza, Benvenuto Cellini and Machiavelli, Pope Alexander
VI and Sir Thomas More, Lucrezia Borgia and Beatrice d'Este. Few
centuries can match the sixteenth for its galaxy of great names. The list
includes Erasmus (1466–1536) and Martin Luther (1483–1546), Rabelais (1483?–1553) and Cervantes (1547–1616), Marlowe (1564–93)
and Shakespeare (1564–1616).

With these men we find ourselves in a world that speaks our language. The Renaissance marks the birth of the modern European
temper and of Western man as we have come to know him. In that
turbulent time was shaped the moral and cultural climate we still
inhabit.

CHAPTER 60

Sixteenth-Century Music

"He who does honor and reverence to music is commonly a man
of worth, sound of soul, by nature loving things lofty."
                    Pierre de Ronsard to Francis II (1560)

THE PAINTING and poetry of the Renaissance abound in references to
music. Nothing more clearly attests to the vast importance of the art
in the cultural life of the time. The pageantry of the Renaissance unfolded to a momentous musical accompaniment. Throwing off its medi-

eval mysticism, music moved toward clarity, simplicity, and a frankly sensuous appeal through beauty of sound.

Art music was cultivated extensively in the homes of the middle and upper classes. To be able to take part in a vocal or instrumental ensemble was a requisite of good breeding. A literature sprang up of intimate social music suited to the needs of the cultivated amateur. Much of it was "apt for voices or viols," the line between vocal and instrumental music not being as clearly drawn as was later the case. The sharp timbres of the medieval instrumental ensemble gave way to gentler sounds. Renaissance music moved steadily toward refinement of tone.

The age achieved an exquisite appreciation of *a cappella* music. (Literally, "for the chapel." This term denotes a vocal work without instrumental accompaniment.) The sixteenth century has come to be regarded as the golden age of the a cappella style, which represents the purest type of choral music. Its vocal polyphony was based on a principle called *continuous imitation*. The motives wandered from vocal line to vocal line within the texture, the voices continuously imitating one another. There resulted an extremely close-knit musical fabric that was capable of the most subtle and varied effects.

The composers of the Flemish school were pre-eminent in European music from around 1450 to the end of the sixteenth century. They came from the southern Lowlands, which is now Belgium, and from the adjoining provinces of northern France and Burgundy, a territory that formed the natural meeting ground of French and Germanic culture. Emigrating to other countries, they held key positions in cathedrals and courts throughout the Continent. In their number were several outstanding figures in the history of music, from among whom we may single out two.

Josquin des Prez

Josquin des Prez (c. 1450–1521) was the representative musician of his time. The modern phase of Western music, using the term in its broadest sense, may be said to begin with him. He inherited the canonic techniques of the earlier Flemish masters. During his stay in Italy his northern art absorbed the classical virtues of balance and moderation, the sense of harmonious proportion and lucid form that found their archetype in the radiant art of Raphael. He advanced to a free and continuous imitation of themes that left room for the imaginative development of musical ideas. His music is rich in sentiment; his serene melodiousness, clarity of structure, and humaneness of spirit bespeak the man of the Renaissance. Martin Luther, who admired him greatly,

Leonardo da Vinci, *Mona Lisa*. (The Louvre Museum, Paris)

"Medieval painting dealt in types; the Renaissance concerned itself with individuals."

Titian, c. 1477-1576, *Pope Paul III and His Nephews*. (The National Museum, Naples)

Rembrandt, 1606-1669, *The Night Watch*. (The Rijksmuseum, Amsterdam)

"The leaders of the Dutch school embodied the vitality of a new burgher art that reached its high point in Rembrandt."

Peter Paul Rubens, 1577-1640, *The Garden of Love*. (The Prado, Madrid)

"The opulence of baroque art, its reveling in the sensuous beauty of brocade and velvet, marble, jewels, and precious metals..."

Paolo Veronese, 1528–1588, *Wedding at Cana.*

"The pageantry of the Renaissance unfolded to a momentous musical accompaniment."

Detail from Veronese's *Wedding at Cana.*

The painter and his friends are shown playing instruments of the period.

said, "He is the master of his notes. They have to do as he bids them; other composers have to do as the notes will."

Josquin's motet *Ave Maria* exemplifies the technique of continuous imitation as practiced in the High Renaissance. (A motet is a choral work, with or without accompaniment, of either sacred or secular character, and originally intended to be performed at religious or festive occasions.) The thematic material is drawn from the Gregorian melody *Ave Maria, gratia plena* which is not quoted literally, however, but is treated with great freedom.

Ave Maria, gratia plena, Dominus tecum;	Hail Mary, full of grace, the Lord is with thee;
benedicta tu in mulieribus,	blessed art thou among women,
et benedictus fructus ventris tui,	and blessed the fruit of thy womb,
Jesus Christus Filius Dei vivi.	Jesus Christ, Son of the living God.
Et benedicta sint beata ubera tua	And blessed be thy breasts,
quae lactaverunt regem regum,	that have suckled the King of Kings,
et Dominum Deum nostrum.	and the Lord our God.

The motet is for four voices; the two middle ones lie in the same range. The uppermost voice is made to stand out occasionally through rhythmic differentiation, as when it sings the words *gratia plena* in longer notes than the other voices. Characteristic is the way in which the two lower voices at times are pitted against the two upper. Each phrase of the text is set separately. A continuous fabric is achieved, however, by causing the phrases to overlap; that is, a new phrase is begun in one voice while the others are finishing the old. Although the texture is predominantly contrapuntal, there are passages in chordal style, as on the words *et benedictus fructus ventris tui.* On the words *Et benedicta* the music changes to triple meter. Throughout the piece the learned devices of counterpoint are subordinated to the expressive content of the music, whose seraphic calm accords with the meaning of the verse. Josquin brought to his art a new vision of beauty. His age justly named him "the Prince of Music."

Roland de Lassus

The Flemish tradition culminates in the towering figure of Roland de Lassus (c. 1532–94). A citizen of the world, Lassus consummated the union of Flemish polyphony with the main currents of renaissance music—the elegance and wit of the French, the profundity and rich detail of the Germans, the sensuous beauty of Italian music. His works number over two thousand, from impetuous love songs whose texts are too erotic for the concert hall, to noble Masses, motets, and the profoundly felt *Penitential Psalms.* In his panoramic view of life, as in his feeling for vivid detail, Lassus's cyclopean personality elicits comparison with another great Fleming—his contemporary, Brueghel (1525–69). His music is compounded of passion, tenderness, brilliance, humor, and—at the last—mysticism.

The mystical mood pervades his motet *Tristis est anima mea.*

Tristis est anima mea usque ad
    mortem:
sustinete hic, et vigilate mecum:
nunc videbitis turbam, quae circum-
    dabit me;
vos fugam capietis, et ego vadam im-
    molari pro vobis.

My soul is exceeding sorrowful, even
    unto death;
Tarry ye here, and watch with me:
Now ye will see the multitude that
    will surround me;
Ye will take flight, and I shall go to
    be sacrificed for you.

The flowing contours of the counterpoint move in free flexible rhythms that follow the natural inflection of the words. The motet is for five voices that intertwine in a closely knit texture. The topmost voice, somewhat removed in range, stands out from the rest, adding to the music a sense of space. Lassus sought a direct relationship between the words and the music. To this end he deployed all the expressive resources of his art. Notable, for example, is the setting of the key word *tristis* (sad) with which each voice enters in succession, building up to the feelingful entrance of the soprano. In similar kind is the moving rendition of the word *mortem* (death). Phrases are repeated two or even three times, which sets them off from those that occur only once. Lassus underlines the thought *nunc videbitis turbam* (now ye will see the multitude) by stopping the contrapuntal flow in favor of chords. The thought *quae circumdabit me* (that will surround me) calls forth pungent harmonies. The excitement of the crowd is suggested by the voices entering in quick succession on a theme that begins with short notes. A similar effect is achieved by close imitation on the words *vos fugam capietis* (ye will take flight). Again massive chords emphasize the announcement *et ego vadam immolari* (and I shall go to be sacrificed); with a florid expansion of a single syllable in the final phrase.

Lassus's art brings to its final statement a century and a half of Flemish polyphony. It incarnates the verve and splendor of the Renaissance. It well merits the judgment carved on his tomb: "Here lies that Lassus who refreshes the weariness of the world, and whose harmony resolves its discord."

Palestrina and the Catholic Reform

The desire for a return to true Christian piety brought about a reform movement within the Catholic Church. After the revolt of Martin Luther, this movement became part of the Counter-Reformation whereby the Church strove to recapture the minds of men. Among its manifestations were the activities of Franciscans and Dominicans among the poor; the founding of the Society of Jesus (Jesuits) by St. Ignatius Loyola (1491–1556); and the deliberations of the Council of Trent, which extended—with some interruptions—from 1545 to 1563.

In its desire to regulate every aspect of religious discipline, the Council took up the matter of church music. The cardinals were much concerned over the corruption of the traditional chant by the singers, who added all manner of embellishments to the sacred melodies. They objected to the use of instruments other than the organ in the religious service. They pointed out that in polyphonic settings of the Mass the sacred text was made unintelligible by the overelaborate contrapuntal texture. Certain zealots advocated abolishing counterpoint altogether and returning to Gregorian chant, but there were many music lovers among the cardinals who opposed so drastic a step. The committee assigned to deal with the problem contented itself with issuing general recommendations for a more dignified service. The authorities favored a pure vocal style that would respect the integrity of the sacred texts, that would avoid virtuosity and encourage piety.

Giovanni Pierluigi, called da Palestrina after his birthplace (c. 1525–94), met the need for a reformed church music in so exemplary a fashion that for posterity he has remained *the* Catholic composer. To this great musician attached itself one of the most persistent legends in music history, to the effect that when the Council of Trent considered abolishing the polyphonic setting of the Mass, certain cardinals appealed to him to save church music, whereupon he responded with a Mass so beautiful that the authorities reconsidered their decision. It is a good story but untrue. As a matter of fact, Palestrina was only one of several composers who created the new devotional style. None, however, achieved anything like his eminence with the generations that came after.

Palestrina served as organist and choirmaster at various churches including that of St. Peter's in Rome. His patron Pope Julius III appointed him a member of the Sistine Chapel choir even though, as a married man, he was ineligible for the semi-ecclesiastical post. He was dismissed by a later Pope but ultimately returned to St. Peter's, where he spent the last twenty-three years of his life. Palestrina's art was almost exclusively devoted to the service of the Church. His music gives voice to the religiosity of the Counter-Reformation, its transports and its visions. He created a universal type of expression ideally suited to moods of mystic exaltation. The contemplative beauty of his music does not exclude intense emotion; but this is emotion directed to an act of faith.

A true Italian, Palestrina was surpassingly sensitive to the sensuous
loveliness of the voice. His melodious counterpoint is eminently singable. The voices proceed for the most part stepwise or with narrow
leaps. Passages in simple chord style are set off against the gentle flow
of counterpoint; the texture is light and transparent. The music unfolds
in a process of continuous imitation, dignified, mellifluous, surcharged
with feeling.

Palestrina's most celebrated work, the Mass for Pope Marcellus II, is
the one associated with the legend of his role as "the savior of church
music." The master shows himself aware in this work of the objections
that had been raised against polyphonic settings of the Mass. He sets the
text clearly and distinctly. He enhances the meaning of the words without flooding them with music. He keeps to a minimum the florid expansion of single syllables that renders a word unintelligible. He emphasizes the central thought of each prayer by having all the voices unite
in singing the key words or by assigning these to each of the voices in
turn. The musical expansion is kept within modest limits. Only the most
important words are repeated.

The Pope Marcellus Mass is for six voices—soprano, alto, two tenors,
and two basses. The opening Kyrie is predominantly contrapuntal. It
unfolds a motive marked by the interval of an ascending fourth (at ×)
which appears in one form or another in all the parts.

Ky - rie e - lei - - - - - son

In the next movement the opening phrase, *Gloria in excelsis Deo* (Glory
to God in the highest), is intoned by the priest alone, as is customary;
the choir responds, voices joined, *Et in terra pax hominibus bonae voluntatis* (And peace on earth to men of good will). Notable is the elasticity
of rhythm, which can only be approximated in modern notation owing
to the free intermingling of groups of three and two. There is a change
of intensity at the *Qui tollis peccata mundi* (Who taketh away the sins
of the world). The harmonic elements are subtly balanced against the
contrapuntal. In the Credo we find the characteristic joining of the
voices in chordal style on the crucial words *Et incarnatus est* (And He
was incarnate) as well as on *Et homo factus est* (And He was made
man). At the *Crucifixus*, Palestrina reduces the voices to four—soprano,
alto, tenor, bass—setting the text for the most part one note to a syllable,
in a harmonic style that points to the future. There is an access of joy
at *Et resurrexit* (And He arose). Yet the changes in mood and emotion
are in no sense as great as we shall find, say, in the B-minor Mass of
Bach. With the *Et in Spiritum Sanctum* (And in the Holy Spirit) Pales-

trina returns to the six-voice setting. The Sanctus, with its positive opening, displays the luminous sense of sound that underlay Palestrina's
conception. Characteristic is the way in which a theme heard in one
voice furnishes the motives that are imitated in the others. The *Hosanna*
begins with strong chords that serve as supporting pillars for the
counterpoint. The calm and remote *Benedictus* (Blessed is He), in
four voices, is marked by greater expansion of single syllables than in
the earlier movements. The rest of the Mass is in the usual six voices.
The first Agnus Dei flowers from the same interval of the ascending
fourth as was heard at the beginning of the Mass. The second Agnus
Dei is a triple canon; that is, three voices instead of two follow one
another in strict imitation. The master here revives the virtuosity of the
great Flemish contrapuntists, adapting it to the expressive needs of the
Latin genius.

Palestrina's style incarnates the pure a cappella ideal of vocal polyphony, in which the individual voice fulfilled its destiny through submergence in the group. His music remains an apt symbol of the greatness art can aspire to when it subserves a profound moral conviction.

The Renaissance Madrigal

In the *madrigal* the Renaissance found one of its chief forms of secular music. The sixteenth-century madrigal was an aristocratic form of
poetry-and-music that came to flower at the small Italian courts, where
it was a favorite diversion of cultivated amateurs. The text was a short
poem of lyric or reflective character, rarely longer than twelve lines,
marked by elegance of diction and refinement of sentiment. Conspicuous in it were the affecting words for weeping, sighing, trembling, dying
that the Italian madrigalists learned to set with such a wealth of expression. Love and unsatisfied desire were by no means the only topics of
the madrigal. Included too were humor and satire, political themes,
scenes and incidents of city and country life; with the result that the
madrigal literature of the sixteenth century presents a vivid panorama
of renaissance thought and feeling.

Instruments participated, duplicating or even substituting for the
voices. Sometimes only the top part was sung while the other lines were
played on instruments. During the first period of the renaissance madrigal—the second quarter of the sixteenth century—the principal leaders
were the Flemish musicians who had settled in Italy. The composer's
chief concern at this stage is to give pleasure to the performers, without
much thought of an audience. The writing is simple and restrained, as
befits an intimate type of vocal chamber music. In its middle phase
(c. 1550–80), the renaissance madrigal becomes a conscious art form

directed toward the listener. It takes on the elaborateness of concert
music, with much contrapuntal imitation and development of musical
ideas. Also, there is a closer relationship between words and music. In
this phase leadership is divided between the Flemings and the Italians.
Both Lassus and Palestrina—the latter wrote sacred and secular madrigals—enriched the literature of the form during these years.

The final phase of the Italian madrigal (1580–1620) extends beyond
the late Renaissance into the world of the Baroque. The form achieves
the height of sophistication both in poetry and music. It becomes the
direct expression of the composer's personality and feelings. Certain
traits are carried to the point of mannerism: rich chromatic harmony,
dramatic declamation, vocal virtuosity, and vivid depiction in music of
emotional words. The final group of Italian madrigalists includes three
great names: Luca Marenzio (c. 1553–99); Gesualdo, Prince of Venosa
(1560–1613); and Claudio Monteverdi (1567–1643), whose art belongs
to the new age.

Marenzio: S'io parto, i' moro

Luca Marenzio is generally regarded as the greatest master of the
Italian madrigal. His contemporaries called this imaginative artist
"the divine composer" and "the sweetest swan." Legend has it that
Marenzio died of a broken heart. The tale accords with the romantic
character of his music.

A native of Brescia, Marenzio seems to have spent his early twenties
in Rome. He entered the service of Cardinal d'Este, a brother of the
Duke of Ferrara. He also served the Medici; visited the court of Sigis-
mund III, King of Poland; and died in Rome. Marenzio's choice of texts
from Dante, Petrarch, Tasso and other leading Italian poets reveals his
fastidious literary taste. His extraordinary feeling for mood and atmosphere, his sense of the dramatic, his sensitive declamation, his lyric invention, and his mastery of contrapuntal devices—a mastery that did
not preclude his responding to the new harmonic style—amply justify
his great reputation both during his lifetime and afterward.

Marenzio's madrigal S'io parto, i' moro illustrates his poignantly expressive writing. The piece is in five voices—soprano, alto, two tenors,
and bass. The text is set phrase by phrase, in a continuous texture whose
flow is defined by frequent cadences. Contrapuntal imitation plays a
far less important part in the artistic scheme than was common at the
time. Marenzio's piece looks to the future in its chordal style and its
direct expressivity. Despite the modal atmosphere, the music foreshadows later harmonic conceptions in its fluctuations from G modal-
minor to D major (the Dominant) and B-flat (the relative major); the

final cadence is in the home key. The free plastic rhythm is subtly molded to the words, giving rise to occasional bars of varying lengths, a characteristic of renaissance music. The elegance of the whole bespeaks a courtly art. The last lines of the poem are repeated to allow for musical expansion.

S'io parto, i' moro, e pur partir conviene.	If I leave, I die; and yet I must leave you.
Morrò dunque, il mio bene, e questa mia partita	I shall die, my treasure, and this departure,
Che mi ti toglie mi torrà la vita.	That tears me from you, will take my life.
Dolorosa partita che m'uccidi.	O sad parting that slays me!
Quei che congiuns' Amor, perche dividi?	Whom love has joined—why must they be parted?

Notice the poignancy of the downward inflection of the soprano on the word *moro* in the first line. The affective quality of this phrase is heightened by the rest that precedes it, as though the singer were choking with emotion—an effect much prized in the madrigals of that time. Key words are expanded to give them heightened expressiveness: *vita* in the alto part; *m'uccidi* in the first tenor, and with a perceptible rise in tension when the word returns in the second tenor part; *perche dividi?* in the alto, then in the second tenor, and in the final phrase again in the alto. Worthy of note is the questioning upward inflection on *perche,* which becomes the key word of the closing section that ends with an eloquent cadence on a G-major chord.

In Marenzio's madrigal we encounter the intimacy and refinement of a subtle court art: a union of music and poetry as sensitive as it is moving.

The English Madrigal

As in the case of the sonnet, England took over the madrigal from Italy and developed it into a native art form. All the brilliance of the Elizabethan age is reflected in the school of madrigalists who flourished in the late sixteenth century and on into the reign of James I. To the humanist impulses emanating from the Italian Renaissance they added the traditional sweetness of English song.

Chief figures among the first generation of madrigalists were William Byrd (1543–1623) and Thomas Morley (1557–c. 1603). Despite the strong Italian influence, the English madrigal developed a character of its own, shaped by the rhythms and inflections of the English language, the sights and sounds of the English countryside, and the expressive needs of the English temperament.

Morley was active in cultivating a type of madrigal known as the *ballett* which, imported from Italy, took on a characteristically English stamp in the hands of the Elizabethans. This was a light choral piece which, as its name implies, was in the character of a dance-song. Where the madrigal was through-composed the ballett was strophic in structure, the same music being repeated for each stanza. Where the madrigal leaned toward sophistication and subtlety, the ballett favored freshness of feeling, and all the charm and lightness of the popular style. The fa-la refrain was a characteristic feature of this wholly English type of song.

A delightful example of Morley's art is the perennial *Sing We and Chant It*. The first stanza establishes the mood.

> Sing we and chant it, while love doth grant it.
> Fa-la-la-la-la-la, fa-la-la-la.
> Not long youth lasteth, and old age hasteth.
> Now is best leisure to take our pleasure.
> Fa-la fa-la la-la-la,
> Fa-la fa-la la-la-la.

This is a ballett for five voices, in binary form and lively triple meter. The regular structure of four-bar phrases indicates the dance character of the piece. For variety there is a three-bar phrase in the last line—a charming asymmetry—followed by one of four bars. The harmonizing in parallel thirds was typical of English choral song from time immemorial. The chordal texture shows the predominantly harmonic nature of popular music, which from this time on was to exert an increasing influence upon the "learned" contrapuntal style. With its unpretentiousness and spontaneity, its pastoral charm and lilting rhythm, this piece is in the finest vein of English lyricism.

The second generation of madrigalists included such masters as Thomas Weelkes (c. 1575–1623), John Wilbye (1574–1638), and Orlando Gibbons (1583–1625). Gibbons is one of the greatest of English church composers. He was less active as a madrigalist than most of his contemporaries. His work in this area is contained in a single volume, published in 1612 as *The First Set of Madrigals and Mottets of 5. Parts: apt for Viols and Voyces*. The inclusion in the title of "and Mottets" was unusual, and indicates the serious character of the volume. Its first number, *The Silver Swan*, became the most celebrated madrigal of the Elizabethan period. The piece is set for soprano, alto, alto (or tenor), bass (or tenor), and bass.

> The silver Swan who living had no note,
> When death approached unlocked her silent throat:
> Leaning her breast against the reedy shore
> Thus sung her first and last, and sung no more:
> "Farewell all joys, O death come close mine eyes,
> More geese than swans now live, more fools than wise."

Although quite short and simply written, *The Silver Swan* reveals the finely wrought facture of Gibbons's art. The madrigal unfolds with the full-throated lyricism—of a decidedly contemplative cast—that was native to this composer's style. Characteristic are the overlapping phrases, the plasticity of rhythm, the modal harmony, the melodious counterpoint that flows so effortlessly within a chordal texture, and the compact formal frame that bespeaks a master of the miniature. Gibbons pits the voices against one another—sometimes two against three—in a highly effective manner. The distribution of the text is exceedingly artful. After the opening chords, the voices rarely sing the same word together; which enables the composer to make a capital effect when they do, as on the final word of four of the six lines: *note, shore, more,* and *wise.* The music communicates its message despite the emotional reserve with which this is stated. It speaks well for the taste of the Elizabethans that a work so understated and so subtly nuanced should have achieved such enormous popularity.

England's madrigals remain a rich legacy of her golden age. They enriched her centuries-old tradition of choral song. They released the lovely music of which our language is capable. Their enchanting strains still echo through the choral pieces of English composers today.

❦ CHAPTER 61 ❦

The Baroque

"Nothing is beautiful but the true. The true alone is to be loved."
Boileau (1636–1711)

THE PERIOD of the Baroque stretched across a turbulent century and a half of European history. It opened shortly before the year 1600, a convenient signpost that need not be taken too literally; and may be regarded as having come to a close with the death of Bach in 1750.

The term *baroque* was probably derived from the Portuguese *barroco*, a pearl of irregular shape much used in the jewelry of the time. During the nineteenth century the word acquired a derogatory sense, indicating a style that was ornate and showy. The notion prevailed that the painting, sculpture, and architecture of the Baroque represented a debasing of the pure renaissance style. Since then a more just estimate has been arrived at. Baroque now stands for one of the great style periods in European art.

The Baroque is of special interest to present-day music lovers, for it is the first period to be consistently represented in the concert repertory. The twentieth century has witnessed a great revival of interest in the forms of baroque music and in neglected masters such as Monteverdi, Lully, Purcell, Vivaldi. The century and a half of baroque art divides itself into three fifty-year periods: early, middle, and late Baroque. Since public interest until recently concentrated on the late phase, many came to think of Bach and Handel as the first great composers. Viewed against the total panorama of their era, these masters are seen rather to have been the heirs of an old and surpassingly rich tradition.

The period 1600–1750 bridged the transition from the Renaissance to the modern era. It was a time of change and adventure. The conquest of the New World stirred the imagination and filled the coffers of the Old. The middle classes gathered wealth and power in their struggle against the aristocracy. Empires clashed for mastery of the world. Appalling poverty and wasteful luxury, magnificent idealism and savage oppression—against contradictions such as these unfolded the pomp and splendor of baroque art: an art bold of gesture and conception; vigorous, decorative, monumental.

The transition from the classically minded Renaissance to the Baroque was foreshadowed by Michelangelo (1475–1564). His turbulent figures, their torsos twisted in struggle, reflect the baroque love of the dramatic. The dome he designed for St. Peter's in Rome embodies baroque striving for the grandiose. In like fashion the Venetian school of painters— Titian, Tintoretto, Veronese—captured the dynamic spirit of the new age. Their crowded canvases are ablaze with color and movement. They glory in the tension of opposing masses. They dramatize the diagonal. Their rows upon rows of columns open on limitless vistas.

The Baroque was the era of absolute monarchy. Princes throughout Europe took as their model the splendor of Versailles. Louis XIV's famous "I am the State!" summed up a way of life in which all art and culture served the cult of the ruler. Courts large and small maintained elaborate musical establishments including opera troupes, chapel choirs, and orchestras. Baroque opera, the favorite diversion of the aristocracy, aimed at a lofty pathos that left no room for the frailties of ordinary men. It centered about the gods and heroes of antiquity, in whom the occupant of the royal box and his courtiers found a flattering likeness of themselves.

The Baroque was also an age of reason. Adventurers more bold than the conquistadors set forth upon the uncharted sea of knowledge. The findings of Kepler, Galileo, and Copernicus in physics and astronomy,

The High Altar of the Theatine Church, Munich.

". . . the pomp and splendor of baroque art: an art bold of gesture and conception; vigorous, decorative, monumental."

of Descartes in mathematics and Spinoza in philosophy were so many milestones in the intellectual history of Europe. Harvey discovered the circulation of the blood. Locke laid the foundation for a scientific study of the workings of the mind. Newton's theory of gravitation revealed a universe based upon law and order. The growing towns and cities were centers of a forward-looking culture. Descartes expressed the confidence of a brave new world when he wrote, "Provided only that we abstain from receiving anything as true which is not so, there can be nothing so remote that we cannot reach to it, nor so obscure that we cannot discover it."

Excluded from the salons of the aristocracy, the middle classes created a culture of their own. Their music-making centered about the home, the church, and the university group (known as *collegium musicum*). For them came into being the comic opera which, like the prose novel, was filled with keen and witty observation of life. For them painting forsook its grandiose themes and turned to intimate scenes of bourgeois life. The leaders of the Dutch school—Vermeer, Frans Hals, Ruysdael—embodied the vitality of a new burgher art that reached its high point in Rembrandt (1609–69), a master whose insights penetrated the recesses of the soul. Under the leadership of merchant princes and financiers, the culture of the city came to rival that of the palace. These new connoisseurs vied with the court in their love of splendor, responding to the opulence of baroque art, to the sensuous beauty of brocade and velvet, marble and jewels and precious metals. This aspect of the Baroque finds expression in the art of Peter Paul Rubens (1577–1640), whose canvases exude a driving energy, a reveling in life. His voluptuous nudes incarnate the seventeenth-century ideal of feminine beauty. He himself was a symbol of the rising order: rugged individualist, dreamer, and man of action; entrepreneur and conqueror all in one.

Peter Paul Rubens, 1577–1640, *The Abduction of the Daughters of Leucippus by Castor and Pollux.*

"His canvases exude a driving energy, a reveling in life. His voluptuous nudes incarnate the baroque ideal of feminine beauty."

The Baroque was an intensely devout period. Religion was a rallying cry on some of the bloodiest battlefields in history. The Protestant camp included England, Scandinavia, Holland, and the north German cities, all citadels of the rising middle class. On the Catholic side were the two powerful dynasties, Habsburg and Bourbon, who fought one another no less fiercely than they did their Protestant foes. After decades of struggle, the might of the Spanish-Habsburg empire was broken. France emerged as the leading state on the Continent; Germany was in ruins; England rose to world power. Europe was ready to advance to the stage of modern industrial society.

Protestant culture was rooted in the Bible. Its emphasis upon the individual promoted a personal tone and strengthened the romantic tendency in the Baroque. Milton (1608–74) in *Paradise Lost* produced the poetic epic of the Protestant world view, even as Dante three and a half centuries earlier had produced that of the Catholic. Bunyan (1628–88) in *Pilgrim's Progress* traced the spiritual journey of the common man. The heroic hymn tunes of the Reformation nourished the profoundly spiritual art of Bach. The oratorios of Handel harnessed baroque splendor to an ethical ideal. The two composers mark the supreme musical achievement of the Protestant spirit.

The Catholic world for its part tried to retrieve the losses inflicted by Luther's secession. The Counter-Reformation mobilized all the forces of the church militant. The Jesuits, recognizing faith to be a matter of the whole personality, strove to fire the hearts and minds and senses of the faithful. They made music, sculpture, architecture, painting, and even the theater arts tributary to their purpose. Jesuit art sought direct communication with the spectator by overwhelming and exalting him. The churches of Spain and Austria testify to its impact. Their crowded decorations, pictorial clouds, and floating draperies defy both the laws of gravity and of restraint. This is an art that summons the worshiper to beatific visions. The rapturous mysticism of the Counter-Reformation found expression in the canvases of El Greco (c. 1542–1614). His elongated ash-gray figures, bathed in an unearthly light, are creatures of a visionary mind that distorts the real in its search for a reality beyond. Baroque theatricalism and pathos came to fullness in the sculptor Lorenzo Bernini (1598–1680). His famous *Ecstasy of St. Theresa* captures in marble all the restlessness and drama of the Baroque.

Between the conflicting currents of absolute monarchy and rising bourgeois power, Reformation and Counter-Reformation, the Baroque fashioned its grandiose art. Alien to its spirit were restraint and detachment. Rather it achieved its ends through violent opposition of forces, lavish creativity, and abandon. With these went the capacity to organize

Giovanni Lorenzo Bernini, 1595–1680, *The Ecstasy of Saint Theresa.*

". . . captures in marble all the restlessness and drama of the Baroque."

a thousand details into a monumental, overpowering whole.

Some view the history of art as an alternation between ethos and pathos: between a noble classicism controlled by intellect and an unruly romanticism given over to emotion. We may trace the alternation of ethos and pathos (with a multitude of overlappings and exceptions, to be sure) through a thousand years of Western art: from the intense religious emotion of the Gothic to the serene classicism of the Renaissance; from the turbulent and massive Baroque to the poise and lucidity of the classical era; from the subjective feeling of the nineteenth century to the objectivity of the twentieth. Over the one presides the temperate ideal of the Greeks. Over the other—an infinitude of longing, ecstasy, passion.

The artist played a variety of roles in baroque society. He might be an ambassador and intimate of princes, as were Rubens and Van Dyck;

or a priest, as was Vivaldi; or a political leader, like Milton. He functioned under royal or princely patronage, as did Corneille and Racine; or, like Bach, was in the employ of a church or free city. He might dabble in business and make a fortune, as Lully did; or launch his own enterprises and lose them, as was the case with Handel. In social status he ran the gamut from favorite at court to something just above the valet or cook. To the aristocrats whom he served he might be little more than a purveyor of elegant entertainment. Yet, beneath the obsequious manner and fawning dedications demanded by the age, there was often to be found a spirit that dared to probe all existing knowledge and shape new worlds; a voice addressing itself to those who truly listened —a voice that was indeed "the trumpet of a prophecy."

CHAPTER 62

Main Currents in Baroque Music

"The end of all good music is to affect the soul."
Claudio Monteverdi

Monody

WITH the transition from Renaissance to Baroque came a momentous change: the shifting of interest from a texture of several independent parts of equal importance to music in which a single melody predominated; that is, from polyphonic to homophonic texture. The new style, which originated in vocal music, was named *monody*—literally, "one song," music for one singer. (Monody is not to be confused with monophony, see p. 355.) The year 1600 is associated with the emergence of the monodic style. Like many such milestones, the date merely indicates the coming to light of a process that was long preparing.

The victory of the monodic style was achieved by a group of Florentine writers, artists, and musicians known as the Camerata, a name derived from the Italian word for "salon." Among their number were Vincenzo Galilei, father of the astronomer, and the composers Jacopo Peri and Giulio Caccini. The men of the Camerata were aristocratic humanists. Their aim was to resurrect the musical-dramatic art of ancient Greece. Since almost nothing was known of the music of the Athenian tragedy, they imagined it in terms of their own needs and desires. Instead of resurrecting something dead the Camerata came forth with an idea that was very much alive.

El Greco, c. 1548-1614, *Saint Andrew and Saint Francis* (The Prado, Madrid)

"His elongated ash-gray figures, bathed in an unearthly light, are creatures of a visionary mind that distorts the real in its search for a reality beyond."

Francisco Goya, 1746-1828, *Carnival Scene* (The San Fernando Royal Academy of Fine Arts, Madrid) and *Execution of the Rioters, May 3, 1808* (The Prado, Madrid)

"The greatest painter of the late eighteenth century stands outside the classical stream. His passionate realism anticipates a later age."

This idea was that music must heighten the emotional power of the text. The Florentine humanists dreamed of bringing their music into close relationship with poetry, and through poetry with life itself. They hoped to achieve their goal through a free musical declamation that rendered the text clearly and followed the meaning and inflection of the words. "I endeavored," wrote Caccini in 1602, "the imitation of the conceit of the words, seeking out the chords more or less passionate according to the meaning." He underlines his opposition to the old contrapuntal style which, "not suffering the words to be understood by the hearers, ruins the verse, now lengthening and now shortening the syllables." Thus came into being what its inventors regarded as the *stile rappresentativo* (representational style), consisting of a recitative that moved freely over a foundation of simple chords.

The Camerata soon realized that the representational style could be applied not only to a poem but to an entire drama. In this way they were led to the invention of opera, considered by many to be the single most important achievement of baroque music. The first complete opera that has come down to us, *Euridice,* was presented in 1600 at the marriage of Henry IV of France to Maria de' Medici. The libretto was by Ottavio Rinuccini, the music by Peri (with the addition of some arias by Caccini).

The polyphonic style, in which many voices commingled, symbolized the submergence of the individual in the group. The new dramatic style, on the other hand, represented the clash of individual wills in the symbolic world of the theater. The change from one to the other signified a movement from religious to secular art, from mystic submissiveness to assertive ego; also from pure musical thinking that overpowered the words, to a music that served the requirements of poetry. Opera became a force of immense social significance in the Baroque. It established the theater as a center of musical art alongside the palace, church, and home.

The Camerata appeared at a time when it became necessary for music to free itself from the complexities of counterpoint. The year 1600, like the year 1900, bristled with discussions about the New Music—*le nuove musiche*—and what its adherents proudly named the *expressive style.* As sometimes happens with inventors, the noble amateurs of the Florentine salon touched off more than they realized.

The Thorough-bass

The melody-and-chords of the New Music was far removed from the intricate interweaving of voices in the old. Since musicians were soon familiar with the basic chords, it became unnecessary to write those out in full. Instead the composer put a numeral above or below the bass note that indicated the chord required. For example, the figure 6 under a bass note indicated a chord whose root lay a sixth above the note. Thus, a 6 below the note A called for the F-major chord. The application of this principle on a large scale resulted in "the most successful system of musical shorthand ever devised"—the *thorough-bass*. (From *basso continuo*, a continuous bass, "thorough" being the old form of "through." Also known as *figured bass*.) The actual filling in of the harmony was left to the performer. A similar practice obtains in jazz music today, where the player fills in elaborate harmonies from the skeletal version on the page.

So important was this practice for a century and a half that the Baroque is often referred to as the period of thorough-bass. The figured bass required at least two players: one to perform the bass line on a cello, double bass, or wind instrument, and the other to fill in or "realize" the chords on a harmonic instrument such as harpsichord, organ, lute, or guitar. The player was expected not only to pick out the correct chords but to improvise a full accompaniment in keeping with the general style of the piece. The thorough-bass style emphasized two voices: the soprano that carried the melody, and the bass that generated the harmony. The inner voices were reduced to a secondary role. The bass took on enough importance to show a melodic profile of its own, and usually served as a counterpoint to the melody. Seventeenth-century monody, consequently, combined two styles. The contrapuntal interplay between melody and bass retained something of the polyphonic art of the past. Yet the preoccupation with chordal texture— that is, with harmony—looked forward to the homophonic style of a later age.

The shorthand made possible by thorough-bass was particularly valuable at a time when printing was an involved and costly process. Since most works were intended for a single occasion or season they were left in manuscript, the parts being copied out by hand. It was a boon to composers to be able to present their music in abbreviated fashion, knowing that the performers would fill in the necessary details. When we read of an old master producing hundreds of cantatas and dozens of operas, we may be sure that "there were giants in the earth in those days." But the thorough-bass helped.

Improvisation

Improvisation played a prominent part in the musical practice of the Baroque. The realizing of the thorough-bass would have been impossible if musicians of the period had not been ready to "think with their fingers." A church organist was expected as a matter of course to be able to improvise an intricate contrapuntal piece. The ability in this regard of great organists such as Bach and Handel was legendary. This abandonment to the inspiration of the moment suited the rhapsodic temper of the Baroque, and even influenced the art of composition. Many passages in the fantasias and toccatas of the time, with their abrupt changes of mood, bear the mark of extemporaneous speech.

Improvisation functioned in baroque music also in another way. The singer or player was expected to add his own embellishments to what was written down (as is the custom today in jazz). This was his creative contribution to the work. The practice was so widespread that baroque music sounded altogether different in performance from what it looked like on paper.

This partnership between composer and player was not without its dangers. The opera stars of the seventeenth and eighteenth centuries considered it their privilege to bury the melodies of the masters under an avalanche of trills, graces, and roulades. The composer had sooner or later to stand up for his music. It took all the authority of a Lully, Handel, or Gluck to cow the singers into submission. But the progress of musical art demanded the victory of careful planning over improvisation. The composer ultimately established his right to choose the notes, the performer being limited to playing, or at most to interpreting them.

One wishes to have heard the fabulous improvisations of the masters. It is one of the ironies of history that today, when we at last possess the equipment to record improvisation, the art—outside of jazz—has died.

Emergence of the Major-Minor System

The Baroque witnessed one of the most significant changes in all music history: the transition from the medieval church modes to major-minor tonality. As music turned from vocal counterpoint to instrumental harmony, it demanded a simplification of the harmonic system. The church modes gave way to two standard scales: the major and the minor. These two scales had been prominent in folk and popular music for generations. They served as the basis of Western art music from around 1650 to the opening of the twentieth century. With the establishment of major-minor tonality, the thrust to the keynote or *do* became the most powerful force in music.

Now each chord could assume its function in relation to the key center. Composers of the Baroque soon learned to exploit the opposition between the chord of rest, the I (Tonic), and the active chord, the V (Dominant). Many a work of the period opens with a hammer-stroke announcement of the I-V-I and ends with an emphatic repetition of the two basic chords at the final cadence. So, too, the movement from home key to contrasting key and back became an important element in the shaping of musical structure. Composers developed larger forms of instrumental music than had ever been known before.

The growing harmonic sense brought about a freer handling of dissonance. Baroque musicians used dissonant chords for emotional intensity and color. In the setting of poetry the composer heightened the impact of an expressive word through dissonance. Such harmonic freedom could not fail to shock the conservatives. The Italian theorist Artusi, writing in 1600 *On the Imperfections of Modern Music*—an attack on Monteverdi and his fellow innovators—rails against those musicians who "are harsh to the ear, offending rather than delighting it," and who "think it within their power to corrupt, spoil, and ruin the good old rules."

The "seven out of twelve" way of hearing music introduced a sharp contrast between the tones included in the key, that is, the diatonic tones, and the five foreign or chromatic tones. Moods of well-being were linked with diatonic harmony, anguish with chromatic. In similar fashion the major came to be connected with joy and the minor with sorrow, an association that persisted for more than two hundred years.

The major-minor system was the collective achievement of several generations of musicians. It expressed a new dynamic culture. By dividing the world of sound into definite areas and regulating the movement from one to the other, it enabled the composer to mirror the exciting interplay of forces in the world about him.

Equal Temperament

If an instrument is tuned according to the natural laws of acoustics, certain discrepancies occur. For example, the interval of a perfect fifth such as C-G is represented by two strings vibrating in the proportion 2:3. If, beginning with C, we tune accurately in this proportion an ascending series of fifths—C-G, G-D, D-A, A-E, E-B, B-F♯, F♯-C♯— the upper C♯ will not be altogether in tune with a C♯ several octaves below. As long as music was mainly vocal, this phenomenon was not too disturbing. The increasing use of instruments, which had to be tuned (as the voice did not), complicated the situation. For example, a tone that was perfectly in tune with the keynote of one scale might be out of tune with the keynote of another. An F-sharp on the keyboard might sound right in the key of G but would be off pitch in the key of B. This made it practically impossible to use keys with a large number of sharps or flats, and imposed similar limitations in regard to harmony and modulation. To free themselves from these restrictions, composers (as well as mathematicians and scientists) experimented through the ages with ways of *tempering* the intonation, so as to adjust the raw material of sound to the artistic purposes of music.

The increased use of keyboard instruments—that is, instruments of fixed pitch such as the organ, harpsichord, and clavichord—during the Baroque made it imperative to find an over-all solution of the problem. In the eighteenth century a system of tuning was adopted that divided the octave into twelve equal parts (semitones). This compromise was known as *equal temperament*. Now, instead of having certain intervals perfectly in tune in the simple keys but distressingly off pitch in the remote ones, they were all ever so slightly mistuned. In this way the discrepancy in nature was distributed evenly throughout the scale. As a result, F-sharp became identical with G-flat on the harpsichord, organ, and piano. (On the string instruments this is not so. The violinist who plays F-sharp rising to G sounds it a little higher than when he plays G-flat descending to F.) The system of equal temperament made it possible to use all the major and minor keys and to move freely from one to the other. The adoption of equal temperament in European music went hand in hand with the triumph of the major-minor system.

Composers of the Baroque produced cycles of pieces that used an ever greater number of the twelve major and twelve minor keys. The most important circumnavigation of the tonal globe was that by Johann Sebastian Bach in the *Well-Tempered Clavier*, in which he wrote a Prelude and Fugue in each of the twelve major and twelve minor keys. (He wrote a second volume, hence the forty-eight Preludes and Fugues in this work.) "Well-tempered" refers not to amiable disposition but to the new adjusted, or tempered, system of tuning.

It follows that when we speak of having our piano tuned we really mean that we want it to be slightly mistuned. If the pitches were set in pure intonation we should be unable to play a good deal of the music of the past two hundred years. As it is, nature is adjusted to art and the ear is made happier thereby.

CHAPTER 63

Further Aspects of Baroque Music

"Musick hath 2 ends, first to pleas the sence, & that is done by
the pure Dulcor of Harmony, & secondly to move ye affections
or excite passion."

Roger North: *The Musicall Grammarian* (1728)

The Doctrine of the Affections

Now that man was become the measure of all things, there was much
speculation concerning the passions and affections, by which were
meant the deep-lying forces that determine our emotional life. It was
realized that these are peculiarly responsive to music. The *doctrine of
the affections* related primarily to the union of music and poetry, where
the mental state was made explicit by the text. The Baroque developed
an impressive technique of what is known as tone painting, in which
the music vividly mirrored the words. Ideas of movement and direction
—stepping, running, leaping, ascending, descending—were represented
graphically through the movement of the melody and rhythm. Bach
exhorted his pupils to "play the chorale according to the meaning of
the words." He associates the idea of resurrection with the rising interval of a fifth. The sorrow of the Crucifixion is symbolized by a bass line
that descends stepwise along the chromatic scale. Temptation is allied
to a sinuous theme that suggests the serpent. Once the musical figure
is brought into being, it abandons its picture quality. It becomes abstract musical material to be developed according to purely musical
procedures. In short, the imagination of the pure musician takes over.

The Baroque consequently developed a double relationship between
poetry and music. On the one hand, the words determined the affection
of the music. On the other, the music asserted its supremacy. This
supremacy shows itself in two traits that strike the listener when he
hears baroque music. In the first place, lines, phrases, and individual
words are repeated over and over again in order to allow room for the
necessary musical expansion. (This practice springs from the realization
that music communicates more slowly than words and needs more time
in which to establish its meaning.) In the second place, a single syllable
will be extended to accommodate all the notes of an expressive melodic
line, so that the word is stretched beyond recognition (the style of
setting known as melismatic). Thus, the music born of words ends by
swallowing up the element that gave it birth.

In instrumental music the practice took root of basing a piece upon a single affection—that is, upon one pervading mood. This was established at the outset by a striking musical subject out of which grew the entire composition. In this way composers discovered the imperious gesture that opens a piece of baroque music, of a tension and pathos that permeate the whole movement.

The doctrine of the affections, really a sort of applied psychology, achieved a fruitful union of music and emotion. In this it was of the essence of the Baroque.

Unflagging Rhythm

The Baroque demanded a dynamic rhythm. The time was ripe for regular recurrence of accent and for clear-cut energetic movement. The bass part became the carrier of the new rhythm. Its relentless beat is an arresting trait in many compositions of the Baroque. This steady pulsation, once under way, never slackens or deviates until the goal is reached. It imparts to baroque music its singleness of purpose, its unflagging drive. It produces the same effect of turbulent yet controlled motion as animates baroque painting, sculpture, and architecture.

Composers became ever more aware of the capacity of the instruments for rhythm. They found that a striking dance rhythm could serve as the basis for an extended piece, vocal or instrumental. Popular and court dances furnished an invigorating element to musical art. Nor, in that stately age, were the rhythms necessarily lively. Idealized dance rhythms served as the basis for tragic arias and great polyphonic works. In a time when courtiers listened to music primarily for entertainment, composers had to dress up a good part of their material in dance rhythms. Many a dance piece served to make palatable a profounder discourse. In effect, rhythm pervaded the musical conception of the Baroque and helped it capture the movement and drive of a vibrant era.

Continuous Melody

The elaborate scrollwork of baroque architecture bears witness to an abundance of energy that would not leave an inch of space unornamented. Its musical counterpart is to be found in one of the main elements of baroque style—the principle of continuous expansion. A movement based on a single affection will start off with a striking musical figure that unfolds through a process of ceaseless spinning out. There are no seams in this fabric; none of the balanced phrases and cadences that we know from the classical style. This music moves forward by a process of spontaneous generation, relentlessly pursuing its goal as the figures and motives flower into ever fresh designs. It is constantly in motion, in the act of becoming. When its energy is spent, the work comes to an end.

In vocal music the melody of the Baroque was imbued with the desire always to heighten the impact of the words. Wide leaps and the use of chromatic tones served to emphasize the affections. There resulted a noble melody whose spacious curves outlined a style of grand expressiveness and pathos.

Harmonic Counterpoint

The New Music of the Florentine Camerata seemed to triumph for a brief space over the "Gothic" counterpoint of the past. But professional musicians, unlike those aristocratic amateurs, were not so ready to discard a tradition of polyphony that had lasted for hundreds of years. The renewed interest in the problems of counterpoint testifies to the fascination that pure craftsmanship always holds for the artist. Once single-line melody had established itself, the scene was set for the return of counterpoint.

But this was a counterpoint that had absorbed all the innovations of the age: the gravitational pull of baroque harmony, the forward stride of baroque rhythm, the exuberance of baroque ornamentation, the continuous expansion of baroque melody. These elements were fused in a style that came to full flower in the late Baroque in the art of Bach and Handel. They and their contemporaries created a music of richly woven texture in which the counterpoint was directed by harmony and the harmony came rhythmically alive through the counterpoint. The horizontal movement of the voices and the vertical movement of the chords met in an ideal balance whose like has not been encountered either before or since.

Terraced Dynamics

Baroque music does not know the constant fluctuation of volume that marks the classic-romantic style. The music moves at a fairly constant level of sonority. A passage uniformly loud will be followed by one uniformly soft, creating the effect of light and shade. The shift from one level to the other has come to be known as *terraced dynamics* and is a characteristic feature of the baroque style.

The nineteenth-century composer who desired greater volume of tone directed each instrument to play increasingly louder. The baroque composer wrote instead for a larger number of players. The nineteenth-century composer used the crescendo as a means of expression within a passage. The baroque composer found his main source of expression in the contrast between a soft passage and a loud—that is, between the two terraces of sound. Each passage became an area of solid color set off against the next. This conception shapes the structure of the music, endowing it with a monumental simplicity.

It follows that baroque composers were much more sparing of expression marks than those who came after. The music of the period carries little else than an occasional forte or piano, leaving it to the player to supply whatever else may be necessary. Performers today are so accustomed to the dynamic shadings of nineteenth-century music that they are almost incapable of the grand architectural simplicity of the baroque style. Especially the music of Bach has suffered from romantic interpretation. A modern edition of the *Well-Tempered Clavier* will carry an array of expression marks on every page. The original manuscript contained not one.

Instrumental Color

The Baroque was the first period in history in which instrumental music was comparable in importance to vocal. The interest in this branch of the art stimulated the development of new instruments and the perfecting of old. The spirit of the age demanded increased brilliancy of tone. The gentle lute was ousted by the less subtle guitar. The reserved viol with its "still music," as Shakespeare called it, was supplanted by the more resonant violin. Baroque music made generous use of trumpet and trombone, oboe, bassoon, and flute.

The period boasted three keyboard instruments: organ, harpsichord, and clavichord. The baroque organ had a pure transparent tone. Its stops did not blend the colors into a symphonic cloudburst, as is the case with the twentieth-century organ, but let the voices stand out clearly so that the ear could follow the counterpoint. With its steady volume of sound, which enabled it to play a uniform soft or loud, the organ was eminently suited to the terraced dynamics of the baroque era.

The same held true for the harpsichord. This instrument differs from the piano in two important respects. First, its strings instead of being struck with hammers are plucked by quills, producing a bright silvery tone. Second, the pressure of the fingers on the keys varies the tone only slightly on the harpsichord, whereas the piano has a wide and very subtle range of dynamic gradations. The harpsichord is therefore incapable of the crescendo and decrescendo that are so essential a feature of nineteenth-century music. Nor does it command the personal

A harpsichord of the seventeenth century, showing the elaborate carving of the Italian Baroque.

expressiveness that made the piano the favorite instrument of the romantic era. These are hardly shortcomings from the baroque point of view. Through the use of two keyboards, one above the other, and by means of stops, it is possible to achieve even levels of soft and loud. The harpsichord is an ideal medium for contrapuntal music, for it brings out the inner voices with luminous clarity. It lends itself to a grand style of playing that on the one hand is elevated and dramatic, on the other, rhythmically precise, refined, and playful. It was immensely popular during the Baroque as a solo instrument. The harpsichord was indispensable in the realization of the thorough-bass, and was the mainstay of the ensemble in chamber music and at the opera house.

The clavichord consisted of a wooden oblong box, from two to five feet long, that rested on legs or on a table. The strings were set vibrating by small brass wedges known as tangents. Dynamic gradations were possible, within a limited range, through pressure on the keys. Clavichord tone was tender, subtle, intimate. It was, however, a small tone. By the end of the eighteenth century both clavichord and harpsichord had been supplanted in public favor by the piano.

The word "clavier" was used in Germany as the general term for keyboard instruments, including harpsichord, clavichord, and organ. Whether a certain piece was intended for one rather than the other must often be gathered from the style rather than the title. In any event, the rendering of Bach's *Wohltemperiertes Clavier* as "Well-Tempered Clavichord" is misleading. Closer to the mark is "Well-Tempered Clavier."

Virtuosity

The interest in instruments went hand in hand with a desire to master their technique. Virtuosity on the organ and harpsichord, violin and trumpet had its counterpart in the opera house in a phenomenal vocal technique that has never been surpassed.

Technical mastery brought a growing awareness of what each instrument could do best, and with it a heightened sense of style. Composers differentiated ever more clearly among the various styles: vocal and instrumental; church, theater, chamber; keyboard, string, woodwind, brass; accompanied chorus and a cappella. At the same time they were given to mixing the styles. It was part of the baroque straining for effect to cause one medium to take over the qualities of another: to make Dresden china imitate the daintiness of lace, wrought iron the curl of leaves and flowers. In like fashion instrumental music copied the brilliant coloratura of the voice, while vocal music emulated the arabesques of the instruments. Church music used to advantage the dramatic style of opera and the rhythms of the dance. The delicate ornamentation of harpsichord music influenced the writing for strings. Organ sonority affected the style of the orchestra. Each nourished the other, to the enrichment of all.

Growing Importance of the Orchestra

During the Baroque, composers wrote many more works for instrumental ensembles than had been the case in earlier times. As a result, they began to pay more attention to the blending of timbres and the balance of tone. The first permanent instrumental ensemble was established at the French court as "the twenty-four violins of the King." This ensemble, to which woodwinds and brass were occasionally added, gained great fame in the reign of Louis XIV. Lully, the King's director of music, taught his men a uniform manner of bowing, developed orchestral discipline, and achieved a rhythmic precision unknown till then. His orchestra became the model for all Europe.

It was in the opera house that the most important experiments in orchestration took place. For it was there that composers were obliged to think of color in relation to mood, atmosphere, and dramatic effect. Masters of baroque opera such as Lully and Handel were pioneers in exploiting orchestral color. In their hands the art of orchestration became a potent force in the arousing of the affections.

Transcriptions of Baroque Music

One of the obstacles to an understanding of baroque music is that we often do not hear it on the instruments for which it was written. The clavier works of Bach, for example, are frequently presented in concert transcriptions for the piano or orchestra.

There is nothing to object to in transcription as such. Bach himself was a tireless transcriber of his own and other men's music. Transcription is essential in the case of works for instruments that have dropped out of use, for it keeps music alive that would otherwise be forgotten. The one requirement is that, as in literary translation, the transcription adhere to the spirit of the original.

The men who transcribed the clavier music of Bach grew up in the nineteenth-century style. They proceeded to impose their own idiom on the older music. Works conceived for the pure-toned baroque organ or the crystalline sound of the harpsichord were decked out in the thick sonorities of the modern grand piano or the flamboyant colors of the nineteenth-century orchestra. A music designed for the intimacy of the chamber was blown up to fill a huge concert hall. The lover of baroque music cannot but regard this touching up as a distortion of the composer's meaning. Such concert versions may be exciting in their own right and may afford much pleasure; but they must not be permitted to supplant the originals.

It is a sign of improved musical taste that more and more people today are eager to hear the masterpieces of the Baroque exactly as they were written. The revival of interest in the harpsichord and baroque organ, and the growing number of recordings on these instruments make it increasingly possible for us to do so.

Types of Patronage

The Baroque was a period of international culture. National styles existed—without nationalism. Lully, an Italian, created the French lyric tragedy. Handel, a German, gave England the oratorio. There was free interchange among national cultures. The sensuous beauty of Italian melody, the pointed precision of French dance rhythm, the luxuriance of German counterpoint, the freshness of English choral song—these nourished an all-European art that absorbed the best of each.

The baroque composer was employed by a court, a church, a municipal council, or an opera house. He was therefore in direct contact with his public. As like as not he was his own interpreter, which made the contact even closer. He created his music for a specific occasion—it might be a royal wedding or a religious service—and for immediate use: in a word, for communication. He was an artisan in a handicraft society. He functioned as a religious man fired by the word of God, or as a loyal subject exalting his king. He was not troubled overmuch by the problem of self-expression, but because he spoke out of passionate conviction he expressed both himself and his era. He had never heard of art for art's sake; but because he created for his fellows and was part of their collective aspiration, he ascended the pinnacles of art. He did not discuss esthetics or the nature of inspiration; but, impelled by a lofty moral vision, he united superb mastery of his craft with profound insights into the nature of experience. He began by writing for a particular time and place; he ended by creating for the ages.

CHAPTER 64

Musical Forms of the Baroque (Vocal)

"I was aware that it is contraries which greatly move our mind. Where I have been able to find no variety in the affections I have at least sought to bring variety into my music."

Claudio Monteverdi

The Opera

THE DRAMATIC spirit of the Baroque lives for us, paradoxically, in its nontheater forms: oratorio, cantata, instrumental music. The vast literature of its music for the stage has ceased to be part of our heritage. One reason for this is that opera by its nature is more subject to the fashions of the moment than are most other forms of music. The formal or serious opera of the Baroque, the *opera seria,* is not easily adapted to the modern temper. Its conventions were attuned to the social order that ended with the French Revolution. The court opera of the Baroque, the favorite diversion of Habsburgs, Bourbons, Medici, and the rest, embodied the world-view of a feudal caste whose gaze was directed to the past. Seeking an escape from the disintegrating order about them, they found refuge in a dream-world where heroes torn between love and honor declaimed to noble music while time stood still in an enchanted grotto out of antiquity or the medieval age. For all its lofty rhetoric, the lyric drama of the Baroque is alien to the conventions that govern the modern theater; alien, too, to present-day notions of what constitutes valid human motivation. The plots are too complicated; the characters are idealized types rather than individuals; the passions are elevated and correct.

Baroque opera was a vital force whose influence extended far beyond the theater. It created the great forms of the lyric drama—recitative and aria, ensemble and chorus—that served as models to every branch of the art. The *da capo* aria, in which the first part was repeated after the middle section, established A-B-A as a basic formula of musical structure. Baroque opera within its own conventions taught composers to depict the passions and the affections, the lyric contemplation of nature, the quintessence of love, hate, fear, jealousy, exaltation. It invigorated the stately music of the courts with popular song and dance, and established new standards of vocal and instrumental performance. Through the opera house of the Baroque, music attained a dramatic-expressive power such as it had never possessed before.

The Lutheran Chorale

A *chorale* is a hymn tune, specifically one associated with German Protestantism. The chorales served as the battle hymns of the Reformation. Their sturdy contours bear the stamp of a heroic age.

Martin Luther (1483–1546) established as one of his reforms that the congregation must participate in the service. To this end he inaugurated services in the vernacular. Music, he saw, could be made to play a prime role in religious experience by means of congregational singing. "I wish," he wrote, "to make German psalms for the people, that is to say sacred hymns, so that the word of God may dwell among the people also by means of song."

Luther and his aides created the first chorales. They adapted a number of tunes from Gregorian chant, from popular sources as well as from secular art music. Appropriate texts and melodies were drawn, too, from Latin hymns and psalms. In the course of generations there grew up a body of religious folk song that was in the highest sense a national heritage. Originally sung in unison, the chorales soon became familiar in four-part harmony. The melody was put in the soprano, where all could hear it as it moved in four-square rhythm to the pause at the end of the line. The chorales greatly strengthened the trend to clear-cut melody, harmony, and rhythm. Since they often had to be sung by the musically untutored, they assumed the elemental simplicity and universality that, as in myth and fairy tale, are the essence of folk art.

In the elaborate vocal forms that presently appeared in the Protestant church service, the chorale served as a unifying thread. When at the close of an extended work the chorale unfolded in simple four-part harmony, its granitic strength reflected the faith of a nation. One may imagine the impact upon an audience attuned to its message. The chorale nourished centuries of German music. It came to full flower in the art of Johann Sebastian Bach, an art whose spiritual roots reach back to the Reformation.

The Cantata

A *cantata* (from the Italian *cantare*, "to sing"—that is, a piece to be sung) is a work for vocalists, chorus, and instrumentalists based on a poetic narrative, either religious or secular, of a lyric or dramatic nature. It generally contains several movements, such as arias, recitatives, duets, and choruses.

The cantata in Germany developed into the most important type of Lutheran sacred music. It was enriched by all the instrumental and vocal forms of the Baroque. It absorbed the recitative, aria, and duet of the opera; the pomp of the French operatic overture; and the dynamic instrumental style of the Italians. The various elements were cemented into a unity by the all-embracing presence of the Lutheran chorale.

The sacred cantata was an integral part of the service. It was related, along with the sermon and prayers that followed it, to the Gospel for the day. Every Sunday of the church year required another. What with some extra works for holidays and special occasions, an annual cycle came to about sixty cantatas. Cantors of Lutheran churches were required to furnish such cycles. Bach composed four or five cycles— approximately two hundred and forty to three hundred cantatas, of which only about two hundred have come down to us. The rest were lost, as a result of the casual attitude toward masterpieces—and posterity—of that superabundant age.

Oratorio and Passion

An *oratorio*—the name comes from the Italian word for a place of prayer—is a large-scale musical work for solo voices, chorus, and orchestra, set to a libretto of sacred or serious character. It is longer than a cantata and, unlike the latter, is not part of a religious service, although it is often based on a biblical story and imbued with devotional feeling. It is performed in a concert hall or church without scenery, costumes, or acting, in which respect oratorio differs from opera. The narrative unfolds in a series of recitatives and arias, ensemble numbers and choruses. There is much greater emphasis on the chorus. The poem, although cast in dialogue form, is of a contemplative rather than dramatic nature. No use is made of the rapid question-and-answer that serves to build tension in the opera house.

The oratorio grew out of the sacred operas of the Italian Counter-Reformation. It was introduced into Germany in the seventeenth century and absorbed the spirit of Lutheran church music. The baroque oratorio reached the peak of its development through the genius of Handel. He brought to it the gripping quality of operatic music and endowed it with its massive architecture, its shattering choruses, its dramatic power. He removed it from its churchly surroundings, imparting to it a universal quality that embraced all faiths. The best-known of his oratorios is, of course, *Messiah*.

The *Passion* is a musical version of that portion of the Gospels which deals with the suffering and death of Christ. In the Middle Ages it was a kind of liturgical play sung in plainchant. This gave way in the fifteenth and sixteenth centuries to a polyphonic setting. By the time of the Protestant late Baroque the Passion did not differ technically from the oratorio. Both featured chorales and impressive choral scenes. Both drew on the recitative and aria of the operatic theater and the dramatic force of the new orchestral style. Where they differed was in the subject matter of the libretto. Also, the Passion was performed at church during Holy Week, while the oratorio was a musical entertainment presented in a public hall.

Bach occupies the same commanding position in regard to the Passion as Handel does to the oratorio. The two great Passions of Bach are those according to St. Matthew and St. John.

The Baroque Mass

The taste for overpowering effects invaded even the musical setting of the Mass. The pure devotional style of the age of Palestrina gave way to the vogue of the "colossal Baroque." Masses were composed for quadruple choir—that is, for four choirs accompanied by orchestras that included woodwind and brass instruments and organs. With their vast dimensions and dynamic contrasts these works captured in tone all the flamboyance of baroque architecture. Never did music come closer to the monumental art of stone that has been called "frozen music."

Musicians of the Baroque did not draw the distinction between sacred and secular that is customary nowadays. They held that the composer worshiped God best by speaking the language of his time and by using all the resources of his art. Inevitably the new dynamic instrumental style and the spirit of opera found their way into this most hallowed of art forms. As in the case of baroque opera, the rich literature of the baroque Mass has not survived in the repertory. The one example that has become part of our heritage, Bach's Mass in B minor, amply attests to the magnificent vitality of baroque music.

✱✱ CHAPTER 65 ✱✱

Musical Forms of the Baroque (Instrumental)

"For by exactly observing this opposition or rivalry of the slow and the fast, the loud and the soft, the fullness of the great choir and the delicacy of the little trio, the ear is ravished by a singular astonishment, as is the eye by the opposition of light and shade."

Georg Muffat (1701)

Two-Part Form

THE CLASSIC-ROMANTIC period, we saw, was partial to the three-part or ternary form based on the principle of statement-departure-return (A-B-A). The Baroque, for its part, was inclined to two-part or binary structure (A-B). This is the question-and-answer type of structure which is found, in its simplest form, in a tune such as *London Bridge*. The principle gave rise to a tightly knit structure in which the A part moved from home to contrasting key while the B part made the corresponding move back. Both parts used closely related or even identical material. The form was made apparent to the ear by a full stop at the end of the first part. As a rule each part was repeated, giving an A-A: B-B structure.

In the three-part form contrast is injected by the middle section. Binary form, on the other hand, is all of a piece in texture and mood. It embodies a single affection, for which reason it was favored by a musical style based on continuous expansion. Binary form prevailed in the short harpsichord pieces of dance character that were produced in quantities during the seventeenth and early eighteenth centuries. It was a standard type in the suite, one of the favorite instrumental forms of the Baroque.

The Suite

The *suite* consisted mainly of a series of dance movements which were all in the same key. It presented an international galaxy of dance types: the German allemande, French courante, Spanish sarabande, English jig (gigue). These had been popular dances, but by the time of the late Baroque they had left the ballroom far behind and become abstract types of art music. The two sections of these little binary forms might be of approximately equal length, each being rounded off by a cadence.

The harpsichord suite as cultivated by Bach consisted of four principal numbers: an allemande in moderate duple meter, a courante in moderate triple, a stately sarabande in slow triple meter, and a lively gigue in $\frac{6}{8}$ or $\frac{6}{4}$. Between sarabande and gigue might be inserted a variety of optional numbers of a graceful song or dance type—minuet or gavotte, lively bourrée or passepied. These dances, of peasant origin, introduced a refreshing earthiness into their more formal surroundings. The harpsichord suite occasionally opened with a prelude. For additional contrast, the orchestral suite took over the operatic overture and aria. The best-known examples of the baroque orchestral suite are the four by Bach and the *Water Music* of Handel.

The essential element of the suite was dance rhythm, with its imagery of physical movement. The form met the needs of the age for elegant entertainment music. At the same time it offered composers a wealth of popular rhythms that could be transmuted into art.

Basso Ostinato

The principle of unity in variety was embodied in an important procedure of baroque music, the *basso ostinato* (obstinate bass) or *ground bass*. This consists of a short phrase, either melodic or accompanimental, that is repeated over and over in the bass while above it the upper parts change with each repetition, weaving an ever fresh texture of melody, harmony, and counterpoint. Basso ostinato consequently was a unifying device: the repeated pattern, like the repeated patterns of dance rhythm, enabled composers to impose structural coherence upon their instrumental pieces and to achieve ever more extended forms. The ostinato supplied the fixed framework within which the composer's imagination freely disported itself. Baroque musicians developed a consummate technique of variation and embellishment over the ground bass.

The upper parts were frequently improvised. This technique was especially popular in England where, since it involved breaking up or dividing the melody into quick rhythmic figures, it was known as *divisions on a ground*. The principle has reappeared in modern jazz as the basis of boogie-woogie piano playing, in which the left hand repeats a rhythmic ostinato while the right engages in free improvisation. The ostinato is little short of infallible both as a unifying device and as a means of building tension. We shall find it playing a prominent part in twentieth-century music.

Passacaglia and Chaconne

One of the most majestic forms of baroque music is the *passacaglia,* which utilizes the principle of basso ostinato. In this case a melody is introduced alone in the bass, generally four or eight bars in length, in a stately triple meter. The theme is repeated again and again, serving as the foundation for an intricate polyphonic structure based on continuous variation.

With each repetition the composer has to reveal the theme in a new light. He must also see to it that the variations as a whole sustain interest and mount cumulatively to the climax. One way of building up tension is to have the other voices proceed in ever faster notes within the measure: eighths, sixteenths, thirty-seconds. The theme may be transferred to the upper voices. It may be combined with counterthemes and presented in various guises. In the building of his edifice the composer marshals all the resources of melodic, harmonic, and rhythmic variation and all the devices of counterpoint. The famous example of the form is Bach's Passacaglia in C minor for organ, a magnificent example of the baroque art of variation.

In the *chaconne,* a related type, a fixed succession of chords in a characteristic rhythm is repeated as the basis for each variation. In other words, the unifying element in the chaconne is the harmony rather than melody. Chaconne and passacaglia are by no means exclusively instrumental forms. As a matter of fact, the principle of the ostinato figured in numerous arias in the operas and cantatas of the period.

Passacaglia and chaconne exemplify the baroque urge toward abundant variation and embellishment of a given musical idea. They embody the desire to make much out of little that is the essence of the creative act.

The Fugue

From the art and science of counterpoint issued one of the most exciting types of baroque music, the *fugue.* The name is derived from *fuga,* the Latin for "flight," implying a flight of fancy, possibly the flight of the theme from one voice to the other. A fugue is a contrapuntal composition, generally in three or four voices, in which a theme or subject of strongly marked character pervades the entire fabric, entering now in one voice, now in another. The fugue consequently is based on the principle of imitation. The subject is often rather short and constitutes the unifying idea, the focal point of interest in the contrapuntal web.

A fugue may be written for a group of instruments; for a solo instrument such as organ, harpsichord, or even violin; for several solo voices or for full chorus. Whether the figure is vocal or instrumental, the several lines are called voices, which indicates the origin of the type. In vocal and orchestral fugues each line is articulated by another performer or group of performers. In fugues for keyboard instruments the ten fingers—on the organ, the feet as well—manage the complex interweaving of the voices.

The *subject* or theme is stated alone at the outset in one of the voices —soprano, alto, tenor, or bass. It is then imitated in another voice— this is the *answer*—while the first continues with a *countersubject* or countertheme. Depending on the number of voices in the fugue, the subject will then appear in a third voice and be answered in the fourth, while the first two weave a free contrapuntal texture against these. (If a fugue is in three voices there is, naturally, no second answer; that is, no fourth voice.) When the theme has appeared in each voice once, the first section of the fugue, the Exposition, is at an end. The Exposition may be repeated, in which case the voices will enter in a different order. From there on the fugue alternates between exposition sections that feature the entrance of the subject and less weighty interludes known as *episodes* which serve as areas of relaxation.

The subject of the fugue is stated in the home key. The answer is given in a related key, that of the Dominant, which lies five tones above the Tonic. There is free modulation to foreign keys in the course of the fugue, which builds up tension against the return home. The baroque fugue thus embodied the contrast between home and foreign keys that was one of the basic principles of the new major-minor system. However, it did not develop this contrast to the same degree as did the later sonata form.

As the fugue unfolds there must be not only a sustaining of interest but the sense of mounting urgency that is proper to an extended art work. The composer throughout strives for continuity and a sense of organic growth. Each recurrence of the theme reveals new facets of its nature. It may be presented in longer or shorter note values, turned upside down, presented backwards, or upside down and backwards.

It may be combined with new subjects or with some other version of itself. It may be presented softly or vigorously. The composer manipulates the subject as pure musical material in the same way that the sculptor molds his clay. Especially effective is the *stretto* (from the Italian *stringere,* "to tighten"), in which the theme is imitated in close succession, with the subject entering in one voice before it has been completed in another. The effect is one of voices crowding upon each other, creating a heightening of tension that brings the fugue to its climax. There follows the final statement of the subject, generally in triumphal mood. The mission has been accomplished, the tension released.

A frequent feature of the fugue—generally towards the end—is the pedal point. This, it will be recalled, is a sustained tone in the bass while the harmonies change in the other parts.

The fugue is based on a single affection, or mood—the subject that dominates the piece. Episodes and transitional passages are woven from its motives or from those of the countersubject. There results an astounding unity of texture and atmosphere. Another factor for unity is the unfaltering rhythmic beat (against which, however, the composer may weave a diversity of counter-rhythms). The only section of the fugue that follows a set order is the Exposition. Once that is done with, the further course of the fugue is bound only by the composer's fancy. Caprice, exuberance, surprise—all receive free play within the supple framework of this form.

It is therefore an error to consider the fugue, as many have done, "the strictest of musical forms." We may even question whether it is a form at all; rather is it a procedure, a type of texture, a manner of thinking. The fundamental traits of fugal style are concentration of thought, purity of expression, and organic unity achieved through the process of continuous imitation and expansion.

Fugal technique reached unsurpassable heights at the hands of Bach and Handel. In the classic-romantic period the fugue was somewhat neglected, although fugal writing became an integral part of the composer's technique. Passages in fugal style occur in many a symphony, quartet, and sonata, especially in the development section. Such imitative passages inserted in a nonfugal piece are known as *fugato.* They afford the composer the excitement of fugal writing without the responsibilities.

Composers of the Baroque found in the fugue a unique combination of qualities. The form represented a mode of thought rooted in the past, into which they poured the living substance of their own time. It mobilized the resources, on the one hand of contrapuntal skill, on the other of imagination, feeling, and exuberant ornamentation. There re-

sulted a form of musical art that may well be accounted one of the
supreme achievements of the Baroque.

The Concerto Grosso

No less important than the principle of unity in baroque music was
that of contrast. This found expression in the *concerto grosso,* a form
based on the opposition between two dissimilar masses of sound. (The
Latin verb *concertare* means "to contend with," "to vie with.") A small
group of instruments known as the *concertino* was pitted against the
large group, the concerto grosso or *tutti* (all). The contrast was one of
color and dynamics, a uniform level of soft sound being set off against
loud. In other words, the orchestra here took over the terraced dynamics
of organ and harpsichord.

The concertino, or solo group, might consist of a string trio such as
two violins and a cello, or any combination that caught the composer's
fancy. The large group as a rule was based on the string choir, but might
be supplemented by winds. The harpsichord furnished harmonic support for both groups. The composer was able to write more difficult
music for the solo group than for the full ensemble. This was a signal
advantage in an age when expert players were none too plentiful.

The concerto grosso was fed by many streams. It was influenced by
the echo effects inherited from choral music and by the rhythms of
popular dance. It assimilated the clarity of the Italian instrumental
forms and the disciplined orchestral playing developed at the French
court, also the dramatic tension of the opera and the broad outlines of
the operatic overture. It manifested the baroque love of virtuoso playing. Above all it adapted itself to the idiom of the violin. The resultant
form embodied what one writer of the time called "the fire and fury
of the Italian style."

Two Italian masters were outstanding in this field, Arcangelo Corelli
and Antonio Vivaldi. Both strongly influenced the Germans, especially
Bach and Handel. The fact is worth noting. Because of the pre-eminence
of German orchestral music during the classic-romantic period, a popular myth has been built up that instrumental music is the exclusive
achievement of German genius. As a matter of fact, the concerto grosso
was one of several important instrumental forms that originated in
Italy, whence they passed to France, Germany, and England for further
development.

Prelude, Toccata, Fantasia

A *prelude* is a piece in imaginative style based on the continuous
expansion of a melodic or rhythmic figure. The prelude originated in

improvisation on the lute and keyboard instruments. In the late Baroque it served to introduce a group of dance pieces or a fugue. Bach's *Well-Tempered Clavier*, we saw, consists of forty-eight Preludes and Fugues.

The prelude achieved great variety and expressiveness during the Baroque. It assimilated the verve of dance rhythm, the lyricism of the aria, and the full resources of instrumental style. Since its texture was for the most part harmonic, it made an effective contrast with the contrapuntal texture of the fugue that followed it.

The baroque *toccata* (from the Italian *toccare,* "to touch," referring to the keys) was a composition for organ or harpsichord that exploited the resources of the keyboard in a glittering display of chords, arpeggios, and scale passages. It was free and rhapsodic in form, marked by passages in a harmonic style alternating with fugal sections. In the hands of the north German organists the toccata became a virtuoso piece of monumental proportions, either as an independent work or as companion piece to a fugue.

By *fantasia* we understand a type of composition in which the play of fancy takes precedence over regularity of structure. The term includes a variety of pieces imbued with the spirit of improvisation. In the great fantasias of Bach massive sonorities, abrupt changes of mood, poetic expression, and luxuriant ornamentation are contained within an architecture at once grandiose and supple. Like the toccata, the fantasia may be either an independent piece or coupled with a fugue.

Church organists, in announcing the chorale to be sung by the congregation, fell into the practice of embellishing the traditional melodies. In so doing they drew upon the wealth of baroque ornamentation, harmony, and counterpoint. There grew up a magnificent body of instrumental art—*chorale prelude* and *chorale variations*—in which organ virtuosity of the highest level was imbued with the spirit of inspired improvisation.

Other Instrumental Forms

The sonata was widely cultivated throughout the Baroque. It consisted of several sections or movements that contrasted in tempo and texture. Sonatas were written for from one to six or eight instruments, with a thorough-bass that required a cello or similar instrument to play the figured bass line while the harpsichordist or organist realized—that is, filled in—the suggested harmonies. A distinction was drawn between the *sonata da camera* or chamber sonata, which was a suite of stylized dances intended for performance in the home, and the *sonata da chiesa* or church sonata. This was more serious in tone and more polyphonic in texture. Its four movements, arranged in the sequence slow-fast-slow-fast, were supposed to make little use of dance rhythms.

In practice the two types somewhat overlapped. Many church sonatas ended with one or more dancelike movements, while many chamber sonatas opened with an impressive introductory movement in the church-sonata style.

The operatic overture was an important type of large-scale orchestral music. The *French overture* was a ceremonious one-movement form associated with Lully. It opened with an impressive slow introduction based on dotted rhythms, which was followed by an allegro in loosely fugal style. Sometimes the form was rounded off with a return to the stately pace of the opening, which resulted in the pattern slow-fast-slow. The *Italian overture* consisted of three sections too: fast-slow-fast. The opening section was not in fugal style; the middle section was lyrical; there followed a vivacious, dancelike finale. This pattern, expanded into three separate movements, was later adopted by the concerto grosso and the solo concerto. We have referred to the opera house as a center of experimentation that had a fruitful effect on all branches of music. The operatic overture of the Baroque was one of the ancestors of the symphony.

An *invention*—the word signifies an ingenious idea—is a short piece for the keyboard in contrapuntal style. The title is known to pianists from Bach's collection of fifteen Inventions in two voices and a like number in three. Bach called the latter group *Sinfonias*, which shows how flexible was musical terminology in those days. His purpose in the Inventions, he wrote, was "upright instruction wherein the lovers of the clavier, and especially those desirous of learning, are shown a clear way not alone to have good *inventiones* but to develop the same well."

The instrumental forms of the Baroque manifest great diversity and venturesomeness. In this they epitomize the spirit of the era that shaped their being.

Baroque and Classical: A Comparison of Styles

In comparing the baroque and classical styles, it becomes apparent that the baroque was the more romantic period in its emphasis on emotion and expressivity. Its turbulent nonsymmetrical forms are at the opposite end from classical symmetry and poise. It had a far greater interest in religious music than did the classical era. The Baroque gave equal importance to instrumental and vocal forms. During the classical era the emphasis shifted steadily to the instrumental branch of the art.

The great instrumental forms of the classical era—solo and duo sonata, trio and quartet, symphony and concerto—traced their ancestry to the baroque sonata, concerto and concerto grosso, suite and overture. But between the baroque and classical eras there interposed a momentous shift of interest from polyphonic to homophonic texture. Baroque music exploited the contrapuntal—that is, the linear-horizontal aspect of music, even as the classical era developed the harmonic or chordal-vertical aspect. This basic difference affected every aspect of musical style.

In baroque music, a movement was shaped by a single affection or mood. Thus, the chief instrumental form of the Baroque, the fugue, was based on a single theme presented within a contrapuntal texture. The classical sonata-allegro, on the other hand, centered about two contrasting themes presented in a harmonic texture. The fugue depended on theme imitation, the sonata form on theme development. The fugue theme remains basically the same throughout; the sonata themes undergo substantial changes as the material is developed. The fugue presents a continuous texture, while the sonata movement consist of three contrasting sections—Exposition, Development, and Recapitulation. As someone has well said, the sonata is sewn together, the fugue is woven together.

The baroque concept of the "single affection" influenced instrumental color. An oboe will accompany the voice throughout an entire movement of a cantata or Mass. The classical style, on the other hand, demanded continual changes of tone color. So too, the relentless single rhythm that dominates an entire movement of baroque music gives way in the classical era to more flexible patterns. Composers of the Baroque did not mix timbres as the classical composers did. They used the different instruments to trace the lines of the counterpoint. For this reason they needed pure colors that would stand out against the mass. Since their orchestral texture was primarily a web of contrapuntal lines, they were not concerned with the capacities of the different instruments. Their conception of music allowed them to give the same kind of line to a flute, a trumpet, or a violin.

The classical era, influenced by the spirit of rationalism, tried to systematize musical forms. One way of doing this was to give the composer a greater control over his material than was the case during the Baroque. As long as the thorough-bass figured in music, the performer participated—through his improvisation—in creating the music. The classical composers wrote out all the parts, limiting improvisation to the cadenza of the concerto. They specified what instruments were to be used in the performance of their scores, as well as the dynamic markings; composers of the Baroque were inclined to leave such matters to the taste and discretion of the performer. Hence it was only in the classical era that the orchestra was stabilized in the four sections that we know today. Music founded on the thorough-bass emphasized soprano and bass; the classical composers aimed for a more equable distribution of the parts. Once the thorough-bass was eliminated, the harpsichord disappeared from the orchestra. Now the other instruments shared in the responsibility of filling in the harmonies, a circumstance that spurred the development of an orchestral style. The terraced dynamics of the Baroque resulted in even levels of soft and loud alternating in areas of light and shade. The classical era exploited the crescendo and decrescendo, as well as the dramatic surprise inherent in explosive accents, sudden fortissimos and sudden rests.

Although four-bar structure is present in the dance forms of the Baroque, it was only in the classical era that symmetrical formations came into their own. Indeed, the grandiose gesture of the Baroque, as manifest in the toccatas, fantasias, and chorale preludes of the period, was clearly alien to the neatly defined symmetries of the classical era. The Baroque was a period of rhapsodic improvisation. Hence its music, in its massiveness and wealth of ornamentation, its tumultuous piling-up of sonorities and its rapturous outpouring, was far closer to the romantic spirit than to the classical. For this reason we are able to trace a certain parallelism in the history of art: from the visionary mysticism of the Middle Ages to the classicism of the Renaissance; from the pathos and passion of the Baroque to the ordered beauty of late eighteenth-century classicism; and from the romanticism of the nineteenth century to the neoclassicism of the twentieth.

CHAPTER 66

Old Masters

Claudio Monteverdi (1567–1643)

"The modern composer builds upon the foundation of truth."

THE INNOVATIONS of the Florentine Camerata awaited the composer who would infuse life into them and enrich them with the resources of the past. That composer was Claudio Monteverdi, in whom the dramatic spirit of the Baroque found its spokesman. Monteverdi stands in history as the first exponent of the direct relationship between music and the life of the heart. He injected into his operas, even as did his contemporary Shakespeare into the spoken drama, an elemental intensity that superimposed modern psychological attitudes upon a landscape still haunted by the shapes of a feudal past.

Claudio Monteverdi.

Monteverdi welded the new-born lyric drama of the Florentines into a coherent musical form. He tightened their shapeless recitative into an expressive line imbued with dramatic urgency. He originated what he called the *stile concitato* (agitated style) to express the hidden tremors of the soul. Dramatic conflict was the essence of his art. Above all, he made his music express the emotional content of poetry. "The text," he declared, "should be the master of the music, not the servant."

Monteverdi used dissonance and instrumental color for dramatic expressiveness, atmosphere, and suspense. He emphasized the contrast between characters by abrupt changes of key. He held that rhythm is bound up with emotion. A master of polyphonic writing, he retained in his choruses the great contrapuntal tradition of the past. There resulted a nobly pathetic art rooted in the verities of human nature, whose high aim it was to capture for music the ebb and flow of the passions. The personages on the stage were neither puppets nor abstractions but men and women who gave vent to their joys and sorrows through song. When his patron the Duke of Mantua suggested a libretto on a mythological subject of the kind fashionable at the time—a dialogue of the winds—the composer of *Orfeo* (1607) and of *Arianna* (1608) protested: "How shall I be able to imitate the speaking of winds that do not speak; and how shall I be able to move the affections by such means? Arianna was moving because she was a woman, and likewise Orfeo was moving because he was a man and not a wind. The harmonies imitate human beings, not the noise of winds, the bleating of sheep, the neighing of horses."

The qualities of Monteverdi's art are well exemplified in the recitative from *Orfeo, Tu se' morta*. Orfeo, having learned of Eurydice's death, decides to follow her to the nether regions:

Tu se' morta, se' morta, mia vita,	You are dead—dead, my darling,
ed io respiro; tu se' da me partita,	And I live. You have left me,
se' da me partita per mai più,	Left me forevermore,
mai più non tornare, ed io rimango—	Never to return, yet I remain.
nò, nò, che se i versi alcuna cosa ponno,	No, no! If verses have any power,
n'andrò sicuro al più profondi abissi,	I shall go boldly to the deepest abysses,
e intenerito il cor del rè dell'ombre,	And having softened the heart of the king of shadows,
meco trarotti a riveder le stelle,	Will take you with me to see again the stars,
o se ciò negherammi empio destino,	Or if cruel fate will deny me this,
rimarrò teco in compagnia di morte!	I will remain with you in the presence of death!
addio terra, addio cielo, e sole, addio.	Farewell earth, farewell sky and sun, farewell.

The recitative is accompanied by a small portable organ and a bass lute that realized the harmonies from the bass. With what economy of means Monteverdi transforms the text into a grandly pathetic declamation! The vocal line is the epitome of simplicity, yet it floods

the words with emotion. Notice how the repetition of key words and phrases heightens the pathos; how the voice descends on the words *profondi abissi,* and rises again on the phrase *meco trarotti a riveder le stelle* (will take you with me to see again the stars). The harmony is for the most part composed of simple triads, with dissonances used sparingly and most expressively to generate tension. Chromatic intervals and an occasional wide leap project the tragic mood. Wholly Italian is the sensitivity to the beauty and affective power of the voice. Wholly Monteverdian is the poignancy of the emotion conveyed, a poignancy that music henceforth was never to forget. The master seems to unlock the music hidden in the Italian language. More important, with unerring instinct he strikes the essentially operatic tone.

When an art form genuinely reflects the soul of a nation its history manifests a striking unity of outlook and achievement. From Monteverdi the heritage descends through two hundred and fifty years of Italian opera to Giuseppe Verdi. In the plaint of Orfeo we hear the throb of passion, the profoundly human quality that echoes in more familiar guise through the measures of *Aïda* and *Otello*.

Monteverdi established the opera on the eternally valid principle of dramatic truth. Time and again, operatic composers were lured away from the dramatic element by the beauty of the purely musical. But sooner or later they returned to the Monteverdian ideal. He foreshadowed in his art the evolution of this irresistible and exasperating form toward ever profounder levels of awareness. One of the great pioneers in the communication of feeling through tone, he was indeed—as his contemporaries called him—a "Prophet of Music."

Jean-Baptiste Lully (1632–1687)

"The assurance of pleasing you has lifted me above myself and filled me with those divine transports which I could feel only in the service of Your Majesty. Indeed, Sire, there is no end I could not reach if it were necessary to obey you."

Lully to Louis XIV

Lully was one of those dominating personalities who have the good fortune to appear precisely when the time is ripe for their gifts. He captured in his music the impulses of the era of French absolutism. In so doing he stamped his image upon a century.

Born in Florence of humble parentage, he displayed in boyhood a gift for singing and dancing. His talent attracted the notice of a French nobleman who offered to take him to France. At the age of fourteen the miller's son Gianbattista Lulli set forth on the eventful journey that was to transform him into Jean-Baptiste Lully, supreme arbiter of musical entertainment at the most sumptuous court in Europe.

Lully's art must be viewed against the resplendent milieu for which it was created. His ballets and operas were performed at the famous festivities of Versailles, in the open-air marble court lined with silver candelabras and rows of orange trees in silver tubs. Here was an enchanted pleasure dome created out of the misery of a nation for a monarch whose whim it was to transform his life into a work of art. In this setting music was meant to soothe the ear and delight the senses; to be elegant, clear, and well-ordered. Lully's goals remained valid for French music for the next two hundred years. We shall meet them again in the pronouncements of Claude Debussy.

But Versailles subserved also another ideal: the aggrandizement of the king as the symbol of absolute power. It testifies to Lully's capacity for growth that he was able to pass from the comedy-ballets of his early years at court to the *tragédie lyrique* in which was incarnated the lofty formalism of the age of Louis XIV. Just as Monteverdi created a style of pathetic expressivity for the Italians, Lully established for the French an art of restraint and decorum. This music aimed for grandeur rather than ecstasy. It preferred polish to passion. Good taste held the reins; the head controlled the heart.

Lully's emphasis on chorus and ballet pervaded French opera for the next two hundred years. His flair for descriptive music remained a specifically French trait. He created a musical recitative shaped to the natural inflections of French speech; his style of setting the language served as the model for all Frenchmen after him. In rhythm, in melody, and in harmony he aimed for simplicity and clarity. His color scheme expressed the affections in a way that persisted for generations: flutes for sad or nocturnal scenes, oboes for pastoral moods, trumpets for martial. His dance movements were the essence of French *esprit*. He popularized the minuet, gavotte, march. Although he was in every sense an artist of the court, his melodies were sung by all France—as a contemporary put it, "from the princess to the serving maid in the tavern."

Lully is particularly associated with the development of the French overture. The Overture to his lyric tragedy *Armide* (1685) exemplifies the type. It opens with a majestic section in duple meter. The stately dotted rhythms, the forthright harmonies, easy melodiousness, and full sonority of the strings are Lullian characteristics. This is music commanding of gesture and ample of gait; its theme is pomp and power. The opening motive, announced by the first violins, is effectively imitated and expanded by the lower strings. This section is repeated softly. The lively middle section, in sextuple meter, opens in fugal fashion; but Lully does not pursue this in any methodical way. His melodious counterpoint is not meant to burden the mind. He puts most of the imitation in the outer parts, where the ear will hear it most easily. The opening motive of the section is made much of, and is occasionally inverted. The final section, in slow duple meter, resembles the first in its stately pace and massive sound. The texture is rather chordal. The second and third sections are repeated, rounding out the form in a clear and concise manner.

Lully was one of a number of foreign musicians who at various times settled in Paris and created a style that the world came to regard as typically French. His dance forms and overtures affected the development of instrumental music all over Europe. His operas ruled the French stage for a long time after his death. The boy who left Florence as a penniless tumbler gave his adopted country the grand manner of

her golden age. For her he remained, as Molière called him, "the incomparable M. de Lully."

Henry Purcell (1659–1695)

"As Poetry is the harmony of Words, so Musick is that of Notes;
and as Poetry is a Rise above Prose and Oratory, so is Musick
the exaltation of Poetry."

Henry Purcell occupies a special niche in the annals of his country.
He was last in the illustrious line that, stretching back to pre-Tudor
times, won for England a foremost position among the musically creative nations. With his death the ascendancy came to an end. Until
the rise of a native school of composers almost two hundred years after,
he remained for his countrymen the symbol of a power they had lost.
His position as national artist is indicated by Dr. Charles Burney, one
of the leading chroniclers of things musical in the following century:
"PURCELL is as much the boast of England in music as Shakespeare in
the drama, Milton in epic poetry, Locke in metaphysics, or Sir Isaac
Newton in mathematics."

Purcell's brief career unfolded at the court of Charles II, extending
through the turbulent reign of James II into the period of William and
Mary. He held various posts as singer, organist, and composer. His was
an art based on an inexhaustible fund of melody; his lyricism issued
from the great tradition of Tudor choral song. Purcell's works cover a
wide range, from the massive contrapuntal choruses of the religious
anthems and the odes in honor of his royal masters, to popular ditties
such as *Sawney Is a Bonny Lad,* or patriotic songs like *Britons, Strike
Home* which stir his countrymen even as do the patriotic speeches that
ring through the histories of Shakespeare.

Yet this national artist realized that England's music, no matter how
indigenous, must not remain insular. A European figure, he linked his
art to the mainstream of baroque music. It was his historic role to assimilate the achievements of the Continent—the dynamic instrumental
style, the movement toward major-minor tonality, the recitative and
aria of Italian opera and the pointed rhythms of the French—and to
acclimate these to his native land.

Purcell's odes and anthems hit off the tone of solemn ceremonial in
an open-air music of great breadth and power. This virile style, taken
over by Handel, laid the foundation for the huge festivals of choral
singing that are still the backbone of musical life in England. His instrumental music ranks with the finest achievements of the middle

Baroque. His songs display the charm of his lyricism no less than his
gift for setting our language. In the domain of the theater he produced,
besides a quantity of music for plays, what many of his countrymen
still regard as the peak of English opera—*Dido and Aeneas.*

The work, presented shortly before 1690 "at Mr. Josias Priest's
boarding-school at Chelsey by young Gentlewomen . . . to a select
audience of their parents and friends," takes little over an hour to perform. Purcell functions here within the limits imposed by a school performance. Recitatives and arias, duets, choruses, and instrumental interludes are noteworthy for their concentration and roundness of form.
Remarkable is the advanced conception of characterization through
music, and a sense of pathos for which there was no precedent in
England.

From the Overture, whose stately dotted rhythms point to the influence of Lully, this gem of a chamber opera abounds in felicitous strokes.
Dido's first aria, "Ah! Belinda, I am prest with torment," wreathes the
lovelorn queen in the atmosphere of noble grief that surrounds her
throughout the work. A favorite with Purcell devotees is the chorus
"To the Hills and Vales"; as is the Laughing Chorus of the Witches.
In Vergil's epic the departure of Aeneas is motivated by the hero's
manifest destiny. The libretto by Nahum Tate, one of the drearier poets
laureate of England, simplifies this into a malicious plot of the Witches
against Dido, a twist presumably more easily understood by the young
ladies of Chelsea. In any case, one of the witches brings Aeneas a faked
command from Jove to be on his way. The sailors of the final scene are
as English a lot as ever sailed from Troy. Their chorus contains one of
Tate's happiest lines: "Take a boozey short leave of your nymphs on the
shore." Hardly less memorable is the Witches' comment: "Our plot has
took, the Queen's forsook."

The culminating point of the opera is Dido's lament after Aeneas's
departure: "When I am laid in earth." This majestic threnody unfolds

laid, ___ am laid _____ in earth,

over a ground bass that descends along the chromatic scale. The aria
builds steadily to the searing high G on "Remember me"—one of those
strokes of genius that, once heard, is never forgotten. The design of
the whole is here consummated; all that preceded is seen to have led
inexorably to this plangent outcry.

Purcell in this work struck the true tone of lyric drama. *Dido and
Aeneas* is an English opera in the sense that its supple melody line takes
life from the inflections and rhythms of English speech. Purcell might
have established opera in England, even as Lully did in France, had
he lived twenty years longer. As it was, his masterpiece had no progeny.
It remained as unique a phenomenon in history as the wonderful musician whom his contemporaries named "the British Orpheus."

Arcangelo Corelli (1653–1713)

Arcangelo Corelli was one of the leaders of the Italian violin school.
He was educated at Bologna and spent the major part of his career at
Rome, where he was vastly admired both as a violinist and composer.
Corelli was an unpretentious man of the most amiable disposition who,
despite his fame, retained his simplicity of manner and true humility
as an artist. His compositions were printed throughout Europe, and
students flocked to Rome to study with him. Among them were such
musicians as Geminiani and Locatelli, who became leading figures in
the next generation of the Italian violin school. Toward the end of his
life Corelli found himself superseded in public favor and took this
eclipse so much to heart that his health began to fail. He died at the
age of sixty and was buried in a magnificent tomb in the Pantheon, not
far from Raphael.

Himself a great violinist, Corelli developed a pure style of violin
playing that exploited to the full the technical and lyrical capacities of
the instrument. His compositions were of major importance in exploring the possibilities of the violin both as a solo and an orchestral

instrument. His sonatas and concerti grossi are marked by an exemplary clarity of thought, compactness of form, and nobility of style. Of special merit are the slow movements, conceived with a dignity and pathos that eloquently exhibit the violin's capacity for songful expression.

Corelli's chamber and church sonatas were written for what was the most popular combination for such works—two violins and basso continuo. Because of the three printed staves in the music, such compositions came to be known as *trio sonatas*. Yet the title is misleading, because it refers to the number of parts rather than to the number of players. Actually the basso continuo needed two performers—a cellist or bass violinist to play the figured bass, and a harpsichordist or organist to realize the implied harmonies.

Corelli's *Sonata da chiesa* in E minor, Opus 3, No. 7 (1689), is a fine specimen of the church sonata of the middle Baroque. The basso continuo is played by cello and organ. The opening Grave, in common time, takes wings from the affecting tone of the violin. The lofty pathos of this slow movement is characteristic of the Italian master. The texture is based on imitation, as is apparent from the opening line, where first violin, second violin, and cello enter in succession with the same motive. Both violins play in the same register, their parts frequently

crossing, so that the effect is that of a continuous dialogue between them.

The second movement, an Allegro in duple meter, has a fugal texture. The two violins and cello enter successively with the theme, after which the movement proceeds in free style. Here too the violins play in the same register, their parts intertwining, the result being a flowing melodiousness in which both share equally. The cello participates in the thematic work, and the organ lends both support and dimension to the proceedings. Third is an Adagio in triple time which has a lyric line of great plasticity. Again the two solo instruments unfold a loosely imitative texture in which the cello takes part now thematically, now as supporting instrument. The finale is a melodious Allegro in $\frac{3}{4}$ with a dancelike lilt. This movement is a binary or two-part form, each part being repeated. The first section, in the Tonic key of E minor, reaches a cadence on the Dominant chord of B major. The second part modulates to the related key of G major, whence it returns to E minor.

Corelli with unerring instinct built his art on what conformed to the true nature of the violin. He was thus able to lay a foundation on which his pupils and successors built an Italian school of instrumental music that remains one of the glories of the Baroque.

Antonio Vivaldi (c. 1675–1741)

For many years interest in the Baroque centered about Bach and Handel to such an extent that the earlier masters were neglected. None suffered more in this regard than Antonio Vivaldi, who has been rediscovered by the twentieth century. Amazingly prolific even for that prolific age, he produced quantities of concertos and sonatas, operas and choral pieces, many of them still unknown. Only with the publication of his complete works—a number of volumes have already appeared—will it be possible fully to evaluate the achievement of this strikingly original musician.

Vivaldi was born in Venice, the son of a violinist. He was ordained in the Church in his twenties and came to be known as "the red priest," an epithet which in that distant age referred to nothing more than the color of his hair. Some years thereafter he took up a musical career, during the greater part of which he was connected with the educational institutions of his native city.

Vivaldi's instrumental music marks one of the high points of the Italian violin school. His novel use of rapid scale passages, extended arpeggios, and contrasting registers contributed decisively to the development of violin style. He also played a leading part in the history of the concerto grosso, exploiting with vast effectiveness the contrast in sonority between large and small groups of players. The Venetian school, in music as in painting, was distinguished by its love of brilliant color. In his devotion to sonority and color Vivaldi was a true son of the Adriatic city. A powerful rhythmic conception captures for his music the relentless drive of the Baroque. Hardly less notable are the clarity and grace of his forms. The concise themes, instinct with dramatic tension, reveal the operatic composer. They inject into the language of the instruments the pathos of the lyric theater.

Characteristic of Vivaldi's style is the Concerto Grosso in D minor for two violins and cello with string orchestra. This is the eleventh of a set of twelve that the composer fancifully named *L'Estro armonico* (The Harmonic Whim). Six of these works were transcribed—or better, adapted—by Bach, who assiduously studied Vivaldi's music: three for organ and three for harpsichord. So completely was the Venetian master forgotten after his death that for generations these transcriptions were regarded as original works by Bach.

The Concerto Grosso in D minor opens with an introduction based on an arpeggio figure. The Allegro proper consists of a fugue. The subject, with its sharp rhythmic profile, is in Vivaldi's happiest vein.

The writing is violinistic and full of dash. Since both the concertino (the solo group) and the accompanying body consist of string instruments, the composer cannot rely on tone color for his contrasts. He obtains these through variety of dynamics and rhythm, echo effects, and by skillfully pitting high register against low.

The Largo e spiccato (very slow and with bouncing bow) is a singing movement in the grand tradition of the classical Italian school. The $\frac{12}{8}$ meter with its dotted rhythms is characteristic of the *siciliano*, a melodious dance type much favored by the Baroque. The melody is carried by solo violin and unfolds in a vaulting arch over an accompaniment of affective harmonies. The focusing of interest on a single instrument indicates Vivaldi's role in drawing the concerto grosso closer to the solo concerto.

The finale corresponds in weight to the first movement, completing the arch of the work. It is one of those busy allegros that vividly conjure up the world of the eighteenth century. Worthy of note are the passages for two solo violins in thirds, in the mellifluous manner of Italian opera; the terraced dynamics that rapidly alternate areas of light and shade; the arpeggios that nourished a century of virtuoso writing for the violin; the sturdy chords in the tutti that support the passage work of the solo group; the lucid counterpoint; the continuous motion and forward thrust of the music. This is a tissue woven without effort and without seams. Vivaldi gets the movement under way, keeps it going, and brings it to a close without wasting a note. Such economy bespeaks a surpassing sense of style.

Vivaldi's music flowered from a noble tradition. His dynamic conceptions pointed to the future. We see him today as one of the great figures of the Baroque.

CHAPTER 67

Johann Sebastian Bach (1685-1750)

"The aim and final reason of all music should be nothing else but the Glory of God and the refreshment of the spirit."

JOHANN SEBASTIAN BACH was heir to the great polyphonic art of the past. This he vitalized with the passion and humanity of his own spirit. He is the culminating figure of baroque music and one of the titans in the history of art.

His Life

He was born at Eisenach of a family that had supplied musicians to the churches and town bands of Thuringia for upwards of a century and a half. Left an orphan at the age of ten, he was raised in the town of Ohrdruf by an older brother, an organist who prepared him for the family vocation. From the first he displayed inexhaustible curiosity concerning every aspect of his art. "I had to work hard," he reported in later years, adding with considerably less accuracy, "Anyone who works as hard will get just as far."

His professional career began when he was eighteen with his appointment as organist at a church in Arnstadt. The certificate of appointment

Johann Sebastian Bach.

427

admonishes the young man to be true, faithful, and obedient to "our Noble and Most Gracious Count and Master . . . to conduct yourself in all things toward God, High Authority, and your superiors as befits an honorable servant and organist." High Authority soon had cause to reprove the new organist "for having made many curious *variationes* in the chorale and mingled many strange tones in it, and for the fact that the Congregation has been confused by it." The church elders were inquiring shortly after "by what right he recently caused a strange maiden to be invited into the choir loft and let her make music there." The maiden was his cousin Maria Barbara, whom he married.

After a year at a church in Mühlhausen, Bach—at twenty-three—received his first important post: court organist and chamber musician to the Duke of Weimar. His nine years at the ducal court (1708–17) were spent in the service of a ruler whose leaning toward religious music accorded with his own. The Weimar period saw the rise of his fame as an organ virtuoso and the production of many of his most important works for that instrument.

Disappointed because the Duke had failed to advance him, Bach decided to accept an offer from the Prince of Anhalt-Cöthen. He needed his master's permission to take another post. This the irascible Duke refused to give. The musician stood up for his rights; whereupon, as the court chronicle relates, "on November 6, the former Concertmeister and court organist Bach was placed under arrest in the County Judge's place of detention for too stubbornly forcing the issue of his dismissal and finally on December 2 was freed from arrest with notice of his unfavorable discharge."

At Cöthen, Bach served a prince partial to chamber music. In his five years there (1717–23) he produced suites, concertos, sonatas for various instruments, and a wealth of clavier music; also the six concerti grossi dedicated to the Margrave of Brandenburg. The Cöthen period was saddened by the death of Maria Barbara in 1720. The composer subsequently married Anna Magdalena, a young singer in whom he found a loyal and understanding mate. Of his twenty children—seven of the first marriage and thirteen of the second—half did not survive infancy. One son died in his twenties, another was mentally deficient. Four others became leading composers of the next generation: Wilhelm Friedemann and Carl Philipp Emanuel, sons of Maria Barbara; and Anna Magdalena's sons Johann Christoph and Johann Christian.

Bach was thirty-eight when he was appointed to one of the most important posts in Germany, that of Cantor of St. Thomas's in Leipzig. The cantor taught at the choir school of that name, which trained the choristers of the city's principal churches (he was responsible for nonmusical subjects too); and served as music director, composer, choirmaster, and organist of St. Thomas's Church. Several candidates were considered before him, among them the then much more famous composer Georg Philipp Telemann, who declined the offer. As one member of the town council reported, "Since the best man could not be obtained, lesser ones would have to be accepted." It was in this spirit that Leipzig received the greatest of her cantors. He undertook to "set the boys a shining example of an honest, retiring manner of life . . . show all proper respect and obedience to the Honorable and Most Wise Council . . . so arrange the music that it shall not last too long, and shall be of such a nature as not to make an operatic impression but rather impel the listeners to devotion"; also to teach the boys their Latin.

Bach's twenty-seven years in Leipzig (1723–50) saw the production of stupendous works. The clue to his inner life must be sought in his music. It had no counterpart in an outwardly uneventful existence divided between the cares of a large family, the pleasures of a sober circle of friends, the chores of a busy professional life, and the endless squabbles with a host of officials of town, school, and church who never conceded that they were dealing with anything more than a competent choirmaster. The city fathers were impressed but also disquieted by the soul-shattering dramaticism of his religious music. Besides, like all officials they were out to save money and not averse to lopping off certain rights and fees that Bach felt belonged to him. He fought each issue doggedly, with an expenditure of time and emotion that might have gone to better things. He describes himself as living "amidst continual vexation, envy, and persecution; accordingly I shall be forced, with God's help, to seek my fortune elsewhere." Even the wind seemed to be against him. "When there are rather more funerals than usual, the fees rise in proportion; but when a healthy air blows, they fall accordingly, as for example last year when I lost fees that would ordinarily come in from funerals to an amount of more than 100 thaler." Despite his complaints he remained in Leipzig. With the years the Council learned to put up with their obstinate cantor. After all, he was the greatest organist in Germany.

The routine of his life was enlivened by frequent professional journeys, when he was asked to test and inaugurate new organs. His last and most interesting expedition was to the court of Frederick the Great at Potsdam, where his son Carl Philipp Emanuel served as accompanist to the flute-playing monarch. Frederick on the memorable evening announced to his courtiers with some excitement, "Gentlemen, old Bach has arrived." He led the composer through the palace showing him the new pianos that were beginning to replace the harpsichord. Upon Bach's invitation the King gave him a subject on which he improvised one of his astonishing fugues. After his return to Leipzig he further

elaborated on the royal theme, added a sonata for flute, violin, and
clavier, and dispatched *The Musical Offering* to "a Monarch whose
greatness and power, as in all the sciences of war and peace, so especially in music everyone must admire and revere."

The prodigious labors of a lifetime took their toll; his eyesight failed.
After an apoplectic stroke he was stricken with blindness. He persisted
in his final task, the revising of eighteen chorale preludes for the organ.
The dying master dictated to his son-in-law the last of these, *When in
the Hour of Direst Need*. In the final moment faith triumphed over
anguish. He renamed it *Before Thy Throne, My God, I Stand*.

His Music

The artist in Bach was driven to conquer all realms of musical thought.
His position in history is that of one who consummated existing forms
rather than one who originated new ones. Whatever form he touched
he brought to its ultimate development. He cut across boundaries, fus-
ing the three great national traditions of his time—German, Italian,
French—into a convincing unity. His sheer mastery of the technics of
composition has never been equaled. With this went incomparable
profundity of thought and feeling and the capacity to realize to the
full all the possibilities inherent in a given musical situation.

Bach was the last of the great religious artists. He considered music
to be "a harmonious euphony to the Glory of God." And the glory of
God was the central issue of man's existence. It was more than convention that made him inscribe at the head of his cantatas, "Jesus, help
me!" and at their close, "To God alone be the praise." Given this exalted
conception of the purpose of art, grandeur and sublimity were as native
to his thought as were charm and elegance to that of more worldly musicians. Not without reason has he been called "the greatest of preach-
ers."

Bach's music issued in the first instance from the Lutheran chorale.
The indestructible tunes of the Reformation imparted to his art its
strength and universality. Through the chorale the most learned composer of the age was united to the living current of popular melody, to
become the spokesman of a faith. The prime medium for Bach's poetry
was the organ. His imagery was rooted in its keyboard and pedals, his
inspiration molded to its majestic sonorities. He created for the instrument what is still the high point of its literature: chorale preludes, fantasias, preludes, toccatas, fugues, and the great Passacaglia in C minor,
which dates from the Weimar period. In his own lifetime he was known
primarily as a virtuoso organist, only Handel being placed in his class.
When complimented on his playing he would answer disarmingly,

"There is nothing remarkable about it. All you have to do is hit the right notes at the right time and the instrument plays itself."

The fugue is closely associated with Bach. He transformed it into a fantasy piece in which contrapuntal art was suffused with expressive elements. What sets Bach's fugues apart is the absolutely personal stamp of his themes, those chiseled patterns of melody that engrave themselves indelibly upon mind and heart. In the field of keyboard music his most important work is the *Well-Tempered Clavier*. The forty-eight preludes and fugues in these two volumes (1722, 1744) have been called the pianist's Old Testament (the New, it will be recalled, being Beethoven's sonatas). The suites for clavier transform the conventional dance forms of the time into abstract movements as diversified as they are appealing. Here the Leipzig cantor dons the grace and elegance of the French style. Two sets of six each (c. 1722, c. 1725) came to be known as the *French* and *English Suites;* they were not so named by the composer. Another six dating from the Leipzig period were named Partitas (1731). The keyboard music includes a variety of preludes, toccatas, fantasias, inventions, fugues, and fughettas. Two popular works in this category are the *Chromatic Fantasy and Fugue* (c. 1720) and the *Italian Concerto* (1735). A favorite with young pianists is the collection of little dance pieces known as *Anna Magdalena's Notebook* (1725). At the other extreme are the *Goldberg Variations* (1742), so called after a virtuoso of the time. Over a ground bass in triple meter Bach constructs a gigantic edifice that sums up the art of variation as his age knew it.

Of the sonatas for various instruments, a special interest attaches to the six for unaccompanied violin (c. 1720). The master creates for the four strings an intricate polyphonic structure—the celebrated Chaconne is an example—and wrests from the instrument forms and textures of which one would never have suspected it capable. Whether writing for instruments or voices, Bach as often as not forced his medium to transcend its natural limitations. The instrument served his ideas; the idea was never made subservient to the instrument.

The *Brandenburg Concertos* (1721) present various instrumental combinations pitted against one another. The four Suites for Orchestra contain dance forms of appealing lyricism. We will discuss in detail the Suite No. 3 and the *Brandenburg Concerto* No. 2.

The two hundred-odd cantatas that have come down to us form the centerpiece of Bach's religious music. They constitute a personal document of transcendent spirituality; they project his vision of life and death. Despair, exultation, the burden of sin, the hope of redemption, the wonder of heaven and earth unfold before us in a vast canvas that can be compared only to those of the great mystical painters of an older time—Albrecht Dürer, Lucas Cranach, Hieronymus Bosch. The drama of the Crucifixion inspired Bach to plenary eloquence. His Passions are epics of the Protestant faith. That according to St. John (1723) depicts the final events in the life of Christ with almost violent intensity. The Passion according to St. Matthew (1729), a work of grand proportions, is more contemplative in tone. Its double choruses embody all the splendor of the Baroque. The intensity of the music laid the composer open to the inevitable charge of being operatic. "When this theatrical music began," a contemporary critic wrote, "all were thrown into the greatest bewilderment. An old widow of the nobility said, 'God save us, my children! It's just as if one were at an Opera Comedy!' " Despite the widow—and the critic—the *St. Matthew Passion* represents the artistic pinnacle of the Lutheran oratorio-passion.

The Mass in B minor occupied Bach for a good part of the Leipzig period. The first two movements, the Kyrie and Gloria—these two movements constitute a Lutheran Mass—were written in 1733, and were dedicated to Friedrich Augustus, Elector of Saxony. The greatest of Protestant composers turned to a Catholic monarch in the hope of being named composer to the Saxon court, a title that would strengthen him in his squabbles with the Leipzig authorities. The honorary title was eventually granted. To the Kyrie and Gloria originally sent to the monarch "as an insignificant example of that knowledge which I have achieved in musique" he later added the other three movements required by Catholic usage, the Credo, Sanctus, and Agnus Dei. The dimensions of this mightiest of Masses make it unfit for liturgical use. In its mingling of Catholic and Protestant elements the work symbolically unites the two factions of Christendom. It has found a home in the concert hall, a place of worship to whose creed all that come may subscribe.

In his final years the master, increasingly withdrawn from the world, fastened his gaze upon the innermost secrets of his art. *The Musical Offering* (1747), in which he elaborated the theme of Frederick the Great, runs the gamut of fugal and canonic thinking. The work culminates in a six-voice fugue that makes live again the wizardry of the medieval contrapuntists. Bach's last opus, *The Art of the Fugue* (1748–50), constitutes his final summation of the processes of musical thought. As if to emphasize the abstract nature of his inquiry he did not specify the instrument or instruments on which the music was to be played, writing it as so many independent lines in open score. He was taken ill just when he had for the first time introduced the fugal subject B-A-C-H (the German letters for B-flat, A, C, and B-natural). This encyclopedic work, "the eternal monument of polyphony," brings to a close the history of the fugue as the central musical type of an epoch.

There is a symbol in the fact that he did not live to finish it: the ultimate question had still to remain unanswered.

Organ Fugue in G Minor

The G-minor Fugue known as "the Little," to distinguish it from a longer fugue in the same key called "the Great," is one of the most popular of Bach's works in this form. This organ fugue is in four voices. The subject is announced in the soprano and is answered in the alto. Next it enters in the tenor and is answered in the bass. In accordance with fugal procedure these entries alternate between the home key (G minor) and the contrasting key (D minor). The subject *is* a sturdy melody that begins by outlining the Tonic chord and flowers into fanciful arabesques.

The Exposition completed, an episode appears in which a characteristic motive is heard in imitation between alto and soprano. This motive takes on increasing significance as the fugue proceeds.

Dating from the early Weimar period, the piece is marked by compactness of structure and directness of speech. The subject, as is customary in fugues in the minor mode, is presently shifted to the major.

After a climactic expansion of the material the theme makes its final appearance on the pedals, in the home key. The work closes with a triumphant major chord.

A brilliant if overblown transcription for orchestra has made this fugue a favorite with the public. It will be instructive, in point of style, for the reader to compare the orchestral version with the original.

Suite No. 3, in D Major

Bach wrote four orchestral suites. He called them *Ouvertures*, according to the practice of the time, because the opening movement, the overture, was the longest and weightiest. The first two suites are supposed to have been written during the Cöthen period (1717–23), the last two at Leipzig. In his orchestral suites Bach responded to the international currents of his time. The pomp of the French overture and the grace of French dance forms are here fused with the dash of the Italian instrumental style. The overture, in these suites, is followed by a variety of *galanteries*—fairly short song and dance forms. The Suite No. 3 is scored for two oboes, three trumpets, drums, first and second violins, violas, and basso continuo. The bass line is played by cellos while the implied harmonies are realized on the harpsichord.

1. *Overture.* The stately opening, in common time, with its dotted rhythms and sweeping gesture, is in the tradition of the overtures of Lully. The oboes play along with the violins. Trumpets, in the upper part of their range, and timpani introduce a note of grandeur that is quite astonishing when one considers the economy of means wherewith it is produced. Bach's sound-image serves other esthetic aims than those of the classic-romantic style. He does not attempt to blend the instrumental colors. Quite the contrary, the different timbres are individualized throughout, the contrast serving to bring out the lines of the texture.

The massive introduction is followed by a lively fugato that unfolds in the effortless, self-generating contrapuntal lines of which the old masters had the secret. The subject is compact and full of animation.

Bach occasionally presents its motives in sequence—that is, the same pattern at a higher or lower pitch. Based as it is on a "single affection," the movement displays the highest degree of organic unity. The steady beat of the rhythm, the dynamic impulsion of the counterpoint, and the unflagging tension show the baroque style at its most characteristic.

There follows a return to the stately pace of the opening. Bach places a repeat sign at the end of the first section, another at the end of the second and third sections. These are not always observed in recordings of the work.

2. *Air.* This movement has won universal popularity in an arrangement for the violin by the nineteenth-century virtuoso August Wilhelmj, under the title *Air for the G String*, a rather sentimentalized version of Bach's noble melody. That the romantic era should have felt such affinity for the baroque master—among the Bach worshipers were Chopin, Liszt, Mendelssohn, Schumann, Brahms, and César Franck—underlines the fact that the old Cantor's art has in it a strong romantic strain. Nineteenth-century composers responded to the powerful emotion that surges through his music, as in the Air of this suite. The seamless melody unfolds in a continuous flow and well justifies Debussy's remark about "the adorable arabesque of Bach." It is presented by the first violins over the steady pizzicato of the cellos. The

Air is a two-part form. The first part modulates from D major to A and is repeated. The second part, twice as long as the first, touches on a number of related keys before the final cadence in D. It too is repeated. Deeply felt and deeply moving, this Air could have been conceived only by a great melodist.

3. *Gavotte.* A sprightly dance piece in quick duple time, the Gavotte displays the terraced dynamics of the baroque style. A phrase for full ensemble—oboes, trumpets, timpani, and strings—alternates with one scored solely for oboes and strings. This movement is in A-B-A form. The A section is a two-part structure, each part being repeated. The first modulates from D major to A; the second from D to B minor and back to D. The second section opens with an inversion of the basic motive. The Trio or middle part also consists of two sections, each of which is repeated. The terraced dynamics of the orchestration continue to present contrasting areas of light and shade. The key scheme of the Trio parallels that of the Gavotte proper: from D to A in the first part, while the second makes a cadence in B minor before returning to the home key. A *da capo* sign at the end of the Trio indicates that the first section is to be repeated.

4. *Bourrée.* A light-hearted dance form in duple meter and two-part structure. The same motive serves as point of departure for both sec-

tions. The first section modulates from D to A. The second goes from D to B minor and touches briefly on G major before returning to the home key, D.

5. *Gigue*. A sprightly dance piece to which the $\frac{6}{8}$ time imparts a most attractive lilt. The formal scheme is similar to that of the other dance numbers: a two-part structure in which each part is repeated. (As has been pointed out, not all the repeat signs are likely to be observed in recording.) The first part modulates from D to A major; the second part modulates farther afield, from D to B minor, to F-sharp minor, and touches briefly upon G major before the return to D. The piece is notable for Bach's use of melodic patterns in sequence.

This Suite in D, like its companions, shows the lighter side of Bach's genius. Its courtly gestures and ornate charm evoke a vanished world.

Brandenburg Concerto *No. 2, in F Major*

In 1719 Bach had occasion to play before the Margrave Christian Ludwig of Brandenburg, son of the Great Elector. The prince was so impressed that he asked the composer to write some works for his orchestra. Two years later Bach sent him the six pieces that have become known as the *Brandenburg Concertos*, with a dedication in flowery French that beseeched His Royal Highness "not to judge their imperfection by the strictness of that fine and delicate taste which all the world knows You have for musical works; but rather to take into consideration the profound respect and the most humble obedience to which they are meant to bear witness." It is not known how the Margrave responded to the works that have immortalized his name.

Like the suites for orchestra, the six concertos belong to the Cöthen period. In these works Bach captured the spirit of the concerto grosso, in which two groups vie with each other, one egging on the other to sonorous flights of fancy. The freedom with which Bach treats the form is no more remarkable than the abundance of his invention, the boldness of his writing for the wind instruments, and the imagination with which he combines those with the strings.

The second of the set, in F major, has always been a favorite, probably because of the brilliant trumpet part. The solo group—the concertino—consists of trumpet, flute, oboe, and violin, all of them instruments in the high register. The accompanying group—the tutti—includes first and second violin, viola, and double bass. The basso continuo is played by cello and harpsichord, the harmonies being realized on the latter.

The opening movement is a sturdy Allegro, bright and assertive. The broad simple outlines of its architecture depend on well-defined areas

of light and shade—the alternation of the tutti and the solo group.
The virile tone of the opening derives from the disposition of the
parts. Flute, oboe, and violin play the theme in unison with the first

violin of the accompanying group, while the trumpet goes its own
way. The contrapuntal lines unfold in a continuous, seamless texture,
powered by a rhythmic drive that never flags from beginning to end.
The movement modulates freely from the home key of F major to the
neighboring major and minor keys. When its energies have been fully
expended it returns to F for an affirmative cadence. Here is the baroque style at its freshest and most vigorous.

The slow movement is a deeply felt Andante in D minor, a soulful
colloquy among flute, oboe, and violin. Each in turn enters with the
theme:

Harpsichord and cello articulate the affective harmonies of the accompaniment, while the solo instruments trace serenely flowing lines
marked by true inwardness of spirit. This profoundly moving Andante
is informed with the noble pathos of the Baroque, lofty of gesture,
contemplative, yet not devoid of a romantic tenderness all its own.

Third and last is an Allegro assai (very fast). Trumpet, oboe, violin,
and flute enter in turn with the jaunty subject of a four-voiced fugue.

The contrapuntal lines are tightly drawn, with much crisscrossing of
parts. The lively interchange is in the nature of a gay conversation
among four equals, abetted in frothiest fashion by the members of the
tutti. The movement reaches its destination with the final pronouncement of the subject by the trumpet.

Cantata No. 140: Wachet auf, ruft uns die Stimme
(*Awake, a Voice Is Calling*)

Wachet auf, which dates from the Leipzig period (1731), is one of the finest examples of the chorale cantata as Bach perfected it. The work was composed for the twenty-seventh Sunday after Trinity.

The Gospel for the day (Matthew 25, 1–13) tells the parable of the five wise and the five foolish virgins. "Then shall the kingdom of heaven be likened unto ten virgins, which took their lamps and went forth to meet the bridegroom. . . . And at midnight there was a cry made, Behold, the bridegroom cometh; go ye out to meet him." Bach appropriately based the cantata on the chorale *Wachet auf, ruft uns die Stimme* (Awake, a Voice Is Calling) by the mystic poet-composer Philipp Nicolai (1556–1608), who wrote both the words and music of the famous hymn. The three verses of the chorale form the supporting pillars of Bach's structure. They occur at the beginning, middle, and end of the cantata. Between these are two recitatives and two duets. It is not known who wrote the text for these. The image of Christ as Heavenly Bridegroom stirred Bach's imagination to a work of poetic mysticism which, both in the words and the music, reveals the strain of pietism that dominated the religious thought of Lutheran Germany in his time.

1. Chorale Fantasia. E-flat major, $\frac{3}{4}$ time.

Wachet auf, ruft uns die Stimme!	Awake, a voice is calling—
Der Wächter sehr hoch auf der Zinne,	The watchman high on the tower,
Wach' auf, du Stadt Jerusalem!	Awake, thou city Jerusalem!
Mitternacht heisst diese Stunde;	This is the hour of midnight;
sie rufen uns mit hellem Munde:	They call us with shining faces:
wo seid ihr klugen Jungfrauen?	Where are you, wise Virgins?
Wohl auf, der Bräutgam kommt,	Cheer up, the Bridegroom cometh.
steht auf, die Lampen nehmt! Alleluja!	Arise, take your lamps! Alleluja!
Macht euch bereit zu der Hochzeit,	Make yourselves ready for the wedding,
ihr müsset ihm entsprungen gehn.	You must go forth to greet him.

A majestic dotted rhythm, established at the outset, derives from the French overture and evokes the image of a stately procession. This is counterposed to the syncopated figure introduced in the fifth measure by the violins and imitated in the oboes:

Some commentators have professed to see in these two motives the approach of the Bridegroom's procession and the impatience of the Virgins. Be that as it may, the instrumental introduction establishes the proper mood of expectancy. The music is scored for two oboes and a tenor oboe; first and second violins and *violino piccolo* (a small violin tuned a minor third higher than the ordinary violin); and the thoroughbass, whose figured harmonies are realized on the organ.

The chorus is in the usual four parts, with a cornett playing along with the sopranos. This was a gentle-voiced instrument much admired during the Baroque, made of wood or ivory, which combined the fingerholes of the woodwinds with the cup-shaped mouthpiece of the brass. The chorale is sung by the sopranos in notes of equal value, with a few intermediate notes omitted. Heard in this skeletal version, the melody takes on a kind of hieratic aloofness, standing apart from the

other voices, which sing the same text in livelier rhythms. This distinction between the soprano and the three other voices is maintained throughout the movement.

A similar distinction is drawn between the material entrusted to the instruments and that presented by the voices. Besides maintaining the basic dotted rhythm, the instruments present a more florid counterpoint. The two streams of sound, vocal and instrumental, advance side by side, the instrumental coming to the fore during the interludes that set off the lines of the chorale. There are fine examples of the tone painting dear to the Baroque. The word *hoch* (high) in line 2, for example, occurs on the highest note of the phrase. So too the lower voices generate excitement by leaping upward on such words as *wach' auf* (wake up); *wo, wo, wo seid ihr* (where, where are you?); *wohl auf* (cheer up) and *steht auf* (arise). The word *Alleluja!* is treated melismatically, with the voices executing exuberant roulades on a single syllable. The altos enter first, the tenors in imitation, then the basses, in a fugal passage that serves as interlude between two lines of the chorale. Here, for the first time, the voices take over a running figure derived from the instrumental countersubject shown above. Now the sopranos enter with the Alleluja, still maintaining their steady, unvarying rhythm.

The music for the first three lines of the poem is repeated for the next three. From then on the movement proceeds by the process of continuous expansion that is so characteristic of the Baroque. The key scheme underlines the architecture: the music modulates from the home key of E-flat to G minor, B-flat major, back to E-flat, C minor, finally to A-flat, which serves as springboard for the inevitable return to E-flat. The instrumental introduction is repeated *da capo* at the end, enclosing the spacious design within a frame. This fantasia is unrivaled for richness of detail within a highly coordinated scheme.

2. Recitative for Tenor.

Er kommt, er kommt, der Bräutgam kommt!	He comes, he comes, the Bridegroom comes!
ihr Töchter Zions, kommt heraus,	O daughters of Zion, come out,
sein Ausgang eilet aus der Höhe	Hasten his departure from on high
in euer' Mutter Haus. Der Bräutgam kommt,	To your dwelling place. The Bridegroom comes,
der einem Rehe und jungem Hirsche	Like a roe, a young deer
gleich auf denen Hügeln springt,	Who leaps lightly among the hills,
und euch das Mahl der Hochzeit bringt.	Who brings you the wedding feast.
Wacht auf, ermuntert euch!	Wake up, be of good cheer
den Bräutgam zu empfangen;	And receive the Bridegroom.
dort! sehet, kommt er hergegangen.	There, see how he comes hitherward.

This is a *secco* ("dry") recitative, supported by the double bass and the figured harmonies on the organ. The vocal line follows the inflections of the language, with wide leaps on such words of action as *er kommt*. Again the highest note in the vocal line is associated with the idea of height—*Höhe*. The recitative leads to a cadence in C minor, the relative of E-flat, thus setting the scene for the next number.

3. Aria (Duet, Soprano and Bass). C minor. $\frac{6}{8}$ time.

Sop. Wann kommst du, mein Heil?	When will you come, my salvation?
Bass. Ich komme, dein Teil.	I am coming, your appointed one.
Sop. Ich warte mit brennendem Öle.	I wait, with the lamp lit.
Eröffne den Saal zum himmlischen Mahl,	Open the hall to the heavenly banquet.
komm, Jesu!	Come, Jesus!
Bass. Ich öffne den Saal zum himmlischen Mahl.	I open the hall to the heavenly banquet.
Ich komme; komm', liebliche Seele!	I come. O come, lovely Soul!

The instrumental prelude is a solo for *violino piccolo,* which presents not only the principal melodic idea but also the fanciful arabesques that it will subsequently execute as contrapuntal figuration behind the voices. The tender tone of the small violin establishes the "basic affection" of this duet. The interchange between soprano and bass—first a phrase for each, then the two voices overlapping—creates the effect

of a sweet, intimate dialogue. The florid line of the solo instrument is
in the nature of a rhapsodic improvisation. Present throughout, the
violino piccolo becomes a unifying element, enveloping both voices
in its pervasive timbre. The music modulates to closely related keys:
from C minor to the Dominant, G minor, and to the relative major,
E-flat; then to A-flat, and back to C minor. The instrumental prelude
is repeated at the end.

4. Chorale. E-flat major, $\frac{4}{4}$.

Zion hört die Wächter singen,	Zion hears the watchmen singing,
das Herz tut ihr vor Freuden springen,	Her heart leaps for joy,
sie wacht und steht eilend auf.	She awakes and quickly rises.
Ihr Freund kommt von Himmel prächtig,	Her friend comes from heaven, resplendent,
von Gnaden stark, von Wahrheit mächtig,	Strong in grace, powerful in truth;
ihr Licht wird hell, ihr Stern geht auf.	Her light shines bright, her star rises.
Nun komm, du werte Kron,	Now come, thou precious crown,
Herr Jesu Gottes Sohn, Hosianna!	Lord Jesus, Son of God, Hosanna!
Wir folgen all' zum Freudensaal	We follow to the hall of joy
und halten mit das Abendmahl.	To partake of the banquet.

The second verse of the chorale is sung by the tenors in a more
melodious version than was heard before. The chorale strides along in
more rhythmic fashion; it is based on shorter note values; and the intermediate notes are included, giving the full outline of the tune. The
chorale is presented in combination with a most arresting counter-

Zi - on   hört   die Wäch - ter   sin -   gen,

melody, which is played by violins and violas and is introduced alone
in the brief instrumental prelude before being combined with the
chorale.

This movement, essentially, is a trio for tenor voices, strings, and
basso continuo. It is the best-known movement of the cantata, because
Bach also wrote it as a chorale prelude for organ, in which form it has
been widely played.

5. Recitative for Bass.

So geh herein zu mir, du mir er-wählte Braut!	So come to me, my chosen bride!
Ich habe mich mit dir in Ewigkeit vertraut.	I have plighted my troth to you in eternity.
Dich will ich auf mein Herz, auf meinen Arm	On my heart, on my arm,
gleich wie ein Siegel setzen,	I will set you as a seal,
und dein betrübtes Aug' ergötzen.	And will delight your sorrowful eyes.
Vergiss, o Seele, nun die Angst,	Forget, dear Soul, your anguish,
den Schmerz den du erdulden müssen;	The pain that you must bear;
auf meiner Linken sollst du ruh'n,	May you rest at my left,
und meine Rechte soll dich küssen.	And be kissed on my right.

This recitative for bass is supported by first and second violins, *violino piccolo*, and the continuo. The music modulates from E-flat to a cadence in B-flat.

6. Aria (Duet for Soprano and Bass). B-flat major, $\frac{4}{4}$.

Sop. Mein Freund ist mein!	My friend is mine!
Bass. Und ich bin dein!	And I am thine!
Both. Die Lieb soll nichts scheiden.	Let nothing part true lovers.
Sop. Ich will mit dir, du sollst mit mir,	I with you, you with me,
Both. In Himmels Rosen weiden, da Freude die Fülle, da Wonne wird sein.	We'll delight in the roses of heaven, In the fullness of joy, of rapture.

This aria-duet is colored by the tone of the oboe solo, whose florid counterpoint accompanies the feelingful interchange between soprano and bass. The mood is one of quiet joy and fulfillment. The two voices not only alternate in brief phrases but also join in extended passages, now imitating, now contrasting with each other. Bach cast this number in the form of the traditional *da capo* aria of the opera house; the first part of the duet is repeated. Notice how a few lines of text are expanded into a sizable number by the simple expedient of repeating the words.

7. Chorale. E-flat major, $\frac{4}{4}$.

Gloria sei dir gesungen	May Gloria be sung to Thee
mit Menschen- und englischen Zungen,	With the tongues of men and angels,
mit Harfen und mit Cymbeln schon.	With lovely harps and cymbals.
Von zwölf Perlen sind die Pforten	Of twelve pearls are wrought the gates
an deiner Stadt; wir sind Konsorten	Of Thy city; we are companions
der Engel hoch um deinen Thron.	Of the angel high above Thy throne.
Kein Aug' hat je gespürt,	No eye has ever beheld,
kein Ohr hat je gehört solche Freude	No ear has ever heard such joy

| Des sind wir froh, io, io! | As we feel, ee-o, ee-o, |
| ewig in dulci jubilo. | Forever *in dulci jubilo* (in sweet jubilation), |

The chorale is now sung in the four-part harmonization of Bach. Each voice is supported by instruments. Thus, at the climax of the cantata, the four-square melody stands revealed in all its simplicity and grandeur, granitelike, indestructible, a song for the ages.

Excerpts from the Mass in B Minor

The quality of sublimity that is the salient characteristic of the B-minor Mass informs the conception as a whole. Excerpts may serve as an introduction to the work. Only a hearing of it in its entirety will reveal the vast terrain that has here been subjugated to the creative will.

The first chorus of the Gloria (No. 4) is set to the text *Gloria in excelsis Deo, et in terra pax hominibus bonae voluntatis* (Glory to God in the highest and peace on earth to men of good will). The movement, in a bright D major, calls for three high trumpet parts that wreathe the chorus in luminous sound. To the Baroque, the trumpet symbolized power and glory. Also used in this section of the Mass are two flutes, two oboes, bassoons, timpani, strings, and organ.

The movement opens with a striking motive that derives its vigor from the brisk triple meter and wide leaps. The chorus is in five parts: first and second sopranos, altos, tenors, and basses. Luxuriant counterpoint unfolds in flowing lines molded to the Latin. Words like *gloria* and *excelsis* (highest) are repeated and expanded until they dissolve in music. As is generally the case in the music of the Baroque, there

Glo - - - ri - a in ex - cel -

is much repetition of text. The words establish the basic affection of the movement, and are then repeated over and over again while the music achieves its proper development. The steady beat of the triple meter provides the framework for a rich diversity of subordinate rhythms. The voices enter in rapid succession and build steadily to the abrupt change of mood and pace at the second idea, "and peace on earth to men of good will." A new motive establishes a mood of supplication. Then the movement gathers momentum and broadens into a majestic stream.

The arias and duets distributed through the Mass supply areas of relaxation between the overpowering choruses. The arias embody a cardinal principle of baroque style, the voice being pitted against the same instrument throughout an entire number. This sameness of color ensures the predominance of a single mood or affection. The vocal arabesques are not especially differentiated from the instrumental. The writing is not necessarily unvocal (although in the hands of any but a first-class singer it may sound so). Rather, as so often in Bach, is the medium made to serve the idea: in short, to surpass itself.

A characteristic aria is that for alto on the text *Qui sedes ad dextram Patris, miserere nobis* (Thou who sittest at the right hand of the Father, have mercy on us). This is the ninth number of the Mass and

Qui ___ se - - - - - des ad ___ dex- tram Pat-ris,

is a part of the Gloria. The solo voice is contrasted with the oboe d'amore, a low oboe whose sweet tone was much prized during the Baroque. The key word *miserere* (have mercy) establishes the basic affection of the music, a mood of entreaty that is admirably underlined by the dark resonance of the alto voice and the plaintive timbre of the oboe. The aria is in B minor, in a gentle $\frac{6}{8}$ that sounds all the better for not being dragged. The vocal line is florid yet impregnated with feeling. The opening phrase returns at the close to round off the form in an abbreviated A-B-A.

Crucifixus etiam pro nobis sub Pontio Pilato, passus et sepultus est (And He was crucified also for us under Pontius Pilate, He suffered and was buried. No. 16). For the most dramatic chorus of the Mass Bach ventured into the territory that lies between church and opera house. This stupendous outpouring of grief, which is part of the Credo, traces its lineage to the operatic laments of the seventeenth century such as that of Dido. The movement unfolds above a chromatic ground bass that strikingly resembles that used by Purcell in the culminating aria of *Dido and Aeneas.*

Bach Grave

Purcell (transposed)

Two symbols of grief—chromatic harmony and descending movement—dominate this choral fresco. The ground bass is stated thirteen times. Minor mode and the use of dissonance reinforce the atmosphere of sorrow, as does the depersonalized sound of two flutes that stand out against the tone mass. When the nethermost point has been reached there is an abrupt modulation to G major. Despair gives way to the jubilant chorus of the Resurrection, in D major: *Et resurrexit tertia die secundum scripturas; ascendit in coelum, sedet ad dextram Dei Patris. Et iterum venturus est cum gloria judicare vivos et mortuos cuius regni non erit finis* (No. 17). (And the third day He rose again in accordance with the Scriptures, and He ascended into heaven and is seated at the right hand of the Father. And He shall come again in glory to judge the living and the dead, and of His kingdom there shall be no end.) Three trumpets and kettledrums help announce the joyful tidings. The basic affection is established by brisk triple meter, vigorous triplets, and the bold upthrust of the theme.

The high trumpet parts require virtuoso playing. The voices pile one upon the other in intricate imitation as the central word *resurrexit* expands into florid arabesque. Orchestral interludes set off the spacious architecture. This is music to resound over hills and valleys: the pronouncement of one who saw God enthroned in heaven and translated the vision into an enduring memorial to the divinity in man.

The notion may be dismissed that Bach was unappreciated in his lifetime. He could not have continued to write cantatas for thirty-five years if he had not reached his public. He was known and admired by his generation even if his greatness was not realized in full. It was the following generations that neglected him. The Lutheran world out of which he stemmed ceased to be a living force even while he was immortalizing its spirit. Great changes were impending, in life and art alike. In this new climate his polyphony seemed pedantic, his baroque monumentality heavy and oppressive. Rejected by fashionable taste, his music disappeared from the scene. Manuscripts of his were suffered to be lost. The plates of *The Art of the Fugue* were sold for the price of the metal when the work failed to attract purchasers. For fifty years after his death no single work of his was deemed worthy of separate publication. To the musical public of the 1760s the name Bach meant his four sons, whose success as composers far exceeded his. Even they considered his music old-fashioned. One of them, with engaging lack of filial piety, referred to him as "the old Wig."

Yet the memory of him did not wholly die. It was kept alive in the decades after his death by his sons, his pupils, and by those who had heard him play. Then the revival began, tentatively at first but with increasing force until it had become a veritable renascence. Scholars, composers, and performers alike contributed to this extraordinary re-instatement. The romantic age felt akin to his fervor, his chromatic harmonies, his vaulting architecture, the surge and splendor of his polyphony. The *St. Matthew Passion,* forgotten for more than three-quarters of a century, was resurrected by the twenty-year-old Mendelssohn in an epochal performance in 1829. Chopin practiced Bach before his concerts. Liszt transcribed the organ works for the piano. Schumann was one of the founders of the Bach Society, an organization that undertook the monumental task of publishing a complete edition of the master's works. The Cantor of Leipzig at last came into his own.

His spirit animated not only the nineteenth century but, in even more fruitful manner, the twentieth. We see him today not only as a consummate artist who brought new meanings to music, but as one of the gigantic figures of Western culture.

₼ₜₐₙₖₐ *CHAPTER 68* ₼ₜ₱ₗ

George Frideric Handel (1685-1759)

"Milord, I should be sorry if I only entertained them. I wished to make them better."

IF BACH represents the subjective mysticism of the late Baroque, Handel incarnates its worldly pomp. Born in the same year, the two giants of the age never met. The Cantor of Leipzig had little point of contact with the redoubtable Saxon who from the first was cut out for an international career. Handel's natural habitat was the opera house. He was at home amid the intrigues of court life. A magnificent adventurer, he gambled for fame and fortune in a feverish struggle to impose his will upon the world; and dominated the musical life of a nation for a century after his death.

His Life

He was born at Halle in Saxony, son of a prosperous barber-surgeon who did not regard music as a suitable profession for a young man of the middle class. His father's death left him free to follow his bent. After a year at the University of Halle the ambitious youth went to Hamburg, where he gravitated to the opera house and entered the

George Frideric Handel.

orchestra as second violinist. He soon absorbed the Italian operatic style that reigned in Hamburg. His first opera, written when he was twenty, created a furor. Its full title echoes the grandiloquence of the Baroque: *The Changes of Fortune undergone by the Crown;* OR *Almira, Queen of Castille.*

Handel's thoughts turned to Italy. Only there, he felt, would he master the operatic art. He reached Rome shortly before his twenty-second birthday; the three years he spent in Italy unfolded against a splendid background peopled by music-loving princes and cardinals. His opera *Rodrigo* was produced in Florence under the patronage of Prince Ferdinand de' Medici. The libretto of his opera *Agrippina* was written by the Viceroy of Naples, Cardinal Grimani. Presented at Venice in 1709, the work sent the Italians into transports of delight. The theater resounded with cries of "Long live the dear Saxon!"

At the age of twenty-five, Handel was appointed conductor to the Elector of Hanover. He received the equivalent of fifteen hundred dollars a year at a time when Bach at Weimar was paid eighty. A visit to London in the autumn of 1710 brought him for the first time to the city that was to be his home for well-nigh fifty turbulent years. *Rinaldo,* written in a fortnight, conquered the English public with its fresh tender melodies. A year later Handel obtained another leave and returned to London, this time for good. With the *Birthday Ode for Queen Anne* and the *Te Deum* (hymn of thanksgiving) for the Peace of Utrecht he entered upon the writing of large-scale works for great public occasions, following in the footsteps of Purcell. Anne rewarded him with a pension; whereupon nothing would make him go back to his Hanoverian master. By an unforeseen turn of events his master came to him. Anne died and the Elector ascended the throne of England as

George I. The monarch was vexed with his truant composer; but he loved music more than protocol, and soon restored him to favor.

Handel's opportunity came with the founding in 1720 of the Royal Academy of Music. The enterprise, launched for the purpose of presenting Italian opera, was backed by a group of wealthy peers headed by the King. Handel was appointed one of the musical directors and at thirty-five found himself occupying a key position in the artistic life of England. For the next eight years he was active in producing and directing his operas as well as writing them. His crowded life passed at a far remove from the solitude we have come to associate with the creative process. He produced his works in bursts of inspiration that kept him chained to his desk for days at a time. He would turn out an opera in from two to three weeks.

Hardly less feverish was the struggle for power inseparable from a position such as his. Overbearing, obstinate when crossed, the Saxon was no mean master of the art of making enemies. His fiery temper found much to exercise it. He was at the mercy of the cliques at court, and he was subject to pressure from the peers who had invested in the enterprise. He was viewed with suspicion by the leaders of English thought who saw in his operas a threat to native music and theater. Addison and Steele, in the pages of the *Spectator* and *Tatler,* missed no opportunity to attack his ventures. It must be said that other men of letters more justly estimated his stature. Pope in the *Dunciad* (1742) thus describes his monumental style:

> Strong in new Arms, lo! Giant HANDEL stands,
> Like bold Briareus, with a hundred hands;
> To stir, to rouze, to shake the Soul he comes,
> And Jove's own Thunders follow Mars's Drums.

Handel functioned in a theater riddled with the worst features of the star system. When the celebrated soprano Cuzzoni refused to sing an aria as he directed, Handel, a giant of a man, seized her around the waist and threatened to drop her out of a window if she would not obey. The rivalry between Cuzzoni and the great singer Faustina Bordoni culminated in a hair-pulling match on the stage, accompanied by the smashing of scenery and fist fights throughout the house. A rivalry no less fierce developed between Handel and his associate in directing the Academy, the composer Marc' Antonio Bononcini. The supposition that genius resided in one or the other, which brought to the arena of art the psychology of the prize-ring, appealed strongly to the fashionable hangers-on of the Royal Academy. Bononcini was the protégé of the Tory Duchess of Marlborough; whereupon Handel, whose interest in British politics was—to say the least—limited, became *the* Whig composer. The feud was immortalized in a jingle that made the rounds of the coffee houses.

> Some say that Signor Bononcini
> Compared to Handel is a ninny;
> Whilst others say that to him Handel
> Is hardly fit' to hold a candle.
> Strange that such difference should be
> 'Twixt Tweedledum and Tweedledee.

It was amid such distractions that Handel's operas—he produced forty in a period of thirty years—came into being. Some were written too hastily, in others he obviously accommodated himself to the needs of the box office; yet all bear the imprint of a genius unfolding his powers within the frame of a dying art form. Despite his productivity the Royal Academy tottered to its ruin, its treasury depleted by the extravagance of the peers, its morale sapped by mismanagement and dissension. The final blow was administered in 1728 by the sensational success of *The Beggar's Opera*. Sung in English, its tunes and humor related to the experience of the audience, this ballad opera was the answer of middle-class England to the gods and heroes of the aristocratic *opera seria*. Ironically, even a bit of Handel's *Rinaldo* found its way into the score.

It should have been apparent to the composer-impresario that a new era had dawned; but, refusing to read the omens, he invested thousands in the New Royal Academy of Music. Again a succession of operas rolled from his pen, among them *Orlando Furioso* (1733), "the boldest of his works." But not even Handel's colossal powers could indefinitely sustain the pace. He was fifty-two when he crashed. "This infernal flesh," as he called it, succumbed to a paralytic stroke. His mind buckled. He owed thousands of pounds, and for a space he stood in the shadow of debtors' prison. Desperate and grievously ill, he acknowledged defeat and went abroad to recover his health. His enemies gloated: the giant was finished.

They underestimated his powers of recovery. He came back to resume the battle. It needed five more expensive failures—among them *Serse* (Xerxes, 1738), whence the famous Largo—to make him realize that *opera seria* in London was finished. At this lowest point in his fortunes there opened, by chance, the road that was to lead him from opera in Italian to oratorio in English, from ruin to immortality. Many years before, in 1720, he had written a masque entitled *Haman and Mordecai*, on a text by Pope adapted from Racine's *Esther*. In 1732 some admirers of his organized a private performance of the piece, now renamed *Esther*, to celebrate Handel's forty-seventh birthday.

The combination of Pope's text and Handel's music pleased so greatly that he decided to bring this "sacred opera" before the public. When the Bishop of London forbade the representation of biblical characters in a theater, Handel hit upon a way out. "There will be no acting upon the Stage," he announced in the advertisement, "but the house will be fitted up in a decent manner, for the audience." In this way London heard its first Handelian oratorio.

He could not remain indifferent to the advantages of a type of entertainment that dispensed with costly foreign singers and lavish scenery. *Deborah* and *Athalia* were composed in 1733. The next six years witnessed his final struggle on behalf of *opera seria*. Then, in 1739, there followed two of his greatest oratorios, *Saul* and *Israel in Egypt,* both composed within the space of a little over three months. Many dark moments still lay ahead. He had to extricate himself from the debts of the past, and to find his way to his new middle-class public. That indomitable will never faltered. *Messiah, Samson, Semele, Joseph and His Brethren, Hercules, Belshazzar* (1742-45), although they did not conquer at once, were received sufficiently well to encourage him to continue on his course. Finally, with *Judas Maccabaeus* (1746), the tide turned. The British public responded to the imagery of the Old Testament. The suppression of the last Stuart rebellion created the proper atmosphere for Handel's heroic tone. He kept largely to biblical subjects in the final group of oratorios (1748-52)—*Alexander Balus, Joshua, Susanna, Solomon, Jephtha*—an astonishing list for a man in his sixties. With these the master brought his work to a close.

There remained to face the final enemy—blindness. But even this blow did not reduce him to inactivity. Like Milton and Bach, he dictated his last works, which were mainly revisions of earlier ones. He continued to appear in public, conducting the oratorios and displaying his legendary powers on the organ. A contemporary account tells how, when *Samson* was performed, at Milton's famous lines on the blinded hero, "Total eclipse—no sun, no moon; All dark amid the blaze of noon," "the view of the blind Composer then sitting by the Organ affected the audience so forcibly that many persons present were moved to tears."

Shortly after his seventy-fourth birthday he began his usual oratorio season, conducting ten major works in little over a month to packed houses. The *Messiah* closed the series. He collapsed in the theater at the end of the performance and died some days later. The nation he had served for half a century accorded him its highest honor. "Last night about Eight O'clock the remains of the late great Mr Handel were deposited at the foot of the Duke of Argyll's Monument in Westminster Abbey . . . There was almost the greatest Concourse of People of all Ranks ever seen upon such, or indeed upon any other Occasion."

His Music

Himself sprung from the middle class, Handel made his career in the land where the middle class first came to power. A vast social change is symbolized in his turning from court opera to oratorio. In so doing he became one of the architects of the new bourgeois culture and a creator of the modern mass public. Like Bach, he stood in the mainstream of European music, assimilating to his art German, Italian, French, and English elements. Bach and he complement each other as the representative figures of the late Baroque. Bach's art is introspective; Handel is the man of action. Bach rhapsodizes in the organ loft; Handel is the courtier. Bach is the meticulous artist who brings to perfection every form he touches; Handel, tossing off his scores for the theater, is a magnificent improviser. Bach is a master of detail; Handel works with sweeping brush strokes. Bach's mystic gaze is turned upon the world to come; Handel hymns the pomp and power of this world. Both men were inspired by an ethical ideal; but Bach was a Lutheran, while Handel was a man of the Enlightenment whose moral sense was bound to no creed or dogma.

The oratorios of Handel are choral dramas of overpowering vitality and grandeur. Vast murals, they are conceived in epic style. Their soaring arias and dramatic recitatives, stupendous fugues and double choruses consummate the splendor of the Baroque. With the instinct of the born leader he gauged the need of his adopted country (whose language, in forty-seven years of residence, he never wholly mastered). He created in the oratorio an art form replete with the blood and thunder of the Old Testament, ideally suited to the taste of England's middle class. In the command of Jehovah to the Chosen People to go forth and conquer the land of Canaan they recognized a clear mandate to go forth and secure the British Empire.

Handel made the chorus—the people—the center of the drama. Freed from the rapid pace imposed by stage action, he expanded to vast dimensions each scene and emotion. The chorus now touches off the action, now reflects upon it. As in Greek tragedy it serves both as protagonist and ideal spectator. The characters are drawn larger than life-size. Saul, Joshua, Deborah, Judas Maccabaeus, Samson are archetypes of human nature; creatures of destiny, majestic in defeat as in victory, through whom is proclaimed the redemption of the strong and the rejection of the weak. The oratorios are folk dramas of monumental cast in which are fused dramatic, lyric, contemplative, and descriptive elements. Through them surges the rhetoric of a heroic age and a heroic temperament.

The Handelian oratorio emerged as England's national art form soon
after the master's death. The hundredth anniversary of his birth was
marked by a celebration in Westminster Abbey in which over five hundred singers and players participated. This number was enlarged in
subsequent Handel festivals until a chorus of three and a half thousand
drowned out an orchestra of five hundred, occasioning Horace Walpole's lovely remark: "The Oratorios thrive abundantly; for my part
they give me an idea of Heaven, where everybody is to sing whether
they have voices or not." Handel, be it remembered, produced his
oratorios with a chorus of about thirty singers and a like number of
instrumentalists. To increase the size of this group more than fiftyfold
meant sacrificing many subtleties of his writing. Yet his art, with its
grand outlines and sweeping effects, was able to take such treatment.
It was indeed "the music for a great active people," inviting mass par-
ticipation even as it demanded mass listening.

Handel's rhythm has the powerful drive of the Baroque. One must
hear one of his choruses to realize what a simple $\frac{4}{4}$ time can achieve in
the way of momentum. He leaned to diatonic harmony even as Bach's
more searching idiom favored the chromatic. His melody, rich in mood
and feeling, unfolds in great majestic arches. His is a basically vocal
conception, whereas Bach's is instrumental. In respect to form he was
conservative, his kind of communication demanding a clear, elegant
simplicity rather than experiment. His fluent, singing counterpoint
comes from Italian rather than German sources. Nor does it seek the
transcendental regions of Bach's. His thinking is based on massive
pillars of sound—the chords—within which the voices interweave. His
fugues are impulsive and free. They do not hesitate to abandon contrapuntal logic for the massed harmonies that fired his imagination.

Rooted in the world of the theater, Handel made use of tone color
for atmosphere and dramatic expression. In *Saul*, for example, trombones suggest the majesty of the King; two bassoons accompany the
utterances of the prophet Samuel's ghost. Trumpets and horns impart
a baroque opulence to his music. His wonderful sense of sound comes
out in the pieces intended for outdoor performance, the *Water Music*
and *Royal Fireworks Music*. In the latter work he realized the dream of
many a later composer, scoring for forty trumpets, twenty horns, sixteen oboes, sixteen bassoons, and eight kettledrums; also a cannon!

The big choral pieces to celebrate occasions of national rejoicing
exemplify what has been called Handel's "big bow-wow" manner. Most
famous are the Coronation Anthems for the accession of George II, one
of which—*Zadok the Priest*—has helped crown every subsequent ruler
of England. The operas contain some of the composer's finest measures.
They have not maintained themselves on the stage chiefly because they

demand a kind of vocal virtuosity that no longer exists. Also, as we indicated in our discussion of baroque opera, they were conceived for a theater whose conventions are alien to our own.

Besides his dramatic works Handel produced an impressive amount of instrumental music. Best known in this category are the twelve concerti grossi Opus 6, which with Bach's *Brandenburg Concertos* represent the peak of baroque orchestral music. The concertos for organ and orchestra are brilliant showpieces that he performed between the acts of the oratorios. He wrote down only a skeletal version of what he improvised in public. His keyboard pieces are undeservedly neglected. One, a theme and variations known as *The Harmonious Blacksmith*, has achieved universal popularity. There never was a blacksmith who sang the tune as he smote the anvil, nor a thunderstorm during which Handel found shelter in the smithy and heard him sing it—another good Handel story that never happened.

Handel's music contained the elements of popular art. Several of his tunes became song hits of the time. The March from *Rinaldo* turned up in *The Beggar's Opera* as "Let's take the road." In *Polly*, the sequel to that work, a minuet from the *Water Music* became "Cheer up, my lads." The official march of England's Grenadier Guards comes from a processional in the opera *Scipione*. In a letter of the time we find: "The great Handel has told me that the hints of his very best songs have several of them been owing to the sounds in his ears of cries in the streets." Given his temperament, it was inevitable that the rhythms of life, the accents of song and dance, the inflections of living speech would nourish his warmly human art.

Messiah

"For the Relief of the Prisoners in the several Gaols, and for the Support of Mercer's Hospital in Stephen's-street and of the Charitable Infirmary on the Inn's Quay, on Monday the 12th of April, will be performed at the Musick Hall in Fishamble-Street, *Mr Handel's new Grand Oratorio, called the Messiah*, in which the Gentlemen of the Choirs of both Cathedrals will assist, with some Concertos on the Organ, by Mr Handel." In this fashion Dublin was apprised in the spring of 1742 of the launching of one of the world's most widely loved works.

The music was written down in twenty-four days, Handel working as one possessed. His servant found him, after the completion of the Hallelujah Chorus, with tears streaming from his eyes. "I did think I did see all Heaven before me, and the great God Himself!" Upon finishing *Messiah* the master went on without a pause to *Samson*, the first part of which was ready two weeks later. Truly it was an age of giants.

With its massive choruses, tuneful recitatives, and broadly flowing arias *Messiah* has come to represent the Handelian oratorio in the public mind. Actually it is not typical of the oratorios as a whole. Those are imbued with dramatic conflict, while *Messiah* is cast in a mood of lyric contemplation. Although it has been ranked with the religious masterpieces, *Messiah* in no way partakes of the mysticism of a Palestrina Mass or of the *St. Matthew Passion*. It expresses rather the humane faith of a man of the world—the eighteenth-century world—who happened to be a great musician.

The libretto is a compilation of verses from the Bible that appeared under the name of Charles Jennens, a wealthy dabbler in the arts. (There is reason to believe that Jennens's chaplain more than took a hand in the task.) The first part treats of the prophecy of the coming of Christ and His birth; the second of His suffering, death, and the spread of His doctrine; and the third of the redemption of the world through faith. The verses are drawn from various prophets of the Old Testament, especially Isaiah; from the Psalms, the Evangelists, and Paul. Upon this assorted material the music imposes a magnificent unity. The great choruses become the pillars of an architectonic structure in which the recitatives and arias serve as areas of lesser tension.

Handel's original orchestration was extraordinarily modest and clear in texture. He wrote mainly for strings, with oboes and bassoons regularly employed to strengthen the choral parts. Trumpets and drums are reserved for special numbers. The work was conceived, in terms of baroque practice, for a small group of players supplemented at the climactic moments by a larger group. The harmonies of the thoroughbass were realized on harpsichord or organ. Handel specified the latter instrument for only a few numbers—as distinct from the present-day habit of playing the organ throughout, which spreads a dulling uniformity over his instrumental colors. The orchestration we hear in performances today was augmented to keep pace with the ever-growing size of the chorus. Various musicians produced these additional accompaniments, Mozart among them.

The Overture, in the French style, opens with a *grave* (slow, solemn) in dotted rhythms, in a somber E minor, and passes over into a sturdy three-voiced fugue. The recitative *Comfort ye, my people* is a tenor arioso in E major, larghetto e piano, over one of those broadly flowing accompaniments of which Handel knew the secret. Characteristic is the majestic span of the melody. There follows the aria *Every valley shall be exalted*, with baroque expansion of the word "exalted." In this and later arias the architecture is broadened by orchestral intro-

ductions, interludes, and postludes. The music unfolds continuously
from the opening figure, embodying that single affection which imparts
to each number its sovereign unity of thought and expression.

The first chorus, *And the glory of the Lord shall be revealed,* is an
Allegro in A major. The vision of divine glory fires Handel's imagination to a spacious choral fresco in which an exciting contrapuntal
texture alternates with towering chords. The vigorous triple meter assumes the character of a festal dance. From the opening motive and

And the glo - ry, the glo -ry of the Lord,

those that follow is fashioned a fabric of continuous imitation and expansion, with much repetition of text. The forward stride of the bass
never slackens. Highly dramatic is the grand pause before the end.
In the final chords, as often happens with Handel, the choral writing
is influenced by organ sound.

The bright A-major sound gives way to a somber D minor in the
accompanied recitative for bass, *Thus saith the Lord of Hosts: Yet
once a little while, and I will shake the heav'ns and the earth.* The
florid expansion on the word "shake" is worthy of note. Handel's operatic background is revealed by the expressive accompaniment with its
urgent dotted rhythm and repeated chords. This leads into a bass aria,
But who may abide the day of His coming? with a dramatic change
from larghetto to prestissimo at the words *For He is like a refiner's fire.*
The fugal chorus in G minor, *And He shall purify the sons of Levi,* is
one of four choral numbers in *Messiah* whose themes Handel drew from
an earlier work. There follows a gracious group in D major. The recitative for alto, *Behold! a virgin shall conceive,* leads into the aria *O thou
that tellest good tidings to Zion.* The expressive melody in flowing $\frac{6}{8}$
meter is one of Handel's happiest inspirations. It is taken over, in
subtly altered guise, by the chorus: the emotion projected at first
through the individual is now experienced by mankind as a whole.

An affecting change from major to minor comes with the arioso for
bass, *For behold, darkness shall cover the earth.* The idea of darkness
is projected through a sinuously chromatic figure in the following aria,
The people that walked in darkness have seen a great light. We encounter at this point a memorable example of Handel's sensitivity to
key. The movement from darkness to light is marked repeatedly by a
modulation from minor to major.

There follows one of the highlights of the score, the chorus *For unto
us a Child is born.* The theme, taken from one of the master's Italian
duets, is of Handelian sturdiness.

For un - to us   a Child is   born,

The piece displays the unflagging rhythmic energy of the Baroque. Harmonic and contrapuntal elements are fused into a stalwart unity. There is joyously florid expansion on the word "born." Unforgettable is the pomp and glory at "Wonderful, Counselor . . . ." The words peal forth in earth-shaking jubilation; yet with what economy of means the effect is achieved.

The Pastoral Symphony is the only orchestral number in *Messiah* outside the Overture. It is cast in the gently flowing, dotted $\frac{12}{8}$ rhythm that recurs throughout the work as a unifying thread. Generally associated with bucolic moods, this is derived from an Italian folk dance (the siciliano that we noted in the slow movement of Vivaldi's Concerto Grosso) and sets the scene for the following recitatives, of which the first is *There were shepherds abiding in the field, keeping watch over their flocks by night.* Wonder and tenderness pervade this music. There follows the chorus *Glory to God* in the key of D major, where for the first time in the work Handel calls for trumpets. This number is often begun in a bright fortissimo, as befits good tidings; yet Handel intended rather a mood of reverence and awe, for he marked the trumpets Da lontano e un poco piano (as from afar and somewhat softly). The soprano aria *Rejoice greatly, O daughter of Zion!* is a brilliant allegro. The basic affection, an exalted joy, is established at the outset by the leaping figure in the vocal line.

A brief recitative for alto is followed by one of the most beautiful arias of the oratorio, *He shall feed His flock like a shepherd*, in the pastoral siciliano rhythm. An infinite quietude of spirit informs this promise of rest to the heavy-laden. The chorus *His yoke is easy* is a finely wrought fugal piece marked by lively interplay of the voices. Handel derived the subject from one of his Italian duets. A dramatic pause in the coda interrupts the expansive mood, after which the voices unite in the grandiose chords that bring the first part of *Messiah* to an end.

The tone of the second part is established by the sorrowful chorus *Behold the Lamb of God*, with its slow dotted rhythm and drooping inflection. The tragic mood continues with the aria for alto, *He was despised and rejected of men*. The affective words "sorrows" and "grief" inspire chromatic harmony and modulations to dark keys such as B-flat minor and F minor. The vocal declamation takes on dramatic intensity in the part that follows, *He gave His back to the smiters*, as does the agitated orchestral accompaniment. Personal grief broadens into collective expression in a grandly pathetic chorus in F minor, *Surely He hath borne our griefs and carried our sorrows*—the first of three consecutive choruses. Plangent discords underline the thought *He was bruised for our iniquities*. The tone of anguish is carried into the second chorus, *And with His stripes we are healed.* The subject of this spacious fugue is marked by the downward leap of a diminished seventh—an emotionally charged interval—on the word "stripes."

This compact theme was common property in the eighteenth century. Among the masters who used it were Bach, in his *Well-Tempered Clavier* (Book II, No. 20); Haydn, in the String Quartet Opus 20, No. 5; and Mozart, in the Kyrie of the Requiem.

The third chorus, *All we like sheep have gone astray*, completes the majestic fresco. It is marked by characteristic rhythm, relentless contrapuntal energy, and briskly moving harmonic masses. But this is one of the spots where Handel's ear for his adopted language goes astray. "All we like sheep" could not possibly sound right, no matter who set it to music.

Concerts today are considerably shorter than they were in the leisure-class society of Handel's time. It is customary to reduce *Messiah* in length by omitting some numbers, especially from the second and third parts. A favorite in Part II is the chorus *Lift up your heads, O ye gates!* The question "Who is the King of Glory?" elicits a reply of Handelian grandeur. Another popular number is the deeply felt soprano aria in G minor, *How beautiful are the feet of them that preach the gospel of peace,* in which we find again the $\frac{12}{8}$ siciliano rhythm. Hardly less popular is the bass aria *Why do the nations so furiously rage together?* in which the florid expansion of the word "rage" demands some virtuoso singing.

The climax of the second part is of course the Hallelujah Chorus. The musical investiture of the key word is one of those strokes of genius that resound through the ages. The triumphal outburst has been compared to the finale of Beethoven's Fifth Symphony. (It is significant that Beethoven, himself the orator of a heroic age, admired Handel profoundly.) A grand effect is the sustained "King of Kings and Lord of Lords" in the upper voices against the jubilant Hallelujahs of the lower. The drums beat, the trumpets resound. This music sings of a victorious Lord, and His host is an army with banners.

The third part opens with *I know that my Redeemer liveth*, a serene expression of faith that is one of the great Handel arias. When on the

I   know   that___   my   Re - deem -   er   liv - eth,

crucial words "For now is Christ risen from the dead" the soprano voice ascends stepwise to the climactic G-sharp on "risen," there is established unassailably the idea of redemption that is the ultimate message of the work. The thought triumphs with the three final choral sections, *Worthy is the Lamb that was slain, Blessing and honor* . . . , and the Amen Chorus. Of the last, one need only say that it meets the supreme challenge of following the Hallelujah Chorus without a sense of anticlimax. With this is consummated a work as titanic in conception as in execution.

Messiah today is popularly associated with a religious setting. Yet it was in no way written for a church service. The work was meant to be an Entertainment, as its librettist described it. That is, it was intended for the commercial concert hall by a bankrupt impresario-composer eager to recoup his losses. That so exalted a conception could take shape in such circumstances testifies to the nature of the age whence it issued —and to the stature of the master of whom Beethoven said, "He was the greatest of us all."

⚜⚜ *CHAPTER 69* ⚜⚜

Aftermath of the Baroque: the Rococo

"There are harmonies that are sad, languishing, tender, agree-
able, gay, and striking. There are also certain successions of
harmonies for the expression of these passions."

Jean Philippe Rameau (1722)

As FAMOUS as Louis XIV's "I am the State" is his successor's "After me,
the deluge." In the reigns of the two Louis, which lasted for more than
a hundred years, the old regime passed from high noon to twilight. The
gilded minority at the top of the social pyramid exchanged the goal of
power for that of pleasure. Art moved from the monumentality of the
Baroque to the playfulness of the Rococo.

The word derives from the French *rocaille*, a "shell," suggesting the
decorative scroll- and shell-work characteristic of the style. The Rococo
took shape as a reaction from the grandiose gesture of the Baroque. Its
elegant prettiness is familiar to us from the Dresden china shepherd-
esses, the gilt mirrors and graceful curves of the Louis XV style. Out of
the disintegrating world of the Baroque came an art of feminine allure
centered about the salon and the boudoir—a miniature, ornate art
aimed at the enchantment of the senses and predicated upon the attractive doctrine that the first law of life is to enjoy oneself.

The spirit of elegant trifling manifest in a work such as Pope's *Rape
of the Lock* pervades the art of the mid-eighteenth century. But the
pace is not uniform in the different areas within a culture. Even as the
Baroque was reaching its final phase with Bach and Handel, the Rococo
was already firmly entrenched in France. The greatest painter of the
French Rococo, Jean Antoine Watteau (1684–1721), and his counterpart in music, François Couperin, not only were slightly older than the
two German masters but died considerably before them.

The Rococo found its musical expression in what is known as the
style galant. We may consider this to have extended from around 1725
to 1775, remembering, however, that it came to flower about a quarter-
century earlier in France.

François Couperin (1668–1733)

To the dream-world of love and gallantry that furnished the themes
for his art, Watteau brought the insights and the techniques of his

459

Flemish heritage. Similarly Couperin, although he spoke the language of the Rococo, was rooted in the illustrious past. He was one of a family of distinguished musicians and the greatest of the French school of clavecinists. (The harpsichord is known in France as *clavecin*.) His art crystallizes the miniature world of the Rococo and the attributes of Gallic genius—wit, refinement, pointed rhythm and scintillating ornament, clarity and precision. This music is "French without tears." Its goal is the goal of his nation's music from Lully to Debussy and on down to Milhaud and Poulenc today: to charm, to delight, to entertain.

A French trait is Couperin's love of literary titles. *The Prude, The Harvesters, Tender Nanette, The Seductress*—these are finely drawn portraits in tone, eighteenth-century miniatures that depict the world Couperin knew. Like Debussy, who admired him intensely, he sought inspiration outside himself. A tender sentiment pervades his music; but it is sentiment of an objective—more exactly, of a descriptive— kind. Of his harpsichord pieces he remarked, "I always had in view different incidents that guided me in their composition. Hence the titles correspond to the ideas I had." All the same, some of his fanciful titles bear little relationship to the music itself. These delicious sketches are

Jean Antoine Watteau, 1684–1721, *Embarkation for Cythera* (Isle of Love).

"To the dream-world of love and gallantry that furnished the themes for his art, Watteau brought the insights and the techniques of his Flemish heritage."

lovely of proportion, limpid of texture, exquisitely adapted to the crystalline sonority of the harpsichord. Many are in binary, or two-part, form (A-B), the first part modulating from the home key to a contrasting key, the second effecting the return. In this regard, and also in the fact that most of his pieces are cast in dance rhythms, they resemble the movements of the early eighteenth-century suite. They are built up of two- and four-bar fragments in a kind of mosaic style that avoids bigness of line. Everything is said intimately—and twice. We shall meet the trait again in Debussy.

Characteristic of Couperin's style is *La Galante*, which amply displays the trills and other ornaments—what the French call *agréments* or graces—of the keyboard music of the gallant style. These graces not only epitomized the dainty elegance of *galanterie* but served also to emphasize and prolong the melody notes. (The harpsichord tone, being of the plucked-string variety, does not have much sustaining power.) The piece starts out with the left hand imitating the right. Although this pattern recurs at the beginning of each period, the contrapuntal manner is not maintained in any real sense. Couperin's pseudo-polyphony requires neither consistency of texture nor inner tension among the voices, for its principal aim is to delight the ear.

The piece is in two-part form, each part being repeated. The first modulates from E major to B major; the second wanders farther afield, touching on C-sharp minor (the relative of E), A major, and B major before it returns to E. Like the finale of Bach's Suite No. 3, *La Galante* is written in the $\frac{6}{8}$ meter of the gigue.

Listening to these supremely civilized measures, one understands Debussy's remark: "French music aims first of all to give pleasure. Couperin, Rameau—these are true Frenchmen."

The Gallant Style in Germany and Italy

The Rococo witnessed as profound a change in taste as has ever occurred in the history of music. In turning to a polished entertainment music, composers embraced a new ideal of beauty. The learned counterpoint of the past seemed to them heavy and overly serious. Elaborate polyphonic texture yielded to a single melody line with a simple chord accompaniment. The intellectual power of the Baroque and its emotional fervor could no longer be sustained. The great toccatas and fugues, cantatas and oratorios gave way to graceful song and dance forms. This age desired its music above all to be simple, natural, reasonable.

The change was already apparent in the lifetime of Bach. It manifests itself in the graces and "gallantries," as he called them, of his harpsichord suites. He himself pointed out to the Most Wise Council of Leipzig that "the state of music is quite different from what it was. . . . Taste has changed astonishingly, and accordingly the former style of music no longer seems to please our ears." His fame during his lifetime was eclipsed by the representatives of the new manner. The gallant style reached its apex in Germany in the mid-eighteenth century, a period that saw the activity of his four composer sons— Wilhelm Friedemann, Carl Philipp Emanuel, Johann Christoph, and Johann Christian. They and their contemporaries consummated that revolution in taste which caused Bach's music to be neglected after his death. His pupil Johann Friedrich Doles, who held his post as Cantor of St. Thomas's, considered the fugue to be an outmoded form of scholastic exercise.

Italy in the eighteenth century produced an important group of composers whose art combined elements of both the Baroque and the Rococo. Passages in fugal or basso ostinato style alternate in their works with the graces of the *style galant* and the simple lyricism of the Age of Sensibility. While some movements are based on a single affection, like the monothematic fugue, in others the two contrasting keys are underlined by two contrasting themes. So too these men moved from the continuous expansion of the Baroque style to the four-bar phrase and the symmetrical sections of the new style.

Domenico Scarlatti (1685–1757)

The towering figure among eighteenth-century Italians was Domenico Scarlatti, one of the most original spirits in the history of music. Born in the same year as Bach and Handel, he was the son of Alessandro Scarlatti (1659–1728), a leading figure of the middle Baroque who was a prolific composer of operas, Masses, and cantatas. The younger Scarlatti left Italy in his middle thirties to take a post at the court of Portugal. When his pupil, the Infanta of Portugal, married the heir to the Spanish throne, the composer followed her to Madrid, where he spent the last twenty-eight years of his life.

Scarlatti's genius was as subtly attuned to the harpsichord as was that of Chopin, a century later, to the piano. His art was rooted in baroque tradition. At the same time it looked forward to the classical style. Scarlatti's fame rests upon his over five hundred sonatas, of which only thirty were published by the composer himself under the unassuming title of *Essercizi per gravicembalo*—exercises or diversions for harpsichord. The individual pieces in the collection were labeled sonatas. The Scarlattian sonata is a one-movement form in two parts.

The first modulates from home to related key, the second marks the return. In many of these movements Scarlatti underlines the two key areas by contrasting themes. At the end of the second part, he presents the final section of the first part transposed from the Dominant to the Tonic. His sonatas thus bear the seed of the sonata-allegro form that was about to come into being.

Scarlatti's sonatas are written in an epigrammatic style of great vivacity. They abound in beguiling melody, piquant harmonies, and daring modulations. Characteristic are the abrupt contrasts of polyphonic and homophonic texture, and the equally arresting changes from rococo playfulness to baroque drama and intensity. The brilliant runs and scale passages, crossing of hands, contrasts of low and high register, double notes, repeated notes, trills and arpeggio figures, managed with inimitable grace and ingenuity, established the composer as one of the creators of the true keyboard idiom.

Almost any one of the sonatas that have been recorded exemplifies Scarlatti's wholly personal style. The music is built up from pointed ideas generally arranged in symmetrical two- or four-bar structure. As with Couperin, each thought is apt to be repeated, either at the same pitch or another. The movement proceeds meticulously from one thought to the next, like a song that is set line by line. It avoids extended development. Marked by inexhaustible invention and rhythmic verve, it captures the sparkle of the *opera buffa* finale and the accents of lyric song. This is an aristocratic music projected in beautifully rounded forms.

Domenico Scarlatti is beginning to come into his own. As his works come to be known to the public, he stands revealed as one of the great musicians of his time: an artist of boundless imagination whose fastidious taste led him to a superb sense of style.

Jean Philippe Rameau (1683–1764)

The desire to systematize all knowledge that characterized the Enlightenment made itself felt also on the musical scene. Jean Philippe Rameau, the foremost French composer of the eighteenth century, tried to establish a rational foundation for the harmonic practice of his time. His theoretical works, such as the *Treatise on Harmony Reduced to Its Natural Principles* (1722), set forth conceptions that furnished the point of departure for modern musical theory. In his music for the harpsichord Rameau achieved that union of lucid thinking and refined feeling which is the essence of French sensibility. A leader among his contemporaries, he is a distinguished representative of the thought and feeling of his time.

As an opera composer Rameau inherited the grand gesture of Lully's lyric tragedy, for which he substituted the charm and tenderness of a less heroic age. His was a conception of symphonic drama in which chorus and orchestra, ballet and song united in a complex fabric. Unfortunately he functioned within the limitations of the rococo theater; his powerful dramatic instincts were defeated by the fondness of the gallant style for entertainment and the miniature. Also he never correctly estimated the importance of a good libretto in the creating of an effective music drama, with the result that most of his operas have disappeared from the stage.

The music of the Rococo sang of the pleasures of life. It achieved an elegance of diction and a refinement of feeling that were destined to become important ingredients of the late eighteenth-century style; also a beauty of structure and clarity of thought that endear it to all who respond to the subtle values in art.

CHAPTER 70

Opera and Symphony in the Pre-Classical Era

"Simplicity, truth, and naturalness are the great principles of beauty in all forms of art."

Gluck (1769)

The Changing Opera

THE VAST social changes taking shape in the eighteenth century were bound to be reflected in the lyric theater. Baroque opera, geared to an era of absolute monarchy, had no place in the changing scene. Increasingly its pretensions were satirized by men of letters all over Europe. The defeat of *opera seria* in London by *The Beggar's Opera* in 1728 had its counterpart in Paris a quarter century later. In 1752 a troupe of Italian singers presented in the French capital Pergolesi's famous comic opera *La Serva padrona* (The Servant as Mistress). Immediately there ensued the "War of the Buffoons" between those who favored the traditional French court opera and those who saw in the Italian *opera buffa* a new realistic art. The former camp was headed by the King, Mme. de Pompadour, and the aristocracy; the latter by the Queen and the Encyclopedists—Rousseau, d'Alembert, Diderot—who hailed the comic form for its expressive melody and natural sentiment, and because it had thrown off what they regarded as the outmoded "fetters of counterpoint." In the larger sense, the "War of the Buffoons" was a contest between the rising bourgeois art and a dying aristocratic art (even if Louis XV's Queen, for personal reasons, sided against him and with the Encyclopedists).

Rousseau's celebrated *Letter on French Music* was an outcome of the controversy. More important, he put theory into practice and composed an *opéra-comique*, *Le Devin du village* (The Village Soothsayer, 1752), to exemplify his doctrines. The versatile philosopher-humanist was a limited composer. But his little operetta with its fresh melodies, its pastoral background, and its fund of feeling gave impetus to the trend toward simplicity and naturalness, qualities that were to take a central place in the new middle-class art.

Christoph Willibald Gluck (1714–1787)

It was a German-born composer trained in Italy and writing for the imperial court in Vienna who brought lyric tragedy into harmony with the temper of the times. Gluck's momentous achievement took shape even as the aristocratic culture of the past met with the humanist impulses of the future. Out of their commingling he fashioned an art truly classical in its harmonious proportions, nobility of style, and unity of mood.

Gluck began his work within the tradition of the Italian opera based on florid vocal virtuosity. From there he found his way to a style that met the new need for dramatic truth and expressiveness. In effect he led the return to that ideal fusion of musical and dramatic elements which had been established by Monteverdi as the eternally valid goal of the lyric theater. This does not mean that, as it is commonly put—and as Gluck himself expressed it—he made the music subservient to the poetry. A great composer, no matter what he says about his aims, is the last person on earth to make music subservient to anything. What it does mean is that Gluck severely curtailed the purely musical elements that had attached themselves to opera and were thwarting its dramatic purpose. "I have striven to restrict music to its true office of serving poetry by means of expression and by following the situations of the story, without interrupting the action or stifling it with a useless superfluity of ornaments."

Gluck's principles were embodied in three works written for the imperial theater at Vienna: *Orfeo ed Euridice* (1762), *Alceste* (1767), *Paride ed Elena* (Paris and Helen, 1770). There followed the lyric dramas with which he conquered the Paris Opéra, the most important being the two based on Homeric legend—*Iphigénie en Aulide*

(Iphigenia in Aulos, 1774) and *Iphigénie en Tauride* (Iphigenia in
Tauros, 1778). In these works he successfully fused a number of elements: the monumental choral scenes and dances that had always been
a feature of French lyric tragedy, the animated ensembles of comic
opera, the verve and dynamism of the new instrumental style in Italy
and Germany, and the broadly arching vocal line that was part of
Europe's operatic heritage. There resulted a music drama whose dramatic truth and expressiveness profoundly affected the course of operatic history.

There can be no better introduction to Gluck's art than to listen, with
libretto, to the complete recording of *Orfeo*. From the grand opening
chorus of lamentation, in C minor, to the final tableau when Eurydice
is restored to Orpheus—the mood is joyous, the key is D major, and
the horns are much in evidence—the score is full of charm and invention. Gluck issued from the miniature world of the Rococo. He rose
above its shortness of breath in the most ingenious way, by combining
several units into one well-rounded section. Therewith he achieved
a breadth of architecture that is most impressive, considering his
natural affinity for the smallish frame of the gallant style. What sustains
the work, besides its fund of melody, is his sense of dramatic characterization through sound; and that sure intuition for what will go in the
theater which makes the true opera composer. Handel might sneer
that Gluck knew no more counterpoint than his cook, but for what
Gluck had to do he had little need of counterpoint. He needed singable
tunes, expressive declamation, and colorful orchestration. These he had
in abundance. He was thus able to create a statuesque art which fully
encompassed the "beautiful simplicity" that was his goal; an art that
has carried conviction to three such dissimilar eras as the late eighteenth,
the nineteenth, and the twentieth centuries.

Pre-Classical Sonata and Symphony

The decades that comprised the aftermath of the Baroque were
among the most momentous in music history. They witnessed the birth
of that whole new manner of thinking which came to fruition in the
classical symphony.

At stake was nothing less than a revolution in musical syntax and
structure. In the course of it composers traveled all the way from an
idiom rooted in the vocal polyphony of the past to the modern language
of the orchestra. They gave up the elaborate contrapuntal imitation
that was at the heart of the fugue. They enriched the new symphonic
style with elements drawn from the operatic aria and overture, from

the tunes and rhythms of *opera buffa*. To the charm of the gallant style they added the emotional urgency of a world in ferment. From all these was born a new thing—the idiom of the classical sonata-symphony. So sweeping a change, we pointed out in our discussion of sonata form, was not engineered by one or two men. The new art form was the collective achievement of several generations of musicians who were active in Italy, France, and Germany throughout the pre-classical period (c. 1740–75).

One of the outstanding figures of the late Rococo was Carl Philipp Emanuel Bach (1714–88), the second son of Johann Sebastian. He deepened the emotional content of the abstract instrumental forms and played a decisive part in the creation of the modern piano idiom. His dramatic sonata style exerted a powerful influence upon Haydn, Mozart, and Beethoven. Besides more than two hundred clavier works and fifty-two clavier concertos he produced eighteen symphonies, a quantity of chamber and church music, and about two hundred and fifty songs; also a theoretical work, the *Essay on the True Art of Playing Keyboard Instruments,* which throws much light on the musical practice of the mid-eighteenth century.

One listens with amazement to Philipp Emanuel's Piano Sonata in F minor. In the ascending broken chord of the opening measure, with its dotted rhythm, we seem to be in the neighborhood not only of Beethoven's First Piano Sonata but, even more, of the grandly solemn beginning of the *Appassionata.* A number of Carl Philipp Emanuel's works —symphonies, concertos, chamber and piano compositions—have been made available on records. They reveal his singing fluency, the freshness of his thematic material, and the poetic slow movements that endeared him to the masters of the classical era. In ideas, in expression, and in execution this pre-classical master rose above the limitations of gallant entertainment music. He could truthfully say, "It seems to me that it is the special province of music to move the heart."

Of major importance too was Carl Philipp Emanuel's half-brother Johann Christian Bach (1735–82), the youngest son of the great Cantor. Johann Christian at nineteen went to Italy, where he was converted to Catholicism and to the Italian ideal of suavely beautiful melody. Known as the "London Bach"—a good part of his artistic career unfolded in that city—he was a prolific composer of operas in the Italian manner and of instrumental music, symphonies, overtures, clavier pieces, and chamber music. His tender songfulness and meticulous forms are the essence of Rococo. Johann Christian's influence upon Mozart was as marked as was Carl Philipp Emanuel's upon Beethoven.

It was the historic task of the composers of the mid-eighteenth century to pilot their art through a period of vast change in all branches of life as well as in musical taste. When they had completed their work the stage was set for the emergence of the classical school, and for the magnificent flowering of the large instrumental forms that we associate with Haydn, Mozart, and Beethoven.

PART SIX

The Twentieth Century

"The century of aeroplanes has a right to its own music. As there are no precedents, I must create anew."

Claude Debussy

$$
\begin{array}{r}
2 \\
89 \\
73 \\
89 \\
\end{array}
$$

$$
3\,\overline{\smash{\big)}\,25\ 1}
$$

$$
8\quad 3
$$

$$
\begin{array}{r}
320 \\
251 \\
\hline
69 \\
\end{array}
$$

The Postromantic Era

"I came into a very young world in a very old time."

Erik Satie

IT BECAME clear in the final decades of the nineteenth century that the romantic impulse had exhausted itself. The grand style had run its course, to end in the overblown gestures that mark the decline of a tradition. The composers who were born in the 1860s and reached artistic maturity in the last decade of the century could not but feel, as did Satie, that they had come into the world in a "very old time." It was their historic task to bridge the gap between a dying romanticism and the twentieth century.

Three leaders of German postromanticism became international figures: Richard Strauss, Gustav Mahler, and Hugo Wolf. In Italy the operatic tradition was carried on by Giacomo Puccini. His generation included Ruggiero Leoncavallo, remembered for *I Pagliacci* (The Clowns, 1892), and Pietro Mascagni, whose reputation likewise rests on a single success, *Cavalleria rusticana* (Rustic Chivalry, 1890). These Italians were associated with the movement known as *verismo* (realism), which tried to bring into the lyric theater the naturalism of Zola, Ibsen, and their contemporaries. Instead of choosing historical or mythological themes, the realists picked subjects from everyday life and treated them in down-to-earth fashion. The action was swift, ofttimes brutal, and emphasized tragedies of peasant life.

The national schools of the late romantic period ended the supremacy of German musical culture. This development came to a head with the First World War, when Germany and Austria were cut off from the rest of Europe. In the postromantic period several newcomers appeared on the musical horizon. Besides Finland these included England, Spain, and the United States. A school of French orchestral composers came into prominence; national schools continued to flourish in Russia and Bohemia. And there emerged the movement that more than any other ushered in the twentieth century—impressionism.

The decades that framed the turn of the nineteenth century are of paramount interest to music lovers. They not only brought the art from the twilight of one epoch to the dawn of another, but also contained the seeds of much that is important to us today.

CHAPTER 72

Giacomo Puccini (1858-1924)

"Almighty God touched me with his little finger and said, 'Write for the theater—mind you, only for the theater!' And I have obeyed the supreme command."

GIACOMO PUCCINI was the foremost composer of Italian opera at the turn of the century. He was one of those fortunate artists who combine a refined sensibility with the popular touch. Coming out of a great tradition, he was able to communicate directly and easily with the varied public that the romantic period had brought into being.

His Life

He was born in Lucca, son of a church organist in whose footsteps he expected to follow. It was at Milan, where he went to complete his studies, that his true bent came to the fore. He studied at the Conservatory with Amilcare Ponchielli, composer of *La Gioconda*. The ambitious young musician did not have to wait long for success. His first opera, *Le Villi* (The Vampires, 1884), produced when he was twenty-six, was

Giacomo Puccini.

received with enthusiasm. *Manon Lescaut* (1893), based on the novel of Abbé Prévost—it was the source also of Massenet's *Manon*—established him as the most promising among the rising generation of Italian composers. In Luigi Illica and Giuseppe Giacosa, he found an ideal pair of librettists and with this writing team he produced the three most successful operas of the early twentieth century: *La Bohème* in 1896;

472

Tosca in 1900; and *Madame Butterfly,* after a play by David Belasco, in 1904. The dates should dispel the popular notion of Puccini as a facile melodist who tossed off one score after another. Each of his operas represented years of detailed work involving ceaseless changes until he was satisfied.

The Girl of the Golden West (1910) was based, like its predecessor, on a play by Belasco. The world premiere, at the Metropolitan Opera House, was a major event. Despite its brilliant launching the work did not maintain itself in the repertory. A more substantial achievement was the trio of one-act operas: *Il Tabarro* (The Cloak), *Suor Angelica* (Sister Angelica), and the comic opera *Gianni Schicchi* (1918). The first two are not heard frequently. The third is a masterpiece.

Handsome and magnetic, Puccini was idolized and feted wherever he went. His wife was jealous not without reason. "I am always falling in love," he confessed. "When I no longer am, make my funeral." As he entered middle age this singer of youth and love began to feel that his time was running out. "I am growing old and that disgusts me. I am burning to start work but have no libretto and am in a state of torment. I need work just as I need food." After much seeking he found a story that released the music in him and embarked on his final task—*Turandot.* He labored for four years on this fairy-tale opera about the beautiful and cruel princess of China. A work of consummate artistry, it is his most polished score. Puccini, ill with cancer, pushed ahead with increasing urgency. "If I do not succeed in finishing the opera someone will come to the front of the stage and say, 'Puccini composed as far as this, then he died.'"

He was sent to Brussels for treatment, accompanied by his son and the rough draft of the final scene. He succumbed after the operation, at the age of sixty-six. *Turandot* was completed from his sketches by his friend Franco Alfano. However, at the first performance at La Scala on April 25, 1926, the composer's wish was fulfilled. Arturo Toscanini, his greatest interpreter, laid down the baton during the lament over the body of Liù. Turning to the audience he said in a choking voice, "Here ends the master's work."

His Music

Puccini was a practical man of the theater with a wonderful instinct for what "goes" on the stage. Like Verdi before him he functioned within the requirements of a living tradition, striving with endless ingenuity to adapt those requirements to the needs of his public. Comparisons with Verdi are dangerous, for Puccini had none of the elemental grandeur that made the older man the mouthpiece of a nation.

He was quite clear as to the scope of his talent. "I am not made for heroic gestures. I love the souls that feel, that know hope and illusion, that respond to bright joy and tearful melancholy."

Puccini was a natural musician, but he was also a sophisticated artist of the end of the century. His unerring sense of dramatic pacing and continuity enabled him to achieve development and movement in his dramas—the "long line." He was not untouched by the tendency toward brutal realism out of which came Leoncavallo's *Pagliacci* and Mascagni's *Cavalleria rusticana*. *Tosca* certainly reflects the Italian *verismo*. All the same, unlike Leoncavallo and Mascagni, Puccini was not drawn to tragedies based on peasant life. Nor, despite his flair for evoking atmosphere, was he a poet of nature. His refined style needed an urban setting, be it Paris or Tokyo, Rome or Peking. True, his operas could not have come into being without the realistic theater of the late nineteenth century. He thought of collaborating with such arch-naturalists as Émile Zola and Maxim Gorki; but the fact remains that he never did. He was a romantic at heart whose desire was to poetize reality, to cast enchantment over the commonplaces of life. Within the framework of the realistic theater he achieved the magic of dream and illusion.

The problem of the libretto was crucial for Puccini. With the completion of each work began anew a frantic search for the right story. He was able to create only out of utter conviction and enthusiasm. "Without fever there is no creation. For emotional art is a kind of sickness, an abnormal mental state accompanied by overexcitement of every fiber and atom of a man's being." He shaped each detail of the drama; his letters to his librettists cajole, instruct, spur on to further effort. "There are certain fixed laws in the theater—to interest, to surprise, to move. . . . Put all your strength into it, all the resources of your hearts and heads, and create me something that will make the world weep. . . . I want a libretto that can move the world. Let it be passionate, stirring, not of vast but of varied scope." He drove his collaborators frantic; Giacosa and Illica vowed times without number that they would never work with him again. But he refused to let be, lashing them on to version after version until they had turned out librettos that remain models of achievement for all future aspirants in this impossible branch of literary composition.

Italian to the core, Puccini had the gift of melody—a flowing amorous melody shaped to the curve of the voice, that pervades the entire musical fabric, recitative as well as aria. He often transforms recitative into the more tuneful arioso—that is, into a free and finely molded vocal line that makes even his dialogue and action melodious. The harmonies are pungent and rich in atmosphere. The orchestration is full

Scenes from *La Bohème:*

Act I, the attic; Act II, Christmas Eve in the Latin Quarter; Act III, wintry dawn at the toll gate; Act IV, the attic.

of light and shade, effective without being obtrusive. Suddenly violins, violas, and cellos unite with the voice; and we are launched on one of those flowing sensuous tunes that Puccini's instinct rightly told him would be hummed and whistled everywhere. All this moves in rhythms animated and varied, it never lags, it never stops to teach or preach or philosophize. It is theater pure and simple. Puccini had the supreme wisdom of the operatic composer: he never permitted the music to stop the drama.

La Bohème

Puccini's best-loved work is based on Henri Murger's *La Vie de Bohème* (Bohemian Life). The novel depicts the joys and sorrows of the young artists who flock to Paris in search of fame and fortune, congregating in the Latin Quarter on the Left Bank of the Seine. "A gay life yet a terrible one," Murger called their precarious existence woven of bold dreams and bitter realities. Puccini's characteristic vein —vivacity shot through with melancholy—was peculiarly suited to this atmosphere of "laughter through tears." Remembering his own life as a struggling young musician in Milan, he recaptured its wistfulness and its charm.

The Bohemian mood is set by the exuberantly rhythmic motive with which the opera opens.

The curtain rises at once, disclosing the attic in which live Rodolfo the poet, Marcello the painter, and their two comrades-in-arms, the young philosopher Colline and the musician Schaunard. Rodolfo's first arietta, *Nei cieli bigi* (High over Paris, rings of smoke ascending from every roof and chimney), is associated with him throughout the work. Its mixture of ardor and dreaminess well characterizes the young poet.

mi   gno - li   Pa - ri - gi, __
ev   ery roof   and chim - ney.__

Marcello and Rodolfo try to work, but can think of nothing but the cold. They are presently joined, first by Colline, then by Schaunard, who by a stroke of luck has come on some money. The landlord arrives with a nasty word—rent!—and is got rid of. The young men go off to the Café Momus to celebrate Christmas Eve, Rodolfo remaining behind to finish an article he is writing.

There is a knock on the door. Enter Mimi and romance. Her arrival is heralded in this act as in later ones by a poignant phrase in the orchestra. Her candle has gone out. Will Rodolfo light it? Their dialogue, bathed by the orchestra in a current of emotion, exemplifies the spell that Puccini casts over the homeliest sentiments. "A little wine? . . . Thank you . . . Here it is . . . Not so much . . . Like this? . . . Thank you."

Mimi returns, having missed her key. Their candles are extinguished by a gust of wind; they search for the key, on the floor, in the dark. Rodolfo, finding it, has the presence of mind to slip it into his pocket. When their hands touch it is time for an aria. First Rodolfo's—*Che gelida manina* (How cold your little hand, let me warm it here in mine). Here is the Italian *cantabile*, the melody gliding along the scale and rising in a broad golden curve to its crest. Three centuries of operatic tradition stand behind an aria such as this.

Her reply, the aria *Mi chiamano Mimì* (I'm known as Mimi), is

Andante lento ♩ = 40

Mi chia - ma - no   Mi - mì,   ma il mio   no - me è Lu - ci - a __
I'm known __   as   Mi - mi,   I'm not   sure __   just why. __

followed by the duet. This is based on a phrase from Rodolfo's aria, which now becomes the love theme of the opera.

(with emotion)
con anima

Ah!   tu sole co - man-di, a - mor! __
Ah,   this won - drous ec - sta - sy __

Rodolfo, smitten, invites her to the café, to phrases that have become part of the Italian folklore of flirtation. "Give me your arm, my little one . . . I obey you, signor." The act ends on the word *amor*, as it should, with a high C for the soprano and tenor to bring down the curtain.

Act II—Christmas Eve in the Latin Quarter—is a festive street scene in which Puccini's Italian sensibility blends with the Parisian setting. His feeling for atmosphere is manifest in the bright brassy parallel chords with which the act opens. Rodolfo, having bought his new flame a rose-colored bonnet, brings her to the table where his friends are waiting. The appearance of Musetta causes a stir, proving especially agitating to her former love Marcello. This pert young lady is accompanied by an elderly councilor named Alcindoro, whom she persists in calling, in the tone of addressing a pet dog, Lulù. Marcello's agitation increases visibly as she sings her coquettish waltz song *Quando me'n vo'* (Smiling and gay, I stroll along the avenue alone).

Having decided to get rid of "the old boy," she sends him on an errand. A grand reconciliation ensues between her and Marcello. The waiter brings the bill. The young men realize to their dismay that they haven't enough to pay it, whereupon the resourceful Musetta instructs the waiter to add it to Alcindoro's and present it to that gentleman upon his return. The young people disappear in the crowd as the act ends with great éclat.

In dramatic contrast the next act opens in a pallid wintry dawn. We see a toll gate outside Paris. Peasant women enter bringing butter and eggs. From the tavern sound the voices of the last carousers, including Musetta's. Mimi appears, seeking Marcello. She confides to him her difficulties with Rodolfo, who is insanely jealous and makes their life unbearable. In this dialogue and the next the voices occasionally move in a free plastic declamation while the orchestra sings the melody. It is a favorite device with Puccini, and one that he uses with infallible effectiveness.

Rodolfo awakes within. To avoid a scene Mimi hides to one side behind some trees. Rodolfo appears and pours out his heart to Marcello; he is helpless against his jealousy and fears. Mimi is ill, she is dying. He is too poor to provide her with the care she needs. Mimi's tears and coughing reveal her presence. She bids farewell to Rodolfo in a touching aria.

The peak of the act is the quartet—better, double duet—at the close. Mimi and Rodolfo melodiously resign themselves to the parting they dread; while Marcello and Musetta quarrel violently backstage, he accusing her of flirting, she retaliating with lively epithets. Upon this Puccinian combination of pathos and comedy the curtain descends.

Act IV is introduced by the Bohemian motive of the opening. We are back in the attic. Marcello and Rodolfo try to work, as they did in the opening scene; but their thoughts revert to their lost loves. Schaunard and Colline arrive with rolls and a herring for their scanty meal. The young men indulge in horseplay that builds up to the agitated entrance of Musetta. She tells them that Mimi is below, too weak to climb the stairs. They help her in.

The friends depart on various errands to lighten Mimi's last moments. Now the lovers are alone. "Ah, my lovely Mimi . . . You still think me pretty? . . . Lovely as the sunrise . . . I fear you are mistaken. You should have said, 'Lovely as the sunset . . .'" They recollect the night they met. The scene derives its impact from Puccini's masterful use of reminiscence. How better underline their blasted hopes than by quoting the music of that first encounter?

The others return, Marcello with medicine, Musetta with a muff to warm Mimi's hands. Rodolfo weeps. Mimi comforts him. "I feel so . . . so happy . . . Now I will sleep . . ." Musetta prays. Schaunard whispers to Marcello that Mimi is dead. Rodolfo's outcry "Mimi . . . Mimi!" is heard against the brief and terrible postlude of the orchestra. Puccini wrote the final scene with tears in his eyes. It has been listened to in like fashion.

"I love small things. And the only music I can or will make is the music of small things, so long as they are true and full of passion and humanity and touch the heart." But when small things are true and full of passion and humanity they become big things. *La Bohème* has retained its freshness for more than half a century. Within its genre it is a masterpiece. Its creator, if he is not among the greatest composers, is certainly one of the most lovable.

CHAPTER 73

Richard Strauss (1864-1949)

"I work very long on melodies. The important thing is not the beginning of the melody but its continuation, its development into a fully completed artistic form."

His Life

THE MOST publicized composer of the early twentieth century was born in Munich. His father was a virtuoso horn player who belonged to the court orchestra. His mother was the daughter of Georg Pschorr, a successful brewer of Munich beer. In this solid middle-class environment, made familiar to American readers by the novels of Thomas Mann, a high value was placed on music and money. These remained Strauss's twin passions throughout his life.

Richard Strauss.

The boy played the piano when he was four and composed his first pieces at the age of six. His father, a confirmed anti-Wagnerite, saw to it that he was brought up "in a strictly classical way." As a result, his early instrumental works show an allegiance to chamber music, concerto, and symphony. In conservative musical circles the gifted youth was hailed as the future successor to Brahms. But at the age of twenty-one Strauss, groping for a type of expression that would suit his temperament, found his way into the camp of program music. It became his aim "to develop the poetic, the expressive in music as exemplified in the works of Liszt, Wagner, and Berlioz."

Macbeth (1886–90), his first tone poem, was followed by *Don Juan* (1888), an extraordinary achievement for a young man of twenty-four. Then came the series of tone poems that blazed his name throughout the civilized world: *Tod und Verklärung* (Death and Transfiguration, 1889), *Till Eulenspiegels lustige Streiche* (Till Eulenspiegel's Merry Pranks, 1894–95), *Also sprach Zarathustra* (Thus Spake Zarathustra, 1896), *Don Quixote* (1897), *Ein Heldenleben* (A Hero's Life, 1898), and two program symphonies, the *Domestic* and the *Alpine*. These works shocked the conservatives and secured Strauss's position, around the turn of the century, as the *enfant terrible* of modern music, a role he thoroughly enjoyed.

In 1894 Strauss married the singer Pauline de Ahna, daughter of a Bavarian general. A colorful personality, she devoted herself to the performance of her husband's songs, often with him as accompanist. Strauss came to be much in demand as a conductor. He toured the capitals of Europe and in 1898 was summoned to the Berlin opera. Kaiser Wilhelm II found Strauss's music too advanced for his taste, but he saw in the composer an international proponent of German culture and favored him with his friendship. In 1904 Strauss and his wife visited the United States, where he conducted the world premiere of his *Sinfonia domestica* and she presented his songs.

In the early years of the century Strauss conquered the operatic stage with *Salome* (1906), *Elektra* (1909), and *Der Rosenkavalier* (The Knight of the Rose, 1911). The international triumph of the last-named on the eve of the First World War marked the summit of his career. He collected unprecedented fees and royalties for his scores. Strauss had an excellent business sense. He did not approve of the fact that publishers piled up fortunes from the works of composers who had lived and died in poverty, and he was active in forming an alliance of German composers that would look after their interests. He was eager to dispel the romantic notion that the artist is better off starving in a garret. On the contrary, he insisted that "worry alone is enough to kill a sensitive man, and all thoroughly artistic natures are sensitive."

Strauss's collaboration with Hugo von Hofmannsthal, the librettist of *Elektra* and *Rosenkavalier*, continued until the latter's death in 1929. They turned out opera after opera; but Strauss's later works did not attract the public in nearly the same degree as had the earlier ones. New conceptions of modernism had come to the fore in the years of

the Weimar Republic; the one-time bad boy of music, now entrenched
as a conservative, was inevitably left behind. The coming to power of
the Nazis in 1933 confronted Strauss with a challenge and an opportunity. He was by no means reactionary in his political thinking; his
daughter-in-law was Jewish, and the cosmopolitan circles in which he
traveled were not susceptible to Hitler's ideology. Hence the challenge
to speak out against the Third Reich—or to leave Germany as Thomas
Mann, Hindemith, and other intellectuals were doing. On the other
hand the new regime was courting men of arts and letters. Strauss saw
the road open to supreme power, and took the opportunity. In 1933, on
the threshold of seventy, he was elevated to the official hierarchy as
president of the Reichsmusikkammer (State Chamber of Music). His
reign was brief and uneasy. He declined to support the move to ban
Mendelssohn's music from Teutonic ears. His opera *Die schweigsame
Frau* (The Silent Woman, 1935) was withdrawn after its premiere
because the librettist, Stefan Zweig, was non-Aryan; whereupon Strauss
resigned.

The war's end found the eighty-one-year-old composer the victim
of a curious irony. He was living in straitened circumstances while huge
sums owing him for performances of his works in England and America
were impounded as war reparations. He was permitted to return to his
villa at Garmisch, in the Bavarian Alps. To his friends Strauss explained
that he had remained in Nazi Germany because someone had to protect
culture from Hitler's barbarians. Perhaps he even believed it.

There were speeches at the Bavarian Academy of Arts on the occasion of his eighty-fifth birthday. He died shortly after.

His Music

Strauss carried to its extreme limit the nineteenth-century appetite
for story-and-picture music. He lived in a realistic age, and his vivid
imagination leaned toward action and movement. He went much
farther than either Liszt or Berlioz in allowing the course of the music
to be affected by the program. His tone poems are a treasury of orchestral discoveries. In some he anticipates modern sound effects—the clat-
ter of pots and pans, the bleating of sheep, the gabble of geese, hoof-
beats, wind, thunder, storm. Much more important, these works are
packed with movement and gesture, with the sound and fury of an
imperious temperament.

Strauss transformed the orchestra of Berlioz, Liszt, and Wagner into
a mammoth virtuoso ensemble in which all the instruments participated
on an equal basis. Even those hitherto used mainly for support—double
basses, trombones, tubas—were now brought into solo prominence.

With *Elektra* the grandiose orchestra of the postromantic period reached its peak. The score includes twelve trumpets, four trombones, eight horns, six to eight kettledrums. Strauss's orchestration springs from an individual sense of sound and gives an effect of riotous color. To the sober palette of the German masters he added French verve and Italian sensuousness. His scores show the most intricate interweaving of the separate instrumental parts; page after page is strewn with notes that the ear cannot possibly unravel. When chided for his complexity he would exclaim, "The devil! I cannot express it more simply."

The secret of Strauss's art is its furious rhythm. He is a master of timing, of shock and surprise. He whips the sound mass into unheard-of speed. His melodies are tense, nervous, alive. He does not always escape banality; but when he is at his best those great vaulting themes of his have immense sweep and power. Accused in his day of deliberately courting the sensational, he knew that the unorthodox harmonies in his music would in time become acceptable, as indeed they did. The boldest of innovators in his youth, in later life he mistrusted innovation. After hearing an advanced work by the youthful Hindemith he remarked to him, "You don't need to write like that. You have talent!"

Strauss's tone poems dominated the international repertory up to the Thirties; however, they are less in evidence today. On the operatic front he holds his own. *Salome,* to Oscar Wilde's famous play, and *Elektra,* based on Hofmannsthal's version of the Greek tragedy, are long one-act operas. In them Strauss explores the dark caverns of the soul. The princess of Judaea who dances for Herod and demands the head of John the Baptist on a silver charger is the incarnation of psychopathic lust. Elektra, demoniacal figure of revenge, bursts into an exultant dance when Orestes kills their mother Clytemnestra. Both lyric tragedies are swiftly paced, moving relentlessly to their climax. They are intimate with evil, frightening, and superb theater.

"I always wanted to write an opera like Mozart's," Strauss is reported to have said at the opening of *Rosenkavalier,* "and now I've done it." He was mistaken. *Rosenkavalier* has neither the wholeness of *Figaro* nor the grandeur of *Don Giovanni.* But it possesses attractions of its own: sensuous lyricism, sophistication, entrancing waltzes. The scene is Vienna in the reign of Maria Theresa. The theme is eternal: the fading of youth and beauty. The aging Marschallin, waging her losing battle with time; the disreputable Baron Ochs; Sophie and Octavian awaking to the wonder of young love—they ring true in the theater, they come alive through music. Strauss here summoned all his wizardry of orchestral color, his mastery of the stage, his knowledge of the human heart. There comes a time, alas, when *Rosenkavalier* seems a trifle long. It is a sign that one's youth is over.

Till Eulenspiegel's Merry Pranks

Till Eulenspiegel (literally, "Till Owl-Glass") was a lovable rogue of the fourteenth century who "visited all cities and plied all trades." His escapades reflect the lusty comedy of the Middle Ages, and the struggle of the eternal rebel against bourgeois respectability. Till was put into a book a century after his death and ended as a folklore figure known to every German child.

The annotations that Strauss appended to the score afford some clue to the episodes he had in mind. Till rides his horse into the midst of a crowd of market women. He joins a group of priests, disguised as one of them, and engages in theological disputation, only to horrify them with his irreverence. He declares his love to a damsel who sends him packing. His nonconforming shocks the Philistines, those staid pillars of society. He proceeds on his way singing a gay street song. But as he watches the life about him he experiences the loneliness that is the lot of the outsider. Why cannot he be like those about him—why cannot he change? But no—he realizes that Till he is and Till he must remain no matter what the cost. He discovers the cost when he is brought to trial for his misdeeds. His cockiness deserts him: this time there is no escaping. "Up the ladder! There he swings. He gasps for air. A final shudder. The mortal part of Till is no more."

Strauss's brilliant tone poem is fashioned out of two basic motives, one lyric, the other rhythmic. These, as the composer says, "pervade the whole in the most manifold disguises, moods, and situations." The first, given out by the violins, is tender and reflective. The downward leap in the melody becomes a characteristic feature of the work.

The other Till motive is the celebrated theme for French horn. A subtle syncopation, achieved by shifting the accent repeatedly within the phrase, suggests the mischief-loving side of the rogue.

The two themes are subjected to a process of continuous transformation. It is their merry pranks rather than Till's, ultimately, that concern our ears.

The lyric theme is set forth at the outset, establishing a Once-upon-a-time atmosphere. Immediately the "mischief" theme sends the rascal off on his adventures. We hear the lyric theme transformed from tenderness to cocky impudence by the simple device of reducing the time values of the notes (diminution).

The commotion of the frightened market women and their wares gives Strauss an opportunity for one of those passages of orchestral hubbub so dear to his heart. The encounter with the priests is introduced by a hymn tune in popular style. Strauss's occasional ventures into the folk manner stand out sharply against his sophisticated style. A descending glissando on solo violin ushers in the section devoted to Till's amours. The music takes on an Italianate sensuousness. You would

never suspect it, but this glowing serenade is a clever transformation of the "mischief" motive. To express the emotions of the rejected lover the lyric theme, with its downward leap, is transformed into a furious fortissimo. Till's rage passes quickly; he is ready for the next escapade.

The plodding rhythms of the Philistines sound deep in the bass, against which is hurled the defiance of the two Till motives in the treble. Tension sags in this episode, which is the weak link in the work. Momentum resumes with Till's cocky street song—the song of the eternal gamin. Here too the popular style stands out against its sumptuous surroundings. Till's self-questioning imparts to the music an upward inflection. The orchestra weighs the possibility of his reforming. But no, the horn theme returns to remind him of his destiny. His decision to remain true to himself is proclaimed by horns and trombones, which give out the "mischief" theme in longer note values (augmentation).

The orchestra crackles with defiance. Suddenly Till is summoned to his doom—by eight horns and six trumpets. Sentence is pronounced to the roll of the drum and harmonies that Strauss marked "menacing" in the score. At the climax of his tale he is a master of economy. The basic descending interval, enlarged, becomes a grim portent given out by the bass instruments. A trill on the flutes, woodwinds fluttering over a dark curtain of sound—and Till has paid the penalty. There is a long pause. We hear the Once-upon-a-time of the opening as the Epilogue bids Till a gentle farewell. At the very end his motive flares into life. Till is gone—but the spirit of youthful rebellion lives on.

The question arises: What would we make of the music if Strauss had given us the piece without title or program, simply as a rondo or as a set of Variations on Two Themes? One thing is certain. We should never, from the sounds, have deduced either Till or his escapades.

Strauss was just such a rebel as Till when the comet of his genius blazed over the musical horizon. Years later a critic wrote of him, "He was not a meteor but a falling meteorite"; yet one that gave off a dazzling light in its passage across the sky. A world figure, he dominated his era as few artists have done. He may have suspected toward the end that the world had been too much with him. "We are all of us children of our time," he said, "and can never leap over its shadows."

Let there be no mistaking. He was one of the major artists of our century.

CHAPTER 74

Jan Sibelius (1865-1957)

> "I love the mysterious sounds of the fields and forests, water and mountains. It pleases me greatly to be called a poet of nature, for nature has truly been the book of books for me."

FINLAND, in the final decades of the nineteenth century, was swept by agitation for independence from tsarist Russia. Out of this ferment flowered the art of Jan Sibelius, whose work served notice of his country's musical coming of age.

A National Artist

Sibelius's identification with his people was so complete that his music, even at its most personal, bore the stamp of their spirit. Such nationalism goes deeper than the quotation of folk tunes. "There is a mistaken impression among the press abroad," he wrote, "that my themes are often folk melodies. So far I have never used a theme that was not of my own invention." The important point is that some of them could have been folk melodies, and at least one of them—the chorale from *Finlandia*—became one.

Sibelius, like Grieg before him, revealed the northern landscape. The more fanciful of his listeners like to discover in his music the brooding forests and lakes of his native land or the legendary heroes of its sagas. Sibelius's rugged strength and his command of the large forms enabled him to win and to hold the attention of the world—or at least part of it. England and the United States became the centers of his cult, where he was acclaimed as enthusiastically as in his homeland. Neither in Paris, Berlin, Vienna, nor Rome has he achieved a comparable eminence.

Sibelius's reputation in serious music circles rests upon his seven symphonies. The first two are in the romantic tradition and pose no special problems. Their successors show a steady development toward refinement of style, conciseness of thought, and tightness of structure. In these works Sibelius discourses upon the great themes of nineteenth-century music—nature, man, destiny. His idiom is sparse and avoids sensuous brilliance. He exploits the somber colors and low registers of the orchestra. He uses short incisive motives that lend themselves to symphonic expansion and development. His speech is direct, abrupt, pithy.

It is in the orchestral and choral works of his first period that Sibelius is most explicitly national. The bardic *En Saga* (1892) was followed by the orchestral legends *The Swan of Tuonela* (1893) and *Lemminkäinen's Homefaring* (1895), and the symphonic fantasy *Pohjola's Daughter* (1906). These appeared during the years of tsarist oppression when to be patriotic was tantamount to being a revolutionary. Conceived in epic mood, they accorded with the temper of the liberation movement and brought Finnish culture to the attention of the world.

This phase of the composer's activity is summed up in the symphonic poem *Finlandia* (1899). The mood of defiance is established at the outset by the snarling of massed brass in lower register, andante sostenuto. There follows an organlike passage in the woodwinds solemnly answered by the strings, leading to an allegro moderato based on a persistent rhythm. The stirring trumpet calls are of a character designed to appeal to national emotion, as is the exultant phrase in the strings

punctuated by the rhythmic interjection of the brass. The famous tune
that appears at first in prayerful quiet, in the violins and cellos, returns
at the close as a triumphal chorale. The melody has become practically

a national anthem in the composer's homeland, where the work occupies the same position as does *The Moldau* in Smetana's. Such music
can be judged critically only by foreigners. The artist's compatriots
hear it through a mist of pride and fervor. Admirers of Sibelius resent
the frankly popular *Finlandia* for having obscured, for masses of listeners, the more elevated aspects of his art. Despite them the piece has
established itself both in Finland and abroad as a popular classic.

Sibelius was the last survivor of the generation of Richard Strauss, a
generation whose historic role it was to bridge the transition from the
romantic era to the twentieth century. Although his works are not
played nearly as much as they were a quarter century ago, the best
among them are well established in the current repertory. In Finland
he is regarded with the special reverence that a small nation lavishes
on the favorite son who became a world figure. A sincere and high-
minded musician, Jan Sibelius is assured a place in the annals of his art.

CHAPTER 75

Impressionism

For we desire above all—nuance,
Not color but half-shades!
Ah! nuance alone unites
Dream with dream and flute with horn.
                                    Paul Verlaine

The Impressionist Painters

IN 1867 Claude Monet, rebuffed by the academic salons, exhibited under less conventional auspices a painting called *Impression: Sun Rising*.
Before long impressionism had become a term of derision to describe
the hazy, luminous paintings of this artist (1840–1926) and his school.

A distinctly Parisian style, impressionism counted among its exponents Camille Pissarro (1830–1903), Édouard Manet (1832–83), Edgar Degas (1834–1917), and Auguste Renoir (1841–1919). Discarding those elements of the romantic tradition that had hardened into academic formulas, they strove to retain on canvas the freshness of their first impressions. They took painting out of the studio into the open air. What fascinated them was the continuous change in the appearance of things. They painted water lilies, a haystack, or clouds again and again at different hours of the day. Instead of mixing their pigments on the palette they juxtaposed brush-strokes of pure color on the canvas, leaving it to the eye of the beholder to do the mixing. An iridescent sheen bathes their painting. Outlines shimmer and melt in a luminous haze.

The impressionists abandoned the grandiose rhetoric of romanticism. The hero of their painting is not man but light. Not for them the pathos, the drama-packed themes that had inspired centuries of European art. They preferred "unimportant" material: still life, dancing girls, nudes; everyday scenes of middle-class life, picnics, boating and café scenes; nature in all her aspects, Paris in all her moods. The impressionists, it has been said, presented nature glimpsed through a keyhole; more prop-

Edgar Degas, 1834–1917, *The Foyer.*

"The impressionists preferred 'unimportant' material, dancing girls, boating and café scenes."

erly, nature glimpsed through the temperament, dreams, and desires of the individual painter. Derided at first—"Whoever saw grass that's pink and yellow and blue?"—they ended by imposing their vision upon the age.

The Symbolist Poets

A parallel revolt against traditional modes of expression took place in poetry under the leadership of the symbolists, who strove for direct poetic experience unspoiled by intellectual elements. They sought to suggest rather than describe, to present the symbol rather than state the thing. Symbolism as a literary movement came to the fore in the work of Charles Baudelaire (1821–67), Stéphane Mallarmé (1842–98), Paul Verlaine (1844–96), and Arthur Rimbaud (1856–91). These poets were strongly influenced by Edgar Allan Poe (1808–49), whose writings were introduced into France by his admirer Baudelaire. They used a word for its color and its music rather than its proper meaning, evoking poetic images "that sooner or later would be accessible to all the senses."

The symbolists experimented in free verse forms that opened new territories to their art. They achieved in language an indefiniteness that had hitherto been the privilege of music alone. Characteristic was Verlaine's pronouncement: "Music above all!" Like the impressionist painters, the symbolists discarded the grand pathos of romanticism. They emphasized the manner rather than the matter; they rejected the humanism—and the rhetoric—of the poetry of the early nineteenth century; they glorified the tenuous, the intimate, the subtle. "Nothing more dear," sang Verlaine, "than the gray song where the indefinite meets the precise." The symbolists discarded the story element in poetry. They avoided the moral, either expressed or implied. Nourished by art rather than life, their exquisite idiom leaned toward the precious. They expressed the moral lassitude of their time, its longing for enchantment of the senses, its need for escape.

The essentially musical approach of the symbolists was not lost upon the musicians. The composer Paul Dukas, in reminiscing about his friend Debussy and their circle, states: "Verlaine, Mallarmé, and Laforgue provided us with new sounds and sonorities. They conceived their poetry or prose like musicians. It was the writers, not the musicians, who exerted the strongest influence on Debussy."

Impressionism in Music

When young Debussy submitted to the authorities of the Conservatory his cantata *The Blessed Damozel* they stated in their report: "It is much to be desired that he beware of this vague impressionism which is one of the most dangerous enemies of artistic truth." Therewith was transferred to the domain of music a term that was already firmly established in art criticism. Debussy himself never liked the word and expressed himself acidly concerning "what some idiots call impressionism, a term that is altogether misused, especially by the critics." But the label stuck, for it seemed to describe what most people felt about his music.

Impressionism came to the fore at a crucial moment in the history of European music. The major scale—the "seven out of twelve" way of hearing music—had served the art since the seventeenth century. Composers were beginning to feel that its possibilities had been exhausted. Debussy's highly individual tone sense was attracted to other scales, such as the medieval modes that impart an archaic flavor to his music. (The reader will recall the church modes given on p. 365.) Debussy emphasized the primary intervals—octaves, fourths, and fifths—which he used in parallel motion. This style of writing somewhat resembled a medieval procedure known as *organum*, in which a melody was harmonized by another that ran parallel to it at a distance of a fifth or

fourth. Notice the resemblance to ninth-century organum in the opening measures of *La Cathédrale engloutie* (The Sunken Cathedral), a passage that evokes an impression of powerful austerity, of old and remote things:

Debussy was also sympathetic to the novel scales introduced by Russian and Scandinavian nationalism, and lent a willing ear to the harmonies of Borodin, Musorgsky, Grieg. He responded to the Moorish strain in Spanish music. Especially he was impressed by the Javanese and Chinese orchestras that were heard in Paris during the Exposition of 1889. In their music he found a new world of sonority: rhythms, scales, and colors that offered a bewitching contrast to the stereotyped forms of Western music.

The major scale, as we saw, is based on the pull of the active tones to the Tonic or rest tone. Debussy regarded this as a formula that killed spontaneity. We do not hear in his music the triumphal final cadence of the classic-romantic period, in which the Dominant chord is resolved to the Tonic with the greatest possible emphasis. His fastidious ear explored subtle harmonic relationships; he demanded new and delicate perceptions on the part of the listener. Classical harmony looked upon dissonance as a momentary disturbance that found its resolution in the consonance. But Debussy used dissonance as a value in itself, freeing it from the need to resolve. He enriched his harmony by overlaying the consonant chords with dissonant intervals. In other words, sounds that were considered dissonant he heard as consonances. In the following example—the closing measures of his piano prelude *Ce qu'a vu le vent d'Ouest* (What the West Wind Saw)—he creates a type of cadence in which the final chord takes on the function of a rest chord not because it is consonant, but because it is less dissonant than what pre-

ceded. Through these and kindred procedures Debussy strengthened the drive toward the "emancipation of the dissonance." He thus taught his contemporaries to accept tone combinations that had hitherto been regarded as inadmissible, even as the impressionist painters taught them to see colors in sky, grass, and water that had never been seen there before. Obviously this expansion of musical resources was not the result of his effort alone. But he was without question the most important among the leaders of harmonic advance in the postromantic era.

Debussy is popularly associated with the whole-tone scale. This is a pattern built entirely of whole-tone intervals, as in the sequence C-D-E-F♯-G♯-A♯-C. The whole-tone scale avoids the semitone distances 3–4 and 7–8 (*mi-fa* and *ti-do*) of the major scale. Thereby it sidesteps the thrust of *ti* to *do* that gives the traditional scale its drive and direction. The newer scale also avoids the fifth step *sol*, the Dominant that represents the active harmony; for in the whole-tone scale the fifth step is G♯, whereas in the C-major scale it would be G. In this way the whole-tone scale avoids the clear-cut resolution of active harmony to rest. There results a fluid scale pattern whose elusive charm can be gauged only from hearing it played. Debussy did not invent the whole-tone scale nor did he use it as frequently as many suppose. It lent itself admirably, however, to the nuances of mood and feeling that haunt his music; as in the following magical passage from the third act of *Pelléas et Mélisande:*

Several other procedures have come to be associated with musical impressionism. One of the most important is the use of parallel or "gliding" chords, in which a chord built on one tone is duplicated immediately on a higher or lower tone. Here all the voices move in parallel motion, the effect being one of blocks of sound gliding up or down. In the following measures from *Soirée dans Grenade* (Evening in Granada), the entire passage consists of a single chord structure which is duplicated on successive tones. Such parallel motion was prohibited in

the classical system of harmony; but it was precisely these forbidden progressions that fascinated Debussy. Also, he sustains a chord in the bass that suggests a definite key while the chords above it give the impression of having escaped to another key. Such "escaped" chords point the way to twentieth-century harmony. In the following example—the opening of *General Lavine—Eccentric* from the second book of Preludes—C-major tonality is established in the first measure, against which is heard a series of triads alien to the tonality.

The harmonic innovations inseparable from impressionism led to the formation of daring new tone combinations. Characteristic was the use of the five-tone combination known as *ninth chords*. These played so prominent a part in *Pelléas* that the work came to be known as "the land of ninths." Here is a characteristic sequence of parallel ninth chords from *Pelléas*.

As a result of the procedures just outlined, impressionist music wavered between major and minor without adhering to either. In this way was abandoned one of the basic contrasts of classical harmony. Impressionism advanced the disintegration of the major-minor system. It floated in a borderland between keys, creating elusive effects that might be compared to the misty outlines of impressionist painting.

These evanescent harmonies demanded colors no less subtle. No room here for the thunderous climaxes of the romantic orchestra. Instead there was a veiled blending of hues, an impalpable shimmer of pictorial quality: flutes and clarinets in their dark lower register, violins in their lustrous upper range, trumpets and horns discreetly muted; and over the whole a silvery gossamer of harp, celesta, and triangle; glockenspiel, muffled drum, and cymbal brushed with a drumstick.

So too the metrical patterns of the classic-romantic era, marked by the regular recurrence of accent on the first beat of the measure, were hardly appropriate for this new dreamlike style. In many a work of the impressionist school the music glides from one measure to the next in a gentle flow that discreetly veils the pulse of the rhythm.

Impressionism inclined toward the miniature. Debussy's turning away from the grand form led him to short lyric pieces: preludes, nocturnes, arabesques—the titles indicate his leaning toward intimate lyricism.

Édouard Manet, 1832-1883, *Boating*. (The Metropolitan Museum of Art, Bequest of Mrs. H. O. Havemeyer, 1929. The H. O. Havemeyer Collection)

Claude Monet, 1840-1928, *Vétheuil*. (The Metropolitan Museum of Art, Bequest of William Church Osborn, 1951)

Claude Monet, *Iris Beside a Pond.* (The Art Institute of Chicago)

"An iridescent sheen bathes impressionist painting. Outlines shimmer and melt . . ."

The question arises: Was impressionism a revolt against the romantic tradition or simply its final manifestation? Beyond question Debussy rebelled against certain aspects of romanticism, notably the Wagnerian gesture. Yet in a number of ways impressionism continued the fundamental tendencies of the romantic movement: in its love of beautiful sound, its emphasis on program music, its tone painting and nature worship, its addiction to lyricism; its striving to unite music, painting, and poetry; and its emphasis on mood and atmosphere. In effect, the impressionists substituted a thoroughly French brand of romanticism for the German variety.

Impressionist music enjoyed an enormous vogue during the first three decades of the twentieth century. It attained the proportions of an international school. In France a whole generation of musicians came either partly or wholly under its spell, among them Maurice Ravel, Paul Dukas, and Albert Roussel. Its influence in England is manifest in the works of Frederick Delius and Arnold Bax. Among the American impressionists may be mentioned Charles Martin Loeffler, John Alden Carpenter, and Charles Griffes. Isaac Albéniz and Manuel de Falla in Spain, Ottorino Respighi in Italy, and Karol Szymanowski in Poland testify to the extent of its orbit. Nor was it without influence on the leaders of the next generation—Stravinsky, Schoenberg, Bartók.

Yet from our vantage point impressionism turns out to have been largely a one-man movement. No one else of Debussy's stature found in it the complete expression that he did. In this respect it differed from the romantic style that allowed room for so many diverse personalities. The procedures of impressionism worked in a limited area; they became stereotyped and soon lost their novelty. It grew to be practically impossible to write impressionist music without sounding like Debussy. Composers were consequently forced to seek other idioms.

Also, by excluding pathos and the heroic element impressionism narrowed its human appeal. It valued elegance above passion, refinement and chic above intellectual content. It was therefore unable to muster the spiritual energy that alone transforms an artistic movement into a universal force.

But on its own premises it created a finely wrought, surpassingly decorative art. It opened up to music a world of dream and enchantment. And it captured a vision of fragile beauty in a twilight moment of European culture.

CHAPTER 76

Claude Debussy (1862-1918)

"I love music passionately. And because I love it I try to free it from barren traditions that stifle it. It is a free art gushing forth, an open-air art boundless as the elements, the wind, the sky, the sea. It must never be shut in and become an academic art."

His Life

THE MOST important French composer of the early twentieth century was born near Paris in the town of St. Germain-en-Laye, where his parents kept a china shop. He entered the Paris Conservatory when he was eleven. Within a few years he shocked his professors with bizarre harmonies that defied the sacred rules. "What rules then do you observe?" inquired one of his teachers. "None—only my own pleasure!" "That's all very well," retorted the professor, "provided you're a genius." It became increasingly apparent that the daring young man was.

He was twenty-two when his cantata *L'Enfant prodigue* (The Prodigal Son) won the Prix de Rome. Like Berlioz before him, he looked upon his stay in the Italian capital as a dreary exile from the boulevards and cafés that made up his world. Already he discerned his future bent. "I shall always prefer," he wrote a friend, "something where the action

Claude Debussy.

will be subordinated to a long and patient expression of feelings and states of mind. The music I desire must be supple enough to adapt itself to the lyrical effusions of the soul and the fantasy of dreams."

Back in Paris, Debussy frequented the advanced artistic circles where were discussed the latest theories in literature and painting. He was extraordinarily sensitive to the stimulus of the other arts and came to the conclusion that "perfumes, colors, and sounds correspond to one another." At the home of Mallarmé—the poet's "Tuesday evenings" were famous—he met the painters and writers whose search for new avenues of expression coincided with his own. He was thus peculiarly fitted to become the leader of a movement in music that owed so much to painting and poetry.

The 1890s, the most productive decade of Debussy's career, culminated in the writing of *Pelléas et Mélisande*. The work, based on the symbolist drama by the Belgian poet Maurice Maeterlinck, occupied him for the better part of ten years. He continued to revise the score up to the opening night, which took place on April 3, 1902, at the Opéra-Comique. *Pelléas* was attacked as being decadent, precious, lacking in melody, form, and substance. Nevertheless, its quiet intensity and subtlety of nuance made a profound impression upon the musical intelligentsia. It caught on and embarked on an international career.

After *Pelléas* Debussy was famous. He was the acknowledged leader of a new movement in art, the hero of a cult. "The Debussyists," he complained, "are killing me." He appeared in the capitals of Europe as conductor of his works and wrote the articles that established his reputation as one of the most trenchant critics of his time. In the first years of the century he exhausted the impressionist vein and found his way to a new and tightly controlled idiom, a kind of distillation of impressionism.

His energies sapped by the ravages of cancer, he worked on with remarkable fortitude. The outbreak of war in 1914 rendered him for a time incapable of all interest in music. France, he felt, "can neither laugh nor weep while so many of our men heroically face death." After a year of silence he realized that he must contribute to the struggle in the only way he could, "by creating to the best of my ability a little of that beauty which the enemy is attacking with such fury." He was soon able to report to his publisher that he was "writing like a madman, or like one who has to die next morning." To his perturbation over the fate of France were added physical torment and, finally, the realization that he was too ill to compose any longer. His last letters speak of his "life of waiting—my waiting-room existence, I might call it—for I am a poor traveler waiting for a train that will never come any more."

He died in March 1918 during the bombardment of Paris. The funeral procession took its way through deserted streets as the shells of the German guns ripped into his beloved city. It was just eight months before the victory of the nation whose culture found in him one of its most distinguished representatives.

His Music

For Debussy, as for Monet and Verlaine, art was primarily a sensuous experience. The epic themes of romanticism were distasteful to his temperament both as man and artist. In art for art's sake he recognized the triumph of Latin grace over Teutonic "spirituality" and love of the grandiose. "French music," he declared, "is clearness, elegance, simple and natural declamation. French music aims first of all to give pleasure."

Upholding the genius of his race, he turned against the grand form that was the supreme achievement of the Germans. Exposition-Development-Restatement he regarded as an outmoded formula, "a legacy of clumsy, falsely interposed traditions"; thematic development was for him a species of dull "musical mathematics." At a concert he whispered to a friend, "Let's go—he's beginning to develop!" He summed up his attitude by quoting Fontenelle's famous question, "Sonata, what do you want of me?"

But the Viennese sonata-symphony was not the only form alien to the Gallic spirit. A greater threat was posed by the Wagnerian music drama, which at that time attracted the intellectuals of France. "The French forget too easily the qualities of clarity and elegance peculiar to themselves and allow themselves to be influenced by the tedious and ponderous Teuton." Wagner's grandiose drama he finds false from the French point of view. "The idea of spreading one drama over four evenings! Is this admissible, especially when in these four evenings you always hear the same thing? . . . My God! how unbearable these people in skins and helmets become by the fourth night." In the end, however, he paid moving tribute to the master whose fascination he had had to shake off before he could find his own way. Wagner, he writes, "can never quite die." He calls him "a beautiful sunset that was mistaken for a dawn," and speaks with feeling of "the past greatness of this man who, had he but been a little more human, would have been great for all time."

From the romantic exuberance that left nothing unsaid Debussy sought refuge in an art of indirection, subtle and discreet. He substituted for the sonata structure those short flexible forms that he handled with such distinction. Mood pieces, they evoked the favorite images of impressionist painting: gardens in the rain, sunlight through the leaves, clouds, moonlight, sea, mist. A true nature poet, he turned from subjective brooding to the world without. Significant is his use of names

borrowed from the painters: *images, estampes* (engravings), *esquisses*
(sketches). Titles such as *The Snow is Dancing* or *Sounds and Perfumes
Waft in the Evening Air* create an atmosphere, a frame within which
the picture takes shape. But we should not be misled by the nebulous
outlines. Debussy was a master craftsman. He traced his lineage from
the French masters of the past who imprinted on their material a crystalline clarity. His music has a capricious quality; yet its impulses are
directed by an artistic intelligence that is conscious of its resources and
calculates to the minutest detail how best to use them.

Debussy worked slowly, and his fame rests on a comparatively small
output. Among the orchestral compositions the *Prélude à l'après-midi
d'un faune* (Prelude to the Afternoon of a Faun) is firmly established
in public favor, as are the three Nocturnes (1893–99)—*Nuages*
(Clouds), *Fêtes* (Festivals), *Sirènes* (Sirens); *La Mer* (The Sea, 1905)
and *Ibéria* (1908). His handling of the orchestra has the French sensibility. He favors pure colors rather than mixtures, and individualizes
each instrument. There are surprisingly few notes in his scores; the
lines are widely spaced, the texture light and airy.

Debussy is one of the important piano composers. His manner is unmistakably his own. The widely spaced chords with their parallel successions of seconds, fourths, and fifths create a sonorous halo. He exploits the resources of the instrument with infinite finesse—the contrast of low and high registers, the blending of sonorities through the
use of pedal, the clash of overtones. His piano pieces form an essential
part of the modern repertory. Among the best-known are *Clair de
lune* (Moonlight, 1890), the most popular piece he ever wrote; *Soirée
dans Grenade* (Evening in Granada, 1903); *Reflets dans l'eau* (Reflec-
tions in the Water, 1905), and *La Cathédrale engloutie* (The Sunken
Cathedral, 1910).

Debussy was one of the most important among the group of composers who established the French song as a national art form independent of the lied. In his settings of Baudelaire, Verlaine, and Mallarmé—to mention three poets for whom he had a particular fondness
—the natural inflections of the French language are released in a music
of exquisite refinement. Debussy's songs are poetic meditations that
demand a special sensitivity on the part of the singer, the pianist, and
the listener. In chamber music he achieved an unqualified success with
his String Quartet in G minor (1893). The three chamber sonatas of
his last years—for cello and piano; flute, viola, and harp; violin and
piano—were described by certain critics as indicating a falling-off of
his powers; and ever since, commentators have gone on repeating the
phrase. But one has only to hear these works to feel oneself in the presence of a master.

Finally there is *Pelléas et Mélisande*. This "old and sad tale of the woods" captures the ebb and flow of the interior life. The characters move in a trancelike world where a whisper is eloquence: Mélisande of the golden hair and the habit of saying everything twice; Pelléas, caught in the wonder of a love he does not understand; Golaud, who marries Mélisande but never fathoms her secret, driven by jealousy to the murder of his younger half-brother; and Arkel, the blind king of this shadowy land. The orchestra provides the frame, creating an atmosphere steeped in nature poetry within which the action takes on the muted quality of a dream. "There is too much singing in music drama," wrote Debussy. "My ambition is to find poems in which the characters will not argue but live their lives and work out their destinies." Maeterlinck's drama gave him his ideal libretto. The result was a unique lyric drama that justifies Romain Rolland's description of him as "this great painter of dreams."

Prélude à L'Après-midi d'un faune
(*Prelude to the Afternoon of a Faun*)

Debussy's best-known orchestral work was inspired by a pastoral of Stéphane Mallarmé that evokes the landscape of pagan antiquity. The poem centers about the mythological creature of the forest, half man, half goat. The faun, "a simple sensuous passionate being," in Edmund Gosse's phrase, awakes in the woods and tries to remember. Was he visited by three lovely nymphs or was this but a dream? He will never know. The sun is warm, the earth fragrant. He curls himself up and falls into a wine-drugged sleep.

Debussy completed the tone poem in 1894 when he was thirty-two. In it we encounter full-fledged his personal idiom. "The music of this prelude," he tells us, "is a very free illustration of the beautiful poem of Mallarmé. It makes no pretensions to being a synthesis of the poem. It projects rather a changing background for the dreams and desires of the faun in the heat of that summer afternoon." Debussy's imagination was attuned to the pagan setting, and his music invokes emotions as voluptuous as they are elusive. It unfolds what he well called his "harmonious harmony."

The piece opens with a flute solo in the velvety lower register. The melody glides along the chromatic scale, narrow in range, languorous.

Glissandos on the harp usher in a brief dialogue of the horns. Of these sounds it may be said, as of the opening chords of *Tristan,* that their like had never been heard before. The dynamic scheme is discreet; pianissimo and mezzo-piano predominate. There is only one fortissimo. The whole-tone scale is heard. Notable is the limpid coloring. The strings are muted and divided. Flute and oboe, clarinet and horns are used soloistically, standing out against the orchestral texture.

The work is in sections that follow the pattern of statement-departure-return. Yet the movement is fluid, rhapsodic. Debussy here achieves his goal of a music "free from motives and themes, founded in reality on a single continuous theme which nothing would interrupt and which would never return upon itself." This continuity of theme imparts to the piece an extraordinary unity of mood and texture.

Almost every fragment of melody is repeated forthwith, a trait that the composer carries to the length of mannerism. Characteristic is the relaxed rhythm which flows across the bar line in a continuous stream. By weakening and even wiping out the accent Debussy achieved that dreamlike fluidity which is a prime trait of impressionist music.

A contrasting motive emerges, marked *Même mouvement et très soutenu* (same tempo and very sustained). Played in unison first by woodwinds, then by the strings, it is an ardent melody that carries the composition to its emotional crest.

The first melody returns in altered guise. At the close, antique cymbals are heard, *ppp.* (Antique cymbals are tiny metal discs attached to thumb and forefinger and struck together.) "Blue" chords sound on the muted horns and violins, infinitely remote. The work dissolves in silence. It takes nine minutes to play. Rarely has so much been said with so little.

Fêtes (*Festivals*)

That Debussy's music also commands forceful rhythms is made plain by *Fêtes,* the second of his Nocturnes for Orchestra. Debussy used the term "nocturne" in much the same way as did Whistler for his evocative canvases. The composer explained: "The title *Nocturnes* is to be understood here in a general, more especially in a decorative sense. It is not intended to denote the usual form of the nocturne, but rather all that this word suggests of diversified impressions and the special effects of light."

In *Fêtes,* he stated, he tried to capture movement and rhythm "dancing in the atmosphere with sudden bursts of light. There is also the episode of a procession—a dazzling and fantastic vision—which passes through the festive scene and becomes a part of it. But the background remains the same—ever the festival and the music blending with it—luminous dust participating in the rhythm of the universe."

Certainly this music captures the play of light, the "luminous dust" that pervades and envelops Debussy's canvas. The piece opens in $\frac{4}{4}$ time, *Animé et très rhythmé* (lively and very rhythmical). Violins establish the provocative triplet rhythm against which English horn and clarinets trace a gliding figure. An ascending glissando on the harp gives the effect, in this coloristic setting, of nothing less than a shower of sparks. There follows a motive that becomes a structural element in the work.

Debussy here attains his ideal of a music that unfolds freely and flexibly, untrammeled by a preconceived mold: the fluid form of the prelude. Motives emerge out of the orchestral haze, melodious fragments that are stated and immediately repeated. The form has the charm and intimacy of the miniature, proceeding in a kind of mosaic work, step by step, that reminds one of the Rococo and of the master whom Debussy hailed as a true exponent of the French spirit—Couperin. Suddenly the orchestral sonority is hushed. Harps, kettledrum, and the lower strings set up a curtain of sound, *ppp,* against which the muted trumpets whisper a fanfare. The procession sets forth, shadowy and remote but coming ever closer, powered by a rhythmic ostinato based on the underlying triplets, whose ceaseless repetition outlines a steady growth in the volume of sound. This is an orchestral crescendo of irresistible verve and power. The procession arrives on the crest of it; the shadowy shapes and revels deploy before us and, as the music is hushed again, move off in the distance, infinitely mysterious and remote. The pianissimo ending is wonderfully suggestive, with its veiled triplets and flickerings of light: oboe, flutes, bassoons, a stippling of string tone, muted horns and trumpet, and a cymbal ever so lightly brushed by a drumstick. It was Couperin's contemporary, Watteau, who painted

Embarkation for Cythera, that serene canvas bathed in golden light which epitomizes Rococo art (p. 460). In *Fêtes* Debussy captures the grace and elegance of the great Fleming whose amorous figures so discreetly follow the summons to the pleasure island of the foam-born goddess.

A sensitive tone poet who was relentlessly exacting with himself, Debussy looms as the first major composer of our era. He bridges the gap between romanticism and the twentieth century. His is a domain limited in scope but replete with beauty. Every note he set down justifies the proud title he assumed in the time of his country's peril: Claude Debussy, *musicien français.*

⟅⟅ *CHAPTER 77* ⟆⟆

Maurice Ravel (1875-1937)

"Does it never dawn on these people that I may be artificial by nature?"

MAURICE RAVEL had to make his way in a milieu dominated by Debussy. He succeeded in remaining himself. Ravel may be accounted a post-impressionist. As in the case of Cézanne, a classical streak in his make-up led him to impose form and order on what, he feared, might otherwise degenerate into amorphous fantasy.

His Life

Ravel was born in Ciboure, near Saint-Jean-de-Luz, in the Basses-Pyrénées region at the southwestern tip of France. The family moved to Paris shortly after Maurice was born. His father, a mining engineer who had aspired to be a musician, was sympathetic to the son's artistic proclivities. Maurice entered the Conservatory when he was fourteen. He remained there for sixteen years—an unusually long apprenticeship.

Ravel's career at the Conservatory was enlivened by his repeated failure to win the Prix de Rome, the official prize that has been held by some of France's most distinguished composers—as well as by a number of nonentities. At his fourth attempt he was eliminated in the preliminary examination, even though his work had already begun to command respect in progressive musical circles. This high-handed

Maurice Ravel.

action on the part of the professors caused a public scandal. The Director of the Conservatory was forced to resign, and Gabriel Fauré—Ravel's teacher in composition—was appointed in his place. Ravel never forgot the affront. In later life he accepted honors from several foreign states, but refused the decoration of the Legion of Honor from a government that had withheld the Rome prize from a deserving young musician.

Ravel's artistic development was greatly stimulated by his friendship with a group of avant-garde poets, painters, and musicians who believed in his gifts long before those were recognized by the world at large. Youthful enthusiasts, they called themselves the "Apaches." In this rarefied atmosphere the young composer found the necessary intellectual companionship, as had Debussy a decade earlier in the salon of Stéphane Mallarmé. Ravel's career followed the same course, more or less, as that of almost all the leaders of the modern movement in art. At first his music was hissed by the multitude and cried down by the critics. Only a few discerned the special quality of his work, but their number steadily grew. Ultimately the tide turned, and he found himself famous.

Ravel, like Debussy, was profoundly shaken by the outbreak of war in 1914. After making a vain attempt to join the air force, he became a driver in the motor transport corps and was sent to the Verdun sector. To his surprise, the horrors of war aroused no fear in him. On the contrary, they cast a terrible spell. "And yet I am a peaceful person," he wrote from the front. "I have never been brave. But there it is, I am eager for adventure. It has such a fascination that it becomes a necessity. What will I do, what will many others do, when the war is over?"

Having fallen seriously ill, he was discharged and returned to Paris just before the death of his mother. Her loss was a heavy blow. In a mood of severe depression he resumed his work with *Le Tombeau de*

Paul Cézanne, 1839–1906, *Mont St. Victoire.*

"Ravel may be accounted a post-impressionist. As in the case of Cézanne, a classical streak in his make-up led him to impose form and order on what, he feared, might otherwise degenerate into amorphous fantasy."

Couperin. (*Tombeau,* literally a tomb, denotes a lyric form of the age of Louis XIV, offered as homage to a deceased person.) "In reality it is a tribute not so much to Couperin himself," he stated, "as to eighteenth-century French music in general." Grief is here transformed into six serenely graceful dance pieces, each dedicated to the memory of a fallen comrade.

In the years after the war Ravel came into his own. He was acknowledged to be the foremost composer of France and was much in demand to conduct his works throughout Europe. In 1928 he was invited to tour the United States. Before he would consider the offer he had to be assured of a steady supply of his favorite French wines and of French Caporals (he was a chain smoker). Ravel and America took to one another, although he tired first. "I am seeing magnificent cities, enchanting country," he wrote home, "but the triumphs are fatiguing. Besides, I was dying of hunger."

With the passing of the Twenties there began for the composer, as for the world about him, a period of depression. His overrefined, stylized art was not the kind that renews itself through a deepening contact with life. Hence he found it increasingly difficult to compose. "I have failed in my life," he had written in a moment of depression. "I am not one of the great composers. All the great ones produced enormously. But I have written relatively very little, and with a great deal of hardship. And now I can not do any more, and it does not give me any pleasure." In these words we hear the self-induced impotence of an artist who ended as "a prisoner of perfection."

Toward the end of his life Ravel was tormented by restlessness and insomnia. He sought surcease in the hectic atmosphere of the Parisian night clubs, where he would listen for hours to American jazz. As he approached sixty he fell victim to a rare brain disease that left his faculties unimpaired but attacked the centers of speech and motor coordination. It gradually became impossible for him to read notes, to remember tunes, or to write. Once, after a performance of *Daphnis et Chloé*, he began to weep, exclaiming: "I have still so much music in my head!" His companion tried to comfort him by pointing out that he had finished his work. "I have said nothing," he replied in anguish. "I have still everything to say."

So as not to watch himself "go piece by piece," as he put it, he decided to submit to a dangerous operation. This was performed toward the end of 1937. He never regained consciousness.

His Music

Ravel shared with Debussy an affinity for the scales of medieval and exotic music. Both men were attracted by the same aspects of nature—daybreak, the play of water and light. Both exploited exotic dance rhythms, especially those of Spain. Both loved the fantastic and the antique, and the old French harpsichordists. Both were repelled by the passion of nineteenth-century music, and believed the primary purpose of art to be sensuous delight. Ravel too was inspired by the symbolist poets and had a gift for setting the French language to music. Both men in surpassing degree exemplified Gallic sensibility. And both considered themselves rebels against the nineteenth-century spirit, although it is apparent to us now that romanticism was the soil out of which their music flowered.

The differences between the pair are as pronounced as the similarities. There is an enameled brightness about Ravel's music that contrasts with the twilight softness of Debussy's. He is less visionary. His rhythms are more incisive and have a verve, a drive that Debussy rarely strives for. His mind is more precise, his humor drier, his harmonies crisper. He goes beyond Debussy's conception of dissonance. Ravel's sense of key is firmer, the harmonic movement more clearly outlined; he is far less partial to the whole-tone scale than Debussy. He is more conventional in respect to form, and his melodies are broader in span, more direct. His texture is contrapuntal, often being based on the interplay of lines rather than on the vertical blocks of sound that fascinated Debussy. Ravel's orchestration derives in greater degree from the nineteenth-century masters; he stands in the line of descent from Berlioz, Rimsky-Korsakov, and Richard Strauss. Whereas Debussy aimed to "decongest" sound, treating each instrument as a soloist, Ravel handled the huge postromantic orchestra with brilliant virtuosity, and with special emphasis on what has well been called the "confectionary department"—harp glissandos, glockenspiel, celesta, triangle.

Ravel ranks as one of the outstanding piano composers of the twentieth century. He extended the heritage of Liszt, even as Debussy was the spiritual heir of Chopin. Among his most widely played works for the piano are *Pavane pour une Infante défunte* (Pavane for a Dead Infanta, 1899), *Jeux d'eau* (Fountains, 1901), and the *Sonatine* (1905). The French art song found in Ravel one of its masters. *Trois Poèmes de Stéphane Mallarmé* (1913) and the sensuous *Chansons madécasses* (Songs of Madagascar, 1926) exemplify the twentieth-century interest in chamber music with voice.

But it was through his orchestral works that Ravel won the international public. The best known of these are *Rapsodie espagnole* (Spanish Rhapsody, 1908); *Ma Mère l'Oye* (Mother Goose, 1912); the ballet *Daphnis et Chloé*, one of his strongest works (1912); *La Valse*, which we will discuss; the ever popular *Boléro* (1928), which exploits the hypnotic power of relentless repetition, unflagging rhythm, steady crescendo, and brilliant orchestration; the classically oriented Piano Concerto in G (1931); and the dramatic Concerto for the Left Hand (1931), a masterpiece. *L'Heure espagnole* (The Spanish Hour, 1907) is a delicious comic opera in one act concerning an elderly clockmaker and his faithless wife. *L'Enfant et les sortilèges* (Dreams of a Naughty Boy, 1925), a one-act fantasy on a text by Colette, combines whimsy and elegance. Mention should be made too of the distinguished Trio for piano, violin, and cello (1914); the Introduction and Allegro for harp, string quartet, flute, and clarinet (1906); the graceful String Quartet (1903), which Ravel dedicated to his teacher Gabriel Fauré; and *Tzigane* (1924), a rhapsody for violin and piano (or orchestra).

Ravel, like Debussy, has always been immensely popular in the United States. His harmonies and orchestration have exercised a particular attraction for jazz arrangers and Hollywood composers. As a result his idiom (somewhat watered down, to be sure) has become part of the daily listening experience of millions of Americans.

La Valse

The idea of writing a piece to glorify the Viennese waltz came to Ravel as early as 1906. "It is not subtle—what I am undertaking at the moment," he wrote to a friend. "It is a Grande Valse, a sort of homage to the memory of the Great Strauss, not Richard but the other—Johann."

Thirteen years—and a world war—later, Ravel returned to the project. He had still not recovered his health after his war experiences; he was depressed. The dance that originally was to have given utterance to his joy in life now returned to his mind in the guise of a *danse macabre;* as the composer described it, "an impression of a fantastic and macabre kind of Dervish dance." The external stimulus came from Serge Diaghilev, who suggested that Ravel turn his symphonic poem on the waltz into a ballet. The piece was completed in 1920.

Ravel's conception of this ballet—a scene at the imperial palace, around 1855—is explained in a note that he appended to the score: "Through whirling clouds we catch a glimpse of couples waltzing. The clouds gradually lift, revealing an immense hall filled with dancers. The scene is gradually lit up. There is a burst of light from the chandeliers." It is worthy of note, in view of the vividly pictorial character of Ravel's orchestration, that he closely associated an upsurge in sound with an upsurge of light.

In *La Valse* a number of disparate elements are deftly intertwined. The spirit of Vienna (as evoked by a sensibility that is wholly French) is combined at the beginning with the mistiness of impressionism, at the end with the dazzling sonorities of the postromantic orchestra. The radiant waltz of Johann Strauss becomes a symbol here of a dying world indulging in its last dance. Hence the duality of the emotion, that strange bittersweet quality so characteristic of Ravel. Like *Boléro, La Valse* is a study in orchestral crescendo—but a crescendo more capricious, more subtle.

The piece opens pianissimo with tremolos in the muted cellos and basses. Wisps of melody float out of an impressionist haze and dissolve before we can fully apprehend them. We seem to be on the verge of hearing a waltz tune which, tantalizingly, never emerges. The only thing the ear can make out is Ravel's tempo, *Mouvement de Valse viennoise.* Finally a melody takes shape in the bassoons and violas:

Then another, a caressing tune on the violins and violas:

From then on the music unfolds one seductive waltz tune after another, now gathering momentum, now returning to the pianissimo sonorities of the opening. Ravel artfully husbands his resources until the frenzied climax, when he unleashes all the clashing dissonances of which the orchestra of his time was capable. It is in these frenetic final measures that his alluring "apotheosis of the waltz" becomes a dance of terror and destruction. The harsh dissonances, *fff*, pass beyond what a recording is able to convey. One must hear the piece in the concert hall, under the baton of a dynamic conductor, to experience fully the grinding sonorities brought into being by Ravel's score. This steep rise in dissonance content, abetted by a crescendo and accelerando, brings the work to an electrifying close. *La Valse* is a virtuoso piece for everyone concerned—the composer, the conductor, the player, and— of course—the listener.

Every movement in history engenders a reaction. Because of the enormous prestige that accrued to the music of Debussy and Ravel in the second quarter of the century it is currently the fashion to deprecate their achievement. As we noted, their art limited the emotional-spiritual ambit of music. Yet it is important not to underestimate what they accomplished. They created an image of French music that incarnated the sensibility of their nation's genius. They held up an ideal of sonorous beauty that electrified a generation. And they opened wide the door to the twentieth century.

CHAPTER 78

Other Postromantic Composers

Gustav Mahler (1860–1911)

"I am thrice homeless. As a Bohemian born in Austria. As an Austrian among Germans. And as a Jew throughout the world."

GUSTAV MAHLER was the last in the memorable line of Viennese symphonists that included Haydn, Mozart, Beethoven, Schubert, Bruckner.

His tone imagery was permeated by the jovial intimacy of Austrian popular song and dance and by the melodious folk song of his native Bohemia. Through his music resound the great themes of an age that was drawing to its close—worship of nature, love and faith, destiny and death. "Only when I experience intensely do I compose. Only when I compose do I experience intensely." Music for him was symbol, vision, intoxication—"a mysterious language from beyond."

He tried to breathe vitality into a world of thought and feeling that was already in process of disintegration. The attempt was doomed to fail. Mahler was a lyricist who shaped mammoth symphonic songs. But the symphony is an epic-dramatic form. He never solved the nineteenth-century conflict between classical form and romantic content, between symphonic tightness and lyric diffuseness. The circumstance imparts to his music its fevered unrest, its extravagant pathos. His nine symphonies dissolve in a stream of fervid song lyricism, and look nostalgically to the past.

Yet in one regard Mahler made a significant contribution to contemporary technique. Faced with the cloud of sound of the hundred-piece orchestra, he moved toward clarity and lightness of texture. He based his style on an orchestral counterpoint in which several melodies pursue their course simultaneously, each setting off the others. This lyrical polyphony gave his symphonies, despite their huge dimensions, a transparency of fabric that was not without its influence upon the contemporary scene.

Mahler's masterpiece is *Das Lied von der Erde* (The Song of the Earth). This symphony for solo voices and orchestra—or better, this symphonic song cycle—was composed in 1908 but received its first performance under the direction of Bruno Walter in 1911, after Mahler's death. Mahler found his text in Hans Bethge's reconstruction of a group of old Chinese poems. In their emphasis on the transience of life these verses bear some resemblance to FitzGerald's adaptation of the *Rubáiyát* of Omar Khayyám. Mahler responded to their imagery of joy and despair. The lyricist in him molded the conception to the voice, while the symphonist expanded the material in the orchestra. There resulted a work that is very special and that reveals his gifts at their best. (See Appendix I for a suggested list of recorded works by the composers discussed in this chapter.)

Other Austro-German Composers

The generation of Richard Strauss and Mahler sought to reconcile the classical tradition with the idiom of Wagner. Hugo Wolf (1860–1903) was the master of the lied in the postromantic era. He introduced the methods of Wagnerian music drama into the domain of song lyricism.

His miniature tone dramas are notable for their concentration of thought and feeling. Songs such as *Verborgenheit* (Secrecy) and the moving *Geh', Geliebter, geh' jetzt* (Go, my love, go now) offer a splendid introduction to Wolf's highly personal art.

Max Reger (1873–1916) preached a gospel that assumed increasing importance as the twentieth century wore on: the return to Bach (although he preached it from the romantic rather than classical point of view). To the rich texture of baroque polyphony he added a Brahmsian strain and an overwrought chromatic harmony that derived from Wagner. Although he has his devotees outside his homeland, Reger is fundamentally in the category of composers that are nonexportable. He stands in the German tradition and speaks most directly to the German mind.

French Composers

The postromantic generation in France continued the efforts of César Franck to create a well-rounded musical culture that would not be tied to the opera house. A leading figure was Gabriel Fauré (1845–1924), a composer who commands extraordinary admiration in his homeland. Abroad he is best known for his Requiem (1887), a lovely work whose inner quietude of spirit reveals Fauré's characteristic trait of "intimate limpidity." His chamber music and songs too are frequently performed. Important too was the pupil and chief disciple of Franck, Vincent d'Indy (1851–1931). A traditionalist in outlook, he believed that the great forms of the past—fugue, sonata, variation—could still serve as the vehicles for a vital and personal expression. His *Symphony on a French Mountain Air* and *Istar Variations* are still played. Paul Dukas (1865–1935) was one of those artists who with a single work achieve an international success that they never again duplicate. In the eyes of the world he is the composer of the brilliantly colored orchestral scherzo *The Sorcerer's Apprentice,* an extremely attractive example of postromantic program music.

Erik Satie (1866–1925) exerted a pronounced influence on twentieth-century thinking. He was persuaded, in Virgil Thomson's phrase, "that the only healthy thing music can do in our century is to stop trying to be impressive." His attempt to deflate music through "spoofing" was aimed both at the remnants of the romantic tradition and the preciousness of the impressionists. Characteristic are such titles as *Pieces in the Shape of a Pear, Sketches and Annoyances of a Wooden Man, Disagreeable Impressions.* Satie's example spurred composers who came after toward a sane, sensible "music for every day." Behind his banter lurks a curious loneliness of spirit and a sensibility wholly modern.

Albert Roussel (1869–1937) emerges as one of the most significant figures of the transition period. He was an aristocratic artist whose music bears the imprint of a mind endowed with sensitive perceptions and insights. Best known among his works are the Second and Third Symphonies, the orchestral suites, and the ballet *Le Festin de l'araignée* (The Spider's Feast).

Two gifted pupils of César Franck won recognition beyond the borders of their native land. Henri Duparc (1848–1933) ranks as one of the creators of the modern French art song. *Extase, Invitation au voyage,* and *Soupir* (A Sigh) are superb examples of intimate lyric art. Ernest Chausson (1855–99) is remembered for several appealing works that show a strong Wagnerian influence. The Symphony in B-flat, the *Poème* for violin and orchestra, and his songs reveal the poetic qualities of the composer's style.

The Russians

The mantle of Tchaikovsky and Rimsky-Korsakov descended to a numerous progeny, the majority of whom were known mainly in their own land. Some, however, won wider popularity through their piano pieces. In this category were Anatole Liadov (1855–1914) and Anton Arensky (1861–1906). The songs of Alexander Gretchaninov (1864–1956) achieved wide currency, as did the showy violin concerto of Alexander Glazunov (1865–1936). And two among this group became international figures: Scriabin and Rachmaninov.

Alexander Scriabin (1872–1915) experimented with the construction of chords in intervals of a fourth instead of, as was the rule in traditional harmony, a third. He was one of those who ushered in new conceptions of dissonance and tonality. Essentially a piano composer and miniaturist, he combined the heritage of Chopin and Liszt with his own chromaticism in a refined salon art. He was also a religious mystic who saw the artist as Messiah come to redeem the world through beauty. His grandiose symphonic poems of a post-Wagnerian cast, such as the *Poem of Ecstasy,* have all but disappeared from view, as have the ten piano sonatas. Still played are the short piano pieces—preludes, études, mazurkas, and the like.

Sergei Rachmaninov (1873–1943) became the accredited voice of Slavic pessimism in the post-Tchaikovsky generation. He captured the sense of futility and longing that hung over the Russian intelligentsia in the dark years leading to the Revolution of 1905, a mood made familiar to Americans through the plays of Chekhov. His compositions unite Slavic intensity and the atmosphere of German romanticism within a traditional frame. They display broadly spun voluptuous melodies, somber marching rhythms, a flair for the piano and its massive chord sonorities, and an expert sense of theatrical effect. Characteristic are his Piano Concertos Nos. 2 and 3, and the *Rhapsody on a Theme by Paganini.*

The English

For almost two hundred years after the death of Purcell, England produced no major composer of her own. With the rise of a native school in the postromantic period the nation's confidence in its ability to create music was restored. The renascence expressed itself in a nationalist movement that cultivated folk song and dance as an expression of rural England. A strengthening factor was the revival of the great church music of the time of the Tudor monarchs, of the Elizabethan madrigal and the art of Purcell.

Sir Edward Elgar (1857–1934) was the first of his generation to achieve international fame. He loved England, her past, her countryside; and became the unofficial musician-laureate of the late Victorian and Edwardian eras. "It is my idea," he declared, "that music is in the air all around us and that at any given time you just take as much as you want." What he took was not always distinguished; but he shaped it lovingly into something that had enormous gusto, that made sense to his countrymen, that shone with all the tints of the postromantic orchestra, and that every now and again had a rousing tune thrown in. Of his major works the *Enigma Variations* and Violin Concerto are still performed, and offer a good introduction to his music. The rest of his large output is to be heard mainly in his native land, where he is something of a national institution.

Frederick Delius (1862–1934) represents another aspect of the British character—its quietude and inwardness of spirit. His is a gentle lyricism compounded of dreams and longing, a lyricism whose sensuous sweetness links him to the great poets of his land. An eloquent example of his art is *Sea Drift,* a work for baritone solo, chorus, and orchestra based on the poem by Walt Whitman.

It has been said about Ralph Vaughan Williams (1872–1958) that he was an Englishman first and a musician afterward. Be that as it may, he combined the twin passions of his life in a manner wholly satisfactory to himself and his admirers. His is the speech of a natural man, blunt, rugged, honest. The national community furnished the framework for his art. But at his best, as in the Symphony No. 4 in F minor, the *London Symphony,* and the Mass in G minor, he reaches beyond his island. The British regard him as one of their foremost musicians.

Others

It will suffice to mention a few other characteristic figures of the time. Ottorino Respighi (1879–1936) was one of a group of Italian composers who tried to establish a symphonic art in the land above all dedicated to operatic music. He was a facile and prolific composer whose scores are notable for their brilliant orchestration. Two of his large orchestral works, *Fountains of Rome* and *Pines of Rome*, achieved a vogue in the 1920s and are still performed.

Ferruccio Busoni (1866–1924), a man of brilliant intellect and versatile gifts, was active as pianist, conductor, teacher, and writer on music as well as composer. Busoni disliked nineteenth-century music, but adored Bach, Mozart, and the closed forms of classical opera. He was one of the first to formulate the neoclassic bent of the new age and to adapt eighteenth-century forms to the modern temper. Characteristic of his style are the *Fantasia contrappuntistica* for piano (1910) and the opera *Arlecchino* (1916).

Spain produced two musicians of charm in Isaac Albéniz (1860–1909) and Enrique Granados (1867–1916). They based their art on the song and dance types of their country, and produced picturesque piano pieces that attained wide currency.

A period of transition, being less stable than the noontide of an era, is markedly less conducive to the production of enduring works. It testifies to the vitality of the postromantic generation that so much of their music continues to delight the public. For it was the unique mission of this group of composers not only to write the coda to the achievements of nineteenth-century musical culture, but also to set the scene for the new music.

CHAPTER 79

The New Music

"The entire history of modern music may be said to be a history of the gradual pull-away from the German musical tradition of the past century."

Aaron Copland

As WE look back over the history of art we find that one thing never changes, and that is the element of change itself. What does vary from age to age is the rate of change. At certain times the cultural process moves so rapidly as to assume the character of a revolution. There were three occasions in the history of music, as it happens at equal intervals from one another, when the change was so abrupt that the word *new* became a battle slogan. The year 1300 is associated with the rise of the *Ars nova* (new art), the year 1600 with the *Nuove musiche,* and the year 1900 with the New Music.

Each of these caused bewilderment and heated polemics, as the chronicles of the time attest. After the initial shock came a period of adjustment; the new concepts were assimilated to the old. The twentieth-century revolution caused the greatest dislocation of all. Changes that in former times would have been spread over generations were now telescoped into a few years. As a result, thousands who had learned to love the melodies of Chopin and Puccini felt themselves to be victims of a gigantic conspiracy known as "this modern stuff"—a conspiracy perpetrated by a band of musicians (also poets and painters) who seemed to have set out to destroy all the values in art that one had come to cherish.

Metropolitan Opera House, Lincoln Center for the Performing Arts. An example of contemporary architecture.

"Changes that in former times would have been spread over generations were now telescoped into a few years."

Now that a good part of the century is behind us, the process of adjustment is well under way. Composers whose first performances forty or fifty years ago touched off riots are today accepted as masters. Their disciples occupy key posts in our universities and critical journals. Their works are disseminated through concerts, broadcasts, recordings.

Twentieth-century music stands revealed not as a temporary aberration of mind and heart, but as the newest and therefore most spectacular link in the chain that binds the present to the past.

The Reaction Against Romanticism

"Epochs which immediately precede our own," writes Stravinsky, "are temporarily farther away from us than others more remote in time." The first quarter of the twentieth century was impelled before all else to throw off the oppressive heritage of the nineteenth. Composers of the new generation were fighting not only the romantic past but the romanticism within themselves.

The turning away from the nineteenth-century spirit was manifest everywhere. Away from the subjective and the grandiose; from pathos and heaven-storming passion; from the romantic landscape and its picture-book loveliness; from the profound musings on man and fate; from the quest for sensuous beauty of tone—"that accursed euphony," as Richard Strauss called it. The rising generation viewed the romantic agony as Wagnerian histrionics. It considered itself to be made of sterner stuff. Its goal was a sweeping reversal of values. It aimed for nothing less than "to root out private feelings from art."

Primitivism

The new music came of age just before the First World War. The spiritual exhaustion of Western culture showed itself in an indefinable restlessness. European art sought to escape its overrefinement, to renew itself in a fresh and unspoiled stream of feeling. There was a desire to capture the spontaneity, the freedom from inhibition that was supposed to characterize primitive life. People idealized brute strength and the basic impulses that seemed to have been tamed by an effete civilization. Even as the fine arts discovered the splendid abstraction of African sculpture, music turned to the dynamism of primitive rhythm. Composers ranged from Africa to Asia and eastern Europe in their search for fresh rhythmic concepts. Out of the unspoiled, vigorous folk music in these areas came primitive rhythms of an elemental fury that tapped fresh sources of feeling and imagination, as in Bartók's *Allegro barbaro* (1911) and Stravinsky's *The Rite of Spring* (1913).

Machine Music

With the mechanization of Western society came a widespread feeling that man had surrendered his soul to forces he neither understood

African sculpture.

"Even as the fine arts discovered the splendid abstraction of African sculpture, music turned to the dynamism of primitive rhythm."

nor controlled. The machine became a symbol of power, motion, energy; a symbol too of what one writer well called "the dehumanization of art."

A manifesto emanating in 1913 from the circle of the Italian futurist poet Marinetti hymned the Art of Noises: "the purring of motors, the throbbing of valves, the pounding of pistons, the screeching of gears." The postwar period saw the production of musical works glorifying locomotive and iron foundry, dynamo and turbine. Characteristic of this trend are such works as Honegger's *Pacific 231*, John Alden Carpenter's *Skyscrapers*, Antheil's *Ballet mécanique*, Mossolov's *Iron Foundry*, and Chavez's *HP* (Horsepower), all dating from the 1920s. Composers regarded such works as the necessary antidote to the birds, waterfalls, and twilights of the romantics. They did not realize that they had merely exchanged one set of picturesque symbols for another.

Europe after the First World War found surcease for its shattered nerves in athletics and sports. The body itself came to be viewed as a rhythmic machine. It is no accident that the ballet came to provide an important platform for the new music, and that some of the foremost musicians of the twentieth century won success in this field.

Under the influence of primitivism, machine music, sports, and ballet, romantic introspection gave way to twentieth-century physicality. Emotion was replaced by motion. Melody, the stronghold of sentiment, yielded to the irresistible propulsion of rhythm. The shift of emphasis

Charles Sheeler, b. 1893, *American Landscape*. Collection, The Museum of Modern Art, New York. Gift of Mrs. John D. Rockefeller, Jr.

"The machine became a symbol of power, motion, energy; a symbol too of what was aptly called 'the dehumanization of art.'"

is expressed in Stravinsky's dictum that "rhythm and motion, not the element of feeling, are the foundation of musical art."

Satire

Humor and parody offered another way out from romanticism—one especially congenial to the Parisian disciples of Erik Satie, who were determined not to let music take itself seriously, to reject all that smacked of what they called "rhetoric." To be avoided at all costs were the oratory and heroic affirmation of Beethoven, the grandiloquence of Wagner, the self-pity of Mahler. Satie's spiritual heirs—Darius Milhaud, Francis Poulenc, Georges Auric—desired a return to what had always been the courtly ideal of French music: to be pretty, clear, and well-ordered; to please and to entertain.

The trend toward humor and satire found adherents also among other composers, among them Hindemith and Kurt Weill, Stravinsky and Prokofiev, Shostakovich and Walton. There came into being a witty music that made light of the idols of the past; one in which clever-

ness and spoofing took the place of passion. Shostakovich's Polka
from the ballet *The Golden Age* (1930) and Walton's *Façade* (1922),
on poems by Edith Sitwell, illustrate this tendency. Whereas the
nineteenth-century artist was overwhelmed by the world's sorrow, his
twentieth-century counterpart shrugged his shoulders and grinned.
Such an attitude could not produce works to fire the hearts of men,
which indeed was the last thing it desired. It did, however, clear the
air of much that was dated and brought into fashion an objective
everyday music that met certain needs of the new age.

Objectivism

Romantic art was based on the "pathetic fallacy" that the world exists
in our minds. The romantic artist saw nature as the mirror of his moods;
when the heroine was melancholy, it rained. The twentieth century
rejected this sort of subjectivity. It glorified the scientific spirit and
tried to see the world as it really is. The vivid colors of the romantic
imagination were toned down to a sober detachment. Objectivism became still another means of shaking off the grip of the past.

Artists now learned that an object exists independently of their personalities and feelings. They came to believe that a work of art is not
simply a projection of its creator's fantasy, as the romantic period assumed, but that it is rather a self-contained organism obeying laws
and purposes of its own. The artist sets it going and sees that it gets
to its destination. He remains outside his creation; he respects its nature
as pure art. This attitude pervades such works as Stravinsky's *Symphonies for Wind Instruments* and Piano Concerto, and the various
compositions that Hindemith entitled *Kammermusik* (Chamber Music).

Once this point was reached, the stage was set for the neoclassic
attitude that soon took a dominant position in contemporary musical
esthetics.

The New Classicism

One way of rejecting the nineteenth century was to return to the
eighteenth. The movement "back to Bach" assumed impressive proportions in the early Twenties. There was no question here of duplicating
the accents of the Leipzig master; the slogan implied rather a reviving
of certain principles that appeared to have been best understood in his
time. Instead of worshiping at the shrine of Beethoven and Wagner, as
the romantics had done, composers began to emulate the great musicians of the eighteenth century—Handel, Scarlatti, Couperin, Vivaldi—

and the detached, objective style that was supposed to characterize their music.

There was a misconception here. Only the social music of the eighteenth century, the concerti grossi, harpsichord pieces, serenades, and divertimenti, may be said to embody sweet reasonableness and detachment. In their great works Bach and Handel marshaled all the expressive power of which music in their time was capable. But each age re-creates the past in its own image. To the nineteenth century, Bach was a visionary and mystic. For the twentieth he became the model for an amiable counterpoint that jogged along as crisply as ever did a piece of dinner music for a German prince.

Basic to the new esthetic was the notion that the composer's function is not to express emotions but to manipulate abstract combinations of sound. This view found its spokesman in Stravinsky. "I evoke neither human joy nor human sadness," he declared. "I move toward a greater abstraction." A classicist by temperament and conviction, he upheld the rule of law and order in art. Music, he maintained, "is given to us with the sole purpose of establishing an order among things." This order, to be realized, requires a construction. "Once the construction is made and the order achieved, everything is said."

The neoclassicists rid the art of the story-and-picture meanings with which the nineteenth century had endowed it. "People will always insist," Stravinsky points out, "upon looking in music for something that is not there. They never seem to understand that music has an entity of its own apart from anything it may suggest to them." Neoclassicism spelled the end of the symphonic poem and of the Wagnerian "union of the arts" which Stravinsky called "a terrible blow upon music itself." It led composers from program music back to absolute forms.

Having arrived at this position Stravinsky was impelled to reject the connection between music and life. In the heat of polemics he made one of the most amazing statements ever to come from a musician: "I consider that music is by its very nature essentially powerless to express anything at all." In effect, what the composer feels while writing the piece and what the listener feels while hearing it are totally irrelevant to its nature as pure music, as a piece of "sonorous material" that has to be fashioned into a craftsmanlike design.

That Stravinsky was impelled to overstate his case is understandable when we realize that nothing less than a revolution in taste was at stake. Art cannot be separated from human experience to the degree that he would wish. Nor would music have played the part it has in the history of civilization if it were only an objective manipulation of sonorous patterns. As a matter of fact there is more expression in Stravinsky's music than is dreamed of in his philosophy. What he was trying to do was to distinguish as clearly as possible between the expressive content of music, which is an intangible and subjective thing, and its formal content, which exists as an objective fact.

Neoclassicism focused attention on craftsmanship, elegance, taste. It concentrated on technique rather than content and elevated the *how* over the *what,* as generally happens in periods of experimentation. It strove for the ideal balance between form and emotion. It went even further, proclaiming that form *is* emotion. It pointed up the intellectual rather than emotional elements in art, rejecting the idea of passion in favor of a passion for ideas. Future generations will find it significant that in a period of social, political, and artistic upheaval there should have been affirmed so positively the classical virtues of detachment, serenity, and balance.

The New Nationalism

Neoclassicism advocated a return to an international musical culture such as had prevailed in the eighteenth century. At the same time the impulse toward nationalism unleashed by the nineteenth century was too strong to be disregarded. The two tendencies existed side by side, now the one predominating, now the other.

Nationalism in the twentieth century pursued different aims from what it had in the nineteenth. The romantic composers had idealized the life of the people. They fastened on those elements of local color and atmosphere that were picturesque and exportable. The new nationalism went deeper. It approached folk song in the spirit of scientific research, separating authentic peasant music from the watered-down versions of the café musicians. It sought the primeval soul of the nation and encouraged the trend toward primitivism. We shall find this point of view very much to the fore in the works of such men as Béla Bartók, Manuel de Falla, and Ralph Vaughan Williams. In addition, a new type of nationalism came into being that emanated from the culture of cities rather than the countryside and sought to capture the pulse of modern urban life.

Twentieth-century nationalism uncovered the harsh dissonances, percussive rhythms, and archaic modes that became elements of a new tonal language. Its discoveries enriched the resources of music and encouraged the breaking away from nineteenth-century ideals.

Expressionism

If Paris was the center of the new classicism, Vienna remained the stronghold of dying romanticism. From the city of Freud emanated the attempt to capture for art the shadowy terrain of the subconscious.

Expressionism was the German answer to French impressionism. Whereas the Latin genius rejoiced in luminous impressions of the outer world, the Germanic temperament preferred digging down to the subterranean regions of the soul. Expressionism set up inner experience as the only reality. It enthroned the irrational. Through the symbolism of dreams it released the primitive impulses suppressed by the intellect. "There is only one greatest goal toward which the artist strives," declared Arnold Schoenberg: *"To express himself."*

As with impressionism, the impulse for the movement came from painting. Wassily Kandinsky (1866–1944), Paul Klee (1879–1940), Oskar Kokoschka (1886–), and Franz Marc (1880–1916) influenced Schoenberg and his disciples even as the impressionist painters influenced Debussy. The distorted images of their canvases issued from the realm of the unconscious—hallucinated visions that defied conventional notions of beauty in order to achieve the most powerful expression of the artist's inner self. So, too, musical expressionism defied the laws of what had hitherto been accepted as beauty and gave birth to new conceptions of melody, harmony, tonality, rhythm, and form.

Within a twentieth-century framework, expressionism retained certain nineteenth-century attitudes. It inherited the romantic love of overwhelming effect and intensity, of the strange, the macabre, the grotesque. The demonic forces of nature, personified in the romantic theater by sinister villains, were replaced by the demonic forces hidden in the human personality. Like the romantic movement itself, expressionism in music triumphed first in the central European area that lies within the orbit of Germanic culture. The movement reached its peak in the period of the Weimar Republic. It is familiar to Americans through the paintings of Kandinsky and Klee, the writings of Franz Kafka (1883–1924), the dancing of Mary Wigman (made familiar in the United States through the art of Martha Graham), the acting of Conrad Veidt, and through such films as *The Cabinet of Dr. Caligari*. Expressionist tendencies entered European opera through Richard Strauss's *Salome* and *Elektra*, and reached their full tide in the dramatic works of Schoenberg and his disciple Alban Berg. Within the orbit of our own culture, expressionistic elements are to be discerned in the work of such dissimilar artists as James Joyce, William Faulkner, and Tennessee Williams.

Expressionism was the suppressed, the agonized, romanticism of an antiromantic age. Its violence was the violence of a world overwhelmed, one that turned to the unconscious and the irrational in its flight from a reality no longer to be controlled or understood. The musical language of expressionism took its point of departure from the ultrachromatic idiom of *Tristan und Isolde*. It favored a hyperexpressive harmonic language linked to inordinately wide leaps in the melody and to the use of instruments in their extreme registers. Composers hitherto had always set texts in accordance with the natural inflections of the language; expressionist composers deliberately distorted the normal accentuation of words, just as expressionist actors distorted the normal pattern of gesture, in order to secure a heightening of tension, a reality transcending the real. Expressionism allied music to "strong" plots replete with violence and unusual behavior, the best example of which is the hallucinatory atmosphere of Alban Berg's expressionist opera *Wozzeck*. Most important of all, expressionism aspired to maximum intensity all the time, an unflagging, unrelenting intensity; hence it had to reject those elements—such as the consonance in music—which represented a slackening of tension. In its preoccupation with states of soul, expressionism sought ever more powerful means of communicating emotion, and soon reached the boundaries of what was possible within the tonal system. Expressionist music was inevitably impelled to push on to atonality.

CHAPTER 80

Style Elements in Contemporary Music

"Music is now so foolish that I am amazed. Everything that is wrong is permitted, and no attention is paid to what the old generation wrote as composition."

Samuel Scheidt (1651)

The Revitalization of Rhythm

PRIMITIVISM, machine music, ballet, the influence of sports and gymnastics, the hectic pace of city life—all these called into being rhythms more complex than had ever been known before. The new music turned away from the standard patterns of duple, triple, or quadruple meter. Composers explored the possibilities of nonsymmetrical patterns based on odd numbers: five, seven, eleven, thirteen beats to the measure.

In nineteenth-century music a single meter customarily prevailed through an entire movement or section. Now the metrical flow shifted constantly, sometimes with each bar, as in the following excerpt from

Stravinsky's *The Rite of Spring*. Formerly music presented to the ear

one rhythmic pattern at a time, sometimes two. Now composers turned to *polyrhythm*—the use of several rhythmic patterns simultaneously. As a result of these innovations, Western music achieved something of the complexity and suppleness of Asiatic and African rhythms. The music of Stravinsky and Bartók revealed to their contemporaries an explosive, elemental rhythm of enormous force and tension. Both men were partial to the rhythmic ostinato—the use of a striking rhythmic pattern which, by being repeated over and over again, takes on an almost hypnotic power.

Nineteenth-century rhythm was subject to the regular recurrence of accent. Twentieth-century rhythm was emancipated from the "tyranny of the bar line"—that is, from the regular beat. One might say that the new music turned from the rhythmic patterns of metrical poetry to those of free verse, or to the flexible rhythm of prose. The listener will not respond to these new rhythms as he would to a Strauss waltz or a Sousa march, by tapping his foot or waving his hand with the beat. As compensation, he will find rhythms that are plastic in the highest degree, of an almost physical power and drive. The revitalization of rhythm is one of the major achievements of twentieth-century music.

Melody

Rhythm was not the only element in which symmetrical structure was abandoned. Melody was affected too. In the nineteenth century, melody was often based on regular phrases of four or eight measures set off by evenly spaced cadences. This expansive rhetoric is not congenial to the contemporary style.

Composers today do not fill out a phrase to last eight measures because the phrase before was that long. Nor do they develop the neatly balanced repetitions and contrasts that prevailed formerly. Their ideal is a direct forward-driving melody from which all nonessentials have been cut away. They assume a quicker perception on the part of the hearer than did composers in the past. A thing is said once rather than in multiples of four. The result is a taut angular melody of telegraphic conciseness which bears the same relation to the rounded melody of the romantic era as does the lean hard prose of a Hemingway to the rolling cadences of Walter Scott. A splendid example of twentieth-century melody is this wiry, resilient theme from the finale of Bartók's Concerto for Orchestra:

Nineteenth-century melody was fundamentally vocal in character; composers tried to make the instruments "sing." Twentieth-century melody is based primarily on an instrumental conception. It is neither unvocal nor anti-vocal; it is simply not conceived in relation to the voice. Melody today abounds in wide leaps and dissonant intervals; it aims for expressiveness but avoids the obvious; it addresses the mind as well as the heart. The second theme in the opening movement of Shostakovich's First Symphony illustrates the instrumental character of a twentieth-century melody.

Contemporary music is often accused of being unmelodious. This is because it has departed from the romantic ideal. As the public grows familiar with the modern idiom it begins to recognize melodies in many works that at first seemed lacking in melody. Composers have in no sense abandoned melody. Now as in the past, melody is the soul of music. What twentieth-century composers have done is to expand our concept of melody. In so doing they have demonstrated that a melody is a more flexible thing than had been supposed.

Harmony

The triads of traditional harmony, we saw, were formed by combining three tones on every other degree of the scale: 1–3–5 (for example, C-E-G), 2–4–6 (D-F-A), 3–5–7 (E-G-B), and so on. Such chords are based upon intervals of a third. (The interval from step 1 to 3, 2 to 4, or 3 to 5 is known as a third—that is, a distance of three tones counting the lower, the middle, and the upper tone.) By carrying this process of construction farther, composers developed four-tone combinations known as *seventh chords* (steps 1–3–5–7), so-called because there is an interval of seven steps from the lowest to the highest tone of the chord. Also five-tone combinations known as *ninth chords* (steps 1–3–5–7–9).

Carrying the traditional method of building chords one step farther, twentieth-century composers added another "story" to the chord, thus forming highly dissonant combinations of six and seven tones—for instance, chords based on steps 1–3–5–7–9–11 and 1–3–5–7–9–11–13 of the scale. The emergence of these complex "skyscraper" chords imparted a greater degree of tension to music than had ever existed before.

chord   chord
of the 11th   of the 13th

A chord of seven tones, such as the one shown above, hardly possesses the unity of the classical triad. It is composed of no less than three separate triads: the I chord (steps 1–3–5), the V chord (steps 5–7–9), and the II chord (steps 2–4–6 or 9–11–13). In this formation the Dominant chord is directly superimposed on the Tonic, so that Tonic and Dominant, the two poles of classical harmony, are brought together in a kind of montage. What our forebears were in the habit of hearing successively, we today are expected to hear—and grasp—simultaneously. Such a chord, which contains all seven steps of the major scale, not only adds spice to the traditional triad, but also increases the volume of sound, an effect much prized by composers. Here are two effective examples.

Bruckner   Milhaud

A seven-tone "skyscraper" is, in effect, a *polychord*. It is a block of sound that is heard on two or three planes. A succession of such chords creates several planes of harmony. One of the outstanding achievements of the new age is a kind of *polyharmony* in which the composer plays two or more streams of harmony against each other, exactly as in former times single strands of melody were combined. The interplay of the several independent streams adds a new dimension to the harmonic space. The following is a famous example of polyharmony from Stravinsky's *Petrushka*. The clash of the two harmonic currents produces a

Pierre August Renoir, 1843-1919, *Lady at the Piano*. (The Art Institute of Chicago) "They preferred everyday scenes of middle-class life."

Edgar Degas, 1834-1917, *The Millinery Shop* (The Art Institute of Chicago)

"Derided at first, the impressionists soon emerged as the most important school of European painting."

bright, virile sonority that typifies the twentieth-century revolt against the sweet sound of the romantic era:

The interval of a third was associated with the music of the eighteenth and nineteenth centuries. To free themselves from the sound of the past, composers cast about for other methods of chord construction; they began to base chords on the interval of the fourth. This turning from *tertial* to *quartal* harmony constitutes one of the important differences between nineteenth- and twentieth-century music. Chords based on fourths have a pungency and freshness that are very much of the new age, as the following examples demonstrate.

Schoenberg, *Chamber Symphony*, Opus 9.

Composers also based their harmonies on other intervals. Here is a chord of piled-up fifths from Stravinsky's *Rite of Spring,* and cluster chords based on seconds from Bartók's *Mikrokosmos.*

The Emancipation of the Dissonance

The history of music, we have seen, has been the history of a steadily increasing tolerance on the part of the human ear. Throughout this long evolution one factor remained constant. A clear distinction was drawn between dissonance, the element of tension, and consonance, the element of rest. Consonance was the norm, dissonance the temporary disturbance. Twentieth-century harmony has wiped out this distinction. In many contemporary works tension tends to become the norm—a clear case of art imitating life. The difference between consonance and dissonance is considered nowadays to be only a difference in degree. "Dissonant tones," Schoenberg taught, "appear later among the overtones, for which reason the ear is less acquainted with them. Dissonances are only the remote consonances." In other words, the distinction is relative rather than absolute. A chord is no longer held to be consonant because of its intrinsic character, but because it is less dissonant than the chords that preceded it. Which means that it can serve as a final cadence only because it is less dissonant than what came before (see the example on p. 492).

Twentieth-century composers emancipated the dissonance, first, by making it more familiar to the ear; second, by freeing it from the obligation to resolve to consonance. Thereby they expanded the traditional notion of what is beautiful in music. They no longer sought the "harmonious harmony" of which Debussy dreamed. They preferred percussive harmonies, of a degree of friction never known before. To ears that only recently had fed on the harmonies of Brahms and Tchaikovsky, the new procedures seemed like the most brutal cacophony. The works of Schoenberg, Stravinsky, Bartók, and their fellows evoked sensations verging on physical pain. Human nature, however, is more adaptable than we realize. Today the same music is listened to with pleasure by a rapidly growing public.

Texture: Dissonant Counterpoint

The nineteenth century was preoccupied with harmony; the twentieth emphasizes counterpoint. The romantic composer thought in terms of vertical mass; the contemporary composer thinks largely in terms of horizontal line. Where the romantics exalted the magic sonority of the chord, their successors stress a neat fabric of tightly woven lines. This is part of the movement "back to Bach" and to the earlier masters of contrapuntal art.

By substituting line for mass, composers lightened the swollen sound of the postromantic period. The new music swept away both the romantic cloudburst and the impressionist haze. In their stead was installed a well-ventilated texture of widely spaced lines from whose interplay the music derived its tension; a texture suitable for a neo-classic age.

Consonance unites, dissonance separates. Composers began to use dissonance to separate the independent lines, to set them off against one another. Counterpoint in Bach's time centered about the euphonious intervals—the third and sixth. Twentieth-century counterpoint turned to the astringent seconds and sevenths, as in the following example from Hindemith's *Ludus Tonalis:*

Or the independence of the voices might be heightened by putting them in different keys.

Thus came into being a linear texture based on dissonant counterpoint, objective, logical, powered by motor rhythms, and marked by solid workmanship as by sober sentiment. This new style is to be found in many modern works, for example in the Piano Concerto and Piano Sonata of Stravinsky, in the String Quartets of Bartók and the chamber works of Hindemith.

Orchestration

Orchestral writing followed the same antiromantic direction as prevailed in other departments of the art. The rich sonorities of nineteenth-century orchestration were alien to the modern temper. The trend was toward a smaller orchestra and a leaner sound, one that was hard, bright, sober. "One is tired," wrote Stravinsky, "of being saturated with timbres." Similarly Schoenberg: "Perhaps the art of orchestration has become too popular, and interesting-sounding pieces are often produced for no better reason than that which dictates the making of typewriters and fountain pens in different colors."

The decisive factor in the handling of the orchestra was the change to a linear texture—the texture, for example, of Stravinsky's *Symphony of Psalms* or Schoenberg's *Variations for Orchestra*. Color came to be used in the new music not so much for atmosphere or enchantment as for bringing out the lines of counterpoint and of form. Whereas the nineteenth-century orchestrator made his colors swim together, the neoclassicist desires each to stand out against the mass. Instruments are used in their unusual registers. The emotional crescendo and diminuendo of romantic music gives way to even levels of soft or loud. This less expressive scheme revives the solid areas of light and shade of the age of Bach. The string section loses its traditional role as the heart of the orchestra. Its tone is felt to be too personal. Attention is focused on the more objective winds. Because of improvements in construction and technique, the woodwind and brass achieve added importance. Their music abounds in special effects such as muted tubas and the trombone glissando. There is a movement away from brilliancy of sound. The darker instruments come to the fore—viola, bassoon, trombone. The romantic horn is supplanted in favor by the more incisive trumpet. The emphasis on rhythm brings the percussion group into greater prominence than ever before. Percussion sound sometimes pervades the entire orchestra. The piano, which in the romantic era was pre-eminently a solo instrument, finds a place for itself in the orchestral ensemble, where its timbre contributes a distinctive color to the tone mass. Both in solo and ensemble music, composers explore the piano's capacity for percussive rhythm, frequently treating it as a kind of xylophone in a mahogany box and in this way opening up new possibilities for the favored instrument of Chopin and Liszt.

The new music revives the eighteenth-century practice of pitting one instrument against another; that is, the *concertante* principle. Since the instruments function more and more as soloists rather than as part of a group, orchestral sound draws steadily closer to the chamber-music ideal. The chamber orchestra becomes a mainstay of the new classicism. Also, contemporary composers place great emphasis on chamber music. The most diverse ensembles are cultivated—strings, winds, or combinations of both. All in all, the new music rejects the romantic use of sonority as an end in itself. Twentieth-century musicians have restored color to its classical function, as the obedient handmaiden of idea, line, structure, and design.

Revival of Absolute Forms

Neoclassicism led the way back to the abstract forms. The symphony, concerto, solo sonata, and various types of chamber music took a new lease on life, as did a number of old forms: theme and variations, suite, toccata, fugue, passacaglia and chaconne, concerto grosso, and the social forms of the Viennese period, the divertimento and serenade.

The preoccupation with form that tends to elevate it above expressive values is known as formalism. Ours, it goes without saying, is a formalist age. Purity of line and proportion are the aim of the new classicism as they were of the old. The contemporary composer strives for the classical ideal: the unity of content and form. Stravinsky's rejection of emotional expression through music goes hand in hand with his emphasis upon formal beauty: "One could not better define the sensation produced by music than by saying that it is identical with that evoked by contemplating the interplay of architectural forms. Goethe thoroughly understood this when he called architecture frozen music."

Twentieth-century music has altered materially the sonata form of Haydn and Mozart. The movement from home key to contrasting key and back means far less today than when the major-minor system was at its height. Contemporary composers have cut away many details of the Exposition-Development-Restatement pattern. What they retain is the impressive architecture and the flexibility of a form that enables them to present purely musical ideas in a purely musical way. They prize the sonata and symphony as a construction. They feel that it suits the abstract nature of their material. Their attitude is summed up in Prokofiev's observation, "I want nothing better than sonata form, which contains everything necessary for my purpose."

There were times during the romantic period when the grand form was in danger of being swamped by program music and the short lyric forms. Today, in an astonishing renewal of vitality, it has re-established its supremacy.

The Influence of Jazz

America's specific contribution to world music invaded Europe shortly after the First World War. Immediately it claimed the attention of serious musicians. Composers through the ages vitalized their art by using popular dance forms. Now, at a time when a new rhythmic conception was taking shape, the syncopations and polyrhythms of the jazz band opened up fascinating perspectives.

The vogue of primitivism made Europeans particularly susceptible to the exotic. They were enchanted by a music whose ancestry went back to the African drums, that reflected both the restless American temperament and the Negro's genius for rhythm. The excitement of jazz seemed to echo the pulse of big-city life. Also, the chamber-music character of the jazz band appealed to the time. Here was a strictly functional ensemble of soloists in which piano, string bass, banjo, and drums supplied the rhythmic-harmonic background while clarinet, saxophone, trumpet, and trombone carried the melody. The absence of string tone in many bands produced a particular sonority characteristic of the twentieth century. Instruments favored by the new music, such as trumpet and trombone, attained a level of virtuoso playing in the jazz band that was never known before. Here originated all sorts of experiments with mutes and special ways of playing that are now finding their way into the symphony orchestra.

Jazz music, with its independent melody lines and rhythms, wove a contrapuntal tissue as complex as it was transparent. The linear texture of jazz, its unconventional sound and its rhapsodic improvising made a strong impact on the European mind. Pieces embodying the spirit of ragtime and the blues appeared in the instrumental literature of the 1920s as well as in opera. Among the works that reflected the jazz influence were *Golliwog's Cakewalk* by Debussy, Erik Satie's ballet *Parade*, Stravinsky's *Ragtime for Eleven Instruments* and *Piano Rag*, and Darius Milhaud's ballets *Le Boeuf sur le toit* and *La Création du monde*. Composers as diverse as Ravel, Honegger, Hindemith, Krenek, Kurt Weill, and Constant Lambert were among the Europeans who fell under the lure of the importation from America. It is worthy of note that musicians abroad were ahead of their American colleagues in realizing the possibilities of jazz as an art form.

Jazz assumed some strange shapes as soon as it left American hands. Nevertheless, the new classicism for a time advanced under the twin banners of Bach and jazz—a formidable combination.

Composer and Public

The changes we have just described swept away the landmarks that had guided listeners for decades through the maze of sound. A gap ensued between composer and public whose like had never been before. The composer found himself in a dilemma. On the one hand he was resolved to exclude from his art the rhetoric that had enabled Handel, Beethoven, and Verdi to address the multitude. On the other he found himself creating in a vacuum, writing advanced works for a coterie of musicians like himself. Lacking a mass base, the new music was soon the exclusive concern of the advance-guard. The public, excluded, found its nourishment in the music of the past.

This cultural lag was aggravated by the rise of the radio, which brought the masses into the ranks of the music-consuming public. Millions were discovering the works of Beethoven, Chopin, and Tchaikovsky even as, at the other end, an isolated group of composers was demolishing the foundation on which this music rested. The new music-lovers, having just entered the gate, could hardly be expected to explore uncharted territory beyond. Equally impervious to the new music was the generation of concert-goers who knew their Brahms and were content with same. A vicious circle ensued. The more the composer was cut off from the life about him, the freer he felt to experiment. The more he experimented, the greater was his isolation.

The new music encountered another serious obstacle in the powerful music industry. Concert managements, record companies, publishing houses, radio stations, and coast-to-coast broadcasts sponsored by giant corporations represent huge investments and have to reach the widest possible audiences. This can be done only by presenting music that has won approval. Here was an even more vicious circle. Modern music could become popular only if the public had the opportunity to hear it again and again. But those in control did not permit it to be heard at all on the ground that it was not popular.

It was in the face of such difficulties that the new music had to make its way. And make its way it did, in accordance with the law which throughout history has decreed that change be always resisted yet always prevail. The more venturesome performers and conductors began to present the new works. The festivals and concerts devoted to contemporary music came to reach an ever wider audience. Certain compositions caught on and paved the way for others. What had seemed strange and difficult in the first quarter century became less so in the second.

A parallel development took place among composers. The wild experimentation of the 1910s—the period of breaking away from tradition —was followed, around 1920, by the new classicism. After 1930 the tide turned. The public began to accept contemporary music; a more relaxed atmosphere prevailed: one no longer had to be modern at all costs. Besides, the advances had been so breath-taking that it was necessary to pause and consolidate one's gains. A new conservatism set in, with the curious result that composers born after 1900 were markedly less radical than the earlier generation had been. It even ceased to be fashionable to sneer at the romantic period. Stravinsky announced his admiration for such nineteenth-century musicians as Gounod and Delibes, Weber and Rossini, Glinka, Verdi, Tchaikovsky. The pendulum began to swing toward a reinstatement of flowing melody, toward a simplification of means and an emphasis upon the emotional element in music; in short, toward a new romanticism.

More important, composers began to break through their isolation. There was a turning to mass-audience forms such as ballet, opera, and film music. A widespread attempt took shape to bring music back into contact with life. The gap between composer and public began to close, each moving to meet the other halfway. Gradually contemporary music took its place as a rounded expression of our culture. And the creative musician affirmed anew that deep need to reach out to one's fellows which no artist, being human, can ever escape.

ﾟﾟﾟ CHAPTER 81 ﾟﾟﾟ

New Conceptions of Tonality

"Every tone relationship that has been used too often must finally be regarded as exhausted. It ceases to have power to convey a thought worthy of it. Therefore every composer is obliged to invent anew, to present new tone relations."

Arnold Schoenberg

In the major-minor system seven tones were chosen out of the twelve to form a key. This "seven out of twelve" way of hearing music has been expanded in the twentieth century to a "twelve out of twelve"—that is,

the free use of twelve tones around a center. The new approach retains
the basic principle of traditional tonality, loyalty to the Tonic; but, by
considering the five chromatic tones to be as much a part of the key as
the seven diatonic ones, it immeasurably expands the borders of tonality. In other words, the chromatic scale of seven basic tones plus five
visitors has given way to a scale of twelve equal members.

This expanded conception of tonality has not only done away with
the distinction between diatonic and chromatic, but also wiped out the
distinction between major and minor that was so potent a source of
contrast in the classic-romantic era. The composers of the eighteenth
and nineteenth centuries presented major-minor in succession; contemporary composers present them simultaneously. A piece today will
be, let us say, in the tonality of F (F major-minor), using all the
twelve tones around the center F, instead of dividing them, as was
done in the past, into two separate groups of seven. This serves to
create an ambiguous tonality which is highly congenial to the taste of
our time.

In general, the key is no longer so clearly defined an area in musical
space as it used to be, and the shift from one key center to another is
made with a dispatch that puts to shame the most exuberant modulations of the Wagner era. Transitional passages are dispensed with. One
tonality is simply displaced by another, in a way that keeps both the
music and the listener on the move. An excellent example is the popular
theme from *Peter and the Wolf*. Prokofiev is extremely fond of this kind
of displacement. (The asterisk indicates change of tonality.)

In similar fashion chords utterly foreign to the tonality are included,
not even as modulations but simply as an extension of the key to a new
tonal plane. As a result a passage will sound A-majorish, shall we say,
rather than in A major.

Expansion of tonality was encouraged by a number of factors: interest in the exotic scales of Bali, Java, and other Far Eastern cultures; use
of scales derived from the folk music of areas more or less outside the
major-minor orbit, such as those of Russia, Scandinavia, Spain, Hungary and other Balkan countries; revival of interest in the medieval

church modes and in composers who wrote long before the major-minor
system evolved, such as the masters of fifteenth- and sixteenth-century
counterpoint. The musicians of our era have gone far afield both in
time and space in order to find new means of revitalizing their art.

Polytonality

Tonality implies the supremacy of a single key and a single tone center. Composers in the past made the most out of the contrast between
two keys heard in succession. The next step was to heighten the contrast
by presenting them simultaneously.

To confront the ear with two keys at the same time means to depart
radically from the basic principle of traditional harmony. *Polytonality*
—the use of two or more keys together—came to the fore in the music
of Stravinsky and Milhaud, whence it entered the vocabulary of the
age. Toward the end of a piece one key is generally permitted to
assert itself over the others. In this way the impression is restored of
orderly progression toward a central point.

Polytonality is used to bring out the different levels or planes of the
harmony. By putting two or more streams of music in different keys
the friction between them is immeasurably heightened. Piano music
especially lends itself to this usage, the right and left hands playing
in different keys. An example is the following passage from Prokofiev's
Sarcasms:

Since the tension comes from the clash of keys, each stream of harmony must be rooted solidly in its own key. Stravinsky's *Petrushka,* for
example, despite its daring harmonic combinations has a surprisingly
C-major look—that is, comparatively few sharps or flats: what is
nowadays referred to as "white" music. The tendency toward "white-
ness" was one of the characteristics of Parisian neoclassicism.

By the same token Vienna, the center of expressionism, inherited the
fondness for chromatic harmony that was at the heart of German
romanticism.

Atonality

Although the principle of key was flexible enough in adjusting to the needs of the new music, there was bound to appear a musician who questioned whether such adjustment was at all possible. This was Arnold Schoenberg, who proclaimed that the concept of key had outlived its usefulness.

Schoenberg rebelled against the "tyranny" of the Tonic. He maintained that as long as the tones of the key, whether seven or twelve, were kept subordinate to a central tone, it was impossible to utilize all the resources of the chromatic scale. He advocated doing away with the Tonic—in other words, treating the twelve tones as of equal importance. In this way, he maintained, music would be freed from a number of procedures that had ceased to be fruitful.

To do away with the Tonic means abandoning a principle as fundamental in the musical universe as gravitation is in the physical. How fundamental is evident in the upward pull of the seventh step of the major scale, *ti*, to the *do*. Schoenberg pointed out that since the major-minor system had not existed longer than three centuries, there was no reason to suppose that it could not be superseded. "Tonality is not an eternal law of music," he asserted, "but simply a means toward the achievement of musical form." The time had come, according to him, to seek new means.

To the music of Schoenberg and his school there attached itself the label *atonality*. He disliked the term as strongly as Debussy did impressionism. "I regard the expression atonal as meaningless. Atonal can only signify something that does not correspond to the nature of tone." However, the name has persisted.

Atonal music is much more of an innovation than is polytonal, for it rejects the framework of key. It excludes consonance which, according to Schoenberg, is no longer capable of making an impression. Its starting point is dissonance; it moves from one level of dissonance to another. There results a music that functions always at maximum tension, without areas of relaxation. This circumstance imparts to it its furious restlessness, what Schoenberg's biographer Dika Newlin calls "its well-nigh hysterical emotionality." Dissonance resolving to consonance was, symbolically, an optimistic act. It affirmed the triumph of rest over tension, of order over chaos. Atonal music, significantly, appeared at a time in European culture when belief in that triumph was sorely shaken.

Having accepted the necessity of moving beyond the existing tonal system, Schoenberg sought a unifying principle that would take the place of the key. He found this in a strict technique that he had worked

out by the early 1920s. He named it "the method of composing with
twelve tones."

The Twelve-Tone Method

"I was always occupied," Schoenberg declared, "with the desire to
base the structure of my music *consciously* on a unifying idea." The
twelve-tone technique made it possible for him to achieve coherence
and unity in a musical composition without recourse to traditional
procedures such as tonal organization, harmonic relationships, expansion and development of themes, and the articulation of symmetrical
phrases. According to Schoenberg's method, every composition is based
on an arbitrary arrangement of the twelve chromatic tones which is
called a *tone row*—or, as he terms it, a basic set. This row or set is
the unifying idea that is the basis of that particular composition, and
serves as the source of all the musical events that take place in it.
The term *serial technique* is often used in this connection, an allusion
to the series of twelve tones. European writers prefer the expression
dodecaphonic, which is the Greek equivalent of *twelve-tone.*

The twelve-tone set differs from a scale in one important respect.
A scale is a traditional pattern that serves as the basic series for
hundreds of composers and thousands of compositions. It soon becomes
familiar to the listener; any departure from the pattern is at once perceptible to the ear. The tone row, on the other hand, is the basic series
of a particular composition, constituting a unique configuration of the
twelve tones not to be found in any other piece. Since the twelve tones
of the row are regarded as equally important, no one of them is allowed
to appear more than once in the series lest it take on the prominence
of a Tonic. (The tone may be repeated immediately, but this is regarded as an extension, not a new appearance.) When the basic set
has unfolded it is repeated throughout the work, with the twelve tones
always in the same order. The row may be turned upside down (inversion); it may be presented backward (retrograde); or upside down
and backward (retrograde of the inversion). Each of these four versions—the original row and its three variants—may begin on any one
of the twelve tones of the scale, giving forty-eight possibilities. The
movement from one level to a higher or lower is loosely analogous to
the passing from one key to another (modulation) in the old tonal
architecture. The tone row, in fine, pervades the entire fabric of the
composition, engendering not only the melody but the contrapuntal
lines that unfold against it; also the harmony, since segments of the row
may appear in vertical formation as chords. Thus, the unifying idea
creates all the other ideas within a piece.

The twelve-tone method represents Schoenberg's concept of "perpetual variation," according to which the maximum diversity of musical forms is derived from a minimum of material. It is a kind of variation technique, perhaps the most highly integrated that ever was. "The main advantage of this method of composing with twelve tones," Schoenberg declared, "is its unifying effect. I believe that when Richard Wagner introduced his *Leitmotive*—for the same purpose as that for which I introduced my Basic Set—he may have said, 'Let there be unity!'" Since the possible combinations of twelve tones in forty-eight positions have been calculated to add up to almost half a billion, dodecaphonic composers have a long way to go before they exhaust the possibilities of the system.

The basic set, of course, establishes not only a series of pitches but —even more important—a series of interval relationships. The persistence of this series of intervals in the melodies, harmonies, and counterpoints of an extended composition cannot but result in the closest possible relationship among these three dimensions of the musical tissue. The old distinction between melody and accompaniment is thereby done away with, the result being a texture of unparalleled homogeneity. Twelve-tone music, in short, seeks the utmost variety within the most stringent unity.

The following example shows the four versions of the basic set of Schoenberg's Wind Quintet, Opus 26. O stands for the original form, R for retrograde, I for inversion, and RI for the retrograde of the inversion. E-flat in the original version is the equivalent of D-sharp in the inversion.

All this, you will object, is quite arbitrary. To which your Schoenbergian will retort that all art is arbitrary. Precisely its artifice makes it art. Musical composition has always had its rules of the game. If they seem to be more in evidence here, it is only because the system is new and its procedures are unfamiliar. The only valid criterion is: are Schoenberg's rules such as to enable a creative musician to express his thoughts, his feelings, and his time? Schoenberg's followers answer with an emphatic yes.

Dodecaphonic melody differs from the traditional kind in one im-

portant respect. Melody as we have come to know it springs out of what
the voice can do. Therefore it generally lies in one register. But in
twelve-tone music the octaves are regarded as interchangeable. The
seven C's of the tone-range are no longer regarded as so many individual tones, but rather as representatives of the "pitch class" C. The same
holds for the D's, the E's, and the rest. From the dodecaphonic point
of view, consequently, music no longer consists of the eighty-eight
tones that make up the piano keyboard. Rather, only the twelve basic
tones exist, no matter in which octave they happen to appear.

This octave equivalence destroys the conventional relationships we
have attached to tones, giving them a new kind of meaning. The successive notes of a melody may appear in different octaves—even in
vocal music—which produces the enormous leaps and zigzag melody
line so characteristic of dodecaphonic music. In addition, the gravita-

tional pull attaching to tones in the traditional harmonic system is
weakened or wholly destroyed. For example, the strongest drive in
tonal music is that of the seventh tone of the scale to the Tonic (*ti* to
do; for example, B ascending to C). This drive is circumvented in
twelve-tone music if the B ascends a ninth to the C of the octave above,
or descends a seventh to the C below. As a matter of fact, intervals of
the seventh and ninth are extremely prominent in twelve-tone music,
as are augmented and diminished intervals. The major, minor, and
perfect intervals are too fraught with tonal implications to be ad-
mitted freely into the dodecaphonic realm.

Twelve-tone thinking is essentially contrapuntal thinking. It represents a horizontal-linear conception of music, with emphasis on melodic
line rather than on the harmonic mass. This conception is implemented
by the devices of counterpoint: canonic and fugal imitation; augmentation and diminution (the duplication of a motive in longer or shorter
note values); inversion; and crab canon or *cancrizans* (the imitation
of a motive backward). The twelve-tone method eliminates the repetitions and sequences, the balanced phrases and cadences of the older
style. The dynamic of this music requires that no thought ever be
repeated or duplicated save in some new form. As Schoenberg advised
his students: "Never do what a copyist can do instead." His esthetic
calls for a terse language of telegraphic compression which says "the

most important things in the most concentrated manner in every fraction of the time."

The tone row is not to be regarded as the theme of the piece. By the time a dodecaphonic composer has presented it in inverted and retrograde forms, and derived from it all his melodies, harmonies, and contrapuntal lines, in constantly varied rhythms, the row will have lost its identity as far as the ordinary ear is concerned. You will hardly be able to follow its peregrinations as you can follow the course of a theme in a symphony. Actually, the tone row is what you do *not* hear (or if you do, it is mainly at the beginning of the piece, where the row is generally presented in its basic form). However, since the row determines the choice and succession of the intervals, it inevitably shapes the over-all sound. More important, it pervades the thinking of the composer, providing him with the framework for his piece, even if that framework is no more visible to the beholder than is the steel skeleton that holds up a building. In recent developments the serial concept—that is, the concept of a series of musical phenomena in a predetermined order—has been applied not only to melody but also to rhythm, dynamics, timbres, and densities.

Twelve-tone music, clearly, unites two contradictory elements. On the one hand it embodies an intensely expressive content based on an ultrachromatic idiom. On the other, it follows strict forms and objective procedures. It is almost as if Schoenberg had united in his art the two opposites in the German character: its love of the hyperemotional and the irrational, and its equally strong love of logic and order. One may detect here a good example of overcompensation. Precisely because the idiom is so supercharged with feeling and the sound is so volatile, the sonorous flow is chained within successions of notes calculated to the minutest detail, controlled by as rigorous a set of formal devices as ever artist imposed upon himself. The first masters of the style display all the logic of this rigidly organized system; yet over their music brood the troubled visions that agonized the consciousness of Europe in the aftermath of the First World War.

The Schoenbergian method resembles Stravinskyan neoclassicism in several ways: both emphasize the abstract nature of music, and both focus attention on an elaborate scheme of structural devices. Both represent a phase in which the enjoyment of music has become increasingly intellectual, and in which emotional factors are subjected to an elaborate formalism. Both too return to the kind of thematic-motivic work to which the impressionists and post-impressionists were so bitterly opposed.

To Schoenberg's adherents, twelve-tone music is a concept of truth and beauty to which they are dedicated with an almost religious fervor.

In a few decades, they are persuaded, twelve-tone music will be the only music; for it alone makes possible further advance. "Indeed," writes Schoenberg, "tonal is perhaps nothing else than what is understood *today* and atonal what will be understood in the future."

All the same, many musicians have great difficulty in forming a connection with it, for they suddenly find themselves in a realm where all the landmarks of music as they know it have been swept away. Some, like Hindemith, oppose the twelve-tone style because it repudiates what they regard as the immutable law of any organized musical art—gravitation to the Tonic. Others reject it because it is completely unrelated to folk and popular song; and because its jagged melody lines, with their enormous leaps, are antivocal. They maintain that the formal procedures of twelve-tone music bear no relation to what the ear can hear, that dissonance unrelieved by consonance becomes monotonous, and that twelve-tone music moves within an extremely narrow expressive range.

Despite these strictures, the devotees of the twelve-tone method have gained tremendous influence in the past few years. If their music does not reach the big public (any more than does *Finnegans Wake*), it does challenge the musical intelligentsia, and it is exerting a fruitful influence even on those composers who do not accept its ideology *in toto*. For it opens up exciting new ways of utilizing the resources of the twelve-tone scale. Today dodecaphonic thinking represents the most advanced line of thought in musical esthetics, and has emerged as a profoundly significant movement on the contemporary scene.

CHAPTER 82

Igor Stravinsky (b. 1882)

"I hold that it was a mistake to consider me a revolutionary. If one only need break habit in order to be labeled a revolutionary, then every artist who has something to say and who in order to say it steps outside the bounds of established convention could be considered revolutionary."

IT IS granted to certain artists to embody the profoundest impulses of their time and to affect its artistic life in the most powerful fashion. Such an artist is Igor Stravinsky, the Russian composer who for half a century has given impetus to the main currents in contemporary music.

His Life

Stravinsky was born in Oranienbaum, a summer resort not far from St. Petersburg (Leningrad), where his parents lived. He grew up in a musical environment; his father was the leading bass at the Imperial

Igor Stravinsky, a portrait by Pablo Picasso, b. 1881.

Opera. Although he was taught to play the piano, his musical education was kept on the amateur level. His parents wanted him to study law. He matriculated at the University of St. Petersburg and embarked on a legal career, meanwhile continuing his musical studies. At twenty he submitted his work to Rimsky-Korsakov, with whom he subsequently worked for three years.

Success came early to Stravinsky. His music attracted the notice of Serge Diaghilev, the legendary impresario of the Russian Ballet, who commissioned Stravinsky to write the music for *L'Oiseau de feu* (The Firebird), which was produced in 1910. Stravinsky was twenty-eight when he arrived in Paris to attend the rehearsals. Diaghilev pointed him out to the ballerina Tamara Karsavina with the words, "Mark him well—he is a man on the eve of fame."

The Firebird was followed, a year later, by *Petrushka*. Presented with Nijinsky and Karsavina in the leading roles, this production secured Stravinsky's position in the forefront of the modern movement in art. In the spring of 1913 was presented the third and most spectacular of the ballets Stravinsky wrote for Diaghilev, *Le Sacre du printemps* (The Rite of Spring). The opening night was one of the most scandalous in modern musical history; the revolutionary score touched off a near-riot. People hooted, screamed, slapped each other, and were persuaded that what they were hearing "constituted a blasphemous attempt to destroy music as an art." A year later the composer was vindicated when the *Sacre*, presented at a symphony concert under Pierre Monteux, was received with enthusiasm and established itself as one of the masterpieces of the new music.

The outbreak of war in 1914 brought to an end the whole way of life on which Diaghilev's sumptuous dance spectacles depended. Stravinsky, with his wife and children, took refuge in Switzerland, their home for the next six years. The difficulty of assembling large bodies of performers during the war worked hand in hand with his inner evolution as an artist: he moved away from the grand scale of the first three ballets to works more intimate in spirit and modest in dimension.

The Russian Revolution had severed Stravinsky's ties with his homeland. In 1920 he settled in France, where he remained until 1939. During these years Stravinsky concertized extensively throughout Europe, performing his own works as pianist and conductor. He also paid two visits to the United States. In 1939 he was invited to deliver the Charles Eliot Norton lectures at Harvard University. He was there when the Second World War broke out, and decided to live in this country. He settled in California, outside Los Angeles, and in 1945 became an American citizen. The observance of his eightieth birthday in June 1962 showed that he was revered not only in his adopted country but throughout the world.

His Music

Stravinsky has shown a continuous development throughout his career. With inexhaustible avidity he has tackled new problems and pressed for new solutions. It happened several times that a certain phase of his development pointed in the opposite direction from what had come before. Seen in retrospect, however, the various periods reveal themselves to have been stages in a steady growth toward greater abstraction of style and refinement of thought.

This evolution led from the post-impressionism of *The Firebird* and the audacities of *The Rite of Spring* to the austerely controlled classicism of his maturity. In the course of it he has laid ever greater emphasis upon tradition and discipline. "The more art is controlled, limited, worked over, the more it is free." He consistently extols the element of construction as a safeguard against excess of feeling. "Composing for me is putting into an order a certain number of sounds according to certain interval relationships." A piece of music is for him first and foremost a problem. "I cannot compose until I have decided what problem I must solve." The problem is esthetic, not personal. As one of his biographers points out, "We find his musical personality in his works but not his personal joys or sorrows."

Stravinsky's doctrine is of course a projection of the needs—and the limitations—of his temperament. What makes it significant is that this personal creed has become the leading esthetic of our time, even as Wagner's became that of the nineteenth century. For all his emphasis upon the artist's detachment, Stravinsky's is a personal style. Every bar of his music bears the signature of one who is a natural, a spontaneous musician. His esthetic outlook belongs in the framework of his time. His music reaches beyond it.

Stravinsky, we noted, was a leader in the revitalization of European rhythm. His first success was won as a composer of ballet, where rhythm is allied with body movement and expressive gesture. His is a rhythm of unparalleled dynamic power, furious yet controlled. It has the elemental force that creates forms and ideas. In harmony Stravinsky has reacted against the restless chromaticism of the romantic period. No matter how daring his harmony, he retains a robust sense of key. He achieves excitement by superposing streams of chords in different keys. For all its explosive force his harmony, like his rhythm, is immensely refined. Stravinsky's subtle sense of sound makes him one of the great orchestrators. Unmistakably his is that enameled brightness of sonority, and a texture so clear that, as Diaghilev remarked, "One could see through it with one's ears." Stravinsky was one of those who led contemporary music to purity of color. The classicist in him demands that color serve form and design. He achieves his effects with astonishing economy of means. Whereas a Richard Strauss puts down as many notes as possible, Stravinsky writes as few.

The national element predominates in his early works; as in *The Firebird* and in *Petrushka,* in which he found his personal style. The *Sacre du printemps* re-creates the rites of pagan Russia. To the fashionable audience that frequented Diaghilev's dance entertainments this savage score came as an electrifying shock. Its primitive force, set forth by a powerful creative imagination, brought to the fore what was practically a new tonal language.

The decade of the First World War saw the turn toward simplification of means. *L'Histoire du soldat* (The Soldier's Tale, 1918) is a dance drama for four characters who speak, mime, and act. The action is based on a Russian folk tale about the deserter who sells his soul and his fiddle to the Devil. It is an intimate theater work accompanied by a seven-piece band consisting of violin and double bass, clarinet and bassoon, cornet and trombone, and a drummer who plays various percussion instruments. Rich in fantasy and possessed of an uncanny atmosphere, this poetic theater piece is one of the distinguished works of our time.

The works written after the First World War show the composer moving away from the Russian style of his first period toward the French-international orientation of his second. In the ballet *Pulcinella* (1919) he affirmed his kinship with the past. Scored for voice and small orchestra, the piece was based on themes drawn from several instrumental works ascribed to Giovanni Battista Pergolesi (1710–36). At the same time his "passion for jazz," as he called it, gave rise to the *Ragtime for Eleven Instruments* (1918) and the *Piano-Rag Music* (1919). There followed the "burlesque tale" *Le Renard* (The Fox, 1922), for four vocalists, dancers, and chamber orchestra, based on a folk story that was put into dramatic form by Stravinsky himself. *Les Noces* (The Wedding, 1923) is a stylization of a Russian peasant wedding. Four singers and a chorus support the dancers, accompanied by four pianos and a diversified percussion group. This ballet-cantata, with its clear glacial sound and its percussive use of the piano, boasts one of Stravinsky's most powerful scores.

The neoclassical period was ushered in by the *Symphonies of Wind Instruments* (1920), dedicated to the memory of Debussy. The instrumental works that followed incarnate the principle of the old concerto grosso—the pitting against each other of contrasting tone masses. This "return to Bach" crystallized in the Concerto for Piano and Wind Orchestra and the Serenade in A, which date from the years 1924–25. To this period belongs also the Piano Sonata. Stravinsky's writing for the piano derives from the crisp harpsichord style of the eighteenth century rather than from the singing Chopin style of the nineteenth.

His devotion to neoclassicism was hailed in certain quarters as conclusive proof that the romantic spirit finally was dead; but the master surprised his disciples by proclaiming his admiration for a number of nineteenth-century composers. He paid homage to Weber and Mendelssohn in the Capriccio for piano and orchestra (1929), a brilliant concert piece. The ballet *Le Baiser de la fée* (The Fairy's Kiss, 1922) was "inspired by the Muse of Tchaikovsky." A more successful score is that of the one-act *opera buffa Mavra* (1922), dedicated "to the memory of Pushkin, Glinka and Tchaikovsky." This genial little work is based on Pushkin's tale about the enterprising soldier who makes his way into his sweetheart's house by disguising himself as a maidservant, only to be discovered in the act of shaving.

Stravinsky's classical period culminated in several major compositions. *Oedipus Rex* (1927) is an "opera-oratorio." The text is a translation into Latin of Cocteau's French adaptation of the Greek tragedy. Stravinsky's comment on his preference for the Latin is revealing. "What a joy it is to compose music to a language of convention, almost of ritual, the very nature of which imposes a lofty dignity! One no longer feels dominated by the phrase, the literal meaning of the words." From the shattering impact of the opening chords, *Oedipus Rex* is an unforgettable experience in the theater. The archaic Greek influence is manifest too in the ballet *Apollon Musagète* (Apollo, Leader of the Muses, 1928), which marked the beginning of his collaboration with the choreographer George Balanchine; *Perséphone* (1934), a choral dance drama on a text by André Gide; and the ballet *Orpheus* (1947), a severely classical work that ranks with the master's most distinguished creations.

The *Symphony of Psalms,* which looks back to the great polyphonic art of Bach, is regarded by many as the chief work of Stravinsky's maturity. The Symphony in C (1940), a sunny piece of modest dimensions, pays tribute to the spirit of Haydn and Mozart. With the Symphony in Three Movements (1945), Stravinsky returns to bigness of form and gesture. The Mass in G (completed in 1948) is in the restrained, telegraphic style that he favored after his middle years. In 1950 there followed *The Rake's Progress,* an opera on a libretto by W. H. Auden and Chester Kallman, after Hogarth's celebrated series of engravings. Written as the composer was approaching seventy, this is a mellow, radiantly melodious score.

Stravinsky, imperturbably pursuing his own growth as an artist, had still another surprise in store for his public. In the works written after he was seventy, he has shown himself increasingly receptive to the serial procedures of the twelve-tone style, to which in earlier years he was categorically opposed. This preoccupation comes to the fore in a number of works dating from the middle Fifties, of which the most important is the *Canticum sacrum ad honorem Sancti Marci nominis* (Sacred Song to Honor the Name of St. Mark, 1956) for tenor, baritone, chorus, and orchestra. The piece was written for St. Mark's Cathedral in Venice and received its premiere there in 1956. There followed the ballet *Agon* (1957) and *Threni—id est Lamentationes Jeremiae Prophetae* (Threnodies: Lamentations of the Prophet Jeremiah, completed 1958). In these works, as in the *Movements* for piano and orchestra (1958–59), *A Sermon, a Narrative and a Prayer* (1960–61), and *The Flood* (1961), Stravinsky assimilates the twelve-tone technique to his personal style and turns it with utter freedom to his own use.

Stravinsky's aphorisms display his gift for trenchant expression. "We have a duty to music, namely, to invent it. . . . Instinct is infallible. If it leads us astray it is no longer instinct. . . . It is not simply inspiration that counts. It is the result of inspiration—that is, the composition . . ."

Speaking of his Mass: "The Credo is the longest movement. There is much to believe." When asked to define the difference between *The Rite of Spring* and *Symphony of Psalms:* "The difference is twenty years." Of the innumerable anecdotes to which his ready tongue has given rise it will suffice to quote one. After the out-of-town opening of *Seven Lively Arts* the managers of the show, apprehensive as to how his music would be received on Broadway, wired him: "Great success. Could be sensational if you authorize arranger Mr. X to add some details to orchestration. Mr. X arranges even the works of Cole Porter." To which Stravinsky wired back: "Am satisfied with great success."

Petrushka

One of the most widely enjoyed of contemporary ballets, *Petrushka*, a burlesque in four scenes, occurred to the composer as a strictly musical rather than dance idea. He intended, he tells us, to compose an orchestral piece in which the piano would play the most important part. "In composing the music I had in my mind a distinct picture of a puppet suddenly endowed with life, exasperating the patience of the orchestra with diabolical cascades of arpeggios. The orchestra in turn retaliates with menacing trumpet blasts. The outcome is a terrific noise which reaches its climax and ends in the sorrowful and querulous collapse of the poor puppet." From this point of departure the figure of Petrushka steadily took on dimension, while the piano surrendered much of its importance to the orchestra. "Having finished this bizarre piece, I struggled for hours while walking beside the Lake of Geneva to find a title that would express in a word the character of my music and, consequently, the personality of this creature. One day I leaped for joy. I had indeed found my title—Petrushka, the immortal and unhappy hero of every fair in all countries . . . the poor, funny, ugly, sentimental, and misguided creature, constantly shaken with rebellious rage, whether justified or not, who is known in France as Pierrot, in Germany as Kasperl, and in Russia as Petrushka."

The setting—a street fair during carnival week in St. Petersburg in the 1830s—enabled the composer lovingly to evoke the colorful atmosphere of his native city. The score is a legitimate offspring of the Russian national school. Although manifesting all the sharp gesture and movement of the ballet, the music leads its independent lyrical life and has found as important a place in the concert hall as in the theater.

The opening scene shows the crowds milling about the booths and stalls of the fair ground. A troop of drunken men pass by. An Italian organ grinder accompanies a dancer while near by a rival dancer performs to the strains of a music box. The crowd is summoned by a drum roll to the marionette theater. The Charlatan, a shrewd showman if ever there was one, plays his flute. The curtain of his diminutive theater rises, disclosing three puppets—Petrushka, the Ballerina, and the Moor. The Charlatan touches the dolls with his flute; whereupon, to the delight of the crowd, they spring to life and perform a Russian dance.

The second tableau takes place inside the marionette theater, in Petrushka's room. Petrushka is kicked unceremoniously into the room. On the wall hangs a portrait of his heartless master; he curses it. "Although the Showman's magic has imbued all three puppets with human feelings and emotions, it is Petrushka who feels and suffers most." He is only too aware of his unprepossessing appearance; he resents his dependence on his master. At thought of the Ballerina he is filled with tenderness; a love song takes shape in his heart. When she appears Petrushka, overwhelmed by emotion, declares his love. The Ballerina flees, leaving Petrushka in despair.

Third is the scene in the Moor's room. Stretched on the divan, the sumptuously attired Moor toys with a coconut. "Although he is brutal and stupid, his magnificent appearance charms the Ballerina." She enters; they dance together. Petrushka appears, mad with jealousy. The Moor throws him out; the Ballerina swoons.

The fourth tableau returns us to the fair ground. It is evening. Nursemaids dance. A peasant plays his pipe and leads a dancing bear. A merchant in jovial mood, accompanied by two Gypsy girls, throws bank notes to the crowd. Coachmen and grooms dance and are joined by the nursemaids. A group of masked figures appear. Their antics amuse the crowd, which joins in a frenzied dance led by a masked devil. Suddenly there is a commotion in the puppet theater. Petrushka rushes out from behind the curtain, followed by the Moor, whom the Ballerina vainly tries to hold back. The Moor overtakes the luckless Petrushka and strikes him with his sword. Petrushka falls, mortally hurt. To the consternation of the crowd, he dies.

A policeman fetches the Charlatan who, to reassure the bystanders, picks up and shakes the little body, showing them that it is only a doll stuffed with sawdust. The crowd disperses. The Charlatan begins to drag the puppet to his room. Above the little theater, however, he catches sight of Petrushka's ghost, grimacing and menacing. He had not foreseen that his creation, through suffering, would achieve a soul. Stricken with fear the Charlatan drops the doll and steals away. . . .

The opening measures evoke the "big accordion" sound of the folk music that surrounded Stravinsky in his childhood. The orchestra teems with movement and animation. A solo flute, supported by the second flute, presents a theme that is etched precisely against a background of clarinet and horn tremolos. This melody recurs as a unifying element throughout the score.

At the rise of the curtain we encounter Stravinsky's rhythmic suppleness. The meter alternates between $\frac{3}{4}$ and $\frac{2}{4}$. Suddenly we hear the percussive harmonies, imbued with rhythmic élan, that are the hallmark of this composer. The motive of the drunkards is typical of the melodies in *Petrushka:* it is compact, strong, rooted in the key. It moves stepwise along the scale, with an occasional narrow leap, and remains within a narrow range, outlining the basic interval of a fifth and repeat-

ing fragments of itself. It bears the imprint of the folk yet is thoroughly assimilated to Stravinsky's personal style.

The hurdy-gurdy sound is well simulated by flute and piccolo, clarinet and bass clarinet. A triangle marks the beat for the dancer and casts a tinsel charm over her wistful little melody, which Stravinsky derived from a French street song piquantly entitled *She Had a Wooden Leg.* The Charlatan's flute solo sets the scene for miraculous doings. After he animates the dolls the orchestra breaks into the Russian Dance, another compact, scalewise tune of primitive strength whose repeated fragments stress the interval of a fifth. The C-major sound of this music announced to the world that the turning away from post-Wagnerian

chromaticism had begun, while the closely bunched dissonant chords on the piano point up the new percussive style of writing for that instrument. The dance is wholly of the twentieth century. Yet when the theme in its final appearance is repeated slowly and plaintively, we are thrust back for a moment into the fairy-tale world of Rimsky-Korsakov.

The second scene presents the famous Petrushka chord, the harmonic kernel out of which the work grew: a C-major arpeggio superposed upon one in F-sharp major that serves it as a kind of "double."

It is a strikingly original sonority, and pointed the way to the polyharmony and polytonality that were to play so important a part in the new music. Petrushka's love song, whimsical and tender, makes a fine contrast to his despair after the Ballerina's departure. At this point in the score Stravinsky comes closest to his original intention of creating a piece in which the piano would exasperate "the patience of the orchestra with diabolical cascades of arpeggios."

The third tableau, *At the Moor's*, contains a series of charming numbers. The percussive harmonies that introduce this vain and brutal character are followed by the Moor's languid dance, an exotic theme presented by clarinet and bass clarinet against tricky syncopated rhythms on the bass drum and cymbal. The entrance of the Ballerina makes for a gay bit on the trumpet and snare drum. Her dance with the Moor is marked Lento cantabile: a staid duet for flute and trumpet that veers into a Viennese waltz, allegretto. The familiar trumpet fanfare announces the appearance of Petrushka. The quarrel between him and the Moor turns on agitated harmonies and colors that stem out of the romantic heritage—but with a difference!

The final tableau brings back the "big accordion" sound of the opening scene. Out of the swarming orchestral voices emerges the Dance of the Nursemaids, a memorable tune out of the heart of the Russian national school. It moves through the two fundamental intervals—octave and fifth—a circumstance that imparts to the melody its quality of simplicity and strength.

The peasant and his bear are characterized by clarinet and tuba against heavy chords in the lower strings. The dance of the coachmen and grooms gives the composer opportunity for those dark percussive harmonies that he was to exploit so brilliantly in *The Rite of Spring*. When the nursemaids join the dance, their theme is given a sumptuous orchestral garb. The carnival reaches its height with the dance of the masked figures. The appearance of Petrushka pursued by the Moor is accompanied by provocative sonorities, including chromatic scales on trumpet, xylophone, and strings. Petrushka's death is depicted with wonderful economy of means: harmonics on the violas, a flicker of piccolo sound, tremolo on muted violins, with the melody line traced in turn by clarinet, violin solo, and bassoon. The C-major chord appears against its F-sharp major "double"; and the work ends with a suggestion of the bitonal harmony from which it sprang.

It was Stravinsky's historic role to incarnate a phase of the contemporary temper. In upholding the Apollonian discipline in art he revealed the age to itself. His spirit was one with the spirit of our time. This is made plain in the closing lines of his *Autobiography:* "I live neither in the past nor in the future. I am in the present. I cannot know what tomorrow may bring forth. I can only know what the truth is for me today. This is what I am called upon to serve, and I serve it in all lucidity."

CHAPTER 83

Arnold Schoenberg (1874-1951)

"I personally hate to be called a revolutionist, which I am not. What I did was neither revolution nor anarchy."

IT IS worthy of note that, like Stravinsky, the other great innovator of our time disclaims revolutionary intent. Quite the contrary, his disciples regard him as having brought to its culmination the thousand-year-old tradition of European polyphony.

His Life

Arnold Schoenberg was born in Vienna. He began to study the violin at the age of eight, and soon afterward made his initial attempts at composing. Having decided to devote his life to music, he left school while he was in his teens. The early death of his father left him in

Arnold Schoenberg.

straitened circumstances. For a time he earned his living by working in a bank, and meanwhile continued to compose, working entirely by himself. Presently he became acquainted with a young musician two years older than himself, Alexander von Zemlinsky, who for a few months gave him lessons in counterpoint. This was the only musical instruction he ever had.

Through Zemlinsky young Schoenberg was introduced to the advanced musical circles of Vienna, which at that time were under the spell of *Tristan* and *Parsifal*. In 1899, when he was twenty-five, Schoenberg wrote the string sextet *Verklärte Nacht* (Transfigured Night). The following year several of Schoenberg's songs were performed in Vienna and precipitated a scene. "And ever since that day," he once remarked with a smile, "the scandal has never ceased."

It was at this time that Schoenberg began a large-scale work for voices and orchestra, the *Gurre-Lieder*. For the huge forces, choral and instrumental, required for this cantata he needed music paper double the ordinary size. Work on the *Gurre-Lieder* was interrupted by material worries. To earn a livelihood, Schoenberg turned to orchestrating popular operettas. In 1901, after his marriage to Zemlinsky's sister, he moved to Berlin and obtained a post in a theater, conducting operettas and music-hall songs. He even wrote a cabaret song, but it was too difficult to be performed. Schoenberg's early music already displayed certain traits of his later style. A publisher to whom he brought a quartet observed, "You must think that if the second theme is a retrograde inversion of the first theme, that automatically makes it good!"

Upon his return to Vienna Schoenberg became active as a teacher and soon gathered about him a band of disciples, of whom the most gifted were Alban Berg and Anton Webern. The devotion of these advanced young musicians sustained Schoenberg in the fierce battle for recognition that lay ahead. An important adherent was Gustav Mahler, who exercised considerable influence upon Schoenberg's development. When Schoenberg's Chamber Symphony Opus 9 was first presented and the audience responded by whistling and banging their seats, Mahler sprang up in his box to command silence. He recognized the creator in Schoenberg. But he knew too that the younger man—they were separated by fourteen years—belonged to a future in which he himself had no part. To his wife Alma he confided, "I do not understand his work. But then he is young and may well be right. I am old, and perhaps I do not have the ear for his music."

Despite the hostility of the public, Schoenberg's music and doctrines slowly made their way. The tide turned in 1913 with the first performance of the *Gurre-Lieder*, which was received with wild enthusiasm by the Viennese. In this long-delayed moment of triumph Schoenberg was unable to forget the years of rejection that had been inflicted on him by his native city. Called to the stage again and again, he bowed to the conductor Franz Schreker and to the orchestra, but would not acknowledge the ovation tendered him by the public. "For years those people who greeted me with cheers tonight refused to recognize me. Why should I thank them for appreciating me now?"

With each new work Schoenberg moved closer to as bold a step as any artist has ever taken—the rejection of tonality. "I already feel," he wrote in 1909, "the opposition that I shall have to overcome. I suspect that even those who have believed in me until now will not be willing to see the necessity of this development. It is not lack of invention or of technical skill that has urged me in this direction. I am following an inner compulsion that is stronger than education, and am obeying a law that is natural to me, therefore more powerful than my artistic training." True, he was not the only one who at this time was moving toward an atonal idiom. But it was he who set the seal of his personality upon this development, and who played the crucial role in creating a new grammar and syntax of musical speech.

The First World War interrupted Schoenberg's creative activity. Although he was past forty, he was called up for military service in the Vienna garrison. He had reached a critical point in his development. There followed a silence of seven years, between 1915 and 1923, during which he clarified his position in his own mind, and evolved a set of structural procedures to replace tonality. The goal once set, Schoenberg pursued it with that tenacity of purpose without which no prophet can prevail. His "method of composing with twelve tones" caused great bewilderment in the musical world. All the same, he was now firmly established as a leader of contemporary musical thought. His fiftieth birthday was marked by a performance of his *Friede auf Erden* (Peace on Earth, 1907) by the chorus of the Vienna Opera, an address by the mayor of the city, as well as a "birthday book" of appreciative articles by his disciples and by leading figures in the world of art. The following year he was appointed to succeed Ferruccio Busoni as professor of composition at the Berlin Academy of Arts. The uniquely favorable attitude of the Weimar Republic toward experimental art had made it possible for one of the most iconoclastic musicians in history to carry on his work from the vantage point of an official post.

This period in Schoenberg's life ended with the coming to power of Hitler in 1933. Like many Austrian-Jewish intellectuals of his generation, Schoenberg had been converted to Catholicism. After leaving Germany he found it spiritually necessary to return to the Hebrew faith. He arrived in the United States in the fall of 1933. After a short period of teaching in Boston, he joined the faculty of the University of Southern California, and shortly afterward was appointed professor of composition at the University of California in Los Angeles. In 1940 he became an American citizen. He taught until his retirement at the age of seventy, and continued his musical activities till his death in 1951. A seeker after truth until the end, to no one more than to himself could be applied the injunction he had written in the text of his cantata *Die Jakobsleiter* (Jacob's Ladder, 1913): "One must go on without asking what lies before or behind."

His Music

Schoenberg stemmed out of the Viennese past. He took his point of departure from the final quartets of Beethoven, the lyricism of Hugo Wolf, the richly wrought piano writing of Brahms, and the orchestral sonority of Bruckner and Mahler—behind whom, of course, loomed the un-Viennese figure of Wagner.

Given this background, Schoenberg may be regarded as the antipodal figure to Stravinsky. Stravinsky rejects the concept of art as personal expression; Schoenberg adheres to it with romantic fervor. "I write what I feel in my heart—and what finally comes on paper is what first coursed through every fibre of my body. A work of art can achieve no finer effect than when it transmits to the beholder the emotions that raged in the creator, in such a way that they rage and storm also in him." Stravinsky rigidly separates art from the experiences of life; Schoenberg upholds their connection. "What else can I do than express the original word, which to me is a human thought, a human word, a human aspiration." Stravinsky is spokesman for the classical view of life; Schoenberg as steadfastly upholds the opposite. "I warn you of the danger lurking in the die-hard reaction against romanticism. The old romanticism is dead; long live the new!" Stravinsky recoils in distaste from any attempt to attach metaphysical meanings to music; for Schoenberg, the mystical approach is most congenial. "My personal feeling is that music conveys a prophetic message revealing a higher form of life towards which mankind evolves. There is only one content which all great men wish to express: the longing of mankind for its future form, for an immortal soul, for dissolution into the universe."

The paradox at the root of Schoenberg's thinking lies in the fact that the emotional, visionary elements in his personality were allied with a strong taste for abstract speculation and intellectual control. He had the true German reverence for the Idea. Music to him was "not another amusement but a presentation of musical ideas." For all his passion, he was an intellectual. "It is really only in the mental realm—where musical thought must be rich in variety—that an artistic expression is possible." His aim above all was "to join ideas with ideas." Here then is the strange duality at the heart of Schoenberg's music: a hyperexpressive content descended from the turbulently chromatic idiom of *Tristan*, controlled by as rigidly intellectual a system of formal procedures as artist ever devised.

Schoenberg's first period may be described as one of post-Wagnerian romanticism; he still used key signatures and remained within the boundaries of tonality. The best-known work of this period is *Verklärte Nacht*, Opus 4. *Pelleas und Melisande*, Opus 5, after Maeterlinck's symbolist play, was written in 1902, the year in which Debussy's opera on the same subject was first produced. Lasting almost an hour, this fervid symphonic poem exploits to the full the expressive possibilities of the mammoth orchestra of the Strauss-Mahler period. The post-romantic orchestral style is carried to its farthermost limits in the *Gurre-Lieder*, a work that occupied Schoenberg intermittently from 1900 until 1911. The work, cast in a hyperemotional post-*Tristan* idiom, calls for an orchestra of about a hundred and forty players; five soloists; and four choruses—three male choirs singing in four parts and a mixed choir in eight parts: all in all, almost four hundred performers.

During these years Schoenberg also produced works along quite different lines. The songs of Opus 2 and 3 set forth the vein of lyricism in Schoenberg's art. The *Eight Songs* of Opus 6 (1905) already display the dislocation of the vocal line through the use of wide intervals which became one of the hallmarks of his school. The First String Quartet, in D minor, Opus 7 (1904–05), embodies the preoccupation with chamber-music style that came to have an ever greater influence on Schoenberg's orchestral writing. This tendency comes to the fore in the First Chamber Symphony for fifteen instruments, Opus 9 (1906). The tonal period ends with the String Quartet No. 2, in F-sharp minor, Opus 10 (1907–08), the last work—until his American period—in which Schoenberg used a key signature. He introduced a voice in the final movement which sings—significantly—Stefan George's *Ich fühle Luft von anderen Planeten* (I feel the air of other spheres).

Schoenberg's second period, the atonal-expressionist, gets under way with the *Three Piano Pieces*, Opus 11 (1909), in which he abolishes the distinction between consonance and dissonance, and also the sense of a home key. During this period Schoenberg turns to the utmost condensation of utterance. His output centers about the short lyric forms —piano and orchestral pieces, and songs. On the one hand he was reacting against the overextended forms of the Mahler-Strauss period as well as his own *Pelleas* and *Gurre-Lieder*. On the other, the new atonal idiom was so concentrated and intense, its future direction as yet so uncertain, that he could best work out its structural problems in abbreviated forms.

The fifteen songs to Stefan George's expressionist poems *Das Buch der hängenden Gärten*, Opus 15 (The Book of the Hanging Gardens, 1908), show the increasing complexity of Schoenberg's vocal writing. The voice is no longer supported by the accompaniment but must negotiate the zigzag vocal line on its own, sustained only by the singer's stout heart and (a prerequisite!) absolute pitch. To this phase of Schoenberg's career belong two expressionist works for the theater— they can hardly be called operas: *Erwartung* (Expectancy, 1909), on a libretto by Marie Pappenheim, and *Die glückliche Hand* (The Lucky Hand, 1913), on a libretto by Schoenberg himself.

The *Five Orchestral Pieces*, Opus 16, constitute one of the high points of this period. Another is *Pierrot Lunaire* (Pierrot of the Moon, Opus 21, 1912), for female reciter and five instruments—flute, clarinet, violin, cello, and piano (with three alternating instruments—piccolo, bass clarinet, viola). The work is written in free rhythms and unequal measures—what Anton Webern called "the prose of music." It introduces an eerily expressive kind of declamation midway between song and speech, known as *Sprechstimme* (speaking voice). This was the first composition to carry Schoenberg's name beyond his immediate circle. The atonal-expressionist phase of Schoenberg's career ended with the *Four Songs* for voice and orchestra, Opus 22 (1914).

Schoenberg's third period, that of the twelve-tone method, was ushered in—after the long silence we referred to—by the *Five Piano Pieces* of Opus 23 (1923). In the last of the set the new technique is revealed in all its features. It should not be supposed that Schoenberg completely changed his musical language when he adopted the twelve-tone method. The serial manner of writing merely enabled him to organize the intuitions that had been present in his earlier works, to systematize the aims toward which he had been moving for years. The twelve-tone method is in evidence in the Serenade for seven instruments and bass voice, Opus 24 (1923), whose third and fourth movements, the *Variationes* and *Sonett*, are based on tone rows. The constructive logic of the twelve-tone method made it possible for Schoenberg to undertake longer works than those of his atonal period. Among these is the Quintet for flute, oboe, clarinet, bassoon and horn, Opus 26 (1924); and the Variations for Orchestra, Opus 31 (1927–28), the first twelve-tone composition for orchestra and one of Schoenberg's most powerful works.

The fourth and last period of Schoenberg's career—the American phase—brought to light several interesting tendencies in the evolution of his art. On the one hand he carried the twelve-tone technique to further stages of refinement. On the other, he modified his doctrine sufficiently to allow tonal elements to coexist with the twelve-tone style, and on occasion even returned to the major scale and to key signatures. In the category of tonal works we find the Suite for String Orchestra in G major (1934), intended for the use of students; also the *Kol Nidre* for speaker, chorus, and orchestra, Opus 39 (1939), an impressive setting of the ancient Hebrew prayer. Several among the late works present the twelve-tone style in a manner markedly more accessible than earlier pieces, often with tonal implications. Among these are the brilliant Piano Concerto (1942); the *Ode to Napoleon* (1944), a setting of Byron's poem for string orchestra, piano, and rhythmic narration; and the cantata *A Survivor from Warsaw* (1948), for narrator, men's chorus, and orchestra, with a text in English by Schoenberg himself— the composer's tribute to the Jews who perished in the Nazi death camps.

The strict use of twelve-tone technique is represented by such compositions as the lyrical String Quartet No. 4, Opus 37 (1936), his last work in this medium; the String Trio, Opus 45 (1946), one of his pro-

Paul Cézanne, 1839-1906, *Landscape with Viaduct*. (The Metropolitan Museum of Art, Bequest of Mrs. H. O. Havemeyer, 1929. The H. O. Havemeyer Collection)

"Ravel stands to Debussy somewhat as Cézanne does to Monet. He was a post-impressionist.

Pablo Picasso, b. 1887, *Three Musicians*. (Collection, The Museum of Modern Art, New York. Mrs. Simon Guggenheim Fund)

"This painting, regarded by many as the masterpiece of cubism, sums up the final stage of the movement."

Piet Mondrian, 1872-1944, *Composition, 1935-42*. (Collection: Mr. and Mrs. Burton Tremaine)

". . . the desire of our age for condensation of style and purity of expression, for athletic movement, economy, and architectonic unity."

foundest works; and the Fantasy for Violin and Piano, written in 1949 when the composer was seventy-five. Also the Violin Concerto, Opus 36 (1936), which is in Schoenberg's most uncompromising manner. Mention should be made too of the Biblical opera *Moses and Aaron,* a most stirring work. The first two acts were finished by 1932, but the work was interrupted by his emigration to the United States; he never went back to it.

Schoenberg was a tireless propagandist for his ideas, a role for which his verbal gifts and his passion for polemics eminently fitted him. Essays and articles flowed from his pen, conveying his views in a trenchant, aphoristic style which, late in life, he transferred from German to English. The following observations are characteristic: "Genius learns only from itself, talent chiefly from others. . . . One must believe in the infallibility of one's fantasy and the truth of one's inspiration. . . . Creation to an artist should be as natural and inescapable as the growth of apples to an apple tree. . . . The twelve tones will not invent for you. When you find that something you have written is very complicated, you should at once be doubtful of its genuineness." (It cannot be said that he always adhered to this maxim.) "No art has been so hindered in its development by teachers as music, since nobody watches more closely over his property than the man who knows that, strictly speaking, it does not belong to him. . . . It is said of many an author that he has indeed technique, but no invention. That is wrong: either he also lacks technique or he also has invention. . . . Mannerism is originality in subordinate matters. . . . An apostle who does not glow preaches heresy. . . . The laws of nature manifested in a man of genius are but the laws of the future."

Verklärte Nacht (*Transfigured Night*), Opus 4

THIS early work (1899) relates the origins of Schoenberg's art to Wagnerian chromaticism. It stands in direct line of descent from *Tristan.* Originally written for string sextet, the piece was later arranged by Schoenberg for string orchestra. *Verklärte Nacht* brought the spirit of program music into the "pure" realm of chamber music, for it was inspired by a poem of Richard Dehmel. This tells of two who wander through a moonlit grove. The woman confesses that she is with child by another man. Now that she has found love, she is tormented by guilt. The man bids her cast away despair. He will raise the child as his own, for their love has made him even as a child. Through his forgiveness he is transfigured. They embrace in the moon-drenched night.

The music is steeped in nature poetry. The chromatic harmonies, restless modulations, and impassioned climaxes make for an utterly romantic tone poem. Schoenberg exploits the possibilities of the medium, the piercing sweetness of the strings in their high register, the dark resonance of the low, and the rich palette of colors between. The material is overextended, an interesting circumstance in view of his later striving for the utmost concision of speech. Although the piece derives its emotional ambience from Wagner, its sensibility is wholly Viennese. Certain turns of the harmony remind one of Franz Liszt, a composer who is never mentioned as having exerted an influence on Schoenberg. *Verklärte Nacht* became something of a hit as the score for Antony Tudor's ballet *Pillar of Fire,* bringing Schoenberg a measure of the popular approval from which he turned away in his later works.

The opening melody, a descending motive in D minor played by violas and cellos, evokes a brooding landscape.

Certain devices dear to the romantic imagination are much in evidence: the tremolo in lower register, a solo violin soaring high above the harmony, imitation between one instrument and another in a manner suggesting tender dialogue. The work unfolds through a continuous flowering of themes and motives, presenting an admirable unity of texture. The seven lines—two groups each of violins, violas, and cellos, supported by double bass—unite in a finely spun fabric. The sound has the nervosity, the light and luminous quality characteristic of Schoenberg's later works. Despite its sensuous harmony, his music even at this early stage leans toward counterpoint. After much restless wandering and building up of tension, the piece reaches its resolution in a Lisztian cadence in D major.

Verklärte Nacht is a sweet, tender work. It reveals the vast technical adroitness with which Schoenberg began his career, and forcefully refutes the oft-repeated contention that the master turned to the iron-clad logic of his twelve-tone method because he lacked the lyric gift.

Piano Concerto, Opus 42

The Piano Concerto (1942) belongs to Schoenberg's final period. The relaxation of strict dodecaphonic procedure that manifested itself during his American sojourn is reflected in this work. Although the writing is dodecaphonic, we find a vaguely tonal atmosphere.

Schoenberg retains some of the traditional features of the piano concerto in his Opus 42. There are three movements—really four, since

the last is subdivided into two sections. The instrument's technical resources are fully exploited. The work boasts two cadenzas. Yet pyro-
technical display for its own sake is sedulously avoided. Piano and orchestra are integrated in a symphonic whole, with a constant interchange of ideas between them. As so often with Schoenberg, the
writing for the piano, in its rich texture and sweeping use of the keyboard, bears some resemblance to the piano style of Brahms. Indeed, the
look of the notes on the page—the spread of the left-hand part, the
double notes and full chords in the right—would remind one of that
master, were it not for the accidentals and for the fact that this, really,
is another language.

The piece has a high emotional content. The continual shifting from
quiet lyricism to impassioned utterance suggests its romantic provenance. The orchestral writing fully justifies Virgil Thomson's description of the Concerto as "chamber music for a hundred players." There
is no attempt at the grand gesture in this rather intimate work, written
when the master was approaching seventy.

I. *Andante*, $\frac{3}{8}$. The tone row with which the Concerto opens per-

vades all three movements. The piano announces the row in a quietly
lyrical mood. Notice that in this presentation Schoenberg departs from
strict twelve-tone procedure, since he repeats several notes before all
twelve have been heard:

The row is immediately heard in an inversion of the retrograde, transposed; then a retrograde version on the original pitch; and then a transposed inversion. These four forms constitute a thirty-nine-measure statement of the theme. The meditative mood is continued as the violins take over the row and carry it to the high register against the figuration of the piano.

The first five tones of the row (under the bracket) serve as a motive that pervades the work. Schoenberg called it the *Kopfmotif* or "head-motive" and used it as a structural element in the Concerto. The customary fragmentation of texture associated with the dodecaphonic style gives way, in this work, to a continuity of line and movement closer to traditional norms. The orchestral writing musters his favorite devices, such as harmonics on the strings, trills in the extreme registers, and fluttertonguing on the muted brass. The transformations of the row are carried out with great imagination. Writing such as this could be done only by one who envisioned the possibilities of the twelve-tone idiom in the way that, let us say, Keats envisioned the possibilities of the sonnet.

II. *Molto Allegro.* The second movement is in $\frac{2}{2}$ time, with excursions to $\frac{3}{2}, \frac{3}{4}$, and $\frac{6}{4}$. The opening measures present an animated interchange among xylophone, brass, and piano. The frequent changes of meter and tempo impart rhythmic flexibility to the movement. A stringendo passage builds up to the climax. Tension subsides in a transitional passage that leads into the third movement.

III. *Adagio,* $\frac{3}{2}$. One of the most lyrical movements that Schoenberg ever wrote, this Adagio opens with an expressive duet between oboe and bassoon which is a transposition of the basic row, accompanied by its inversion in the trombones and violas. The opening passage for orchestra leads into a piano cadenza requiring agile fingers. Another evocative passage for the orchestra introduces delicate figuration on the piano against a subtle background of winds and strings. A brief cadenza for the piano ushers in the last movement.

IV. *Giocoso* (moderato), $\frac{2}{2}$. The finale is a lively movement in rondo style. The opening phrase is an inverted version of the first six notes of the piano theme, while the next six notes present the second half of the row arranged backward.

A vigorous orchestral passage in triplet rhythm is followed by an animated exchange with the piano. The movement mounts in tension until the coda, which is taken at an increased speed. The "head-motive" appears in a new guise, and in the furious final measures is combined,

in the piano part, with its inversion.

The Piano Concerto is a mellow work of the master's maturity. It embodies Schoenberg's majestic attempt to unite the emotional, intellectual, and technical aspects of his art in a single embracing synthesis.

꽃ᆇᆇᆇ CHAPTER 84 꽃ᆇᆇᆇ

Béla Bartók (1881-1945)

"What is the best way for a composer to reap the full benefits of his studies in peasant music? It is to assimilate the idiom of peasant music so completely that he is able to forget all about it and use it as his musical mother tongue."

IT WAS the mission of Béla Bartók to reconcile the folk melody of his native Hungary with the main currents of European music. In the process he created an entirely personal language and revealed himself as one of the major prophets of our age.

His Life

Bartók was born in a district of Hungary that is now part of Rumania. The sensitive, studious lad—he was rather frail in health—soon revealed a serious musical talent. When he was seventeen he was offered a scholarship at the Vienna Conservatory, but he decided instead to follow his friend Ernö Dohnányi to the Royal Academy of Music in Budapest. There young Bartók acquired a reputation as a brilliant pianist. He also came in contact with a strong nationalist movement that strove

Béla Bartók.

to shake off the domination of Austro-German culture. His first important work for orchestra was a symphonic poem on the life of the Hungarian patriot Louis Kossuth.

Bartók soon developed an absorbing interest in native folklore. He became aware that what passed for Hungarian folklore in the eyes of the world was either the Gypsy music that had been romanticized by Liszt or the popular tunes of the café musicians, which were overlaid with elements of Austro-German music. Impelled by what he later described as "an urge towards the unknown, a dim inkling that true folk music was to be found only among the peasant class," he undertook to collect the native songs before they died out. In company with his fellow composer Zoltán Kodály, and armed with the indispensable recording equipment, he set out on a series of investigations that took him to the remotest villages of the country. From these expeditions Bartók derived the basic element of his art. "Those days I spent in the villages among the peasants," he recalled later, "were the happiest of my life. In order really to feel the vitality of this music one must, so to speak, have lived it. And this is possible only when one comes to know it by direct contact with the peasants." He also explored the folk music of neighboring countries—Slovakia, Rumania, Bulgaria, and what is now Yugoslavia—and subsequently extended his investigations to include Turkish and Arab folk song. Bartók later published a great deal on ethnomusicology and became one of the leading authorities in this field—a rare example of artistic creativity going hand in hand with a gift for scientific research.

His attainments as a pianist were recognized when, in 1907, he was appointed professor of piano at the Royal Academy in Budapest. His compositions, however, were much too advanced for a public accustomed to the standard German repertory. In 1911, along with Kodály and other young musicians, Bartók formed the New Hungarian Musical Society, which was dedicated to the goal of disseminating modern music. The project was defeated by the apathy of the public and the hostility of the critics. Bartók became so discouraged that for a time he gave up composing.

The tide turned when Hungary was declared independent of Austria. The resultant upsurge of national feeling created a favorable climate for Bartók's music. His ballet *The Wooden Prince* was presented with great success at the Budapest Opera, and was followed by his opera *Duke Bluebeard's Castle*. However, when Admiral Horthy came to power, Bartók's librettist—who had been active in the left-wing regime of Béla Kun—had to flee Hungary. The two works were dropped from the repertory. *The Miraculous Mandarin*, a ballet, was rejected by the authorities because of its subject, which they considered immoral. Bartók undertook no further works for the stage.

In the ensuing years he was acclaimed throughout Europe as one of the leading figures of his generation. But he was less successful in his own country. Bartók was out of sympathy with the Horthy regime and did nothing to ingratiate himself with those who might have furthered his career. The alliance between Horthy and Nazi Germany confronted the composer with issues that he faced without flinching. His physical frailty had no counterpart on the moral plane. He spoke out against Hitler in a political climate where it was inexpedient to do so, protested the playing of his music on the Berlin radio, and lost no opportunity to make clear his abhorrence of Nazism. "In Hungary," Bartók wrote, "the 'civilized' Christian folk are almost entirely devoted to the Nazi system. I am really ashamed that I come from this class." To go into exile meant surrendering the official status he enjoyed in Hungary, and the economic security that went with it. But he would not compromise. "He who stays on when he could leave may be said to acquiesce tacitly in everything that is happening here." Bartók's friends, fearing for his safety, prevailed upon him to leave the country while there still was time. He arrived in the United States in 1940 and settled in New York City.

He embarked on a concert tour, playing two-piano music with his wife and onetime pupil, Ditta Pasztory-Bartók. He also received an honorary doctorate from Columbia University and an appointment there to do folklore research. (Bartók throughout his life refused to teach composition.) Despite this fair beginning, his life in America yielded little in the way of happiness. His retiring personality was not one to make an impact on the American public. He felt increasingly isolated in his new surroundings. His letters, some of them written in English, trace a mounting curve of discouragement. "Concerts are few and far between. If we had to live on those we would really be at the end of our tether. Our situation is getting daily worse and worse. I am rather pessimistic. I lost all confidence in people, in countries, in everything. Until now we had two free pianos, a baby grand and an upright. Just today I got the news the upright will be taken from us. So we will have no possibility to study two-piano works. And each month brings a similar blow. I am wondering and asking myself what next?" With the entry of the United States into the war, such income as Bartók still received from Hungary was cut off. "At Columbia," he wrote at the end of 1942, "I am 'dismissed' from Jan. 1 on. They seem to have no more money for me. Otherwise my career as a composer is as much as finished: the quasi boycott of my works by the leading orchestras continues; no performances either of old works or new ones. It is a shame—not for me, of course."

The onset of leukemia made it impossible for Bartók to appear in public any longer. Friends appealed for aid to ASCAP (American Society of Composers, Authors and Publishers). Funds were made available to provide the composer with proper care in nursing homes and to enable him to continue writing to the end. A series of commissions from various sources spurred him to the composition of his last works. They rank among his finest. When he realized that he was dying he worked feverishly to finish his Third Piano Concerto, in order to leave his wife the only inheritance within his power. The Viola Concerto was left unfinished, to be brought to completion from his sketches by his friend and disciple Tibor Serly. "The trouble is," he remarked to his doctor shortly before the end, "that I have to go with so much still to say." He died in the West Side Hospital in New York City.

The tale of the composer who dies in poverty only to be acclaimed after his death would seem to belong to the romantic past, to the legend of Mozart, Schubert, Musorgsky. Yet it happened in our time. Bartók had to die in order to make his success in the United States. Almost immediately there was an upsurge of interest in his music that soon assumed the proportions of a boom. As though impelled by a sense of guilt for their previous neglect of his works, conductors, performers, record companies, broadcasting stations, and even his publishers rushed to pay him the homage that might have brought him comfort had it come in time.

His Music

Like Stravinsky and Schoenberg, Bartók disclaimed the role of revolutionary. "In art there are only fast or slow developments. Essentially it is a matter of evolution, not revolution." Despite the newness of his language he was rooted in the classical heritage. "In my youth my ideal was not so much the art of Bach or Mozart as that of Beethoven." He adhered to the logic and beauty of classical form, and to Beethoven's vision of music as an embodiment of human emotion. In this latter respect he parts company with the Stravinskyites. "I cannot conceive," he wrote, "of music that expresses absolutely nothing." His art recaptures the heroic lyricism of an earlier age. In his adagios is to be encountered something of the Beethovenian pathos.

Bartók found authentic Hungarian folk music to be based on ancient modes, unfamiliar scales, and nonsymmetrical rhythms—elements, he pointed out, "almost unknown to so-called romantic music." His investigations brought him to new conceptions of harmony and rhythm and freed him from what he called "the tyrannical rule of the major and minor keys." Folk music taught him "to cultivate the utmost excision of all that is nonessential." The time had passed for embedding folk songs in large-scale movements according to the Austro-German formula. "What we had to do was to divine the spirit of this unknown music and to make this spirit, so difficult to describe in words, the basis of our works."

Classic and romantic elements intermingle in Bartók's art. His classicism shows itself in his emphasis on construction. His idiom is concentrated, reticent, austere. The powerful melodic line flowers into rhapsodic curves. It can also be angular and taut. Characteristic is a type of melody that, like Stravinsky's, moves in a narrow range and creates an effect of primitive force. His harmony can be bitingly dissonant. In the popular *Allegro barbaro*, written in 1911, we find the percussive treatment of dissonant chords that was to come into vogue with Stravinsky's *The Rite of Spring*. Polytonality abounds in his work;

his *Bear Dance* (No. 10 of *Ten Easy Pieces for Piano*, 1908) has four
keys going at once. Despite a tendency toward atonalism, he never
wholly abandoned the principle of key.

Bartók's is one of the great rhythmic imaginations of modern times.
His pounding, stabbing rhythms constitute the primitive aspect of his
art. Passages in his scores have a Stravinskyan look, the meter changing almost at every bar. Like the Russian master, he is fond of syncopation and repeated patterns (ostinati). Bartók played a major role in
the revitalization of European rhythm, infusing it with earthy vitality,
with kinetic force and tension.

He was more traditional in respect to form. His model was the
sonata of Beethoven, even as Stravinsky adopted the continuous expansion of Bach. In his middle years he came under the influence of
pre-Bach music and turned increasingly from harmony to linear thinking. His complex texture is a masterly example of modern dissonant
counterpoint. It sets forth his development toward greater abstraction,
tightness of structure, and purity of thought.

In orchestration Bartók exemplifies the contemporary tendency to
make color serve idea. From the orchestra of Richard Strauss and Debussy he found his way to a palette all his own. He ranges from brilliant mixtures to threads of pure color that bring out the intertwining
melody lines; from a hard bright glitter to a luminous haze. A virtuoso
pianist himself, Bartók is one of the masters of modern piano writing.
He typifies the twentieth-century use of the piano as an instrument of
percussion and rhythm. The most important work for piano of his later
years is *Mikrokosmos* (1926–37), a collection of one hundred and fifty-
three pieces ranging from simplest grade to virtuoso playing.

The six string quartets may very well rank among the major achievements of our century. These are uncompromising and extraordinarily
expressive works, certain of them impregnated with the brooding
pessimism that was the aftermath of the First World War. Bartók is
best known to the public by the three major works of his last period.
The *Music for Strings, Percussion, and Celesta*, written in 1936, is regarded by many as his masterpiece. Tonal opulence and warmth characterize the Concerto for Orchestra (1943), a favorite with American
audiences. The master's final statement, the Third Piano Concerto
(1945), is an impassioned and broadly conceived work, its three movements by turn dramatic, contemplative, satanic. The last-named quality
connects him with the Hungarian master of the romantic period, Franz
Liszt.

Bartók's music encompasses the diverse trends of his time, the polytonal and atonal, expressionism and neoclassicism, folk dance and ma-

chine music, lyricism and the dynamic. It reaches from primitivism to
the intellectual, from program music to the abstract, from nationalism
to the universal. Into all these he infused the high aim of a former
age: to touch the heart.

Concerto for Orchestra

In the summer of 1943 Bartók was confined in Doctors Hospital in
New York City. One day he received a visit from Serge Koussevitzky,
who came offering a thousand-dollar commission and a first performance
by the Boston Symphony Orchestra for any piece he would write. The
knowledge that his music was wanted and that a major orchestra was
waiting to perform the as yet unwritten score had a beneficent effect
on the incurably ill composer. He was able to quit the hospital, and set
to work on the Concerto for Orchestra, which was completed in Octo-
ber of that year. "The general mood of the work," he wrote, "represents,
apart from the jesting second movement, a gradual transition from the
sternness of the first movement and the lugubrious death-song of the
third to the life-assertion of the last."

Of symphonic dimension, the work is called a concerto because of its
tendency, as Bartók explained, "to treat the single instruments in a
concertante or soloistic manner." In other words, he used the term as
the eighteenth century did. The element of virtuosity prevails, but the
virtuoso is the entire orchestra. The work exemplifies Bartók's wonderful sense of sound, his mastery of the grand form, and his passion for
folklore. Written in his most communicative mood, the Concerto was
the first of his compositions to establish itself with the American public.

I. *Introduzione. Andante non troppo—Allegro vivace.* The Introduction is spacious of gesture. It prepares the listener for a large work. In
the composer's best vein are the sonorities of the opening passage, a
solemn statement by cellos and basses set off by tremolos on upper
strings and flute. The theme is based on the interval of the fourth (indicated by brackets), which occupies a prominent position in the melodic formations of this composer.

The first subject of the Allegro vivace consists of a vigorously syncopated figure that ascends to a climax and as briskly subsides. Here too the

fourth is prominent. A contrasting idea in folklore style consists mainly
of two notes. The Development builds up tension through contrapuntal
imitation. The Restatement is abbreviated, as is customary in twentieth-
century works. The movement has the quality of inevitable progression
that is the essence of symphonic style.

II. *Giuoco delle coppie* (Game of Pairs). So called because the wind
instruments are paired at specific intervals, bassoons in sixths, oboes in
thirds, clarinets in sevenths, flutes in fifths, muted trumpets in seconds.
This "jesting second movement," as Bartók called it, is marked Allegretto
scherzando. The side drum, without snares, ushers in music of a pro-

cessional nature that is filled with teasing ideas. In evidence is the element of the bizarre that appealed to Berlioz and Mahler no less than
to Bartók. The form is a "chain" of five little sections, each featuring
another pair of instruments. There is a chorale for brass. The five sections are then restated with more elaborate instrumentation.

III. *Elegia. Andante non troppo.* This movement is the "lugubrious
death song." An oboe traces a long line of lamentation against Bar-
tókian flickerings of clarinet, flute, and harp tone. The music is rhapsodic, visionary; it rises to a tragic climax. This is a heroic canvas in the
great line of the hymnic adagios of Beethoven.

IV. *Intermezzo interrotto* (Interrupted Intermezzo). A plaintive tune
in folk-song style is introduced by the oboe and continued by the flute.
The nonsymmetrical rhythm, an alternation of $\frac{2}{4}$ and $\frac{5}{8}$, imparts to the
movement a wayward charm. There follows a broadly songful theme
on the strings, one of the great melodies of the twentieth century. The

mood is interrupted as the music turns from folk lyricism to the sophisticated tone of the cafés. The return of the lyric theme on muted strings makes a grandly poetic effect. The movement is replete with capriciousness and tender sentiment.

V. *Finale. Pesante—Presto.* There is an introduction of seven bars marked pesante (heavily), in which the horns outline the germinal theme. The movement of "life-assertion" gets off to a whirlwind perpetuum mobile (perpetual motion) in the strings. The fugue that follows parades intricate devices of counterpoint; yet so lightly does Bartók wear his learning that there is nothing here to tax the untutored ear. The fugue subject is presented by the second trumpet. Notice again the decisive role played by the interval of a fourth.

The answer, played by the first trumpet, is an inversion of the theme. The folk tone as Bartók uses it here has nothing in common with the prettified peasant dances of the nineteenth century. Its harmonies are acrid, its rhythms imbued with primitive strength. The movement rises to a mood of heroic affirmation.

The work follows the progression "through suffering to the stars" that formed the epic theme of Beethoven's symphony-dramas. Like those, the Concerto for Orchestra moves from a sense of the tragic to indomitable optimism. Like those, too, it seeks to "embrace the millions." The composer's intention was realized. At the first international Bartók festival held in Budapest in the fall of 1948 his works were applauded by tens of thousands of his countrymen. The mass sale of Bartók recordings in England and America testifies similarly to the wide appeal and profoundly human quality of his art.

Bartók's prime characteristic both as musician and man was the uncompromising integrity that informed his every act—what a compatriot of his has called "the proud morality of the mind." He was one of the great spirits of our time.

CHAPTER 85

Paul Hindemith (1895-1963)

"A composer's horizon cannot be far-reaching enough; his desire
to know, to comprehend, must incite, inspire, and drench every
phase of his work. Storming the heavens with artistic wisdom
and practical skill must be his least ambition."

EVERY age has its artists who, acutely sensible of their heritage, find in
it the point of departure for their own work. In the late nineteenth century this retrospective role was played by Brahms. In our time it is
Paul Hindemith who has striven most consistently to preserve, within
the framework of contemporary thought, a sense of kinship with the
past.

His Life

Hindemith was the most substantial figure among the composers who
came up in Germany after the First World War. Defeat, revolution, and
inflation had shaken the social structure and loosened the grip of tradition. Hindemith's early works embodied the boldly experimental spirit
that prevailed under the Weimar Republic. In 1927 he was made professor of composition at the Berlin Hochschule, where he put into practice his progressive theories of education.

Although the Nazi leaders were eager to encourage German art,
Hindemith was too "modern" for a regime that recognized the Wagnerian as the only proper path. Propaganda minister Goebbels accused
him of "atrocious dissonance" and "cultural bolshevism." Hindemith's
music was banned as being "unbearable to the Third Reich." The composer arrived in the United States shortly before the outbreak of the
Second World War and in 1942 joined the faculty of Yale University.
Many young musicians came under his influence there and at the summer school of the Berkshire Music Center in Tanglewood, Massachusetts. A notable feature of his teaching was the revival of medieval and
renaissance music, which he had his students play on the old instruments for which it was written. In 1949–50, Hindemith delivered the
Charles Eliot Norton lectures at Harvard. He subsequently expanded
these into a book, *A Composer's World*, that gives the essence of his
artistic creed.

Hindemith exerted a strong influence on the American scene during
the decade and a half he spent here. With the restoration of peace he
felt the need of returning to the pattern of life in which he had his
roots. In 1953 he went to live in Zurich. During the ensuing years he

was ever more active as a conductor. In 1959 he came back to the
United States for a series of concerts and conducted several of his recent works, the most important of which was the *Pittsburgh Symphony*
—*1958*, written for that city's two-hundredth anniversary. He died in
Switzerland in December, 1963.

His Music

Hindemith's roots go back to the Reformation. The Lutheran chorale,
the contrapuntal art of the sixteenth century, the cantatas and fugues
of Bach are sources of his style. He was influenced, too, by Brahms
and Reger. Dissonant counterpoint supplies tension and mobility to his
tightly woven scores. His melody is descended from the popular song
of medieval Germany, and emphasizes fundamental intervals such as
the fifth and fourth. Now ornate and discursive, now terse and muscular,
it is a freely unfolding melody that lends itself to polyphonic treatment.
His harmony is based on the free use of twelve tones around a center.
Certain daring formations result from his superposing chord upon chord
rather than note against note. Still, he never abandons the principle
of key. The crackling dissonance of his early works mellows in the later
ones to a rich chromaticism. His rhythm is tense and vigorous, although
less spectacular than that of either Stravinsky or Bartók. Significantly,
he was one of those who in the Twenties came under the spell of jazz.

Hindemith emulates the old masters whose complete works fill an
impressive space on the shelves. He has written an enormous amount of
music. Of necessity its quality is uneven. His best ranks with the best
of his time. His less-than-best plays its part in the scheme by preparing
the way for something better. Chamber music holds the central place
in his work. The several compositions entitled *Kammermusik* are for
diverse combinations of strings and winds. These works are flanked by a
mass of solo sonatas and concertos. The vocal works range from solo
song to cantata, oratorio, and opera. In the first-named category an outstanding work is *Das Marienleben* (The Life of Mary, 1922–23, revised
1948), a cycle of fifteen songs for soprano and piano to poems of Rainer
Maria Rilke, in the composer's characteristic vein of reflective lyricism.

Hindemith would seem to belong to the class of composers whose
dramatic powers exist apart from the stage and are even hampered by
scenic representation. His earlier stage works were too experimental to
hold the scene. His finest achievement in the lyric theater is *Mathis der
Maler* (Matthias the Painter, 1934).

Hindemith was one of several German composers—others were
Ernst Krenek, Kurt Weill, and Hanns Eisler—who were associated
with what is known as *Gebrauchsmusik.* The term may be translated
as "workaday" or "everyday" music—literally, music to be used. "The

days of composing for the sake of composing are perhaps gone for-ever," wrote Hindemith in 1927. "A composer should write today only if he knows for what purpose he is writing." The trend toward Ge-brauchsmusik produced such works as Hindemith's "musical game for children," *Wir bauen eine Stadt* (We're Building a City, 1930); his Opus 45, "Music to Sing or Play—for amateurs or music lovers" (1928); his pieces for teaching young violinists the first position; and his music for community singing. Compositions such as these em-bodied the conviction of the younger generation of German composers that a healthy musical culture depended not on the much publicized virtuoso, but on a broad base of amateurs, young and old, who ought to take part themselves in every phase of musical activity. Most of the works produced under the banner of Gebrauchsmusik soon faded from view. But the movement itself sprang out of a healthy desire on the part of composers to reach out to the public, and to reestablish the connection between their art and the life around them.

Coming to maturity in the decade following Germany's defeat, Hindemith in his early scores caught the echo of a bitter time. Sardonic humor and parody pervade the youthful works. With the passing of the years his poetic lyricism increasingly asserted itself, leading in the end to a reconciliation with the romantic spirit. "Nothing is more wearisome or more futile," he has stated, "than the most antiquated of all manias: the rage to be modern. We should minimize the word 'new' in the term *new art* and emphasize rather the word 'art.'"

This attempt to reconcile the new and the old has been interpreted by some as an abandonment of the progressive views he espoused in the Twenties. Others regard it rather as the mellowing that comes with maturity; the necessary retreat in order to consolidate one's gains and move on the more firmly.

Symphony Mathis der Maler (*Matthias the Painter*)

The hero of Hindemith's opera is the painter Matthias Grünewald (active 1500–1530). An artist of impassioned eloquence, Grünewald encompassed both the mysticism of the dying Middle Ages and the realism of the oncoming Renaissance. His masterpiece is the series of paintings for the altar at Isenheim executed for the Brothers of St. Anthony. These display an intensity of vision that places him in the company of Albrecht Dürer, Lucas Cranach, and Hieronymus Bosch.

The peasant revolts that marked the end of medieval serfdom and the beginnings of the Reformation confronted Mathis with a moral issue: How could the artist serenely pursue his work amid the suffering of his fellow men? Should he not rather abandon his art and join the struggle against oppression? Mathis leaves the service of his patron

Cardinal Albrecht and casts his lot with the peasants. Also, in good
operatic fashion, he falls in love with the peasant leader's daughter
Regina. (The libretto, which was written by Hindemith, here comes
to the assistance of history. Almost nothing is known of Grünewald's
personal life.) Mathis soon becomes aware of the gulf that separates
him from his companions in arms. When the peasants suffer defeat he
flees with Regina, vainly seeking inner peace. In his disturbed state he
relives in a kind of allegorical vision the subject of his grandest painting,
the Temptation of St. Anthony. He doubts his genius, he questions the
validity of art. As Hindemith puts it, "All the promptings of conscience
within his tortured soul rise to assail and plague him and call him to
account for his actions. The knowledge of being condemned to utter
uselessness overwhelms him." He passes through the crisis and comes
to realize that only by creating beauty can he serve his fellow men.
The final scene shows the aging artist, the turbulence of life and love
far behind him, tranquilly awaiting his end.

For his symphony Hindemith extracted three orchestral movements
from the score, each named after one of Mathis's paintings. First is
the *Concert of Angels* hymning the birth of Christ, which in the opera
serves as overture. Second is *The Entombment of Christ* and the Lament
of Mary. This music comes from an intermezzo in the last scene and
accompanies Mathis's final withdrawal from life. Last is *The Temptation
of St. Anthony,* a movement that accompanies the climax of the drama,
the sixth scene.

Needless to say, we have here no symphony in the conventional sense.
Nor is this program music of the descriptive variety. The work seeks
rather to evoke in twentieth-century terms certain soul-states that went
into the painting—and the beholding—of the Isenheim pictures. It is
one of the powerful scores of our time.

I. *Concert of Angels. Ruhig bewegt* (moving quietly). The Introduction is based on modal harmonies. A religious folk song of the
Middle Ages, *Es sungen drei Engel* (Three Angels Sang) is intoned by
three trombones, creating an archaic atmosphere.

Wholly characteristic are the serene chords that establish points of
repose within the forward movement.

The Allegro proper, in $\frac{2}{2}$ time, is a tone poem of breadth and energy.
Noteworthy is the composer's gift for creating long-lined melodies
that expand naturally into a flowing texture. The main theme, played

by flutes and violins, bears the composer's personal stamp. Stepwise movement along the scale is enlivened by decisive intervals at the points of stress. The leap of a fifth (at ×) is typical of Hindemith, as is the modal harmony.

The second theme is more placid. A true contrapuntist, Hindemith fashions this idea with a view ultimately toward combining it with the first. Here too we find an upward leap of a fifth (at ×) and a modal atmosphere.

The Development derives its excitement from the devices of imitative counterpoint. A heightening of emotional temperature culminates in the return of the chorale on the trombones. Against it we hear an elaborate orchestral tissue woven out of the two main themes.

II. *The Entombment. Sehr langsam* (very slowly) $\frac{4}{4}$. Muted strings, answered by flutes and clarinets, set the elegiac tone. As in the first movement, Hindemith uses no key signature, indicating sharps or flats wherever he needs them. Pizzicato chords on the strings accompany a broadly arching lament on the oboe, which is imitated by the flute. There follows a mournful dialogue between both instruments. Tension is sustained through the persistent dotted rhythm, which serves as a unifying element. At the climax, wind sonority is pitted against the strings, with superb use of trumpet tone. The music is withdrawn, inward. The serene major chord at the close achieves a Hindemithian effect of finality.

III. *The Temptation of St. Anthony.* In Grünewald's painting the Saint is tormented by noisome beasts. These become, in the scene that constitutes the emotional peak of the opera, the symbol of his own doubts and desires. The score bears the motto (in Latin): "Where wert Thou, good Jesus, where wert Thou, wherefore didst Thou not give aid and heal my wounds?"

The introduction consists of a rhapsodic declamation of the strings in unison, which is imbued with dramatic gesture. The bold arch of the melody is in the great tradition. The movement proper, a frenetic Allegro in $\frac{9}{8}$, opens with a broad characteristic melody. Tension mounts steadily. There is brutal strength in the brass sound. A sustained trill on the violins, with a suggestion of the diabolical, ushers in a languorous episode in which the orchestra takes on a Straussian sensuousness. Clearly the holy man is sorely tried.

Matthias Grünewald, flourished 1500–1530. *The Temptation of St. Anthony* from the Isenheim Altar piece.

The movement resumes with a furiously syncopated section in $\frac{2}{4}$ marked *Lebhaft* (lively). This culminates in a fugato, out of which emerges the Gregorian melody *Lauda Sion Salvatorem* (O Zion, praise the Savior). This is a vast tone painting replete with fantasy and inventiveness. The massed brasses sing a hallelujah as Anthony-Mathis (and presumably Hindemith) achieve the faith that conquers anguish and banishes doubt. It is all very grand, and very German.

✿✿✿ *CHAPTER 86* ✿✿✿

Alban Berg (1885-1935)

"When I decided to write an opera, my only intention was to give to the theater what belongs to the theater. The music was to be so formed that at each moment it would fulfill its duty of serving the action."

IT WAS the unique achievement of Alban Berg to humanize the abstract procedures of the Schoenbergian technique, and to reconcile them with the expression of feeling. Upon a new and difficult idiom he imprinted the stamp of a lyric imagination of the first order.

His Life

Berg was born in Vienna. He came of a well-to-do family and grew up in an environment that fostered his artistic proclivities. At nineteen he made the acquaintance of Arnold Schoenberg, who was sufficiently impressed with the youth's manuscripts to accept him as a pupil. During his six years with Schoenberg (1904–10) he acquired the consummate mastery of technique that characterizes his later work. Schoenberg was not only an exacting master, but also a devoted friend and mentor who shaped Berg's whole outlook on art.

The outbreak of war in 1914 hurled Berg into a period of depression. "The urge 'to be in it,'" he wrote to Schoenberg, "the feeling of helplessness at being unable to serve my country, prevented any concentration on work." A few months later he was called up for military service, despite his uncertain health (he suffered from asthma and attacks of nervous debility). He was presently transferred to the War Ministry in Vienna. Already *Wozzeck* occupied his thoughts; but he could not begin writing the music until the war was over. In December 1925 *Wozzeck* was presented at the Berlin State Opera. At one stroke Berg was lifted from comparative obscurity to international fame.

In the decade that remained to him he produced only a handful of works; but each was a significant contribution to his total output. During these years he was active as a teacher. He also wrote about music, propagandizing tirelessly on behalf of Schoenberg and his school. With the coming to power of Hitler, the works of the twelve-tone composers were banned in Germany as alien to the spirit of the Third Reich. The resulting loss of income was a source of worry to Berg, as was, to a far greater degree, the rapid Nazification of Austria. Schoenberg's enforced emigration to the United States was a bitter blow.

Exhausted and ailing after the completion of the Violin Concerto, Berg went to the country for a short rest before resuming work on his opera *Lulu*. An insect bite brought on an abscess that caused infection. Upon his return to Vienna he was stricken with blood poisoning. He was taken to the hospital and given a transfusion. On catching sight of the donor, a typical young Viennese, he remarked jokingly, "Let's hope I don't become a composer of operettas." During the final delirium his mind was occupied with *Lulu;* he went through the motions of conducting the music, exhorting the orchestra to play more firmly. He died on Christmas Eve 1935, seven weeks before his fifty-first birthday.

His Music

Berg's art issued from the world of German romanticism—the world of Schumann, Brahms, Wagner, Richard Strauss, and Mahler. The romantic streak in his temperament bound him to this heritage even after he had embraced the dodecaphonic style. Berg's was the imagination of the musical dramatist. For him the musical gesture was bound up with character and action, mood and atmosphere. Like his teacher, he leaned toward the formal patterns of the past—fugue and invention, passacaglia, variations, sonata, and suite. He was master of a colorful orchestral palette, which he employed with classical economy and precision. We find in his works the rarefied sonorities of the dodecaphonic school, and all the devices native to it—the evanescent glissandos, trills, harmonics, and muted passages. These and kindred devices were synthesized into an extremely personal style marked by lyric feeling and dramatic élan.

The list of his published works begins with the Piano Sonata Opus 1 (1907–09), a highly charged work in a post-Wagnerian idiom. The four songs of Opus 2 (1909) reveal the composer in a period of transition from Mahlerian romanticism to the expressionist tendencies of his later years. In the last of the four, the young composer abandons key signatures. The *Three Orchestral Pieces*, Opus 6 (1913–14), consist of a *Prelude, Round,* and *March.* With the third piece of this set we find ourselves in the atmosphere of *Wozzeck.* Berg's most widely known composition, after *Wozzeck,* is the *Lyric Suite,* written in 1925–26. The work is in six movements. The first and last follow strictly "the method of composing with twelve tones." The dodecaphonic technique appears also in parts of the third and fifth movements. The last movement, a Largo desolato, contains an allusion to the Prelude of *Tristan and Isolde.* Originally written for string quartet, the *Lyric Suite* achieved such popularity that in 1928 the composer arranged the three middle movements for string orchestra.

Berg spent the last seven years of his life on the opera *Lulu.* The work is based on a single twelve-tone row. The composer fashioned the libretto himself from two dramas by Frank Wedekind—*Earth Spirit* (1893) and *Pandora's Box* (1901). Lulu is the eternal type of *femme fatale* "who destroys everyone because she is destroyed by everyone." Berg was in the midst of orchestrating *Lulu* when he interrupted the task to write the Violin Concerto (1935). The opera remained unfinished at his death. However, the sketches he left behind made it possible to complete the work according to his intentions. *Lulu* has been recorded, and in years to come may very well take its place alongside *Wozzeck* as one of the challenging works of the modern lyric theater.

Alban Berg is today one of the most widely admired masters of the twelve-tone school. His premature death robbed contemporary music of a major figure.

Wozzeck

In 1914 Berg saw the play that impelled him to the composition of *Wozzeck.* He finished the draft of the libretto by the summer of 1917. Most of the music was written from 1918 to 1920 and orchestrated the following year. The vocal score was published in 1923 with the financial help of Alma Mahler, to whom *Wozzeck* was dedicated.

The author of the play, Georg Büchner (1813–37), belonged to the generation of intellectuals who were stifled by the political repressions of Metternich's Europe. His socialist leanings brought him into conflict with the authorities. After his death at twenty-four, the manuscripts of *Danton's Tod* (The Death of Danton) and the unfinished *Woyzeck* (this was the original spelling) were found among his papers.

In the stolid infantryman Wozzeck he created an archetype of "the insulted and the injured" of the earth. Though it issued from the heart
of the romantic era, Büchner's stark drama is surprisingly contemporary
in thought and feeling. Above all—as Berg, with the intuition of genius,
immediately recognized—the play was ideally suited to the emotional
atmosphere of the expressionist theater and the atonal music of the
twentieth century.

Berg's libretto tightened the original play. He shaped the material
into three acts, each containing five scenes. These are linked by brief
orchestral interludes whose motivic facture serves to round off what
has preceded as well as to introduce what follows. As a result, Berg's
"opera of protest and compassion" has astonishing unity of texture and
mood.

The action centers around Wozzeck's unhappy love for Marie, by
whom he has had an illegitimate child. Wozzeck is the victim of the
sadistic Captain and of the Doctor, a coldly scientific gentleman who
uses Wozzeck for his experiments—to which the soldier submits because he needs the money. (Wozzeck is given to hallucinations. The
Doctor is bent on proving his theory that mental disorder is related to
diet.) Marie cannot resist her infatuation with the handsome Drum
Major. Wozzeck slowly realizes that she has been unfaithful to him.
Ultimately he kills her. Driven back to the death-scene by guilt and
remorse, he drowns himself. The tragedy unfolds in three acts. The
first is the Exposition of the theme: "Wozzeck in relation to his environment." The second is the Development of the theme: "Wozzeck
becomes more and more convinced of Marie's infidelity." The third act
is the Catastrophe: "Wozzeck murders Marie and atones by suicide."

The vocal line sensitively portrays characters and situations. Har-
monically, the greater part of the opera is cast in an atonal idiom. Berg
anticipates certain procedures of the twelve-tone system; he also looks
back to the tonal tradition and puts a number of passages in major and
minor keys. He uses diatonic and nondiatonic scales to unify the work,
as well as serial rows and leitmotives in the Wagnerian manner. The
snatches of popular song in the score create an effective contrast to
their atonal surroundings. Appearing in so special a context, they take
on a strange wistfulness.

In the opening scene, Wozzeck is shaving the Captain. From the
hysterical Captain's opening remark—*Langsam, Wozzeck, langsam*
("Slow, Wozzeck, go slow!")—the jagged vocal line, with its wide
leaps and brusque inflections, projects the atmosphere of German expressionism. Wozzeck's music is more sustained in manner. His reply
introduces the chief motive associated with him, on the words *Wir
arme Leut* ("We poor folk!").

Wir ar - me Leut! Sehn Sie, Herr Haupt-mann, Geld, Geld!   Wer kein Geld hat!

This motive in various guises underlines the key statement of the scene, beginning with *Ja, wenn ich ein Herr war:* "Yes indeed, if I were a fine gentleman and had a silk hat and watch and an eyeglass, and could talk fancy, I would be virtuous too. But I'm a poor nobody. Our kind is unlucky in this or any other world! I really think that if we got to Heaven we'd be put to helping with the thunder."

Scene 2, in which Wozzeck and his friend Andres are seen cutting branches in a field, is one of several in which Berg conjures up an atmosphere of fear through his handling of the orchestra. Flickerings of sound on piccolos, oboes, and clarinets admirably prepare Wozzeck's *Du, der Platz ist verflucht!* ("Say, this place is haunted!"). In this scene we have the first of the songs, that of Andres. It is an example of Berg's evocative distortion of popular elements. The following scene, which takes place in Marie's room, shows her growing interest in the Drum Major. Berg here uses military music in a most poignant way. Marie's song *Soldaten sind schöne Burschen* ("Soldiers are handsome fellows!") is one of the tonal passages in the opera: in A-flat major. The lullaby that follows—*Mädel, was fangst Du jetzt an?* ("Girl, what song shall you sing? You've a little child but no husband!")—is a hauntingly lovely bit. When the child falls asleep, Marie remains lost in thought. The strings intone a motive of fifths closely associated with her. "Their

harmonic immobility," Berg wrote, "expresses, as it were, her aimless waiting, which is only terminated with her death."

In Scene 4, between Wozzeck and the Doctor, we return to the atmosphere of obsession. The music takes the shape of a passacaglia. How better express the Doctor's *idée fixe*—the connection between

nutrition and insanity—than by twenty-one variations on a theme? The
theme of the passacaglia is a twelve-tone row, a most interesting cir-

cumstance in view of the fact that the dodecaphonic technique had
not yet been worked out when Berg wrote it. In the final scene of Act
I—the climax of the action thus far—Marie yields to the Drum Major.

The first scene of Act II involves another motive of fear, this time
felt by the child, when Marie bursts out impatiently *Schlaf, Bub!* ("Go
to sleep, boy!"): a minor second on the xylophone, which returns in
various forms throughout the scene.

When Wozzeck begins to suspect Marie, this motive (x) reappears
in slow tempo as a canon on the muted trombones:

The second scene, in which the Captain and the Doctor torment
Wozzeck with veiled references to Marie's infidelity, is an invention
and fugue on three subjects. This scene culminates in Wozzeck's
agonized outcry, *Himmel! Man könnte Lust bekommen sich aufzu-
hängen!* ("God in Heaven! A man might want to hang himself!"). There
follows the brooding Largo during which Wozzeck threatens Marie.
When he raises his hand against her, Marie's words point to the tragic
outcome—*Mensch! Ruhr mich nicht an:* "Man don't touch me. Better
a knife in my flesh than a hand on me. My father didn't dare when I
was ten." There follows a scene at the inn, in which Wozzeck is enraged at seeing Marie dance with the Drum Major. The music begins
with a slow *Ländler* in $\frac{3}{4}$ and brings into prominence the popular elements of Berg's score. The song of the two young workingmen, the
waltz, the chorus, the song of Andres, Wozzeck's jealousy, and the
mock sermon of the drunken young fellow are welded into a vivid
scene in which Berg skillfully exploits the clash between the band

onstage and the orchestra. Equally memorable is the scene in the guard house, which opens with the snores of the sleeping soldiers. The Drum Major boasts of his new conquest. Wozzeck throws himself at the Major, but is beaten down by his burly opponent.

Act III opens with Marie's reading of the Bible, a profoundly moving scene. She tells her child about a poor little orphan; the passage is in F minor. A fugue unfolds as she reads about Mary Magdalen and pleads that the Lord forgive her frailty. The murder scene abounds in ominous sonorities, as at Marie's words *Wie der Mond rot aufgeht* ("How red the moon is!"), where the strings hold a B-natural spread out over five octaves against muted trombones and fluttertonguing on muted trumpets. Unforgettable is the repeated stroke on the timpani, going from a whisper to a spine-chilling fortissimo as Wozzeck cries *Ich nicht, Marie! und kein Andrer auch nicht!* ("If not me, Marie, then no other!") just before he kills her. The drum stroke returns to a pianissimo. In the interlude that follows, the note B is sustained by the orchestra for thirteen bars in a dramatic crescendo, punctuated by the brutal rhythm that symbolizes the catastrophe.

In Scene 3 Wozzeck returns to the tavern and dances with Marie's friend Margaret, who notices blood on his hands. The scene opens with a wild polka accompanied by an out-of-tune piano.

The haunted atmosphere returns as Wozzeck goes back to the pond. How poignant is his *Marie! Was hast du für eine rote Schnur um den Hals?* ("Marie, what is that red string around your neck?")! His last words, *Ich wasche mich mit Blut . . .* ("I wash myself in blood—the water is blood . . . blood . . ."), usher in ghostly chromatic scales that, starting in the strings, pass over to the woodwinds and brass.

There follows a symphonic meditation in D minor, a passionate lament for the life and death of Wozzeck. This inspired fantasy indicates how richly Berg's art was nourished by the romanticism of Mahler. The final scene takes place in the morning in front of Marie's house. Children are playing. Marie's little boy rides a hobbyhorse. Other children rush in with news of the murder, but Marie's son does not understand. The children run off. The little boy continues to ride and sing. Then, noticing that he has been left alone, he calls *Hopp, hopp* and rides off on his hobbyhorse, to the sound of clarinet, drum, xylophone, and strings *ppp*. For sheer heartbreak this final curtain has few to equal it in the contemporary lyric theater.

What *Carmen* revealed to the nineteenth century—"the tragic irony that constitutes the kernel of love," to borrow Nietzsche's famous phrase—*Wozzeck* brought to the twentieth. Like *Carmen* and *Boris Godunov, Pelléas,* and *Salome, Wozzeck* creates an atmosphere all its own. It envelops the listener in a hallucinated world in which the hunters are as driven as the hunted. *Wozzeck* could have come only out of central Europe in the Twenties. But its characters reach out beyond time and place to become eternal symbols of the human condition.

CHAPTER 87

Other Contemporary Composers

Toward the end of the nineteenth century there arose in Spain a movement to create a national art based on authentic folklore. Its culminating figure was Manuel de Falla (1876–1946), whose individuality was strong enough to lift the native idiom into the mainstream of twentieth-century music. He is remembered chiefly for the ballet *El Amor brujo,* generally translated "Love the Magician"—although "Love Bewitched" would be closer to the mark (1915); *Nights in the Gardens of Spain,* three impressionist nocturnes for piano and orchestra (1916); the ballet *The Three-Cornered Hat* (1919); and the Concerto for Harpsichord (or Piano) and Five Instruments—flute, oboe, clarinet, violin, and cello (1926). The best-known of these is *El Amor brujo.*

Ernest Bloch (1880–1959) differs from other composers of Jewish extraction such as Mendelssohn, Meyerbeer, Saint-Saëns, or Mahler, who were assimilated to the musical culture of the country in which they lived. He found his personal style through mystic identification with what he conceived to be the Hebraic spirit. In works such as the Hebrew Rhapsody *Schelomo* for cello and orchestra (1915)—the title is the Hebrew name of the poet-king Solomon—he evokes a biblical landscape with all the force of a temperament given to sensuous abandon and exaltation. In his chamber works, on the other hand, rhapsodic content submits to the discipline of classical form. His Quintet for Piano and Strings (1923) and String Quartet No. 2 (1945) have made a secure place for themselves in the music of our time. Bloch was born in Geneva. In 1916 he settled in the United States. His pupils include several of our prominent composers, among them Roger Sessions, Randall Thompson, and Douglas Moore.

Of the disciples of Schoenberg, none is exerting a stronger influence on our time than Anton Webern (1883–1945). He cut himself off from the tonal past in greater degree than either Schoenberg or Berg. Webern's scores call for unusual combinations of instruments. Each tone is assigned its specific function in the over-all scheme. The instruments, used in their extreme registers, frequently play one at a time, and very little. This technique results in an extreme attenuation —one might call it atomization—of the musical fabric, conferring upon the individual sonority an importance it never had before. This sensitivity to timbre is matched by the subtle dynamic level at which Webern pitches his discourse. There are passages that are no more than a whisper. A superabundance of rests serves to set off the individual tones. His is music in which silence is hardly less expressive than sound.

Within the framework of the dodecaphonic system Webern evolved a style of writing based upon the most intellectual disciplines of the art of counterpoint. The close-knit texture of his music represents the summit of musical economy. In this motivic fabric, concentration of thought and purity of style are carried to the farthest point. In his Symphony, Opus 21 (1928), and the works that followed, the twelve-tone technique is used with unprecedented strictness; the material is made to create its own forms. To this last period belong the Quartet for violin, clarinet, tenor saxophone, and piano, Opus 22 (1930); the songs of Opus 23 (1934) and Opus 25 (1935); the Concerto for Nine Instruments, Opus 24 (1934); and Opus 26, *Das Augenlicht* (The Light of Our Eyes, 1935), for mixed chorus and instrumental ensemble. Also the Piano Variations, Opus 27 (1936); String Quartet, Opus 28 (1938); the two cantatas for solo voice, chorus, and orchestra, Opus 29 (1939) and Opus 31 (1943); and the Variations for Orchestra, Opus 30 (1940). In these works Webern extended Schoenberg's serialism, which concerned itself with a fixed order of pitches, to include also timbre and rhythm. Therewith he moved toward complete control of the sonorous material—in other words, total serialization. His disciples, such as Pierre Boulez and Karlheinz Stockhausen, have carried the implications of Webern's practice to its farthest consequences by applying the serial concept to pitches, rhythms, timbres, dynamics, and densities. As a result, Webern has emerged as the dominant figure in the dodecaphonic thinking of the mid-century. Dedicated to his austere vision of sonorous beauty, he was content to go his way, an obscure figure in the musical circles of his time, overshadowed by those who made a bigger noise in the world. He had no way of knowing that, little over a decade after his death, avant-garde musicians in Europe and America would think of themselves as belonging to "the age of Webern."

The French School

Darius Milhaud (born 1892) is the leading figure in contemporary French music. He is one of the most prolific composers alive. His opus numbers run well past the three-hundred mark. Milhaud is essentially a lyricist. He is associated specifically with polytonality, having explored in greater detail than almost any of his confreres the possibilities of several keys sounding at once. Among his better-known works may be mentioned the ballet *Le Boeuf sur le toit* (named after a famous Parisian cabaret, "The Ox on the Roof," 1919); *Saudades do Brasil* (Brazilian Moods, 1921), a suite of piano pieces which the composer also arranged for orchestra; *La Création du monde* (The Creation of the World, 1923), a Negro ballet based on jazz rhythms; *Suite provençale* (1936–37); the popular two-piano suite *Scaramouche* (1937); and Symphony No. 1 (1939). Also the operas *Christophe Colomb* (1928), *Maximilien* (1930), and *Bolivar* (1943).

Arthur Honegger (1892–1955), born in Le Havre of Swiss parents, spent the greater part of his professional life in Paris and was justly regarded as one of the French school. At the same time he was the least Gallic among them. The spacious lines of the classical sonata and the rhetoric of Wagnerian drama, neither of which flourishes in the Parisian atmosphere, appealed to his imagination. Honegger had a natural affinity for the choral idiom. *King David* (1921), a "symphonic psalm" for chorus and orchestra, and the biblical opera *Judith* (1925) manifest a Handelian bigness of gesture. *Jeanne d'Arc au bûcher* (Joan of Arc at the Stake, 1938) is a kind of oratorio with a speaking part for the heroine amid vivid frescoes for chorus and orchestra. Much publicity accrued to Honegger because of his symphonic movement *Pacific 231* (1923), an orchestral depiction of a locomotive that was the last word in modernism in the Twenties. His Symphony No. 5 (1950), a profoundly felt and powerful work, may be regarded as his finest achievement.

Francis Poulenc (1899–1963) belonged, with Milhaud and Honegger, to a group of six young musicians who attracted much attention in Paris after the First World War. *Les Six* were opposed to romantic grandiloquence as to impressionist haziness. Their spiritual godfather was Erik Satie, their literary propagandist Jean Cocteau. They wanted a "music for everyday" that would be simple, natural, and free from pretentiousness. *Les Six* never had the singleness of aim of the Russian "Five" after whom they were named. Milhaud, Honegger, and Poulenc soon went their separate ways. The other half of the coterie —Georges Auric, Louis Durey, and Germaine Tailleferre—did not attain the fame of their comrades.

Poulenc's music is urbane, Parisian. His piano pieces form a twentieth-century brand of salon music. The *Mouvements perpetuels* for piano, written in 1918 when he was nineteen, are precisely right for what Anatole France called "the intimate conversations of five o'clock." Poulenc's chamber music shows the sympathetic handling of the woodwinds for which French composers are noted. His rich vein of lyricism is to the fore in his songs and in the distinguished choral works that display his gift at its top level. His two operas—*Dialogues des Carmélites* (Dialogues of the Carmelites, on a libretto by Georges Bernanos, 1953–55) and *La Voix humaine* (The Human Voice, based on a one-act play by Jean Cocteau, 1958)—have established him as one of the most important representatives of the trend toward a new romanticism.

The Russians

Contemporary Russian music produced a world figure in Serge Prokofiev (1891–1953). His clean muscular music, bubbling over with wit and whimsy, struck a fresh note. "I love melody," he declared, "and I regard it as the most important element in music. One must be especially careful to make sure that the melody retains its simplicity without becoming cheap, saccharine, or imitative. It is easy to say but not so easy to do." Beyond dispute he managed to do it. Characteristic are the athletic march rhythms, the harmonies pungently dissonant but rooted in the key, the sudden modulations, the unexpected turns of phrase, and the orchestral color that manifests all the brilliance we associate with the Russian school.

Prokofiev himself enumerated the elements of his style. First is the classical, second an eagerness for novelty and experimentation. The third is dynamism, what he called "the toccata or motor element." Fourth is his bent for strong emotional expression, which reaches its culmination in his Fifth Symphony, a heroic work composed toward the end of the Second World War and dedicated "to free and happy Man." Last is the penchant for the comic, the grotesque, and the satanic, a trait that links him to Berlioz, Liszt, Mahler, and the romantic tradition. "In application to my music I should like to replace the word

grotesque by 'scherzo-ness' or by the three words that give its gradations: jest, laughter, mockery."

A greater number of Prokofiev's works have established themselves
as "classics" with the international public than those of any of his
contemporaries save Stravinsky. Among these are *Sarcasms* (1912) and
Visions fugitives (1917) for piano; *Scythian Suite* (1914), with its
deliberate primitivism; the *Classical Symphony* (1917); the Third Piano
Concerto, a masterpiece (1921); *Lieutenant Kije* (1934), a suite
arranged from his music for the film; *Peter and the Wolf* (1936);
Alexander Nevsky (1938), a cantata arranged from the music for the
celebrated Eisenstein film; the ballets *Romeo and Juliet* (1935) and
Cinderella (1944); the two Violin Concertos (1914, 1935); the Seventh
Piano Sonata (1939–42); the Fifth Symphony (1945) and the Seventh
(1953). Several of Prokofiev's operas have found favor outside his
homeland—*Love for Three Oranges* (1919); *The Duenna* (1941), a
sprightly work based on Sheridan's comedy; and *War and Peace*
(1941–42), after Tolstoi's novel. Prokofiev was one of those fortunate
artists who achieve popularity with the masses and at the same time
win the admiration of their fellow musicians. He was among those
who led the way to the reinstatement of melody, the simplification of
technique, and the rapprochement between contemporary music and
the public. His wit, his verve, his melodic gift, and his brilliance of
imagination place him among the masters of our time.

Dmitri Shostakovich (b. 1906) is the first Russian composer of international repute who is wholly a product of Soviet musical culture.
He was trained at the Leningrad Conservatory. His First Symphony
(1925), written as a graduation piece when he was nineteen, won
instant success both at home and abroad. There followed a stream of
works in all branches of music, the most important being the Fifth
Symphony (1937) and the Seventh, the *Leningrad Symphony* (1941);
the ballet *The Golden Age* (1930); the opera *Lady Macbeth of Mzensk*
(1934); six string quartets (1936–56) and the Quintet for Piano and
Strings (1940); the Concerto for Piano, Trumpet and Strings (1933)
and the Violin Concerto (1955). His facility makes for unevenness of
quality, but behind his output stands a vigorous creative personality
in command of a big style that has caught the attention of the world.

The Armenian composer Aram Khatchaturian (b. 1903) bases his art
on the folklore of his native republic. In his love of the exotic he follows
in the footsteps of Rimsky-Korsakov, Borodin, and Ippolitov-Ivanov.
Khatchaturian's Piano Concerto (1936) combines Armenian folk elements with the grand virtuoso tradition of Liszt. Similarly his Violin
Concerto (1940) displays lavishness of melody, sumptuous color, and

the bravura style. Both works are favorites with the American public; as is the suite from the ballet *Gayane* (Happiness, 1942), whose final number, the *Saber Dance*, for a season or two was played so relentlessly that one hoped never to hear it again. Khatchaturian is one of those warm, outgoing artists whose work is destined for popularity. He pursues the goal of bold emotional utterance and sweeping line, within the limitations of a temperament that is impassioned if not always profound.

The English

William Walton (b. 1902) assimilated the ample choral style that is England's inheritance, and drew inspiration from the Tudor church composers and the Elizabethan madrigal. Walton's reputation in this country rests on three serious works. The Viola Concerto (1929) is one of the most convincing among contemporary compositions for that instrument. *Belshazzar's Feast* (1931), a sane and virile work, evokes the spacious line of the Handelian oratorio. The Violin Concerto (1939), written for Jascha Heifetz, is such as to delight the virtuoso who needs a novelty for his concerts that is up to date without being too advanced. Walton is also appreciated here as a film composer. He is now known as Sir William Walton. The title goes well with a music that is polished, urbane, and thoroughly English.

Benjamin Britten (b. 1913), a musician of great invention, technical mastery, and charm, is the most important English composer of his generation. At an age when most artists are just beginning to break through the wall of public indifference, he was already firmly established in the musical world. Britten's music is polished, fluent, and adroit. It has taste and elegance.

Besides a quantity of orchestral, choral, and chamber music, Britten has written several operas, of which the most impressive is *Peter Grimes* (1945). *The Rape of Lucretia* (1946) is a work of rare elegance and classical stylization. *Albert Herring* (1947), like *Lucretia,* is a chamber opera, and belongs to that unlucky class of works which demand the deftest interpretation but invariably attract amateur groups. *Billy Budd* (1951), from the story by Melville—the libretto was prepared with the collaboration of the novelist E. M. Forster—received its American premiere on television in 1952 and made a strong impression. *The Turn of the Screw* (1954) captures the eerie atmosphere of Henry James's famous story. *A Midsummer Night's Dream* (1960), after Shakespeare, affirms Britten's position as one of the foremost operatic composers of our time. These works issue from what one of his countrymen has well called "an unusually compassionate and English heart."

Wassily Kandinsky, 1866-1944, *Composition No. 3, 1914.* (Collection, The Museum of Modern Art, New York. Mrs. Simon Guggenheim Fund.)

"The images on the canvases of expressionist painters issued from the realm of the unconscious: hallucinated visions that defied the traditional notion of beauty in order to express more powerfully the artist's inner self."

Joan Miró, b. 1893, *The Hunter* (Catalan Landscape). (Collection, The Museum of Modern Art, Purchase)

"Expressionism, like surrealism, set up inner experience as the only reality. Through the symbolism of dreams and the glorification of the irrational, it aspired to release the primordial impulses that intellectual men too long had suppressed."

From Central Europe

Zoltán Kodály (b. 1882) was associated with Béla Bartók in the collection and study of peasant songs. The folklore element is paramount in his music. Two works of Kodály's have won international success: the *Psalmus Hungaricus* (Fifty-fifth Psalm, 1923) for tenor solo, mixed chorus, children's voices, and orchestra; and *Háry János* (1926), a folk play with music centering about a retired soldier of exuberant imagination, one of those quixotic and lovable characters in whom is embodied the wit and fantasy of peasant lore.

Bohuslav Martinu (1890–1959) is one of several Czech musicians who have tried to reconcile the native idiom with contemporary Western trends. Martinu has written prolifically in all the forms. In works such as the *Mass at Camp* for baritone, male chorus, winds, and percussion (1939) and the Double Concerto for two string orchestras, piano, and kettledrums (1940), which were written after the betrayal of his country at Munich, or the *Memorial to Lidice* (1943), he echoes the mood of a tragic time. Like many of his colleagues Martinu found a haven in the United States, where he lived from 1941 until his return to his native land at the end of the Second World War. He was a substantial figure on the contemporary scene and a worthy representative of an eminently musical nation.

Ernst Krenek was born in Vienna in 1900. In the 1920s he fell under the spell of jazz. In 1927 he was catapulted into international fame by the sensational success of his jazz opera *Jonny spielt auf!* (Johnny Strikes Up), which centered about a Negro jazz band leader, the Parisian chambermaid who succumbs to his charms, and the sensitive composer Max who symbolizes the dying world of romanticism. Krenek subsequently found his way to the new romanticism emanating from Vienna: the twelve-tone method. Schoenberg's doctrines appealed strongly to his intellectual proclivities. The new technique, he maintains, offers "a very high amount of logical coherence and intelligible significance . . . it enlarges the region of spiritual freedom." When the Nazis took over Austria, Krenek came to the United States, where he has since taught at several colleges. His book *Music Here and Now* reveals an intellect that probes the complexities of contemporary musical thought. Krenek is one of the most prolific composers of our time. Among his works are eleven operas, three ballets, incidental music for seven plays; about thirty choral pieces, including *Lamentations of the Prophet Jeremiah* (1942) and *The Santa Fé Time Table* (1947); six piano sonatas, five symphonies, four piano concertos, and eight string quartets. Krenek is a severely intellectual composer, most of whose music is neither intended nor suited for the casual listener. It bristles with problems, makes no concessions, and is an impressive manifestation of twentieth-century thinking.

Kurt Weill (1900–1950) was one of the most arresting figures to emerge in Germany in the Twenties. He won recognition as an opera composer while still a young man. After Hitler's rise to power he found a haven in the United States, where he fashioned a second career for himself as the composer of a number of Broadway successes, among them *Johnny Johnson, Knickerbocker Holiday, Lady in the Dark, One Touch of Venus,* and *Street Scene;* also *Down in the Valley,* an opera for young people based on folk song. But to the international public his name is indissolubly linked with *Die Dreigroschenoper* (The Three-Penny Opera) that he and the poet Bertolt Brecht adapted from John Gay's celebrated *Beggar's Opera.* Upon the lusty antics of Gay's work, Weill and Brecht superimposed the despair, the agonized outcry of a Germany in the aftermath of the First World War. This stark and sardonic theater piece, with its overtones of social protest, captured the mood of a nation on the threshold of spiritual breakdown. Launched in 1928, the work was a fabulous success; it achieved more than two thousand performances in Germany and was presented all over Europe. Revived in New York City in 1954 in an English version by Marc Blitzstein, with Weill's widow Lotte Lenya singing the role she created in the original production, it proved to be an extraordinary experience in the theater. Weill's score combines arias, duets, trios, quartets, and choruses with such scholarly procedures as the canon and such unscholarly rhythms as the shimmy, blues, march, and tango. The supporting chamber ensemble conjures up all the flavor of the period. *The Ballad of Mack the Knife* is one of the indestructible tunes of the twentieth century. And Jenny's pirate song, the *Ballad of the Black Freighter,* with its mingling of loneliness, hate, and sheer poetic imagination, is as compelling a moment as the contemporary lyric theater has to offer. It is sometimes given an artist to capture the temper of an era, to lift it from its place in time and by an act of creative insight to endow it with meaning for those who come after. The moment that Kurt Weill was fated to illumine—when butter cost a hundred thousand marks a pound and the brown shirts were beginning to march—can never cease to have meaning for our generation.

PART SEVEN

The American Scene

CHAPTER 88

The Past

"Music . . . the favorite passion of my soul."
Thomas Jefferson

THE FIRST publication to appear in the New World was an almanac.
Second was the Bay Psalm Book, which was published in Cambridge
in 1640. Its appearance underlines what was the chief function of
music in early New England: the singing of psalms and hymns.

In Virginia, on the other hand, there evolved a society of planters
who adhered to the social amenities of Cavalier England. As in the
aristocratic circles of Europe, music served for polite and elegant entertainment. Jefferson was an amateur violinist, played string quartets at
the weekly musicales of Governor Fauquier, and invented an ingenious
violin stand which when folded did duty as an end table. Years later,
in planning Monticello, he inquired of a friend in France whether there
might not be found a gardener, weaver, cabinetmaker, and stone cutter
who could double on French horn, clarinet, oboe, and bassoon. "The
bounds of an American fortune," he writes, "will not admit the in-
dulgence of a domestic band of musicians, yet I have thought that a
passion for music might be reconciled with that economy which we
are obliged to observe."

In the absence of an aristocracy to act as patrons, music in colonial
America found an outlet in public concerts, which began to be given
in such cities as Boston and Charleston in the 1730s. Ballad opera too
found favor with the public. The ordinance against theater in Boston
stated that such entertainments discouraged industry, frugality, and
piety (in that order). To get around the law, stage shows masqueraded
as "moral lectures" and "readings." By the end of the century the Bos-
tonians had succumbed to several dozen ballad operas.

The best-known of our early composers was an aristocratic amateur.
Francis Hopkinson (1737–91) came from the same stratum of society
in Philadelphia as did his friend Jefferson in Virginia. Composing was
but one of the many interests of this jurist, writer, statesman, signer
of the Declaration of Independence and framer of the Constitution.

Hopkinson's best-known song is *My Days Have Been So Wondrous
Free*. In 1788 he published a collection of songs "in an easy, familiar
style, intended for young practitioners on the harpsichord or forte-
piano"; he was responsible also for the texts. The work was dedicated
to Washington, to whom he wrote, "However small the Reputation may

595

be that I shall derive from this work, I cannot, I believe, be refused the
Credit of being the first Native of the United States who has produced
a Musical Composition." To which Washington replied, "I can neither
sing one of the songs, nor raise a single note on any instrument to
convince the unbelieving. But I have, however, one argument which
will prevail with persons of true estate (at least in America)—I can tell
them that *it is the production of Mr. Hopkinson."*

A more substantial composer was William Billings (1746–1800). A
tanner by trade, this exuberant figure was the product of a pioneer culture. The little knowledge he had was gleaned from the rudimentary
treatises contained in the hymn books of the time. Billings is specifically
associated with the lively "fuguing pieces" in which he treated psalm
and hymn tunes contrapuntally. The fugal treatment—actually, merely
a sort of simple imitation—produced a music that was, he claimed,
"twenty times as powerful as the old slow tunes. Each part striving
for mastery and victory. The audience entertained and delighted. Now
the solemn bass demands their attention; next the manly tenor. Now
here, now there, now here again! O ecstatic! Rush on, you sons of
harmony." Such ebullience was not to be resisted. Billings's psalms,
anthems, humorous pieces, and patriotic songs were widely performed
in the late eighteenth century. He was rewarded for his efforts with a
pauper's grave near Boston Common. His memory lived on, however,
to inspire some twentieth-century Americans. Otto Luening's *Prelude
on a Hymn Tune by William Billings*, William Schuman's A *Billings
Overture,* and Henry Cowell's *Hymns and Fuguing Tunes* pay homage
to this extraordinary American primitive.

The Nineteenth Century

The young republic attracted an influx of musicians from England,
France, and Germany, who brought with them a tradition and a level
of technique beyond any that existed here. In consequence, the new
generation of American musicians was better equipped than their
predecessors. A typical figure was Lowell Mason (1792–1872), who
wrote *Nearer, My God, to Thee* and other standard hymns. It was
Mason's great achievement to establish music in the public-school
curriculum. His son William Mason (1829–1908) studied with Liszt
at Weimar and became one of the foremost pianists and teachers of his
day. The circle was now complete—Europeans had come to the New
World to live, Americans were returning to Europe to study.

The vogue of the visiting virtuoso began. The Norwegian violinist
Ole Bull was followed, in 1850, by Jenny Lind. What with her gift for
song and P. T. Barnum's genius for publicity, Jenny was a sensation.

Jenny Lind at Castle Garden.

"The vogue of the visiting virtuoso began."

Toward the middle of the century, America produced its own virtuoso in Louis Moreau Gottschalk (1829–1869). Born in New Orleans, the son of an English Jew and a Creole, Gottschalk was one of the adored pianists of the romantic period. Handsome and magnetic, he was a Lisztian figure who left his white gloves on the piano to be torn to shreds by overwrought ladies in need of a little something to press between the pages of a book. Gottschalk left behind some salon pieces such as *The Last Hope* and *The Dying Poet* that nourished several generations of pupils and parents. More important were the exotic miniatures he wrote during the 1840s—*Bamboula, Le Bananier, The Banjo*—which, by exploiting the New Orleans locale, pointed the way to an awakening nationalism.

The revolutions of 1848 caused thousands of liberals to emigrate from central Europe. German musicians came over in large numbers. They formed the backbone of the symphony orchestras, singing societies, and chamber-music groups. In this way the traditions of Weimar and Leipzig, Munich and Vienna were established in our midst and became a decisive factor in shaping our musical taste.

But the great American composer of the pre-Civil War period did not issue from the tradition of Haydn and Mozart. He came out of the humbler realm of the minstrel show. Stephen Foster (1826–64) was born in Lawrenceville, Pennsylvania. His was a substantial middle-class environment in which music was not even remotely considered to be a suitable career for a man. His parents took note of his talent but did nothing to encourage or train it. Foster's lyric gift, unassimilated to any musical culture, found its natural outlet in the sphere of popular song.

Foster's was a temperament unable to accommodate itself to the bourgeois ideal of success. He was, as his biographer John Tasker Howard has written, "a dreamer, thoroughly impractical and . . . never businessman enough to realize the commercial value of his best songs." His course led with tragic inevitability from the initial flurries of good fortune, through the failure of his marriage, to the hall bed-room on the Bowery and the alcoholic's lonely death at the age of thirty-eight. In that time he managed to write some two hundred songs, a half dozen of which have imprinted themselves on the American soul.

Seen in the perspective of history this lovable weakling, the despair of his parents, his wife, and his brothers, emerges as one of our great artists. He stands among the very few musicians whose personal vision created the songs of a nation.

The Postromantic Period

The decades following the Civil War witnessed an impressive expansion of musical life throughout the country. Most important, there appeared a native school of trained composers. First to achieve more than ephemeral fame was John Knowles Paine (1839–1906), who for thirty years was professor of music at Harvard, and mentor of the so-called Boston or New England group that included leading American composers at the turn of the century. Among these was George W. Chadwick (1854–1931), Horatio Parker (1863–1919), Mrs. H. H. A. Beach (1867–1944), and Edgar Stillman Kelley (1857–1944). The Boston group issued from a cultural environment that since the days of Emerson was rooted in German philosophy and culture. They finished their studies in Leipzig, Weimar, or Berlin and worked within the German tradition. It was their historic role to raise the technical level of American music to that obtaining in Europe.

A more striking personality was Edward MacDowell (1861–1908), the first American composer to achieve a reputation abroad. He studied composition in Germany and came to the notice of Liszt, who secured performances of his works. MacDowell settled in Germany and taught there for several years. In 1888 he returned to the United States.

The four piano sonatas and two concertos for piano and orchestra reveal MacDowell to have been at home in the large forms. He was at his best, however, in the small lyric pieces that are still favorites with young pianists. The *Woodland Sketches* (whence the perennial *To a Wild Rose*), the *Fireside Tales*, and *New England Idyls* are the work of a miniaturist of great charm and sensibility.

The composers just mentioned were really belated romanticists. The postromantic label is more properly applied to the Alsatian-born Charles Martin Loeffler (1861–1935), who came to this country when he was twenty. He is remembered chiefly for *A Pagan Poem* (1901), a work for thirteen instruments which he later rewrote for piano and orchestra. Loeffler was a recluse and a mystic. His was a music of shadowy visions, betraying an affinity for Gregorian chant, medieval modes, and impressionist harmonies. His style resembles that which came to be associated with Debussy; yet he found his way to it in the 1890s, before he could have heard much of the Frenchman's music. Loeffler anticipated what was to become the most important development in American music of the twentieth century: the turning from German to French influence.

The American composers of the late nineteenth century ill deserve the oblivion we have permitted to overtake them. Our present-day musicians feel little kinship with these disciples of Liszt, Schumann, and Mendelssohn. And in the world arena they have been overshadowed by their European contemporaries, compared to whom they appear to take second place. Yet comparisons are hardly in order. The European postromantics were heirs to a rich past. The Americans were building for a rich future. They were pioneers dedicated to a noble vision. We have every reason to remember them with pride.

CHAPTER 89

The Present

"The way to write American music is simple. All you have to do is to be an American and then write any kind of music you wish."

Virgil Thomson

Three Generations of American Composers

AMERICAN composers of the early twentieth century faced a difficult task. They had to effect the transition from the postromantic era to the modern. And they had to discover what an American music would be

like. Some of them continued more or less in the path of their predecessors. Frederick Shepherd Converse (1871–1940), Henry Hadley
(1871–1937), Daniel Gregory Mason (1873–1953), and David Stanley
Smith (1877–1949) carried on the genteel tradition of the earlier New
England group. Although they and their fellows had an occasional success, the fact remains that during the first quarter of our century the
serious American composer was something of a stepchild in his own
country. His music faced a twofold handicap: it was contemporary, and
it lacked the made-in-Europe label that carries such weight with our
public. He had no powerful publishers to champion his cause, no system of grants and fellowships to give him the leisure to compose, no
famous conductors to bring him the performances he needed. On the
rare occasions when a work of his was played, as like as not it was sand-
wiched between two masterpieces of the ages, almost as if to point up
the fact that we had no Bach or Beethoven in our midst. As we follow
the careers of the older generation of modern American composers—
those, that is, who were born between 1870 and 1890—we cannot help
feeling that they appeared upon a scene that was not quite ready for
them.

The middle generation—composers born between 1890 and 1910
—had an easier time. The gradual victory of contemporary music in
Europe could not but have repercussions here. Besides, the emergence
of a strong native school became a matter of national pride and found
support in various quarters. The era of prosperity in the Twenties encouraged private patronage in the form of grants and fellowships. Of
enormous value to the members of this generation were the Guggenheim fellowships, the Prix de Rome (which gives the recipient up to
three years at the American Academy in Rome), the Pulitzer Prize, and
the grants of the National Academy of Arts and Letters. Equally helpful were the commissions for new works offered by the League of Composers, the Alice M. Ditson Fund of Columbia University, and the Elizabeth Sprague Coolidge Foundation.

Of great help was the forward-looking policy of conductors like
Serge Koussevitzky, Leopold Stokowski, and Dimitri Mitropoulos, who
made a point of giving the American composer a hearing. The conservatories too, which had hitherto concentrated on the training of instrumentalists and singers, began to turn their attention to the needs of
young composers. So too the music departments of our colleges and
universities took on new importance as centers of progressive musical
activity. The fact that American composers began to occupy chairs at
our leading universities further underlined the growing prestige of the
modern American school.

During this time our composers were actively experimenting with the techniques of contemporary musical speech. In craftsmanship, their scores began to bear comparison with the best of Europe's. They mastered the symphony, chamber music, and choral music; they made progress in conquering what has always been the last stronghold to resist a native art—the opera. And they created an environment in which a young American who wished to compose could receive the finest possible training without having to go abroad. The decade before the Second World War saw this country emerge as the musical center of the world. The presence here of Stravinsky, Schoenberg, Bartók, Hindemith, Milhaud, Krenek, Martinu, and their confreres had a tremendous impact on our musical life. Many of our younger musicians studied with these masters and came directly under their influence.

In the years after the Second World War our native music made important strides forward. Publishing houses and recording companies assumed an ever more receptive attitude toward contemporary American works. Another significant trend was the emergence of the opera workshop, which has offered a strong incentive to the writing of American operas. The government came to the assistance of deserving musicians through the Fulbright grants; during the Fifties the large foundations began to contribute to our musical life in ways that helped composers. As a result of these and kindred developments, especially the emergence of a public interested in hearing American works, the third generation of the contemporary American school—composers, that is, born since 1910—have found an incomparably more favorable climate for their work than did their forebears.

Toward an American Music

As American composers became more sure of themselves, they aspired in ever greater measure to give expression to the life about them. At first they concentrated on those features of the home scene that were not to be found in Europe: the lore of the Indian, the Negro, and the cowboy. They became increasingly aware of a wealth of native material that was waiting to be used: the songs of the southern mountaineers, which preserved intact the melodies brought over from England three hundred years ago; the hymns and religious tunes that had such vivid associations for Americans everywhere; the patriotic songs of the Revolutionary period and the Civil War, many of which had become folk songs; the tunes of the minstrel shows which had reached their high point in the songs of Foster. There were, in addition, the work songs from various parts of the country—songs of sharecroppers, lumberjacks, miners, river men; songs of prairie and railroad, chain gang and frontier. Then there was the folklore of the city dwellers—

Thomas Hart Benton, b. 1889, *The Cotton Pickers.*

"As our artists became more sure of themselves they aspired in ever greater measure to give expression to the life about them."

commercialized ballads, musical-comedy songs, and jazz: a world of melody, rhythm, and mood.

Certain composers, on the other hand, resisted this kind of local color. They preferred the international idioms of twentieth-century music that had been stripped of folk elements: impressionism, neoclassicism, atonality, and twelve-tone music. Others managed to reconcile the two attitudes. They revealed themselves as internationally minded in certain of their works, but employed folklore elements in others. It was gradually realized that Americanism in music was a much broader concept than had at first been supposed: American music could not but be as many-faceted as America itself. A work did not have to quote a Negro spiritual, an Indian harvest song, or a dirge of the prairie in order to qualify for citizenship.

The music of the contemporary American school follows no single formula. Rather, it reflects the contradictory tendencies in our national character: our jaunty humor, and our sentimentality; our idealism, and our worship of material success; our rugged individualism, and our wish to look and think like everybody else; our visionary daring, and our practicality; our ready emotionalism, and our capacity for intellectual pursuits. All of these and more are abundantly present in a music that has bigness of gesture, vitality, and all the exuberance of youth.

CHAPTER 90

The Senior Group

THE POPULARITY of impressionism in America broke the grip of the German conservatory. The new generation of composers looked to Paris, even as their predecessors had taken their cue from Leipzig or Weimar. This trend, strengthened by the boycott of all things German during the First World War, occasioned a major change of orientation during the Twenties.

Charles Tomlinson Griffes (1884–1920)

"It is only logical that when I began to write I wrote in the vein of Debussy and Stravinsky; those particular wide-intervaled dissonances are the natural medium of the composer who writes today's music."

The most gifted among the American impressionists was Charles Tomlinson Griffes, who was born in Elmira, New York. At nineteen he went to study in Berlin. His four years there brought him into contact with a rich musical culture; yet it was only after he outgrew the German influence that he found his true path. Upon his return to the United States Griffes accepted a teaching job at a boy's preparatory school in Tarrytown, New York. His chores at the Hackley School interfered seriously with his composing, but he was never able to escape; he remained there until his death.

Recognition finally came to Griffes in the last year of his life, when his works were accepted for performance by the Boston, New York, and Philadelphia orchestras. *The Pleasure Dome of Kubla Khan*, presented by the Boston Symphony in its home city and in New York, scored a triumph. A few days later, the accumulated strain of years took its toll; Griffes collapsed. The doctors diagnosed his illness as pleurisy and pneumonia; the deeper cause was physical and nervous exhaustion. He failed to rally after an operation on his lungs, and died in New York Hospital at the age of thirty-six.

Griffes represents the current in American music most strongly oriented to foreign influence. His dreamlike art could not be nurtured by indigenous folk song. A nostalgic yearning, a gently elegiac quality informs his music. Stimulated by far-off places and remote times, his imagination turned to moods and fancies rooted in romantic longing. He admired the composers who at that time were attracting the attention of progressive musicians—Debussy, Ravel, Musorgsky and Scriabin, Busoni, Stravinsky, Schoenberg. Another liberating influence was his preoccupation with the music of the Far East.

Griffes's fame rests on a comparatively small output. He favored the short lyric forms. Songs like *By a Lonely Forest Pathway* and *The Lament of Ian the Proud* reveal a lyricist of exquisite sensibility. He was no less successful with the short piano piece, and brought to American piano music a subtlety of nuance that had hitherto been found only among the French composers. Characteristic are the *Three Tone Pictures—The Lake at Evening, The Night Winds,* and *The Vale of Dreams* (1910–12); and the *Four Roman Sketches—The White Peacock, Nightfall, The Fountain of Acqua Paola,* and *Clouds* (1915–16). Of the orchestral works, the most important are *The Pleasure Dome of Kubla Khan* (1912), the *Poem* for flute and orchestra (1918), and *The White Peacock,* which Griffes transcribed for orchestra in 1919.

The White Peacock stems from the years when the Debussyan influence was strongest. The music is languid, capricious; it discourses of strange and lovely things. It wears the jeweled raiment of the impressionist orchestra: oboes and flutes gliding along the chromatic scale, the shimmer of harps, the flash of trumpet tone at the single climax, the whispered ending. Debussy's disciples never found it easy to retain their own individuality. Griffes succeeded. His music displays a fastidious lyricism not devoid of melancholy. It bears the promise of important things to come, a promise cheated of fulfillment by his early death.

Edgard Varèse

Edgard Varèse, born in Paris in 1885, came to the United States when he was thirty-one. He settled in New York City and became an ardent propagator of the new music. Varèse was one of the extreme radicals of his generation. Music for him was an organization of pure sound, a material to be molded rather than a state of soul. "The world of sound is infinite," he stated, "and only a small and arbitrary portion has been used by composers." He set himself the task of expanding this portion with all the wit, clarity, and elegance of his French heritage.

Like Stravinsky, Varèse was interested in sound for sound's sake. But he went even further in rejecting traditional concepts. As he put it, "I refuse to submit myself only to sounds that have already been heard." Melody, harmony, and thematic development were subordinate, for him, to primal rhythm and timbre. His attention focused on that group in the orchestra which stands closest to sheer sonority, the percussion. Varèse was one of the leaders, along with Stravinsky and Bartók, in the twentieth-century discovery of percussive rhythm. His "subject" is the pure composition of planes and volumes of sound whose interplay generates the tension and thrust of the music. When the tension is resolved the piece comes to an end. "I do not use sounds impressionistically as the impressionist painters used colors. In my music they are an intrinsic part of the structure."

This lapidary music unfolds in geometrical patterns based on the opposition of sonorous planes and volumes—patterns that, in their abstraction, are the counterpart in sound of the designs of cubist painting. Varèse's music was utterly revolutionary in its day. It sounded like nothing that had ever been heard before. Varèse's is music for a machine age. It has the hard tensile quality of steel, the rasp of pistons and turbines. It stems out of the climate of disillusionment in the Twenties when intellectuals found themselves facing a mechanistic world seemingly driven by forces beyond human control. Romantic emotion is alien to this music. But its naked clarity arouses another kind of emotion, as compelling as that which the nineteenth century fed on. Varèse gave his works fanciful titles that smack of the foundry or the laboratory: *Hyperprism* (1923), *Octandre* (1924), *Intégrales* (1925), *Ionisation* (1931), *Density 21.5* (1935).

The best known of these, *Ionisation,* is a study in percussion sound. It is written for thirteen players who handle thirty-five instruments, most of which are of indefinite pitch. Tubular chimes, celesta, and piano represent those of fixed pitch. There are also two sirens that slide across and between the degrees of the scale. The freshness of the rhythmic patterns, the projection of dynamic tension, and the illusion of space created by the several planes of sound attest to a musical imagination of the first order.

"I have been waiting a long time for electronics to free music from the tempered scale and the limitations of musical instruments. Electronic instruments are the portentous first step toward the liberation of music." Varèse was one of the first composers to realize the potentialities of the new world of sound that science is opening for the musician. In *Deserts* (1954) and *Poème électronique* (1958) Varèse addressed himself to the problems of electronic music. Thus, in his seventies, the intrepid explorer was still pursuing new paths, bringing back to his less venturesome fellows the shapes and sounds of the music of the future.

Others

Carl Ruggles, "the Cape Cod composer" (b. 1876, Marion, Massachusetts), produced a handful of works whose nobility of style and meticulous craftsmanship have won the admiration of the musical fraternity: *Men and Angels* (1920), *Men and Mountains* (1924), *Portals* (1926), and *The Sun Treader* (1933). Wallingford Riegger (1885–1961) was a dedicated atonalist whose symphonies and string quartets made a strong impact upon our music. Among his important works are *Study in Sonority* for ten violins (or any multiple of ten, 1927); *Dichotomy*, for chamber orchestra (1932); Symphony No. 3 (1948, revised in 1957); and Symphony No. 4 (1957). Charles Ives we will discuss in a separate chapter.

The rise of a national school in the United States had its parallel in Latin America. This movement united contemporary trends with folk elements drawn from Indian, Negro, and Spanish-Portuguese sources. The first composer of South America to command the attention of the world was the Brazilian nationalist Heitor Villa-Lobos (1887–1959), an exuberant musician who turned out music with a tropical abundance. He left behind him over two thousand works, among them twelve symphonies, five operas, eighteen ballets, ten symphonic poems; church music, choral and orchestral pieces, music for band, for solo instrument and orchestra, for voice and orchestra, chamber music, works for violin and piano and for cello and piano, also piano pieces, guitar music, and songs. In an artist of this type, for whom creating is as natural as breathing, a raft of indifferent works paves the way for the few that represent his top level. In his *Bachianas brasileiras*, a series of works in which he pays homage to the spirit of Bach, he created a form intended to forge a link between the art of his homeland and the Western tradition. The most popular of the series is No. 5, for soprano and eight cellos. Villa-Lobos had the faults and virtues of a young culture. He was spontaneous, uninhibited, and not self-critical. His collected works, whenever that project is put through by a grateful nation, will cover a wall in the library at Rio de Janeiro. Out of that mass of notes enough will survive to keep his memory green.

CHAPTER 91

Charles Ives (1874-1954)

"Beauty in music is too often confused with something that lets the ears lie back in an easy chair. Many sounds that we are used to do not bother us, and for that reason we are inclined to call them beautiful. Frequently, when a new or unfamiliar work is accepted as beautiful on its first hearing, its fundamental quality is one that tends to put the mind to sleep."

CHARLES EDWARD IVES waited many years for recognition. Today he stands revealed as the first truly American composer of the twentieth century, and one of the most original spirits of his time.

His Life

Ives was born in Danbury, Connecticut. His father had been a bandmaster in the Civil War, and continued his calling in civilian life. George Ives was the ideal father for anyone who was to become an experimental composer. He was a singularly progressive musician with endless curiosity about the nature of sound. He listened carefully to church bells; and when he found that he could not duplicate their pitch on the piano, he built an instrument that would play the tones "in the cracks between the keys"—that is, quarter tones. Or he made his family sing *Swanee River* in the key of E-flat while he played the accompaniment in the key of C, "in order," his son later wrote, "to stretch our ears and strengthen our musical minds."

Charles at thirteen held a job as church organist and already was arranging music for the various ensembles conducted by his father. At twenty he entered Yale, where he studied composition with Horatio Parker. Ives's talent for music asserted itself throughout his four years at Yale; yet when he had to choose a career he decided against a professional life in music. "Assuming a man lives by himself and with no dependents, he might write music that no one would play prettily, listen to or buy. But—but if he has a nice wife and some nice children, how can he let the children starve on his dissonances? So he has to weaken (and if he is a man he *should* weaken for his children) but his music more than weakens—it goes 'ta-ta' for money! Bad for him, bad for music!" Ives thus began by assuming that society would not pay him for the kind of music he wanted to write. He was not mistaken.

Charles Ives.

He therefore entered the business world. Two decades later he was head of the largest insurance agency in the country. The years it took him to achieve this success—roughly from the time he was twenty-two to forty-two—were the years when he wrote his music. He composed at night, on weekends, and during vacations, working in isolation, concerned only to set down the sounds he heard in his head.

The few conductors and performers whom he tried to interest in his works pronounced them unplayable. Some smiled, persuaded that such writing could come only from one who was ignorant of the rudiments. Others, accustomed to the suavities of the postromantic period, concluded that the man was cracked. After a number of these rebuffs Ives gave up showing his manuscripts. When he felt the need to hear how his music sounded, he hired a few musicians to run through a work. Save for these rare and quite inadequate performances, Ives heard his music only in his imagination. He pursued his way undeflected and alone, piling up one score after another in his barn in Connecticut. When well-meaning friends suggested that he try to write music that people would like, he could only retort, "I can't do it—I hear something else!"

Ives's double life as a business executive by day and composer by night finally took its toll. In 1918, when he was forty-four, he suffered a physical breakdown that left his heart damaged. The years of unrewarded effort had taken more out of him emotionally than he had suspected. Although he lived almost forty years longer, he produced nothing further of importance.

When he recovered he faced the realization that the world of professional musicians was irrevocably closed to his ideas. He felt that he owed it to his music to make it available to those who might be less hidebound. He therefore had the *Concord Sonata* for piano privately printed, also the *Essays Before a Sonata*—a kind of elaborate program note that presented the essence of his views on life and art. These were followed by the *114 Songs*. The three volumes, which were distributed free of charge to libraries, music critics, and whoever else asked for them, caused not a ripple as far as the public was concerned. But they gained Ives the support of other experimental composers who were struggling to make their way in an unheeding world. Henry Cowell, Wallingford Riegger, and Nicolas Slonimsky espoused his cause, as did the critic Paul Rosenfeld. The tide finally turned in this country when the American pianist John Kirkpatrick, at a recital in Town Hall in January, 1939, played the *Concord Sonata*. Ives was then sixty-five. The piece was repeated several weeks later by Kirkpatrick and scored a triumph. The next morning Lawrence Gilman hailed the *Concord Sonata* as "the greatest music composed by an American."

Ives had already begun to exert a salutary influence upon the younger generation of composers, who found in his art a realization of their own ideals. Now he was "discovered" by the general public and hailed as the grand old man of American music. In 1947 his Third Symphony achieved performance, and won a Pulitzer Prize. This story of belated recognition was an item to capture the imagination, and was carried by newspapers throughout the nation. Ives awoke at seventy-three to find himself famous. Four years later the Second Symphony was presented to the public by the New York Philharmonic, exactly half a century after it had been composed. The prospect of finally hearing the work agitated the old man; he attended neither the rehearsals nor the performances. He was, however, one of millions who listened to the radio broadcast.

He died in New York City three years later, at the age of eighty.

His Music

Charles Ives, both as man and artist, was rooted in the New England heritage, in the tradition of plain living and high thinking that came to flower in the idealism of Hawthorne and the Alcotts, Emerson and Thoreau. The sources of his tone imagery are to be found in the living music of his childhood: hymn tunes and popular songs, the town band at holiday parades, the fiddlers at Saturday night dances, patriotic songs and sentimental parlor ballads, the melodies of Stephen Foster, and the medleys heard at country fairs and in small theaters.

This wealth of American music had attracted other musicians besides Ives. But they, subservient to European canons of taste, had proceeded to smooth out and "correct" these popular tunes according to the rules they had absorbed in Leipzig or Munich. Ives was as free from subservience to the European tradition as Walt Whitman. His keen ear caught the sound of untutored voices singing a hymn together, some in their eagerness straining and sharping the pitch, others just missing it and flatting; so that in place of the single tone there was a cluster of tones that made a deliciously dissonant chord. Some were a trifle ahead of the beat, others lagged behind; consequently the rhythm sagged and turned into a welter of polyrhythms. He heard the pungent clash of dissonance when two bands in a parade, each playing a different tune in a different key, came close enough together to overlap; he heard the effect of quarter tones when fiddlers at a country dance brought excitement into their playing by going a mite off pitch. He remembered the wheezy harmonium at church accompanying the hymns a trifle out of tune. All these, he realized, were not departures from the norm. They *were* the norm of popular American musical speech. Thus he found his way to such conceptions as polytonality, atonality, polyharmony, cluster chords based on intervals of a second, and polyrhythms. All this in the last years of the nineteenth century, when Schoenberg was still writing in a post-Wagner idiom, when neither Stravinsky nor Bartók had yet begun their careers, when Hindemith had just been born. All the more honor, then, to this singular musician who, isolated alike from the public and his fellow composers, was so advanced in his conceptions and so accurate in his forecast of the paths that twentieth-century music would follow.

The central position in his orchestral music is held by the four symphonies. The First (1896–98) dates from the period when he was evolving his style. The Second (1897–1902) is a romantic work in five movements. The Third (1901–04) quotes the old hymn *Take It to the Lord*, as well as the Welsh battle song known as *All Through the Night*, and is the most fully realized of Ives's symphonies. Fourth is the Symphony for orchestra and two pianos (1910–16), in which the composer introduces the hymn tune *Watchman, Tell Us of the Night*. Of similar dimension is *A Symphony: Holidays* (1904–13), based upon the "recollections of a boy's holidays in a Connecticut country town." The four movements are *Washington's Birthday, Decoration Day, Fourth of July,* and *Thanksgiving Day*.

Among his other orchestral works are *Three Places in New England,* which we will discuss; and *Three Outdoor Scenes* (1898–1911), consisting of *Hallowe'en, The Pond,* and *Central Park in the Dark,* the last-named for chamber orchestra; also *The Unanswered Question* (1908). The Sonata No. 2 for piano—"Concord, Mass., 1840–1860"—which occupied him from 1910 to 1915, reflects four aspects of the flowering of New England. *Emerson* is an apocalyptic evocation of Ives's beloved philosopher. Second is the scherzo, *Hawthorne,* which conjures up some of that writer's "wilder, fantastical adventures into the half-childlike, half-fairylike phantasmal realms." Third is *The Alcotts,* a gentle slow movement that evokes "the memory of that home under the elms—the Scotch songs and the family hymns that were sung at the end of each day . . . a conviction in the power of the common soul which, when all is said and done, may be as typical as any theme of Concord and its transcendentalists." Fourth is *Thoreau.* The *114 Songs* (1884–1921) range from works in folk style to those that express passion, anger, and poetic feeling. Ives chose texts from Keats, Stevenson, Browning, and Landor, as well as from modern poets. Some of the texts he wrote himself; others are by his wife. The songs are as unequal in quality as they are diverse in character. But the collection as a whole, which includes such striking things as the rugged cowboy ballad *Charlie Rutlage* and the evocative *Serenity, Evening,* and *Ann Street,* vividly reflects the personality behind it. Ives also wrote a variety of chamber, choral, and piano compositions.

There are crudities and rough spots in Ives's style, as there are in the prose of Theodore Dreiser, in the verse of Whitman. His desire to express all the facets of life precluded his developing a homogeneous style. Nor did he ever acquire that solidity of technique which marks the professional composer. Aaron Copland, in a perceptive essay on Ives, has well summed up his predicament: "He lacked neither the talent nor the ability nor the metier nor the integrity of the true artist—but what he most shamefully and tragically lacked was an audience. 'Why do you write so much—which no one ever sees?' his friends asked. And we can only echo, 'Why, indeed?' and admire the courage and perseverance of the man and the artist."

Three Places in New England

In this work (1903–11) Ives evokes three place-names rich in associations for a New Englander. The score specifies the instruments but not the number of each, leaving it to the conductor to decide: piccolo, flute, oboe and English horn, clarinet, bassoon; horns, trumpets, trombones, tuba; percussion, piano, organ (optional), and strings.

I. *The "St. Gaudens" in Boston Common: Col. Shaw and his Colored Regiment. Very slowly.* It will suffice to quote the opening lines of the poem that Ives wrote into the score:

> Moving,—Marching—Faces of Souls!
> Marked with generations of pain,
> Part-freers of a Destiny,
> Slowly, restlessly—swaying us on with you
> Towards other Freedom! . . .

An atmosphere of solemn dedication envelops the opening measures. No familiar tunes are actually quoted in this movement, yet the melodic line unmistakably suggests the world of the Stephen Foster songs and the range of emotions attached to the Civil War. The ostinato patterns in the bass, the urgency of the brass, the complex chord structures on the piano used for their color value, the fluid polyrhythms, and the polytonal effects are all characteristic of the composer; as are the wide-apart instrumental lines and the effect of distance that Ives achieves at the emotional climax by pitting high woodwinds against low brass. The texture is predominantly homophonic. The form is free, in the manner of a prelude or fantasy. The piece ends, as it begins, *ppp*.

II. *Putnam's Camp, Redding, Connecticut. Allegro* (Quick-Step Time). "Near Redding Center," Ives wrote, "is a small park preserved as a Revolutionary Memorial; for here General Israel Putnam's soldiers had their winter quarters in 1778–9. Long rows of stone camp fireplaces still remain to stir a child's imagination." The scene is a "4th of July" picnic held under the auspices of the First Church and the Village Cornet Band. The child wanders into the woods and dreams of the old soldiers, of the hardships they endured, their desire to break camp and abandon their cause, and of how they returned when Putnam came over the hills to lead them. "The little boy awakes, he hears the children's songs and runs down past the monument to 'listen to the band' and join in the games and dances."

In this genre painting Ives conjures up the frenetic business of having a good time on a holiday picnic in a small American town: the genial hubbub, the sweating faces, the parade with its two bands that clashingly overlap. The ardent nationalism that breathes from this music is due not so much to the actual quotation of popular tunes—although one or two do appear—as to the deep love of all things American that lies at the heart of this movement. There is an exciting polymetric passage where two march rhythms clash, four measures of the one equaling three of the other. The intricate polyrhythms in the final measures lead to a daringly dissonant ending, *ffff*. This is one of those works that spring from the soil and soul of a particular place, and could have been conceived nowhere else.

III. *The Housatonic at Stockbridge. Adagio molto* (Very slowly).
Ives quotes the poem of that name by Robert Underwood Johnson:

> Contented river! in thy dreamy realm—
> The cloudy willow and the plumy elm . . .
> Thou hast grown human laboring with men
> At wheel and spindle; sorrow thou dost ken. . . .
>
> . . . . Wouldst thou away!
> I also of much resting have a fear;
> Let me thy companion be
> By fall and shallow to the adventurous sea!

The strings set up a rippling current of sound that serves as background for the melody that presently emerges, divided between the

horn and English horn. It is a serene, hymnic tune that evokes the prayer meetings of Ives's boyhood. The fluid rhythms of this contemplative nature piece impart to it an engaging plasticity. The music flows calmly and steadily to the *fff* climax, then subsides to a pianissimo ending.

Ives holds a unique place in our musical life. Certainly no other composer has so vividly captured the transcendental quality of the New England heritage. Charles Ives is our great primitive. Like the writers he admired most, he has become an American classic.

CHAPTER 92

The Second Generation

DOUGLAS MOORE (b. 1893)

"The particular ideal which I have been striving to attain is to write music which will not be self-conscious with regard to idiom, and will reflect the exciting quality of life, traditions, and country which I feel all about me."

DOUGLAS MOORE has been a consistent advocate of a wholesome Americanism in music. He was born in Cutchogue, on Long Island, and is a descendant of both Miles Standish and John Alden. He attended Yale University, where he studied with David Stanley Smith and Horatio Parker. His *Good Night, Harvard* became Yale's favorite football-rally song. Moore served in the First World War as a lieutenant in the navy. Out of this experience came a collection of songs, in collaboration with the ballad singer John Jacob Niles, under the provocative title *Songs My Mother Never Taught Me.* The war over, Moore went to Paris, where he studied with Vincent d'Indy at the Schola Cantorum. He subsequently was appointed curator of music at the Cleveland Museum of Art.

His four years in Cleveland gave him his first experience as an educator and organizer of musical events. More important, he came in contact with a group of young American composers who were students of Ernest Bloch—Roger Sessions, Bernard Rogers, Quincy Porter, and Theodore Chanler. He too studied with Bloch and considers him the most inspiring teacher he ever had. A Pulitzer Traveling Fellowship enabled Moore to return to Paris and work with Nadia Boulanger. In 1926 he joined the faculty of Columbia University, and in time succeeded Daniel Gregory Mason as Edward MacDowell Professor and head of the music department. At Columbia, in addition to his more specialized duties, Moore developed a flair for making music understandable to the layman. Out of his very popular courses came two books—*Listening to Music* (1937) and *From Madrigal to Modern Music* (1942).

Moore's career moved forward steadily through the years. He had his greatest success when he was in his sixties, with the production of his opera *The Ballad of Baby Doe.* This work, along with those that preceded it, placed him in the forefront of our present-day nationalists.

Moore had to shake off the French influence before he could find his true bent. This he was able to do only by going back to his roots. "I cannot believe," he wrote in the Twenties, "that the fashions decreed by such elegant couturiers as the Parisian Stravinsky or Ravel, successful as they are in permitting a post-war Europe to express herself in music, are likely to be appropriate or becoming for us."

Moore is a romantic at heart. He regards romanticism as a characteristic American trait. "We are incorrigibly sentimental as a race, and our realism in the drama and literature usually turns out to be meltingly romantic in execution. The best of what we accomplish is usually achieved by dint of high spirits, soft-heartedness, and a great deal of superfluous energy." He defends his conservatism on national grounds. "If we like a good tune now and then, if we still have a childish love for atmosphere, is it not well for us to admit the fact and try to produce something which we like ourselves?" His music is honest, unpretentious and clear. When he sets the verses of our poets—among his favorites are Stephen Vincent Benét, Vachel Lindsay, and Archibald MacLeish—his melodic line projects the rhythms and inflections of American speech. The national quality is implicit too in his orchestral pieces. *The Pageant of P. T. Barnum* (1924), a suite that ends with a roistering *Circus Parade; Moby Dick* (1928), after Melville's masterpiece; and the *Overture on an American Tune* (1931), which conjures up the boisterous optimism of Sinclair Lewis's *Babbitt*, exemplify Moore's sympathetic handling of Americana. In the same vein is *Village Music* (1942), and an engaging suite for chamber orchestra called *Farm Journal* (1947). Even his absolute music, such as the Symphony in A (1945), the jaunty String Quartet (1933), or the Quintet for Clarinet and Strings (1946), echoes the native scene, although of course in more stylized form.

"I've always liked setting words better than any other form of composition," Moore declared fairly early in his career, "and I've always had a passion for the theater." This double affinity leads a composer in one direction—opera. Moore states his predilection with gusto. "I love to write operas. To me it is the most spontaneous form of expression. The music writes itself if the book is good." This is a big "if." Moore's first opera, *White Wings* (1934), after Philip Barry's play, did not get off the ground. *The Devil and Daniel Webster* (1938), with a libretto by Stephen Vincent Benét, based on his celebrated short story, did. This exuberant one-acter, which shows Daniel Webster matching his wits and eloquence against the Devil's, has established itself as an American classic. *Giants in the Earth* (1950), on a libretto by Arnold Sundgaard after the novel by O. E. Rölvaag, brought Moore a Pulitzer Prize; but his music was not able to surmount the handicap of a cumbersome book.

The experience he gained, however, prepared him for his most ambitious efforts in the theater—the opera about Baby Doe, and *The Wings of the Dove* (1961), after Henry James's novel.

The Ballad of Baby Doe

The Ballad of Baby Doe (1956) is based on an American legend that really happened: the rise and fall of Horace Tabor, who struck silver in Leadville, Colorado, became one of the wealthiest men of his time, and was ruined when the United States abandoned the silver

A scene from *The Ballad of Baby Doe.*

standard for gold. The action unfolds in a turbulent period of American history against the background of a Colorado mining town. The eternal triangle involves Horace; Augusta, his domineering and strait-laced wife, who accompanied him from his humble beginnings to wealth and power; and Baby Doe, as she was known among the miners —a twenty-year-old beauty with an uncertain past, for whose sake the middle-aged magnate divorced Augusta. John LaTouche provided a beautiful libretto—dramatically compelling, with characters who are three-dimensional and true. The story line is one that has been infallible in the drama ever since the Greeks—the destruction of the hero through the fatal flaw he carries within him. The intertwining of personal destiny with vaster issues is as imaginative as it is deft.

There are eleven scenes. The first takes place in 1880, on the night of the opening of the Tabor Opera House—Horace's gift to Leadville and culture. It is also the night of Baby Doe's arrival in Leadville.

Moore's music, noisy and brash, projects the atmosphere of the Colorado mining town.

Scene II. Outside the Clarendon Hotel, later that evening. Baby Doe's song, "Willow, where we met together," establishes the sweet-

Wil-low, where we meet to-geth-er.___ Wil-low when our love was new.___

Wil-low, if he once should be re-turn-ing, Pray tell him I am weep-ing too.

ness of the girl. It enraptures Horace and impels him to a lyric outburst: "Warm as the autumn light, soft as a pool at night, the sound of your singing, Baby Doe. . . ." In both arias Moore's melodic line, sensitively attuned to LaTouche's text, is unmistakably American.

Scene III. The Tabor apartment several months later. Augusta confronts Horace with proof of his infidelity. Both characters are clearly limned, musically and dramatically. Altogether admirable is Moore's handling of what has always been the thorniest problem of opera in English—the recitative.

Scene IV. The lobby of the Clarendon Hotel, shortly thereafter. Baby Doe has decided to leave Tabor and writes her mother to explain why. This adaptation of the "letter scene" of European opera comes to a dramatic climax when Augusta enters to confront her rival. Baby Doe pleads with her to understand Horace and not to judge so great a man by the usual standards. Augusta mocks this naive idealization of her husband and leaves haughtily. Baby Doe realizes that Augusta's domination must ultimately destroy everything in Horace that is clamoring for fulfillment, and decides to stay. In a tender duet she and Horace affirm their love.

Scene V. Augusta's parlor in Denver, a year later. Four of Augusta's friends inform her of Horace's intention to divorce her. Moore makes effective use of the women's voices in this scene, which reaches its peak with Augusta's declaration that Horace will rue the day if he should ever attempt to humiliate her in this fashion.

Scene VI. The Willard Hotel, Washington, D. C., 1883. Tabor, serving a thirty-day interim term as United States senator, marries Baby Doe. It transpires at the reception that both Baby Doe and Tabor have been divorced. The Catholic priest who has just performed the ceremony, realizing that he was not told the truth, leaves in horror. The reception is about to break up when the footman announces the President of the United States, Chester A. Arthur. This *deus ex machina* brings the first act to a theatrically effective close.

Act II, Scene 1. The Windsor Hotel in Denver, 1893, on the night of the Governor's Ball. A diatonic waltz nostalgically conjures up the Nineties. Baby Doe is startled by the arrival of Augusta, who has swallowed her pride in order to warn her that the country is about to abandon the silver standard. She pleads with Baby Doe to persuade Horace to sell his mines. Horace enters, misunderstands Augusta's motives, and orders her to leave. He makes Baby Doe promise that she will never sell the Matchless Mine.

Scene 2. A Club Room in Denver, 1895. Horace appeals to his wealthy cronies for financial help and informs them of his decision to support William Jennings Bryan, who is campaigning for the presidency on a free silver platform. They turn a deaf ear to his appeal. He gives vent to his sense of betrayal in an impassioned aria.

Scene 3. The Matchless Mine, summer, 1896. A campaign rally for Bryan. The atmosphere of brass-band festivity is evoked with a wealth of picturesque detail. Bryan's famous "Cross of Gold" speech is transformed into a big aria for bass-baritone. The great orator, hailed by the crowd, christens Horace's little daughter Silver Dollar.

Scene 4. Augusta's home in California. She hears the newsboys shouting the news of Bryan's defeat—which means Tabor's ruin—and is visibly moved. Baby Doe's mother arrives to ask her to help Horace; but Augusta has been too deeply hurt to be able to forgive him.

Scene 5. The stage of the Tabor Opera House, 1899. Tabor, a crushed old man, returns to the scene of his former glory. He relives the chief moments of his life in a strange kaleidoscope of past and future. The grimly accusing figure of Augusta fills him with a sense of failure. Baby Doe arrives to help the dying man. She sings of the one real thing among the shadows—their love. "Always through the changing of sun and shadow, time and space, I will walk beside my love in a green and quiet place. . . ." As the aria unfolds, we see her as a white-haired old woman by the Matchless Mine, keeping her promise to Horace. (The real Baby Doe guarded the mine, a solitary eccentric wearing castoff men's clothing, with gunnysacks wrapped around her feet, until she was found frozen to death on the floor of her shack in March, 1935.)

The Ballad of Baby Doe—"The Girl of the Silver West," as it was called by the critic Jay Harrison—unites lyric and dramatic elements in a fine theater piece. The music is rich in atmosphere. The characterization is vivid, the scoring adroit, the melodic line simple and relaxed. Here is an American opera that recreates our past in a literate way, that belongs to us in every word and note.

WALTER PISTON (b. 1894)

"The self-conscious striving for nationalism gets in the way of
the establishment of a strong school of composition and even of
significant individual expression . . . The composer cannot afford the wild-goose chase of trying to be more American than
he is."

Walter Piston is a leading representative of the international outlook
among American composers. Art limits itself, he believes, through exclusive preoccupation with native themes. "Is the Dust Bowl more
American," he asks, "than, say, a corner in the Boston Athenaeum?" An
intellectual by temperament, a humanist by profession, he leans rather
to those values in art that transcend the local. This does not mean that
American elements are wholly absent from Piston's style; but they are
there only as part of a larger, a universal conception.

Piston speaks the current language of neoclassicism, which is understood with equal readiness in Paris, London, or Berlin. Such art, from
the nationalist point of view, lacks the raciness that comes from contact
with the soil. By the same token it gains, in the eyes of its devotees,
dignity and universality of outlook. Piston's music is urbane, polished,
witty, controlled. It is to be admired no less for the distinction of its
ideas than for the perfection of its workmanship. "Piston's music, if
considered only from a technical viewpoint, constitutes a challenge to
every other American composer. It sets a level of craftsmanship that is
absolutely first-rate in itself and provides a standard of reference by
which every other American's work may be judged." This is praise indeed, coming from a fellow composer—Aaron Copland.

Walter Piston was born in Rockland, Maine, where his grandfather,
an Italian sailor named Antonio Pistone, settled, married an American
girl and dropped the *e* from the family name in token of his acclimatiza-
tion. The composer's first ambition was to become a painter. While at
art school he learned the piano and supported himself by playing in
dance bands, restaurants, and theaters. He enlisted in the navy band at
the outbreak of the First World War and acquired some knowledge of
the saxophone. Subsequently he went to Harvard, where he soon made
up for his late start as a composer. A fellowship enabled him to continue
his studies in Paris, where he came under the influence of Nadia
Boulanger, a remarkable teacher who played an important role in
training the postwar generation of young Americans in Paris. Upon
his return from Paris in 1926 Piston joined the music faculty of Harvard
University. He was head of the music department for several years;

and in 1951 was appointed to the newly endowed Naumburg professorship, which left him more time for composing. He retired in 1960. Piston's teaching aimed to reconcile modern concepts with tradition. Out of it came four books—*Principles of Harmonic Analysis* (1933), *Harmony* (1941), *Counterpoint* (1947), and *Orchestration* (1955)—which are used as college texts throughout the country.

Producing slowly but steadily throughout the years, Piston has turned out a body of works that exemplify his fondness for the absolute instrumental forms. His natural habitat is a music free from "pictorial, narrative, political, or philosophical intent," as he puts it. "Each new work is for me the start of a new problem, a new adventure the outcome of which I am never able to predict. It is in a sense another study towards the perfect balance between expression and form." This balance was at first weighted on the side of form. Typical of his earlier period is the brilliant Concerto for Orchestra (1933), the witty Concertino for piano and chamber orchestra (1937), and the First Symphony of the same year, with its dissonant counterpoint and elaborate fugal devices. Piston thenceforth moved toward directness of utterance, simpler textures, more melodious phraseology, and, above all, a more personal lyricism. This development is manifest in the Second Symphony (1943); it comes fully into its own with the new expansiveness of the Third (1947), which received a Pulitzer Prize, and the Fourth (1949). The Fifth (1954), a thoughtful, sensitive work, was followed in 1955 by the relaxed and songful Sixth and in 1961 by the deftly wrought Seventh.

Notable for their structural logic, breadth of conception, and purity of speech, the symphonies form the center of Piston's output. His list includes three string quartets, two orchestral suites; the Violin Concerto of 1939, and a Quintet for piano and strings (1949) that is a distinguished addition to the limited contemporary literature for that combination.

The Incredible Flutist

The work by which Piston is best known to the American public is the gay and tuneful concert suite drawn from his ballet *The Incredible Flutist*, which was written for Hans Wiener's dance group and first performed in Boston in 1938. The suite contains about half the music of the ballet.

The scene is laid in a Spanish village in carnival time. The siesta hour is over, the shop reopens. The merchant's daughters display their father's wares to the customers. Various village characters appear. Suddenly a march is heard announcing the arrival of the circus. The grand parade files past, led by the circus band—barker, jugglers, snake

charmer, monkey trainer, and the star attraction of the show, the Incredible Flutist, whose playing charms even the circus animals. He
charms also one of the merchant's daughters, who meets him that evening in the village square. They are not alone; other couples have been
lured out by the romantic night. The merchant courts a rich widow
who has resisted his suit for years. Love is in the air: she suddenly yields
and grants him a kiss. They are discovered by their prying neighbors.
The lady from sheer embarrassment swoons, but is revived by a little
music from the Incredible Flutist. The enchanted moment is over, the
circus must be on its way. The band strikes up. The Incredible Flutist,
so gallant and debonair, is off for new adventures.

The introductory melody, marked Lento, establishes the Spanish
atmosphere, its languid arabesques suggesting the siesta hour in the
market place. The Dance of the Vendors (Allegro moderato), with its
tart dissonances, has a Stravinskyan flavor: the Stravinsky of *Petrushka*.
The Tango of the Four Daughters is a suave tune in $\frac{5}{8}$ that displays
Piston's hitherto unsuspected flair for popular melody. The villagers

greet the circus with shouts of joy (Allegro moderato). These noisy
measures well suggest the expectancy of the crowd. The Circus March
is followed by the solo of the flutist, who weaves his spell with trills
and roulades (Lento). The widow and the merchant mark their ren-
dezvous with a brief minuet, which is followed by a gay Spanish waltz.
The flutist and the merchant's daughter have their romantic moment
to the tender measures of a siciliano, an Andante in $\frac{6}{8}$. In the brilliant
finale (Tempo di polka, $\frac{2}{4}$), Piston has recourse to a device that is
always effective: a catchy tune repeated over and over, each time a
bit faster.

This music is tender and gracious. It has the feel of the theater, the
balletic suggestion of body movement and gesture. Its gay measures
offer a charming introduction to Walter Piston's more serious works.

VIRGIL THOMSON (b. 1896)

"I wrote in Paris music that was always, in one way or another,
about Kansas City. I wanted Paris to know Kansas City, to
understand the ways we like to think and feel on the banks of
the Kaw and the Missouri."

Virgil Thomson's art is rooted in the homespun hymns and songs,
many of Civil War vintage, that were the natural inheritance of a boy
growing up in Missouri. On this was superimposed the cultural tradition of Harvard; and upon that, during a fifteen years' residence in
Paris, the Gallic approach to art and life whose foremost American
spokesman he is.

A group of American composers. From left to right, seated: Virgil Thomson,
Gian Carlo Menotti, William Schuman. Standing: Samuel Barber, Aaron
Copland.

Thomson's esthetic derives from Erik Satie. (For him the three S's
of contemporary music, in descending order of importance, are Satie,
Schoenberg, and Stravinsky.) Like *Les Six*, he represents a turning
away from the grandiloquence of the postromantic era. He is no less
opposed to the intellectuality of much that was done in the name of

neoclassicism. He desires music to return to the age-old French ideal of a sweet and reasonable art whose goal it is to charm, please, and entertain—a neoromantic art aimed at the heart rather than the mind, and never pretentious. Thomson seeks coziness of spirit as well as elegance. The new romanticism, as he conceives it, is marked by "the wish to express sincere personal sentiments with a maximum of directness and of spontaneity."

The *Symphony on a Hymn Tune* (1928) was followed by a Second Symphony (1931), both based on folk material. *The Seine at Night* (1947), a symphonic sketch, has for its companion pieces an American landscape composed a year later, *Wheatfield at Noon,* and *Sea Piece with Birds* (1952). A melodious Concerto for Cello and Orchestra (1949) has been widely played. The concert suites that Thomson fashioned from his film scores, such as *The Plough that Broke the Plains* and *Louisiana Story,* reveal him in a genre in which he has always been at his best. Thomson has produced much vocal music to French and English texts, and a number of choral works. A Mass of 1959 is his major achievement in this area. His ear is remarkably sensitive to the inflections of American speech, a gift that enables him to set our language with great effectiveness. He lets the words float on the music without ever submerging them.

Thomson came into prominence with the production in 1934 of *Four Saints in Three Acts* on a libretto by Gertrude Stein. The work received over fifty performances, a run never before achieved by an American opera. Nobody quite knew what it was about save the Stein experts— and how many of those have you? But the superb acting and singing of the Negro cast, the cellophane wrappings designed by Florine Stettheimer, the free-association prose of the ineffable Gertrude informing her public that "pigeons on the grass, alas," and a nostalgic score unabashedly based on the three major chords of traditional harmony combined to delight a world that had very little at the moment to be delighted about.

Collaboration with Miss Stein produced a second work, *The Mother of Us All* (1947), dealing with the life and career of the feminist leader Susan B. Anthony. An odd assortment of characters from different periods of American history are fancifully juxtaposed in the various scenes. General Grant, expressing himself in excellent Steinese, declares bravely, "As long as I sit I am sitting." Miss Anthony sings persuasively, "You're entirely right but I disagree with you," and is informed that "a Cause is a Cause because." *The Mother of Us All* is a vivid bit of Americana that proved to possess ample vitality when it was revived in New York in 1959. It is clear from these two operas that Thomson needs very special material to be able to function in the lyric theater.

The association with Miss Stein came to an end with her death. One wonders what their next would have been like.

As critic of the New York *Herald Tribune* (1940–54) Thomson became known as one of the most provocative writers of our time. His was an inimitable blend of seriousness and wit flavored with French sauce. He was outspoken and, a great asset in a critic, he was not afraid to be wrong. He had his prejudices and his blind spots; but even those who disagreed with his columns could not resist reading them. Whatever the future of his music—and posterity is notoriously unreliable in this regard—he is assured his place in music history as the wittiest chronicler of our era.

Louisiana Story

Robert Flaherty's documentary film *Louisiana Story* (1948) dealt with the impact of the oil industry upon the bayou country as seen through the eyes of a boy. The concert suite consists of four pieces.

I. *Pastoral* (The Bayou and the Marsh Buggy) is an impressionistic tone painting. In the film this music accompanies the boy's paddling through his beloved bayou. The piece evokes a lonely landscape of sky, water, and giant trees. The mood is embodied in a modal folk tune, which is first heard on the English horn.

The music gathers momentum as the boy's canoe approaches the marsh buggy—an amphibious tractor used in prospecting—and is almost overturned.

II. *Chorale* (The Derrick Arrives). A vivacious folk song alternates with the chorale that is associated in the score with the derrick. The chorale, based on a twelve-tone row, depicts the boy's wonder as he gazes at the lofty mesh of steel that thrusts against the sky.

III. *Passacaglia* (Robbing the Alligator's Nest). A ground bass in $\frac{5}{4}$ time is repeated over and over, now with a countertheme, now without. The music creates an atmosphere of suspense as the boy, in the act of stealing the alligator's eggs, is confronted by the enraged beast.

IV. *Fugue* (Boy Fights Animal). The fourth piece, which accompanies the dramatic struggle at the climax of the film, is in the form of a fugue. The subject is announced by bassoons, trombones, tuba, cellos, and double basses, fortissimo. The chromatic idiom employed here, descended from the harmonic language of Liszt and Franck, is manifest in the use of chords traditionally associated with suspense and excitement. It is to be noted that Thomson, in so descriptive a score, employs three of the forms of the Baroque—chorale, passacaglia, and fugue. This underlines the tendency of twentieth-century composers, like those of the eighteenth, to impose musical forms on the drama rather than to allow the drama to shape musical form.

Longing, we have seen, is the essence of romantic art. A great longing pervades Thomson's music and motivates its glances to the past. Is this the nostalgia of the sophisticate for a simplicity forever lost? Be that as it may, Virgil Thomson is a profoundly American romantic.

ROGER SESSIONS (b. 1896)

"I am not trying to write 'modern,' 'American,' or 'neoclassic' music; I am seeking always and only the coherent and living expression of my musical ideas."

The eminence of Roger Sessions does not depend upon the number of performances his works receive or their popularity with the public. It derives from the fact that he concerns himself with problems which are fundamental to contemporary musical thought, and does so on the highest level of responsibility. He has been called a musicians' musician; his art is not calculated to win easy approval. In this connection he states, "I would prefer by far to write music which has something fresh to reveal at each new hearing than music which is completely self-evident the first time and though it may remain pleasing makes no essential contribution thereafter."

Roger Sessions was born in Brooklyn, New York, of a New England family that returned soon afterward to Massachusetts. It was there that the composer spent the greater part of his boyhood. Precocious not only in music, he entered Harvard at fourteen. After his graduation he studied with Horatio Parker at Yale; then with Ernest Bloch, whose assistant he became at the Cleveland Institute of Music (1921–25). Several prizes and grants made it possible for him to spend the next eight years in Europe. He returned in 1933 and speedily made a place for himself on the American scene. For ten years he was a member of the music department of Princeton University. In 1945 he was appointed professor of composition at the University of California in Berkeley, a post he retained until his return to Princeton in 1953.

Along with Piston, Roger Sessions is the chief representative of the international trend in contemporary American music. He thinks of himself as an American writing music rather than as a composer of American music. He is an exponent of the neoclassic esthetic, which upholds the primacy of pure musical forms and ideas. In an article written in 1927 Sessions formulated the ideals of his generation in a paragraph that became a kind of manifesto of the new classicism: "Younger men are dreaming of an entirely different kind of music— a music which derives its power from forms beautiful and significant by virtue of inherent musical weight rather than intensity of utterance; a music whose impersonality and self-sufficiency preclude the exotic; which takes its impulse from the realities of a passionate logic; which, in the authentic freshness of its moods, is the reverse of ironic and, in its very aloofness from the concrete preoccupations of life, strives rather to contribute form, design, a vision of order and harmony."

The classicist bent in Sessions is combined with a romantic streak. He has responded not only to the objectivity of the French tradition but also to the emotional expressiveness of the German. This inter-mingling of classic and romantic elements is indicated in his remark, "My music is always expressive in intent, and often has concrete associations for me. In composing, however, I follow not the associations but the impulsion of the musical ideas themselves."

The central place in Sessions's output is held by his four symphonies (1927, 1946, 1957, 1958). These bear the imprint of profound thought and concentrated emotion so characteristic of the composer. The Third belongs to a group of works marked by a more personal lyricism and a more accessible style than his earlier compositions. This group includes the Second String Quartet (1951), the brilliant Concerto for Piano and Orchestra (1956), the *Idyll of Theocritus* for soprano and orchestra (1954), and the Mass of 1958. Also *The Trial of Lucullus* (1947), based on a play by Bertolt Brecht in which the celebrated Roman general stands trial after his death, his jury consisting of the little people whose lives were shattered by his triumphs.

Symphony No. 1

The First Symphony (1927) is a sunny, unproblematic piece that sums up the characteristics of Sessions's neoclassic period. It is scored for an orchestra of usual size, including piano.

I. *Giusto*, $\frac{2}{4}$, E minor. The imperious flourish with which the movement opens leads into a closely woven texture of imitative counterpoint with propulsive force and vigor. This Allegro takes its point of departure from a compact idea that lends itself admirably to motivic treatment.

The emphasis on winds rather than strings makes for the bright "objective" sonority that was in vogue in the Twenties. The frequent dislocation of accent engenders a foreshortening of the measure which adds to the rhythmic tension. A contrasting motive emerges in the brass. But a movement such as this depends upon the principle of continuous expansion as practiced by the Baroque rather than on the sectional contrasts of the Haydn-Mozart period. In the Recapitulation Sessions adroitly varies the musical fabric, especially in regard to the distribution of the thematic material among the voices.

II. *Largo*, $\frac{2}{4}$, C major. This slow movement in A-B-A form is steeped in manly lyricism. The florid singing line draws inspiration from the arabesque of Bach. The emphasis is on the vibrant expressiveness of the

strings. The soloistic treatment of the instruments results in a chamber-music texture. In the middle part, clarinet and piano set up a diaphanous background of triplets for the traceries of oboe and flute. The A section is repeated in curtailed form.

III. *Allegro vivace*, $\frac{2}{4}$, E major. The finale captures the dancelike impulsion of the classical rondo. Here lighthearted rhythm is released into the pure joy of pattern-making. The strong tonal feeling in this movement, as in the rest of the symphony, nourishes the energy of the music and the clarity of its drive. The rondo theme is properly vivacious, the texture is limpid, the color bright. A rhythmic intensification leads to a forthright coda and vigorous cadence in E.

The complexity of Sessions's writing, like that of Proust's, springs from a mind subtle and allusive, which sees all the ramifications of an idea and delights in tracing these to their ultimate consequence. His is a music surcharged with nobility of thought and feeling. It presents distinguished ideas in a distinguished way.

ROY HARRIS (b. 1898)

"I am trying to write a music which expresses our time and
period in America. What I am trying to say in music is related
principally to the region of the West where I was born and
where I understand life best."

In the early Thirties Roy Harris was hailed as the white hope of American music, a young genius come out of the West to reveal to us our soul.
For a decade he was the most played and most publicized composer in
America. Then, quite suddenly, he dropped from the limelight. Such
vagaries of fortune make the hazards of a public career among us. They
in no way affect the ultimate value of Harris's contribution to his art.

He was born in a log cabin in Lincoln County, Oklahoma, of Scotch-
Irish stock. His parents moved shortly afterward to less rigorous surroundings near Los Angeles; but the log cabin remained part and parcel
of the Harris legend. The youth was torn between his artistic leanings
and an environment that had little room for art. At eighteen he was
working his own farm. After two years in the army during the First
World War he enrolled at the University of California. He drove a
truck, delivering butter and eggs; worked as usher in the Los Angeles
Auditorium so that he could hear music; and wandered about the
country doing odd jobs, on one occasion acting as gatekeeper at a
rodeo. When he was twenty-four his musical impulse was no more to
be denied. He began to study with the composer Arthur Farwell in
Los Angeles. The young man's passionate eagerness made a deep impression on the teacher. Years later, when writing about his astonishing
pupil, Farwell remembered Schumann's famous tribute to the young
Chopin: "Hats off, gentlemen—a genius!" He began his own article
with "Gentlemen, a genius—but keep your hats on!"

Harris's rise to fame was as spectacular as his start was halting.
In the summer of 1926 Hoogstraten performed his Andante for Orches-
tra at the Hollywood Bowl, and repeated it at a Stadium concert in New
York. In the meantime the piece had come to the notice of Howard
Hanson, who accepted it for performance by the Rochester Symphony.
The attention of the musical world was suddenly focused on this new
voice from the west. Harris was given an opportunity to study in Paris,
and returned after three years to find himself *the* American composer.
With his spare frame and soft drawl, looking "like a midwestern farmer
in city clothes," he captured the imagination of his contemporaries as
no American musician had done. He saw himself as a national artist,
a kind of Walt Whitman who was the voice, whether for exhortation

or prophecy, of a young and vital civilization. As Virgil Thomson quipped, "One would think, to read his prefaces, that he had been awarded by God, or at least by popular vote, a monopolistic privilege of expressing our nation's deepest ideals and highest aspirations."

Harris's music is American in its buoyancy and momentum, its expansiveness and manly strength. Its epic quality suggests to some the vastness and loneliness of the prairie. Others are attracted by its intimate lyricism. Harris belongs to the spontaneous type of artist who is apt to appear during the youth of a culture. Such artists yield without inhibition to the creative impulse within; and even their awkwardness imparts to their style an element of strength. They are likely to do their most arresting work fairly early in their career; for their gift, being essentially lyric, loses in freshness by as much as it gains in technique.

Harris's seven symphonies (1933–51) form the core of his output. Of the shorter pieces for orchestra the most popular are the *Chorale for String Orchestra* (1932); the overture *When Johnny Comes Marching Home* (1934); and the *Time Suite* (1936). Chamber music occupies an important place in Harris's work. The Quintet for Piano and Strings (1936) and the Third String Quartet (1937) are among his strongest compositions. His two major choral works—the *Song for Occupations* (1934) and *Symphony for Voices* (1935)—are on texts by Walt Whitman.

Third Symphony

Harris's most frequently performed work (1938) reveals the composer at the peak of his "singing strength." The symphony is in one movement made up of contrasting sections. The composer's description indicates its content and scope. "Section I: *Tragic*—low string sonorities. Section II: *Lyric*—strings, horns, woodwinds. Section III: *Pastoral* —emphasizing woodwind choir. Section IV: *Fugue*—dramatic. A. Brass, percussion predominating. B. Canonic development of Section II material, constituting background for further development of fugue. C. Brass climax. Rhythmic motif derived from fugue subject. Section V: *Dramatic-Tragic*. A. Restatement of violin theme of Section I: tutti strings in canon with tutti woodwinds against brass and percussion developing rhythmic motif from climax of Section IV. B. Coda—development of materials from Section I and II over pedal timpani."

The opening motive expands into a long-breathed line on the cellos that accords with Harris's goal of a self-generating melody. The even quarter-note movement is spaced at the end of the phrase by a longer note or a rest—a rhythm derived, of course, from the imagery of the congregational hymn. The full orchestra then presents a kind of chorale. In the section identified by Harris as lyric, his songful counterpoint asserts itself in the fluent, overlapping lines and in his antiphonal treatment of strings and winds. The word "section" is used loosely here. For the symmetrical, sectional structure of the classical symphony Harris substitutes a seamless, continuously evolving texture. His contemplative lyricism has an affinity with the music of such symphonists as Brahms and Sibelius. The dark resonance is also related to the orchestral sound of those two masters.

The pastoral section evokes the "nature sound" of the romantic era in a twentieth-century environment. The warbling of the strings and the mounting animation of the brass conjure up a lovely landscape. The music abounds in free flexible rhythm. The harmonic idiom, for all its tensions, is diatonic.

The fugue subject is a commanding idea, with a sharp melodic profile and rhythmic urgency. The elaborate fugal development builds

up into what Harris calls the "brass climax." The restatement of the chorale-like theme broadens into a spacious coda based upon the steady beat of the drum. Although Harris thinks of the mood as "dramatic-tragic," this processional strikes the epic tone, and justifies those of Harris's admirers who find in his Third Symphony echoes of "the dark fastness of the American soul, of its despair and its courage, its defeat and its triumph."

Roy Harris was a vital force in our musical coming of age. His Third is still one of the finest symphonies produced by an American.

GEORGE GERSHWIN (1898–1937)

"Jazz I regard as an American folk-music; not the only one, but a very powerful one which is probably in the blood and feeling of the American people more than any other style of folk-music. I believe that it can be made the basis of serious symphonic works of lasting value."

The first attempts to bridge the gap between "popular" and "classical" stemmed from the classical side. Jazz musicians for their part came more and more to adopt the procedures of serious music. This development culminated in the vogue of "symphonic jazz" associated with Paul Whiteman, who "took jazz and made an honest woman of her." The elevation to respectability took place at the historic concert given by Whiteman in New York's Aeolian Hall on February 12, 1924. On that occasion he introduced the piece that was to carry the name of George Gershwin, then twenty-six, around the globe: the *Rhapsody in Blue*.

George Gershwin.

The Brooklyn-born composer came out of the musical world of Broadway. Whereas serious composers used the jazz idiom with some degree of self-consciousness, it was his natural speech. His success in musical comedy made him all the more determined to bridge the distance between Tin Pan Alley and Carnegie Hall. This aim was achieved in 1925 when he played his Concerto in F with Walter Damrosch and the New York Symphony Orchestra.

Having amalgamated jazz with the Lisztian rhapsody and the romantic concerto, Gershwin next tackled the Lisztian tone poem and produced *An American in Paris* (1928). He was not equipped to handle the large forms. But he had the gift of song; and this, like the talisman in fairy tales, guided him safely through dangers that might have felled another. His ambition to make jazz, as he said, "the basis of serious symphonic works" was rather naive, considering that jazz and symphony issue from two unrelated worlds. What he did was to fill his orchestral works with the wonderful Gershwin tunes, falling back on the good old technique of repetition and sequence to round out the frame. The formula worked. Whereas dozens of correctly constructed symphonies and tone poems fell by the wayside, his *Rhapsody*, Concerto, and *American in Paris* have retained their vitality and charm.

So, too, he failed to solve the problem of operatic recitative in *Porgy and Bess* (1935). But he had tenderness and compassion, and the instinct of the musical dramatist, and the lyrics of his brother Ira. And so he captured, as Lawrence Gilman put it, "the wildness and the pathos and tragic fervor that can so strangely agitate the souls of men." A dozen operas launched by the Metropolitan, with recitative and arias in the most approved German or French manner, have fallen into limbo; while this "folk opera" has established itself as an American classic.

An American in Paris

Gershwin was thirty when he visited the French capital. One purpose of his trip abroad—he was increasingly aware of his deficiencies in the technique of composition—was to study with one or another of the European masters. But the composers he approached were chary about accepting as a pupil one whom they regarded as the wonder boy of American music. Ravel asked, "Why do you want to become a second-rate Ravel when you already are a first-rate Gershwin?" Stravinsky, always practical, inquired how much Gershwin made a year. When told that the young man's annual income was well over a hundred thousand he remarked, "In that case perhaps it is I who ought to take lessons from you!"

An American in Paris captures the insouciant gayety associated in the tourist's mind with the city on the Seine. The work is cast in the loose form in which Gershwin felt most at home. "This new piece," he stated, "really a rhapsodic ballet, is written very freely and is the most modern music I've yet attempted. My purpose here is to portray the impressions of an American visitor in Paris as he strolls about the city, listens to the various street noises, and absorbs the French atmosphere. The rhapsody is programmatic only in a general impressionistic way, so that the individual listener can read into the music such episodes as his imagination pictures for him." The passages of hectic animation, about midway between jazz and the cancan, are set off against a "blues"—one of those warm-hearted sweeping melodies of which Gershwin held the secret. This tune symbolized for the composer an access of homesickness; or was it perhaps that teasing nostalgia which even in Paris may make one long to be somewhere else?

George Gershwin, dead at thirty-nine—when he was on the threshold of important advances in his art—has remained something of a legend among us. Because he was so close to us we are inclined to view him within the Broadway frame. It is well to remember that so severe a judge as Arnold Schoenberg said of him, "I grieve over the deplorable loss to music, for there is no doubt that he was a great composer."

AARON COPLAND (b. 1900)

"I no longer feel the need of seeking out conscious American-isms. Because we live here and work here, we can be certain that when our music is mature it will also be American in quality."

Aaron Copland is generally recognized as the representative figure among present-day American composers. He manifests the serenity, clarity, and sense of balance that we regard as the essence of the classical temper. He is describing his own point of view when he writes, "The typical contemporary composer prefers an objective, impersonal approach; a complex, contrapuntal texture; a concentration on perfection of line and beauty of proportion." Yet, as he makes clear, the new classicism implies the disciplining rather than the rejection of emotion. "Every artist's work," he states, "is of course an expression of himself, but none so direct as that of the creative musician. He gives us, without relation to exterior 'events,' the quintessential part of himself."

Copland was born of Russian-Jewish parentage "on a street in Brooklyn than can only be described as drab. . . . Music was the last thing anyone would have connected with it." During his early twenties he studied in Paris with Nadia Boulanger, whose first full-time American pupil he was. When Boulanger was invited to give concerts in America, she asked Copland to write a work for her. This was the Symphony for Organ and Orchestra. Contemporary American music was still an exotic dish to New York audiences. After the first performance (1925) Walter Damrosch found it necessary to assuage the feelings of his subscribers. "If a young man at the age of twenty-three," he announced from the stage of Carnegie Hall, "can write a symphony like that, in five years he will be ready to commit murder." Damrosch's prophecy, as far as is known, was not fulfilled.

Copland was soon active as propagandist for the new American music. He organized concerts, festivals, and composers' groups. He lectured, turned out magazine articles, and wrote several eminently readable books. His prose has the qualities of his music. It is simple, lucid, spare, direct; it avoids rhetorical effect; it is personal.

In his growth as a composer Copland has mirrored the dominant trends of his time. After his return from Paris he turned to the jazz idiom, a phase that culminated in his Piano Concerto (1927). Leaving behind him the opulent sonorities of his early works, he moved toward a manner he has well described as "more spare in sonority, more lean in texture." There followed a period during which the neoclassicist experimented with the abstract materials of his art; he produced his *Piano Variations* (1930), *Short Symphony* (1933), and *Statements for Orchestra* (1933–35). "During these years I began to feel an increasing dissatisfaction with the relations of the music-loving public and the living composer. It seemed to me that we composers were in danger of working in a vacuum." He realized that a new public for contemporary music was being created by the radio, phonograph, and film scores. "It made no sense to ignore them and to continue writing as if they did not exist. I felt that it was worth the effort to see if I couldn't say what I had to say in the simplest possible terms." In this fashion Copland was led to what became a most significant development after the Thirties: the attempt to simplify the new music so that it would communicate to a large public.

The decade that followed saw the production of the scores that established Copland's popularity. *El Salón México* (1936) is an orchestral piece based on Mexican melodies and rhythms. The three ballets are *Billy the Kid* (1936), *Rodeo* (1942), and *Appalachian Spring* (1944). Copland wrote two works for high-school students—the "play-opera" *Second Hurricane* (1936) and *Outdoor Overture* (1941). Among his film scores are *Quiet City* (1939), *Of Mice and Men* (1939), *Our Town* (1940), *The North Star* (1943), *The Red Pony* (1948), and *The Heiress* (1948), which brought him an Academy award. Two important works written in time of war are *A Lincoln Portrait* (1942), for speaker and chorus, on a text drawn from the Great Emancipator's speeches; and *Letter from Home* (1944).

In the Third Symphony (1944–46) Copland achieved a notable fusion of the personal and the universal, the emotional and the intellectual. His later works include an opera, *The Tender Land* (1954); *Twelve Poems of Emily Dickinson* for voice and piano (1948–50), in the composer's characteristic vein of contemplative lyricism; the starkly dissonant Fantasy for Piano (1958) and *Connotations* for orchestra (1962), in which Copland shows himself receptive to the serial techniques of the twelve-tone school.

Billy the Kid

For the ballet based on the saga of Billy the Kid Copland produced one of his freshest scores. In it are embedded either in whole or in part such cowboy classics as *The Old Chisholm Trail, The Dying Cowboy,* and *Git Along Little Dogies.* These are not used literally. They are assimilated to the composer's style and flavor the work without subjugating it.

Billy the Kid—the Brooklyn-born William Bonney—had a brief but intense career as desperado and lover, in the course of which he became one of the legends of the Southwest. The ballet touches on the chief episodes of his life. We see him first as a boy of twelve when, his mother having been killed by a stray bullet in a street brawl, he stabs the man responsible for her death. Later, during a card game with his cronies, he is accused of cheating and kills the accuser. Captured after a running gun-battle, he is put in jail. He murders his jailer and gets away. A romantic interlude ensues when he rejoins his Mexican sweetheart in the desert. But the menacing shadows close in on him. This time there is no escaping. At the close we hear a lament for the death of the dashing outlaw.

The concert suite contains about two-thirds of the music of the ballet. *The Open Prairie,* which serves as a Prologue, evokes a spacious landscape. The mingling of tenderness and strength is typical Copland, as is the climax of blocklike masses of tone with emphasis on the winds. *Street Scene* conjures up the square of a frontier town. The tune in cowboy style blends with Copland's sophisticated harmony and strutting syncopations. *Card Game* (Molto moderato) has the quality of

wistful lyricism that marks Copland's later works. The setting is a starry night in the desert. The music projects a mood of gentle contemplation. In violent contrast is *Fight* (Allegro), with its overtones of brutality. The literal imitation of gunfire, legitimate in the theater, is less effective in the concert hall, for the more vividly music depicts, the less it suggests. The *Celebration* that follows Billy's capture is properly brassy

and gay. Altogether lovely is the Epilogue (Lento moderato) in which the prairie music of the opening returns. The physical landscape is transformed into a poetic symbol, a brooding expanse that is incalculably vast, changeless, remote.

It is in passages such as these that Aaron Copland shows himself to be, as he has often been described, the most American of our composers. What is local or regional is dissolved in personal lyricism, thereby assuming a value that extends beyond the particular time or place. At work here is the unconscious nationalism referred to in the quotation at the head of this section—an inevitable nationalism that comes about when the artist has achieved oneness with his environment and its people.

OTHERS

Howard Hanson (b. Wahoo, Nebraska, 1896) made a contribution of prime importance to our musical scene during the Twenties and Thirties, when American music needed championing. As head of the Eastman School of Music at Rochester and conductor of its orchestra, he took the initiative in organizing annual festivals of American music that helped to launch some of our most important composers upon their careers. His own music stems out of the romantic heritage of Franck and Sibelius. The most important of his five symphonies are the First (the *Nordic*, 1922) and the Second (the *Romantic*, 1930). He has also written symphonic poems; choral works such as *The Lament for Beowulf* (1925) and *Three Songs from "Drum Taps,"* on Walt Whitman's stirring lines about the Civil War (1935); and the opera *Merry Mount* (1934).

The music of Quincy Porter (b. New Haven, 1897) draws its sustenance from the realm of chamber music, where subtlety of nuance goes hand in hand with delicacy of thought and feeling. His eight string quartets (1923–50) occupy the central place in his output. They are flanked by a variety of instrumental works, among them the Viola Concerto of 1948 and the *Concerto Concertante* for two pianos and orchestra, which brought the composer a Pulitzer Prize in 1954. Porter's music speaks the international language of neoclassicism, yet in a way that is very much the composer's own.

Henry Cowell (b. Menlo Park, California, 1897) attracted attention during the Twenties with his "tone-clusters" on the piano. By pressing down a number of keys with his palm or forearm he was able to wreathe his melody in the sonorous halo of which the instrument is uniquely capable. Such an aggregate of tones exploited the percussive possibilities of the piano in a way that had not been envisaged before, and was in line with the experiments in dissonant harmony that were in the air at that time. Cowell subsequently composed an enormous amount of music, the chief item on his list being fifteen symphonies of a romantic cast abounding in folklore elements.

Randall Thompson (b. New York City, 1899) set himself to create an art that expressed, as he put it, "our own genuine musical heritage in its every manifestation, every inflection, every living example." His tuneful Second Symphony (1931), with its jazz-like rhythms, the "blues" of the slow movement, and the broad melody of the finale, displays the essentially American traits of his music. Thompson's flair for choral writing is manifest in *The Peaceable Kingdom* (1936), a work inspired by one of the paintings of the early American folk artist Edward Hicks, and *The Testament of Freedom* (1943), based on four excerpts from the writings of Thomas Jefferson.

Carlos Chávez (b. Mexico City, 1899) has played the same decisive part in the musical life of his homeland as Villa-Lobos did in that of Brazil. Chávez, along with his friend Diego Rivera, became a leading figure among the dedicated band of musicians, painters, and poets who captured in their work the spirit of the Mexican Revolution. The two pieces by which he is best known—*Sinfonía de Antígona* (1933) and *Sinfonía India* (1936)—date from his nationalist period. In his later works Chávez moved toward a classical orientation and produced a number of instrumental works in the large forms.

☙ CHAPTER 93 ❧

The Third Generation

SAMUEL BARBER (b. 1910)

"I began composing at seven and have never stopped."

COMPOSERS in the past two centuries, if performers at all, as a rule were instrumentalists. Samuel Barber is that comparatively rare phenomenon, a singer-composer. For a time he considered a concert career. The fact that his contact with music came through vocal lyricism has played its part in shaping his melodic imagery.

Barber is one of the best known among his generation of American composers. He owes his popularity in equal measure to innate musicality and to the circumstance that he is a conservative. Barber is an avowed romantic; his music is poetic and suffused with feeling. Nor is it averse to the grand rhetoric of the nineteenth-century tradition. Its gentle melancholy alternates with passages that have brilliancy and dramatic impact.

Barber was born in West Chester, Pennsylvania. A nephew of the singer Louise Homer, he grew up in a musical environment. He entered the Curtis Institute in Philadelphia when he was fourteen, and soon distinguished himself in composition. In 1935 Barber won both the Prix de Rome and a Pulitzer Traveling Scholarship. He spent several years in Europe, where he appeared both as a singer and conductor.

In 1943 Barber was inducted into the Army. As the result of an unusually enlightened policy, he was commissioned to write a symphony for the Air Force. The work was performed by the Boston Symphony Orchestra under Koussevitzky in March, 1944. The event brought Barber the most memorable piece of fan mail he ever received. "Dear Corporal," the note ran, "I came to hear your symphony. I thought it was terrible, but I applauded vociferously because I think all corporals should be encouraged."

Barber's qualities are manifest in the light-hearted Overture to *The School for Scandal,* Opus 5 (1932), a work of youthful exuberance, which was followed in 1933 by *Music for a Scene from Shelley.* Inspired by lines from the second act of *Prometheus Unbound,* this poetic piece aptly evokes Shelley's flamelike incorporeality. The *Adagio for Strings* (1936) is one of Barber's best-known works; another is the first *Essay for Orchestra,* which we will discuss. The Symphony No. 1, Opus 9, was written in 1936 and revised by the composer six years later. The four movements of the traditional symphonic form are synthesized into a single movement (the piece is occasionally referred to as the *Symphony in One Movement*). To this period belong *Dover Beach,* Opus 3 (1931), a setting of Matthew Arnold's poem for solo voice and string quartet; the *Three Songs,* Opus 10, set to poems from James Joyce's *Chamber Music* (1936); and the Concerto for Violin and Orchestra, Opus 14 (1939).

In the second decade of Barber's career a significant change took place in his style. The romanticism of the first years was enriched by elements that betokened a deepening awareness of contemporary procedures. The *Symphony Dedicated to the Air Forces,* Opus 19 (1944), bears the marks of this turbulent period in its dissonant harmonies and the wide leaps in its melodic lines. This development in Barber's style is already to be observed in several works that preceded the Symphony. A *Stopwatch and an Ordnance Map,* Opus 15 (1940), for men's voices and three kettledrums (with optional accompaniment for brass instruments), is a deeply felt setting of Stephen Spender's poem about the death of a soldier in the Spanish Civil War. The *Second Essay for*

Orchestra, Opus 17 (1942), retains the epigrammatic character of the First, but is broader in scope. The *Capricorn Concerto* for flute, oboe, trumpet, and strings, Opus 21 (1944), is a witty concerto grosso—the composer's bow to Stravinskyan neoclassicism. The Cello Concerto, Opus 22 (1945), is an important addition to the literature of that neglected instrument.

Knoxville: Summer of 1915 for soprano and orchestra, Opus 24 (1947), is a setting of a prose poem by James Agee which appeared first in *Partisan Review.* (This is also the opening chapter of Agee's book *A Death in the Family.*) Barber invested this Proustian evocation of childhood in an American town with a remarkably sensitive vocal line. In the Sonata for Piano, Opus 26 (1949), Barber achieved a notable synthesis of his earlier and later manner. *Prayers of Kierkegaard* for mixed chorus, soprano solo, and orchestra, Opus 30 (1954), a cantata surcharged with mystical feeling, is one of Barber's strongest works, as is *Medea's Meditation and Dance of Vengeance* (1955), a tone poem he fashioned from his ballet *Medea* (1946). His Piano Concerto made a strong impression when it was heard during the festival inaugurating Philharmonic Hall in the Lincoln Center for the Performing Arts in 1962.

Barber for many years was eager to write an opera, but could not find a suitable libretto. The problem was solved by Gian Carlo Menotti, who wrote the libretto of *Vanessa* for him. The opera received its premiere at the Metropolitan Opera House in 1958. Barber was somewhat tentative in the first act, as though he had to find his bearings. Thereafter he was carried along by his ability to spin a long melodic line.

Essay for Orchestra, *No. 1*

Lyric composers come into their basic style almost from the beginning of their career, as is apparent from the *Essay for Orchestra,* which was written in 1938, when Barber was twenty-eight. The use of the word *essay* as a title conjures up the literary form in which ideas are developed concisely within an intimate framework.

The introductory section, Andante sostenuto, opens with the main theme on the violas and cellos. This contains a three-note motive that becomes a germinating force within the work. For example, it appears repeatedly in the melody, both in the original pattern and in inversion.

The music mounts in urgency through an effective passage for the brass that culminates in a flourish. There follows the charming Allegro molto that constitutes the main body of the piece. This section captures the elfin lightness of the Mendelssohnian scherzo, but infused with the satanism that descended through the romantic era from Liszt and Berlioz to Mahler, whence it passed into the mainstream of twentieth-century music. The germinal motive appears in longer note values (augmentation) beneath the warblings of woodwinds and strings. A brilliant climax leads into the Largamente sostenuto which presents the initial theme in a mood of affirmation. The music subsides. At the very end the first violins present the basic motive in inverted form.

Barber avoids the knotty problems of contemporary musical thought. He stems out of the romantic past, and uses his heritage with taste, imagination, and elegance.

WILLIAM SCHUMAN (b. 1910)

"A composer must create on his own terms, not simply write what the public thinks it wants at the moment. If his music has worth, the world will subsequently come to understand it."

William Schuman was born in New York City. Whatever music his boyhood contained belonged to the sphere of jazz. In time he formed a dance band in which he played the violin and banjo and sang. Together with a childhood friend, Frank Loesser, he turned out about forty songs, of which one—a ditty called *In Love with a Memory of You*—was published. (Loesser subsequently achieved success on Broadway with such musicals as *Where's Charley?* and *Guys and Dolls*.) Schuman worked for a time as a song plugger for a music publishing house. At the same time he enrolled in a business course at the New York University School of Commerce. He was almost twenty when he heard his first symphony concert. It opened up a new world for him. The next day he left the School of Commerce and quit the job he had taken with an advertising agency. Having heard that composers began with the study of harmony, he forthwith enrolled in a course in that subject.

At the age of twenty-three he entered Teachers College at Columbia University, and two years later received his degree. Schuman had unconventional ideas about how music should be taught and found a congenial outlet for them at Sarah Lawrence College, where he went in 1935. Of great importance at this time was the influence of Roy Harris, with whom he studied for two years. "Harris helped me to formulate my point of view," Schuman has stated. "Basically our esthetic springs from the same direction."

Despite his late start, Schuman forged ahead rapidly. His First Symphony was performed at a Composer's Forum Laboratory concert in the fall of 1936. Two years later the Second was played by Serge Koussevitzky and the Boston Symphony Orchestra. The Third Symphony, conducted by Koussevitzky in 1941, achieved an extraordinary success. The works that followed established Schuman in the forefront of the composers of his generation. He was performed by major orchestras in this country and abroad, and received his share of prizes and honors. Recognition came in another sphere when, in 1945, the board of directors of the Juilliard School of Music invited him to become president of the institution. At the age of thirty-five Schuman was the head of one of the most important music schools in the country. He introduced sweeping reforms into the curriculum, and transformed the school into a center for the propagation of contemporary music. In 1961 he entered upon a broader sphere of activity when he was appointed president of Lincoln Center for the Performing Arts in New York City.

Schuman's earlier works betrayed a reticence bordering on shyness when it came to the revelation of private emotion. With maturity came a deeper perception of the expressive aspects of his art. There is an undercurrent of somber intensity beneath the bright surface of Schuman's music. This duality adds dimension to his later works and constitutes one of the interesting features of his style.

Schuman's eight symphonies form the central item in his output. The Third (1941) is the most widely played of the series. To the category of large-scale works belong the Concerto for Piano and Small Orchestra (1942); the Concerto for Violin and Orchestra (1947); and the Fourth String Quartet which, from the arresting measures of the opening, shows a fine feeling for this purest of musical genres. The *American Festival Overture* (1939) is a bright, festive piece. In the *New England Triptych* (1956) Schuman pays homage to the American "primitive" who has aroused such interest among our present-day composers. The piece draws upon three anthems of Billings— *Be Glad Then, America; When Jesus Wept;* and *Chester,* one of the battle songs of the Revolution. Schuman's penchant for sturdy sonorities and sweeping lines found a natural outlet in choral music. He is at his best with the kind of poetry—for example, Walt Whitman's —that enables him to communicate manly, exuberant emotions. Whitman's verse inspired *Pioneers,* for eight-part unaccompanied chorus (1937), as well as the "secular cantata" *A Free Song* (1942). Another favored poet is Genevieve Taggard, whose poems Schuman set in *Prologue for Chorus* (1939); *This Is Our Time* (1941); and *Holiday Song* (1942).

Schuman has written several ballets. *Undertow* (1945) is rich in mood and atmosphere, as are the two ballets he wrote for Martha Graham—*Night Journey* (1947) and *Judith* (1948), a dramatic treatment of the biblical story. His one-act opera *The Mighty Casey* (1953), after Ernest L. Thayer's immortal *Casey at the Bat*, did not quite come off. It was more difficult to transfer Thayer's classic to the opera house than either the composer or his librettist, Jeremy Gury, supposed.

Symphony No. 3

Schuman's Third Symphony sets forth in compelling fashion the essential characteristics of his style. The instrumental investiture is of surpassing brilliance. Yet—a classical trait, this—his virtuoso handling of the orchestra serves throughout to highlight his ideas and clarify the form. Athletic rhythms, with an abundance of dotted patterns, impart to the music its headlong drive. Schuman's fondness for unmixed colors—especially his reliance on the pure full brass tone—makes for a texture in which the interweaving lines stand out with radiant clarity even when the orchestra is playing fortissimo.

The themes exemplify the composer's ability to mold plastic, long-breathed melodies into a large design. The lyricism of the work has been well described as "strong but nonsubjective." What stands out about the piece, apart from the saliency and vigor of its ideas, is Schuman's capacity to think and feel instrumentally. The Third Symphony bases itself on the capacities for dramatic expression inherent in instrumental sonority. This sonority becomes the form-building element that nourishes the ideas and creates the continuum within which they freely disport themselves.

The symphony is divided into two parts, each containing two movements that are connected: Passacaglia and Fugue, Chorale and Toccata. In other words, the composer has based his structure on four musical procedures that reached their full flower in the age of Bach. He uses these, however, with no antiquarian intent. His desire rather is to explore the possibilities of these procedures in relation to the expressive needs of his own time. As a result he brings to the devices of canonic imitation and thematic variation an engaging freshness that lends the symphony a quality of spontaneous and uninhibited expression.

The entire work is derived from the theme of the Passacaglia, a circumstance that makes for an extraordinary degree of organic unity. The theme is stated at the outset by the violas. Several of its interval

relationships take on significance as the symphony evolves, such as the octave leap at the beginning; the two consecutive fourths which together outline a seventh, in measures 2 and 6; the two rising sixths in measures 4-5; and the rising fifth in measures 2-3 and 6. The theme is rich in motives that lend themselves to the processes of variation.

The initial statement of the theme, beginning on E, is imitated canonically by the second violins entering on F, the cellos entering on F-sharp, the first violins entering on G, the double basses on A-flat, the horns on A, and the upper woodwinds on B-flat. This succession of entrances in rising semitones serves as the initial build-up, in the course of which the movement steadily gains momentum. The balance of the movement is given over to four variations of the material. In the first of these the theme, given out by trumpets and trombones, is combined with a highly mobile counterpoint in the strings. The second variation opens with polychordal formations in low register that move in propulsive dotted-rhythm patterns derived from the theme. In the third variation the initial idea is metamorphosed into a long-breathed melody that unfolds serenely against a running accompaniment of sixteenth notes in the cellos, which are reinforced first by the violas then by the double basses. In the fourth variation the theme is artfully distributed between first and second violins, in a series of dotted figures, against the stentorian proclamation of a quartet of trombones.

The subject of the Fugue is related intervallically to the Passacaglia

theme, albeit rhythmic alteration gives it a different character. It enters in a series of rising semitones, this time moving from E to B-flat. This Exposition completed, the fugue unfolds in lithe, sinewy counterpoint, gradually building up tension until the climactic passage when the subject is proclaimed by the brass in augmentation.

The second part of the symphony opens with the chorale which, after a brief prelude, is announced by solo trumpet. The chorale is then subjected to variation through changes in rhythm, register, instrumental color, and through contrapuntal elaboration. The Toccata begins dramatically with the announcement of the underlying rhythm of the theme on the snare drum. The theme itself is presented by the

bass clarinet. The Toccata is a motoric piece in which the orchestra is handled with virtuosity. In the closing pages the materials of the Passacaglia, Fugue, and Chorale are brought together in a rousing peroration.

Stemming from a temperament that is optimistic, assertive, and thoroughly at home in the world, this music has vigor and assurance. It is planned on a large scale, and combines classical form with American content in a personal, forceful way.

❦❦ CHAPTER 94 ❦❦

Other Composers of the Third Generation

THE WORKS of Elliott Carter (b. New York City, 1908) are not the kind that achieve easy popularity; but their sureness of line, profundity of thought, and maturity of workmanship bespeak a musical intellect of the first order. Carter was educated at Harvard and worked in Paris with Nadia Boulanger. He has taught at various colleges, but his chief activity in the past two decades has been composing. Carter started out with a musical idiom rooted in diatonic-modal harmony. His gradual assimilation of a dissonant chromaticism went hand in hand with his response to the influences that directed his development. He has absorbed dodecaphonic no less than Stravinskyan elements; but he uses both in an independent fashion. Among the earlier works, the ballet *Pocohantas* (1939) manifests his rhythmic invention. In the First Symphony (1942), written for an orchestra of classical size, Carter moved toward a simplification of style. The Piano Sonata of 1946 is a broadly conceived work noteworthy for careful detail, imaginative use of piano figuration, and the irregular scansion of metrical patterns. In his ballet *The Minotaur* (1947) Carter projects somber moods with an intensity of feeling new to his music. The Sonata for Cello and Piano (1948) is a darkly expressive piece that displays the composer's subtle insights into the problems of metrics, sonority, and balance. *Eight Etudes and a Fantasy* (1950) for woodwind quartet—flute, oboe, clarinet, bassoon—are studies in sonority that reveal the more fanciful side of Carter's style. The Variations for Orchestra (1955) is one of his finest achievements, and introduces the listener to a very special world of sound. The String Quartet No. 2 (1959) received extraordinary critical acclaim when it was first heard in New York in 1960, and brought Carter a Pulitzer Prize. Cast in a tensely expressionistic idiom that demands the highest virtuosity from the players, this is a work of striking invention and brilliance of execution. The Double Concerto for Harpsichord, Piano and Orchestra (1961) confirms Carter's position as one of the most important composers in America today.

Gian Carlo Menotti's inclusion in the American school stretches a point, since he has never renounced his Italian citizenship. But he has spent the greater part of his life in this country; he generally writes his librettos in English; and—perhaps the best reason for considering him one of our own—he has won his greatest success in the United States. He was born in Cadegliano, near Lake Lugano, in 1911, and showed great musical talent while still a child. At the age of seventeen he came to the United States and studied at the Curtis Institute in Philadelphia. Menotti's works have their roots in the tradition of Italian opera. *Amelia Goes to the Ball* (1934), an astonishingly deft piece for a man of twenty-three, shows his ingenious adaptation of the *opera buffa* manner to the modern theater. *The Old Maid and the Thief*, a "radio opera" written in 1938 on a commission from the National Broadcasting Company, attractively combines lyricism and romantic comedy. *The Medium* (1946), a melodrama for five singers, one dance mime, and an orchestra of fourteen, has achieved close to two thousand performances since its premiere. It is generally presented on a double bill with *The Telephone*, an airy bit of persiflage. In *The Consul*, which brought Menotti a Pulitzer Prize in 1950, he movingly evoked the human condition in our troubled time.

Amahl and the Night Visitors (1951), the first opera to have been commissioned expressly for television, has established itself as a Christmas classic. *The Saint of Bleecker Street* (1954) is one of several Menotti works that ran on Broadway, thus bridging the gap that had always separated the American theater public from opera. From a purely musical standpoint this piece is one of Menotti's most important achievements, although the theme—which moves somewhere between religious mysticism and hysteria—repelled many who saw it. *Maria Golovin*, which received its premiere at the Brussels World's Fair in the summer of 1958, traces with almost Proustian subtlety the love affair of a young man blinded in the war and an older woman. Menotti's is not an epic gift; rather it is sweet and tender and heartwarming. And behind it is an extraordinary flair for what is dramatically effective. The composer is well represented on records. A hearing of either *The Medium* or *The Consul* will introduce the listener to the exciting art of this born man of the theater.

Norman Dello Joio (b. New York City, 1913) represents a phenomenon uniquely characteristic of our cultural life: a first-generation American who assimilates the heritage of his fathers to the thought and feeling of the land of his birth. His father, a church organist who had emigrated from a small town near Naples, raised him in the Italian tradition; to which were added more indigenous elements. The future composer led his own jazz band; studied at the Juilliard School; and worked with Hindemith. Hence Dello Joio's style assimilated several important influences: Gregorian chant, American jazz, Italian opera, and Hindemithian neoclassicism. Upon these he brought to bear an essentially romantic temperament. In *Concert Music* (1944), a kind of symphonic rondo in three sections, we find the composer's fully formed language. *To a Lone Sentry* (1943) shows Dello Joio's penchant for lyricism of a contemplative kind. His ability to make the orchestra sing is exemplified by the Serenade (1948), *Epigraph* (1951), and *Meditations on Ecclesiastes*, which brought him a Pulitzer Prize in 1957. Dello Joio's most ambitious orchestral work to date is the *Variations, Chaconne and Finale* (1947). Of his several concerto-like compositions, the most important is the Fantasy and Variations for Piano and Orchestra (1962). His chamber music includes the Trio for Flute, Cello and Piano (1943) and the Variations and Capriccio for Violin and Piano (1948), an attractive piece in the neoclassic manner. The Second Piano Sonata (1943) and the Third (1947) display the composer's idiomatic writing for his own instrument. Dello Joio's rhythmic invention makes him a natural ballet composer. His best-known work in this category is *On Stage* (1945). His choral works include three on texts by Walt Whitman—*Vigil Strange, Mystic Trum-*

peter, and *Jubilant Song*—and *A Psalm of David* (1950), a searching work on a Latin text, in which the composer pays obeisance to the sixteenth-century polyphonists, notably Josquin. He has also written three operas—*The Trial at Rouen* (1955), *The Ruby* (1955), and *Blood Moon* (1961). For Dello Joio, the prime purpose of composing is the communication of feeling. This circumstance makes him one of the leading proponents of the new romanticism.

Leonard Bernstein (b. Boston, 1918) is having a brilliant career. As conductor and pianist, composer of serious works as well as of successful Broadway shows, educator and television personality extraordinary, he is easily the best-known musician of his generation. He was educated at Harvard, became the favorite pupil of Serge Koussevitzky at the Berkshire Music Center in Tanglewood, and finally—after several years as a struggling young musician—was appointed assistant conductor of the New York Philharmonic. He leaped to fame when Bruno Walter, the guest conductor, fell ill and was unable to conduct a Sunday afternoon performance. Bernstein took his place and, without a rehearsal, gave an extraordinary performance. Next morning the story was carried by newspapers all over the country. In 1958 Bernstein succeeded Dimitri Mitropoulos as director of the Philharmonic, the first American-born conductor—and the youngest—to occupy the post. As a composer, Bernstein speaks the language of contemporary music with great fluency. He has been influenced on the one hand by Stravinsky and Copland, on the other by Mahler and Richard Strauss. His style consequently is a blend of classical and romantic elements. He has an immense aptitude for orchestration; his harmonic idiom is spicily dissonant; his jazzy rhythms have gusto and drive. Among his serious works are the *Jeremiah Symphony* (1942), an impressive achievement for a composer in his middle twenties; *The Age of Anxiety,* for piano and orchestra (1949), based on W. H. Auden's poem of that name; *Trouble in Tahiti,* a one-act opera on the composer's libretto, which satirizes life in suburbia (1952); and the Serenade for Violin Solo, Strings and Percussion (1954), after Plato's *Symposium.* In his scores for Broadway musicals Bernstein achieves a sophisticated kind of musical theater that explodes with movement, energy, and sentiment. The list includes *On the Town,* a full-length version of his ballet *Fancy Free* (1944); *Wonderful Town* (1953); *Candide,* on a book by Lillian Hellman after Voltaire's celebrated satire (1956); and the spectacularly successful *West Side Story* (1957).

Leon Kirchner (b. Brooklyn, New York, 1919) grew up on the West Coast and studied with Schoenberg at the University of California in Los Angeles. After teaching at the University of Southern California and Mills College, he went to Harvard. His music, as Aaron Copland has aptly put it, is "charged with an emotional impact and explosive power that is almost frightening in intensity." Kirchner takes his stand with those who regard music as an expression of thought and emotion. He has been influenced not only by Schoenberg but also by Roger Sessions, Mahler, Bartók, Alban Berg; his roots, consequently, are to be found in the tradition of central European expressionism. The most important of his earlier compositions are the Piano Sonata of 1948, a work of unmistakable creative afflatus; the String Quartet No. 1 (1949), which he dedicated to Roger Sessions; and the *Sinfonia* of 1950, in which his mature orchestral writing stands fully revealed. The evolution of his highly personal style may be traced in the five major works that followed: *Sonata Concertante* for violin and piano (1952); the Piano Concerto of 1953, a large-scale, visionary work; the Trio for violin, cello, and piano (1954); the Toccata for strings, solo winds, and percussion (1955); and the String Quartet No. 2 (1957). These reveal a composer who has reinterpreted the great tradition in terms profoundly relevant to our own time.

Lukas Foss was born in Berlin in 1922. His parents left Germany immediately after Hitler's accession to power. After some years in Paris, the family came to the United States in 1937. Foss studied at the Curtis Institute in Philadelphia and with Koussevitzky at the Berkshire Music Center. For several years he served as pianist of the Boston Symphony Orchestra. Foss succeeded Schoenberg as professor of composition at the University of California in Los Angeles; he also teaches at the Berkshire Music Center, where his own career as composer-pianist so auspiciously began. The over-all effect of Foss's music is one of communicative lyricism and dramatic verve. *The Prairie,* a cantata for four soloists, large chorus, and orchestra, on the poem by Carl Sandburg (1943), was an astonishing production for a youth of twenty-one. The Symphony in G (1944), a joyous work, was followed by two biblical cantatas—the *Song of Anguish,* from the Book of Isaiah, for baritone and orchestra (1945), and the *Song of Songs,* for soprano and orchestra (1946). Foss's theater works include a ballet, *The Gift of the Magi* (1945); *The Jumping Frog of Calaveras County* (1950), a one-act opera on a libretto by Jean Karsavina based on Mark Twain's celebrated tale; and the fantasy-opera *Griffelkin,* commissioned by the NBC Opera Theater and presented on television in November 1955. A *Parable of Death* (1953), for narrator, chorus, and orchestra, on a text by Rainer Maria Rilke, is characteristic of the composer's lyricism; as is the *Symphony of Chorales* (1958), a work that shows the increasing complexity of Foss's thought. In *Time Cycle* (1960), for soprano and orchestra, he moves in new directions. The tonality, while clearly defined in some places, is wholly destroyed in others. Foss in recent years has developed an interest in ensemble improvisation. He has formed a chamber ensemble that plays without written or memorized music, creating harmony, melody, and counterpoint on the spur of the moment—within a system of controlled chance. This new form of music-making transfers to the concert hall the excitement of the "jam session," and is one of a number of attempts by composers both here and abroad to recapture for art music the random, spontaneous elements of improvisation.

Peter Mennin (b. Erie, Pennsylvania, 1923) studied at the Eastman School of Music. He taught at the Juilliard School from 1947 to 1958, when he was appointed director of the Peabody Institute in Baltimore. In 1962 he succeeded William Schuman as head of the Juilliard School. Mennin's music is characterized by high spirits and a relentless forward drive. His works have established themselves because of his assured handling of the large forms and the sense of bustling energy that flows from his writing. Mennin is a natural contrapuntist. In his music the harmonies are determined by the interweaving of the melodic lines, rather than the other way around. His orchestral writing is clear and economical. The form and the color scheme unfold in broad outlines. Mennin's seven symphonies (1942–55) show his steady growth in the manipulation of ideas. They are flanked by a variety of pieces, among them the Fantasy for Strings, the Violin Concerto, and the *Sinfonia* for chamber orchestra, all dating from 1947; the Partita for Piano of 1950; and *The Christmas Story*, a cantata in nine parts (1951). The weightiest items among Mennin's later works are the String Quartet No. 2 (1952); *Concertato for Orchestra* (1954); the Cello Concerto of 1956; the *Sonata Concertante* for violin (1958), which shows Mennin moving toward a simplification of style; and the dashing Piano Concerto (1958). Among the composers of his generation, Peter Mennin must be accounted one of the most successful practitioners of the grand form.

We leave off without having mentioned many talented members of the contemporary American school. To give anywhere near a full account of their work would carry us far beyond the limits of this book. Enough has been said, however, to indicate the diversity of our composers and the tendencies they represent.

A musical culture depends not on the foreign performers and composers whom a nation attracts to its shores but on what it brings forth by its own efforts. Our present situation indicates that we have established in this country all the preconditions for a mature musical culture. Our conservatories and colleges turn out musicians whose technical equipment is second to none anywhere. We have literally hundreds of composers functioning throughout the land, writing, teaching, organizing musical activities in their schools and communities. It would be unrealistic to suppose that all their works are of first rank; but that is hardly the point. History shows that a Bach, a Beethoven, or a Stravinsky emerges only out of a tradition that is flourishing and a climate that is ready. There can be no question that our efforts in the past half century have given us such a tradition and climate.

Postscript

WE HAVE included in these pages a variety of facts, historical, biographical, and technical, that have entered into the making of music and that must enter into an intelligent listening to music. For those who desire to explore the subject further we include a list of books that will guide the music lover in his reading. But books belong to the domain of words, and words have no power over the domain of sound. They are helpful only insofar as they lead us to the music.

The enjoyment of music depends upon perceptive listening. And perceptive listening (like perceptive anything) is something that we achieve gradually, with practice and some effort. By acquiring a knowledge of the circumstances out of which a musical work issued, we prepare ourselves for its multiple meanings; we lay ourselves open to that exercise of mind and heart, sensibility and imagination that makes listening to music so unique an experience. But in the building up of our musical perceptions—that is, of our listening enjoyment—let us always remember that the ultimate wisdom resides neither in dates nor in facts. It is to be found in one place only—the sounds themselves.

A List of Records

THE FOLLOWING discography lists the basic works discussed in the text, which are marked by an asterisk (*), as well as supplementary titles for those readers interested in further study. These will be found in the standard catalogues of records. Because new recordings are constantly being issued, it was not found expedient to list specific recordings here. For guidance in choosing among the several recordings of a work the reader is referred to the annual series called *Records in Review* (Great Barrington, Mass., The Wyeth Press, 1955 on) and the summaries of record reviews in the magazine of the Music Library Association, *Notes*.

The required items in the following list represent specific categories such as short lyric forms, program music, etc. However, once a composer is introduced, we have taken the opportunity to suggest in the supplementary listings other aspects of his total output.

Chapter 2. Music and Life: The Sources of Musical Imagery

I. SONG

FOLK SONG:
  Greensleeves
  Black is the Color of My True Love's
    Hair
  Water Boy
  Lord Randall
  Barbara Allen
  I Gave My Love a Cherry

ART SONG:
  Schubert, *Serenade*
  Brahms, *Lullaby*
  Schumann, *The Two Grenadiers*
    (Die beiden Grenadiere)
  Grieg, *Ich liebe dich* (I Love Thee)

II. THE DANCE

Bach, J. S., Suite No. 3, in D, Gavotte
Mozart, Symphony No. 39, Minuet
Beethoven, Country Dance in E-flat
Chopin, Waltz in C-sharp minor
Bartók, Rumanian Dances
Ravel, *Pavane for a Dead Princess*
Stravinsky, *Circus Polka*

Haydn, Symphony No. 104 (*London*),
  Minuet and Finale
Strauss, Johann, *Emperor Waltz*
Brahms, Hungarian Dances
Musorgsky, Hopak
Dvořák, Slavonic Dances
Shostakovich, Polka from *The Age of Gold*

III. THE MARCH

Sousa, *The Stars and Stripes Forever*
Verdi, Triumphal March from *Aïda*
Schubert, *Marche militaire*
Chopin, *Polonaise militaire*
Beethoven, March from *The Ruins of Athens*
———, Symphony No. 3 (*Eroica*),
  second movement: Funeral March

Mendelssohn, March of the Priests
  from *Athalie*
Elgar, *Pomp and Circumstance*
Ippolitov-Ivanov, *Procession of the Sardar* from *Caucasian Sketches*
Prokofiev, March from *Love for Three Oranges*

IV. OF RELIGIOUS INSPIRATION

Palestrina, Kyrie from the *Mass for Pope Marcellus*

Bach, J. S., Chorale, *Jesu, Joy of Man's Desiring*

Handel, Hallelujah Chorus from *Messiah*
———, *I Know that My Redeemer Liveth* from *Messiah*
Go Down, Moses and *Deep River*
Schubert, *Ave Maria*
Wagner, Prelude to *Lohengrin*

———, Good Friday Music from *Parsifal*
Brahms, *Blest Are They that Mourn* from *A German Requiem*
Berlioz, *The Farewell of the Shepherds* from *The Childhood of Christ* (L'Enfance du Christ)

Chapter 3. Melody: Musical Line

CONTRAST IN DEGREE OF ACTIVITY OF MELODY LINE:
Brahms, Hungarian Dance No. 5
Schubert, *Ave Maria*
Verdi, Triumphal March from *Aïda*
Ravel, *Pavane for a Dead Princess*

CLIMAX IN MELODY LINE:
Schumann, *Träumerei* (final phrase)

Chopin, Nocturne in E-flat (final section)
Londonderry Air

MELODY PERVADED BY A RHYTHMIC FIGURE:
Handel, Hallelujah Chorus from *Messiah*

Chapter 4. Harmony: Musical Space

INCREASING DEGREE OF HARMONIC DISSONANCE:
Mozart, Piano Sonata in C major, K. 545, first movement

Wagner, *Liebestod* from *Tristan und Isolde*
Debussy, *La Soirée dans Grenade*
Bartók, *Allegro barbaro*

Chapter 5. Rhythm and Meter: Musical Time

$\frac{2}{4}$ TIME:
*Brahms, Hungarian Dances Nos. 5 and 6
*Schubert, *Marche militaire*
*Shostakovich, Polka from *The Age of Gold*

$\frac{3}{4}$ TIME:
*Mozart, Symphony No. 39, Minuet
*Strauss, Johann, *Emperor Waltz*

$\frac{4}{4}$ TIME:
*Verdi, Triumphal March from *Aïda*

*Prokofiev, March from *Love for Three Oranges*

$\frac{6}{8}$ TIME:
*Mendelssohn, *Venetian Boat Song* in F-sharp minor
*Grieg, *Morning* from *Peer Gynt Suite* No. 1
*Rimsky-Korsakov, *Scheherazade*, first movement

$\frac{5}{4}$ TIME:
Tchaikovsky, Symphony No. 6 (*Pathétique*), second movement

Chapter 6. Tempo: Musical Pace

LARGO:
Handel, Largo from *Xerxes*
Dvořák, Symphony No. 5 (*New World*), second movement

ADAGIO:
Beethoven, Piano Sonata in C minor, Op. 13 (*Pathétique*), second movement

———, Piano Sonata in C-sharp minor, Op. 27, No. 2 (*Moonlight*), first movement

ANDANTE:
Haydn, Symphony No. 94 (*Surprise*), second movement

ANDANTINO:
Rimsky-Korsakov, *Scheherazade,* second movement (*Kalendar Prince*)

ALLEGRETTO:
Franck, Symphony in D minor, second movement

ALLEGRO:
Beethoven, Symphony No. 5, fourth movement

ALLEGRO MOLTO:
Mozart, Symphony No. 40, first movement

VIVACE:
Mendelssohn, Scherzo from *A Midsummer Night's Dream*

PRESTO:
Haydn, Symphony No. 104 (*London*), finale

Chapters 7–9. Timbre: Musical Color—The Instruments—The Orchestra

°Prokofiev, *Peter and the Wolf*
°Tchaikovsky, *Nutcracker Suite*
Saint-Saëns, *Carnival of Animals*
Britten, *The Young Person's Guide to the Orchestra*
Spotlight on Keyboard and Strings (Vox)

Spotlight on Winds and Brass (Vox)
Spotlight on Percussion (Vox)
The Instruments of the Orchestra (Vanguard)
Instruments of the Orchestra (RCA Victor)

Chapter 10. Dynamics: Musical Volume

INTENSIFICATION (CLIMAX) THROUGH STEADY CRESCENDO, ACCELERANDO, OR RISE IN PITCH:
Rossini, Overture to *The Barber of Seville* (final section)
Ravel, *Bolero*
Wagner, Prelude to *Lohengrin*

Debusy, *Fêtes* from Three Nocturnes for Orchestra
Honegger, *Pacific 231*
Tchaikovsky, Waltz of the Flowers (final section) from the *Nutcracker Suite*
Grieg, *In the Hall of the Mountain King* from *Peer Gynt Suite* No. 1

Chapter 11. Form: Musical Structure and Design

THREE-PART OR TERNARY FORM (A-B-A):
Schubert, *Marche militaire*
Chopin, Nocturne in F-sharp major
Brahms, Hungarian Dance No. 5
Mozart, Symphony No. 40, Minuet
Beethoven, Country Dance in E-flat

TWO-PART OR BINARY FORM (A-B):
Couperin, *La Galante* †
Bach, J. S., Suite No. 2, in B minor, for Flute and Strings, Saraband, Minuet, Badinerie

Chapter 17. Franz Schubert

°*Der Erlkönig*
°*Heidenröslein*
°Impromptu in A-flat, Op. 90, No. 4
°*Moment musical* in F minor, Op. 94, No. 3
Die Forelle (The Trout)

Der Tod und das Mädchen (Death and the Maiden)
Hark, Hark, the Lark
Die Winterreise
Die schöne Müllerin
Impromptu in B-flat, Op. 142, No. 3
Piano Sonata in B-flat (posthumous)

† *Masterpieces of Music before 1750* (Haydn Society).

Chapter 18. Robert Schumann

*The Two Grenadiers (Die beiden Grenadiere)
*Ich grolle nicht (I'll Not Complain)
*Aufschwung (Soaring)
*Romance in F-sharp major
Im wunderschönen Monat Mai (In the Lovely Month of May)

Frauenliebe und -Leben
Dichterliebe
Carnaval
Symphonic Etudes
Piano Quintet
Symphony No. 1 (Spring)

Chapter 19. Frédéric François Chopin

*Etude in E major, Op. 10, No. 3
*Prelude in D minor, Op. 28, No. 24
*Polonaise in A-flat, Op. 53
Etude in C minor, Op. 10, No. 12 (Revolutionary)
Waltz in C-sharp minor, Op. 64, No. 2
Ballade in G minor, Op. 23

Fantasy in F minor, Op. 49
Nocturne in F minor, Op. 55, No. 1
Fantasie-Impromptu in C-sharp minor, Op. 66
Nocturne in F-sharp major, Op. 15, No. 2
Scherzo in B-flat minor, Op. 11

Chapter 20. The Short Lyric Forms in the Late Romantic Period

*Brahms, Die Mainacht (May Night)
*———, Vergebliches Ständchen (Futile Serenade)
*———, Intermezzo in B-flat minor, Op. 117, No. 2
———, Sechs Clavierstücke (Intermezzi and Rhapsody), Op. 118

Grieg, Ich liebe dich (I Love Thee)
———, Ein Traum (A Dream)
Tchaikovsky, None but the Lonely Heart
Dvořák, Songs My Mother Taught Me
Musorgsky, The Flea

Chapter 22. Felix Mendelssohn

*Overture and Incidental Music, A Midsummer Night's Dream
Hebrides Overture (Fingal's Cave)

Symphony No. 4, in A (Italian)
Songs Without Words (for piano)
Octet in E-flat, Op. 20

Chapter 23. Hector Berlioz

*Symphonie fantastique
Overture, Roman Carnival
Symphony, Romeo and Juliet

Oratorio, L'Enfance du Christ
Requiem
Symphony, Harold in Italy

Chapter 24. Franz Liszt

*Les Préludes
Faust Symphony
Sonata in B minor
Mephisto Waltz

Valse oubliée
Waldesrauschen (Forest Murmurs)
La Campanella

Chapter 25. Nationalism and the Romantic Movement

Chopin, Polonaises and Mazurkas
Liszt, Hungarian Rhapsodies
Dvořák, Slavonic Dances
Grieg, Norwegian Dances
Tchaikovsky, *Overture 1812*

EXOTICISM:
  Rimsky-Korsakov, *Capriccio espagnol*

Chabrier, *España*
Lalo, *Symphonie espagnole*
Borodin, Polovetzian Dances from
  Prince Igor
————, *In the Steppes of Central Asia*
Ippolitov-Ivanov, *Caucasian Sketches*

Chapter 26. Bedřich Smetana

The Moldau
From Bohemia's Meadows and Forests

Overture to *The Bartered Bride*

Chapter 28. Nicholas Rimsky-Korsakov

Scheherazade
Russian Easter Overture

Coq d'or Suite

Chapter 29. Peter Ilyich Tchaikovsky

*Overture-Fantasy, *Romeo and Juliet*
Capriccio italien

Swan Lake

Chapter 31. César Franck

*Symphony in D minor
Variations symphoniques

Prelude, Chorale, and Fugue for piano
Sonata for Violin and Piano

Chapter 32. Johannes Brahms

*Symphony No. 3
Symphonies Nos. 1, 2, and 4
Variations on a Theme by Haydn

A German Requiem
Academic Festival Overture
Clarinet Quintet

Chapter 33. Antonín Dvořák

*Symphony No. 5, *From the New World*

Symphony No. 4
Quartet in F, Op. 96 (*American*)

Chapter 34. A Late Romantic Symphony

*Tchaikovsky, Symphony No. 6 (*Pathétique*)

————, Symphonies Nos. 4 and 5

Chapter 36. Three Romantic Concertos

*Mendelssohn, Violin Concerto
*Schumann, Piano Concerto
*Brahms, Piano Concerto No. 2
Chopin, Piano Concertos Nos. 1 and 2
Liszt, Piano Concertos Nos. 1 and 2

Brahms, Violin Concerto
Tchaikovsky, Piano Concerto No. 1
————,Violin Concerto
Dvořák, Cello Concerto

Chapter 37. Edvard Grieg

*Piano Concerto

Peer Gynt Suites Nos. 1 and 2

Chapter 39. Opera in the Romantic Period

Gounod, *Faust*
Massenet, *Manon*
Offenbach, *The Tales of Hoffmann*
Rossini, *The Barber of Seville*

Donizetti, *Lucia di Lammermoor*
Bellini, *Norma*
Weber, *Der Freischütz*

Chapter 40. Richard Wagner

*Overture to *Tannhäuser*
Tristan und Isolde: Prelude, Love
    Duet, *Liebestod*
Overture to *The Flying Dutchman*
Die Meistersinger: Prelude, Prize
    Song, Closing Scene
Die Walküre: Siegmund's Love Song
    and Closing Scene, Act 1; Ride of

the Valkyries; Wotan's Farewell
    and Magic Fire Scene
Götterdämmerung: Siegfried's Rhine
    Journey, Siegfried's Funeral March,
    Immolation Scene
Parsifal: Prelude and Good Friday
    Music

Chapter 41. Giuseppe Verdi

Aïda
La Traviata
Rigoletto

Otello
Falstaff

Chapter 42. Georges Bizet

Carmen
Symphony No. 1

L'Arlésienne Suites Nos. 1 and 2

Chapter 43. Modest Musorgsky

Boris Godunov
Night on Bald Mountain

Pictures at an Exhibition
Songs and Dances of Death

Chapter 45. The Major-Minor System

DIATONIC HARMONY:
    Mozart, Piano Sonata in A major,
    K. 331

CHROMATIC HARMONY:
    Wagner, Prelude to *Tristan und
    Isolde*

Chapter 51. Joseph Haydn

*Symphony No 94, in G (*Surprise*)
Symphony No. 92, in G (*Oxford*)
Symphony No. 101, in D (*Clock*)

Symphony No. 104, in D (*London*)
Oratorio, *The Creation*

Chapter 52. Wolfgang Amadeus Mozart

Don Giovanni
*Symphony No. 40, in G minor
*Piano Concerto in D minor, K. 466
Eine kleine Nachtmusik

Symphony No. 39, in E-flat
Symphony No. 41, in C (*Jupiter*)
The Marriage of Figaro
The Magic Flute

Chapter 53. Ludwig van Beethoven

*Symphony No. 5, in C minor
*Piano Sonata in F minor, Op. 57
    (*Appassionata*)
*Overture to *Coriolanus*
Symphonies Nos. 3 (*Eroica*), 6
    (*Pastorale*), 7, and 9
Piano Concerto No. 4, in G major

Overture, *Egmont*
Overture, *Leonore No. 3*
Piano Sonata in C minor, Op. 13
    (*Pathétique*)
Piano Sonata in C-sharp minor, Op.
    27, No. 2 (*Moonlight*)

Chapter 54. Classical Chamber Music

*Haydn, Quartet in F, Op. 3, No. 5
*Mozart, Clarinet Quintet, K. 581
*Beethoven, Quartet in C minor, Op.
    18, No. 4
*Schubert, Piano Quintet (*Trout*)
Haydn, Quartet in C, Op. 76, No. 5
    (*Emperor*)
Mozart, String Quintet in G minor,
    K. 516
———, Quartet in C major, K. 465

Beethoven, Quartet in C minor, Op.
    59, No. 2
———, Quartet in A minor, Op. 132
———, Violin Sonata in F, Op. 24
    (*Spring*)
Schubert, Trio in B-flat, Op. 99
———, Quartet in D minor (*Death
    and the Maiden*)
———, String Quintet in C, Op. 163

Chapter 55. From Classic to Romantic

*Schubert, Symphony No. 8, in B
    minor (*Unfinished*)

———, Symphony No. 9, in C major

Chapter 56. Harmony and Counterpoint: Musical Texture

MONOPHONIC:
    Gregorian Chant

POLYPHONIC:
    Bach, Chorale from *Christ lag in
    Todesbanden* †

HOMOPHONIC:
    Chopin, Waltz in B minor, Op. 69,
    No. 2

CANONIC IMITATION:
    Franck, Violin Sonata, third move-
    ment

† *Masterpieces of Music before 1750* (Haydn Society).

Chapter 57. The Remote Past

GREGORIAN CHANT:
Antiphon, *Laus Deo Patri* †

Chapter 58. The Later Middle Ages

Dufay, Kyrie from Mass *Se la face
ay pale* †

Chapter 60. Sixteenth-Century Music

*Josquin des Prez, *Ave Maria* †
*Lassus, *Tristis est anima mea* †
*Palestrina, *Mass for Pope Marcellus*

*Marenzio, *S'io parto, i'moro* †
*Morley, *Sing We and Chant It*
*Gibbons, *The Silver Swan*

Chapter 66. Old Masters

*Monteverdi, *Tu se' morta* from *Orfeo* †
*Lully, Overture to *Armide* †
*Purcell, *Dido and Aeneas*
*Corelli, Sonata da chiesa in E minor, Op. 3, No. 7 †
*Vivaldi, Concerto in D minor, Op. 3, No. 11

Monteverdi, *Il Combattimento di Tancredi e Clorinda*
————, Madrigals
Purcell, Fantasies for Strings
Vivaldi, *The Four Seasons*
————, Gloria

Chapter 67. Johann Sebastian Bach

*Organ Fugue in G minor (Little)
*Suite No. 3, in D major, for orchestra
*Brandenburg Concerto No. 2, in F major
*Cantata No. 140, *Wachet auf*
*Mass in B minor, excerpts
St. Matthew Passion
Cantata No. 4, *Christ lag in Todesbanden*
Chorale, *Jesu, Joy of Man's Desiring*

Toccata and Fugue in D minor for organ
Fantasia and Fugue in G minor for organ
Passacaglia in C minor for organ
Prelude and Fugue in C minor from *The Well-Tempered Clavier*, Vol. 1
Concerto in D minor for Two Violins
Chaconne in D minor for unaccompanied violin

Chapter 68. George Frideric Handel

Messiah
Water Music
Concerto in D minor for Organ

Concerto grosso in G major, Op. 6, No. 1
The Harmonious Blacksmith
Israel in Egypt

Chapter 69. Aftermath of the Baroque: The Rococo

*Couperin, *La Galante* †
Scarlatti, Sonata in C minor †

Rameau, Scene from *Castor et Pollux* †

† *Masterpieces of Music before 1750* (Haydn Society).

Chapter 70. Opera and Symphony in the Pre-Classical Era

Gluck, *Orfeo*
Bach, C. P. E., Symphonies: No. 1, in D; No. 3, in C
————, Clavier Concerto in D minor

————, Clavier Sonatas
Bach, J. C., Clavier Concertos in D major and G major

Chapter 72. Giacomo Puccini

*La Bohème
Tosca

Madame Butterfly

Chapter 73. Richard Strauss

*Till Eulenspiegel
Don Juan
Death and Transfiguration

Der Rosenkavalier
Salome

Chapter 74. Jan Sibelius

*Finlandia

Symphonies Nos. 1, 2, 5, and 7

Chapter 76. Claude Debussy

*Prelude to the Afternoon of a Faun
*Fêtes
La Mer
String Quartet

La Soirée dans Grenade
La Cathédrale engloutie
La Chevelure
Pelléas et Mélisande

Chapter 77. Maurice Ravel

*La Valse
Daphnis et Chloé Suite No. 2
Boléro
Rapsodie espagnole

Le Tombeau de Couperin
Ma Mère l'Oye
Jeaux d'eau
L'Enfant et les sortilèges

Chapter 78. Other Postromantic Composers

Mahler, *Das Lied von der Erde;* Symphonies Nos. 1 and 5
Wolf, Hugo, *Verborgenheit*
Reger, *Variations and Fugue on a Theme by Mozart*
Fauré, Requiem
D'Indy, *Symphony on a French Mountain Air*
Dukas, *The Sorcerer's Apprentice*
Satie, *Gymnopédies*
Roussel, *The Spider's Feast*
Duparc, *Extase*

Chausson, *Poème* for violin and orchestra
Scriabin, *Poem of Ecstasy*
Rachmaninov, Piano Concerto No. 2
Elgar, *Enigma Variations*
Delius, *Sea Drift*
Vaughan Williams, Symphony No. 2 (*London*)
Respighi, *The Fountains of Rome*
Albeniz, *Iberia*
Granados, Spanish Dances

Chapters 79–80. The New Music—Style Elements in Contemporary Music

PRIMITIVISM:
Bartók, *Allegro barbaro*

MACHINE MUSIC:
Honegger, *Pacific 231*

SATIRE:
Shostakovich, Polka from *The Age of Gold*
Walton, *Façade*

OBJECTIVISM:
Hindemith, *Kleine Kammermusik,* Op. 24, No. 2

THE NEW CLASSICISM:
Stravinsky, Capriccio for Piano and Orchestra

THE NEW NATIONALISM:
Bartók, *Hungarian Sketches*
Falla, Dances from *El Amor brujo*
Vaughan Williams, *Greensleeves*
Copland, *A Lincoln Portrait*

EXPRESSIONISM:
Berg, *Wozzeck*, opening scene

REVITALIZATION OF RHYTHM:
Stravinsky, *The Rite of Spring*

REVIVAL OF ABSOLUTE FORMS:
Stravinsky, Symphony in Three Movements
Bloch, Concerto grosso No. 1

INFLUENCE OF JAZZ:
Milhaud, *La Création du monde*

Chapter 82. Igor Stravinsky

*Petrushka
The Firebird
The Rite of Spring

L'Histoire du soldat (The Soldier's Tale)
Symphony of Psalms

Chapter 83. Arnold Schoenberg

*Verklärte Nacht (Transfigured Night)
*Piano Concerto

Five Orchestral Pieces, Op. 16

Chapter 84. Béla Bartók

*Concerto for Orchestra
Music for Strings, Percussion, and Celesta

Piano Concerto No. 3

Chapter 85. Paul Hindemith

*Mathis der Maler

Symphonic Metamorphoses on Themes by Weber

Chapter 86. Alban Berg

*Wozzeck
Lyric Suite

Violin Concerto

Chapter 87. Other Contemporary Composers

Falla, *El Amor brujo*
Bloch, *Schelomo*

Webern, Cantata No. 1, Op. 29
Milhaud, *Scaramouche*

Honegger, Symphony No. 5
Poulenc, *Mouvements perpetuels*
Prokofiev, *Lieutenant Kije Suite;* Piano
   Concerto No. 3
Shostakovich, Symphonies Nos. 1 and 5
Khatchaturian, Piano Concerto
Walton, *Belshazzar's Feast*

Britten, *Peter Grimes*
Kodály, *Háry János Suite*
Martinu, Double Concerto for two
   string orchestras
Krenek, *Lamentations of Jeremiah*
Weill, *The Three-Penny Opera*

Chapter 88. The (American) Past

MacDowell, Piano Concerto No. 2
———, *Indian Suite*

———, *Woodland Sketches*

Chapter 90. The Senior Group

Griffes, *The White Peacock; The
   Pleasure Dome of Kubla Khan*
Varèse, *Ionisation; Poème électronique*
Ruggles, *Portals*

Riegger, Symphony No. 3
Villa-Lobos, *Bachianas brasileiras* No.
   5

Chapter 91. Charles Ives

Three Places in New England

Symphonies Nos. 2 and 3

Chapter 92. The Second Generation

Moore, *The Ballad of Baby Doe*
———, Symphony No. 2
Piston, *The Incredible Flutist*
———, Symphony No. 2
Thomson, *Louisiana Story*
———, *A Solemn Music*
Sessions, *Symphony No. 1*
———, *The Black Maskers*
Harris, *Third Symphony*

———, Symphony No. 4 (*Folksong*)
Gershwin, *An American in Paris*
———, *Rhapsody in Blue*
———, *Piano Concerto in F*
———, *Porgy and Bess*
Copland, *Billy the Kid*
———, *El Salón México*
———, *Appalachian Spring*
———, Symphony No. 3

Chapter 93. The Third Generation

Barber, *Essay for Orchestra*, No. 1
———, *Adagio for Strings*
———, Overture to *The School for
   Scandal*
———, *Piano Sonata*

———, *Medea's Meditation and Dance
   of Vengeance*
Schuman, *Symphony No. 3*
———, *Judith*
———, *New England Triptych*

Chapter 94. Other Composers of the Third Generation

Carter, Variations for Orchestra
———, Quartet No. 2
Menotti, *Amahl and the Night Visitors*
———, *The Consul*
Dello Joio, *Variations, Chaconne and
   Finale*
———, *Meditations on Ecclesiastes*

Bernstein, *Age of Anxiety*
———, *West Side Story*
Kirchner, Piano Concerto
———, Quartet No. 1
Foss, *A Parable of Death*
———, *Song of Songs*
Mennin, Symphonies Nos. 3 and 5

APPENDIX II

A List of Books

THE FOLLOWING is by no means a complete list. Those desiring to pursue the subject further will find specialized bibliographies in many of the works listed below.

ON THE NATURE OF ART

Dewey, John. *Art as Experience*. New York: Putnam, 1934.
Read, Herbert. *Art and Society*. New York: Pantheon, 1945.
Sachs, Curt. *The Commonwealth of Art*. New York: Norton, 1946.

DICTIONARIES

Apel, Willi. *Harvard Dictionary of Music*. Cambridge: Harvard, 1944.
Grove's Dictionary of Music and Musicians, 5th ed. (ed. by Eric Blom). New York: St. Martin's, 1954, 1961.
Baker's Biographical Dictionary of Musicians, 5th ed. (ed. by Nicolas Slonimsky). New York: Schirmer, 1958.
Thompson, Oscar, and Nicolas Slonimsky. *International Encyclopedia of Music and Musicians*. New York: Dodd, Mead, 1953.

THE ELEMENTS OF MUSIC

Copland, Aaron. *What to Listen for in Music*. New York: Whittlesey, 1939.
Grove's Dictionary of Music and *Harvard Dictionary of Music:* articles on melody, harmony, rhythm, meter, tempo, timbre, etc.

MUSIC HISTORY (SINGLE-VOLUME WORKS)

Einstein, Alfred. *A Short History of Music*. New York: Knopf, 1947.
Grout, Donald Jay. *A History of Western Music*. New York: Norton, 1960.
Lang, Paul Henry. *Music in Western Civilization*. New York: Norton, 1941.
Sachs, Curt. *Our Musical Heritage: A Short History of Music*, 2nd ed. New York: Prentice Hall, 1955.

STYLES AND PERIODS

Abraham, Gerald. *This Modern Music*. New York: Norton, 1952.
Bauer, Marion. *Twentieth Century Music*. New York: Putnam, 1947.
Bukofzer, Manfred F. *Music in the Baroque Era*. New York: Norton, 1947.
Copland, Aaron. *Our New Music*. New York: Whittlesey, 1941.
Cowell, Henry, ed. *American Composers on American Music*. New York: Ungar, 1962.
Einstein, Alfred. *Music in the Romantic Era*. New York: Norton, 1947.
Locke, Arthur W. *Music and the Romantic Movement in France*. New York: Dutton, 1920.
Machlis, Joseph. *Introduction to Contemporary Music*. New York: Norton, 1961.
Praz, Mario. *The Romantic Agony*. New York: Oxford, 1951.
Reese, Gustave. *Music in the Middle Ages*. New York: Norton, 1940.
————. *Music in the Renaissance*, revised ed. New York: Norton, 1959.
Reis, Claire R. *Composers in America*. New York: Macmillan, 1947.
Sachs, Curt. *The Rise of Music in the Ancient ·World*. New York: Norton, 1943.
Slonimsky, Nicolas. *Music Since 1900*. New York: Coleman-Ross, 1949.

Stevens, Denis, ed. *A History of Song.* New York: Norton, 1961.
Thompson, Oscar. *Great Modern Composers.* New York: Dodd, Mead, 1941.

BY COMPOSERS

Anderson, Emily (ed. and tr.). *The Letters of Beethoven.* New York: St. Martin's, 1961.
Berlioz, Hector. *Memoirs.* New York: Knopf, 1948.
———. *Evenings with the Orchestra.* New York: Knopf, 1956.
Bernstein, Leonard. *The Joy of Music.* New York: Simon & Schuster, 1959.
Copland, Aaron. *What to Listen for in Music,* revised ed. New York: McGraw-Hill, 1957.
———. *Music and Imagination.* Cambridge: Harvard, 1952.
———. *Copland on Music.* New York: Norton, 1963.
Debussy, Claude. *Monsieur Croche.* New York: Lear, 1948.
Dvořák, Antonín. *Letters and Reminiscences.* Ed. by Otakar Šourek. Prague: Artia, 1954.
Robbins Landon, H. C. *The Collected Correspondence and London Notebooks of Joseph Haydn.* Fair Lawn, N.J.: Essential, 1959.
Hindemith, Paul. *A Composer's World.* Cambridge: Harvard, 1952.
Ives, Charles. *Essays Before a Sonata and Other Writings.* New York: Norton, 1962.
Mahler, Alma Maria. *Gustav Mahler: Memories and Letters.* New York: Viking, 1946.
Milhaud, Darius. *Notes Without Music.* New York: Knopf, 1953.
Anderson, Emily (ed. and tr.). *The Letters of Mozart and His Family.* New York: Macmillan, 1938.
Puccini, Giacomo. *Letters.* Philadelphia: Lippincott, 1931.
Rimsky-Korsakov, Nicholas. *My Musical Life.* New York: Knopf, 1942.
Schoenberg, Arnold. *Style and Idea.* New York: Philosophical, 1950.
Schumann, Robert. *On Music and Musicians.* New York: Pantheon, 1946.
Sessions, Roger. *The Musical Experience of Composer, Performer, Listener.* Princeton: Princeton Univ., 1950.
Smetana, Bedřich. *Letters and Reminiscences.* Ed. by František Bartoš. Prague: Artia, 1955.
Strauss, Richard. *Correspondence with Hugo von Hofmannsthal.* New York: Knopf, 1927.
Stravinsky, Igor. *Poetics of Music.* Cambridge: Harvard, 1947.
———. *An Autobiography.* New York: Steuer, 1958.
Stravinsky, Igor and Robert Craft. *Conversations with Igor Stravinsky.* Garden City, N.Y.: Doubleday, 1959.
———. *Memories and Commentaries.* Garden City, N.Y.: Doubleday, 1960.
———. *Expositions and Developments.* Garden City, N.Y.: Doubleday, 1962.
Thomson, Virgil. *The Musical Scene.* New York: Knopf, 1945.
———. *The Art of Judging Music.* New York: Knopf, 1948.
———. *Music Right and Left.* New York: Holt, 1951.
Vaughan Williams, Ralph. *National Music.* London: Oxford, 1934.
———. *The Making of Music.* Ithaca, N.Y.: Cornell, 1955.
Wagner, Richard. *Prose Works.* London: Kegan Paul, 1892–99.
Verdi: The Man in His Letters. Ed. by Franz Werfel and Paul Stefan. New York: L. B. Fischer, 1942.

ON COMPOSERS

Johann Sebastian Bach. Philipp Spitta. New York: Dover, 1951.
J. S. Bach. Albert Schweitzer. New York: Macmillan, 1935.
The Bach Reader. Hans T. David and Arthur Mendel. New York: Norton, 1945.
The Bach Family. Karl Geiringer. New York: Oxford, 1954.

Samuel Barber. Nathan Broder. New York: Schirmer, 1954.

The Life and Music of Béla Bartók. Halsey Stevens. New York: Oxford, 1953.

Beethoven: Impressions of Contemporaries. O. G. Sonneck. New York: Schirmer, 1926.

The Life of Ludwig van Beethoven. A. W. Thayer, ed. H. E. Krehbiel. New York: Beethoven Association, 1921.

Beethoven: His Spiritual Development. J. W. N. Sullivan. New York: Knopf, 1947.

Beethoven, Schubert, Mendelssohn. George Grove. New York: Macmillan, 1951.

Alban Berg. H. F. Redlich. New York: Abelard-Schuman.

Berlioz and the Romantic Century. Jacques Barzun. Boston: Little, Brown, 1950.

Bizet. Winton Dean. London: Dent, 1948.

Bizet and His World. Mina Curtiss. New York: Knopf, 1958.

Borodin. Gerald E. H. Abraham. London: William Reeves, 1927.

Brahms: His Life and Work. Karl Geiringer. New York: Oxford, 1947.

Benjamin Britten. Donald Mitchell and Hans Keller, eds. New York: Philosophical, 1952.

Bruckner and Mahler. H. F. Redlich. New York: Farrar, Straus & Cudahy, 1955.

William Byrd. Edmund H. Fellowes. London: Oxford, 1948 (2nd ed.).

Ernest Chausson. Jean-Pierre Barricelli and Leo Weinstein. Norman: Univ. of Oklahoma, 1955.

Chopin: The Man and His Music. Herbert Weinstock. New York: Knopf, 1949.

Copland. Arthur Berger. New York: Oxford, 1953.

Aaron Copland. Julia Smith. New York: Dutton, 1955.

Corelli: His Life, His Music. Marc Pincherle. New York: Norton, 1956.

François Couperin and the French Classical Tradition. Wilfrid Mellers. London: Dobson, 1950.

Debussy: Man and Artist. Oscar Thompson. New York: Dodd, Mead, 1937.

Delius. Peter Warlock. New York: Oxford, 1952 (revised ed.).

Antonín Dvořák. Otakar Šourek. New York: Philosophical, 1954.

César Franck. Norman Demuth. New York: Philosophical, 1949.

George Gershwin. Isaac Goldberg. New York: Ungar, 1958.

Gluck. Alfred Einstein. New York: Dutton, 1936.

Grieg: A Symposium. Ed. by Gerald Abraham. Norman: Univ. of Oklahoma, 1950.

Handel: A Documentary Biography. Otto Erich Deutsch. New York: Norton, 1955.

Handel's Dramatic Oratorios and Masques. Winton Dean. London: Oxford, 1959.

Haydn. Karl Geiringer. New York: Norton, 1946.

Charles Ives and His Music. Henry and Sidney Cowell. New York: Oxford, 1955.

Liszt. Sacheverell Sitwell. Boston: Houghton Mifflin, 1934.

Monteverdi: His Life and Works. Henry Prunières. New York: Dutton, 1926.

Monteverdi: Creator of Modern Music. Leo Schrade. New York: Norton, 1950.

Mozart. Eric Blom. London: Dent, 1935.

Mozart: His Character, His Work. Alfred Einstein. New York: Oxford, 1945.

The Musorgsky Reader. Jay Leyda and S. Bertensson. New York: Norton, 1947.

Musorgsky. M. D. Calvocoressi. New York: Dutton, 1946.

Paganini the Genoese. G. I. C. de Courcy. Norman: Univ. of Oklahoma, 1957.

Palestrina. Henry Coates. London: Dent, 1938.

Prokofiev. Israel V. Nestyev. Stanford: Stanford Univ., 1960.

Puccini. Mosco Carner. New York: Knopf, 1959.

Purcell. J. A. Westrup. New York: Dutton, 1937.

Rachmaninov. Victor I. Seroff. New York: Simon & Schuster, 1950.

Jean-Philippe Rameau. Cuthbert Girdlestone. London: Cassell, 1957.

Maurice Ravel. Roland-Manuel. London: Dobson, 1947.

Ravel. Vladimir Jankelevitch. New York: Grove, 1959.

Rossini. Francis Toye. New York: Knopf, 1934.

Erik Satie. Rollo H. Myers. London: Dobson, 1948.

Domenico Scarlatti. Ralph Kirkpatrick. New York: Knopf, 1953.

The Schubert Reader. Otto Erich Deutsch. New York: Norton, 1947.

Schubert. Maurice J. E. Brown. New York: St. Martin's, 1958.

William Schuman. Flora Rheta Schreiber and Vincent Persichetti. New York: Schirmer, 1954.

Schumann. Joan Chissell. London: Dent, 1948.

Stravinsky. Roman Vlad. London: Oxford, 1960.

Tchaikovsky. Herbert Weinstock. New York: Knopf, 1943.

Virgil Thomson. Kathleen Hoover and John Cage. New York: Yoseloff, 1959.

Ralph Vaughan Williams. Hubert J. Foss. London: Oxford, 1950.

Giuseppe Verdi. Francis Toye. New York: Knopf, 1931.

Vivaldi. Marc Pincherle. New York: Norton, 1957.

The Life of Richard Wagner. Ernest Newman. New York: Knopf, 1933–46.

Wagner as Man and Artist. Ernest Newman. New York: Knopf, 1924.

Hugo Wolf. Frank Walker. London: Dent, 1951.

APPENDIX III

Comparative Range of the Instruments

THE HUMAN VOICE

Bass   Baritone   Tenor   Contralto   Mezzo   Soprano

STRINGED INSTRUMENTS

Violin   Viola   Cello   Double - bass

WOODWIND INSTRUMENTS

BRASS INSTRUMENTS

PERCUSSION INSTRUMENTS

OTHER INSTRUMENTS

Complete List of Major and Minor Scales

APPENDIX V

Pronouncing List
of Selected Musical Terms

accompagnato (-pa-nyáh-toh)
assai (ah-sígh)
ballade (bal-láhd)
bourrée (boor-ráy)
cantabile (can-táh-bih-leh)
chorale (co-rál)
clavecin (clav-sá*n*)
clavier (clah-véer)
concertante (con-chehr-táhn-teh)
concerto (con-chéhr-toh)
dodecaphonic (doh-deh-ca-fón-ic)
dodecaphony (-cáff-uh-nee)
dolce (dúll-cheh)
embouchure (om-boo-shóor)
etude (áy-tyood)
Gebrauchsmusik (geh-brówkhs-moo-
  zéek)
gigue (zheeg)
gioioso (joy-óh-zoh)
grave [tempo] (gráh-veh)
pizzicato (pit-sih-cáh-toh)

homophonic (hoh-moh-fón-ic)
homophony (hoh-móff-uh-nee)
marziale (mar-tsyáh-leh)
opera buffa (bóo-fah)
opera seria (séhr-ee-ah)
órganum
ostinato (oh-stih-náh-toh)
passacaglia (poss-ah-cáh-lyah)
polyphonic (poll-ih-fón-ic)
polyphony (poh-líff-uh-nee)
recitative (reh-sih-tah-téev)
rococo (roh-cóh-coh)
scherzo (skéhr-tsoh)
siciliano (sih-chill-yáh-noh)
sonata da chiesa (da kyáy-zah)
stile concitato (stée-leh cone-chih-
  táh-toh)
timbre (tám-br)
vibrato (vih-bráh-toh)
vivace (vih-váh-cheh)
xylophone (zígh-loh-fone)

A Chronological List of Composers, World Events, and Principal Figures in Literature and the Arts, 1400-1962

(The list of composers does not presume to be complete. It includes those mentioned in the text and some additional names.)

Pre-Baroque
RENAISSANCE
(1450–1600)

Guillaume Dufay
(c. 1400–74)

Josquin des Prez ✓
(c. 1450–1521)

Giovanni da Pales- ✓
trina
(c. 1529–94)
Roland de Lassus ✓
(c. 1532–94)
William Byrd ✓
(1543–1623)
Tomás Luis de Victoria
(c. 1549–1611)
Luca Marenzio
(c. 1553–99)
Giovanni Gabrieli ✓
(c. 1555–1612)
Thomas Morley
(1557–c. 1603)
Carlo Gesualdo
(1560–1613)
John Wilbye
(1574–1638)
Thomas Weelkes
(c. 1575–1623)
Orlando Gibbons
(1583–1625)

1415 John Huss burned for heresy. Henry V defeats French at Agincourt.
1453 Constantinople captured by Turks.
1456 Gutenberg Bible.

1492 Columbus discovers New World.
1506 St. Peter's begun by Pope Julius II: Bramante, Raphael, Michelangelo, *et al.*
1509 Henry VIII becomes King of England.
1513 Ponce de Leon discovers Florida. Balboa reaches Pacific.
1517 Luther posts 95 theses on Wittenberg church door.
1519 Cortez begins conquest of Mexico.
1520 Magellan reaches Philippines.
1534 Henry VIII head of Church of England.
1536 Anne Boleyn beheaded.
1541 De Soto discovers the Mississippi.
1558 Elizabeth I becomes Queen of England.
1572 St. Bartholomew's Eve Massacre.
1587 Mary Queen of Scots executed. Virginia Dare, first English child born in New World.
1588 Drake defeats Spanish Armada.
1590 First three books of Spenser's *Faerie Queene* published.
1601–09 Shakespeare's best tragedies (*Hamlet, Othello, Macbeth, Lear, Antony and Cleopatra*) and comedies (*As You Like It, Twelfth Night, Much Ado About Nothing*).

Luca della Robbia
(1400–82)
Giovanni Bellini
(1430–1516)
François Villon
(1431–c. 1465)
Sandro Botticelli
(1447–1510)
Leonardo da Vinci
(1452–1519)
Erasmus (1466–1536)
Niccolò Machiavelli
(1469–1527)
Albrecht Dürer
(1471–1528)
Michelangelo
(1475–1564)
Titian (1477–1576)
Raphael (1483–1520)
François Rabelais
(1490–1553)
Hans Holbein
(1497–1543)
Benvenuto Cellini
(1500–71)
Pierre de Ronsard
(1524–85)
Pieter Brueghel
(1525–69)
Michel de Montaigne
(1533–92)
El Greco (1542–1614)
Miguel de Cervantes
(1547–1616)
Edmund Spenser
(1552–99)
William Shakespeare
(1564–1616)

Baroque

BAROQUE
(1600–1750)

AND ROCOCO
(1700–1775)

Claudio Monteverdi
(1567–1643)

Jean-Baptiste Lully
(1632–87)

Dietrich Buxtehude
(1637–1707)

Arcangelo Corelli
(1653–1713)

Henry Purcell (1659–
95)

François Couperin
(1668–1733)

Antonio Vivaldi
(1676–1741)

Georg Telemann
(1681–1767)

Jean-Philippe Rameau
(1683–1764)
Johann Sebastian Bach
(1685–1750)

Domenico Scarlatti
(1685–1757)

George Frideric Han-
del (1685–1759)

Giovanni Battista Per-
golesi (1710–36)

1607 Jamestown settled.
1609 Henry Hudson explores
Hudson River.
1618–48 Thirty Years' War.
1620 Mayflower Compact. Ply-
mouth settled. Francis Bacon's
Novum Organum.
1626 Manhattan Island purchased from Indians.
1628 Harvey discovers circulation of blood.
1637 Descartes's *Discourse on
Method.*
1642–49 **Puritan Revolution in
England.**
1649–60 Commonwealth and
Protectorate in England.
1651 Hobbes's *Leviathan.*
1661–1715 Reign of Louis XIV.
Absolutism.
1664 New Amsterdam be-
comes New York.
1666 Newton discovers Law of
Gravity.
1667 Spinoza's *Ethics.*
1669 Academy of Music (Paris
Opera) founded.
1682–1725 Reign of Peter the
Great.
1685 Locke's *Two Treatises on
Civil Government.*
1702–14 War of the Spanish
Succession.
1712 Queen Anne succeeded
by George I, Handel's patron.
1715 First Opéra Comique
founded.
1715–74 Reign of Louis XV.
1719 Herculaneum and Pom-
peii rediscovered. Classical
Revival.
1732 Linnaeus's *System of Nature.*
1732–99 George Washington.
1737 San Carlo Opera, Naples, opened.
1740–96 Age of Enlightened
Despots.
1743–1826 Thomas Jefferson.
1751–72 Great Encyclopedia.
Age of Enlightenment. Sensibility.
1752 Franklin's discoveries in
electricity.

John Donne (1573–
1631)

Ben Jonson (1573–
1637)

Peter Paul Rubens
(1577–1640)

Frans Hals (1580?–
1666)

Giovanni Lorenzo Ber-
nini (1598–1680)

Anthony Van Dyck
(1599–1641)

Diego Velázquez
(1599–1660)

Rembrandt van Ryn
(1606–69)

Pierre Corneille (1606–
84)

John Milton (1608–74)

Molière (1622–73)

John Bunyan (1628–
88)

John Dryden (1631–
1700)

Jan Vermeer (1632–
75)

Sir Christopher Wren
(1632–1723)

Jean Baptiste Racine
(1639–99)

Daniel Defoe (1659?–
1731)

Jonathan Swift (1667–
1745)

Joseph Addison (1672–
1719)

Richard Steele (1672–
1729)

Jean Antoine Watteau
(1684–1721)

Alexander Pope (1688–
1744)

Voltaire (1694–1778)

Giovanni Battista Tie-
polo (1696–1770)

William Hogarth
(1697–1764)

François Boucher
(1703–70)

PRE-CLASSICAL
(c. 1740–75)

Christoph Willibald
Gluck (1714–87)

Carl Philipp Emanuel
Bach (1714–88)

Johann Stamitz (1717–
57)

Johann Christian Bach
(1735–82)

Domenico Cimarosa
(1749–1801)

THE CLASSIC
PERIOD
(1775–1825)

Joseph Haydn (1732–
1809)

Wolfgang Amadeus
Mozart (1756–91)

Maria Luigi Cherubini
(1760–1842)

Ludwig van Beethoven
(1770–1827)

1756–63 Seven Years' War (in
America, the French and Indian War).

1759 Wolfe captures Quebec.

1763 Canada ceded to England.

1765 Watt's steam engine.

1767 Hargreaves's spinning
jenny.

c. 1770 Beginning of the factory system.

1771 First edition, *Encyclopedia Britannica.*

1774 Priestley discovers oxygen.

1775–83 American Revolution.

1776 Declaration of Independence.

1776 Adam Smith's *The
Wealth of Nations.*

1778 La Scala Opera opened
in Milan.

1781 Kant's *Critique of Pure
Reason.*

1787 Constitutional Convention.

1788 Fitch's steamboat.

1789–94 French Revolution.

1791 Bill of Rights. Second
Opéra Comique opened.

1793 Eli Whitney's cotton gin.

Henry Fielding (1707–
54)
Samuel Johnson (1709–
84)
Jean Jacques Rousseau
(1712–78)
Laurence Sterne
(1713–68)
Thomas Gray (1716–
71)
Sir Joshua Reynolds
(1723–92)
Thomas Gainsborough
(1727–88)
Oliver Goldsmith
(1728–74)
Pierre Augustin Caron
Beaumarchais (1732–
99)
Jean Honoré Frago-
nard (1732–1809)
Edward Gibbon
(1737–94)
Jean Antoine Houdon
(1741–1828)
Francisco José de
Goya (1746–1828)
Jacques Louis David
(1748–1825)
Johann Wolfgang von
Goethe (1749–1832)
William Blake (1757–
1827)
Robert Burns (1759–
96)
Johann Christoph
Friedrich von Schil-
ler (1759–1805)
Charles Bulfinch
(1763–1844)
William Wordsworth
(1770–1850)
Sir Walter Scott (1771–
1832)
Samuel Taylor Cole-
ridge (1772–1834)
J. M. W. Turner
(1775–1851)
John Constable (1776–
1837)
Jean Auguste Domi-
nique Ingres (1780–
1867)
George Gordon Byron
(1788–1824)

Gasparo Spontini
(1774–1851)

THE ROMANTIC
PERIOD
(c. 1820–1900)

1. *From Classic
to Romantic*
(*1800–c. 1830*)

Carl Maria von Weber
(1786–1826)

Franz Schubert (1797–
1828)

2. *Romanticism,
First Phase*
(*c. 1830–c. 1850*)

Niccolo Paganini
(1782–1840)

Giacomo Meyerbeer
(1791–1864)

Gioacchino Rossini
(1792–1868)

Gaetano Donizetti
(1797–1848)

Vincenzo Bellini
(1801–35)

Johann Strauss (the fa-
ther: 1804–49)
Michael Glinka (1804–
57)

Felix Mendelssohn
(1809–47)

1796   Jenner begins vaccination.

1798   Malthus's *Essay on Population.*

1800   Laplace's mechanistic
view of universe. Volta invents voltaic pile.

1803   Louisiana Purchase.

1807   Hegel's *Phenomenology
of Mind.*

1807   Fulton's steamboat.

1812   Napoleon invades Russia.

1815   Battle of Waterloo. Con-
gress of Vienna.

1817   Ricardo's *Political Economy and Taxation.*

1819   First steamship to cross
Atlantic.

1823   Monroe Doctrine.

1824   Bolivar liberates South
America. Stephenson's locomotive.

1829   Independence of Greece.

1830   First railroad, Liverpool–
Manchester. July Revolution
in France.

1832   Morse invents telegraph.

1833   Slavery outlawed in British Empire.

1834   McCormick patents mechanical reaper.

1837–1901   Victoria's reign.

Alphonse Lamartine
(1790–1869)
Jean Louis Géricault
(1791–1824)
Percy Bysshe Shelley
(1792–1822)
John Keats (1795–
1821)
Thomas Carlyle (1795–
1881)
John Baptiste Camille
Corot (1796–1875)
Alexander Pushkin
(1799–1837)
Honoré de Balzac
(1799–1850)
Ferdinand Victor Eu-
gène Delacroix
(1799–1863)
Alexander Dumas
(1802–70)
Victor Hugo (1802–85)
Ralph Waldo Emerson
(1803–82)
Nathaniel Hawthorne
(1804–64)
George Sand (1804–
76)
Honoré Daumier
(1808–79)
Edgar Allan Poe (1809–
49)
Nikolai Gogol (1809–
52)
Alfred Tennyson
(1809–92)
William Makepeace
Thackeray (1811–
63)
Charles Dickens (1812–
70)
Robert Browning
(1812–89)
Charlotte Brontë
(1816–55)
Henry David Thoreau
(1817–62)
Emily Brontë (1818–
48)
Ivan Sergeevich Tur-
geniev (1818–83)
George Eliot (1819–80)
Herman Melville
(1819–91)
Walt Whitman (1819–
92)

Frédéric François Chopin (1810–49)

Robert Schumann (1810–56)

3. Romanticism, Mid-Nineteenth Century (c. 1840–c. 1880)

Hector Berlioz (1803–69)

Franz Liszt (1811–86)

Richard Wagner (1813–83)

Giuseppe Verdi (1813–1901)

4. Late Romanticism (c. 1870–c. 1900)

Charles Gounod (1818–93)

Jacques Offenbach (1819–80)

César Franck (1822–90)

Édouard Lalo (1823–92)

Bedřich Smetana (1824–84)

Anton Bruckner (1824–96)

Johann Strauss (the son: 1825–99)

Stephen Collins Foster (1826–64)

Johannes Brahms (1833–97)

Alexander Borodin (1834–87)

Camille Saint-Saëns (1835–1921)

Léo Delibes (1836–91)

1839 Daguerreotype invented, beginnings of photography. N. Y. Philharmonic Society founded. Vienna Philharmonic founded.

1842 Long uses ether as anaesthetic.

1843 Leipzig Conservatory founded.

1846 Repeal of Corn laws. Famine in Ireland.

1848 Revolutions throughout Europe.

1848 Gold Rush in California. Mill's *Political Economy*. Marx's *Communist Manifesto*.

1852 Second Empire under Napoleon III. *Uncle Tom's Cabin* appears:

1853 Commodore Perry opens Japan to West. Crimean War.

1855 Charge of the Light Brigade.

1857 Dred Scott decision.

1858 Covent Garden opened as opera house.

1859 Darwin's *Origin of Species*. John Brown raids Harper's Ferry.

1861 Serfs emancipated in Russia.

1861–65 Civil War in America.

1863 Emancipation Proclamation.

1865 Lincoln assassinated.

1866 Transatlantic cable completed.

1867 Marx's *Das Kapital* (first vol.). Alaska purchased.

1870 Franco-Prussian War.

1871 William I of Hohenzollern becomes German Emperor. Vatican Council proclaims papal infallibility. Paris Commune. Unification of Italy complete; Rome becomes capital. Stanley and Livingston in Africa.

1873 Dynamo developed.

1875 New Paris Opera House opened.

1876 Telephone invented. Internal-combustion engine. Bayreuth theater opened.

1877 Phonograph invented.

John Ruskin (1819–1900)

Pierre Charles Baudelaire (1821–67)

Gustave Flaubert (1821–80)

Feodor Mikhailovich Dostoievsky (1821–81)

Dante Gabriel Rossetti (1828–82)

Henrik Ibsen (1828–1906)

George Meredith (1828–1909)

Leo Nikolaevich Tolstoi (1828–1910)

Emily Dickinson (1830–86)

Camille Pissarro (1830–1903)

Édouard Manet (1832–83)

Pedro Antonio de Alarcón (1833–91)

James McNeill Whistler (1834–1903)

Hilaire Germain René Degas (1834–1917)

Mark Twain (1835–1910)

Winslow Homer (1836–1910)

Algernon Charles Swinburne (1837–1909)

William Dean Howells (1837–1920)

H. H. Richardson (1838–86)

Henry Adams (1838–1918)

Paul Cézanne (1839–1906)

Alphonse Daudet (1840–97)

Émile Zola (1840–1902)

Auguste Rodin (1840–1917)

Claude Monet (1840–1926)

Thomas Hardy (1840–1928)

Pierre Auguste Renoir (1841–1919)

Mily Balakirev (1836–1910)

Georges Bizet (1838–75)

Modest Musorgsky (1839–81)

Peter Ilyich Tchaikovsky (1840–93)

Alexis Emmanuel Chabrier (1841–94)

Antonín Dvořák (1841–1904)

Sir Arthur Sullivan (1842–1900)

Jules Massenet (1842–1912)

Edvard Grieg (1843–1907)

Nicholas Rimsky-Korsakov (1844–1908)

POST-
ROMANTICISM
(c. 1890–c. 1910)

Gabriel Fauré (1845–1924)

Henri Duparc (1848–1933)

Vincent d'Indy (1851–1931)

Engelbert Humperdinck (1854–1921)

Leoš Janáček (1854–1928)

Ernest Chausson (1855–99)

Sir Edward Elgar (1857–1934)

Ruggiero Leoncavallo (1858–1919)

Giacomo Puccini (1858–1924)

Hugo Wolf (1860–1903)

Isaac Albéniz (1860–1909)

1880   Irish Insurrection.
1881   Tsar Alexander II assassinated. President Garfield shot.
1881–1914   Panama Canal built. Boston Symphony founded.
1882   Koch discovers tuberculosis germ. Berlin Philharmonic founded.
1883   Brooklyn Bridge opened. Nietzsche's *Thus Spake Zarathustra*. Metropolitan Opera opened. Amsterdam Concertgebouw founded.
1884   Pasteur discovers inoculation against rabies.
1885   First electric street railway in U. S., in Baltimore.
1886   Statue of Liberty unveiled in New York Harbor.
1887   Daimler patents high-speed internal-combustion engine.
1889   Eiffel Tower, Paris World's Fair opened. Brazil expels emperor, becomes republic.
1890   Journey around world completed in 72 days.
1892   Duryea makes first American gas buggy.
1893   World's Columbian Exposition, Chicago.
1894   Nicholas II, last Tsar, ascends throne.
1894–1905   Dreyfus affair.
1895   Roentgen discovers X-rays. Pavlov discovers conditioned reflex. Marconi's wireless telegraphy.
1896   Becquerel finds radioactivity in uranium. Olympic games revived. Gold rush in Alaska.
1897   Queen Victoria's Diamond Jubilee.
1898   Pierre and Marie Curie discover radium. Empress Elizabeth of Austria-Hungary assassinated. Spanish-American War.
1899   Boer War. First International Peace Conference at the Hague.

Stéphane Mallarmé (1842–98)

Henry James (1843–1916)

Paul Verlaine (1844–96)

Friedrich Wilhelm Nietzsche (1844–1900)

Anatole France (1844–1924)

Eugène Henri Paul Gauguin (1848–1903)

Augustus St. Gaudens (1848–1907)

Joris Karl Huysmans (1848–1907)

Guy de Maupassant (1850–93)

Robert Louis Stevenson (1850–94)

Vincent Van Gogh (1853–90)

Arthur Rimbaud (1854–91)

Oscar Wilde (1856–1900)

Louis H. Sullivan (1856–1924)

John Singer Sargent (1856–1925)

George Bernard Shaw (1856–1950)

Joseph Conrad (1857–1924)

Georges Seurat (1859–91)

A. E. Housman (1859–1936)

Anton Chekov (1860–1904)

James M. Barrie (1860–1937)

Aristide Maillol (1861–1945)

Edith Wharton (1862–1937)

Gerhart Hauptmann (1862–1946)

Maurice Maeterlinck (1862–1949)

Paul Signac (1863–1935)

Gabriele D'Annunzio (1863–1938)

George Gray Barnard (1863–1938)

Gustav Mahler (1860–1911)

Edward MacDowell (1861–1908)

Charles Martin Loeffler (1861–1935)

Claude Debussy (1862–1918)

Frederick Delius (1862–1934)

Pietro Mascagni (1863–1945)

Richard Strauss (1864–1949)

Alexander Grechaninov (1864–1956)

Paul Dukas (1865–1935)

Alexander Glazunov (1865–1936)

Jan Sibelius (1865–1957)

Ferruccio Busoni (1866–1924)

Erik Satie (1866–1925)

1900   Boxer Insurrection in China. Count Zeppelin tests dirigible balloon. Philadelphia Symphony founded.

1901   Queen Victoria dies, Edward VII succeeds. De Vries's mutation theory.

1903   Wrights' first successful airplane flight. Ford organizes motor company.

1904–05   Russo-Japanese War. London Symphony founded.

1905   Sigmund Freud founds psychoanalysis. Norway separates from Sweden. First Russian Revolution.

1905–10   Einstein's theories.

1906   San Francisco earthquake and fire.

1907   Second Hague Conference. Triple Entente. William James's *Pragmatism*.

1908   Model T Ford produced.

1909   Peary reaches North Pole.

1910   Discovery of protons and electrons. Edward VII dies, George V succeeds.

1911   Amundsen reaches South Pole.

1912   China becomes republic. *Titanic* sinks.

1912–13   Balkan Wars.

1914–18   World War I.

1915   *Lusitania* sunk.

1916   Battle of Verdun.

1917   U. S. enters World War I. Russian Revolution. Prohibition Amendment.

Henri de Toulouse-Lautrec (1864–1901)
Rudyard Kipling (1865–1936)
William Butler Yeats (1865–1939)
Romain Rolland (1866–1943)
Wassily Kandinsky (1866–1944)
H. G. Wells (1866–1946)
Arnold Bennett (1867–1931)
John Galsworthy (1867–1933)
Luigi Pirandello (1867–1936)
Edmond Rostand 1868–1918)
Stefan Georg (1868–1933)
Maxim Gorky (1868–1936)
Edward Arlington Robinson (1869–1935)
Henri Matisse (1869–1954)
Frank Lloyd Wright (1869–1959)
Stephen Crane (1871–1900)
Ignacio Zuloaga (1870–1945)
André Gide (1870–1951)
John Marin (1870–1953)
John M. Synge (1871–1909)
Marcel Proust (1871–1922)
Theodore Dreiser (1871–1945)
Georges Rouault (1871–1958)
Sergei Diaghilev (1872–1929)
Piet Mondrian (1872–1946)
Willa Cather (1873–1947)
Hugo Von Hofmannsthal (1874–1929)
G. K. Chesterton (1874–1936)

Enrique Granados
(1867–1916)

Albert Roussel (1869–
1937)

CONTEMPORARY
MUSIC
(1910–)

Modern

Alexander Scriabin
(1871–1915)
Ralph Vaughan Wil-
liams (1872–1958)
Max Reger (1873–
1916)
Sergei Rachmaninov
(1873–1943)
Arnold Schoenberg
(1874–1950)
Charles Ives (1874–
1954)
Gustav Holst
(1874–1934)
Maurice Ravel (1875–
1937) – *Bolero*
Manuel de Falla
(1876–1946)
John Alden Carpenter
(1876–1951)
Carl Ruggles
(1876–)
Ottorino Respighi
(1879–1936)
Cyril Scott (1879–)
Ernest Bloch
(1880–1959)
Ildebrando Pizzetti
(1880–)
Béla Bartók (1881–
1945)
Georges Enesco
(1881–1955)
Heitor Villa-Lobos
(1881–1959)
Igor Stravinsky
(1882–)
Zoltán Kodály
(1882–)
Francesco Malipiero
(1882–)
Karol Szymanowski
(1883–1937)
Anton von Webern
(1883–1945)

1918   Kaiser abdicates.

1919   Treaty of Versailles.
League of Nations, formed.

1920   Nineteenth Amendment
(women's suffrage).

1922   Discovery of insulin.
Fascist revolution in Italy.
John Dewey's *Human Nature
and Conduct.*

1924   Lenin dies.

1927   Lindbergh's solo flight
across Atlantic.

1928   First all-talking film.
Graf Zeppelin crosses Atlan-
tic. First radio broadcast N. Y.
Philharmonic Orchestra.

1930   Penicillin discovered.

1931   Japan invades Man-
churia. Empire State Building completed.

1933   Franklin D. Roosevelt
inaugurated. Hitler takes over
German government.

1935   Italy invades Ethiopia.

1936   Sit-down strike first used.
Sulfa drugs introduced into
U. S.

1937   Japan invades China.
Spanish Civil War. Nylon introduced.

1938   Munich appeasement.

1939   World War II starts:
Germany invades Poland.
Britain and France declare
war on Germany. Russia invades Finland. U. S. revises
neutrality stand.

1940   Roosevelt elected to
third term. First radio broadcast of Metropolitan Opera
performance.

Gertrude Stein (1874–
1946)
W. Somerset Maugham
(1874–)
Rainer Maria Rilke
(1875–1926)
Thomas Mann (1875–
1955)
Robert Frost (1874–
1963)
O. E. Rolvaag (1876–
1931)
Constantine Brancusi
(1876–1958)
Maurice Vlaminck
(1876–1958)
Isadora Duncan (1877–
1927)
Marsden Hartley
(1877–1943)
John Masefield (1878–)
Vachel Lindsay (1879–
1931)
Paul Klee (1879–1940)
E. M. Forster (1879–)
Raoul Dufy (1879–
1953)
Jacob Epstein (1880–
1959)
Fernand Léger (1881–
1955)
Pablo Picasso (1881–)
Martinez Sierra (1881–)
Georges Braque
(1881–)
James Joyce (1882–
1941)
Jean Giraudoux (1882–
1944)
Virginia Woolf (1882–
1945)
Franz Kafka (1883–
1924)
Kahlil Gibran (1883–
1931)
José Clemente Orozco
(1883–1949)
Maurice Utrillo (1883–
1955)
José Ortega y Gasset
(1883–1955)
Amadeo Modigliani
(1884–1920)
Georges Duhamel
(1884–)

Alfredo Casella
(1883–1947)
Arnold Bax (1883–
1953)
Charles T. Griffes
(1884–1920)
Alban Berg (1885–
1935)
Edgard Varèse
(1885–)
Wallingford Riegger
(1885–1961)
Jaromir Weinberger
(1896–)
Ernest Toch (1887–)
Bohuslav Martinu
(1890–1959)
Jacques Ibert
(1890–1963)
Sergei Prokofiev
(1891–1952)
Arthur Bliss (1891–)
Darius Milhaud
(1892–)
Arthur Honegger
(1892–1955)
Douglas Moore
(1893–)
Walter Piston
(1894–)
Karol Rathaus
(1895–1954)
Paul Hindemith
(1895–1963)
Leo Sowerby
(1895–)
William Grant Still
(1895–)
Virgil Thomson
(1896–)
Howard Hanson
(1896–)
Roger Sessions
(1896–)
Henry Cowell
(1897–)
Quincy Porter
(1897–)
George Gershwin *Porgy & Bess*
(1898–1937)
Ernst Bacon (1898–)
Roy Harris (1898–)
Carlos Chávez
(1899–)
Randall Thompson
(1899–)

1941   U. S. attacked by Japan,
declares war on Japan, Germany, Italy.

1942   British stop Rommel at
El Alamein. U.S. forces land
in North Africa; U.S. army
lands in Sicily. Bataan Death
March. Corregidor surren-
dered. Six million Jews die in
Nazi extermination camps.
First nuclear chain reaction.

1943   Germans defeated at
Stalingrad and in North
Africa. Italy surrenders.
Roosevelt, Churchill, and
Stalin decide on invasion of
France.

1944   Invasion of France.

1945   United Nations Conference at San Francisco. Germany surrenders. Atom bomb
dropped on Hiroshima. Japan
surrenders.

1946   First meeting of U.N.
General Assembly.

1947   Truman Doctrine. Mar-
shall Plan. India wins independence. Communists take
power in Hungary and Ro-
mania.

1948   Gandhi assassinated.
Communists take over
Czechoslovakia. Israel proclaimed a nation. Soviet
blockade of Berlin; airlift begun. Organization of 21
American states.

D. H. Lawrence (1885–
1930)

Sinclair Lewis (1885–
1951)

François Mauriac
(1885–)

André Maurois (1885–)

Diego Rivera (1886–
1957)

William Zorach
(1887–)

Mary Ellen Chase
(1887–)

Georgia O'Keeffe
(1887–)

Alexander Archipenko
(1887–)

Marc Chagall (1887–)

T. E. Lawrence (1888–
1935)

Giorgio de Chirico
(1888–)

Thomas Hart Benton
(1889–)

Karel Čapek (1890–
1938)

Grant Wood (1892–
1944)

John P. Marquand
(1893–1960)

Carlos Merida (1893–)

Joan Miro (1893–)

Ernst Toller (1893–
1939)

Francis Poulenc
(1899–1963)
Kurt Weill (1900–
1950)
Aaron Copland *Billy the Kid suite*
(1900–)
George Antheil
(1900–1959)
Otto Luening
(1900–)
Ernst Křenek
(1900–)
Sir William Walton
(1902–)
Aram Khatchaturian
(1903–)
Luigi Dallapiccola
(1904–)
Marc Blitzstein
(1905–)
Dmitri Shostakovich
(1906–)
Paul Creston
(1906–)
Ross Lee Finney
(1906–)
Olivier Messiaen
(1908–)
Elliott Carter
(1908–)
Samuel Barber
(1910–)
William Schuman
(1910–)
Gian Carlo Menotti
(1911–)
Arthur Berger
(1912–)
John Cage
(1912–)
Hugo Weisgall
(1912–)
Benjamin Britten
(1913–)
Tikhon Khrennikov
(1913–)
Norman Dello Joio
(1913–)
Morton Gould
(1913–)
David Diamond
(1915–)
Irving Fine (1915–
62)
Robert Palmer
(1915–)

1949   Communists defeat
Chiang Kai-shek in China.
USSR explodes atomic bomb.
North Atlantic Defense Pact.

1950   North Koreans invade
South Korea. U.S. Marines
land at Inchon. U.S. plans
hydrogen bomb.

1951   Schuman Plan pools coal
and steel markets of six European nations.

1952   George VI dies; succeeded by Elizabeth II.
Eisenhower elected Presi-
dent.

1953   Stalin dies. Armistice in
Korea.

1954   First atomic-powered
submarine, *Nautilus,*
launched. War in Indo-
China.

1955   Churchill, at 80, succeeded by Anthony Eden.
Salk serum for infantile pa-
ralysis.

E. E. Cummings
(1894–1962)
Aldous Huxley (1894–
1963)
Edmund Wilson
(1895–)
F. Scott Fitzgerald
(1896–1940)
Robert Sherwood
(1896–1955)
John Dos Passos
(1896–)
William Faulkner
(1897–1962)
Louis Aragon
(1897–)
Sergei Eisenstein
(1898–1948)
Bertolt Brecht
(1898–1956)
Ernest Hemingway
(1898–1961)
Alexander Calder
(1898–)
Stephen Vincent Benét
(1899–1943)
C. S. Forester (1899–)
Hart Crane (1899–
1932)
Eugene Berman
(1899–)
Rufino Tamayo
(1899–)
Federico García
Lorca (1899–
1936)
Thomas Wolfe (1900–
1938)
Antoine de Saint-
Exupéry (1900–44)
Ignazio Silone
(1900–)
André Malraux
(1901–)
John Steinbeck
(1902–)
Langston Hughes
(1902–)
Carlo Levi (1902–)
George Orwell
(1903–50)
Mark Rothko
(1903–)
Salvador Dali
(1904–)

Vincent Persichetti
(1915–)
George Perle
(1915–)
Ben Weber
(1916–)
Milton Babbitt
(1916–)
Alberto Ginastera
(1916–)
Robert Ward
(1917–)
Gottfried von Einem
(1918–)
Leonard Bernstein
(1918–)
George Rochberg
(1918–)
Leon Kirchner
(1919–)
Lukas Foss
(1922–)
Peter Mennin
(1923–)
Mel Powell
(1923–)
Pierre Boulez
(1925–)
Gunther Schuller
(1925–)
Luigi Nono
(1926–)
Hans Werner Henze
(1926–)
Carlisle Floyd
(1926–)
Karlheinz Stockhausen (1928–)

1956 Soviet leaders disavow Stalinism and "cult of personality." Egypt seizes Suez Canal. Russia launches Sputnik, first man-made satellite. Uprising in Hungary.

1957 First underground atomic explosion. USSR announces successful intercontinental missile.

1958 Alaska becomes 49th state. Fifth Republic in France under De Gaulle. Pope Pius XII dies, succeeded by John XXIII.

1959 Castro victorious over Batista. Soviet launches first man-made planet. Hawaii becomes 50th state.

1960 Kennedy elected President.

1962 Opening of Lincoln Center for the Performing Arts in New York City.

1963 Pope John XXIII dies, succeeded by Paul VI. President Kennedy assassinated. Lyndon Johnson becomes 36th President.

George Balanchine
(1904–)
Christopher Isherwood
(1904–)
James T. Farrell
(1904–)
Isamu Noguchi
(1904–)
Willem de Kooning
(1904–)
Lillian Hellman
(1905–)
Jean-Paul Sartre
(1905–)
Arthur Koestler
(1905–)
W. H. Auden
(1907–)
Christopher Fry
(1907–)
Alberto Moravia
(1907–)
Theodore Roethke
(1908–)
Stephen Spender
(1909–)
Jackson Pollock
(1912–56)
Albert Camus
(1913–60)
Dylan Thomas
(1914–53)
Tennessee Williams
(1914–)
Arthur Miller
(1915–)
Robert Motherwell
(1915–)
J. D. Salinger
(1919–)

The Harmonic Series

WHEN A STRING or a column of air vibrates, it does so not only as a whole but also in segments—halves, thirds, fourths, fifths, sixths, sevenths, and so on. These segments produce the *overtones,* which are also known as *partials* or *harmonics.* What we hear as the single tone is really the combination of the fundamental tone and its overtones, just as what we see as white light is the combination of all the colors of the spectrum. Although we may not be conscious of the partials, they play a decisive part in our listening; for the presence or absence of overtones in the sound wave determines the timbre, the color of the tone. Following is the table of the Chord of Nature: the fundamental and its overtones or harmonics:

Half the string gives the second member of the series, the octave above the fundamental. This interval is represented by the ratio 1:2; that is to say, the two tones of this interval are produced when one string is half as long as the other and is vibrating twice as fast. The one-third segment of the string produces the third member of the harmonic series, the fifth above the octave. This interval is represented by the ratio 2:3. We hear it when one string is two-thirds as long as the other and is vibrating one and a half times (3/2) as fast. The one-fourth segment of the string produces the fourth member of the series, the fourth above. This interval is represented by the ratio 3:4, for its two tones are produced when one string is three-fourths as long as the other and vibrates one and a third times (4/3) as fast. One fifth of the string produces the fifth member of the harmonic series, the major third, an interval represented by the ratio 4:5. One sixth of the string produces the sixth member of the series, the minor third, represented by the ratio 5:6; and so on. From the seventh to the eleventh partials we find whole tones; this interval is represented by the ratio 7:8. Between the eleventh harmonic and its octave, 22, the semitone appears. This interval is represented by the ratio 11:12. After partial 22 we enter the realm of microtones (smaller than semitones)—third tones, quarter tones, sixth and eighth tones, and so on.

On the brass instruments, the player goes from one pitch to another not only by lengthening or shortening the column of air within the tube, which he does by means of valves, but he also splits the column of air into its segments or partials, going from one harmonic to another by varying the pressure of his lips and breath. The bugle does not vary the length of the air column, for it has no valves. The familiar bugle calls consist simply of the different harmonics of the same fundamental.

Index

JOSEPH HAYDN 1732–1809
JOHANN CHRISTIAN BACH 1735–1782
FRANCIS HOPKINSON 1737–1791
LUIGI BOCCHERINI 1743–1805
WILLIAM BILLINGS 1746–1800
DOMENICO CIMAROSA 1749–1801
WOLFGANG AMADEUS MOZART 1756–1791
MARIA LUIGI CHERUBINI 1760–1842
LUDWIG VAN BEETHOVEN 1770–1827
GASPARO SPONTINI 1774–1851
NICCOLO PAGANINI 1782–1840
CARL MARIA VON WEBER 1786–1826
GIACOMO MEYERBEER 1791–1864
LOWELL MASON 1792–1872
GIOACCHINO ROSSINI 1792–1868
FRANZ SCHUBERT 1797–1828
GAETANO DONIZETTI 1797–1848
VINCENZO BELLINI 1801–1835
HECTOR BERLIOZ 1803–1869
JOHANN STRAUSS (ELDER) 1804–1849
MICHAEL GLINKA 1804–1857
FELIX MENDELSSOHN 1809–1847
ROBERT SCHUMANN 1810–1856
FREDERIC FRANCOIS CHOPIN 1810–1849
FRANZ LISZT 1811–1886
RICHARD WAGNER 1813–1883
GIUSEPPI VERDI 1813–1901
CHARLES GOUNOD 1818–1893
JACQUES OFFENBACH 1819–1880
CESAR FRANCK 1822–1890
EDOUARD LALO 1823–1892
BEDRICH SMETANA 1824–1884
ANTON BRUCKNER 1824–1896
JOHANN STRAUSS (THE SON) 1825–18
STEPHEN COLLINS FOSTER 1826–1864
WILLIAM MASON 1829–1
LOUIS M. GOTTSCHALK 1829–1869
JOHANNES BRAHMS 1833–1897
ALEXANDER BORODIN 1834–1887
CAMILE
LEO DELIBES 1836–1891
MILY BALAKIREV 183
GEORGES BIZET 1838–1875
MODEST MUSORGSKY 1839–1881
JOHN KNOWLES PAINE 183
PETER ILYICH TCHAIKOVSKY 1840–1893
ALEXIS EMMANUEL CHABRIER 1841–1894
ANTONIN DVORAK 1841–1904
SIR ARTHUR SULLIVAN 1841–1900
JULES MASSENET 1842–
EDVARD GRIEG 1843–190
NICHOLAS RIMSKY-KORS
GAI
ENGEL
ERNEST CHAUSSON 1855–1899
EDGAR STILLMAN KELLEY 1857–1944
RUGGIERO LEONCAVALLO 1858–1919
GIACOMO PUCCINI 1858–1924
HUGO WOLF 1860–1903
ISAAC ALBENIZ 1860–1909
GUSTAV MAHLER 1860–1911
EDWARD MacDOWELL 1861–1908
CHARLES MARTIN LOEFFLER 1861–1935
CLAUDE DEBUSSY 1862–1918
FREDERICK DELIUS 1862–1934
PIETRO MASCAGNI 1863–1945
HORATIO PARKER 1863–1919
RICHARD STRAUSS 1864–1949
ALEXANDER GRETCHANINOV 1864–1956
PAUL DUKAS 1865–1935
ALEXANDER GLAZUNOV 1865–1936
JAN SIBELIUS 1865–1957
FERRUCIO BUSONI 1866–1924
ERIK SATIE 1866–1925
ENRIQUE GRANADOS 1867–1916
MRS. H. H. A. BEACH 1867–1944
ALBERT ROUSSEL 1869–1937
FREDERICK SHEPHERD CONVERSE 1871–1940
ALEXANDER SCRIABIN 1871–1915
HENRY HADLEY 1871–1937
RALPH VAUGHAN WILLIAMS 1872–1958
DANIEL GREGORY MASON 1873–1953
MAX REGER 1873–1916
SERGEI RACHMANINOV 1873–1943
ARNOLD SCHOENBERG 1874–1950
CHARLES IVES 1874–1954
GUSTAV HOLST 1874–1934
MAURICE RAVEL 1875–1937
MANUEL DE FALLA 1876–1946
JOHN ALDEN CARPENTER 1876–1951
CARL RUGGLES b. 1876
DAVID STANLEY SMITH 1877–1949
OTTORINO RESPIGHI 1879–1936
CYRIL SCOTT b. 1879
ERNEST BLOCH 1880–1959
ILDEBRANDO PIZZETTI b. 1880
BELA BARTOK 1881–1945
GEORGES ENESCO 1881–1955
HEITOR VILLA-LOBOS b. 1881
IGOR STRAVINSKY b. 1882
ZOLTAN KODALY b. 1882
FRANCESCO MALIPIERO b. 1882
KAROL SZYMANOWSKI 1883–1937
ANTON VON WEBERN 1883–1945
ALFREDO CASELLA 1883–1947
ARNOLD BAX 1883–1953
CHARLES T. GRIFFES 1884–1920
ALBAN BERG 1885–1935
EDGAR dVARESE b. 1885
WALLINGFORD RIEGGER b. 1885
ERNEST TOCH b. 1887
BOHUSLAV MARTINU 1890–1959
JACQUES IBERT b. 1890
SERGEI PROKOVIEV 1891–1952
ARTHUR BLISS b. 1891
ARTHUR HONEGGER b. 1892
DARIUS MILHAUD b. 1892
DOUGLAS MOORE b. 1893
WALTER PISTON b. 1894
KAROL RATHAUS 1895–1954
PAUL HINDEMITH b. 1895
LEO SOWERBY b. 1895
WILLIAM GRANT STILL b. 1895
VIRGIL THOMSON b. 1896
HOWARD HANSON b. 1896
ROGER SESSIONS b. 1896
JAROMIR WEINBERGER b. 1896
HENRY COWELL b. 1897
QUINCY PORTER b. 1897
GEORGE GERSHWIN 1898–1937
ERNST BACON b. 1898
ROY HARRIS b. 1898
CARLOS CHAVEZ b. 1899
RANDALL THOMPSON b. 1899
FRANCIS POULENC b. 1899
KURT WEILL 1900–1950
AARON COPLAND b. 1900
GEORGE ANTHEIL b. 1900
OTTO LUENING b. 1900
ERNST KRENEK b. 1900
MARC BLITZSTEIN b. 1905
ELLIOTT CARTER b. 1908
SAMUEL BARBER b. 1910
WILLIAM SCHUMAN b. 1910
GIAN CARLO MENOTTI b. 191
HUGO WEISGALL b. 191
NORMAN DELLO JOIO b. 1913
MORTON GOULD b. 1913
LEONARD BERNSTEIN b. 1917
LEON KIRCHNER b. 1919
LUKAS FOSS b. 1922
PETER MENNIN b. 1923
MEL POWELL b. 1923